# Malcolm Arnold:
# Rogue Genius

# Malcolm Arnold: Rogue Genius

The life and music of Britain's
most misunderstood composer

Anthony Meredith
and Paul Harris

With a Foreword by
David Mellor

Thames / Elkin

First published 2004

A Thames/Elkin Publication
Distribution by William Elkin Music Services
Station Road Industrial Estate
Salhouse, Norwich, Norfolk NR13 6NS

Email: sales@elkinmusic.co.uk

ISBN 0 903413 54 X

*British Library Cataloguing-in-Publication Data:*
A catalogue record for this book is available from the British Library

Type management by John Saunders

Printed and bound in the UK by
Thanet Press Ltd, Union Crescent, Margate, Kent CT9 1NU

For
Heather Meredith
Michael Meredith
and Jean Harris

*Forsan et haec olim meminisse iuvabit*

# Contents

# *Foreword by*
# David Mellor

MALCOLM ARNOLD's light music and film scores have always been popular, but at long last his 'serious' music is beginning to enjoy a comeback, which makes this new biography particularly timely. His symphonies, indeed, promise to establish him one day in that shining Pantheon of twentieth-century British music, where Elgar, Vaughan Williams, Britten and Walton currently reign supreme. Not for nothing has Malcolm Arnold been called 'the English Shostakovich'. It is time we rejoiced in his supreme achievements.

Anthony Meredith and Paul Harris make a very convincing case for the importance of his music, and, in particular, the nine symphonies, which they cover in depth but in a most accessible manner which will attract both layman and scholar. One of the joys of the book, indeed, is the easy manner in which they introduce the music alongside the life. It is all so gripping that I guess there will be few readers who will not be inspired to seek out the music straight away, either to listen to it for the very first time or to revisit well-known works, freshly expounded by the authors. So many of the highly dramatic moments of Malcolm Arnold's life are contained within the music that the two main strands of the book, his music and his life, sit very comfortably together, each one gloriously illuminating the other.

Malcolm Arnold's buccaneering and tremendously colourful life is of huge intrinsic interest. Anthony Meredith and Paul Harris have done a wonderful job in their research, with the result that it is not only Malcolm who emerges vividly from these pages, but a whole gallery of friends and relations, most of whom are so interesting in themselves that they would worthily inhabit the pages of a novel! And in the middle distance, backing up these big personalities, are many of the most famous names involved in the cultural life of the twentieth century.

*Malcolm Arnold: Rogue Genius* is both a serious study of an important and much misunderstood composer and a most entertaining book, which, once started, is hard to put down. It seems to me to achieve precisely what Malcolm Arnold himself set out to achieve in his music: to be inclusive, embracing the very broadest appeal possible and determinedly leaping over artificial boundaries of dull categorisation. I can recommend it most warmly to everyone; to the serious (and not-so-serious) musical fraternity; to those who enjoy reading a good biography; and to anyone who wishes to be entertained and, at the same time, learn a little more about human nature. *Malcolm Arnold: Rogue Genius* satisfies on all counts.

# Preface and Acknowledgments

I**T WAS WHILE** we were travelling down by train to London, to see a day's cricket at Lord's, that we had a wide-ranging discussion on Sir Malcolm's life and music, discovered several areas where there were many questions without obvious answers, and took a precipitate decision, somewhere shortly after Watford Junction, to collaborate on this biography. Later that day rain stopped play, but this by no means proved a bad omen, for throughout the entire period of the book's research and writing we have rarely been met with anything but cheerful, whole-hearted co-operation.

Anthony Day, who has looked after Malcolm Arnold for many years, and Katherine, Malcolm's daughter, were our first ports of call, and in both cases we could not have been more generously received. Both set us securely on our way, alerted us to any number of useful points of contact, and kept a kindly watching brief on our endeavours. We have also been extremely fortunate in the unstinted help we have received from other members of Malcolm's family. His son, Robert, has offered us constant wisdom and support from the Scottish isles; his brother, Edward, great clarity of recall; Malcolm's niece, Penny, the poetry and diaries of her mother, Ruth, and much more besides; her sister, Jenny, amplification of Ruth's importance; and Malcolm's nephew, Robin, many other detailed family insights, not least on his father and Malcolm's eldest brother, Aubrey. Sheila, Malcolm's first wife, has been a further source of information and inspiration, while Sir Malcolm himself, from time to time over a number of years, has offered many useful nuggets of information.

We have in addition enjoyed so much goodwill on all sides that we are in serious danger of lapsing into hyperbole before we have even reached the first great piece of music. A few helpers in particular deserve special mention: Michael and Heather Meredith, who not only lived with the project at close hand for a long time (which in itself deserves a medal) but also offered it invaluable constructive criticism; Alan Poulton, whose catalogue of Malcolm's work has been our Bible, and who must have responded to over a thousand emails, always with patience as well as deep knowledge; Dorothy Morris, Malcolm's secretary for several years (as Dorothy Payne), who kindly entrusted us with her fascinating diaries; and Donald Mitchell, who has throughout the project provided a strong musical perspective and a challenging ambition. Outstanding help, often in responses to the text, has also been received from Richard Adeney, John Amis, Piers Burton-Page, Sally Cavender, Jean Cockburn, Irene Duffy-Lynch, David

Ellis, Annetta Hoffnung, Richard King, Martin Kingsbury, Keith Llewellyn, Niamh O'Kelly, Dee Ryan, Fiona Southey and Robert Tucker.

But we also owe gratitude to so many more for their invaluable contributions: Christine Amos, Richard Arnell, Avril Arnold, Barry Arnold Long, Lord Attenborough, Joe Ayers, Richard Baker, Charles Barr, Father Cyril Barratt, Sir Richard Rodney Bennett, Vera Binge, Humphrey Bowles, Howard Blake, Colin Bradbury, Dennis Bloodworth, Alan Blyth, Raymond Boland, Amber Bonham-Carter, Robin Boyle, Roddy Braithwaite, Terry Bracher, Geoffrey Brand, Julian Bream, James Brown, Vincent Budd, Terry Bryan, Rupert Burchett, John Carewe, Tracy Cayton-Smith, Brian Charlton, Mary Charlton, Peter Civil, Edward Clark, Nicholas Clark, Andrew Clarke, Mary Clarke, Bridget Coates, Maurice 'Bill' Cody, Lucy Coker, Colin Coleman, Paul Collen, Anna Connelly, Sue Constable, Frances Cook, Tony Cooper, Bill Copland, Martin Cotton, Noel Cox, Richard Crozier, David Culshaw, Judy Cunningham, Trevor Daniels, Benjamin Davey, John Davies, Claire Devlin, James Diack, Johnny Doyle, David Drew, John Dankworth, Oliver Davies, John Slater Dickens, Stephen Dodgson, Sir Edward Downes,, Leslie East, Giles Easterbrook, Martin Ellerby, Wendy Ellis, Julian Elloway, Terry Emery, Mavis Emery, Mike Fage, Bryan Fairfax, Pat Fisher, Julia Farron, Michael Figgis, Christopher Finzi, Bryan Forbes, Denham Ford, Barry Forshaw, Francesca Franchi, Barry Freeman, Benjamin Frith, Catherine Gale, John Gale, James Galway, John Gardner, Hilary Giles, Rodney Ging, Alessandra Giovenco, Brian Gipps, Jean Glasspool, Olivia Gollancz, Noel Goodwin, John Gould, Alexander Grant, Edward Greenfield, George Greenfield, Beryl Grey, Jenny Gregory, Mike Griffiths, Iain Halliday, Eric Hancock, Robert Hardy, Adrian Harris, Anne Heaton, Ann Henderson, Gavin Henderson, Karen Heward, Barry Hillman, Doug Hillman, Betty Hilliard, Tim Holford, Arden Holford, Norman Hollanders, Joseph Horovitz, John Holles, Peter Horton, Duncan Hyslop, Kenneth Hytch, Phyllis Hunt, Ingrid Ingelbau, Georgina Ivor, Paul Jackson, Michael Jeffrey, Edward Johnson, Karen Jones, Martin Jones, Ursula Jones, Edward Kay, John Kehoe, Robert Kendall, Nicholas Kenyon, Peter Kermani, Anthony King, Dame Thea King, Beresford King-Smith, Richard Knight, Rennie Law, Julian Lloyd Webber, Diane Jones, Martin Kirwan, Eric Lawe, Jacqui Kavangh, Barry Latchem, Topsy Levan, David Liddle, John Lill, Jon Lord, Ian Lowes, Mark Lowther, John McCabe, Hugh Maguire, Jane Mann, Sir Neville Marriner, Pauline Marshall, Jenny Martin, David Mason, Monica Mason, Bernadette Maugham, Franck McQuade, David Mellor, David Alan Miller, Betty Mills, Hayley Mills, Sir John Mills, Tania Mooring, Gareth Morris, Jihad Mortada, Anna Murby, Roger Murphy, Jeremy Noble, Victoria North, Simon Oates, Brendan O'Brien, Margaret O'Sullivan Farrell, Kathryn Oswald, Robin Page, Tony Palmer, Lily Payton, Andrew Penny, Philip Pfaff, Ian Phillips, Edmund Pirouet, James Pople, Ross Pople, Tom Priestley, Nigel Proddow, Mike Purton, Terry Pullen, Imeli Rawson, Suzanne

Rozsa-Lovett, Eleanor Roberts, Sue Robinson, David Rose, Edwin Roxburgh, Kriss Russman, Anya Sainsbury, Chris Sayer, Toni Schoff, Robert Secret, Phyllis Sellick, Paul Serotzy, Richard Shaw, Ned Sherrin, Jill Smallshaw, Howard Snell, Tamsyn Howell Sprent, Alec Strahan, Matthew Taylor, Caroline Theakstone, Ronald Thomas, Sara Thomas, Delma Tomlin, Basil Tschaikov, Malcolm Tyler, Jeff Walden, Nicky Walker, John Wallace, Delma Walsh, Lady Walton, John Warrack, William Waterhouse, Fanny Waterman, Eleanor Warren, Jan Warren, Alexander Waugh, Larry Westland, Pamela Weston, Eric Wetherall, Dennis Wick, Bram Wiggins, Edgar Williams, Stephanie Williams, Sir David Willcocks, Jonathan Willcocks, Sally Willison, Donald Witts, Philip Wood, Stanley Woods, John Woolf, Kay Woollard, Jonathan Wortley, David Wright and Lesley Wright.

Thanks also to the following institutions:

BBC Written Archive Centre, Caversham; BBC Radio Northampton; BMG UK & Ireland Limited; the Britten-Pears Library; the British Library; Camden Local Studies and Archives Centre; Chandos Records; The Cheltenham Festival; The Cheyne Walk Club; The Newspaper Library, Colindale; The Embassy of Lebanon; Faber Music; The City of Birmingham Symphony Orchestra Archive; The Hallé Archive; Alfred Lengnick & Co; The London Philharmonic Orchestra; The Malcolm Arnold Society; Mill Hill School; Milton Keynes Public Library; Naxos Records; News International Limited; Novello; Northampton Museum; Northampton Public Library; Northampton School for Boys; the Padstow Lifeboat Archive; Harry Ransom Humanities Research Centre; Royal College of Music Library and the Royal College of Music Department of Portraits and Performance History; Royal Opera House, Covent Garden; The Savile Club; The Sibelius Society and The Stokowski Society.

We are most grateful to the following for allowing us to use their pictures and photographs: Katherine Arnold, Robert Arnold, Sheila Arnold, John Carewe, Tony Cooper, Brian and Mary Charlton, Anthony Day, Mavis Emery, Jenny Gregory, Annetta Hoffnung, Alan Poulton, Penny Pullen, Mike Purton, Jill Smallshaw and Basil Tschaikov. The cover and first page of the miniature score of *Beckus the Dandipratt* are reproduced by kind permission of Alfred Lengnick & Co (a division of Complete Music Ltd): hire material available from Chester Music. The excerpt from Seamus Heaney's poem 'Elegy' is reproduced by kind permission of Faber and Faber.

We should be delighted to hear from anyone able to shed further light on Sir Malcolm's life. Likewise we should be grateful to be told of any areas in which we have failed to acknowledge properly other people's labours or work, despite our best intentions and efforts. Any such omissions will be rectified in any subsequent editions.

Finally our thanks to all at Thames Publishing and especially Richard Elkin for his great enthusiasm and commitment.

*Anthony Meredith and Paul Harris*
*Akeley and Buckingham, July 2004*

*Musician,*
May you weave
Harmonies as delicate and subtle
As a Summer's eve.

May sorrow never cloud your brow,
And may you never know
The bitter pangs
Of dire futility.

Musician,
May you dream
And may angry voices never
Mar the theme
Of your Divine inheritance.

*RUTH ARNOLD*

# 1
# Myth and Reality

## A Celebration in 1996

MALCOLM ARNOLD was rehearsing for a live broadcast. After the orchestra had run through one item in the programme, the leader raised an understandable query. 'When you conduct this piece on the air, will you be observing the *rallentando* at letter C?' 'How the hell do I know?' Malcolm replied. 'That's one of the great mysteries of live music!'[1]

Malcolm's cavalier spirit made him the stuff of legends. He was a larger-than-life character, strongly left-wing and anti-establishment, a composer who wrote music from the heart, works of wide diversity including nine symphonies and seventy film scores.[2] A hater of pomposity and defender of the underdog, Malcolm saw himself as a people's composer, whose primary job was to communicate and, if possible, make the world a better place. Hyperactive, with a thirst for work and the good things in life, he was hardly going to worry over a *rallentando* at letter C.

Today it is rare to meet musicians of more mature years who do not have good stories about Malcolm. Many involve his prodigious appetite for wine, women and song, and few are repeatable in polite company. As the stories proliferate, so do the questions. Did he really indulge in a non-stop party at the Savile Club for three days? Did he really drink champagne in pint mugs? Did he really have sex with the *au pair* on the kitchen table? And inevitably, as the stories are embellished and the myth grows, it becomes even harder to identify the man beneath the legend and hold on to the fact that he was not just a talented musician but one of the major British composers of the twentieth century.

Malcolm's bohemian and often outrageous life-style was better material for the gossip columns than serious musical journals, militating against the acceptance of his serious work. And he himself, by the breadth of his talent, eluded easy categorisation: a trumpet player-turned-composer, who might write a symphony one month and two film scores the next, with a television theme tune quickly dashed off in between. Nor did his serious musical style settle neatly into any niche, ancient or modern. He was his own man, a breaker of convention,

---

[1] The story is Stanley Hibbert's, quoted in *Arnold at 75*, p.20 (*The Gramophone*, May 1996).
[2] As well as over forty documentaries

disregarding the fads of the day, making his own decisions about tonality and serialism. Nobody knew quite what to make of him and the myth arose that he was merely a clown hankering to play Hamlet.

On the whole, however, Malcolm's professional life has been better documented than his personal life. As his music in all its glorious diversity begins to be properly appreciated again after a long period of neglect, there has been a proliferation of material about him in the media. But the figure re-emerging into the public consciousness is one coated in half-truths and misconceptions. The current story of Malcolm's life is one-sided, largely promulgated by Malcolm himself, an old man with a failing memory, a mischievous sense of humour and vivid creative powers. It ignores many of the people who have been most important to him; some facts are wildly inaccurate; the dates often cavalier. Malcolm's life story, left unchallenged, will soon turn the myths into 'reality'.

The situation is exemplified in the booklet from which the story of Malcolm and the *rallentando* emanates. In May 1996, not long before Malcolm's seventy-fifth birthday, *The Gramophone* published an *Arnold at 75* supplement. The booklet rightly stresses the serious side of Malcolm's writing. Edward Greenfield in the leading article puts the case most firmly:

> The nine symphonies stand at the core of Arnold's achievement. If their weight and importance have too often been undervalued by superficial critics, that is in part because they refuse to follow fashion, on the one hand recognizably the work of the tuneful composer of the *English, Scottish* and *Cornish Dances*, on the other hand mingling melodic writing with disconcertingly gritty and uncompromising arguments that reflect the composer's darker feelings.[3]

Shortly afterwards Ivan March makes a similar case for the importance of the symphonies:

> He offers us a series of musical journeys, always unpredictable, even at times almost bizarre in their emotional contradictions; he places optimism and despair disconcertingly side by side, his moments of repose are regularly punctuated by warnings that nothing can be taken for granted. Yet he is very proud of the fact that the underlying musical arguments with their germinal thematic metamorphoses, not only welcome intellectual analysis, but remain stimulating in their own right.[4]

The importance of Malcolm's serious works with their 'darker feelings' and often disconcerting juxtaposition of 'optimism and despair' is also stressed on the booklet's thought-provoking cover: a moody photographic close-up of the composer in old age, with four-fifths of his face in total shadow. The part which *is* lit looks gloomy and reflective, the one visible eye down-cast, like the face of someone who has lived and largely lost. There are hints of past mishaps. A pencil of light outlines a nose which is as crooked at the bridge as a boxer's. Parallel lines not only run across his creased forehead but upwards, at right angles. It is

---

[3] *Arnold at 75*, p.3
[4] *Ibid*, p.6

a fine photograph, but distinctly glum. This is not the Malcolm Arnold whose lighter music is so well known, not the composer hailed for the 'sheer enjoyment of his music-making' and whose 'compositions have created laughter and happiness' with their 'bright, colourful and gloriously melodious music'.[5] There surely should be some hint of mirth somewhere on that elderly face? But there is none.

By its dramatic cover *The Gramophone* is deliberately reinforcing its message that Malcolm Arnold is essentially a serious composer in whose work there is a constant interplay between light and darkness, with the latter often predominating. Rarely, even in his happiest works, is there not an undercurrent of anxiety.

But although *The Gramophone* offers a shrewd and full assessment of the music, it struggles to offer reliable information on his life, giving instead a potted list of the usual unreliable facts. Malcolm was married twice: first to Sheila Nicholson, in 1942, when he was just twenty, and then Isobel Gray in 1964, when he was forty-two. The booklet gets both dates wrong, and likewise the dates of the two divorces. Neither wife is deemed important enough to have a photograph included, for in Arnold myth the women are only tangential to the great round figure of Malcolm. Both Sheila and Isobel in their different ways were inspirational and very much part of Malcolm's music.

The same is true of his three children. The births of the eldest two, Katherine and Robert, are not included in the potted facts. The third, Edward, *is* included, though the date and place of birth are wrong. They are naturally not included among the booklet's many photographs, for in the Arnold myth all the children have been reduced to ghostly, spear-carrying extras. The booklet *does* tell us that the Seventh Symphony was a musical portrait of Katherine, Robert and Edward, though the important definition of 'portrait' is left unexplored; it also tells that he took the whole family several times to see *Avalanche Patrol*, his first documentary film, though all three children had not been born at this time; and, as an illustration of Malcolm's 'warm-heartedness and generosity', we are told of young Robert driving a go-kart on the Brighton seafront with his father paying for go after go. There is so much more to be said. Malcolm's complicated relationship with his children is of crucial importance to an understanding of his life and music.

The one area of Malcolm's personal life which the booklet covers with depth is the most recent, the years since 1984 when Malcolm has been looked after by his carer and companion, Anthony Day. Of all the many points of interest about Malcolm's life nothing, perhaps, is so remarkable as the devotion of Anthony to the cause of helping Malcolm back from the physical and financial effects of a total breakdown which lasted several years.

In the birthday booklet Edward Greenfield writes in delighted relief:

---

[5] *Arnold at 75*, p.1

To see Sir Malcolm Arnold at home in his modern red-brick house at Attleborough, a few miles from Norwich, is to register the happiness of a man content to enjoy retirement after one of the most active careers of any British composer this century ... The overall picture is of domestic comfort, reflecting the ease of one who has thoroughly earned his relaxation.

And Anthony writes of his pleasure in receiving the dedication of Malcolm's final symphony:

I have now looked after Malcolm for twelve years. I hadn't heard of his music before but after hearing it I developed a deep passion for his work that gets deeper every day. Malcolm's gift to me has been the Ninth Symphony which he wrote and dedicated to me for my birthday in 1986. I adore it and think it stands amongst his greatest works. It tells the story of his life between 1979-84, going from the depth of depression to eternal hope and triumph.

These celebratory comments, written in affection, remind us that even on ground as seemingly secure as the last twenty years inaccuracies are to be found. Edward Greenfield's picture of Malcolm in retirement with 'no emotional stresses any longer to trouble him' is an idealized one, and so too Anthony's vision of Malcolm in his Ninth Symphony moving to 'eternal hope and triumph'. Both stem from the natural human desire for happy endings, but Malcolm all his life has possessed an inner turbulence which militates against the concept of comfortable retirement, disallowing him to return love for love with any consistency. The manic-depressive illness with which he has had to live has brought increasingly wilder swings of mood and, although these are controllable to an extent by medication, they still make him very unpredictable. Anthony knows Malcolm, loves him, makes allowances for him and thereby sustains a relationship which can often be very challenging and wearing. His achievement in providing Malcolm with dignity and stability for twenty years is immense, but it has been at a cost, for living with Malcolm could never be free of 'emotional stresses'.

Another area where the booklet is unintentionally misleading is his 'alcohol dependence'. The two years Malcolm spent in a mental hospital in his late fifties are explained away as 'some months in a recuperation centre' for 'alcohol dependence'. There has always been a determination, for the very best of motives, to cover Malcolm's mental illness with the mask of his alcoholism. There is so much less social stigma in bouts of drunkenness than madness. But the alcohol dependence stems from the mental illness, not vice versa. And Malcolm's mental illness has had its say in his professional achievements. There is well-documented evidence that artistic creativity and manic-depressive illness are often interlinked. Malcolm is just one in a long line of similarly afflicted composers.

There is much in Malcolm's private life, therefore, which needs exploration if the major contribution he made to twentieth-century music is to be properly understood. We cannot divorce the man from his music, however tempting it is to do so, for in Malcolm's case, to understand the one is to understand the other, such is their intense correlation. Malcolm was once asked in a radio interview[6] how much of his private life went into his music. 'Everything,' he replied simply. 'One's whole life.'

Malcolm's will not be a comfortable story. Headstrong and self-destructive, he not only has given millions enormous pleasure with his music but also, paradoxically, has wreaked considerable havoc on his impetuous journey through life. That he is touched with genius is clear. But it is a rogue genius, ungovernable, and sometimes leading him to strange shores and dangerous climes. Many of those closest to Malcolm would have echoed the words which Seamus Heaney wrote of another troubled spirit, the poet Robert Lowell:

> You were our night ferry
> thudding in a big sea,
> the whole craft ringing
> with an armourer's music
> the course set wilfully across
> the ungovernable and the dangerous.[7]

Although the night ferry no longer thuds across dangerous seas, its music continues to ring out, becoming more and more compelling. And the greater Malcolm's reputation grows as one of Britain's leading twentieth-century musical figures, so too the need to extricate reality from the entangling myth of his personal life. A most moving story of triumph and tragedy will emerge, for the reality is even more remarkable than the myth.

---

[6] By Margaret Howard, Classic FM, 21 October 1992
[7] Excerpt from 'Elegy', from *Field Work* by Seamus Heaney (Faber and Faber), quoted by Kay Redfield Jamison (*Touched with Fire*, The Free Press, 1993, p.9)

*Malcolm in his Eaglehurst blazer, with his brother Philip*

*Malcolm with his father at Fairview*

# 2
# An Original Education
## Northampton, 1921-38

MALCOLM WAS BORN on 21 October 1921 in Northampton, where the Arnolds were well-known as the makers of high quality shoes. His birth-place[1] was a detached, ivy-clad Victorian house called Fairview, recently acquired by the Arnolds on profits made from the wartime demand for boots, and standing in an acre of gardens in Cliftonville, a road favoured by prosperous businessmen.[2] There were two family shoe businesses at the time, one run by his father, William Arnold, and one run by his grandfather of the same name, part of a thriving industry in Northampton which boasted hundreds of factories with row upon row of narrow, red-brick terraced houses for the workers, who, though poorly paid, were only too grateful not to be among the country's two million unemployed.

His father, later known in the family as Pappy, was at the height of his pros-perity in the immediate post-war period, selling all the shoes he could make, when short supply had led to rationing. Pappy had little education, having left school at twelve in the year of Queen Victoria's Diamond Jubilee, in order to go into his father's factory and learn about the business. But by the time Malcolm was born the two William Arnolds had fallen out badly and were not on speaking terms.

The story of how Grandfather William had made the family fortune is well documented in the privately printed *Recollections of William Arnold*,[3] an immodest work which attributes his rise from rags to riches to a renunciation of drink and a subsequent walk with God, the result of a dramatic conversion on the Racecourse.[4] Grandfather William, born in 1860, had started life in abject poverty, the son of a shoemaker in the village of Everdon. He had no schooling and as a seven-year-old was working as a ploughboy for two shillings a week. At

---

[1] The car park of Northampton General Hospital's Accident and Emergency Department now covers the site of Fairview. The Arnolds had previously lived, less grandly, at Sunnyholme, Stimpson Avenue.

[2] Two other shoe manufacturers, Church and Barratt, had houses in Cliftonville.

[3] Northampton, 1915. The book was necessarily put together by a friendly 'ghost' as William Arnold senior was barely literate.

[4] By then the Northampton racecourse had become an open public park.

fourteen, he came to Northampton to find menial employment in one of the town's three hundred shoe factories. Ten years later, by forming partnerships with some better-placed relations, he became part of a business which failed,[5] but a second venture, 'A & W Arnold',[6] succeeded triumphantly thanks to a brave investment in revolutionary mechanisation. He moved to new, impressive premises in St Giles Terrace and with a partner opened a second factory at Vernon Terrace. By the First World War the illiterate village boy had become a highly respected big businessman who took his new-found position in local society very seriously. Photographs show him sitting proudly with his six handsome sons,[7] all immaculately dressed, from their shiny starched collars and silk cravats down to their gleaming Arnold footwear.

Grandfather William was still very much in control of his empire at the time of Malcolm's birth, a sprightly sixty-year-old, short and stocky, living in a house overlooking the Racecourse.[8] Although an important figure in Primitive Methodist circles, a fiery lay preacher and well-known philanthropist, Grandfather William was not an entirely sympathetic character. Malcolm's nephew, Robin,[9] remembers him as an absolute tyrant.

> He used to sit in the conservatory, surrounded by his clients, holding court. There was always a bunch of sycophants around him, bowing and scraping.[10]

Malcolm's niece, Penny,[11] on the other hand, has stories of big parties he would give to his sisters' children, showering them with presents. He also would return to Everdon every Christmas to throw in the air large quantities of florins and sixpences for the local children to catch.

Malcolm's father, born in 1886, inherited much from Grandfather William. Like him he was a devoted Primitive Methodist, preaching equally fiercely in the various local chapels each Sunday. So passionate was he indeed for the Protestant cause that on one occasion he hired a boat, filled it with Bibles and sailed to Italy to convert the Catholics. Unfortunately he was arrested almost as soon as he landed and quickly deported. History does not relate what he did with all his Bibles.

Religious fervour was not all that Pappy shared with his father. They both had hot tempers, which led to such a strong disagreement in 1909 that Pappy and his brother, Matthew, left their father's business and founded a rival firm, 'Arnold Brothers'. Pappy was as strongly teetotal as his new partner was not, but the business they founded in Henry Street prospered, Pappy being in charge of sales

---

[5] Arnold and Company

[6] With his uncle Anthony as partner and, no doubt, chief investor.

[7] The four daughters were naturally excluded.

[8] 26 Kingsley Road

[9] The son of Malcolm's eldest brother, Aubrey

[10] August 2003

[11] Penny Pullen, the daughter of Malcolm's sister, Ruth

and administration and Matthew the design and production.[12] The Arnold Brothers's slogan, *Cathedral shoes wear out the pavement,* testified to the high quality of their products.

Malcolm's Uncle Mat was a real character, his favourite haunt the White Elephant overlooking the Racecourse, his favourite tipples beer and whisky chasers. From time to time he would solemnly sign the pledge, more because he enjoyed the drama of the occasions than from any real intention to stop drinking. Pappy and Grandfather William despaired of him.

Pappy soon rivalled his father not just in shoe production but philanthropy, always alert to the needs of those on the streets. Robin Arnold remembers that as a child he used to walk across the Racecourse with Pappy, who would dispense white £5 notes to anyone on the benches who was clearly down on his luck.

Pappy proved the more popular employer, as he had the happy knack of remembering the names of his workers, their wives and their children. He also knew all their interests and where there was a problem he helped with cash and kindness. Accordingly his employees held him in enormous respect and affection. Family relationships, however, were less warm and the rift between father and son did not heal with time, the two not speaking to each other for over ten years. Robin recalls Pappy hurrying him away on the Racecourse because his Grandfather William had been sighted emerging from his house.

Malcolm's father had two distinct personalities, the charitable and the selfish. Totally self-absorbed and preoccupied with what people thought of him, Pappy could not bear being crossed. Highly emotional, he would burst into tears and fly into rages. 'Shocking, terrible, tragic!' he would cry at the merest upsets. Another gambit to get his own way was to dash off letters of complaint. 'Keep away from me!' began one such tirade to his grandson, Robin.

Nevertheless, for all his instabilities, he succeeded as a young man in wooing the amiable and highly cultured Annie Hawes. They had first met, auspiciously, at a church organ, where they were having lessons from the same teacher. Pappy was a keen musician, playing the organ and piano with panache in Chapel, but his wife, Nan (as the younger members of the family always called her), was in a different class. Highly artistic, she sang sweetly and played Chopin and Rachmaninoff on the Bechstein in Fairview with real feeling. In her younger days she was also a good violinist, participating with her sisters in string quartets and quintets, organised by her violinist father, William Hawes. He was a man of many parts. A Professor of Music in Northampton (at least, according to Pappy), he numbered Gervase Elwes,[13] the future tenor, among his pupils and also taught the violin at Oundle School. Pappy tended not to mention that he also tested the gas meters of Northampton.

---

[12] The factory buildings, which occupied all the land between Henry Street and Talbot Road, survive today, although Arnold Brothers have long since ceased trading.

[13] Elwes came from an important Catholic family which had an estate east of Northampton at Billing Hall.

CLIFFORD
7 YEARS

RUTH
12½ YEARS

AUBREY
14 YEARS

PHILIP
2½ YEARS

MALCOLM
6 MONTHS

MAY, 1922

*The five Arnold children were regularly featured on postcards by their proud parents. This one dates to 1922.*

*William Arnold (Pappy) with his children, 1925.*

*Back row: Aubrey, Pappy and Ruth.*

*Front row: Clifford, Malcolm and Philip*

*Malcolm drives cautiously, 1924*

*The young Tam O'Shanter, 1925*

*Malcolm aged 6*

*In the Fairview garden, 1931*

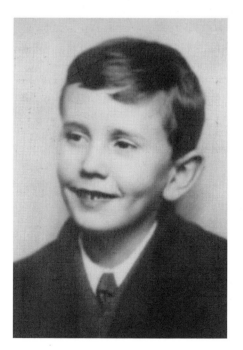

The marriage was successful by dint of Nan's selfless determination to put Pappy's interests and feelings first. There were five children, with Malcolm very much the afterthought. Aubrey was thirteen years older, Ruth twelve and Clifford six. Malcolm was closest to Philip, two years his senior.

Fairview was a delightful house in which to grow up, its attractive gardens overlooking the Nene Valley a constant source of pleasure. Photographs taken at Fairview show Malcolm, the much-spoiled baby of the family, sitting on a swing with a pet dog on his lap; on a sledge in the snow; dressed up as an Indian brave; standing with a toy aeroplane; and motoring around very soberly in his pedal-car. Always on hand for the children were the chauffeur, Linnet, who lived above the garage, five servants and a young, uniformed nanny, Lizzie Witts, who had joined the Arnold family as a thirteen-year-old and was to work for Pappy for over seventy years.[14] The children were all devoted to Lizzie, their friend, playmate and confidante. The idyll of a privileged childhood, however, was sometimes marred by Pappy, who maintained an iron discipline by use of the cane. Tensions created by his moods probably accounted for occasional outbreaks of discord between the five children. During a thunderstorm, for example, Malcolm and Ruth, tied by Aubrey to the foot of a tree, were in terror of their lives.[15]

As he grew up, Malcolm became aware of the different kind of life being lived by less fortunate children. He enjoyed being hugely spoilt by Nan and Lizzie, but working class privations worried him. He felt a desire, like Pappy and Grandfather William, to fling around money to alleviate some of the poverty, but for the moment he contented himself with sweets rather than £10 notes.

Yet the drama and excitement of social change *were* in the air, even in sleepy Northampton. The horrors of war and the disillusion at its aftermath had led to the old ways at last being challenged and the new eagerly embraced. There was a demand not just for better pay and working conditions but for more leisure, entertainment and fun. And amongst the many manifestations of change in this turbulent period came that particular trademark of the Roaring Twenties, jazz.

Malcolm's birth had coincided with its introduction to England.[16] And although Malcolm's conservative parents looked askance at the new music, his grown-up sister, Ruth, rejoiced in it. If the Twenties roared at all in Northampton, they did so most often when Ruth was around, for she was one of the town's Bright Young Things. She wore make-up, bobbed her hair like her screen idol Louise Brooks and boasted a large collection of jazz records. As he was growing

---

[14] Lizzie's world was completely circumscribed by the Arnolds. Most of her closest relations worked in Arnold factories.

[15] Aubrey's action seems totally out of character. 'I never saw him angry,' says his son, Robin, 'nor heard him say an unkind word. His total integrity, sense of honour and honesty actually *worried* me!' (April 2004)

[16] The self-styled 'Creators of Jazz', the Original Dixieland Jazz Band, had recently introduced London to ragtime. The band's leader, cornettist Nick La Rocca, would soon become one of Malcolm's first idols, for in the early 1920s ODJB records sold everywhere.

up the little Malcolm marvelled at his big sister, who could sing a song, dance the Charleston and play the banjolele all at the same time. The fun-loving Ruth very much epitomised the current antipathy of the young towards restrictive Victorian ideals. As an emancipated twenty-year-old, who championed the cause of women's rights and gay minorities long before they became an important issue, she threw off the shackles of convention. She would get engaged one evening only to break it off the next. She had been known to fling back rings at her suitors as dramatically as any heroine of the flickering silent screen. Ruth's advanced views, so admired by the impressionable Malcolm, worried her parents and probably scandalised the genteel neighbours. She even read D.H. Lawrence.

The young Malcolm soon sampled Ruth's jazz collection, guitarist Django Reinhardt becoming a lifelong favourite as well as Sophie Tucker, 'the red hot momma'. But it was Louis Armstrong[17] who impressed most, his trumpet displaying an inspirational vigour and lyricism on the Hot Five recordings which turned simple jazz improvisations into a new art form.[18] Malcolm was so impressed by his first Louis Armstrong record that, at the age of nine, he bought a second-hand trumpet and began teaching himself to play.[19] His mother was immediately anxious about its effect on his asthma. 'If it doesn't kill him,' the doctor told her, 'it will cure him!'

Malcolm's eldest brother, Aubrey, thirteen years his senior and the antithesis of Ruth, was also influential. Aubrey had just started at Mill Hill School when Malcolm was born, and from there he went on to Cambridge, studying the unusual combination of Law and Spanish and becoming friendly with the rich Spanish-American jazz pianist, Fred Elizalde. Aubrey, who had more money than most of his contemporaries, found he and Elizalde had many interests in common. Both were later to visit Spain, Elizalde to fight for Franco and Aubrey to study bull-fighting. So when Elizalde enjoyed meteoric success as a band leader at London's Savoy Hotel, the Arnolds followed his career with enthusiasm, Malcolm listening intently to all his records.

Jazz at this period was all-pervasive, its influence quickly spreading to more serious music. The 1920s saw the composition of Walton's *Façade*, Lambert's *Rio Grande* and Gershwin's *American in Paris*. Satie and Les Six were assimilating the new music and Ravel included a blues in his Violin Sonata of 1923.

---

[17] Constant Lambert in *Music Ho!* called him 'one of the most remarkable virtuosi of the present day'.

[18] Yet he was by no means the only trumpeter to make a lasting impression on the young child. Years later, in 1959, when Malcolm was a celebrity guest on BBC Radio's 'Desert Island Discs', among his highly eclectic selection of records was the jazz standard *Dipper Mouth Blues*, which had associations with three legendary names: Louis Armstrong, who played it regularly; Muggsy Spanier, whose recording Malcolm had chosen; and Joe 'King' Oliver, who wrote the tune for his own Creole Jazz Band.

[19] Malcolm interviewed by Andrew Stewart in *Music Teacher*, June 1989. 'I went on practising the violin and piano, of course.'

With the advent of radio, music of all kinds was enjoying an unprecedented popularity, and contemporary composers could hope to reach into almost every household in the country. The Arnolds looked upon music as an integral part of their lifestyle. Pappy saw to it as a matter of course that the family home boasted a music room, several good pianos, and the very latest in radio and gramophone technology.

There was music on both sides of Malcolm's family. Pappy's piano-playing was much better than Malcolm would later admit; Lizzie Witts's nephew, Donald, described it as 'brilliant', the repertoire ranging from Bach and Mozart to absolutely anything by Malcolm but especially *The Bridge on the River Kwai*. Pappy's sister, Malcolm's Aunt Harriet, was a good pianist and her husband, Uncle Reg,[20] an excellent organist. Most celebrated of all, however, was Malcolm's Aunt Cissie.[21] Boasting a music degree and a Blüthner grand, she was for many years a formidable presence at Northampton music competitions.

But it was also from Pappy's side of the family that Malcolm inherited the genes of mental instability. The strong streak of eccentricity, which was to make Pappy as endearing as he was infuriating, came out more vividly in two of his sisters. The delightful Aunt Joy and Aunt Grace both ended their lives in mental hospitals, the former in St Andrew's, just down the road from Malcolm's birthplace. There was also a wildness about Pappy's brother, Uncle Alf, the black sheep of the family, about whom lips were tightly sealed. Aunt Harriet in old age committed suicide.

Music and eccentricity were both strong, too, on his mother's side of the family. Malcolm always revered his great-great grandfather, William Hawes,[22] a highly versatile musician, proudly remembered by Malcolm as 'the Great William'. He began life as a chorister of the Chapel Royal and stayed at St James' Palace in various important capacities for over fifty years. He was also Master of the Choristers at St Paul's Cathedral and, for many years, simultaneously attached to the Westminster Abbey choir. Living in style in Adelphi Terrace and moving in high circles, he was lutenist to George III and played the organ at Victoria's Coronation. Among his acquaintances he numbered Liszt.

The Great William did not confine himself to sacred music:

From 1801 I commenced private teaching, and had a good share of it, at low prices – singing principally. Shortly afterwards I was appointed as a violin performer at the Covent Garden Theatre, and as Junior of the Orchestra had the task for several

---

[20] Frederick Reginald Harris, a prominent Northampton engineer and mason
[21] Leonora Harris, Reginald's sister
[22] 1785-1846

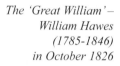

*The 'Great William' –*
*William Hawes*
*(1785-1846)*
*in October 1826*

seasons of sitting in a corner of the stage for six hours, fiddling to the pantomime tricks of Mother Goose etc.[23]

The Great William was also a composer, writing popular glees and songs which sold in their thousands.[24] And he himself appeared as a singer for many years on the stage, making his debut at Drury Lane aged eleven. Later he turned to theatrical management, in which the bad times – involving fires and bankruptcy – very much offset the good. His greatest success was the acquisition of Weber's *Der Freischütz*, which he himself mounted and conducted at the English Opera House, its first genuine performance in England, though he 'improved' it with arias of his own. He also brought Mozart's *Così Fan Tutte* to the English stage for the first time, conducting it himself.

Musical distinction was indeed a Hawes family trait. Malcolm's great-grandmother was a fine contralto called Maria Merest, her greatest success probably being participation in 1846 in the first performance of Mendelssohn's *Elijah*. Her father, the Great William, conducted.

Nan took understandable pride in these achievements of her ancestors and, as soon as Malcolm started to show musical ability at a very early age, she was delighted. He might well be special, even another Great William, so his education should be particularly important.

Resplendent in striped blazer and cap, Malcolm was sent off at the age of five to Eaglehurst College,[25] a private school overlooking the Racecourse, where he

---

[23] From a *curriculum vitae* of 18 November 1835
[24] His arrangement of the Scottish tune *We're a-noddin* sold over 30,000 copies in two years.
[25] 37/38 East Park Parade

joined Clifford and Philip. Eaglehurst, which occupied two of a long line of three-storeyed Victorian terraced houses, was typical of many small, family-run educational establishments which flourished in the days before the need for science laboratories and ministry accreditation.[26] The school, which catered for about a hundred pupils, most of whom left by thirteen, was owned by Robert Philips,[27] the Headmaster, a strong disciplinarian,[28] keen on sport, neither virtue being much of a recommendation to Malcolm. But Mr Philips was also a good pianist and played the organ at St Michael's Church, and some of his staff were musical too. Methuen Clarke, the young curate at nearby St Matthew's Church, had been a choral scholar at King's College, Cambridge, and was the first alto soloist in Britten's *Rejoice in the Lamb*.

Every day Malcolm and his brothers were taken the short distance to school by Pappy's chauffeur, often making a detour to the shops so that Malcolm could stock up with sweets which he would later distribute to all and sundry. This act of cunning self-defence, however, did not prevent him from acquiring the nickname of 'fatty'. He was a difficult pupil. School discipline, he once declared, 'put ideas of study out of my mind'[29] and he sometimes brought in the triangle from his drum set to relieve the tedium of lessons. He hated school so much that when it was raining he would often stand outside Eaglehurst with his shirt off, trying to catch cold. Life at home, where his every whim was indulged by Nan, was just too much of a contrast. He had only to ask and he would be presented with ten shillings and taken by the chauffeur to the sweet shop.

After he had spent a couple of years as an unwilling pupil at Eaglehurst, Nan thought he might be better in the homely atmosphere of a little school just round the corner from Fairview, run by two sisters, Ellen and Alice Strickland.[30] This was a tall, semi-detached house with just a few small classrooms, but he quickly proved too much for the Stricklands and he was sent back to Eaglehurst, staying until 1931. His best friend was Ian Philips, the headmaster's son and a fellow pupil, who was later to take over the school from his father. Ian Philips was often invited to Fairview to play with Malcolm and, on one occasion, when they were about nine, they went up to an attic where Malcolm produced a trumpet and

---

[26] It finally closed in 1973. It had opened in 1886, the year Pappy was born.

[27] He had previously taught at Steyne House, Brighton. He was a good club cricketer, opening the bowling for the Saints, and a Northamptonshire vice-president, which was probably why the school used the nearby county ground rather than the Racecourse for the most important sporting occasions. Old Boys of the school included 'Tubby' Vials, who later captained the county cricket team, the jockey Josh Gifford, and playwright John Whiting. Malcolm's time at Eaglehurst would have briefly overlapped with that of Whiting.

[28] A former pupil, Tony Cooper, remembers the Headmaster (who lived in a house attached to the school building) as very strict.

[29] As quoted by Hugo Cole, *Malcolm Arnold* (Faber Music, 1989), p.1

[30] 18 Billing Road, almost facing the entrance to Cliftonville

asked his friend to have a go. When Ian Philips failed to make a single sound, Malcolm took over and played with considerable confidence.

At nearly ten Malcolm was sent with his brother, Philip, to the Town and Country Grammar School, today's Northampton School for Boys, close to Fairview and not far down the Billing Road. There was still no opportunity to make his mark in music, which had a low profile in most secondary schools in the 1930s. There was an orchestral society, but only six of the six hundred pupils belonged to it. There was also a choir, which sang irregularly, and Gilbert and Sullivan operettas were occasionally performed. Malcolm, however, seems not to have availed himself of these small opportunities. By Easter 1933, when he decided enough was enough, he had progressed only from IIB to IIIB and attracted no plaudits.

In May 1933 we find him, still only eleven, having his third stint at Eaglehurst. 'He was placed in his present form,' wrote Headmaster Robert Philips at the end of this term, 'because I thought he might be happier here.' In other words, he was placed in a form below his intellectual potential, to give him a better chance of relating to his peers. However, co-operation and hard work do not seem yet on his agenda. 'I am rather sorry he couldn't take a higher place in the exams,' continued the Headmaster. 'He could work harder.' His Form Master concurred: 'I think he has made some progress but he needs to work much harder.'

Malcolm took exams that summer in sixteen subjects. His best result was to come third in General Knowledge (though the modest 35% says something about the form's abilities). Alas, he registered a Nil Satis in Divinity, Reading, English History, French and an exam called Repetition.

Malcolm stayed on for one more year at Eaglehurst, preparing for, and passing, Common Entrance to Mill Hill, where Aubrey had been notably successful, ending up as a monitor and captain of the 1st XV.[31] Pappy clearly thought that Mill Hill would be the place to sort out his difficult youngest son, for whom he had plans in accountancy, and off he was dispatched for the autumn term of 1934. But Malcolm had his own ideas on the subject. He spent just four hours at the school before summoning the chauffeur to come down and collect him. The prospect of life as a boarder away from all his creature comforts had brought on an anxiety attack, real or simulated. 'When I was twelve,' he said many years later, 'I left school because of bad health. I had asthma.' It was true that he did suffer from the illness, and on one occasion the attack was so bad that only the alertness of Nan had saved him. Nonetheless, to finish schooling at twelve was every spoilt mother's-boy's dream.

By the time Malcolm's schooling ended prematurely, the highly educated Aubrey had not only married but been selected by Grandfather William to be the London Representative of A & W Arnold, with the promise that the business

---

[31] Clifford had been there briefly too, before moving on to Pangbourne.

*Aunt Belle (left)
and Aunt Bess,
about 1880*

would be his on the old man's retirement. Pappy agreed to this happily enough because his brother Matthew had two sons to come into their business and, of his own sons, the steady Philip would be ideal for guiding the future destiny of Arnold Brothers. Malcolm really seemed good for nothing, and the contrast between his successful eldest son, Aubrey, and his youngest was painful indeed. The spoilt Malcolm would clearly never make an accountant, had little to offer either of the family firms, and could be discounted from all future plans. If Nan wished to waste her time on him, so be it! Fortunately for Malcolm, Nan *did* take an interest at this very crucial time, redoubling her efforts at turning him into a good pianist [32] and enlisting the aid of three of her larger-than-life sisters, Aunt Belle, Aunt Bess and Aunt Alice.

Malcolm had been having violin lessons from the redoubtable Aunt Belle since the age of four:

> I used to be taken round by my mother and dropped on her doorstep, terrified of her, because she was a very, very fine player. She said, 'You're more interested in your trumpet, aren't you?'
>
> 'No,' I replied. 'I want to play the violin like you, auntie.' [33]

[32] Throughout his teenage years he was to have a problem. 'He couldn't get his hands in the right shape to begin playing with any technical facility,' commented his teacher Philip Pfaff. Nan had started teaching Malcolm when he was five (according to a 1991 interview) or three (according to an even less reliable interview, 1996).

[33] Interview with Margaret Howard, Classic FM, 21 October 1992

Belle was a fine musician, who taught the violin for a time at Northampton High School. She would also oblige the large Arnold family with a party piece at Christmas, when, it would seem, some items came off better than others. Her grand-niece, Jenny Gregory,[35] remembers that on one occasion 'when she started playing, I started screaming'. But by then Aunt Belle was probably past her peak.

Malcolm adored her eccentricities. Aunt Belle, who was very rich, owned seven almost derelict terraced houses in Northampton, which she would let out at inflated prices and defiantly refuse to repair or decorate. She also had a large house in Hunstanton, to which she would drive from time to time, ever so slowly, because she rarely emerged from first gear in her Austin Seven. This was perhaps just as well, as the Austin Seven was custom-made with two fluted, silver vases in the back, which Belle would fill lavishly with flowers. Their scent alleviated the smell of petrol. Fearful of being trapped inside after an accident, Aunt Belle had the little car converted to a hatch-back, the special rear door being openable from the inside by her silver-topped walking stick.

Aunt Bess owned a house in Northampton, a bungalow on the Great Orme's Head, Llandudno, and a cottage in the tiny village of Capel Garmon, near Llanrwst, where only Welsh was spoken, and all the children ran around in bare feet until one day a lorry-load of complimentary Arnold shoes arrived. Bess was also musical, playing the viola in the chamber groups of her father, William Hawes. She ended up in old age a little like Dickens's Miss Havisham, sitting in her grand but dingy Northampton back parlour, full of dusty bric-a-brac, usually with a smelly cairn terrier recumbent on an apron on her lap, continually feeding it chicken. Robin remembers being sent to visit her, at the age of eleven, when Aunt Bess would give him a glass of sherry and a piece of Christmas Cake, even in the height of the summer. As the glass was usually dirty, before filling it with sherry Aunt Bess would wipe it with the cairn's apron.

Aunt Alice was perhaps Malcolm's favourite aunt, opening up to him for the first time visions of the good life. Extremely rich, thanks to Hawes brewery money, Aunt Alice was decidedly grand, she and her husband twice becoming Mayor and Mayoress of Northampton. They built a particularly fine house called Eastfield where they would throw lavish parties.

Nan herself was not free of airs and graces. Although she and her youngest son shared a very deep and special affection, it was not to her that Malcolm would go in moments of trouble, but his sister, Ruth, or Lizzie Witts. Nan for all her homely, plump appearance, had ambitions to be gracious and elegant and would be fashionably dressed and sweetly scented with lavender or cologne. Pappy likewise, still slim and dapper, took a pride in his outward appearance. Together he and Nan cut quite a dash when holidaying, as they did regularly, at

---

[34] Ruth's elder daughter

*Pappy with his children in the Craigmore garden, about 1935.*
*Back row: Aubrey, Pappy, Ruth*
*Front row: Malcolm, Clifford, Philip*

*Malcolm, about 1936,*
*outside Craigmore*

*Nan, Malcolm's mother, January 1942*     *Pappy, Malcolm's father*

one of the south coast's more luxurious hotels. The shoe industry might be strug-gling and in recession by the mid-thirties, but Pappy and Nan never let it show.

Nan still loyally supported Pappy, gently calming down his outbursts as best she could, always trying to keep the children's misdemeanours away from him. But even Nan could not save Pappy from a *folie de grandeur* involving the enclosed world of Northampton's Primitive Methodists.

Both Grandfather William and Pappy, having invested much time and money in the movement, tended to feel they owned the chapels. Grandfather William had made two very big benefactions in the 1920s: a new church[35] by the county cricket ground (whose spire was long known as 'Arnold's toothpick') and a delightful Methodist 'Homestead' of sheltered retirement housing, close to the Racecourse. So when a new pastor, the Revd. Reeves, arrived to take charge of the four Primitive Chapels and inadvertently upset them, they reacted haughtily. 'I think I can serve God best,' wrote Pappy to the new minister,[36] 'by not attending any meetings.' Reeves did his best to calm things down but thought

---

[35] Park Avenue Methodist Church. It was built in 1924 in memory of Grandfather William's wife. Perhaps significantly, the tablet puts 'Laid by J.W. Arnold' in capitals and 'in memory of Elizabeth Harries Arnold' in much smaller letters.
[36] In late 1928 when Malcolm was seven.

Pappy 'a difficult man to get on with', disliking his 'tendency to control the church'. The dislike simmered and then came to the boil.

One of the district's four chapels was at Far Cotton, a depressed working-class area, where Reeves, a married man, had become friendly with a Miss Emily Baxter, just fifteen when their four-year friendship blossomed. Grandfather William told Pappy he should take action to safeguard the good name of Primitive Methodism. Pappy, needing little persuasion, foolishly engaged a local printer to produce pamphlets denouncing the Revd. Reeves's adulterous conduct, and a libel suit resulted. Unfortunately for Pappy, he had no hard evidence. 'The couple had been seen in summer evenings frequenting the haunts of courtesans,' declared Pappy's counsel hopefully. Reeves began his defence by quoting a comment Pappy had once made to him: 'I have always been a crank and suppose I shall be to my journey's end.' His friendship with the girl, he declared, had been 'high and pure'. She had become a Sunday School teacher. 'I have discussed sermons with her, for she is a girl of independent views.' Indeed, it was her lively mind, together with her frail, weak body, which had drawn her to him. The jury's sympathy was now aroused. And when Reeves's counsel let slip that little, frail Emily worked for one of the Arnolds' biggest rivals, Barratt's, the case was lost. Pappy had to pay reparations, the large sum of £750. But worse, for a time he was the laughing-stock of the town.

Confidence in Arnold Brothers faltered and Pappy found his profits reduced. It was necessary to live more cautiously and, at around the time Malcolm gave up school, the Arnolds left Fairview and moved the short distance to St George's Avenue, on the far side of the Racecourse from Eaglehurst. Their new home, Craigmore,[38] was at the end of a long row of tall, terraced Edwardian houses. There were to be no more chauffeurs or tennis courts, but Craigmore had four floors and Pappy could still have an impressive front parlour with a good view. There was also a handy sitting-room for Lizzie Witts and her cat, Sally, over-looking the long, narrow walled back garden, patrolled by Joey, her tortoise. Best of all, there was a large basement running right under the house with parquet flooring and fireplaces at both ends, ideal, once a piano was installed, for young people's jazz parties.

The move from Fairview to Craigmore coincided with an event which Malcolm was always to enjoy re-telling, his first meeting with Louis Armstrong. In the Easter of 1934 Pappy and Nan had taken Ruth and the three younger boys to stay at the smart Royal Bath Hotel, Bournemouth. There Armstrong made an appearance at a *thé dansant* in the course of which Armstrong's wife sat down at their table while Louis played 'Sleepy Time Down South':

---

[37] Craigmore still survives, though its name has gone. It is number 106, the last of the long row which stretches down the avenue from Kingsley Road. When the Arnolds lived at Craigmore, a large area of wild ground existed between them and Trinity Avenue. This land has now been built upon.

Louis later came up himself and signed my programme, writing 'Satchmo'. I looked at him in wonder. 'Isn't your name Louis Armstrong?' I said. 'A'hm Satchmo, kid,' he replied.[38]

This meeting is often said to have fired Malcolm's ambition to study the trumpet, but he had, in fact, been studying it for four years already. Nor was the lady at the table, as is sometimes claimed, Lil Armstrong, Satchmo's jazz pianist wife, for she and her husband had long since split up. The 'Mrs Armstrong' the Arnolds met that exciting afternoon was a glamorous young lady called Alpha, who in due course would become Louis' third wife. There were, however, repercussions, for as soon as he was back in Northampton Malcolm insisted on a visit to the instrument makers, Tomkins,[39] to buy a really good trumpet, and one of the Tomkins employees, Frank Burton, who was a good enough trumpet player to be in the Rushden Brass Band[40] and the Northampton New Theatre Orchestra, began giving Malcolm his first formal trumpet lessons in 1935. Malcolm also had some lessons with Burton's friend Sidney Kite, another member of the theatre orchestra.

The inspiration of Louis Armstrong led to constant jazz in the Craigmore cellar, where an Arnold quartet often featured Philip on clarinet or alto-sax alongside Malcolm, with a rhythm section of Ruth on piano and Clifford on guitar. For variety Malcolm would play a swinging violin in a style not encouraged by Aunt Belle, and friends were often recruited to swell the sound. Eric Lowe[41] remembers Malcolm's musicality as 'exceptional', and quotes as an example their listening to a record of the popular 1930s ballad 'I Cover the Waterfront', by the Dutch trumpeter Louis de Vries. Without the use of a piano Malcolm transcribed the trumpet solo straight from the record to manuscript paper. He then played the solo himself, sounding note for note as good as de Vries.

Despite the progress he was making on his three instruments, Malcolm might well have dissipated his musical talents in exuberant basement jam sessions, had it not been for the timely appearance in Northampton of a young musician, Philip Pfaff. A twenty-two-year-old just down from Cambridge, Philip had arrived in October 1936, to become organist of St Matthew's, a church close to the Arnolds' new home, and was living just across the Racecourse in East Park Parade. He had been a choral scholar at St John's, Aubrey's college, and it was this connection which led to Malcolm having lessons with him. Philip Pfaff was always to remember his first impression of Malcolm:

---

[38] *Omnibus*, BBC TV, October 1991

[39] Fred Tomkins & Son was an important shop for the young Malcolm, situated close to Craigmore, at 71 Palmerston Road

[40] Encouraged by local industries, the area was full of brass bands. Northampton had one. So too Wellingborough and Barton. Kettering had at least three.

[41] Writing in *Beckus*, the quarterly journal of the Malcolm Arnold Society (issue 28).

He was a large, clumsy fifteen-year-old, extremely shy and self-conscious.[42]

By contrast, most reminiscences of Malcolm at this period suggest quite a different character: loud, full of fun, ebullient, the life and soul of every party. But this was always to be the façade, and here, on his first meeting with Philip Pfaff, was the real, vulnerable Malcolm. He had long nursed ambitions to be a composer, but with his lack of formal training and limited musical knowledge it seemed an unrealisable dream. As he knocked on the door at East Park Parade, he little realised that he had reached one of the turning-points in his life.

Philip Pfaff's friendly manner and youthful enthusiasm soon restored Malcolm's confidence, rekindled his ambition and made him, for the first time in his life, a model pupil. Philip was soon as excited as Malcolm:

> We arranged initially for him to have two lessons a week in the theory of music. It didn't take me long to realise I was dealing with someone absolutely extraordinary … I encouraged him to compose, but I talked a lot to him about the history of music, I talked to him about Mozart's orchestration, and I introduced him to twentieth-century developments in music – he knew absolutely nothing – the 12-note scale and things like this. He just absorbed it all. Like a sponge.[43]

Malcolm had already taught himself a certain amount. He had, for example, acquired Berlioz's book on orchestration and read most of Prout's books on counterpoint. Philip Pfaff was unconvinced by the latter and at once encouraged Malcolm to explore R O Morris's views on theory, 'in the hope that his under-developed harmony would grow'.[44] Malcolm, with no school to worry about, had huge quantities of time to devote himself to his new life as Philip Pfaff's friend and disciple, thirsting for all manner of cultural enlightenment. He was encouraged to make regular visits to the local repertory theatre, where he gained a useful knowledge of classical and contemporary drama. The dance world became another new interest, Malcolm learning about the *Ballets Russes* and visiting London to see the fledgling Sadler's Wells Ballet, where Constant Lambert was the inspirational music director.

As the weeks went by, Philip Pfaff must have marvelled at what was happening and wondered sometimes if it was all real. Did pupils usually race through the scores of Ravel and Debussy, Schoenberg and Berg with such voracity and enjoyment? Would his own beloved Stravinsky ever again spark off such a barrage of fascinating responses and questions? Did many other fifteen-year-olds get excited by Delius's *Dance* for Harpsichord or discuss with confidence the recordings Beecham made for the Delius Society? Did the book by Sharp and Vaughan Williams on *Lesser Known Folk Songs* usually elicit such interest?

Malcolm's trumpet playing, until the coming of Philip Pfaff, had been confined to chapel bands, which Pappy had encouraged him and Philip to join. In

---

[42] December 2003

[43] BBC radio programme, marking his 80th Birthday (2001)

[44] Paul Jackson, *The Life and Music of Sir Malcolm Arnold* (Ashgate 2003), p.6

January 1937 Malcolm was approached by the Chairman of The Northampton Men's Own,[45] a mission held at Doddridge Castle Hill Church, to rejoin the Men's Own Orchestra:

> I want to say how much we have missed you... and wondered whether you would consider if it is not possible for you to come back again? Your playing was such a great help to us and we have missed you very much all the Session...

After sticking the letter in his scrapbook, Malcolm wrote underneath it: 'Soft Soap From A Christian Gentleman.' He did, however, return, but this time as a soloist. In March 1937 he was greatly praised for his rendition of Brahms' Fifth *Hungarian Dance*, together with *Joyous Bird* and one of Paul Robeson's current hits, 'Trees', with Nan his accompanist. That year Malcolm joined the Northampton Symphony Orchestra, playing in several concerts at the Town Hall and enjoying Wagner's *Tannhäuser* Overture, Tchaikovsky's Fifth Symphony and Bruch's Violin Concerto.

For his sixteenth birthday Malcolm was bought a Bach D trumpet, which allowed him to be the soloist in a chamber concert featuring the Second Brandenberg Concerto,[46] organised by Philip Pfaff and given in Northampton's Carnegie Hall, a large room on the first floor of the Public Library.[47] Among the performers was the oboist Sidney Sutcliffe. The local newspaper, after an encouraging heading of A CLEVER BOY TRUMPETER, did not find Malcolm's playing wholly satisfactory:

> A striking duet between trumpet and oboe revealed some good lip work by Arnold to advantage, marred, however, by lack of attack and cloudy tone due to nervousness. This was overcome to some extent in the last work, the Septet for Trumpet, Strings and Piano by Saint-Saëns, where the forte passages displayed improvement in tone and attack.

Malcolm responded tartly in his scrapbook: 'Music criticism, written by a gentleman that cannot read music', a first small tilt at that body of professionals against whom he would shortly be jousting long and hard. But he was amused by a piece in the *Northampton Independent*, which he ironically headed in his scrapbook 'Celebrity Interview'. His enthusiasm for his new instrument is very obvious and he is certainly not lost for words:

> He laughed apologetically, and his brown eyes were a little uneasy. 'I'm afraid tonight's performance was not so good as it might have been. I could have wished the floor would swallow me up when I had to make noises on this' and he held up his Bach trumpet. 'The sensation is similar to blowing into a gas pipe, but the tone produced by its length is necessary for Bach's music. The instrument is naturally more difficult to play without valves than with, and possessing some technical knowledge

---

[45] George Webb, 20 January 1937
[46] 28 October 1937
[47] The Carnegie Hall still exists, as part of the reference library, but the stage on which Malcolm played has been removed.

of the trumpet I am amazed at the technical feats of the trumpeters of Bach's day, who obtained all their notes by lip pressure. On occasions they were even able to produce half-tones! But in the early orchestras to play one part it was very often necessary to have two trumpeters, one to take the higher register and one in the lower.'

Malcolm's trumpet playing was flourishing. In a Trinity College grade exam (Senior Division), which he took in July 1937, he scored a remarkable 98%. The examiner commented:

> Most artistic and technically excellent work. Intonation and expression excellent. Gifted musically and technically, the player should certainly go on <u>to much higher things</u>.[48]

Trinity College gave him an Exhibition, and Philip Pfaff in November 1937 persuaded the Arnolds to use it for trumpet lessons in London, contacting Ernest Hall, then the principal trumpet of the BBC Symphony Orchestra and Professor of Trumpet at the Royal College of Music.[49] Malcolm was soon visiting Hanover Street for private lessons with Ernest Hall, and it was not long before he was producing an altogether fuller and richer sound. By February 1938 Malcolm had taken a further public exam, Hall enclosing the certificate to Nan with an enigmatic comment which suggests Malcolm had not quite done himself justice:

> He plays very well and I trust he will gain more self-confidence as time goes on, as it is such a drawback these days.

He included entry forms for the Royal College of Music Open Scholarship.

Concentration on the trumpet did not prevent Malcolm from taking tentative steps towards composition. His first known work dates to about a year before Philip Pfaff's arrival. Inspired by newsreel footage of the dignified bearing of the Ethiopian Emperor Haile Selassie arriving in exile in London, the fourteen-year-old Malcolm composed a *Haile Selassie March* for piano solo. In 1935 Ethiopia had been invaded and annexed by Mussolini, and Selassie's plight, as a victim of fascist aggression, appealed to Malcolm's natural sympathy for the underdog. He was pleased enough with the march, which unfortunately has since been lost, to send it to Boosey & Hawkes. It was their printed card of acknowledgement which had inspired him to begin a scrapbook of his musical endeavours:

> We beg to acknowledge with thanks receipt of your manuscript which shall have our most careful consideration.[50]

And underneath, on the first page of the scrapbook, he stuck in – with what feelings we can only imagine – its successor:

---

[48] Dr Henry Coleman of Peterborough Cathedral
[49] 'I could give your pupil a lesson on Tuesday next,' wrote Hall to Pfaff, '23rd Nov. at Weekes Studios Hanover Street. Top of Regent St at 6.15 p.m. I think I told you that my terms are £1-1-0 per lesson …'
[50] 12 August 1936

*Ruth, setting fashions
in Northampton
in the late 1920s*

Messrs. Boosey & Hawkes Ltd. regret that they are unable to make use of the accompanying Manuscript which they beg to return to Mr Arnold with best thanks for his offer.[51]

Around this time Nan created a music room for Malcolm in the Craigmore attic, and he made the most of this, for four piano works survive from 1937, the period of Pfaff's influence, giving us a fascinating insight into Malcolm's compositional skills at the age of fifteen. The earliest work, *Theme and Three Variations*,[52] demonstrates a solid grasp of harmony and a flair and interest in contrapuntal writing,[53] something which was to become extremely important in Malcolm's future work. The *Allegro in E Minor*[54] owes much to Bach's famous prelude in C Major, though there are some hints of originality.[55] The *Three Piano*

---

[51] 8 September 1936

[52] 20 January 1937

[53] As the four-part writing in the Fugato shows

[54] 13 February 1937

[55] The familiar division of notes between the hands and the predominantly two bar phrases are openly imitated. There are, however, two curious, almost bi-tonal, bars towards the end. (In bar 19 a chord of C major in the left hand accompanies a broken chord of A minor in the right; similarly in bar 20, where the same A minor right hand is now set against a chord of E minor.) Yet when Malcolm rewrote this Allegro for Pfaff just two days later (as the Prelude to the *Three Piano Pieces*) the clashes disappeared. The tutor, it seems, was of a more conventional mind than the pupil.

*Pieces* show similar technical competence, the Gigue [56] being another spirited attempt at contrapuntal writing. But six months later, when Malcolm was still only fifteen, comes a much more arresting work, the *Serenade in G*, the first of several piano pieces to be dedicated to his mother on her birthday.[57] The writing has developed in confidence and style, expressing its reflective mood most colourfully.[58] When he heard this strongly atmospheric work, Philip Pfaff knew that his young pupil was specially gifted.

Pfaff was to work with Malcolm for not much more than a year,[59] but it was thanks to all that he had done that Malcolm was ready to take the Scholarship to the Royal College of Music four months before his seventeenth birthday. The exam was another crucial moment in Malcolm's life, but as he walked along the streets of Kensington clutching his trumpet case and talking inconsequentially to Nan, he felt excitement rather than nerves. He had played, after all, in the Northampton Town Hall and Public Library as well as in many a Primitive Methodist Chapel. He had played in the White Elephant, too, where the attention span of listeners was none too predictable. He was not going to be overawed by the Royal College of Music. At 2 pm, the appointed time, he was in Room 32 and master of all he surveyed. He felt a strange exhilaration, a confidence that nothing could go wrong, that he was indeed the finest pupil Ernest Hall had ever had, and, to his mother's tender accompaniment, he played quite beautifully. The scholarship was never in doubt[60] and the very next morning Ernest Hall sent a delighted telegram of congratulations. A few weeks later Nan heard from Edmund Rubbra, whose mother still lived in Northampton:

> May I congratulate him and you. It is really splendid. He could not go to a better place than the RCM and he will find life there very exciting.[61]

That summer, while waiting to go up to college, Malcolm wrote his first songs, a cycle of nine which he called *Kensington Gardens*. For his text he followed the example of Holst and chose the poet Humbert Wolfe, taking six poems from Wolfe's *Kensington Gardens* and three from his *Humoresque*.[62]

---

[56] Including two sets of fugal entries in four parts, the short twenty-one bar piece is lively and effective.

[57] Inscribed rather formally, 'To mother, love from Malcolm', 3 October 1937

[58] Chromatic and seventh chords abound, and the writing, although perhaps still a little awkward, has a greater sophistication.

[59] Approximately from January 1937 to the spring of 1938

[60] For Philip Pfaff it was a double triumph, for another of his pupils, viola player Evelyn Panter who lived close by to Malcolm in Northampton, won another of the twelve scholarships on offer in 1938.

[61] 7 July 1938

[62] Ruth would have been behind the choice of poems, for Wolfe was a favourite poet. She loved his busy rhymes and insouciant wit. In *The Chestnut and the Beech Tree*, for example, the two trees look down on the office workers passing below them in the park and bemoan the fact that hair styles are not what they were.

Malcolm's response to Wolfe's verses is mature and lyrical,[63] the piano writing is sympathetic and the work shows a real feeling for the English song school. *Kensington Gardens* represented a major step forward for the sixteen-year-old.

The Arnold family, meanwhile, was fast splitting up. By the summer of 1938, when Malcolm began thinking of his future life as a student in London, all three of his brothers had left home. The serious-minded Aubrey was now thirty, working for Grandfather William and living in Kenton with his wife Wyn (a former dancer and Tiller Girl), his step-daughter Antoinette and son Robin. The handsome Clifford, now in his early twenties, had gone into the merchant navy and would reappear in Northampton from time to time loaded with exotic gifts from distant parts. His parents noted uneasily, however, that he was trying to get through life on charm, drinking heavily and showing every sign of misusing his abilities. The practical Philip was more encouraging. Still Pappy's hope for the future of Arnold Brothers, he had spent over six months in Germany, studying methods of leather boot manufacture and learning the language. His experiences of Nazi Berlin, however, had convinced him of the inevitability of war and on his return, at the age of eighteen, he had joined the Royal Air Force Voluntary Reserve to train as a pilot.

Malcolm and Ruth were the two survivors at Craigmore, Ruth now in her late twenties and with a chapter of disasters behind her which had alienated her from Pappy and caused Nan great worry. Ruth, like Malcolm, suffered from manic-depressive illness, which resulted in periods of deep gloom and frustration and also impressive creativity in art and poetry. As a young girl she had been sent to a boarding school far away in Kent,[64] which proved a traumatic experience; like Malcolm, at only sixteen, she had won a scholarship, in her case to the Slade School of Art, where things, alas, eventually went wrong.[65] The Slade has always had a reputation for unconventional high spirits, and when Ruth cavorted on a carnival float, scantily dressed, with two almost nude black men, she was only doing what an Iris Tree or a Nancy Cunard might have done. The Slade authorities, however, seemed to have lost their sense of humour on this occasion and expelled her, with predictably dour repercussions at Craigmore.

As Pappy was intensely concerned about what other people thought of him, he reacted very unfavourably to Ruth's blithe contempt for boring middle-class convention; she was a feminist in a male chauvinist world, and sometimes, as Robin has pointed out, her frustrations upset the delicate balance of her emotional stability:

> Ruth was beginning to prove something of a nightmare to her parents. She was found naked in a local church and was found behaving irrationally in other areas. She went

---

[63] As Richard Shaw has pointed out: *Malcolm Arnold: Songs and Arias* (Novello 2004).

[64] Ruth Parker Gray's School, Broadstairs

[65] She was the youngest ever student to gain a scholarship at the Slade.

into hospitals from time to time and had electric shock therapy. It was all highly distressing, for she was such a talented artist.[66]

Ruth craved love and understanding, but her realistic ambitions as a poet and artist were severely blunted by parental cynicism. After certain bad moments she was even sent off to a convent in Belgium,[67] which only intensified her distrust of organised religion and increased her feelings of alienation. This extreme measure may have given Pappy temporary respite from worry about keeping up appearances, but it was hardly in Ruth's best interests.

In Malcolm alone Ruth found total understanding, and her sufferings bound them even closer together as he grew to maturity. He read Ruth's poetry with care and admiration. One poem[68] in particular he loved and, when in contemplative rather than boisterous mood, he sympathised deeply with his sister's darker thoughts:

> I'll take me solemnly to where
> The hills rise pale against the sky,
> And where the magpie pipes his tune,
> His roundelay – 'tis there I'll die.
>
> The snow will bring her offering,
> A moonbeam of a downy dress,
> And that will be my only shroud
> Of bitterness.
>
> And p'raps a twinkling star will fall
> To light the grasses where I lie -
> My lonely heart beats not at all,
> I care for nothing – no, not I.
>
> And if a witch there passing near
> Should spy me, both her eyes aflood
> With thoughts of wicked deeds, my dear,
> And my heart's blood,
>
> And should she clench her bony hands,
> And smoke her cauldron to the sky,
> And weave a magic charm around –
> I'll know not of it – no, not I.

Malcolm, therefore, was the unwitting beneficiary of Ruth's problems, for in the years of his adolescence when he was not at school she was often on hand to introduce him to the pleasures of art, history and literature. Under her influence he grew to know the full range of English poetry, some of his particular favourites including Shelley's 'When the lamp is shattered', Suckling's 'Why so

---

[66] April 2004

[67] One of her stays at the Convent Sœurs Norbertines, Duffel, was in 1936, when Malcolm was fourteen.

[68] *Envoi*, written in 1929

pale and wan, fair lover?', Herrick's 'To Anthea' and Robert Bridges' 'I will not let thee go'. Thomas Hood's 'Ruth', of course, was another favourite ...

Ruth's enthusiasm for the arts was an inspiration. To her Malcolm owed his lifelong love of books and a depth of knowledge which quite transcended his total lack of secondary schooling. He also enjoyed the benefit of Ruth's compassionate perspective on life. He shared her fervent pacifism. He learnt to value minorities. Later on, even at the height of his worldly success, he still ordered the *Daily Worker*.

An interesting cartoon, drawn by Malcolm in 1936, shortly before the abdication of Edward VIII, shows the strong influence of his sister. She loved puncturing the foibles of humanity by witty cartoons and, inspired by this, Malcolm attempted a sardonic comment on growing totalitarian militarism and (as they both believed) the English people's determination to have nothing to do with the current war-mongering. First he depicts in three different drawings huge public enthusiasm generated by three dictators: 'Mussolini reviewing his troops in Rome' – 'Hitler opening a new building in Berlin' – 'Stalin looking over a new factory in Moscow.' And beneath is a fourth drawing: a tiny figure in a completely deserted shipyard with the laconic caption, 'King Edward inspects a new ship at Clydebank (good old Ted). He received a grand welcome.'

In the summer of 1938, as Malcolm prepared to become a student in London and war loomed ever closer, Ruth made a book of poems with the theme of music as a present for the younger brother she loved and admired. *The Pleasures of*

*Music* not only displayed her skills as calligrapher and artist, but also her wide knowledge of English poetry. It was a token of what their relationship had meant to her. The poems she included of her own were particularly precious to both of them. 'The Music that you Saw', written after a period of illness, combines many things brother and sister shared: frequent pain of illness; constant joy in music; and a fragile hope in, if not God, at least a spirit of goodness and wisdom looking after the world.

> The music that you saw within my eyes
> Was dulled for one brief moment.
> Now it springs, happy to live again,
> For I am wise, with pain and joy made holy.
> Earthly things, they capture me.
>
> Am I not part of God's desire?
> Look into my soul. Reach out to me.
> And touch me with your heart.
> For you are by me as
> I see the goal I strive for.
> Bless my hands and blend my eyes
> With those deep pools of wisdom.
>
> All is mine! The freedom I have gained,
> The sacred ties are living melodies
> Of thee and thine.

Ruth's poetry has much in common with Malcolm's music. It comes from the heart. She has an urgent need to set it down. What she has to say may be misunderstood or cause embarrassment, but say it she must. She follows an old tradition, but not slavishly. She breaks with the rule book when the mood invites her to. All that matters is to pour out her thoughts, her anguish and her joy. Communication is all. Her poetry never achieved a public, for circumstances impeded her talent. Yet in a way it does live on. For all the questions she wanted to ask, all the worries she wanted to explore, all the myths she wanted to explode, and all the beauties she wished to share are there in her brother's music. His are 'the living melodies' of which she dreamed.

That Ruth's restlessly creative spirit was the dominant force in Malcolm's adolescence serves to emphasise the essential instability of his early years. Superficially his family background was secure. His parents were well-off and respected. Upper middle-class life in St George's Avenue, Northampton, was distinctly comfortable. Materially he lacked nothing. But emotionally his background was less settled. 'I never remember any hugging or kissing within the family,' comments his niece, Penny.[72] The warm central hub of the family was, by default, the devoted servant, Lizzie Witts. His education, too, had been completely mishandled. Days when his contemporaries would have all been at

---

[72] October 2003

school were spent wandering aimlessly around the town. Philip Pfaff remembers that Malcolm would spend hours each week in Griffin's music shop,[73] close to Pappy's factory, browsing through score after score. He needed the support of a school, learning how to get on with other people. Instead, he was learning in his solitariness to be self-preoccupied. And despite having more freedom than most children ever have, he felt more repressed, hedged in by the uncompromisingly authoritarian figure of Pappy. His father might be able to hold Malcolm in check for the moment. But the harsher Pappy became in his efforts to extract conformity to his own ideals, the more explosive would be the reaction when Malcolm was finally free of paternal oppression.

---

[73] Percy Griffin's was in Cowper Street.

*Malcolm and Nan outside Craigmore around the time he won his
scholarship to the RCM*

# 3
# Master of the Revels

## The Royal College of Music, 1938-41

ALTHOUGH NAN was anxious at saying goodbye to Malcolm in London, she kept her misgivings to herself on the journey home. The last few weeks in Northampton had been particularly difficult and she had struggled to hide it all from Pappy. There was no point in worrying him with the thought that perhaps Malcolm was going the way of Clifford. He was not yet seventeen but already drinking regularly and sometimes to excess, hanging out in the pubs all hours. There was an emotional volatility about him reminiscent of Ruth and his father. He quickly spent every penny of his allowance and then came back to her for more. Lots of girls seemed to be hanging around in the background, and she was surprised, even shocked at his manner of speaking about them. There was also the worry of how he would react to the discipline of college life, having found school so difficult. Perhaps she may have been a little too indulgent? Nan's boundless pride in Malcolm was now matched by her anxiety. And it was an anxious enough world already. Although the Prime Minister, Neville Chamberlain, had just come back from Munich waving that precious piece of paper, Nan found herself detached from the growing mood of optimism. With Malcolm let loose in London at the age of sixteen, 'peace in our time' seemed a remote possibility.

Malcolm, in London and claiming to be eighteen, could not believe his good luck, to be surrounded by other young people with a similar passion for music and full of determination to enjoy themselves before their world fragmented in war. He began noisily and expensively making his mark. Pauline Rawdon-Smith, a fellow student at the College, remembers being part of a weekly pub-crawl led by Malcolm, starting at South Kensington and reaching Piccadilly via Knightsbridge and Marble Arch.[1]

> As one pub closed so we would move on to the next. The drink would usually be champagne. We all quickly recognised Malcolm's brilliance as a musician, but he was eccentric almost to the point of insanity.[2]

---

[1] The group usually included William Blezard, Ivor Slaney, Richard Adeney, Livia Gollancz and Edward Warren.
[2] Pauline Marshall, October 2003

His ebullience was infectious. Another fellow student, flautist Richard Adeney, revelled in a new-found confidence inspired by Malcolm:

> He was full of jokes and jollity and the most daring and extrovert person I'd ever met … We were always laughing, arguing hotly, gossiping and wandering around London looking at the sights and talking to strangers in pubs. With him everything was a light-hearted joke.[3]

Another student, Judy Hill, remembers going out for meals with Malcolm and other friends, after which, like a busker, he would entertain the queues outside the Albert Hall. 'Take a Pair of Sparkling Eyes' was his favourite and usually brought in useful beer money.

Malcolm expected everyone to follow his outrageous example and mocked the faint-hearted. Only he had the audacity to play jazz on Vaughan Williams's piano in the great man's study; only he dared mimic the unpopular College Registrar, Hugo Anson,[4] turning a corner abruptly in one right-angular movement; only he would attempt to tie fellow students to the railings outside the girls' quarters; only he (so it was said) dropped fish down the pipes of the College's Great Hall organ. He would produce his trumpet with a radiant grin at the most inopportune times and places. Many a sleepy voice cried out 'Enough!' after a public fanfare in the early dawn.

Undeterred by any rebuff, the pied piper continued on his compulsive way, leading the revels, buying the drinks, paying the taxis, exulting in 'the glamour of drunkenness'[5] and preaching a gospel of 'the supremacy of youth'. He intended, he said, to live not a moment beyond thirty. Few of his friends realised that he really meant it. For them it was just a brief, hectic binge. They would all sober up later. For Malcolm, however, growing notoriety was itself a form of intoxication. Here was a possible way of life. This was better than standing out in the rain at Eaglehurst. At last people were taking notice of him.

By seventeen Malcolm had shed his earlier chubbiness. Dark and handsome, he was attractive to the girls, even though, when walking, he had something of an old man's slouch, head forward, shoulders hunched, feet distinctively splayed out.[6] His girlfriends were much envied, for his sexual prowess was rapidly achieving legendary status at the College. But with Malcolm, who was so innately creative, facts and fantasy were often intermingled. When he held forth on the latest gossip, it was hard to know what to believe, as Richard Adeney mused:

> Was it *really* true that the fat, jolly soprano paid the handsome New Zealand violin student for sex? Did the pallid girl who played the viola *really* sell her body on the

---

[3] Richard Adeney's unpublished autobiography, *Flute*
[4] The nature of Anson's job opened him up to unpopularity. It was he, for example, who sought out Malcolm when he missed a piano exam. (July 1939)
[5] Richard Adeney, *Flute*
[6] *Ibid.*
[7] *Ibid.*

streets? Had Malcolm *really* been to bed with so many of the girl students? And had he *really* been caught by the police having sex in Hyde Park in full daylight? [7]

There was general agreement, however, that Malcolm had seduced a girl in the Great Hall organ loft while a college orchestra rehearsed below.

Malcolm's vivid, frantic socialising was reflected in his busy musical life and he would turn down few invitations. He was happy to be first trumpet at Glyndebourne, for a performance of *Macbeth*, and third trumpet at the St John's School, Leatherhead summer concert. He appeared at the West London Synagogue,[8] Borough Polytechnic, [9] Victoria and Albert Museum,[10] St Pancras Town Hall,[11] and Goldsmiths' College, where he played in *The Canterbury Pilgrims*, one of the most important works by the College's Principal, George Dyson. That Malcolm was motivated in these travels rather more by the money he earned than the experience gained is suggested by a note penned on the programme while he was playing with the Horsham Orchestral Society:

> Dear Mother and Dad,
>
> Thanks for letter. Sorry I haven't written – but I'm playing in this instead of Woodage who is playing in the London Philharmonic. I'm writing this in the middle of the Mendelssohn Violin Concerto. With love from Malcolm.
>
> PS I'm getting 25/- for it.

Malcolm was much more industrious in College than he would let others believe, responding well to teachers as good as Ernest Hall. The large, bluff Cockney, his trumpet teacher for the past three years, looked on him as an important protégé. 'Very good work,' he was to report.[12] 'A very keen and promising pupil.'

Piano studies were with the equally sympathetic J Hurst Bannister. 'He worked excellently,' reported Bannister, 'but needs much more self-confidence. He always prepares a lot of work and does it well.'

Under Bannister Malcolm made quick improvements, but he spent most of his spare time playing in a more popular style. Neville Marriner, as a fellow student, heard more of him as a jazz pianist than trumpet player. Malcolm also relished some conducting classes under Constant Lambert and it was not long before he was furthering his education in some of Lambert's favourite pubs. Malcolm played in a dozen College concerts in his first year, with Lambert,[13] Sargent and Reginald Jacques among the conductors. Student conductors included Norman del Mar. Malcolm was delighted to be on percussion in a College production of Vaughan Williams's *Sir John In Love*, and even more

---

[8] With the West London Amateur Orchestra
[9] In Stanford's opera *The Travelling Companion*
[10] With the Purley Philharmonic
[11] With the Ernest Read Symphony Orchestra
[12] From the RCM's Christmas Term's Report, 1938
[13] Under Lambert he played in some rarely performed works, such as Balakireff's First Symphony and Dohnanyi's *Cello Konzertstück*.

gleeful to be on the cymbals when Malcolm Sargent was conducting Verdi and Rachmaninoff.

Early on in his time at College Malcolm wrote a piano piece, *Day Dreams*, which he dedicated to Nan on her birthday.[14] It is one of his very best early works, showing in its contrapuntal textures and harmonic language strong indications of a developing voice. Ranging confidently between extremes of mood, it has a strong blues influence, many of its harmonies smacking of the fashionable nightclubs and pianists like 'Hutch' and Turner Layton.[15] The delighted Nan played it over and over on the grand piano in the Craigmore front parlour.

That the excellent *Day Dreams* was not followed by a series of similarly bold enterprises reflects Malcolm's problems with his first composition teacher, Patrick Hadley. A composer of attractive choral music in the tradition of his friend Vaughan Williams, Hadley had suffered the misfortune to lose a leg in the First World War,[16] so he had little time for students, barely out of their cradle, who paraded their pacifist views. He did not take to Malcolm, who found him frightening, and it did not help that their weekly meetings took place at 10.25 in the morning, when neither was at his best. At the end of their first term together Hadley wrote that Malcolm was 'far too diffident for one of his natural talents', but suggested that, when diffidence was overcome, he 'should go right ahead' as he was 'decidedly musical'. He was similarly positive at the end of the second term, calling him a 'good musician' and 'a steady worker' who 'occasionally shows real flights of imagination'.

During this term Malcolm had felt confident enough to show Hadley his song cycle, *Kensington Gardens*, on which his tutor pencilled some interested, if conventional, responses.[17] Malcolm, suitably encouraged, then showed Hadley another song he had written just before arriving in London,[18] his setting of a poem of Ruth's:

> Beauty haunts the woods at night.
> O woods of stillness and delight,
> Of things that love thee only I
> Have wished to rest there when I die.
>
> Beauty and I go hand in hand
> Through this green foliate fairyland.
> And when I wither this I crave
> That Pan will pipe upon my grave.

---

[14] 3 October 1938

[15] It belongs to the same world as the earlier *Serenade*, but this time the late-night club atmosphere is perfectly caught.

[16] Many of his later students remembered how, if they had the first of his morning's tutorials, their duty was to fix on his artificial limb.

[17] Richard Shaw (*Malcolm Arnold: Songs and Arias*, Novello 2004) has identified the marks on the manuscript as Hadley's.

[18] July 1938 is the most likely date.

It was a poem going back deep into Malcolm's childhood; something important which he and Ruth had once shared. He loved the striking juxtaposition of seeming opposites, beauty and death, and the sudden shock of 'I die' and 'I wither', breaking up what was a traditional pastoral ode. In his music he would often pursue the same thought process, the creation of an idyllic world and its speedy demolition only moments later. Pan, too, was very much *their* god, an impish, unconventional deity, piping his cheerful little ditties throughout eternity, so much more fun to have around than Jove or Pluto. Two of Malcolm's favourite instruments were the piccolo and flute, first cousins of Pan's pipes.

Malcolm's 'Beauty Haunts the Woods' is an attractive if unsophisticated song, capturing the poem's mood well. Hadley, however, could see nothing good in either the poem or its setting.

> Another bloody awful song! Why not write a trumpet piece? Aren't you meant to be quite good with the bloody trumpet?

Malcolm bridled. 'No, thank you! If you want something different I'll write you a bloody violin sonata!'[19] And off he stormed, straight into the Principal's office, to demand and be given a change of tutor. George Dyson knew all about Malcolm's promise and had already decided that next term he should have the very best composition tutor, Gordon Jacob.

Dyson was not particularly popular with most of the students. 'He was ice-cold,' remembers Phyllis Hunt, 'with the most piercing blue eyes imaginable. Cold as charity!' He was especially ridiculed by the pacifist majority of students for the pamphlet he had produced on the hand grenade in the First World War which had become the standard Army manual on the subject.

But Dyson was not at all as his students depicted him.[20] Having fought in the Great War and been invalided out with shell shock, he had weighed long and hard his position on Nazi Germany. It was much to his credit that at the beginning of the summer term of 1939, only weeks away from the declaration of war, he gathered all his students together to discuss the issues. He gave a calm, reasoned exposition, but concluded with questions he did not see as open-ended:

> Are we to be moved to what may be a truly righteous indignation? Can we stand by, cool and detached, while wrongs remain unrighted, however uncouthly that wrong may express itself? Is it possible to permit an evil to exist without condoning it? That is the dilemma which faces the peacemaker, whether it be a man or a nation …[21]

Malcolm, still smouldering from Hadley's insensitivity, was outraged at this view and decided to give up college in protest. It was just a question of where to

---

[19] The incident is mentioned in a BBC Norfolk interview, 1991. Malcolm did write the violin sonata over the summer holidays, but it has since been lost.

[20] Christopher Palmer in *George Dyson: A Centenary Appreciation* (1984) describes him as a 'man of peace and goodwill'.

[21] *Ibid.*

go. Northampton was hardly an option, so he headed down to the West Country, leaving behind him a letter which rudely told Dyson of the failings of his teaching staff and precisely what he could do with the scholarship. He chose Plymouth, he explained later, as 'it seemed to me a romantic place', and, this being so, he of course needed female company. He therefore took with him a beautiful red-haired Welsh girl, Eryl, who, prior to being propositioned by Malcolm, had been studying at the nearby Royal College of Art. Inspired by her charms and depressed by what he saw as lack of progress at College, Malcolm now decided he would have nothing more to do with music. Instead, he would lead the life of an artisan.

Nature, alas, had not equipped him for this kind of work. He had the greatest difficulty in knocking a nail into a piece of wood, so he was soon forced to return to the art he had rejected, playing the trumpet. As a member of the Paramount Orchestra, the seventeen-year-old could not believe his luck, for the Paramount Dance Hall was in Union Street, the pulsating heart of Plymouth, awash with sailors and good-time girls. Everyone agreed that this was the liveliest dive in town.[22]

There was consternation at Craigmore when the College rang up to say that he had gone missing. Did the family perhaps know where he was? They didn't. A week went by, and then another, and there was still no sign of him. Malcolm and Eryl had disappeared off the face of the earth. The happy couple meanwhile were enjoying themselves enormously, glorying in the summer weather on daytime excursions to beauty spots like Polperro and making a fine collection of beer-mats. Eventually Pappy and Nan put private detectives on the case – this was, after all, the age of Raymond Chandler's Philip Marlowe – and great was the relief when Malcolm's whereabouts were discovered. Nan sensibly took Ruth with her as she travelled down to confront him in a rented room at Monkley Grange, Plymouth. 'I explained to my mother that we slept tip-to-toe in the bed,' Malcolm said later.[23] 'Of course, she did not believe me.'

They had been away a month[24] and the escapade had made headline news in some of the national papers. The admirable George Dyson, however, instead of taking offence, tersely implored him to return:

Dear Malcolm, You have a brilliant future. Please come back.

Malcolm did so, and, finding the increased attention he now generated from students and staff not wholly displeasing, he quickly settled down as if nothing unusual had happened. He was delighted to find the preparations for war offered new opportunities for merriment. He was soon music-making in the air-raid shelter in Kensington Gardens, often with Livia Gollancz,[25] who played the

---

[22] 'Special summer time dances,' ran a local advertisement of the period, 'every evening at the Paramount (opposite the Gaumont) at 8.00 pm; 6d and 9d. Special King's Birthday dance. Paramount Orchestra. The best in the west.'

[23] *Music & Musicians*, October 1986

[24] From 6 May to 6 June 1939

[25] The daughter of the publisher and founder of the Left Book Club

French horn. They would also practise with vigour in the military trenches in Hyde Park, until chased away by the soldiers. But his tutors were happy enough with his progress.

'Everything OK now,' reported Ernest Hall reassuringly at the end of the term. 'Excellent work and progress,' agreed J Hurst Bannister. 'He has ideas,' wrote Gordon Jacob. 'His work shows considerable imagination.'

That summer a calmer Malcolm joined his family for their second holiday at Llandudno in 1939. At Easter he had played with the Pier Orchestra in a Paul Robeson concert,[26] but such pleasures seemed far away in the current political crisis. With Hitler now threatening Poland, there was a growing acceptance that war was inevitable, and both Malcolm and Ruth were distraught at the prospect. There was further conflict in the family over Ruth's declared intention to marry someone her parents thought socially beneath her. They were highly disappointed that Ruth should have chosen the son of a blacksmith, who lived in a small terraced council house and was training as a barber. But they also believed, with some justification, that the couple were not intellectually compatible. Ruth could only see the class prejudice, and feelings were bitter at Llandudno.

Malcolm and Ruth both found respite in creativity. Malcolm was engaged on the five-part song settings of two Ernest Dowson poems,[27] the second containing Horace's famous *Vitae summa brevis spem nos vetat incohare longam* ('Experience of life teaches us not to entertain hopes for the future that are overlong'), sentiments which would have particularly attracted someone not planning to live beyond thirty.[28] It was Ruth who had introduced Malcolm two years earlier to Dowson's poems and both were attracted by the world-weariness which pervades them.

Ruth was working on a poem called 'Dream World', whose imagery had a flavour of Dowson, *The Yellow Book* and Aubrey Beardsley. Its opening lines comment graphically on the peace and beauty in the world which war would shortly shatter:

> There were pools, full of stars
> Where slim maidens bathed white feet by the moonlight.
> And hair was a long and never-ending poem,
> Dark with dusk and hung with hibiscus flowers.
> Eyes were keen and eager
> And there was no sin, because the world was young.
> For sin was a beggar at the doors

---

[26] He played in seven concerts with John Morava's Pier Orchestra (7-10 April) as well as the special Robeson concert (7 April). Robeson, coming to the end of a four-month tour of Britain, was a highly popular recording star, the concert programme advertising fifty of his records currently available.

[27] Delius had set both of these poems to music (*Songs of Sunset*) and Malcolm's handling reflects his influence.

[28] Horace, Odes I:4. Dowson himself died aged 33.

> Knocking in vain for charity;
> And sin was a creeping reptile,
> Waiting to dart a tongue of flame
> To burn into the freshness of youth;
> And sin was an aged woman, shaking with envy
> For the past to be reborn into her.
> And the future bent down
> And beckoned her in …

Ruth's feelings in this poem may well have been mirrored in a further work Malcolm produced that summer of 1939, a *Rhapsody for Piano*, as another present for his mother. Speculation, however, is idle, for the work has been lost.

War was declared on 3 September. Life might have continued in Britain without much obvious change, in the first instance, but for the Arnolds there was a speedy family fragmentation, hardening existing differences. As pacifists Malcolm and Ruth found themselves strangely at odds with their brothers, for Aubrey at once volunteered for the Army, Clifford for the Navy, while Philip was already training in the RAF. Pappy, unable to resist the opportunity for a little self-advertisement, spoke proudly to the local newspapers of the Arnolds representing all three Services. Three days before the declaration of war Malcolm himself, perhaps feeling the pressure at home, wrote to the recruiting officer at Northampton offering his services in the Royal Navy and Royal Marines Band.

Ernest Hall, called away from the College to play for the BBC Symphony Orchestra, wrote encouragingly to Malcolm:

Dear Arnold,

Many thanks for your letter. I was very interested to read its contents about joining the Marines. I should think they would be only too pleased to have you. You could write to Captain V Dunn of the Plymouth Division Royal Marine Band and mention my name, but I am afraid he would not let you go after War is over. That is the difficulty.

Your playing in the Variety Theatre in Northampton would do you a lot of good. It's the finest experience any young player can get. I had seventeen months of it before I was your age …[29]

Hall had forgotten Malcolm's youth. At an interview shortly afterwards Malcolm was told that, at seventeen, he was too young and should reapply later. It was back to College, therefore, for the start of his second year, but there were compensations. He was sharing a flat with his good friend Wesley Woodage, had several lucrative engagements with the Rudolph Dolmetsch Orchestra[30] and

---

[29] 6 October 1939
[30] He earned £8 11s 0d for a couple of concerts (2 October and 7 December 1939), at a time when a new Austin Seven cost only £107. He played with Dolmetsch again in March 1940, as did Eric Bravington and Livia Gollancz. Another friend, Olive Zorian, was the orchestra's leader. Later in the war Dolmetsch was to die when his ship was torpedoed.

would continue his composition studies with the calm and encouraging Gordon Jacob.

Jacob proved as sympathetic as Hadley had been combative. 'We could joke, we could chat. I enjoyed my lessons with him,' recalled Malcolm.[31] His pacifist views also found some sympathy with his new tutor. Jacob had lost a brother in the First World War and he himself spent many years as a prisoner in Germany, as one of the few survivors from a unit destroyed on the Somme.

Ballet was another, less inflammatory, topic of mutual interest. A few years earlier Gordon Jacob had collaborated with Constant Lambert over the orchestration of arrangements of Liszt for Ashton's *Apparitions*. Now, in 1940, he and Malcolm discussed a fresh orchestration Lambert was doing for Ashton, Liszt's *Dante Sonata*.

Malcolm would always speak most highly of the help Jacob gave to him:

> Composition with Gordon Jacob was marvellous. He let you do free work and would criticise it very thoroughly but in a way that encouraged you. He was very kind and very efficient.[32]

Jacob was forward-looking, at pains in his own compositions to avoid the lush romanticism of his elders. He believed that however much a composer might admire the work of his predecessors and contemporaries, he should not imitate their styles but, rather, strive 'to come near to their spirit of adventure and independence of thought in his own work'.[33] It was something Malcolm very much took to heart. He also learnt much from the careful craftsmanship of Jacob's own works. But he saw that, for all their subtlety and neatness, they were inhibited by a lack of emotion. That was something else for him to ponder.

Christmas 1939 was celebrated in Northampton with a somewhat fevered festivity. It was Ruth's first Christmas since she had become Mrs Charles Dickens, the pair living in a rented bungalow not far from the disapproving family at Craigmore. Aubrey believed that Charles Dickens (or 'Wag' as he was called) was being used by Ruth to upset Pappy and what she saw as his middle-class hypocrisies. Wag was not going to impress those Pappy wanted to impress, as, apart from his humble origins, he was sometimes unkempt and, having suffered from polio as a child, had a bad limp which precluded him from military service. Wag had always been a good friend of Malcolm's, went fishing with him and, as a useful clarinettist, had sometimes joined in the Craigmore jazz sessions. Wag's elder brother, Harry, who was a good trumpet player and a friend of Malcolm's early teacher, Frank Burton, had taken an avuncular interest in his exploits. So Malcolm enjoyed some lively dance music that Christmas at Ruth's bungalow. Both his brother Philip and Harry Dickens were home on leave, and,

---

[31] Radio Norfolk interview, October 1991
[32] *Music & Musicians*, October 1986
[33] Jacob: *Orchestral Technique* (Oxford 1931), a book all RCM students of this period would have known well. Malcolm called it 'a magnificent mine of information'.

with other family and friends crammed in and the barrel of beer on the kitchen table being emptied with rapidity, they recreated something of the carefree, pre-war jam sessions in the Craigmore basement.

Malcolm as a trumpet player was living two distinct lives, at Christmas imitating Satchmo with the Ruth Dickens Hot Seven, and, back at College, playing the Stravinsky Octet under Gordon Jacob. A great admirer of Stravinsky's orchestration, Gordon Jacob conducted two College performances of the Octet in the Spring Term of 1940, which inspired Malcolm to make a start on his own *Suite for Wind Octet*, using exactly the same instrumentation as Stravinsky.[34] Only thirty-one bars of the first movement[35] remain of the orchestrated version, but a piano duet arrangement of the complete movement does survive.[36] Stylistically, Malcolm's Octet is steeped in the jazz-orientated world of Constant Lambert. Emotionally, it expresses outrage at the onset of war. The middle section, with its aggressive chords and heavily accented melodic lines,[37] is an angry response to the world around him.

With the 'phoney war' still on and the fall of Belgium and France only weeks away, the Arnolds again spent Easter in North Wales. Nan took this break at Llandudno as an opportunity to acquire a cottage in Capel Garmon, a remote village near Llanrwst, where her sister, Aunt Bess, already had a small holiday home. The strain of coping with Pappy and her children was telling on Nan, who was smoking heavily and needing time by herself to unwind.

Nan was pleased that Malcolm was again playing for John Morava's Orchestra at the end of the pier, she and Pappy happily joining other holiday-makers in deckchairs, listening to medleys from Edwardian shows like *The Merry Widow* and *The Arcadians*. On Easter Monday Malcolm had a moment of glory with a trumpet solo, Reginald King's 'Song of Paradise'. Patriotic songs inevitably abounded. George Baker's stern rendering of 'There'll always be an England' and 'Plymouth Ho' were enthusiastically encored and Elgar's *Pomp and Circumstance March No 1* went down equally well.

Malcolm countered the growing jingoism by immersing himself in Rabindranath Tagore's *Sadhana*, a collection of essays revealing the ancient spirit of India, chapters including 'The Problem of Evil', 'The Problem of Self' and 'The Relation of the Individual to the Universe'. He was also reading Thoreau's *Walden*, describing the author's two-year experiment in self-sufficiency in the woods near Concord, Massachusetts, in the 1840s. The transcendentalist thinking of Thoreau, which inspired Gandhi to the technique of passive resistance, greatly attracted Malcolm. The advent of war had encouraged him to think deeply.

---

[34] Flute, clarinet, 2 bassoons, 2 trumpets, trombone and bass trombone.
[35] Entitled *Overture*, and dated by Malcolm on the first page, 31 January 1940
[36] Dated 19 April 1940
[37] Based on a scale pattern containing a sharpened fourth

Just a month later, in May 1940, Germany invaded the Low Countries, Neville Chamberlain resigned and Churchill became Prime Minister. Shortly afterwards came the fall of France and the evacuation from Dunkirk. For Ruth it was the realisation of her worst nightmares:

> The war comes nearer every day, and now bombs are being dropped and civilians killed. France has given in and Italy is fighting with Germany. A depressing outlook. It is merely a day-to-day affair. No longer can plans be made for the future.

Fears of a German invasion of Britain were growing and it must have been hard to concentrate on music at College. Malcolm's end-of-term report was mixed. 'Distinctly promising,' wrote Gordon Jacob of his composition work. 'He has music in him and [an] amusing vein of cynicism which must not be allowed to become too predominant.'

John Cozens, a former player with the LPO and now Malcolm's trumpet teacher, was less impressed. 'Technically an excellent student, <u>but he lacks mental stability</u> ...' The underlining is Cozens's. Clearly there had been some tempestuous outbursts in lessons.[38]

Malcolm spent much of the summer of 1940 in the company of Richard Adeney, whose parents by happy chance had moved out to Northampton, where Richard was a frequent visitor at Craigmore and came to know the Arnolds well. He liked Nan, finding her kind and motherly, 'always keen to welcome me in and organise a pot of tea'. Craigmore, however, he remembers as very gloomy, 'typically dark and Victorian. Heavy wood. Everything a sombre colour, too much cluttered furniture, ornaments everywhere'. There were red velvet curtains in the main rooms; an imposing staircase just inside the front door; dark brown embossed wallpapers (with cream at the top); a row of bells outside the kitchen (so Lizzie Witts knew who was calling her); and two big attic rooms, one for Malcolm's music and one for Nan's drawing and painting.

Malcolm went on two holidays that year with Richard Adeney. In the Easter they rented a small cottage in Kent with Richard's sister, where Malcolm composed a trio for trumpet, flute and cello. 'My sister played the cello in a very amateurish way,' remembers Richard, 'so he wrote a simple cello part and a professional standard flute and trumpet part. I remember the piece as a little tango.'[39]

For the summer holidays the two friends persuaded a pretty blonde pianist, Betty, to join them in Cornwall. Thus, in August 1940, during the early weeks of the Battle of Britain, they found themselves on a farm at St Buryan, near Mousehole. The holiday was much against the wishes of all their parents, for there were fears at the time that the Germans might land in the West Country. Each of them knew that their immediate future was likely to be bleak. Richard Adeney wrote in his autobiography:

---

[38] In addition to Hall and Cozens Malcolm was also taught by George Eskdale.
[39] May 2003. The work has since been lost.

I thought that Britain's military position was hopeless, and that the war would soon be lost … It was delicious to be the only holidaymakers around in that unusually hot and dry summer … But we had no idea about what was actually going to happen, so we walked in the sun on empty roads to empty beaches and swam and laughed in the heat. And at night Malcolm and I took turns to go to the pretty pianist's bed, he, I supposed, with the greater enthusiasm. That holiday seemed to be the end of our youth, happiness and freedom.

For Richard, Betty and himself Malcolm wrote an exuberant trio, which he named ironically *Grand Fantasia, Op 973,* a piece of escapism at the time of the Battle of Britain. Trumpet, flute and piano are all handled with panache as Malcolm takes the listener on a European tour, with stops in Italy, Hungary and Austria. And the fantasy is not purely geographical for in a gloriously catholic work he manages to salute the idioms of opera, musical comedy and jazz. It is a helter-skelter affair, full of the joys of a youthful artist who knows he's at ease in his medium. It is no surprise to find the manuscript telling us that it was not composed by Malcolm at all, but by 'A.Youngman'.

The *Suite Bourgeoise*, also written in 1940 and in much the same impudent style, is another token of Malcolm's determination to ignore the horrors of war[40] and another piece expressly created to be played with two friends, this time Richard Adeney and oboist Ivor Slaney.[41] The *Suite Bourgeoise* at face value is a charmingly insouciant diversion in five short movements. But Malcolm has left a few clues along the way, which suggest there may be something of a programme behind it, with sex a dominant theme, for one of the five movements was titled *Whorehouse* and another *Elaine* (otherwise known at the College as 'La Belle Hélène' or Helen), a beautiful girl who, so Malcolm assured Richard Adeney, 'could be fucked by anybody'.

The title of the piece encourages speculation. Is this to be a light-hearted exposé of middle-class morality? The first movement, a Prelude, suggests so, for we hear a tune which has convincingly been said[42] to be akin to the nursery rhyme *Lavender's blue, dilly dilly* yet contained within a movement of great dissonance and some violence. Bourgeois domestic bliss, Malcolm seems to be saying, is something worth fighting hard to escape from. In the second movement, a charming if slightly monotonous tango, he moves from bourgeois married life to bourgeois free love, for this is 'Elaine', offering temporary, raunchy delight but ultimate monotony. Third comes a movement full of jazz syncopations, the 'Whorehouse',[43] bourgeois sex for sale. More fun perhaps than Elaine, and certainly more variety, but hardly a way of life to be contemplated for ever. In the

---

[40] After being lost for many years the manuscript resurfaced in 1996, complete with the illustrated cover which Ruth and a friend had made for it.

[41] Malcolm supported his friends on the piano. Slaney later became a popular bandleader.

[42] Jackson *op.cit.,* p.11

[43] But before showing the work to Gordon Jacob Malcolm stuck a thick piece of brown paper over this provocative title and renamed the piece *Dance.*

fourth movement, *Ballad*, Malcolm climbs the social ladder and takes us to a smarter milieu, an art deco haven, all white tie and tails, the bourgeois celluloid dream, with Fred Astaire elegantly wooing the graceful Ginger Rogers. There is one last clue given, in the final movement, a gracious waltz which is dedicated to 'Ugo', Hugo Rignold, a jazz violinist, amateur racing driver and *bon viveur*, who later converted himself into a classical conductor of repute. Rignold in 1940 was one of the leading players in the orchestra of the exclusive Kit-Kat Club, Mayfair. In the last port of call, therefore, we have at last escaped the bourgeois world and are at one with the upper classes. In such a reading the *Suite Bourgeoise* is a progression, a sexual and social odyssey. Malcolm, it seems, has precociously discovered that life can be lived on a far grander scale than most bourgeois people imagine. Not for him the middle-class values of Pappy and St George's Avenue, Northampton. He proclaims instead the virtues of both the low and the high life.

While Malcolm mocked the bourgeois values, his brothers were staunchly defending them. Aubrey, having volunteered for the Royal Artillery, became an officer in charge of a battery of anti-aircraft guns protecting the London Docks. For a time he and his family were stationed in the Tower of London, which Robin remembers as a terrifying place in perpetual blackout gloom:

> But you got a good view from there of the search lights, barrage balloons, the ack-ack going off and the German bombers overhead ...[44]

Clifford was now serving in Arctic convoys, finding it not at all to his liking, and planning to extricate himself from the whole hideous business. The twenty-one-year-old Philip was a Pilot Officer and married. By the summer of 1940 he and Joan were living at RAF Scampton in Lincolnshire, the airfield made famous later in the war by the Dambusters.

Philip was flying Handley Page Hampdens, four-crew bombers, so confined in cabin space that they were called 'flying suitcases'. His active service began that August with regular night-time bombing sorties against a variety of targets: German invasion barges in channel ports; U-boat bases; and important industrial sites like the Krupp factory at Essen. War escalated that summer with the bombing of cities. After the German attack on London, the War Office ordered the bombing of Berlin, and Philip flew on the first sortie. When Hamburg was attacked in retaliation for the German blitz on Coventry in November, Philip again participated. The fires lighting the skies over Coventry had been visible to Ruth, miles away in Northampton:

> As we stood watching the terrific barrage of anti-aircraft guns, my thoughts were with Philip. I cursed inwardly at the madness of it all.

A month into active service Philip wrote a remarkably candid letter to his parents from Scampton.[45]

---

[44] March 2004
[45] 28 August 1940

Dear Mother & Dad,

Thanks so much for the letters and papers. I'm only sorry I haven't written for some time only I've been flying so much, we are slackening off a bit now that the moons have gone in, and I hope to be on leave in about two weeks' time. I was on the first bombing raid on Berlin on Saturday night, I've got one of the safety pins off one of the bombs we dropped there, which I'll give you when I see you next.

I've also done several mine laying trips in the harbours down the west coast of France, Bordeaux, Brest etc and have visited Leipzig, Hanover, Hamburg and the Ruhr Valley since I wrote you last.

I took Joan to a dance in the mess last Saturday night. It was very good. We go to the pictures quite often in Lincoln when I'm not flying. When I've been on trips to the west coast of France I always fly over Northampton on the way back. Last Wednesday night we saw several bombs dropped on the South Coast, as we were crossing the coast on our way to France.

I do hope everyone is keeping OK at home and that there is plenty of work at the factory. Give my love to everyone.

Love,

Phil

In the air for 10 hours and 10 minutes – a record for Scampton-Berlin and back

Philip tactfully fails to mention that several planes in that first Berlin mission ran out of fuel and perished in the sea. The life expectancy of a bomber crew was very low. By the time he visited the family on leave that September he had already flown more raids over Germany than any other pilot in his squadron.

Back in Northampton Philip found himself something of a hero, interviewed at length in the local newspaper. Malcolm's feelings were confused. Philip was the brother closest to him. But delight in his achievements clashed with his own passionate belief that all war was wrong. When Pappy proudly lined up his children and their spouses for a reunion photograph in the Craigmore garden, Malcolm was characteristically playing the fool. Philip, by contrast, stood behind his young wife, looking extremely preoccupied.

Away from their parents, Philip had some harrowing stories to tell. A wireless operator with whom he had often flown had just won the VC on another Hampden. The pilot had given his crew orders to bale out as he returned from a mission with the plane on fire. The rear gunner and navigator had done so. But the young radio operator had stayed on, using his own bare hands to put the fire out when he had exhausted the two extinguishers. Against all expectation the pilot brought the badly damaged plane home, the radio operator still alive but horribly burned.[46] The pilot, decorated for this feat, perished on a subsequent mission.

---

[46] Philip's friend, John Hannah VC, died seven years later, aged 25, of illness related to his war injuries.

*Family reunion, September 1940. Back row: Aubrey, Wag, Clifford and Philip. Seated: Wyn, Ruth, Doll and Joan. In front: Robin, Malcolm and Gill.*

Malcolm marvelled at Philip's resilience in the face of such tragedies. Privately he and Ruth agreed that they only reinforced their own position as pacifists, Ruth later expressing their feelings in her journal:

War is blood lust, the very worst element in man, let loose on a large scale. It is the lowest instinct in a human being.

The Blitz was in full force when the College began its autumn term of 1940. Malcolm, however, didn't return but spent the next two terms in Northampton, having fallen out with Pappy that summer. He had started dutifully enough, playing trumpet solos at a local Salvation Army concert, but his wild behaviour thereafter caused bitter exchanges. Malcolm should mend his ways at once, thundered Pappy. He was letting the family down. His drunkenness was an acute embarrassment to him, a pillar of the community, known for his strong stance on temperance. How could he preach against the demon drink when his own son was inebriated every night of the week? Malcolm's extravagance in London was equally intolerable. The generous £400 College scholarship, which should have been ample, was proving a pittance against the debts he was incurring. He was not going to subsidise him any more until he changed his ways. He would not return to College.

Malcolm never responded well to criticism, resentment at exclusion from college life only fuelling his determination to live life his own way. He continued to embarrass his father by loud and unruly behaviour, the situation worsening after Nan had fled to Capel Garmon, until, one early morning in November 1940, Malcolm was confronted by an enraged Pappy and had the front door of Craigmore slammed in his face.

Fortunately he could always rely on his sister's sympathy and help. 'The poor boy wandered about all night,' wrote Ruth indignantly, 'sleeping in air-raid shelters and lavatories. He arrived here at a quarter to seven, just as Wag was making tea.' After Wag's cup of tea and a council-of-war Malcolm returned to St George's Avenue. However, when the door opened and he saw Pappy's face, he realised it was an error of judgement. A volley of abuse followed, this time centred on a new point of attack, his refusal to join the army. 'You're a white livered rat!' shouted Pappy, oblivious of the neighbours, before slamming the door in righteous indignation. Malcolm retreated to Ruth's where the three of them agreed with some asperity that Pappy had hardly rushed to the colours himself in the previous war, preferring to man the till, ringing up profits made out of other people's misery. 'Never mind, dear,' said Ruth. 'You can sleep on our sofa as long as you like.'

Later that day Malcolm walked across to the New Theatre with Wag, who worked there as an occasional follow-spot operator. In no time at all Malcolm had fixed up a job playing in the theatre pit. It might not be quite the same as playing under Constant Lambert or Gordon Jacob, but at least the pay gave him a pleasing self-sufficiency.

Pappy was furious when he heard and began exercising sanctions. Lizzie Witts was ordered not to let Malcolm have his Ration Book and the New Theatre Manager was told to dismiss his new trumpeter immediately. He bravely declined. Pappy then turned on Ruth, denouncing her for enticing away his son. Ruth was understandably outraged:

> How weak he is in character, and how lacking in control. Had his remarks not been so hurtful we would have been amused … He has stooped to every mean trick in his power to get Malcolm to go home …

There is something of the bitterness Ruth felt towards Pappy in a poem of this period, a not altogether successful pastiche of W H Auden, called 'The Song of the Profiteer':

The last war was a cosy spot
For us and all our ilk.
We sent our sons to Eton
And dressed our wives in silk.

We learnt to drink the best champagne
And holiday in France
And bought expensive jewelry
Our bodies to enhance.

> Today the ones who take our place
> Provide for Britain's mourning
> With yards and yards of blackout cloth
> In lieu of air-raid warning.
>
> The sons we spent our money on
> Are being killed like flies
> In aeroplanes and on the sea
> Before our very eyes.
>
> Oh! What a bitter, bitter pill
> And very far from funny
> To think we sold our very blood
> For hoards of tainted money.

Very shortly afterwards, in mid-November 1940, the poem took on an extra relevance when Joan phoned from Scampton with the news that Philip had failed to return from a mission to Berlin. Nothing further was known. No-one had seen him crash. He had simply disappeared, and was now posted as missing. Joan came back to Northampton shortly afterwards, bringing his belongings. Malcolm handed in his notice at the theatre and quietly went home, though more out of concern for his sister-in-law than his father. He did not wish to upset Joan, noted Ruth, by prolonging family feuds. It was a time of great mental distress for all of them:

> The uncertainty is so hard to bear. We must wait for weeks before we know whether he managed to bale out.

They duly waited, but nothing further was heard. At Christmas the family gathered as usual at Craigmore, and an empty seat was left symbolically at the table. Malcolm tried hard to raise everyone's spirits, but with little success. Nan was devastated, Ruth red-eyed, Pappy grimly living in his own withdrawn world.

The start of a fragmentary poem by Malcolm dates to this period. He called it 'The Shadow':

> Sloping crucifix,
> Its shadow groping
> For perpendicular,
> Hoping,
> Though not particular
> For
> Eternity...

There was still no news of Philip in the New Year. Nor was there any possibility of Malcolm returning to College, for in addition to Pappy's veto Nan did not want to have Malcolm in London during the Blitz. Fortunately for Malcolm there was release from his frustration and anxiety in music, as he had the company of Richard Adeney, who had completed his course at the College and was a conscientious objector. The two spent much time together, Malcolm writing him a Flute Sonata, now lost, which was performed in February 1941 in the public library. This was one of a series of Saturday afternoon concerts organised by Malcolm and Richard and featuring many of their college friends. These included Maria Donska (advertised as 'that clever Polish piano player'),[47] Peter Halling (a cellist who later played for the LPO), a local viola player 'Molly' Panter, who had gone up to the College as a scholar at the same time as Malcolm,[48] and Sidney Fell, clarinettist of the Hallé. Malcolm and Richard had a great deal of fun in their entrepreneurial role. 'A. Youngman' came before the Northampton public as the composer of Malcolm's Flute Sonata (which Richard remembers as being 'rather good'), presented in the programme in absurdly fractured French: 'Sonate poor flute par A.Youngman'.[49] B.Youngman and C.Youngman were also invented. Richard Adeney wrote tongue-in-cheek reviews of the concerts for the local paper, including scathing criticisms of his own fine playing. Friends not in the know were shocked and offered to sue.

In March 1941 Malcolm distressed his father further by registering as a conscientious objector. It was an informed and carefully considered action. Malcolm had read widely around the issues, taking particular interest in Richard Gregg's *The Power of Non-Violence*, which draws upon literary sources from all the great religions to illustrate the wisdom of non-violence. He also listened regularly on the radio to the pacifist sermons of Dick Sheppard, whom he, Ruth and many of their friends much admired.

Ruth was pleased to have Malcolm in Northampton. Married life was not proving easy, money was scarce and she was now pregnant. Wag had unfortunately lost his job at Sywell Aerodrome, where he had been working as a mechanic, and was for the moment out of work. 'We have enough money for next week's rent and food,' noted Ruth, 'and after that?'

Fortunately Wag soon found work at a garage and later at a barber's shop, but neither job was well paid. Malcolm made a point of visiting their Kingsley Road bungalow and his antics did much to bolster his sister's morale. He could do little, however, when she suffered the indignity of being summoned to the Rates Office to explain non-payment. This was another blow to Pappy's pride:

> How angry my father was with me because of it. Instead of offering to lend me at least part of the money, he sneered at me and accused me of living in a house which is beyond our means! I can only affirm my years-old opinion that he is one of the biggest hypocrites that ever walked in and out of Chapel. My mother lent me the money, of course.

---

[47] Older than the other students, Maria Donska was a fine pianist who had studied in Poland under Schnabel.

[48] Dorothy Evelyn Panter also appeared as part of the Carter Trio (with Mary Carter and Myra Howe). These three became on other occasions part of the Adeney Quartet.

[49] It is very likely, given the presence of 'A.Youngman', that the *Grand Fantasia* was first played in Malcolm's series of Northampton concerts in 1941.

Later that winter, however, things were so bad that, rather than beg again for help, Ruth sold her precious piano.

> I have nowhere now to put the photos of Philip and Joan, but the rates, gas and electric light bills are paid. I can walk out with a clear conscience and can look everyone straight between the eyes.

With Philip's fate still unknown that Easter there were tensions enough for the Arnolds without Luftwaffe planes overhead two nights a week going to and from Coventry. Desultory bombs were dropped on Northampton and the fields around. It was a time for patching up differences. Ruth, whose nerves were particularly affected by constant nights without sleep, gratefully accepted an invitation to stay with Pappy at the Capel Garmon cottage. Malcolm joined the party in Snowdonia shortly after Easter, travelling up with Lizzie Witts and Joan. Malcolm was working hard to support Joan, who had now endured seven months of uncertainty since Philip was posted missing. Ruth too did her best. She had founded a spiritualist club in Northampton some years back, which had enjoyed much successful contact with the spirit world, and she was able to assure Joan that several messages had been received that Philip was safe and well.

Malcolm's truce with his father allowed him to resume his college career at the end of the Easter holidays, 1941. Ruth, disconsolate without him, rummaged through his books and records:

> When I am at my worst, I find the best cure is to play some music. I have found a record of Malc's which calms down my mood considerably, and I'm afraid that when he comes to play it, it will be rather worn! It is a Ballet Suite by Stravinsky called *Baiser de la Fée*. I would never have credited Stravinsky for being able to soothe a pregnant woman's nerves...!

Malcolm's return to London was enlivened by his sharing a flat in Hammersmith with Alex Lindsay, a New Zealander who liked all-night jazz sessions and could swing his violin like Hugo Rignold. Sometimes Lindsay would come back bleary-eyed from a jazz club, don his surplice and go off to join the choir of the nearby Catholic Church. Alex Lindsay was later to play with Malcolm in the London Philharmonic Orchestra before returning to New Zealand where he founded his own orchestra and did much as player and conductor to raise national standards before his early death. An obituary notice tells of his 'fondness for a few beers in congenial company'. He was 'charismatic, charming and sometimes – reflecting his occasional irresponsibility in non-musical matters – a likeable rogue'.[50]

Alex Lindsay played in the quartet[51] which gave a first performance that summer of Malcolm's *Vita Abundans*, his entry for the College's Cobbett

---

[50] *The Dictionary of New Zealand Biography*
[51] The other members of the quartet were Desmond Mitchell, Leonard Lopes-Salzedo and Pamela Hind.

Prize, a prestigious annual award. Walter Willson Cobbett[52] had endowed a composition prize for a chamber work in one movement, stipulating simply that composers could 'write what they like – in any shape – as long as it *was* a shape'. In addition he asked that 'Phantasy' be part of the title, hoping that composers would draw on the early string 'Fantasias' of Tudor and Jacobean times for inspiration. Malcolm instead turned to a popular song of the day, 'Red Sails in the Sunset', though it was cleverly disguised. His *Phantasy for String Quartet*, usually known as *Vita Abundans*,[53] was a last minute entry, written in just five days,[54] and it won the second of the two prizes, the remarkable Ruth 'Widdy' Gipps[55] coming first with her piano quartet, *Brocade*.

'Widdy' Gipps was as big a personality as Malcolm and the two got on famously. A rebellious workaholic, once described by Herbert Howells as 'go-getter Ruth', she had also won the previous year's Cobbett Prize and *Brocade* was already her Opus 17.

Malcolm's *Vita Abundans* is clearly the work of a highly imaginative and fertile mind. It impishly opens with a sensuous Latin-American melody, half tango, half rumba, from the opening bars of which much of the whole work is developed. The central *Andante* is serious and troubled yet lyrical too, and the *Presto*, by contrast, is utterly cheeky. In a short coda Malcolm gives particular prominence to the *Andante*, now presented in unashamedly romantic terms. *Vita Abundans* is precociously sophisticated, contains passages of fine quartet writing,[56] and was so good that even the self-confident 'Widdy' Gipps told him he should have won. Malcolm thought highly enough about the work to contemplate its full orchestration.[57]

A letter survives from this period, written by Malcolm to his parents from Bournemouth:

Dear Mother and Dad,

   Thanks for your letter and money. My string quartet has won the Cobbett Prize – there are two offered every year for the best chamber music by young composers – I have won the second prize which is 5£. I am very pleased. There is a prize of 10£ for

---

[52] 1847-1937

[53] The title *Vita Abundans* is intriguing. A Catholic priest, probably procured by Alex Lindsay, is said to have helped Malcolm with the Latin, which he later crossed out, presumably after reading the competition's rubric at the last minute, substituting *A Phantasy for String Quartet*. It is fascinating to ponder what precisely was the thought which Malcolm wanted to encapsulate in a terse Latin tag, for which he needed expert help. 'To be alive is to be presented with a series of glorious opportunities', perhaps, or maybe 'Cram the very most into your days'. Whatever the precise wording, it was a highly optimistic message. Malcolm was on a high.

[54] It was completed on 17 June 1941.

[55] 1921-1999

[56] The *Presto*, beginning at Bar 169, shows an extensive grasp of quartet textures.

[57] There are instrumentation ideas written all through the manuscript. It is thought he may have been considering this work as a movement for his first symphony.

the string quartet which gives the best performance of it. This is given by the College. I am also given a copy of the score and parts done by an exceptional copyist. The music is then kept in the Library for anyone that wants to play it.

It is too hot to write.

Much love,

Malcolm

PS I shall not enter for the LRAM. If I am still about I should like to do that in September.

Parental delight at Malcolm's success was undercut only days later by the news that they had all been dreading. A letter arrived from the Red Cross in Geneva, telling of Philip's death in action eight months before and his burial in the cemetery of Neuruppin outside Berlin 'with full military honours'. Pappy shut himself away in the Craigmore front room, erecting a shrine there to Philip's memory: an enormous framed photograph, with massed vases of flowers below and a plethora of Union Jacks. Nan mourned inconsolably, spending a long time alone at Capel Garmon. Ruth watched sadly from nearby. Craigmore, for her an important symbol of security in good times and bad, had altered so much:

> The atmosphere in the house is extremely frigid at times, and it's quite a strain even on the strongest nerves. Poor Ma gets so depressed, and we all come in for a fair share of nagging! She and Dad don't hit it off very well these days and he is constantly aware of her disapproval at various foolish and petty deceptions which he is not clever enough to get away with, the main one being the attendant at the Turkish Baths, whom he has asked up here with his wife when Ma is away! She went back to Wales this morning ...

Ruth continued to draw help from Malcolm's library. She was now reading Tagore's *Sadhana* and a new book of modern poetry given her by Malcolm. She was very moved to discover that Malcolm had earmarked in his own *Anthology of Modern Verse* Wilfred Wilson Gibson's *Lament*:

> We who are left. How shall we look again
> Happily on the sun or feel the rain
> Without remembering how they who went
> Ungrudgingly and spent
> Their lives for us, loved too the sun and the rain?

Ruth had been writing her own verses on Philip and she now wrote out a fair copy, folded it up, and placed it inside Malcolm's anthology. It began with an ironic look at their childhood:

> When we were young, we used to play with toy soldiers,
> And dress up as Indians in wild feathers,
> And wave swords and guns madly in the air –
> 'Whiz! Bang! We'll shoot the Germans dead!'
> We had miniature collections of cannons and tanks,
> And ships and shining aeroplanes,
> And our heroes were men who thirst for blood...

It is a long poem with strong imagery:

> Over the battlefields of War and in the Air
> Beauty waits to gather the broken fragments
> Of those whose Souls were searching for reality
> And who saw the treasured flower of Birth and Death
> Buried beneath a heap of human bones.
>
> In distant graveyards the growth of it is springing
> Lifting bright spears of light into the smoke-filled air:
> But the mortal eye can see only the untended plots,
> And ears are listening for the drear tolling of bells,
> And brains are wrapped up in a National Flag,
> And fingers grow cold touching tawdry medals.

Malcolm was similarly sarcastic about the tolling bells, waving flags, colourful medals and all the other empty palliatives of war. He mirrored these sentiments of Ruth's very closely when he came to write a grotesque military march as the mocking culmination of his First Symphony.[58]

For the moment, however, he was still making his way as a composer, writing only chamber music. There had as yet been no works for full orchestra. Philip's death had served to focus his mind on the way forward. Though only nineteen, he had decided to leave college and forego formal qualifications, feeling independence was more important. Hugo Anson kindly put his name forward to John Gardner, who was running the RAF Fighter Command Band. At the audition Gardner and his trombonist, Harry Roche, meeting Malcolm at the College, found him 'a bit mad and unpredictable but very talented'.[59] After he had played through a series of trumpet exercises with great nonchalance, they asked him to busk a chorus of 'Lady Be Good', and he did so in the distinctively fluent style of Bix Beiderbecke.[60] He was offered a job and accepted.

A few days later, however, he was contacted by his former teacher, Johnny Cozens, who had recently returned to the London Philharmonic Orchestra as principal trumpet. There was a vacancy in the orchestra. Why didn't Malcolm take it? He rushed off to see Gordon Jacob: 'What can I do, Dr Jacob? I don't want to spend my time carrying a trumpet around, do I? What about rehearsals at nine and ten in the mornings and all that kind of thing?' Gordon Jacob smiled. 'Well, you could do what I've been doing. Get a job at a college, sit on your backside and do bugger all!'[61]

It was neither true nor possible, but it was what his pupil wanted to hear. Malcolm rushed off to telephone Thomas Russell, who ran the LPO, accepting the offer.

---

[58] They are there, too, in the last movement of the Piano Sonata of 1942.
[59] April 2004
[60] Malcolm hugely admired the legendary 'Bix' Beiderbecke, who was not only a fine cornet player but drank himself to death in 1931 at the age of twenty-seven.
[61] *Music & Musicians*, October 1986

From Malcolm's point of view the job was perfect in several ways. Touring with a professional orchestra was an accepted occupation for a conscientious objector. It also removed him from Pappy's sphere of influence. But, above all, it was a first, tentative step towards the high life, the classy restaurants, clubs and good-time girls to which, even as a paid-up member of the Communist Party, he nonetheless aspired. It was a first lowly rung on the ladder. Somewhere aloft, high up in the clouds maybe but real enough to those with sufficient ambition, was that fashionable milieu he had sketched so fondly in his *Suite Bourgeoise.* If the long climb to the good life meant leaving behind family and old friends, he would have to be content.

*A happy family group: Pappy, Ruth, Malcolm and Nan*

# 4
# The Trumpet Virtuoso
## Sheila and the LPO, 1941-44

FOR A COMMUNIST in 1941 – even a flawed one like Malcolm, nursing an indecent respect for the capitalist good life – the London Philharmonic Orchestra was an ideal organisation for which to work. Only two years earlier, after seven successful years under its founder, Thomas Beecham, the LPO had suffered a severe financial crisis and reinvented itself as a Soviet-style co-operative, Musical Culture Ltd, with each orchestral player a shareholder.[1] Its Secretary and General Manager, Thomas Russell, was a dynamic young Marxist with a passionate belief in the importance of music to wartime morale. Fortunately the government also shared Russell's view, Churchill declaring in May 1941:

> The arts are essential to any complete national life. The state owes it to itself to sustain and encourage them.

The Council for the Encouragement of Music and the Arts, CEMA, later to become the Arts Council, was founded that year. At first its subsidy to the LPO was very modest – 'It would barely cover the expenses of a third-rate provincial revue company,' protested Russell – so he negotiated backing from the impresario, Jack Hylton, who suggested the orchestra gave two or three concerts a day in large industrial centres, using theatres, music halls or even places of work, where there was no concert hall. It was a daunting proposition, especially in wartime, yet the LPO co-operative embraced it willingly. A gruelling routine of non-stop touring began, the orchestra's epic travels matching the national mood:

> A new defiance was in the air; a determination that the Nazis should not rob us of our culture inspired music-lovers to continue their support in spite of personal danger, and with this encouragement the LPO continued to visit all the blitzed towns of Britain regardless of danger, lack of accommodation, the shortage of food in certain areas, the blackout and the inconveniences caused by dislocated railway communications.[2]

When the Queen's Hall was bombed and many of the LPO's instruments stored inside were lost, the public immediately donated money and second-hand instruments, and the concerts continued. The resourceful Russell soon acquired

---

[1] In 1943 Malcolm bought a £1 share in the orchestra's £200 capital.
[2] Donald Brook: *Conductors' Gallery* (Rockliff, 1945), p.180

an alternative venue, a large but struggling theatre in Golders Green, the Orpheum, where the orchestra took responsibility for stoking the boilers and plugging holes in the roof. There was a strong spirit of camaraderie in the LPO. Emotions ran high, and never more so than at a packed Orpheum in 1942 when, with Malcolm as second trumpet and Henry Wood conducting, the orchestra celebrated not just its tenth birthday but its survival against the odds.

Malcolm had joined the LPO several months earlier, in July 1941, just in time for six days of concerts at Cardiff under Malcolm Sargent and Basil Cameron.[3] He then travelled north to Wrexham to meet a new conductor, Richard Tauber, the great Austrian tenor, whose fame on stage and screen ensured good houses at all the ports of call: Rhos, Hanley, Doncaster, Nottingham, Stratford-on-Avon, Coventry, Stafford and Dudley. By the end of this tour, which crammed twenty-eight concerts into seventeen days, Malcolm felt a hardened professional, though he was still only nineteen.[4]

Malcolm could not have had a friendlier conductor with whom to make his touring debut than Tauber.

> He was the most charming, genial person, addressing everyone indiscriminately as 'Schnappelapumpi', which I think must be the Viennese equivalent of 'Thingumajig', and often inviting a few of us back to his hotel after concerts to regale us with drinks and stories.[5]

It was auspicious that Tauber's limited repertoire of just six composers included Weber, and Malcolm was delighted to be playing the overture to *Der Freischütz*, which his great-great grandfather had first presented in England. Tauber seemed equally delighted to hear all about the great Schnappelapumpi, William Hawes.

Rotund and rubicund, with a monocle in one eye, Tauber was as distinctive as he was famous, yet a publicity bill for the concert at the Miners' Institute at Rhos shows the orchestra sharing the star billing:

> Musical Culture Ltd. presents
> For the first time in history
> A special visit of the entire
> London Philharmonic Orchestra.
> Full strength – 70 Master Players.

Of the seventy 'master players' only one, the harpist, was female, for sexual discrimination was rampant in the 1940s, even in a Soviet co-operative. One of

---

[3] Malcolm many years later declared that his first concert was at Rhos, but this would have meant him joining as an emergency replacement in the middle of the Welsh tour and the circumstances of his recruitment do not suggest this. Cardiff seems the more probable first concert.

[4] 14-30 July 1941

[5] Richard Temple Savage: *A Voice from the Pit* (David & Charles, 1988), p.95

the LPO's guest conductors, New Zealander Warwick Braithwaite, was happy to assert that women were 'too individualistic' to be good orchestral players:

> I think their place is more in the women's orchestra. I must say, they are splendid workers, earnest, keen and meticulously careful, but they don't seem to be able to take the long view of orchestral problems ... besides, their discipline is not as good as the men's.[6]

Malcolm would not have lacked female company, however, as he began the relentless rounds of British industrial centres, because young girls would cluster round the artists' entrance after concerts, eager to meet the glamorous musicians. The Orchestra Popsies, as the players called them, did much to alleviate the tedium of touring. As the orchestra developed its provincial links, many venues were visited on a fairly regular basis and it became possible, for those players so minded, to have a girl in every port. One trumpet player is said to have set up two homes and families, one in London and one at St Ives. Malcolm, however, preferred to keep his liaisons casual.

In the early months of touring Malcolm found little time for writing. He did, however, mark his mother's birthday in October with the usual musical gift, this time the *Two Piano Pieces*. The inspiration for these gentle miniatures can be identified from the content. The first piece romps along in playful high spirits; the second is warmly romantic, a nocturne fashioned for a twentieth-century night club. Most unusually for Malcolm, there is not a single bar of conflicting, pessimistic emotion in either piece.[7] The composer sounds contentedly, help-lessly, totally in love. And so he was. He would be married within three months.

Malcolm had met Sheila Nicholson two months earlier, on 22 August, when in Sheffield, her home town. As a violinist about to start her fifth and final year at the Royal Academy of Music, Sheila knew several members of the LPO. One of them, the young, highly talkative cellist, Peter Halling, had played in quartets with her and become a good friend.[8] He was also part of Malcolm's lively LPO circle, which included Richard Adeney, another new member of the orchestra. When they arrived in Sheffield, therefore, to give a concert at the City Hall under Adrian Boult, Peter Halling invited Sheila, who was at home for the summer holidays, to come out with him that afternoon to see a 'flick' and to meet his friend, Malcolm. They duly met up, and after the film had a noisy tea at the Sunshine Café before making their way to the City Hall. Sheila thought the concert 'not too bad', with Moura Lympany the star of the evening in Franck's *Symphonic Variations*.[9] She found the dinner afterwards at the Grand Hotel even

---

[6] Donald Brook, *Conductors' Gallery*, p.31

[7] The writing is remarkable too in its economy. In the second piece Malcolm uses just one melodic idea, at first paraded in a whole series of different harmonic and textural guises before a final simple statement, employing some very poignant harmony.

[8] He was later to be a regular session musician with the Beatles.

[9] The orchestra also played Vaughan Williams's London Symphony, Bach's Third Brandenberg Concerto and Beethoven's Leonora Overture No 3.

*Sheila Nicholson, 1941*

*Malcolm and Sheila on the Racecourse, Northampton, with St George's Avenue in the background, Easter 1942*

more enjoyable than the concert, and she danced with Peter Halling, Richard Adeney, Boris Rickelman and Malcolm until the early hours.

Malcolm, the latest idol of the Orchestra Popsies, the passionate advocate of casual sex and one-night stands, was stopped in his unseemly tracks. Here was somebody different, somebody very special, old-fashioned enough to have just a hint of his mother, high-principled, modest and thoroughly enchanting. Out of the windows of the Grand Hotel, Sheffield, flew all his prejudices about bourgeois marital conformity. Richard Adeney was equally impressed:

> I wanted to marry her myself. We had both met her on the same day and both thought she was absolutely gorgeous. Great charm and beauty. Very feminine. And in spite of my homosexuality I thought that this was someone I really could live with. I took her out a lot. I remember trying to kiss her in an alley off Regent Street. She wouldn't have it! Malcolm was the bigger catch. She preferred him! [10]

Sheila was twenty-two, petite, and pretty as an English rose. She had joined the Academy in 1937 straight from school in Sheffield. She was close to her mother but less at ease with her father, Herbert Nicholson, who was fifty when she was born. 'It was a funny family,' she recalls.[11] 'There was a generation missing.'

The Nicholsons had made considerable amounts of money in steel and shipbuilding, but Herbert was a gritty northern businessman whose income derived from a parade of shops, which he had built and let out, and an insurance business, which he ran from his home, 179 Rustlings Road. To keep himself busy, he supervised the tobacconist's in his block of shops.

The highly musical Sheila had found life in Sheffield uncongenial:

> It was all steelworks, coal mines, businesses. Another world. The people there were terribly unemotional. Very matter-of-fact. It was life without embellishment. My father was in his sixties and didn't want to do much or go anywhere, so we were rather stuck. My elder sister stayed and went to university there, but I got out when I was eighteen and went to London. There was so much more life there! [12]

Sheila's parents, although not particularly musical, did their best to encourage their daughter when they noticed her talent. Herbert bought her an expensive 1812 Ceruti violin, and a specialist violin teacher came in once a week from Hull to augment her local lessons.[13] She was also sent on holiday courses, sometimes with the great violin professor Carl Flesch, whom she impressed.

When she won a scholarship to the Academy, her parents were alarmed at the prospect of her being alone in London, even though she was to live at the Three Arts Club, across the road from the Academy.[14] Sheila herself was both daunted and excited:

---

[10] April 2003
[11] August 2003
[12] August 2003
[13] Her local teacher was Nora Bridge.
[14] 'It was full of actresses, musicians and artists, all female. You could get a good lunch for 1s 3d!'

I'd never seen anything quite like all those musicians!

It was not long before she was winning important prizes at the Academy, beating musicians who later became established figures, as well as playing in any number of orchestras and chamber groups.[15] Dennis Brain was among her fellow students, Henry Wood just one of the eminent conductors under whom she played.

For all her prettiness Sheila was mentally tough. Having taken the decision to leave home, she stayed on as a student throughout the Blitz. Sheffield had also been getting its share of bombing – three thousand homes and shops were destroyed at this time – but the scale of destruction in London was worse:

> There'd be an air-raid one night, and next morning someone would not appear at College. Practising an instrument in such circumstances seemed rather futile, but somehow we all kept going.[16]

Romances flourished amid wartime dangers and uncertainties, and it was not long before Sheila had a serious boyfriend, Sidney Ellison,[17] who was later to enjoy a distinguished career as a trumpet player. Her father was horrified when he heard.

> He didn't approve! I don't think he ever expected me to go out with a man! Not in those days!

So when Sheila wrote that she was engaged to Sidney, a handsome young man with a two-seater sports car, feelings ran high at Rustlings Road. Her father was full of self-pity and anger:

> I was just going out to an appointment with regard to the letting of Blake's shop when your letter came and it quite upset me, and I do not think I got the best out of the transaction …

Having digressed to explain the paltry sum negotiated, he returned to the attack:

> With regard to Sidney, you must not take any notice of him. Take notice of your mother and me. Sidney is only a boy as regards experience. And Sidney should apologise for whatever he's done …[18]

The letter ended with a reminder that it was *he* who was paying the Academy fees. Sidney had to go.

Soon afterwards Sheila fell in love again, this time with a musical Dane called Fritz. Her father, however, was now seriously ill, so an engagement with Fritz went ahead unquestioned. By the time Sheila met Malcolm she was about to

---

[15] She played many chamber works in public, often with her friend Betty Mills. The Franck Violin Sonata, Beethoven's A minor Sonata and the Brahms Trio (with Paul Engel on horn) were favourites.

[16] September 2003

[17] South African born trumpet player and teacher; he was in the RAF during the war, before joining the LPO. He later joined the LSO.

[18] Undated letter from Herbert Nicholson to Sheila

celebrate the second anniversary of this engagement, and Fritz, though still much loved, was long since back in Denmark.

The day after the concert Sheila went to the station to see the boys off. Malcolm, to her surprise, had impulsively decided to stay on in Sheffield for another three days, even though he would miss a concert. They spent their first afternoon together going to another 'flick', which was followed by another supper at the Grand, after which Sheila invited him home to meet her mother and invalid father. They talked, looked at music and books, but she was disappointed to find Malcolm 'very depressed'. Next day they went up on the moors for a bracing walk before picnicking beside an attractive pool where Malcolm talked and talked. Later that night she confided in her diary that Malcolm was 'rather nice', an 'interesting person' and 'good fun'. On their third and final day together they went round the bookshops, saw their third 'flick' (John Gielgud as Disraeli in *The Prime Minister*), played records on the wind-up gramophone at home, took the dog for a walk, and talked. Malcolm left next morning, still talkative as he waved goodbye from the departing train, and suddenly Sheila found life very flat. He had not supplanted Fritz but he had definitely made something of an impact.

Over the next couple of weeks they exchanged letters, Sheila finding Malcolm's first effort 'obscene' and sending it back to him. He tried another tack, which went down much better; 'He's got brains!' she noted. As soon as Sheila returned to London in late September, Malcolm leapt forward. They met for tea at Marble Arch, talked in Hyde Park, saw a 'flick', *The Reluctant Dragon*, which Sheila loved, and ended up in 'a low dive in Charing Cross Road'. It had been 'a very amusing evening,' noted Sheila, back in her flat in Golders Green. Next day they strolled across both Hampstead Heath and Hyde Park, walked to Westminster, stared at the river and sauntered to Victoria, with Malcolm voluble and witty throughout. 'Fun!' declared Sheila. 'I like him!' Twenty-four hours later they were back at Speakers' Corner, where Malcolm and Sheila engaged in a spirited argument on dialectical materialism. 'How about a 'flick'?' asked Malcolm. 'Maybe *The Reluctant Dragon*?' queried Sheila. So they saw it again, found it just as funny and then walked the length of Piccadilly. 'Can't stand many more nights like this!' wrote Sheila. But less than twenty-four hours later there was tea at the Blue Cockatoo in Chelsea and more watching of the river, where Malcolm was 'rather annoying'. He had overstepped the mark, and well-brought-up girls in the 1940s had a firm code of conduct. Malcolm, fascinated, was having to learn a new set of rules.

Sheila's diary shows how much time they were spending together, just a month since their first meeting:

Saturday September 27: Met Malcolm at Hyde Park. Walked to Soho – wonderful morning. Excellent lunch at Chinese restaurant. Fun! Jolly hot. Walked down Charing Cross Road and looked at books. Walked to Marble Arch and saw Marx Brothers film

– funny. Walked in Hyde Park – beautiful evening. Sat by Serpentine. Walked back to Baker Street. Home.

She loved his sense of humour, which, after the dour atmosphere of Rustlings Road, was quite startling. And he gave her little glimpses of a world she had never seen, as they walked round Soho and darted into bohemian pubs to listen to live music. 'Interesting low life,' she commented. Whenever possible they went to lunchtime concerts in the National Gallery, but most of all, they simply walked and talked. Malcolm was beginning to cast a spell which threatened Fritz's monopoly. 'Very pleasant evening, dear me.'

The courtship was briefly halted at the end of September with the sudden news that Sheila's father had died. She spent a week in Sheffield and returned to London in deep gloom. On their reunion, however, they walked around Hyde Park, oblivious of the rain, and, a little afterwards, on a damp bench in St James's Park, Malcolm declared his love. 'He wants to marry me! Incredible!' But she felt worried about the speed of it all and put him off. Shortly afterwards there was further cause for anxiety. They were together on the Chelsea Embankment, watching the river, when Malcolm experienced a lightning change of mood: 'Malcolm suddenly got depressed. Mad! Depressed me too. Damn!' But his spirits returned, the jokes restarted, and by mid-October she was confiding to herself, 'I think I must be in love with him'.

The LPO's concerts became key moments in her life. Albert Sammons's playing of the Brahms Violin Concerto delighted her. But even better was tea afterwards with Malcolm, a 'news flick', a walk around the parks and dinner at the Shanghai. His absences on tour became harder to bear. 'I think I shall marry him,' she resolved at the end of October. 'There is nothing else to do.' But there was still Fritz, a powerful presence even *in absentia*. 'If it weren't for Fritz everything would be so easy.'

Malcolm was nothing if not attentive. In early November, on his day off, he suggested an outing:

Met Malcolm. Train to Windsor. Had lunch – walked in the park – bit cold. V. nice! Train back. Saw 'My Life With Caroline' – not bad. Had supper at Istanbul. It will be awful not seeing him for a week. Jolly tired. Marvellous day.

By early November there were signs that Fritz had been defeated – Sheila had laid aside her Auden and MacNeice and was reading Dowson – and in mid-November an important decision was reached:

Broke off my engagement to Fritz. Oh dear!

The courtship continued serenely with its busy ritual of walks, meals and films. One 'flick' of particular interest was *Ships with Wings*, a propaganda war movie starring John Clements, one of the first films for which Malcolm played. 'Dreadful film,' commented Sheila, whose tastes were not catholic. She found *Follow the Fleet* 'awful' and *Fantasia* 'good in many ways, obscene in many more'. But there were new interests. Sheila shared Malcolm's left-wing sympathies. With Hitler in power and fascism rampant, the Communist Party seemed a logical choice, the only organisation which was saying trenchant things about the treatment of Jews. So together they enthusiastically distributed literature for the Bolshevik cause on street corners. They also began looking for flats for their future together.

Officially engaged on 10 December, they decided it was time to meet Malcolm's family, so just before Christmas they took a train to Northampton, easing the tedium of the journey by playing some live music. Malcolm was drawing Sheila out of herself. She was less at ease playing a duet with Nan in the Craigmore front parlour, but she enjoyed meeting several of the Arnolds – Ruth and Wag, Clifford and his wife Doll – finding the experience 'amazing'. Malcolm himself was in sparkling form:

> Malcolm really is brilliant. Makes me feel a fool. God, I love him. Everything is marvellous with Malcolm. I've never felt like this in my life. He's wonderful.

Pappy and Nan were delighted at the prospect of Sheila as a daughter-in-law. Of all their five children it seemed Malcolm would make the best marriage, both socially and financially. Sheila with her solid Yorkshire good sense could only have a beneficial influence on Malcolm. Sheila, for her part, understood Pappy somewhat better than Malcolm, drew the best from him and forged a good relationship. Given for Christmas a 1943 Arnold Brothers diary, she congratulated Pappy on the William Morris quotation he had chosen for the front page:

> If these hours be dark, at least do not let us sit deedless like fools and fine gentlemen, thinking the common toil not good enough for us, and beaten by the muddle; rather let us work like good fellows trying by some dim candle light to set our workshops ready against tomorrow's light.[19]

Sheila spent Christmas with her mother and sister at Sheffield, as Malcolm was touring, only then breaking the news to them that she was getting married. Neither was best pleased, and when Malcolm arrived at Rustlings Road on 28 December to stay for a night, he failed to impress. His departure left Sheila upset. 'Ma depressing about everything. God, I hope it will be all right.' The next day she went down to London to prepare the flat they were renting, 19 Ovington Mews, in Knightsbridge.

> Felt dreadfully miserable. Oh God, it's dreadful. Unpacked. Did the house up a bit. Pretty lonely. It will be all right with Malcolm.

On 3 January 1942 Malcolm and Sheila were married quietly at Hendon

---

[19] This was a piece of luck for Pappy. Most years he wrote his own vacuous doggerel:
'May every step of this New Year From January to December
Bring you daily, beside good cheer, Something lovely to remember.' (1945)

Registry Office, not far from Sheila's Golders Green flat.[20] Pappy and Nan came down from Northampton and Sheila's elder sister, Gwenol, represented the Nicholson family in her mother's abence. It was all very rushed. Malcolm had been touring in the north, playing in Blackburn on the evening of 1 January. There was no time for a honeymoon. Over the next three days Malcolm was working at the Orpheum, the Pinewood film studios and HMV's recording studios at Abbey Road. Then, after one free day, he was off to the West Country. Sheila, meanwhile, was starting her penultimate term at the Academy on 5 January.

It was ironic that music, which brought them together, now kept them apart, Malcolm playing at venues all over England in the first two months of marriage. For over a quarter of this period he was absent at night, on tour.[21] In London at weekends he played in concerts at the Cambridge Theatre, the Orpheum and the Kingston Empire, as well as six times at the Albert Hall. In these two months, as always, he fitted in some lucrative film work which took him to Denham and Elstree studios. The schedule of travel, demanding enough in peacetime, was made worse by the privations of war. Journeys were all by laborious steam train, the carriages crowded, the corridors packed with standing passengers; the occasional overnight journeys were even worse with the heating seldom working and the light bulbs painted over to avoid the attention of German bombers. On rare occasions instruments and music failed to reach the correct destination in time for a concert; players had been known to spend nights on railway station benches.

Sheila, seeing Malcolm only intermittently, busied herself with all manner of musical activities in her final year at the Royal Academy. She already had her LRAM and teaching certificate and was now studying for her ARCM.[22] As one of the Academy's leading instrumentalists she was much in demand for orchestral and chamber groups – she herself now founded an Arnold Quartet – and, in bringing music to schools and adult groups, she travelled quite widely. In early March[23] she was able to spend five days in Bournemouth where the LPO played several concerts and over the Easter weekend they both visited Malcolm's family at Northampton. There were four happy weeks in the summer when the LPO

---

[21] Coventry-Hanley; Preston-Wakefield-Birmingham; Sheffield-Coventry-Dudley-Chesterfield-Nottingham; Malvern-Cheltenham-Bristol; and Cambridge-Norwich. He also made tiring, one-day visits to Weston-super-Mare, Cambridge, Bristol, Wolverhampton, Oxford, Winchester and Walsall.

[22] Most students took the performing diplomas LRAM (Licentiate of the Royal Academy of Music) and ARCM (Associate of the Royal College of Music) regardless of which institution they were members.

[23] 9-13 March 1942

played every night at the Proms at the Albert Hall, close to their Knightsbridge flat.[24]

In the middle of August, when the orchestra was given a two-week holiday, Malcolm and Sheila enjoyed a delayed honeymoon, taking a train down to Penzance, from where they travelled by horse and cart to their destination, the sleepy village of St Buryan some five miles away. They stayed at Tregurnow, the farmhouse which Malcolm, Richard and Betty had found two years earlier. It is easy to see why, for Tregurnow was beautifully situated high above Lamorna Cove with spectacular views across Mount's Bay to the Lizard Peninsula. It was a part of Cornwall made famous by artists of the Newlyn School, and their holiday reading included Laura Knight's most recent volume of memoirs.[25] It proved wonderful walking country, and Sheila soon became familiar with the Lamorna Valley, the Merry Maidens monolithic stone circle, Mousehole and Land's End. And when they came back from their long walks there was much music to write and discuss.

While they were at Tregurnow, Malcolm completed a Piano Sonata.[26] It is an enigmatic work, reflecting not so much the glories of their Cornish holiday as the war that was raging beyond. The first movement, in traditional sonata form, has a restlessness about it, a strongly dissonant second subject never allowing the calmer first subject to settle. The short *Andante* with its gentle, blues-tinged love theme is desperately sad, and roughly broken into by the third movement, a ghoulish military march,[27] forerunner to the Gothic nightmare with which Malcolm was to conclude his First Symphony. Philip's death was still on his mind.

Sheila's calming influence made this holiday at St Buryan considerably more sober than its predecessor. With no hangovers to fight, Malcolm was more creative. While walking on the headlands and relaxing on the beaches, he and Sheila discussed another work, the two-movement *Divertimento No.1*. Sheila marvelled at the seeming ease with which he, for the very first time, was handling a full orchestra, and shared his belief that in their years together there were to be

---

[24] Under Henry Wood and Basil Cameron. This was the first season of Proms at the Albert Hall, following the destruction of Queen's Hall. A small note in the programmes of these wartime concerts gives an insight into the spirit of the period: 'In the event of an Air Raid warning the audience will be informed immediately, so that those who wish to take shelter, either in the building or in public shelters outside, may do so. The concert will then continue.'

[25] Volume 3 of *Oil Paint and Grease Paint* (Penguin 1941)

[26] It was the only one he was to write. Many years later, in Ireland in 1975, he was engaged on another: 'I am working on a piano sonata at the moment,' he wrote to David Drew on 21 March, intimating that he would not complete it before the summer. In the event, it seems, he never completed it at all.

[27] Asked in September 2001 about this movement, Malcolm simply commented 'I included a few shocks and surprises for the audience, as if to say "Pay attention! No daydreaming!"'

works in abundance to succeed this, his Opus 1.[28] He was already close to completing another work, a chamber piece he would be able to try out with Richard and three other friends in the orchestra, the *Three Shanties for Wind Quintet*.[29] St Buryan had proved an inspired holiday setting, and, as their horse and trap ferried them back along deserted country lanes towards Penzance, they vowed to visit Cornwall every summer.

The day after their return to London, Malcolm was off to Aberdeen on a month-long tour, which had six different conductors,[30] for the LPO, being an autonymous co-operative, preferred not to have a musical director. Such tours, however physically taxing, gave Malcolm a wonderful musical education. He was not just learning the whole classical repertoire but different approaches to it, gaining an illuminating insight into the conductor's art.

From his first days with the LPO he had found that orchestral playing was an incentive to composition:

It was almost as though I thought 'I'd like to write a piece along these lines' or 'I think I could have written that passage to make it sound better', and the three main composers who influenced me most were Beethoven, Berlioz and Sibelius. I didn't say I thought I could write better music than they did, but that their examples inspired me ... I was often thinking of their music and the music I would write when I should have been playing ...

At the end of this tour, Malcolm and Sheila celebrated their reunion at the Lyons' Corner House, Marble Arch, where the most popular drink on offer was a cup of tea. At this early stage Sheila enjoyed a certain moral ascendancy in their relationship. She disliked drunkenness and Malcolm tried hard not to drink in her presence.

Marble Arch was a focal point of their early lives together. It was there that they had often met in the days of their courtship, and where they now found their second home, moving in November 1942 to Queensborough Mews, Bayswater,[31] situated quietly on the north side of Hyde Park. They were to live in their rented flat, 7 Queensborough Studios, for several years and Malcolm was to write

---

[28] The Divertimento No 1 had to wait until May 1945 for its first performance, given by Benjamin Frankel and the LSO under the auspices of the Committee for Promotion of New Music. The score has since been lost.

[29] A month later, while on tour, he made a note in his diary to send the *Three Shanties*, together with the Divertimento No 1 and the Piano Sonata to Henry Wood.

[30] Malcolm Sargent (Leicester); Henry Wood (Harrogate and London); Warwick Braithwaite (Edinburgh, Aberdeen and Newcastle); Basil Cameron (Harrogate and Edinburgh); Edric Cundell (Edinburgh, Glasgow, Aberdeen and Newcastle); and Leslie Heward (Glasgow and Newcastle).

[31] The flat was quaintly positioned at the end of a narrow, high-walled cul-de-sac. Part of a three-storey block of flats with an outdoor terrace on the first floor, the Studio had a bohemian air, appropriate for an aspiring composer.

important works there. It was also in Bayswater that Malcolm made a significant new friendship. He was playing the slow movement of Mahler's Fourth Symphony on the piano and the windows of the flat were wide open.

> I stopped because my fingers got muddled up and a woman's voice outside carried on the melody. I looked out. She was a sculptor, who lived up the road and I said 'Do you know what that is?' 'Of course I do!' she answered. 'My father wrote it.' [32]

The singer was Anna Mahler, who had fled from Vienna in 1938, two days before the Germans arrived. Mahler's music was much less popular in the 1940s than it later became, but Malcolm loved it.

> We played one movement from his Second Symphony just at the beginning of the war.[33] And afterwards I went to Foyles' second-hand department and bought all the Mahler they had.[34]

Anna Mahler was to have a closer link with the LPO when in 1943 her husband, Anatole Fistoulari, became the orchestra's first Principal Conductor.[35] Fistoulari was brought in to try to bring a little discipline into what had become a largely unco-operative co-operative, a guest conductor's nightmare. Vince Burrows, second horn, epitomised the players' unruly attitude, as indulgently described by the LPO's own magazine:

> When his feelings are roused by a verbose conductor, he displays a gift for invective which covers most of the known ground in record time. His blunt remarks and forthright opinions are the terror of boring conductors.[36]

There is a famous story of Malcolm Sargent, stopping a rehearsal to criticise the trumpets. As soon as he had finished and his back was turned, there came from the area of the trumpets a loud, falsetto cry of 'Bollocks'! Sargent, quivering with anger, turned around. Malcolm was looking utterly innocent and faintly shocked, but Denis Egan, beside him, was convulsed with ill-suppressed laughter. Egan, well known for his very high voice, received the full flow of Sargent's outrage. Malcolm meanwhile was looking on placidly, but winking furiously at anyone who dared catch his eye.[37]

Basil Cameron was regularly baited. Whenever he announced the rehearsal of a much-played popular piece, there would be huge groans. 'Oh Basil! For heaven's sake! We *know* exactly what you want! Please let's get *on* with it!'[38] Cameron had been known to flee the rostrum and lock himself in his room.

---

[32] Interview with Christopher Ford, *The Guardian*, 17 April 1971
[33] i.e. Soon after Malcolm joined the LPO in autumn 1941
[34] Ford, *op.cit.*
[35] 1943-44
[36] *Philharmonic Post*
[37] The story was told both by trumpet player Bram Wiggins, a friend of Malcolm's, and Sir Edward Downes, the distinguished conductor who then played the horn in the LPO. It circulated merrily around the orchestras.
[38] Bill Newman: *Episodes from a Memory Bank*

The male camaraderie of orchestral life appealed strongly to Malcolm, who was never short of friends to share his pranks. Basil Tschaikov[39] remembers Malcolm and Denis Egan playing trumpet duets in the middle of the night in Leicester town centre. If Malcolm was drinking too much, Denis Egan would always look after him.[40] Going down by train to Bristol, Malcolm spotted the viola player Wrayburn Glasspool[41] asleep with his shoes half off, so he removed and hid them. On waking up, Glasspool searched everywhere for them, with Malcolm his assiduous assistant, much to everyone else's amusement. Fortunately Glasspool was a very even-tempered individual and walked uncomplainingly in his socks from the station to the hotel. The next day the shoes mysteriously reappeared on the breakfast table. It was Glasspool's avoidance of military service on psychiatric grounds which became one of the LPO's great legends. Glasspool arrived at the tribunal, feigning madness, with an aggressive glint in his eye. Malcolm, dressed up in a smart suit, hovered in the background, playing the part of his anxious attendant. At one stage in proceedings Glasspool suffered a 'psychotic episode' and ran around the office pulling open drawers and causing absolute mayhem until put under restraint by Malcolm. It sounds a well embellished story.

Malcolm had several boisterous friends in Bristol, usually the scene of heavy drinking. Maurice Carpenter, a part-time poet whose work Malcolm once set to music,[42] worked at the BAC factory (which, Malcolm said, stood for 'Buggers Against Conscription') and belonged to the British Aerospace Jazz Group, for whom Malcolm delightedly guested. Another Bristol friend was saxophonist Roger Bennett, a broadcaster from Radio Bristol. All three barely escaped arrest on one occasion when busking somewhat too floridly outside Temple Meads Station. But drinking did not seem to affect Malcolm's playing, his performances of the *Trumpet Voluntary* drawing high praise in the Bristol newspapers.[43] It was a piece Malcolm was to play many times. Congratulated once by an admirer on the breathtaking speed of his playing, he grinned sheepishly. 'I'm so bloody bored with it, I just tried to get it over with as quickly as possible!'

An important, enduring friendship with William Walton had its quiet beginning around this time. Malcolm had played under Walton, his senior by nearly twenty years, in the first performance of the Violin Concerto.[44] Both men shared the same iconoclastic sense of humour, so they were equally amused and

---

[39] Formerly Second Clarinet with the LPO, he later founded the National Centre for Orchestral Studies, where Malcolm's Ninth Symphony received its first performance.

[40] A devoted friend, he would send large presents to Malcolm's children for many years.

[41] Always quoted by Malcolm as the greatest viola player he knew, Glasspool joined the LPO in 1935 and retired in 1992.

[42] 'Morning Noon', one of two Japanese songs written by Malcolm in 1944 (Op 8) under the influence of Constant Lambert's Li Po songs.

[43] 12 March 1943

[44] 1 November 1941

appalled by a concert in the Albert Hall to celebrate the 25th Birthday of the Red Army,[45] a case of art prostituted on the altar of political expediency. Louis MacNeice wrote a Salute to the Red Army, read by Laurence Olivier and John Gielgud, while Ralph Richardson and Sybil Thorndike delivered narrations from steel towers:

> Two thousand people were to participate in the great apotheosis of the performance, spreading themselves over three acting areas. The first of these was the orchestral platform, backed by a huge panoramic perspective of the city of Stalingrad. This magnificent set, 120 feet wide and 60 feet high, gave noble and lofty dimensions to the whole production. The second area consisted of the existing arena, with all seating removed. The third comprised a space at the opposite end of the auditorium created by the further removal of seats: an area which would accommodate the London Philharmonic Orchestra, augmented by the BBC Symphony Orchestra and the Royal Choral Society, with Malcolm Sargent elevated on a high rostrum ...[46]

There were fanfares in honour of the Red Army specially composed by Bax and Walton and the climax of the whole jamboree was a speech by Anthony Eden, the Foreign Secretary. It was an absurdly manic occasion, over which both Malcolm and William Walton would later often chuckle.

Another bizarre entertainment soon followed, a wartime propaganda movie, *Battle For Music*, the story of the London Philharmonic Orchestra, made at the National Studios, Elstree. Malcolm was filming for five days,[47] bringing to the studios not just his trumpet but several changes of costume: tails, dinner jacket, smart day suit and informal day dress. Four conductors were featured – Lambert, Braithwaite, Boult and Sargent – and the two pianists most associated with the orchestra, Moiseiwitsch and Eileen Joyce. One dramatic moment showed Beethoven's Fifth Symphony being interrupted by an air raid, Malcolm Sargent imperturbably turning round to the audience to say that, just as Beethoven's music could not be destroyed by Hitler, so too the orchestra intended to finish the performance. Malcolm is visible, sitting thoughtfully behind Sargent, trumpet on knee.

He had much to preoccupy him. It was all very well dressing up and watching Sargent play up to the cameras, but he wanted to be the one in the limelight. He had been delighted to have been promoted to principal trumpet, but worried about his own work as a composer. Was he doing enough to assert himself? And it was hard to know where the most productive outlets lay. Enthusiastic colleagues like Charles Gregory were helpful. Gregory, the tall and loquacious first horn and Chairman of the LPO Management Committee, was keen to foster chamber groups within the orchestra. It was his LPO wind ensemble[48] which

---

[45] 21 February 1943
[46] Neil Tierney: *William Walton,* pp.104-105 (Robert Hale, 1984)
[47] April 12-16 1943; Jerrold Northrop Moore: *Philharmonic Jubilee* (Hutchinson, 1982)
[48] Richard Adeney (flute), Michael Dobson (oboe), John Clucas (clarinet), Charles Gregory (horn) and George Alexandra (bassoon).

encouraged Malcolm to write two chamber works, the *Three Shanties* and a Wind Quintet.

In the *Three Shanties*, conceived in 1942, Malcolm gives wonderfully inventive treatment to three traditional songs: 'What shall we do with the drunken sailor?', 'Boney was a warrior' and 'Johnny come down to Hilo'. He parades them roguishly in any manner of adroit disguises. There is that rich, skilful blending of sound which is distinctively his, stemming from an exceptional understanding of wind instruments. It is a work of wit and sophistication, full of fun, light of touch, always hurrying on to the next witticism, labouring no point, however clever.[49]

The Wind Quintet,[50] completed late in 1942, has a tuneful first movement, full of surprises and jazz-inspired ideas. The second movement is a fiendish Scherzo of immense energy, bursting with dazzling cross rhythms. The final movement is an emotionally charged March, taking the equivalent movement of the Piano Sonata a stage further. Its severe dissonances, mocking fanfares, and angular, almost brutal melodic and rhythmic shapes cry out angrily against the folly of war. The *Three Shanties* and the Wind Quintet are not just lively, entertaining and extremely skilfully written works, but the first compositions which have the unmistakeable Malcolm Arnold stamp.

Sheila had by now graduated from the Royal Academy of Music, and, with Malcolm so busy, began to augment chamber music with friends by occasional professional engagements, which helped pay the rent. The orchestra she played most regularly for was The London Women's String Orchestra, later renamed the Riddick String Orchestra. Kathleen Riddick, a doughty champion of women's rights in the music profession, had founded the orchestra before the war and was strongly backed by CEMA. Had she been more ambitious for herself, Sheila could have overcome sexual discrimination and moved from Riddick to one of the major national orchestras, like her friend Livia Gollancz, who had recently joined the Hallé as principal horn. However, she had greater ambitions for Malcolm than for herself. The more she knew him, the more she believed she was married to a genius. Her role was to provide the domestic support to enable him to write the great works of which she believed him capable. Sheila's supportive influence is reflected in the nine works which Malcolm produced, despite all the touring, in the first two years of marriage. But there was to be worry for her as well as fulfilment at this period. For in the summer of 1943 he suffered a serious breakdown.

The details are not precisely known. The facts, such as they are, come from Malcolm nearly fifty years after the event:

---

[49] Thus the fleeting tribute to Glenn Miller at the close of the piece seems so far to have eluded notice.

[50] The work was lost for nearly sixty years. It had, in fact, been put away for safe keeping by the clarinettist, Stephen Waters (1914-1989), who had forgotten its whereabouts; and it was only rediscovered in 2003.

When I was twenty-one and I was diagnosed as a schizophrenic, which was a total breakdown, I lost all memory and I think it's so very distressing for one's relations, one's children, one's girlfriends and all one's friends, when one is put away.[51]

Malcolm was never a reliable interviewee. In a good mood, he tended to say what he thought people wanted to hear; in a bad one, he would be as contrary as possible. In old age, muddled and careless, he perpetrated many inaccuracies and half-truths. He may simply have been using 'twenty-one' to mean 'as a young man'. For 'schizophrenia'[52] we could as easily read 'manic-depressive illness', for the two often overlap. His memory of 'being put away' in a mental hospital is probably a blur with a more serious breakdown seven years later, which did indeed have that outcome.

But to be diagnosed with schizophrenia, after a psychotic outburst, is something not easily forgotten, so Malcolm's memory of 1943 is probably correct. There is also some circumstantial evidence, supporting this dating of the illness. By the end of June 1943 Malcolm's diary entries had become chaotic, which was always the case in periods of mental turbulence. It is likely, therefore, that the breakdown lasted some weeks in June and early July. Later in the year bold entries like BALLS TO LPO and HELL ON EARTH may just be reflections of overwork, but that Malcolm was anxious about his state of mind in 1943 is shown by his buying Bernard Hart's *The Psychology of Insanity*,[53] a long-established work exploring the psychological background to mental disorder, as well as a newly published book on mastering depression and anxiety, Dr Harry Fosdick's *On Being a Real Person*. And it is probably not coincidence that for the past year he had been immersing himself in the life and works of William Blake and Robert Burns, two troubled poets. Blake suffered from manic-depressive illness with wild mood swings, severe melancholia, delusions and hallucinations. Burns had a milder form of the illness, dying before its ultimate severity could be established.[54] Malcolm was trying to understand better the nature of his illness.

Sheila's Yorkshire grit was much needed at this trying time, particularly as the social stigma of mental illness in the 1940s exacerbated all the natural feelings of dismay and humiliation.[55] She was also pregnant, and the news of the pregnancy may well be related to the psychotic moment, for although he was to love all his children very much, the concept of paternity aroused within him certain insecurities.

---

[51] BBC TV *Omnibus* programme on his 70th Birthday, 1991.
[52] Schizophrenia, which leads to withdrawal for periods from the rational world, is, unlike manic-depressive illness, not in the genes.
[53] Cambridge University Press, 1912
[54] Malcolm put this interest to good musical effect. *Tam O'Shanter* and *Five William Blake Songs* were written twelve and sixteen years later, respectively.

Shortly after the breakdown, the orchestra's two-week summer holiday allowed a timely return to Cornwall. The previous summer they had gazed each day across to the Lizard Peninsula. This year they stayed upon it, in a remote farmhouse at Gillan,[56] a few miles from Helston, high up on open farmland, from where there were fine distant views of Falmouth Bay and a long stretch of coastline. A walk through the fields took them to the little fishing village of Porthallow, once a busy port engaged in the pilchard industry. Malcolm soon found the Five Pilchards Inn, where he made friends with the fishermen and drank, in careful moderation, the best local cider. He and Sheila also found a farmhouse at which they could get glasses of fresh milk, still warm from the cows, and Cornish cream teas, a luxury at a time of severe food rationing. The rest of the village consisted of just a post office and a few small dwellings nestling between cliff and sea. Porthallow was a down-to-earth village, pretty only in its wild, unspoilt state, but for recuperation from overwork and illness it was perfect.

Life felt less threatening at Gillan, and war had lent the area an even greater tranquillity than usual. There were concrete tank traps and rolls of barbed wire on the cliff tops, an RAF airfield not far away, and at Nare Point there was an observation post for the anti-submarine torpedo range. But somehow these were surreal embellishments on a landscape on which war did not impinge. And it was not long before Malcolm, who always acted like a child at the seaside, was excitedly playing in the waves. Porthallow beach, lying dramatically between granite headlands under the wooded cliffs, has wide expanses of grey shingle when the tide is out. That summer, several children connected with a nearby Naval installation spent much of their time romping along it. One was particularly lively. His father, he said proudly, was serving on a destroyer. In next to no time Malcolm was galloping along the shingle and into the waves, while the boy, on his shoulders, noisily urged him on:

'Come on, Beckus, my old grey mare!'

'Bloody little urchin,' puffed Malcolm. 'Bloody little dandipratt!'

Quite where Malcolm discovered 'dandipratt', an old English word for urchin, is unclear. But this seaside meeting with these extrovert children at Porthallow Bay led to the composition of the work which brought Malcolm his first public success. He wrote it just a couple of months after the holiday, in September 1943, at Nan's cottage in Capel Garmon, while enjoying a short break from the orchestra.[57] Malcolm changed points of detail, giving the urchin, the protagonist in the piece, the name of the horse, but, essentially, the work owes its

---

[55] It was not known then that 90% of all families, if only they were to be able to delve back far enough in their family history, would find some case of mental instability.

[56] The farmhouse was called Menifters, owned by a Mrs Hoskins. They were there in the last two weeks of July 1943.

[57] After coming down from a concert in Derby on 20 September 1943, he had five free days before playing at Kettering on 26 September.

inspiration to the child on Porthallow beach. Malcolm in old age was to declare that its writing was a kind of therapy:

> I had been very depressed and I think it saved my life.[58]

The work, written in sonata form, is often described as a 'comedy overture', but this is misleading, despite the lively beginning and regular outbreaks of high spirits. A cornet first introduces the urchin, a figure with whom Malcolm clearly sympathises: a coarse outsider who cocks a snook at the rest of the world. The glorious tunes of the first two subjects certainly suggest that we are in for quite a romp and at one stage of noisy vulgarity the urchin seems to have become involved with clowns at a circus. But as the development proceeds we can be in no doubt that Beckus' life, which had seemed so jolly, is now in a great deal of turmoil. The melodies get more and more fragmented until there is a virtual breakdown, a most precarious section where everything for a while becomes totally becalmed, almost to the point of silence. It is a surprise and relief when Beckus cheekily re-emerges, triumphant, right at the end. 'Look!' he seems to say. 'Here I am! I haven't vanished! I may have been having some problems, but I'm back!'

*Beckus* is the first orchestral work to show the distinctive new voice which had already emerged in chamber works like the *Three Shanties* and the Wind Quintet. It is a strangely different piece from *Larch Trees*, a tone poem completed only three months before.[59] Celebrating a particular country scene in Yorkshire, *Larch Trees* sounds derivative. Debussy, Delius, Sibelius, Vaughan Williams and William Alwyn have all been suggested as influences. *Beckus*, by contrast, is totally distinctive. There is the lilting main melody, for example, which is pure Arnold in its rollicking exuberance.[60] Likewise the joy and laughter, close to hysteria, have the characteristic sense of fragility. Malcolm's music, as Donald Mitchell has written, 'often sets about qualifying its own happiness'.[61] The overture also shows off Malcolm's clarity and transparency of the orchestration, his textures likened by Hugo Cole to Berlioz:

> He will hold his heavy forces in reserve for long passages of chamber-music transparency, then suddenly throw in the whole brass section in some shock attack.[62]

To have produced such an original and mature work as *Beckus the Dandipratt* at the age of twenty-one was so remarkable an achievement that the connection between this act of creativity and the psychotic illness of that summer seems certain. Dr Kay Jamison [63] has convincingly put the case that 'the fiery aspects of

---

[58] 1991

[59] June 1943

[60] In comparing Malcolm Arnold to the novelist Charles Dickens, Donald Mitchell notes that they both possess this quality of 'rollicking exuberance' in abundance.

[61] Malcolm's sixty-fifth birthday souvenir

[62] Hugo Cole: *Malcolm Arnold*, p.17

[63] Professor of Psychiatry at the Johns Hopkins University School of Medicine

thought and feeling' which trigger a great work of art very frequently carry with them 'the capacity for vastly darker moods, grimmer energies, and, occasionally, bouts of "madness"'.[64] The distinction, she suggests, between what the world sees as 'artistic temperament' and psychiatrists as 'manic depressive illness' is a very fine one. The affliction which was to dog Malcolm's progress through life also contributed to his genius.

*Beckus* was still only forming in his mind when Malcolm rejoined his colleagues at the end of the summer holiday and began his third year with the orchestra. The relentlessness of the travel was awesome.[65] He knew every railway station in London and a great many round Britain. And it was a hand-to-mouth existence. The pay was very modest and his diary was full of IOUs: Johnny Kuchmy 5/-; Boris Rickelman 8/6; Richard Adeney 10/-; Michael Dobson £5/10... Nor was there the compensatory interest of a quick-changing repertoire. It was hard to feel much love for Beethoven's Fifth when it had been heard all the way from Aberdeen to Portsmouth. Analysed soberly, in the cold light of dawn, without a Popsy in sight, it was a dog's life. There was only one redeeming feature – but it was a big one – the audiences were hugely appreciative. Many of them had never heard any classical music before. What the players were doing, as they went round the factories and the variety theatres, was creating a whole new, mass audience. And that was exciting.

Thomas Russell captured the pioneering spirit in a vivid account[66] of one orchestral concert, at a Bristol aircraft factory, given in a large canteen as the workers had their lunch:

> Gradually, their meal finished, the workers edged their way towards the improvised platform so that no sound or movement of the players or conductor should be missed. As I walked slowly round the gaunt, angular building, with its bare tables, rigid iron girders, and the tense mass of working people, the music seemed to take on a special significance. I found I was nervous. More nervous than I should have been at Queen's Hall or the Royal Albert Hall ... Here, anything less than the best would be a breach of faith ... The Londonderry Air began the programme. Even the two groups of four men, playing their daily, after-lunch game of solo, seemed to lay their cards more gently on the table ... Cups and plates ceased to exist, and the silence became deathly. Two thousand human beings, bare floors, bare tables and an echoing roof, but not a sound could be heard beyond the rhythm of the orchestra, the infectious rhythm of the Dances from Prince Igor ...

---

[64] Dr Kay Redfield Jamison: *Touched With Fire* (The Free Press, 1993)
[65] His diary shows: 8.30, St Pancras for Loughborough; 8.20, Liverpool St for Wisbech; 2.10, Paddington for Birmingham; 1.10, King's Cross for Doncaster; 9.50, Euston for Hanley; 9.50, Marylebone for Leicester; 11.30, Waterloo for Southampton; 11.50, Victoria for Chatham ...
[66] *Philharmonic Post*

The Bristol week of August 1943 was a good one for Malcolm, for it signalled the first performance of the *Three Shanties* at a lunchtime concert in an aircraft hangar outside the city at Filton.[67] There was also the first broadcast of his Wind Quintet, an event not without its own excitements. Charles Gregory had arranged with the BBC that his players would broadcast two works, Hindemith's much admired quintet and Malcolm's new one, during their week in Bristol. They had not looked at Malcolm's far from easy piece for five months,[68] but believed they would have three or four days to remind themselves of it. However, when they arrived for their first rehearsal, Charles Gregory rushed in with the news that the quintets were to be broadcast that day, the first almost at once, at 11.00, and the second at 12.00. The oboist Michael Dobson remembered the crisis well:

> Charles had a taxi waiting, and we all piled in and rushed to the studios. Fortunately we had played the Hindemith recently so we decided to broadcast that first … We then had half an hour to rehearse the Malcolm Arnold work and decided it would be safer if Malcolm conducted it. We rehearsed it with him until a few minutes before the hour and then gave it its first broadcast performance. We gave a few subsequent performances at various music clubs but it never went quite so well as at that Bristol broadcast![69]

Now in his third year with the orchestra, Malcolm was working more by instinct than rational thought, exhausted by the demanding work schedule and his own inability to look after himself. Once *Beckus* had been written he let himself go for several months. It was a shock to discover at Christmas that Sheila was expecting her baby any day. By the New Year Sheila's mother had come down from Sheffield to stay in their small studio flat, and Malcolm's immediate request to borrow some money from her hardly settled her anxieties about her son-in-law's lack of thrift. Nor was she impressed when, just two days before the birth of the baby, on 6 January, Malcolm undertook film engagements at Pinewood and Uxbridge. Far worse, he had failed to make definite arrangements for Sheila's confinement. When Sheila was taken to a nursing home in Marble Arch, it was completely booked. So the baby was born at home in the Queensborough Mews flat. Tragically, the little girl died almost as soon as she was born. Malcolm was not in the flat at the time, though he had no engagements booked that day. Mrs Nicholson never forgave him, but he hardly noticed, for he was too full of self-recrimination. He had failed Sheila, of all people, when she most needed him. Nothing else really mattered. The tragedy of 6 January 1944 would eventually recede in time, and was rarely, if ever, mentioned. But it never left him.

---

[67] Some time between 2 and 7 August 1943
[68] The Quintet had received at least one previous performance at the Lourdes Hall, Harpenden, on 20 March 1943.
[69] Michael Dobson to Alan Poulton, 7 December 1983

Three days after the death of his daughter Malcolm was back with the LPO. His diary is a jumble of frantic overnight stops. It must have been hard for him to know whether he was in Hamer's Hotel, Bolton, or the Lion, Guildford; in digs at 8 Jamaica Street, Glasgow, or 12 Windsor Terrace, Newcastle. Every Sunday he was back in London, playing at the Adelphi Theatre, where highlights included Jean Pougnet as soloist in the Elgar Violin Concerto, Walter Goehr conducting the first performance of Michael Tippett's *A Child of Our Time*, and Boult conducting Elgar's *The Dream of Gerontius*. With D-Day and the Normandy landings imminent, the Americans were in England in large numbers, and an unusual programme of American music was conducted by Hugo Weisgall, 'now in England with the US Army'. By the time the regular Easter week at Bristol arrived Malcolm was in a volatile mental state. His feelings of guilt at the death of his daughter had not disappeared with the miles travelled or the bottles emptied. By Easter 1944 he had been on the road for nearly three years. To accentuate his intentions at Bristol, against each of the five days spent there he wrote in his diary in large capital letters: PISS-UP. At the end of the week was the solitary phrase, again in large capitals: VIVE LA GUINNESS!

He found it hard to contain the anger inside him. The baby hadn't asked to be born and it certainly hadn't asked to die. By May he was playing in Northampton for a week, and the anger accelerated. He put off going to Pappy and Nan, and spent the first night with Clifford and Doll, whom Pappy had set up in a house at the back of Craigmore.[70] Clifford and Doll were the best of drinkers, but it still proved an uncomfortable evening. It concerned him that Clifford's eight-year-old daughter, Gill, was sleeping over at Craigmore, looked after by Lizzie, so that her parents could enjoy a proper evening's drinking with no worries about making too much noise. It annoyed him that a daughter who had survived the hazards of being born was then neglected. And it alarmed him that Doll was belching, like a character out of Hogarth. Clifford too seemed less glamorous than before. He still had a fund of hilarious stories which he told with inimitable timing, but Malcolm was not yet drunk enough not to feel uneasy at his tales of cowardice and duplicity, of Clifford living off Pappy and Nan, getting them to create a workshop out of the garage at the bottom of their garden complete with a super-de-luxe lathe, so he could start an engineering business, which had only worked well for a bit ... Now he had some better ideas for making his fortune, and decent old Lizzie was going to let him borrow her savings. Fortunately, he'd always been her favourite …

Malcolm left just as quickly as he could the next morning. But Ruth's at Milton Street proved equally uncomfortable. Ruth was depressed, and silently critical at his neglect. She seemed to think he was making a fortune as a trumpet player, which was hardly the case. Wag seemed dour and discontented. So on to Craigmore, where Nan was as warm as ever, but the anxieties showed in every

---

[70] In Homestead Way

line on her face. She was having to subsidise his father, she said, because he would insist on living beyond his means … Pappy had changed dramatically, wanting to know about every little piece of music he'd written, taking notes about it with a reverential enthusiasm. It was almost as unnerving to be hugely in favour as hugely out of it. The only time Pappy stopped asking about the LPO or the writing was to regale him with Aubrey's latest exploits. Now a Major, Aubrey had just been put in charge of three batteries around Avonmouth, protecting Bristol. Once Pappy had three war heroes to brag about. Now he had one.

It had been bad luck, coming back to Northampton at this particular moment, when his head was bursting and he found it hard to make coherent responses. And he hated the New Theatre, which had too many memories. It was in the interval of the final concert that the explosion occurred. For some months Malcolm had been becoming irritated with an orchestra leader who wasn't up to the job. Jean Pougnet might have Latin good looks and be a fair fiddler, but he had had no orchestral experience before joining the LPO and he was letting them all down! So when Pougnet chose *not* to listen to his explanation of what had just gone terribly wrong in the Beethoven, Malcolm knew it was time to go. Telling Denis Egan to take over as first trumpet for the rest of the programme, he walked out of the theatre, ignored his belongings at Craigmore and made straight for the railway station.

He was twenty-two already. One year older than Philip, so time was no longer on his side. He had better things to do than kow-tow to ignorant French pin-up boys. The main goal was to get clear of Northampton just as quickly as possible. After that he might be able to breathe, and then he could begin to ponder what kind of new life he might be able to make for himself. For the moment he little cared. All he knew was that he was finished with a dog's life. There were the Proms coming up any week now, and he really didn't want to play his *umpteenth* Tchaikovsky 5, his *umpteenth* Brahms 2, and *umpteenth* 'New World'! It was not as if any of them were getting any better! He'd miss Albert Sammons having a go at the Elgar, he'd miss *Der Freischütz*, Sibelius 7, the Delius piano concerto and George Dyson's 'At the Tabart Inn'. But could he really stand *another* Tchaikovsky piano concerto, *another* Grieg, and *another* Schumann? He often woke up in the morning hearing the Tchaikovsky thundering along in some remote corner of his brain, unless of course he'd had a jarful, when he'd hear the Grieg. Either way, it couldn't be good. And, what was worst of all, if he *had* stayed around, there'd have been Pougnet out front, showing off with the fifth Brandenburg, pretending he was Kreisler. Better to cut adrift, catch an early train, and fashion the future by some means or other. At the back of his mind, a curious thought was emerging. Perhaps on the train he'd be able to explore more fully the idea of enlistment?

# 5
# Private Arnold
## In War and Peace, 1944-48

SHEILA WAS TAKEN ABACK by Malcolm's plans to enlist, and nothing she could say would change his mind. When she pointed out that it was a betrayal of everything he had once stood for, he merely shrugged his shoulders and changed the subject. He had decided to enlist, and that was that.

He first explored the possibility of joining the Navy, because, as he said later, 'I wanted a good, clean death'.[1] Turned down on medical grounds, he next applied to a parachute regiment, from which he was also rejected, later claiming jokingly that this was because he was 'too large'.[2] Eventually, however, he met with success and signed up with the 'Buffs', the Royal East Kent Regiment.

It was an extraordinary change of heart, the reasons for which Malcolm tried to gloss over in later life, preferring, if possible, to treat it all as a joke:

> There were many people in the course of my career in the LPO whom I would have willingly have strangled or shot through the temple, so I thought I must volunteer.[3]

Quizzed on the subject by a journalist in 1971, Malcolm prevaricated disarmingly:

> I had exemption as a conscientious objector, not the Christian pacifist sort but an aggressive one, yet I joined the Army. My views were totally cynical and turned out correct.[4]

It was in this confused interview that he increased his length of service from the actual two months to a fictitious two years, a length which is often quoted.

Piers Burton-Page, his first biographer, hard pressed to explain why a passionate pacificist should suddenly don khaki, offered four possible reasons, none wholly convincing: Malcolm was frustrated with wartime orchestral life; inhibited as a composer (despite writing a dozen works in the past three years); sad about Philip's death (which had occurred three years earlier); and alarmed at defeatism in London (though the Americans were now in the war).[5] Paul Jackson,

---

[1] The comment comes from the BBC Television *Omnibus* programme, celebrating his seventieth birthday in 1991.

[2] In photographs of the time he is extremely slim.

[3] BBC Television *Omnibus* programme, 1991

[4] Christopher Ford, *The Guardian*, 17 April 1971

[5] Burton-Page: *Philharmonic Concerto*, p.24

a similarly perplexed biographer, added a fifth possibility, the death of the baby daughter (six months earlier).[6] All these suggestions stem from the premise that Malcolm was mentally stable at the time, making rational decisions, rather than, as was really the case, in a state of mental turmoil, obsessed with death and harbouring self-destructive thoughts. For someone intending to be dead by thirty, active service was an appealing form of Russian roulette. When he talked of the Navy offering 'a good clean death', he may have been inaccurate, but he wasn't joking.

There was some anticipatory excitement for the future soldier with the advent of German flying bombs, which began dropping in large numbers on London that summer, as Malcolm rushed about, attending interviews, seeing friends and picking up part-time work in films and broadcasting.[7] He was in ebullient mood, caring little for danger, looking forward to the glamour of khaki, and delighting temporarily in the fun he was having with Dennis Brain, arranging some early music for a concert at St Peter's Church, Eaton Square.[8]

As the day for reporting for duty drew nearer, however, Malcolm grew more and more nervous and it became clear to Sheila that he was absolutely terrified of the whole business of soldiering. He no longer wished to shoot Nazis or play Russian Roulette; like the twelve-year-old at Mill Hill, he just wanted to stay at home. He was in a pub on the day he was meant to join up, hoping to be forgotten. Not long afterwards, the Military Police came knocking on his door and brusquely took him off to war. There could hardly have been a less promising recruit.

14876218 Private Arnold M did his training at Canterbury in the detail squad of B Company, 62 Platoon. But no amount of training would eradicate a deep-rooted wish to get his own way. When, after only three weeks, Myra Hess included a new work of his, the Quintet for Flute, Bassoon, Violin, Viola and Horn, in one of her lunchtime concerts at the National Gallery, he naturally expected to be there and was outraged at the rejection of his application for leave of absence. How dare the army be so crass as to prohibit his presence at this important première? Sheila was equally indignant and proved a willing accomplice to a carefully planned escape, going down to Canterbury and throwing some civilian clothes to him over a fence. So he was present, after all, at the National Gallery concert[9] and much enjoyed the audience's plaudits, but six days later, up before his CO, he was less happily received. Worse was to

---

[6] Jackson: *The Life and Music of Sir Malcolm Arnold*, p.26

[7] He also played occasionally for the New London Orchestra, with whom Sheila was associated.

[8] Malcolm arranged trios for himself, Dennis Brain and the trombonist George Maxted.

[9] The Quintet Op. 7 was another work encouraged by the horn player Charles Gregory, written shortly after Malcolm's abrupt departure from the orchestra. In addition to Gregory, the participants were Richard Adeney (flute), Albert Chasey (violin), Wrayburn Glasspool (viola) and George Alexandra (bassoon). The first performance took place on 21 December. The Quintet is skilfully written and much in the vein of the *Three Shanties*.

*Private Arnold (centre), 1944, with B Company, 62 Platoon*

follow shortly. On 17 January, 1945, not four weeks after the National Gallery concert, he effectively ended his career as a soldier when he shot himself in the foot in the lavatory of his barracks.

Malcolm has been at pains to put all the blame on the army. There he was, a fully trained fighting man, all ready to mow down Nazis in their hundreds before gallantly expiring in some corner of a foreign field, and, instead, he had been given the humiliating posting of the regimental brass band. But Malcolm, trained or otherwise, would hardly have been an asset in an army platoon requiring unquestioning obedience to orders. On the other hand, his expertise on the trumpet would be given full expression in the band, as he himself had realised at the beginning of the war when he had applied to the Marines. The army had made a sensible and sensitive decision, and Malcolm's first response to it – to go on hunger strike – only underlined the rightness of the decision. Malcolm's second response has been well chronicled:

> I sat in that deserted room and cried. I had five rounds of ammunition left and I thought what shall I do? And I went in my best denims, put a biscuit[10] underneath my foot, or on the top, and shot it. There was this resounding bang and there I was in a pool of blood …[11]
>
> I am not particularly proud of that. It was very painful, and there was a lot of blood around. The man who had been giving us bayonet practice found me and fainted. I was left alone for some time before the medical orderly arranged for a stretcher party, and I went to hospital …[12]

---

[10] An army term for a small mattress
[11] *Omnibus*, BBC TV, 1991
[12] *Contrasts*, Central Television, 1989

This account nimbly passes over Malcolm's possession, against army regulations, of five live rounds, which he must have hidden away after a training exercise. And as Denis Egan had given him instructions on how to shoot himself in the foot, reminding him that it was the commonplace way of getting a 'Blighty' in the First World War, there can be little doubt that Malcolm had decided that only by this painful act of self-mutilation would he be able to extract himself from a situation which he could no longer tolerate. The bizarre nature of his enlisting and withdrawing, with its mixture of risk-taking and impulsiveness, strongly reflects the manic-depressive state.

Sheila was on an ENSA[13] orchestral tour with the Riddick String Orchestra in the Isle of Wight when the news of the shooting came through. She at once gave up her music to help support Malcolm. Unfortunately the reaction in Northampton was less positive. Robin happened to be at Craigmore when the news came through that his uncle had shot himself in the foot:

> Nan took to her room, the middle parlour, crying, and Pappy, also in tears, went off to the front parlour. He was worrying about the family disgrace, not about Malcolm's injury. I was at once sent back to my parents.[14]

Only Ruth was supportive. Seeing the shooting as an act of bravery, she wrote in her journal:

> I am distressed for Malcolm. What a lot of guts it takes to do what he has done.

But she feared for Nan:

> These last few weeks have been a nightmare ... The awful cold and frost and snow and being continually hungry for chocolate! And now the worry over Malc, and wondering what effect it will have on Ma.

After six difficult years of marriage Ruth herself was struggling.

> I long sometimes for someone to talk to. How I wish Sheila and Malc lived nearer. I bottle myself up and my brain fair bursts for want of expression ...

Financial worries were ever present, though it seems that her relationship with Pappy was slightly improved:

> I don't know what will happen to us. When Wag's ill we're fairly stuck for money and spend the rent. Still, dad usually helps us out ...

Malcolm meanwhile, had been taken off to a military hospital at Barming, near Maidstone, from where, six days later,[15] he wrote an extraordinarily matter-of-fact letter to Pappy:

> Dear Dad,
>     Would it be possible to send a pair of shoes to this bloke L/Cpl Buckle, 4 Derwent Manse, Derwent Road, Anerley SE. He has been very decent and I should like to

---

[13] Entertainments National Service Association
[14] April 2004
[15] 23 January 1945

return what he has done for me in some way. He takes size 10. I should think brown would be most acceptable.

It doesn't matter if it is going to be difficult to send them because I haven't said anything to him about this.

He is only a young bloke and was in charge of the Squad I was in and as I said he was very decent to me.

Much love,

Malcolm

After nearly two months at Barming Malcolm was transferred to an army convalescent home, Brookhurst Grange, near Ewhurst, a large and comfortable suburban villa requisitioned for the war. Here his spirits revived so much that he restarted composition, producing in a matter of days a Duo for Flute and Viola. It was written for Richard Adeney and Wrayburn Glasspool, both ardent pacifists, which suggests the Brookhurst Duo may be a restatement of everything Malcolm stood for at the beginning of the war.

The opening slow movement begins with a typically Arcadian tune on the flute. Peace seems to reign. But as the movement progresses the theme is broken into many jagged fragments, and at the end there is no full restatement of Arcady, just the merest hint of its erstwhile tranquillity. In the second movement, an *Allegro*, the two instruments express turmoil and regret in equal measure. A military motif keeps intruding and peace is a thing of the past. The third movement quite eclipses its striking predecessors. It begins with a memorable tune, pastoral and jaunty. Malcolm would have us believe that all at last is well: peace reigns again. But, against all expectations, another process of fragmentation occurs, sections of the melody are pulled this way and that, as both instruments struggle to recapture the atmosphere of Arcadia. Thwarted in our hopes of hearing a recapitulation of the glorious tune, we find the work ending instead on a strong dissonance, followed by a haunting, dying fall. In this remarkable nine-minute miniature Malcolm would seem to be exorcising the traumas of the last few months.

He was able to walk again by 15 May, when he appeared before an Army Board and was given a dishonourable discharge:

> There was great sympathy for me, for the war had ended by this time and they said 'You bloody fool! You could have maimed yourself for life!'[16]

He was fortunate that the hearing coincided with national celebrations over VE Day, the surrender of Germany meaning that at least the war in Europe was over. At such an important time Malcolm's self-inflicted wound seemed a paltry thing and was easily forgiven.

> They thought I was a lunatic. I think they were probably right.[17]

---

[16] Christopher Ford, *The Guardian*, 17 April 1971

[17] *Ibid.*

*Charles Gregory giving the first performance of the First Horn Concerto with the LPO, conducted by Ernest Ansermet, Covent Garden, 8 December 1946*

In his immediate delight at being free of soldiering and war, Malcolm responded enthusiastically to a request from the LPO's Chairman, Charles Gregory,[18] that he should write him a horn concerto. The resultant work was not just the first of many concertos written at the request of distinguished friends, but also the longest, a token of the importance he attached both to the commission and the occasion. Just as the Brookhurst Duo was a very personal statement about the war, the Horn Concerto No 1 responded to it at a more universal level. As he hobbled around his Queensborough Studios flat, still only twenty-three, Malcolm was somehow able to look back on the European conflict with an impressively cool detachment, producing a work which, in its many moods and wide scope, has much to offer soloist, orchestra and listeners.

The first movement, in conventional sonata form, presents a pastoral vision of England at peace, the horn setting an atmosphere of cheerful tranquillity with both first and second subjects. In the development, however, there is an interruption, a steady marching off to war, followed by a short period of utter confusion. The twin pastoral themes in due course reassert themselves, England is at peace once more and the movement ends with some outward expressions of jubilation, though at no stage is the joy unequivocal. There follows a ten-minute *tour de force*, an *Andante* so heartfelt in its expression of long, continuing sorrow that it

---

[18] The Gregorys and the Arnolds were good friends. It was Gregory who had told Malcolm about the farmhouse at St Buryan, Gregory loving the area so much that at the end of his career he settled near there.

is hard not to identify it immediately with Malcolm's grief for all the victims of the past six years of war. The horn leads the way, sounding a ghostly Last Post over the souls of the dead, who cry out from time to time, pitiful and uncomprehending. The movement has a Mahlerian continuity and breadth, though written in Malcolm's economical way, with individual woodwind often having poignant conversation with the soloist as he comments with touching dignity on events too tragic for human understanding.

Malcolm reasserts himself in the final *Allegro*, taking us back to rural England with a cheeky hunting tune, all galloping horses and loud halloos. Here are the ruling classes, at peace again, having a good time. But there is a counter melody, simple and wistful, played on the horn with a ripeness suggesting nostalgia for times past. It is tempting to see it as the quarry, an unruffled fox, keeping an eye on the hunters, sometimes close by, sometimes far off, always cheerful and confident in their unceasing hallooing. From time to time Mr Fox puts in a disdainful appearance, letting the hunt catch good sight of him. But just for once, it seems, he has misjudged things, finds himself cornered and in big trouble, the music expressing thud upon thud as the hunters unfeelingly attempt to administer the *coup de grâce*. That, we are led to believe, will be the conclusion. But not a bit of it. Malcolm has a cheekier ending in store, on the same lines as that in the Brookhurst Duo. For just when we least expect it, back comes Mr Fox's ripe old tune on the horn. He is still alive, after all, only a little dazed, until, most unexpectedly, he sinks with a sigh to the ground, as the concerto ends with a breathless dying fall.

Just as Malcolm was Beckus, so here he was clearly Mr Fox, the victim and cheeky outsider, weary at the end of the war with being so out of tune with the times. And if Mr Fox in the end made a surprising misjudgement, which led to disaster, so too did Malcolm.

As usual, as soon as the euphoria of writing subsided, despondency set in. On the completion of the concerto Malcolm could see how much he was at odds with the national mood. The country, financially and emotionally drained by the war, had little sympathy with those who questioned the sacrifices. Now was not the moment for Malcolm, Ruth or anyone to declare that dying for one's country was 'the old, old lie'. Not that Malcolm could even side with the pacifist cause any more. He had deserted it for a militarist stance, only to desert that too.

In war's immediate aftermath he was close again to Ruth in spirit, questioning like her the stoical patriotism of the time. In a bitter poem called 'Armistice' she imagined a war 'hero' contemplating a photograph of himself in a local newspaper:

> Look at me!
> Or the husk of me!
> My soul remained with the flotsam of war;
> The broken, the slain, the martyred and the tortured …

> Look at my smiling relations!
> They are so glad to have me back
> I was embarrassed at their effusions.
> Because the 'I' they know is no longer with me.
> O God! What a mockery is the aftermath,
> The long drawn-out horror of 'peace',
> The restless lull between battles,
> The artifice, the glamour, the deceit of it!

'The artifice, the glamour, the deceit' were things Malcolm brooded on, and come out strongly in his music. They are also what made Ruth constantly return to the theme of Philip:

> I am but a young airman,
> Afraid to die, because I know
> That Death should be a peaceful reckoning.
> I would like to leave something
> Behind me, a little grain of wisdom,
> But can only be silent …

Malcolm too wanted to leave something behind him. He felt he had much to say but it was a question of finding the time and space. That first summer of peace in 1945, therefore, was a strange, restless world for him. He felt an acute sense of dislocation as he hurried around the bomb-scarred London landscape, infected himself perhaps with that national sense of inner dissatisfaction which had brought in Attlee as Prime Minister for Churchill. To be turned down for a job by the dance band leader Geraldo was a chastening experience, in keeping with the times.

Morale was restored when he took a temporary job with the Liverpool Philharmonic Orchestra, with whom he was playing when news broke of the surrender of Japan. This time he caught the national mood, celebrating long and hard. Later that August, he even exceeded the national mood, with the result that he made a sheepish appearance at Marylebone Magistrates Court.[19]

He quickly redeemed himself in Sheila's eyes, however, by acquiring a position as second trumpet with the BBC Symphony Orchestra, and before taking up this appointment he delighted Nan by staging a conciliatory day out with her and Pappy, including a concert at the Albert Hall.[20] Malcolm's four months[21] with the BBC Symphony Orchestra at the end of 1945 had been engineered by Ernest Hall, his teacher at the RCM, who was the orchestra's long-established principal trumpet. The orchestra had only just returned to London after evacuation and for the moment it was having to use the People's Palace in the Mile End Road as its base. There was very little touring, and a great deal of broadcasting. This should

---

[19] 20 August 1945

[20] 8 September 1945

[21] From 23 September 1945 to 16 January 1946

*In the BBC Symphony Orchestra with Ernest Hall (left) and Jack Macintosh, 1945*

have been ideal for Malcolm, but during much of his time with the BBC Symphony Orchestra he was needing regular medical support for his depression.

He had known all along that the BBC job was only temporary and that he was filling in for somebody still in the army. Nevertheless, the manner of his departure was clumsily handled. He was in the Maida Vale studios one morning, when Adrian Boult, the orchestra's principal conductor, passed by and casually murmured how sorry he was that they would not be seeing much more of each other. Luckily, jobs had become more plentiful. Two great orchestras were being founded in the immediate post-war period. Malcolm, known to be the best trumpet player around, could have found employment at either the Philharmonia or the Royal Philharmonic. He chose instead to accept the offer of Thomas Russell[22] and rejoin the LPO in his old job as principal trumpet. He felt more comfortable back in his group of anarchic friends.

The orchestra's touring was as relentless as ever. In 1946, the LPO gave well over two hundred concerts,[23] and the next year was equally busy. In addition to all their regular venues Thomas Russell was always willing to fit in extra bookings. One of the first concerts Malcolm played in on his return was one

---

[22] A victim of McCarthyism, Russell was to be dismissed from the LPO in 1952 for his communist sympathies.

[23] Basil Cameron conducted a fifth of them: Rankl, Ansermet, Fitelberg and van Beinum also conducted. Malcolm was especially pleased, however, to play under Bruno Walter and Victor de Sabata.

such extra, a hastily arranged trip under Ernest Ansermet to Stowe School. An enthusiastic music master with private means to underwrite the venture had encouraged Boult to bring the LPO to Stowe before the war. Now he was doing so again. Malcolm, therefore, found himself travelling into the Buckinghamshire countryside by an uncomfortable 'utility' coach and playing *Petroushka* and the *Enigma Variations* in a cramped, wooden gym. What he thought of the venue – with the nearest pub three miles away – we don't know. But a moment in the *Leonora Overture*, when 'a sustained note on the trumpets tended to obliterate the rushing scale passages of the woodwind and strings',[24] gives us an indication that Malcolm may have been expressing himself with vigour. Nonetheless, he found time to chat and joke afterwards with members of the youthful audience. Years later, vivid memories of the friendly and zany LPO visit still remain.

The end of the war allowed Malcolm to enjoy the guest appearances of many famous foreign conductors, both in the concert hall and recording studios. He played in the famous Decca recording of Brahms's Second Symphony conducted by Wilhelm Furtwängler, who had controversially stayed in Berlin through the war. Thomas Russell was delighted to have procured him for the 1947-48 season:

> The cycle of concerts directed by Furtwängler attracted very large audiences and provoked keen discussion. The four symphonies of Brahms included in the cycle are rarely presented in a regular succession …[25]

The concerts with Furtwängler enhanced the LPO's standing only if the listeners did not worry too much about the music. The LPO, wrote Richard Adeney, needed a trainer to discipline them out of raggedness. But Furtwängler, used to the highly disciplined Berlin Philharmonic, seemed unaware of the orchestra's technical problems:

> There was an absurd performance of Beethoven's Seventh Symphony when, perhaps to compensate for the inaccuracies from the orchestra, he put in so much rubato that the music sometimes completely stopped, and, because of his vague beat, we didn't know exactly when to start again …[26]

Richard Adeney found Furtwängler both disturbing and hypnotic, his head flopping loose on the end of a long, scraggy neck:

> Tall, thin and bald, like an untidy Giacometti sculpture, he seldom beat to the rhythm of the music, but stood like a puppet on strings, fluttering his baton rapidly up and down.

He hissed like a steam train in faster passages, sending spittle all over the nearest string players. From the safety of the brass, Malcolm beamed happily at their discomforture.

---

[24] *The Stoic*, April 1946

[25] *Philharmonic Post*, June 1948

[26] Adeney, *Flute*

Another German, Carl Schuricht, made a greater impression, not only with the intricacies of Beethoven and Brahms, but also because of his unambiguous political inclinations. 'With a fine record of wartime behaviour,' wrote Russell, 'Schuricht is a welcome visitor to England.'

From Italy came Victor de Sabata, 'a little bald man with a bad limp and a very pale, thin, lined face, like a sad, underfed Italian waiter'.[27] As soon as he had made his painful way to the conductor's rostrum, however, he became mesmerisingly histrionic, with a glistening smile, shining eyes and the acrobatic body of a dancer. The orchestra loved and respected him as a virtuoso orchestral trainer and a conductor with the minutest details of each score etched in his memory. Malcolm often talked nostalgically about de Sabata's LPO recording of Beethoven's *Eroica* 'with the tune doubled at the end of the first movement on the trumpet'.[28] Richard Adeney delighted in the way de Sabata would often whip the orchestra up 'to extraordinary heights of frenzy'. There was a sensational performance of Wagner's *Ride of the Valkyries* in Bristol, for instance:

> At the end there wasn't the usual, immediate applause, but a stunned silence; a woman screamed and the scream was appropriate, and only then did the clapping start.[29]

Other notable guests were Sergiu Celibidache, Ernest Ansermet, Clemens Krauss and Erich Kleiber. Thomas Russell particularly admired a concert in which Kleiber had conducted Berlioz's *Symphonie Fantastique.*

> He was a past master at handling an orchestra … There was an added maturity to the qualities we had remembered from pre-war days … The audience no less than the players were electrified by the result.

Richard Adeney found Kleiber even better in rehearsal than performance:

> A little, bald Napoleon of a man, compact, paunchy and strutting, he had infinite patience in getting balance adjusted, chords in tune, bowings sorted out, phrasing exactly to his liking and rhythms taut and springy …

Malcolm particularly revered Bruno Walter, an admiration which was reciprocated, Walter appreciating not only Malcolm's own playing but the care with which he rehearsed the entire brass section. On one occasion at the Albert Hall Walter surprised Malcolm by insisting he come up and take a bow beside him at the end of Mahler's Fourth.

---

[27] Adeney, *Op. cit.*

[28] *Music & Musicians*, October 1986. Richard Adeney, by contrast, remembers de Sabata in despair during this recording. 'He got the orchestra perfectly trained to be unanimous, perfectly rhythmic and correctly balanced; but the tempos and the interpretation foxed him.' (*Op. cit.*)

[29] Adeney, *Op. cit.*

I had to come to the front, under all those spotlights, feeling an idiot and so exhausted, as I put the trumpet under my arm and bowed. I didn't know what the fuss was about. I'd just played it the best I could.

Malcolm especially liked the way Walter never reacted to errors made in performance:

He always looked the other way if something went wrong, which is what a great conductor should do. He should never look and swear …

He was also amused by Walter's high-handedness in sending the lovely Polish singer Eugenia Zareska away from rehearsal because she was wearing a trouser suit.[30]

Malcolm often told the story of Bruno Walter's subtle changes to the official scores, not to simplify them for the players but to clarify the composer's intentions:

Once we were doing the Schubert 'Great' C Major Symphony with Bruno Walter conducting. He brought his own score, naturally, and also his own set of parts. Basil Cameron, who attended every Bruno Walter rehearsal, came up to him when the rehearsal was finished and asked, 'Maestro, would it be possible for me to look at your score?' 'By all means,' Walter replied, 'but whatever you do, don't give the game away.'[31]

However good the many foreign guest conductors were, Thomas Beecham nonetheless remained Malcolm's ultimate favourite.

He was marvellous to work for. He made the orchestra feel you were all part of the same act, the same joke, as it were, a serious joke. You were all one. He had a fantastic personality …[32]

Malcolm, like most of his colleagues, was hard to please and would not stay silent if a point needed expressing. When the histrionic Victor de Sabata was proving too demanding for his liking, Malcolm visited the Berlitz School of Languages, so he could answer him back in Italian. De Sabata had kept saying 'Not staccato enough!' while rehearsing the Franck Symphony. 'I wanted to say in Italian, "Maestro, if we play it any shorter there won't be any notes left!"'[33] Malcolm likewise was the single member of the orchestra brave enough to make it quite obvious to Wilhelm Furtwängler that he had a problem with BO.

By this time Malcolm's expertise on the trumpet was widely acknowledged. 'He had a way of playing music,' says Basil Tschaikov, 'that would make sense in a way few others could achieve.'[34]

[30] Radio Norfolk interview with Peter Paul Nash, 14 October 1991. She was singing Mahler's *Lieder eines fahrenden Gesellen*.
[31] *Music & Musicians*, October 1986
[32] Mike Purton's Sheridan Morley interview, Anglia TV, 1984
[33] Bill Newman interview in *Classic CD* (October 1991)
[34] December 2003

Denis Wick[35] was a Luton schoolboy when he heard the LPO at the Vauxhall Motors canteen in a concert which included *Beckus* and Tchaikovsky's Sixth Symphony:

> Malcolm's playing towered over everything. I went home inspired to become a professional player.[36]

John Amis thought Malcolm's trumpet sound was 'shining and glorious'. Malcolm's contribution to Shostakovich's First Symphony brought tears to his eyes. Amis has given a vivid word picture of Malcolm at this time:

> Malcolm was a slim boyish young man, quite ordinary in looks but with the peculiarity that when he had a solo his face resembled a Disney creature under pressure. It went pink, red, purple and puce, according to the length and strength of the solo. Once having finished, he would lay the instrument on his lap and regard it, almost with loathing, at the least with icy indifference, as though he bore no responsibility for what had just sounded.[37]

As soloist with the orchestra Malcolm played on a number of occasions the Haydn concerto with great aplomb,[38] and gave fine performances of those by Goedicke, Riisager and Shostakovich.[39]

He might have been featured even more, but for his unreliability. There was always a certain amount of concern as to whether or not he would turn up, and on one tour he disappeared for three days, only to be found playing in a night club. Because he made use of the 'deputy system' quite often, he was always willing to deputise, on one occasion standing in at the New Theatre during an Old Vic Season featuring Laurence Olivier. During the course of *Richard III* he and Bram Wiggins had to leave the pit and play from the wings. The music, he was assured, was always stuck up on the back of the scenery. They arrived with not much time to spare before Olivier enacted some important business on stage during which they were to play. Unfortunately, the music was nowhere to be seen. Totally unconcerned, Malcolm proceeded to improvise in great style. 'It sounded to me,' says Bram, 'considerably better than the original!'[40]

The LPO's hierarchy was taking an interest in the promising composer within its ranks and towards the end of 1946 gave the première of Malcolm's Horn Concerto No 1 at one of their Sunday concerts at the Royal Opera House, Covent Garden.[41] Because Malcolm used no brass in the concerto, to show off the soloist, he was able to sit with Sheila in the Grand Tier, proudly listening as

---

[35] First trombone for the LSO for thirty-one years

[36] December 2003

[37] John Amis: *Amiscellany* (Faber & Faber, 1985), p.192

[38] Notably at the Adelphi Theatre, 3 October 1943

[39] Malcolm played the Shostakovich for the first time very early in his LPO career, with Eileen Joyce on piano and Sidney Beer conducting.

[40] July 2003

[41] 8 December 1946

Charles Gregory made his way through the work with nimble assurance, Ernest Ansermet conducting. The overall impression, said one perceptive critic, was that here was someone 'with a distinct musical personality and something definite to say'.[42] It was the first time that Malcolm had heard an orchestral work of his played in a public concert.

It was an exciting moment late in 1946 when *Beckus* was broadcast. The BBC Reading Panel had found it 'an amusing and light piece in a mildly modern idiom' in November 1945 and a year later the BBC Scottish Orchestra gave it its first broadcast. Thomas Russell then wrote to the BBC, pushing its claims further:

> ... As you probably know, we have a very promising composer in our orchestra, Malcolm Arnold, whose Horn Concerto we performed a short time ago. Assuming that we take part in the Promenade Season, I think it would be fitting if we were able to perform one of his works. I would suggest the overture, Beckus the Dandipratt ...[43]

But the BBC did not agree with Russell and it was not until 1977 that *Beckus* was finally played in the Proms. Eduard van Beinum made up for this disappointment by including it alongside Tchaikovsky's First Piano Concerto and Sixth Symphony at one of the LPO's Albert Hall concerts in 1948.[44]

Malcolm's career as a composer owed much to van Beinum, principal conductor of the Amsterdam Concertgebouw, who began guesting with the LPO in 1946. Van Beinum had exactly the right approach for bringing a headstrong group of renegades into line, treating them as colleagues engaged with him on an important collaboration. Some thought the quiet Dutchman boring, but the LPO loved him and Malcolm had felt able to show him the *Beckus* score. Van Beinum was impressed and persuaded Russell to include it in the LPO's repertoire. It was given its first concert performance under James Robertson at Chatham[45] and a further six provincial performances took place before van Beinum himself conducted it at Covent Garden in late November. Luck then played its part. Van Beinum had taken the LPO through a recording of Brahms's Third Symphony so quickly, that he suggested to Decca that in the spare time he might record *Beckus*.

Inevitably there were disappointments. The BBC Reading Panel, to whom he had submitted his Symphonic Suite in 1945, turned it down in 1947. There was also a second refusal of his Divertimento No 1. And Leonard Isaacs wrote to his panel colleagues in 1948[46] that, although Malcolm's letter about his Trio for Flute, Viola and Bassoon had his sympathy, 'I can't say I like the work. I find it far too clever to be good music.'

---

[42] *The Strad*, January 1947

[43] Thomas Russell to Victor Hely-Hutchinson, BBC Director of Music, 4 March, 1947 (BBC Written Archives, Caversham)

[44] 27 May 1948. Malcolm was the first of the six trumpets at that concert. Sidney Ellison, Sheila's first boyfriend, was the third.

[45] 24 May 1947

[46] 11 June 1948 (BBC Written Archives)

The Trio in question was written early on in his marriage and overflows with happiness, at least in the outer two movements. These *Allegro* movements, exuberant in their rhythms and melodic invention, conjure up the sheer fun he was having on the road with friends Richard Adeney, Wrayburn Glasspool and George Alexandra. Adeney's airy flute and Alexandra's earthy bassoon fight playfully together, with Glasspool's viola the genial referee. These two movements, however, frame an *Andante* whose strange modulations and remote beauty are suggestive of relentless wartime mourning and ghostly, vain memorials. The spirit of Philip seems never far away. It is hard to see how the Trio could be considered 'clever', unless indeed it is the genuine cleverness of contrasting the fun to be had from life on a selfish, personal level against the deep unhappiness of the times. The Trio is a little jewel.

The immediate post-war period was a time of great creativity. Although Malcolm was working full-time as an orchestral player, the Symphonic Suite and the Horn Concerto were just two of many works in the three years after the army fiasco. He also wrote a first Clarinet Concerto, for his friend Jack Thurston;[47] a flute sonatina for Richard Adeney; a *Festival Overture* for his old tutor, Philip Pfaff, then running the Ipswich Symphony Orchestra; viola and violin sonatas; several more piano pieces, including *Variations on a Ukrainian Folk Song*, the song suggested by his friend, LPO violinist Johnny Kuchmy; and two other orchestral works, a Symphony for Strings and a suite, *To Youth*. The Symphony for Strings was given its first performance and broadcast by the Riddick Orchestra, for whom Sheila played.

It is an impressive amount of work, varying considerably in substance and style, for although Malcolm had already, in 1943, discovered a distinctive voice, he was at this early stage of his career determined to keep himself open to the musical world around him. The Symphony For Strings, for example, reflected his admiration for Bartók, a highly influential figure at the time. In other works the influence of Sibelius, Stravinsky and Britten can be discerned, though whatever the stylistic flavour, Malcolm's gift for melodic invention is always in evidence, and so too many of his own stylistic idiosyncracies.

The second movement of the Violin Sonata No 1 is particularly characteristic. The violin is given a beautifully tranquil G major melody over a quiet, rhythmic piano accompaniment, only to be interrupted by a passage of savage violence, the piano leading the dissonant assault the whole way through. The violence eventually departs as abruptly as it arrived and the serene G major tune returns as if nothing unusual has happened. Such abrupt interruptions of an idealised beauty are a reflection of the manic-depressive state. Malcolm's lyricism is never free from the possibility of violent assault.

---

[47] The first performance (29 August 1949), given by its dedicatee, Frederick 'Jack' Thurston, preceded Finzi's similarly scored concerto by just a few days

The suite *To Youth* was one of Malcolm's sunnier pieces, written for the National Youth Orchestra, in its very early days. When Ruth Railton was starting up the orchestra in 1948, Malcolm gave her enthusiastic assistance, running the brass section at some of her courses with a natural ease. She never forgot the help he gave her:

> I learnt most from Malcolm Arnold, so talented; full of ideas, imagination and humour, with the warmest, most generous personality. He explained that the young know when things are wrong but can't always analyse why, and teachers are vague and don't tell them. 'Tell them it's sharp,' said Malcolm, 'and they'll put it right; or that those actual notes were too slow, and they'll respond at once. Teaching is telling them what they don't know.'[48]

Colin Bradbury[49] remembers Malcolm coming down to the first NYO course at Bath as composer/housemaster. 'He was decidedly better in one capacity than the other. As a housemaster he ended up joining in all the pillow fights!'[50] It was for this course that Malcolm wrote *To Youth* (later[51] called *Little Suite No 1*), Reginald Jacques conducting the NYO at its première at the Bath Pavilion.[52] It has remained a great favourite with professional and youth orchestras ever since.

The manic-depressive illness often allows longer periods for work than would normally be possible, the sufferer wanting less sleep and being able, when in an an exalted frame of mind, to sustain considerable feats of concentration. So in addition to everything else, Malcolm also found the time and energy to venture into films. He was later to say[53] that in his final eleven months with the LPO he would get up most mornings at 4am, which allowed him to write the scores of two feature films and eleven documentaries, in addition to a concerto and sonata. The financial rewards from the film scores allowed him in 1948 to give up orchestral playing and devote himself full-time to composition.

Stories of how he got started in films all involve John Hollingsworth, conductor of the Sadler's Wells Ballet and assistant to Muir Matheson, the director of music at Denham Studios. Back in 1943, Hollingsworth had been present at a concert in the Albert Hall, organised by the Society for the Promotion of New Music, where Malcolm's *Larch Trees* made a good impression. Hollingsworth came up afterwards and suggested he write for films, but Malcolm never managed to follow up the offer. However, the violinist Sidney Twinn, who realised what a success Malcolm might make, constantly nagged him: 'Have you sent a score to Denham yet, Malcolm?' Eventually, shortly after acquiring his

[48] Ruth Railton: *Daring to Excel* (Secker and Warburg, 1992), p.67
[49] Distinguished clarinettist and member of the first NYO
[50] January 2004
[51] After some revision
[52] 21 April 1948
[53] To Charles Reid, *Daily Mail*, 2 November 1960

first publisher, Lengnick, Malcolm carried out Twinn's suggestion and was given a film at once. The score he had forwarded was *Beckus*.

Malcolm's last concert with the LPO was at Folkestone on 27 June 1948. If he had any misgivings, the final schedule of touring would have convinced him otherwise. In the fortnight leading to Folkestone he played at thirteen different venues.[54] During the preceding six months the LPO had given one hundred and ten concerts, playing Tchaikovsky's *Pathétique* Symphony no less than thirty-two times. At the end of the Folkestone concert Malcolm symbolically hung up his trumpet in the orchestra pit and walked away from it, never looking back.

Writing for films meant a greatly enhanced life-style. By the summer of 1947 Malcolm had made enough money from his two documentaries[55] to holiday abroad with Sheila at a time when most holidays were taken in England. They went to Yugoslavia, spending happy weeks at Dubrovnik and Split. Sheila, however, would have preferred that Malcolm had stayed out of films, his years with the LPO being the happiest of their marriage. His absences had allowed her to further her own career – she was playing with the Jacques Orchestra as well as the Riddick – and Malcolm's orchestral life gave him a stability he otherwise lacked, keeping him focused on serious music and away from the bright lights and the 'clever' people she distrusted. He might be limited in the amount of music he was able to write, but he was not doing too badly. After five and a half years in the LPO and a few months in other orchestras he already had twenty works to his name. The best of these, she felt, showed just how much benefit he enjoyed, as a composer, by listening, day in day out, to both the great masters and the more recent talents.[56] She knew Malcolm's weaknesses. Essentially she favoured a course of damage limitation.

It was not a point of view, however, to which Malcolm subscribed. He liked 'clever' people and wanted to mix with them. He believed that if he worked hard enough in the film industry, he could be that rare thing, a full-time composer. Enough money was coming in already for them to move out of their small mews flat in Bayswater into a much bigger flat in the leafy suburbs of St Margaret's,

[54] Chatham, Reading, Birmingham, Llangollen, Liverpool, Coventry, Bedford, Dorking, Wimbledon, Watford, the Albert Hall, Wembley and East Ham
[55] *Avalanche Patrol* (for which Hollingsworth conducted the LSO) and *Seven RAF Flashes*
[56] In the Proms of 1942-43, for example, the LPO played works by John Ireland (*Epic March* and Piano Concerto); Arnold Bax (Cello Concerto, Third Symphony and *London Pageant*); Granville Bantock (*Daughter of Zeus* and *Comedy Overture*); Mary Anderson Lucas (*Circus Suite*); Harry Farjeon (*Pannychis*); Constant Lambert (*Rio Grande*); Elizabeth Maconchy (*Dialogue* for Piano and Orchestra); Alan Rawsthorne (Piano Concerto); William Walton (*Crown Imperial*); Alan Bush (Symphony in C); Lamar Stringfield (*A Negro Parade*); Inglis Gundry (*Heyday Freedom*); Lennox Berkeley (Symphony); Benjamin Britten (*Sinfonia da Requiem* and *Scottish Ballad* for Two Pianos and Orchestra); Walter Piston (Sinfonietta); Clive Douglas (Symphonic Sketches); John Gough (*The Wallaby Track*); E J Moeran (Violin Concerto); William Reed (Scherzo for Orchestra); Alec Rowley (*Burlesque Quadrilles*) and Frank Bridge (*The Sea*).

Twickenham.[57] Besides, he had just been awarded a Mendelssohn Scholarship by the Royal College of Music, a travel grant to help promising composers widen their horizons. He had decided to spend the money by staying in Rome, which is what his great idol, Berlioz, had done at exactly the same age of twenty-seven. He too had won a prize, the Prix de Rome, and had met Mendelssohn there.

It was unfortunate that Sheila happened to be expecting another baby, but he would do the decent thing, wait for the birth and check that both of them were all right, before going away. His mother-in-law was already down from Sheffield, and she'd be good at holding the fort. It was at times like this that mothers-in-law had a purpose in life. Meanwhile, when the time was ripe, he would slip away, like Berlioz's Harold, to Italy. He would hardly be missed once the baby was born. While Sheila and her mother doted day and night on the *bambino*, he could be quietly basking under Mediterranean skies, sipping the odd *Campari*. A composer, after all, needed the stimulus of wider horizons. And who could begrudge him a little *dolce vita*?

*Father and daughter, 1948*

---

[57] 6 St Peter's Road. Their flat was on the first floor.

# 6
# Enfant Terrible
## St Margaret's, Twickenham, 1948-52

IT WAS A SUBDUED MALCOLM who crossed the channel on his way to
Italy in late July, 1948, more like Byron's melancholy Childe Harold than the
romantic hero of Berlioz's *Harold in Italy*. He was right to go to Rome to take
up the scholarship, he was sure of that. The example of Berlioz's Prix de Rome
was just one incentive. There was also a clear line of English composers of which
he was now an exciting part. George Dyson had put his name forward for the
scholarship and then suggested Italy: 'Go to Rome and enjoy yourself. You've
done all the hard work. Now go and learn from another culture.'[1] In doing this
he was, Malcolm believed, passing on a precious torch, for, years earlier, when
Dyson himself had won the award, he had been given the same advice by Charles
Stanford: 'Go to Italy, me bhoy, and sit in the sun'.[2] Stanford – Dyson – Arnold.
So he was now the third generation to visit the shrine of Italian musical genius
and it little mattered that Vaughan Williams, when sitting on the Award panel,
had vacuously asked 'Why do you want to be a composer? You're the best
trumpet player in England'.[3] He was right to be going, to have weathered all the
protests and put the music first, and anyway, as he had patiently explained to his
mother-in-law, he had no intention of staying out there for the full year. He would
be back to see little Katherine shortly. Nor could Mrs Nicholson say that he had
failed Sheila this pregnancy. Although he had been side-lined by his mother-in-
law, as she and Sheila explored all ways and means to prevent a second tragedy,
and although he was more than a little perplexed by all the talk of drug-free
living, healthy foods and natural childbirth, he had at least been there for the
drive to the Blackheath hospital, and afterwards he was there again, with a
congratulatory bottle of champagne at the moment of triumph.

His companion on the journey to Rome was a young sculptor, Douglas Wain-
Hobson,[4] who had also won an award that took him there. He was the kind of
'clever' person Sheila so much distrusted, but it was a long journey, Malcolm had

---

[1] Andrew Stewart interview, *Music Teacher*, June 1989, p.25

[2] Christopher Palmer: *Op. cit.* p.18

[3] Paul Jackson: *The Life and Music of Sir Malcolm Arnold*, p.30. Malcolm had been in the
LPO when Vaughan Williams conducted the première of his Fifth Symphony.

[4] He was later to teach at the Slade.

many ideas flooding though his head, and it was good to be with someone who offered the opportunity of stimulating conversation. By the time the train was slowly crossing central France, they had moved on to Byron's *Childe Harold*, Wain-Hobson discovering that Malcolm was something of an authority on the life of the poet:

> Had he not died in Greece, Byron would have probably killed himself. He saw the cause of Greek independence as a possible way out for himself. He was schizophrenic, of course. Had extreme mood fluctuations, was often very irritable and violent. Often couldn't sleep, often in despair. But it was all episodic. For much of the time he was as sane as you or I. Perfectly lucid for months, even years. Then, bugger it! Something snapped!
>
> He wasn't 'Byronic' at all in the accepted sense, all that bloody nonsense about the brooding, theatrical poseur! He wasn't like that at all! He was highly disciplined in his own erratic way, really determined to fight the gremlins in his head, which threatened on and off to bring him crashing down. Just like Berlioz. That's what makes *Harold in Italy* doubly fascinating, the double madness. That and the viola. Such a bloody marvellous instrument … A Byronic instrument if ever there was one![5]

That summer Malcolm and Douglas Wain-Hobson became good friends, both staying at the British School, a Lutyens building close by the Borghese Gardens. Originally catering only for architecture, the British School had by now branched out into the fine arts, literature and history, and its ambience was very much to Malcolm's taste. So too Rome itself, feverishly enjoying its new republican status, only fours years since the end of fascism and its liberation from the Nazis.

Malcolm fell in love with Italy, its people, attitudes, climate and beauty. Society in Rome was still male-dominated, just as it had been in classical times, and he felt at home in it. There was a sense of continuity which he found therapeutic. The cobbled streets and piazzas with their statuary all spoke of a heritage, carelessly yet gently passed on from one generation to another. Death was not so fearful in Italy.

He was too enamoured of the place to do any work; he had far too much to see and assimilate. He made friends with an old German scholar, who was cataloguing the sculpture of the Vatican and who happily left his labours to guide him around the churches and chapels of the city, expertly revealing the inner meaning of so many works of art. Before this, one Madonna and Child had seemed to Malcolm much like another. With the Professor's help he slowly developed an artistic discrimination. Pictures began to communicate to him, as a two-way process, something he had never experienced before, and it was exactly what he most wanted from his music. He stared at the distinctive colours of each Raphael and wondered how they might be transferred to the instruments of an orchestra. Colour and sound, they were one really. What Raphael had discovered from within himself, carefully nurtured and put down on canvas or fresco, he could do with his music. It was all a question of opening oneself up, writing from the soul,

---

[5] As recreated by Duncan Hyslop, October 2003

not being deflected from one's own personal vision, however limited or insignificant it might be when measured against the vastness of time. He would write that first symphony which had been proving so elusive, nothing but a series of screwed up manuscript sheets lobbed irritably into the waste paper basket. It was a question of confidence and determination, he saw that now, a trusting to his own inner voice.

He immersed himself meanwhile in listening to other people's music, spending much time at the opera. Malcolm also made friends with composer and teacher Alexei Haieff,[6] a cultured and hard-drinking Russian who had emigrated to America and was a friend of Stravinsky's. Haieff was currently working at the American Embassy, where there were weekly musical recitals. Malcolm, Haieff, Wain-Hobson and other friends enthusiastically toured the city, attending every concert they could find, large or small. And afterwards, as the hot sun set, they threw themselves into the night life with equal enthusiasm.

Roman delight in opera strengthened Malcolm's resolve to make a success of a project awaiting his return to England. Through his recent involvement in films he had become friendly with a scriptwriter, Joe Mendoza,[7] who had produced an outline libretto for a possible opera on Henri Christophe, the first black ruler of Haiti, who had shot himself with a golden bullet. Malcolm spent many nights outlining the melodramatic plot and assuring anyone who would care to listen that the new work would outdo *Otello* and *Boris Godunov*, neither of which had any Caribbean Voodoo to offer.

Film making was another area of artistic activity which flourished in Rome in 1948. Mussolini's pre-war investment in the huge Cinecittà studio complex was now paying off. Visconti was beginning his career. De Sica and Rossellini were already world famous: 1948 was the year of de Sica's *Bicycle Thieves* and Rossellini's *L'Amore*. Like most of post-war Rome, Malcolm was devoted to that most passionate of actresses, Anna Magnani. He was quick to see that there was a grainy realism about Italian cinema which made the average American and British movie seem static and artificial. It was something else to ponder once he was home.

It is often stated that Malcolm spent a year in Italy, though he himself in one interview[8] modified this to six months. The reality was even less. He was back in London in late October, for a concert at the Albert Hall which included the overture, *The Smoke*, which he had completed on 19 July, just before his departure to Rome, eleven days after Katherine's birth. The concert marked the end of his three months in Italy. He had been prodigal, blowing all his scholarship money on entertaining his friends and living the good life, so he turned back to England where several film documentaries were waiting for him; and, reunited with his daughter, now three and a half months old, he lost the appetite for further travel.

---

[6] Piers Burton-Page: *Philharmonic Concerto,* p.40
[7] A cousin of the pianist Solomon
[8] *Music Teacher*, June 1989

The performance of *The Smoke* by Rudolf Schwarz and the Bournemouth Municipal Orchestra on 24 October was the first time Malcolm's work had been presented at the Albert Hall in a public concert.[9] It is Malcolm's picture of London, as he saw it in 1948. Its background context is the turbulence of the weeks around Katherine's birth: the natural anxieties beforehand; the jubilation afterwards; the sudden dislocation of regular routine; the noises of a new baby; the introduction into a marriage of a demanding third party. It is also the first serious music written after the move from Queensborough Studios to St Margaret's, Twickenham, a move which may well have inspired the piece, Malcolm taking a retrospective look at the city where he and Sheila had lived for the last six years.

But there is no peace or nostalgia in *The Smoke*. Malcolm's London is a violent, fearful place, as frighteningly unreal as a hallucination. The overture opens in noisy chaos. Only a harp occasionally interrupts with snatches of tranquillity. There is some staid, old-fashioned dancing too, but strong dissonant brass and percussion quickly eliminate anything gracious or graceful. We seem to be not so much in London, but with the guys and dolls of Damon Runyon's New York. The main tune is blues-inspired, and in a nervously quiet and mysterious central section it keeps reappearing in various disguises as Malcolm shows off his mastery of orchestral sound. The central section moves us on to the celluloid fantasies of Gene Kelly, *Slaughter on Tenth Avenue*, a luridly-coloured night-club nightmare where sex and death are doled out in equal measure with the cocktails. The air bristles with fear and suspense. It swirls around, like smoke, filling the narrow lanes around Queensborough Studios with menace, Jack the Ripper stalking the fog-filled mews. The piece ends as noisily as it began. But, for his dramatic dénouement, Malcolm now turns his main tune into a New Orleans street parade. Louis Armstrong is marching up Queensborough Terrace from Kensington Gardens, and even Bertram Mills' Circus may be heard parading just around the corner. The ending is equally esoteric – an extended peroration where pounding drums, gong and cymbals bring us several times to a conclusion which only finally materialises when Malcolm has shocked us with one last, violent glimpse of a Soho strip joint. It is an amazing work.

Sheila, brought up on calmer fare like John Ireland's *London Overture* and Vaughan Williams's *London Symphony*, struggled to be enthusiastic about a work which clearly was an expression of Malcolm at his most exalted and dangerous. The orchestration was masterly but the sentiments disturbing. The BBC's Reading Panel, when shortly afterwards offered the work, rejected it.

This made Malcolm angry. The Albert Hall audience had responded with great enthusiasm and it was not long before Adrian Boult and the LPO were eliciting similarly appreciative responses. The work might fail on the grounds of

---

[9] If one discounts the wartime concerts put on by the Committee for the Promotion of New Music, which had sponsored *Larch Trees* at the Albert Hall five years earlier.

good taste, but it always made a big impact in performance. So Malcolm fought against the BBC's decision:

> Please forgive me for troubling you, but as my overture 'The Smoke' has been rejected by the BBC panel as unsuitable for any programme, I wondered if it would be possible for an official from the BBC music department to hear this, when it is played at the Festival Hall on June 30th, conducted by Sir Adrian Boult.
>
> It has been played quite a lot during the last two years and always seems to get a good reception.[10]

The letter did not achieve its object, but made him feel better. This was true of another, earlier letter, written to *The Times* in defence of Rudolf Schwarz, whose conducting at the Albert Hall had been attacked by a *Times* critic. Schwarz, an Austrian Jew working in Berlin at the outbreak of war, had been interned in Auschwitz and miraculously survived three years in various concentration camps before being released from Belsen in 1945. After a slow recovery he had come to England and was now director of the newly reformed Bournemouth orchestra. Malcolm was aware of all that Schwarz had suffered yet was now achieving at Bournemouth. That a critic should get things so wrong offended his sense of justice. The complaint was that Schwarz had given the orchestra little aid, 'preferring simple indication of the beat (and not always that) to more detailed gesticulation'. It was ill-informed, baseless criticism:

> Mr Schwarz communicated so little of himself and his enjoyment of the music to the orchestra that the performance lacked the last-minute touches and leads to the players that ensure an exciting interpretation and put the orchestra at ease.

Malcolm's letter,[11] in which he was joined by Denis Matthews, suggested that Schwarz's lack of histrionics was a matter of praise, not complaint, given his excellent results. The letter elicited an immediate reply from Schwarz and laid the foundation for a lasting friendship:

> Dear Malcolm Arnold,
>
> When I arrived in this country last year I soon realized that English fairness is more than a saying.
>
> Today when I read your and Denis Matthews' letter to The Times my first thought was: this is unique, this could never happen in any country but England, because people have lost your idea of courage, they do not know any more what is right and just.
>
> So you made me feel thankful and happy that I may live and work amongst human beings – I am so proud of you.
>
> Thank you!
>
> Very sincerely yours,
>
> Rudolf Schwarz

---

[10] 20 June 1951 (BBC Written Archives, Caversham)

[11] 5 November 1948. Matthews had played Beethoven's Third Piano Concerto in the same concert.

Now that he was no longer on the road with the LPO, Malcolm had more time to write courageous letters. It was an odd situation for Malcolm to be working at home without the worry of the next concert. Sheila insisted he should take the best room for his study, with a terrace outside, overlooking the long communal gardens with an attractive view of the Thames. For the first few months he devoted himself to film music. Despite the interest aroused by *The Smoke* his priority had to be writing as many scores for as many films as he possibly could, to establish his financial position. He enjoyed the challenge but was troubled by loss of independence. As an orchestral player touring Britain he had been a free spirit. For the past three months in Rome he had even been released from the need for conformity at home; he could drop in on the bars in the Via Veneto and visit the tarts of Trastevere just exactly as he pleased, whereas now he was working in a small Surrey flat where the chief focus each day was the every need of a noisy baby. Their lives were governed by the Truby King System of Child Welfare. Sheila would sit beside Katherine in her cot and let her scream for food, because Sir Frederic Truby King, in *Feeding and Care of Baby,* had declared that there must be no little treats between the regular four-hour feed. Here he was, trying to cope with the mathematical precision needed for a film score and Truby King was obstructing him!

He could understand why Sheila's every thought was for the baby, and, when he didn't have the pressure of a film deadline, he shared her joy. But he missed having Sheila to himself. To achieve that these days meant inviting Granny Nicholson down from Sheffield to look after baby Katherine. Granny needed no second invitation, and she knew her Truby King backwards, so it was worth putting up with a week of her silent scrutiny to enjoy again time out with Sheila. They both loved taking the Tube to the end of the line and going for long country walks.

In this first year as a full-time composer nearly all his film commissions were documentaries, usually with prosaic subject matter, more often than not connected with the industrial rebirth of post-war Britain. But he was always positive about them, when being interviewed:

> The most difficult problem in music is form, and in a film you already have this solved for you.[12]

Writing for films, he said, offered the same kind of fun as solving jigsaw puzzles.

> Sometimes it is difficult, but this stimulates me all the more, especially when I have to work things out in seconds, or fractions of them.

Initially he used a stopwatch, but after a while he was able to work on pure instinct:

> There are basic tempos of music one gets to know so well that one can synchronize without a watch.

---

[12] R M Schafer: *British Composers in Interview* (Faber & Faber) pp.147-154

*Women of Our Time*[13] was typical of the kind of documentary on which he was engaged in 1949. Women were shown working in any number of situations: on the land, in a crane, as despatch riders, watch-making, nursing, flying planes, in a beauty parlour, demonstrating television sets, cleaning the underground and operating barrage balloons. There were interviews with several famous women of the day: Edith Summerskill, Lady Pethick Lawrence and the notable feminist and suffragette, Lady Rhondda. This meant that some of Malcolm's nineteen minutes of music for the twenty minute film was obscured beneath dialogue, but this was a job just like any other and had little to do with art. In his search for appropriate sound he stole unscrupulously whenever the need. *Women of Our Time* had snatches of *Lilliburlero*, Ethel Smyth's *March of the Suffragettes* and even a Beethoven piano sonata. It was a resourceful score with flashes of true invention but essentially a mish-mash.[14]

Fortunately Malcolm worked at an altogether faster rate than was normal. William Blezard used to tell how Malcolm helped him when he was struggling with a commission[15] from John Hollingsworth. 'How's it going?' Malcolm had asked. 'Badly,' replied Blezard. 'In fact the score is needed tomorrow and that's impossible.' 'Bloody nonsense,' said Malcolm breezily. 'I'll give you a hand. After we've had a glass or two.' So Malcolm, Blezard and his girlfriend repaired to the pub and then, a considerable time later, returned to Blezard's Kensington flat. Blezard sat at one desk, Malcolm another. Blezard handed Malcolm page after page of his bare ideas and Malcolm, after a quick assessment, developed and orchestrated them there and then. Before dawn rose on Kensington High Street the crisis was over.

Malcolm's first feature film, R C Sherriff's stage success, *Badger's Green*, was written shortly after his return from Italy. It presented no problems that he had not already solved in documentaries and he had the confidence of having played in several wartime movies, learning much from observing the practicalities in William Walton's scores for *The Foreman went to France*, *Next of Kin* and *Went The Day Well?*[16] *Badger's Green*, a four-reel B-movie lasting an hour, centres around rivalries in the social hierarchy of a small English village. Genial old Dr Wetherby used to run the village cricket team until bluff Major Forrester arrived and took over the captaincy. Their wives also confront each other, over who should run the team teas. But rivalries are sunk at the arrival of a common foe, Mr Butler, a London businessman intent on building bungalows and

---

[13] One of several documentaries Malcolm made for the Rank Organisation's series, *This Modern Age*

[14] He later considered turning the score into a *Divertimento* No 3, possibly for the National Youth Orchestra. He identified four movements: Prelude, Waltz, Ragtime and Blues. It was never written.

[15] *The Astonished Heart*, directed by Noël Coward

[16] All three films featured the LPO, conducted by Ernest Irving, and all were first shown in 1942.

doubling the size of the village. The comedy is all very predictable, but Malcolm's music, written in the style he was shortly to make famous with the *English Dances,* lends strong support both to the comic mood and the charming rustic setting. There are some atmospheric moments early on when, to the sound of the sunniest of waltzes, the camera explores the lovely village. Various little dramas, like the obstructive tactics of the local constables against the developer, are neatly highlighted in the score. Everything Malcolm offers is stylish and appropriate.

Malcolm was delighted to have his music played by John Hollingsworth and the London Symphony Orchestra, but was less pleased with the director, John Irwin, who, having used his score effectively in the film's first two reels, ignored it totally in the third and only allowed it back in the fourth to bring things to a close. The key event of the film, a cricket match, was played in musical silence. Even when the developer wins the match for the locals with a six through a window, Malcolm is silent. He had, however, made his point. His score was written on time and did the job asked of it. That was all that mattered. His work-manlike approach was noted and *Badger's Green* marked the beginning of a twenty-year involvement in feature films.

Malcolm's enthusiasm for documentaries must have flagged as *The Struggle for Oil* was followed by *European Volunteer Workers* and *This Farming Business*. But his friend Joe Mendoza was directing *This Farming Business*, really an extended commercial for the Ferguson Tractor Company, so he gave it particular care:

> Malcolm of course came up trumps. We had a super sequence of four Ferguson trac-tors – like a squadron – ploughing one huge field side by side; each in a quarter section, moving up and down the screen like determined beetles … Malcolm's score for that sequence was super. It started with the ploughshare of each of the four tractors dropping, in turn, into virgin soil: 1, 2, 3, 4 … of course it was a march. I can still remember the tune! Malcolm knew I'd like his 'March of the Little Tin Tractors' but made me promise not to tell Harry Ferguson his title![17]

In 1949 Malcolm wrote no less than fourteen documentaries and two feature films. Financially this was a triumph and resoundingly secured his new way of life. But there were frustrations in other areas. After the success of *The Smoke* he had settled down to write a first symphony and a first string quartet, but could get performances for neither. On top of this the Festival of Britain committee had decided that the opera, *Henri Christophe,* was not for them, despite the Caribbean Voodoo. It was too *avant-garde*. Malcolm, who had written, as required, a significant passage in full score, including the overture, was extremely disappointed.

Pressures were building on Malcolm by the beginning of 1950. His patterns of work became erratic, dictated by current deadlines and his state of mind. He

---

[17] *Beckus*, The Journal of the Malcolm Arnold Society, Summer 2000

*Rehearsing the National Youth Orchestra, 1948*

tended to work for long stretches in the periods when he seemed to have an almost unbridled self-assurance, a powerful flow of energy which sustained him both in the mundane jobs as well as the challenges of creation. On the occasions when the energy ebbed and melancholy set in, he usually could still write, the slower pace offset by a sensitivity and compassion which were otherwise not always there.

When he went to Paris in the Easter of 1950, to help Ruth Railton with her first National Youth Orchestra course abroad, the pressures building up inside him were not obvious. His boundless energy and enthusiasm caught everyone's attention, while his surprising swings to melancholy or anger were thought merely part of his highly developed artistic temperament. He had written a three-movement work for the students to prepare and play in concert, the *Divertimento No 2*[18] which he had crafted specifically with a Parisian audience in mind. It was much admired, and he kept quiet about the midnight oil burned recently on its behalf and the putting off of a commission for a *Serenade for Small Orchestra*, which he would now have to do in a rush on his return from Paris.

But while he was in Paris he intended to enjoy himself. Like a headstrong terrier finding himself surprisingly off the leash, he bounded around in sheer delight. With good friends like Jack Thurston and Reginald Jacques also involved on the course, he felt under obligation to make sure that they had plenty of fun too outside the rehearsal rooms. Above all, he saw it as his duty to Ruth

---

[18] A tuneful and highly approachable work with a brilliantly scored chaconne, a form much favoured by Malcolm, as the last movement.

Railton to ensure that he entertained the sixty-five boys and thirty-five girls of the National Youth Orchestra who were surrendering part of their holidays to give the two concerts in Paris. He was master of the revels again, everybody's favourite prankster, enlivening every hour of every day, putting huge stress on the *entente cordiale* as he over-drank, over-ate and chatted up every pretty *mademoiselle* in sight. The young musicians, who had never encountered such a larger-than-life character, were fascinated by him. When they came back to England, knowing that his cases were as full of taxable bottles as every bulging pocket, they clustered round him protectively through customs.

Physically exhausted, back in England he kept up the frantic pace, rushing down to Brighton where Reginald Jacques and the NYO performed the *Divertimento* at the Dome, and then hurrying back to St Margaret's to write the *Serenade for Small Orchestra* for the New London Orchestra.[19] He produced a little masterpiece, the first movement contrasting rural peace with something of the bustle and pressure of his current life, but in a highly controlled way, without a sense of mania. The *Andante* possesses one of his great tunes, as romantic as his own courtship of Sheila. Inevitably, though, there is a central section souring the relationship, and although the 'Sheila' tune returns there is still some under-cutting of the happiness, the movement ending in ambiguity. The concluding *Vivace* is all boundless energy and enthusiasm, Malcolm off the leash, perhaps, leading the NYO's noisy parties. It is a highly amusing final movement to a hugely enjoyable little work written under enormous pressure.

The score reached his friends in the New London Orchestra just in time for its première in their concert at Hampton Court, where the audience could sit inside the William III Orangery or on the terrace outside. It was a fine summer evening, and all went well except that the blackbirds so enjoyed Malcolm's music that they joined in with gusto.[20]

But Malcolm was not present at William III's Orangery, because four days earlier, on 30 May, he had lost his reason and attacked Sheila. In his younger years Malcolm suffered from psychotic episodes, or fits of madness, very infrequently. The other known breakdown was in 1943, where the evidence is thin and the form it took unknown. It is possible that Malcolm's alcoholism sometimes obscured manic incidents which were just taken as drunken idiocy; for loss of normal judgement and the advent of uninhibited, reckless or violent behaviour could as easily have been induced by mania as drink. Malcolm was also

---

[19] He completed the score on 8 May 1950
[20] But there was no pleasing some of the critics. *The Times* regretted its lack of profundity and the inclusion of 'salon music and American jazz'. *The Scotsman* found it derivative: Sibelius in the first movement, Britten and late Bartók in the second ('with a few sly oleaginous references to Melanchrino') and Prokofiev and Shostakovich in the third. It was left to a local paper, the *Reading Standard*, to describe it as 'a stimulating composition of many moods'.

beginning to have crises which needed two or three days' sleep to overcome; many of them were probably drink-related, but not all.

Much of Malcolm's behaviour was kept within the family. As the children grew up Sheila's priority was to protect them not just from any hurt, but also from the knowledge of their father's problems. Malcolm, too, was a party to this, for he knew the potential he had for physical as well as verbal assault, and was deeply anxious about it. For the very best of reasons a policy of dissimulation began, and it would continue all Malcolm's life.

The attack took place in his study in the St Margaret's flat. Katherine, not yet quite two, was in her cot, having her afternoon sleep, two rooms away. There had been no argument beforehand; Sheila merely came into his study, perhaps interrupting a crucial musical moment, and he seized a knife, then pushed her down on a chair. For a brief moment Sheila thought he was going to kill her. Managing to break away, as Malcolm raged and shouted incoherently, she locked the door and phoned for help. Police and ambulance men arrived, and, quickly assessing a situation beyond easy retrieval, took control of Malcolm, put him under restraint and led him out of the flat.

Malcolm loved and admired Sheila, and it had been, on the whole, a good marriage. But though he wanted a family, he also wanted his relationship with Sheila to be unchanged, as close as in the early days of marriage. When Sheila was attacked, she was over five months pregnant, just as she had been pregnant at his previous breakdown, back in the summer of 1943.

There was to be no quick recovery this time. Malcolm was taken to Springfield Hospital, a Victorian asylum at Tooting Bec, and it was there, some time later, that Richard Adeney visited him:

> It was a huge, dreary place and I found him in a ward of crazy-looking patients. He seemed well and cheerful, but during our conversation he often laughed excitedly. I asked him why. 'Just listen to that music up there,' he said. 'I don't know how it's allowed.' 'Yes, but it's just an orchestra playing a waltz.' 'But the words, they're filthy. How can they get away with it?' and he went on laughing at the words which only he could hear.
>
> We were sitting on a very low sofa in a corner of the ward. He called out to a patient, an enormous thug of a man with red hair and a jutting jowl.
>
> 'Joe,' he said, 'This is Richard. HIT HIM!'
>
> I looked around for help, but none was available, so I just shrank lower on the sofa.
>
> 'Oh, come off it, Malcolm' said Joe, 'You and your jokes!' [21]

It was to be three and a half months before Malcolm was released from Springfield. In the meantime he was subjected to applications of 'Insulin Shock', a treatment which was to be discredited and abandoned not many years later. The idea of inducing convulsions to reduce the symptoms of insanity, which goes

---

[21] Richard Adeney, *Flute*

back to the ancient Greeks, had been developed since the 1920s, doctors injecting unfed patients with insulin on a daily basis, to reduce blood sugar levels in the brain and induce convulsions and coma. The coma lasted several hours before the patient was revived by the re-raising of the blood sugar level. Since the brain normally extracts between sixty to eighty milligrams of glucose per minute from the bloodstream, this method of treatment was highly dangerous. Brain damage had been known; death too. But loss of memory and balance were the usual side-effects. The benefit was the temporary removal of suicidal or murderous tendencies, the patient shocked into a state of calm, becoming, in the jargon of the day, 'less engaged emotionally'. In Malcolm's case it would seem, from Richard Adeney's account, that the insulin treatment had calmed down the mania but engendered an unreal, delusional state of acquiescence with the world.

Although the treatment usually erased the memory of the patient's previous psychotic state, detention in a mental hospital often brought with it a deep humiliation and sense of outrage. Ruth, who had already experienced herself what Malcolm was now enduring, spent the rest of her life inveighing against what she saw as an old-fashioned 'prison system' practising an almost medieval 'casting out of devils'. 'Never in all my experience,' she wrote towards the end of her life, 'have I met one person who has had any sympathy or understanding for the so-called schizophrenic... Not once, in all my detentions, have I even had a kind word from those in charge ... I have been locked up by my husband and various so-called doctors and treated as a criminal ...' Shortly after Malcolm's period at Springfield she wrote a most moving poem, *Mental Home*, in which she viewed her fellow internees with great compassion:

Here then, are the forgotten relics of wars,
And the proofs of man's inhumanity and lust;
The sexes carefully isolated and segregated,
Except myself – who walk beyond the barrier
                    Of time and place,
Taking to my heart these myriad lost souls
Who patiently await their own day of release –
Whether from the body, or merely the grim four walls,
                    It is hard to say.

See, here is a tiny birdlike creature,
Fashioning pink rosebuds from paper
Intertwined with fresh young leaves.
She fastens them here and there upon a lacy shawl
And – draping it around her head
                    Proclaims that she is Queen;
And so she may be for one brief moment!
She saves crumbs for the birds
And carefully secretes a crust of bread
In case some dumb and hungry creature
Should beg – with its pleading eyes at her conscience;
And yet the world wants none of her,
Or her saintliness and pure simplicity.

Springfield at Tooting Bec was conveniently only five miles away from the Twickenham flat. But Sheila was in a state of shock and it would take her some time to come to terms with what had happened. So she took Katherine to spend several weeks in Scotland with her sister, Gwenol, in that troubled summer. Apart from anything else, her absence from St Margaret's saved her from having to answer embarrassing questions as to Malcolm's whereabouts.

Through some bizarre piece of bureaucratic mismanagement Malcolm was released from hospital just a few days before Sheila gave birth to Robert. It was an anxious moment, even though Granny Nicholson was already in place when Malcolm returned. There were no new dramas. Sheila had her baby, Malcolm was delighted and Granny Nicholson held a careful watching brief. It was not long before Malcolm quietly shut himself in his study and began writing. Within two months of his release he had written the first set of *English Dances*, a work which, more than any other concert piece, established his name before the general public.

Malcolm's publisher, Bernard de Nevers, who had run Lengnick[22] since the 1930s and used his income from Brahms and Dvořák to encourage young British composers, had instigated the idea, suggesting a set of English Dances along the lines of Dvořák's popular *Slavonic Dances*. Malcolm's first set of four was completed in early December, a second by June 1951. Light and tuneful,[23] they paint an idealised picture of Olde England, the Northamptonshire of Grandfather William, perhaps, when he was still a boy, a shoemaker's apprentice tramping innocently along mile upon mile of unspoilt countryside. They are so simply and lovingly crafted that it is hard to believe that they were created in the wake of extreme mental anguish.

A month later Malcolm had finished two Sonatinas, highly effective and enduring works for oboe and clarinet, which he had promised Leon Goossens and Jack Thurston.[24] Each colourful work demonstrates an impeccable command and understanding of the instrument. But he did not stop there. In the early months of 1951 he completed four more pieces: *A Sussex Overture*[25] (written as part of the Brighton Philharmonic's celebration of the Festival of Britain); a

---

[22] Northampton's other two composers, William Alwyn and Edmund Rubbra, were already published by Lengnick. Other friends with Lengnick included Humphrey Searle and Francis Chagrin.

[23] Unlike the 'English' works of Vaughan Williams or Holst, the *Dances* do not draw on traditional folk material. The melodies are all Malcolm's own.

[24] The first performance of the Clarinet Sonatina was, in fact, given by Colin Davis accompanied by Geoffrey Corbett at the RBA Galleries, London, on 20 March 1951. Through its inclusion on music exam syllabuses around the world, this is probably Malcolm's most often performed work.

[25] The *Sussex Overture* is full of high spirits and some very sophisticated and inventive developmental writing. Perhaps the big tune is not among Malcolm's most memorable, but the work remains another cheerful example of the popular overture.

Concerto for Piano Duet and Strings;[26] the second set of *English Dances*; and the Symphonic Study *Machines*. Most of this music was gloriously optimistic and buoyant, and it came on top of further film work. It was as if the painful insulin treatment at Springfield had cleared away, temporarily, all distressing thoughts.

Malcolm's life continued to be one of extremes. In July 1951, only a year after his residence at Springfield Hospital, he was conducting the Hallé Orchestra at the Cheltenham Festival of Contemporary Music as they gave the first performance of his First Symphony.[27] Gordon Jacob had persuaded the Festival committee to include the work, which had been written two years earlier, shortly after the return from Rome, in intervals between documentary films.[28] Although the symphony preceded the first set of *English Dances* by only a few months, the two works have little in common.[29] One is dark, the other light, and in between them lies the mental breakdown. The Symphony is overshadowed by the imminent personal catastrophe, the *Dances* carefree in its aftermath. Christopher Palmer suggested the Symphony reflected the world situation, dominated by the Cold War,[30] and certainly the growing hostility between Britain and Russia distressed Malcolm. But the Symphony is essentially a personal vision, a very candid expression of his deepest feelings.

The first movement veers brusquely between two extreme moods, the manic and the depressed. Its opens in high, elevated style, with a strong but tortured statement, brass and unison strings fiercely dominant. The first three bars are crucial, for much in the twelve minute *Allegro* derives from them. As the opening develops, it is not long before we are being taken on a march to war – Malcolm's recurring nightmare – an incessant 'left-right' on the low brass beating its bullying way into our heads, drums pounding, trumpets braying, senses numb. But we move from that ugly scene, in a highly cinematic bridge passage, to a quiet place of retreat, where the belligerence is only in the background, and various wind instruments even suggest the possibility of happiness. Everything has slowed as well as quietened. The music becomes desolate, fragmented, hardly moving anywhere, lost in its own myopic world, and though strings, harp and piccolo at times all try to break in, gently and even caressingly, they do not

---

[26] A very engaging and tuneful work for four hands at one piano which, among many notable features, includes an extraordinarily manic scalic passage for the strings in the central *Larghetto*.

[27] The Festival ran for two weeks. There were new symphonies by Gardner, Jacobson and van Wyk, as well as Rawsthorne's Piano Concerto, Rubbra's String Quartet, Humphrey Searle's *Poem for 22 Strings* and Reizenstein's Wind Serenade. The Hallé Orchestra played four new works in their two concerts.

[28] The score was completed on 16 February 1949, the first performance taking place in the Cheltenham Town Hall on 6 July 1951.

[29] Other than the lyrical tune at the beginning and end of the symphony's second movement.

[30] 'The Cold War was on, and the atmosphere seems as chilly and hostile inside the music as in the world outside.' (Palmer, 1992)

succeed in changing the overall mood of listlessness. Eventually the brass comes crashing into the sanctuary and we are briefly back in tortured mood, only to become depressed again, before finally returning to a noisy turbulence, screwed up tight, near to breaking point. In a spectacular conclusion, a lyrical march, sustained against a savage accompaniment of brass and percussion, carries us off, screaming, to war, and amid a mayhem of further brass and percussion the nightmare ends abruptly. It is a highly dramatic opening movement, but the work of a very troubled spirit.

The *Andantino* comes as a relief. The strings introduce a wistful melody fit for tranquil valleys in the mist of morning. This is not so much St Margaret's Twickenham, as the Roman Campagna as seen by Poussin or Claude, with perhaps Sheila in the foreground, sitting on a stile and nursing Katherine. The melody is repeated, taken up by woodwind, before it moves off into insubstantial realms, landscapes only glimpsed through swirling mists. Tranquillity, even of this surreal kind, now gets subjected to blasts of menace, the brass briefly introducing a reminder of the anguish of the first movement. The strings bravely and quietly carry on regardless, only to find themselves in greater mists and even less substantial landscapes, a kingdom of spirits. A struggle ensues between what have now emerged as two distinct forces, which we might well term sanity and madness, the strings opting to flee from the madness but doing so only in strange, distant keys, until they and the woodwind find themselves totally lost. Where should they now go to extricate themselves from this ghostly muddle? Muted chords in the distance bring reminders of what is lying in wait for them, lurking out there in the shadows. A flute solo endeavours an airy escape. The strings attempt a restatement of a previously known tranquillity, but chords on the brass force their anxious withdrawal. With the outcome still very much in the balance, it is a relief to hear the woodwind restating the main melody. All is calm in the valley again. It is a new day. And yet, as the strings present the melody one final time, all is not quite as it was before. Life has moved on. It is the same landscape, painted in chiaroscuro, all light and shade like a Claude, with the same features and figures, but as the music comes to the softest of conclusions, with one last, long sigh, we are aware that something for us has altered.

This challenging *Andantino* is neatly positioned between two fiery movements, the third being every bit as exciting as Malcolm's direction (*Vivace con fuoco*) might suggest. It begins with a vigorous fugal melody, thrown excitedly around the orchestra, like a game of pass the parcel. It is embellished with an altogether more reflective interlude, and Malcolm seems to have sufficient material here to develop an effective final movement. But he has other, more shocking ideas. Suddenly, two piccolos unexpectedly sing out a bizarre tune, deliberately mis-harmonised, but which otherwise might have come straight from an Edwardian musical comedy. It is a moment of pure theatre, a *coup* of the highest order, introducing visions of overdressed Ruritanian guardsmen, absurd in their colourful finery, the same kind of image Ruth used when attacking human over-eagerness to elevate the trappings of war:

> When we were young, we used to play with toy soldiers ...

The bizarre ditty then gets taken up by the strings, but so grotesquely fast that it flies away almost as quickly and unexpectedly as it had appeared. The toy soldiers have been flung away. There follows a second *coup*, equally brilliant and astonishing, an exaggerated military march, a *marche fantastique* lurching alarmingly between *triomphale* and *funèbre*, its every grotesque distortion an angry denouncement of the glorification of war. 'You can stuff your parades, your medals and your banners,' shouts Malcolm. 'War stinks! Wonderfully brave human beings suffer! Up yours, Field Marshal!' This bitterly ironic and incongruous passage brings the work to a conclusion of such violence that we cannot ignore what he is saying. We are forced to endorse or deny. Malcolm, in his determination to communicate, knows no half measures.

Malcolm's symphony of brilliant light and Stygian shade was unlikely to please the more conservative critics in the immediate post-war era, who, in John Amis's words, were 'trying to keep England free of the moderns, free for Elgar, the Three Choirs Festival, England and St George'.[31] Martin Cooper found it 'disconcerting', Eric Blom 'self-consciously truculent and strident' and Richard Capell 'brutal'. *The Times*' critic, finding it 'loud-voiced' and 'expressed with much wanton harshness', gave Malcolm a schoolmasterly dressing-down:

> The composer would have done well to remember that emotional depth is sometimes expressed more fully and lastingly in reticent passages than in strident ones much encumbered by brass and percussion.

These were honest responses, though disappointingly obtuse. Less impressive were the observations of a new breed of critic, too interested in being entertaining to be thoughtful. The *Observer*'s Desmond Shawe-Taylor was a case in point:

> A good deal of his work sounds like a succession of twiddley bits punctuated by rests. Has anything so fragmentary as this ever before been called a symphony? He treats his ideas like a boy with a coloured top, to which every now and then he gives a careless flick which keeps it spinning.

Britain in 1951 had a reactionary establishment, a self-perpetuating élite which controlled all the arts. The struggle that was awaiting Malcolm is well illustrated in the response of the BBC to his Cheltenham performance. The Third Programme's Music Organiser, Peter Crossley-Holland, had attended the concert and afterwards sent round the following report to the Head of Music:[32]

---

[31] *Amiscellany*, (Faber & Faber, 1985, p.156) But change was in the air. 'There is no longer, thank Heaven,' wrote Hubert Foss, 'a kind of central musical idiom, a polite speech or disembodied Oxford accent without which no new work may be admitted into the circle.' (*Hallé*, June 1951)

[32] Herbert Murrill

This symphony which is in three movements does not give the over-all impression of true symphonic writing. In the first place a real conception was lacking. The aim, of course, is not serious, but the actual material is tawdry and its use sectional and bitty. The long tracts of slow vague-sounding music in the first two movements made it very difficult to keep attention. There is little continuity of texture, and so very often before a phrase or figure has time to establish itself or grow, it is rudely interrupted by some grotesque effect on the percussion. The only time one felt one could settle down without anxiety of being catapulted yet again was in the closing section of the last movement. When the work does at last reach its 'big tune' the result turns out to be blatant and vulgar.

The work aims, it seems, to be humorous. If so, it fails. It is too restricted to the sardonic, vulgar and whimsical to be called humorous. There are, it is true, some moments which give evidence of genuine musicianship, and there are also a few colourful strokes of orchestration, but these effects come in the wrong places. All in all, this is not the product of an adult musical mind and leaves an impression, as did the movements of the composer when conducting it, of the ungracious and the gawky.[33]

The Music Programmes Organiser[34] initialled the report, adding 'I agree with this'.

Peter Crossley-Holland, a former pupil of John Ireland when at the Royal College of Music, was an intellectual, with a B.Mus. in ethnomusicology. He had just written a cantata, *The Visions of Saint Godric*; his most famous song was *The Weather the Cuckoo Likes*; and he wrote in 'an elegiac and almost sentimentally English style'.[35] But such a pedigree in the pastoral tradition hardly justifies the savagery of the attack. It may be that he had taken an active dislike to Malcolm when their paths briefly crossed at College, and this coloured his views. Whatever his motivation, his inability to realise that the symphony was a wholly serious work is very instructive. Fifty years on, in the aftermath of decades of experimental music, the dissonances which Malcolm from time to time chose to introduce into his symphonies no longer seem so arbitrary and wayward. In 1951 they were seen by many as the acts of an *enfant terrible*, sending up or mocking symphonic form.

Fortunately for Malcolm, some critics were more open to new ideas. *Musical Opinion*, for example, did not take sincerity for cynicism, and was full of praise:

It is the most attractive of the many symphonies by British composers that have appeared in recent years. It has sanity of style, clarity of design, thematic material of distinction and its scoring is brilliant and original.

---

[33] 17 July 1951 (BBC Written Archives)

[34] Frank Wade

[35] Robert Beale reviewing *Celtic Magic* (Manchester Music Album Reviews: Manchester online).

*The Musical Times* found it 'original, buoyant, and full of ingenuity of instrumental effect.' It was a 'large-minded piece', wrote Hubert Foss. Malcolm was a fearless 'teller of the truth'.

As if in endorsement, the LPO brought the symphony to London's South Bank that November, asking Malcolm to conduct his old colleagues. It was a great compliment that his symphony should be played in the Festival Hall, which, built as a key component of the Festival of Britain's South Bank showground, had only been opened six months earlier by King George VI. The Festival, which attracted over eight million people to see the Hall, along with Dome of Discovery, the Skylon, a 3-D film cinema and several other exciting expressions of modernity, was an ambitious statement of intent. The days of post-war austerity were over; Britain was now looking forward instead of backwards. Malcolm's First Symphony, as the LPO's management shrewdly realised, was very much in keeping with this pioneering Festival spirit.

It was also becoming clear to concert managers that Malcolm's presence on the podium was an additional asset. His enthusiasm, gaiety and common touch quickly endeared him to the public. He did not subscribe to the Rudolf Schwarz school of self-effacement, as Stanley Bayliss in the *Daily Mail* made clear:

> He showed the audience a beefy figure, a cherubic face, and a wildly exuberant style with the baton. I remember one gesture fit to unleash a deafening tempest of sound: instead it ushered in a modest drum-tap or two.

Others commented on 'a wild over-exuberance of gesture' and 'an immense amount of athletic action'. But it was a style which worked, especially with the LPO. The players clearly enjoyed the symphony. 'They played superbly for the composer,' noted *The Times*.

This Festival Hall concert did much to consolidate Malcolm's growing reputation, the press reaction being extremely favourable. *The Times* completely altered its view. Malcolm's previous compositions, declared *The Times'* critic, had showed distinct promise, a fluent technique and uninhibited emotions. But this time there was something more:

> The composer has ordered his emotions without inhibiting himself. The youthful high spirits are still abundantly evident yet obviously a strong mind controls the symphonic shape.

Malcolm could not have been paid a higher compliment:

> This is a rarity, a contemporary piece of music that is capable of comprehension and yet enjoyment at the same time of hearing.

The symphony disdained padding, offered many novel combinations of sound and was thought-provoking:

> It is entertainment in the best sense of that word, and though some of the audience were shocked by its rumbustuous exuberance nobody was bored.

There was a similarly sensitive response from Mosco Carner in *Time and Tide:*

His sonorities change like the colours of the kaleidoscope and the effect on the listener is both disconcerting and highly intriguing … The work is a curious compound of the picturesque, the grotesque, the sensitive, the crude and the truly inspired. It kept reminding me of Berlioz …

These thoughtful and encouraging responses were all the more valuable, in that Malcolm himself was unable to express himself effectively in interview. Believing that his music made its own meaning clear, he refused to comment on it in any depth, and his programme notes were accordingly often eccentrically deadpan. Of the First Symphony he wrote:

The last movement is a fugue. The fact is not very important because the chief interest of the movement, I hope, lies in its purely emotional excitement.

Far from talking himself up, he was remarkably self-critical:

The symphony ends in D major with a short coda in which, for no reason at all, there is a passing reference to the main theme of the first movement.

Asked in an interview, prior to the LPO concert, what were his ideas in writing the symphony, he embarked on a defensive digression, when others would have promoted themselves much more directly:

Well, the ideal to aim for in any work of art, I suppose, is that it shall be absolutely straight-forward and beautifully done. Take Somerset Maugham, for instance (I admire him tremendously). He has all the technique in the world, and style – no, more than that – elegance of style – and can be read with pleasure by one and all. Now take a composer. If you listen to the music of Berlioz (and I'm one of his warmest admirers) it sounds more clear and contemporary, more up-to-the-minute than most of the music that has been written since or is being written now. Why? Because in Berlioz, as in Sibelius – yes, and sometimes Mahler too – it seems that without any striving they are themselves original. The only comparable modern I can think of at the moment who has the same thing (though his background and national outlook make his stuff completely different) is Bartók. So few composers have a distinctive sound – with air and light.[36]

Pressed by the interviewer, all Malcolm would say about the content of the work was that 'I did get a few things off my chest I'd been wanting to.' He would not be drawn further and, instead of discussing *what* he was saying preferred to dwell on *how* he was saying it:

The general idea was to take out everything (the usual chordal background) but the essential thought in it. It's like one of those drawings done in as few lines as possible, overlaid here and there with patches of strong and brilliant colour. I have tried to treat definite, straight-forward, understandable material with the utmost simplicity in what I hope is an interesting manner, treating every single orchestral sound and note as meaning something and not to be wasted. When you sit in the orchestra, as I have, you can't help seeing and being disgusted with the waste of players' energies and talents on mountains of useless padding.

---

[36] *Philharmonic Post*, November-December 1951

*At a recording session of* The Sound Barrier *with David Lean and Muir Matheson*

At this juncture Malcolm was still coming to terms with his growing fame, which over the next twelve months continued to spread.

In the cinema he quickly established himself in feature films. The success of a hastily written score for *Britannia Mews* led to a prestigious Twentieth-Century Fox production of *No Highway* in 1951, starring James Stewart and Marlene Dietrich.[37] Soon Malcolm was writing for the most important man in the British film industry, Alexander Korda, producing in quick succession three scores for Korda's London Films, all released in 1952: *Home at Seven*[38] with Jack Hawkins and Glynis Johns, *The Holly and the Ivy* with Ralph Richardson and Celia Johnson; and the first of three films directed by David Lean, *The Sound Barrier*.[39]

In the Concert Hall in 1952 Malcolm secured a personal triumph at the Proms with the première of the second set of *English Dances*, played by the BBC Symphony Orchestra, conducted by Malcolm Sargent. The same year Leon Goossens, the dedicatee, gave his Concerto for Oboe a successful première at the Festival Hall. A little earlier Malcolm's String Quartet had been well reviewed on its first public appearance, and a new chamber piece, the *Divertimento* for Wind Trio[40] (for Richard Adeney, Sidney Sutcliffe and Stephen Waters) inadvertently

---

[37] Called *No Highway in the Sky* in America
[38] Called *Murder on Monday* in America
[39] Called *Breaking the Sound Barrier* in America
[40] In July 1952 he forwarded to the BBC his *Divertimento* for wind trio, Op 37, with a fairly terse letter: 'I wish to submit the enclosed work to the BBC Reading Panel. The Wigmore Ensemble included this work which was written two months ago in one of their programmes and were told by the BBC they could not broadcast it because it had been rejected by the panel. This, of course, is impossible, because the panel has never seen the work.'

led to a beneficial association with a new publisher, Michael Diack of Paterson.[41] Only in a one-act opera, *The Dancing Master*, did he not meet with his usual success, but it was not a project to which he devoted much time.[42]

Malcolm also began to be seen on television, for in the early 1950s classical music was strongly featured, watched at peak times by a mass audience. The LPO, now a much more disciplined concern under Sir Adrian Boult, was quick to take advantage of the new opportunities and in 1952 Malcolm was invited to make a guest celebrity appearance with his old orchestra. Boult's letter of invitation[43] survives:

> My dear Arnold,
>
> I am so very glad to hear that you are coming to appear for a moment at our Television show. It will be such a help and it is just that personal touch that they enjoy.
>
> I want to tell you honestly what I propose about [the] fee for they are very hard up, although they are giving me quite a handsome sum. I therefore want to ask whether you will accept ten guineas of my fee and I hope you will think that is adequate and fair. Please do not say that you will not have anything because the labourer is worthy of his hire and I can assure you in this case the undersigned labourer is adequately rewarded.
>
> Yours ever,
> Adrian Boult.

Malcolm always projected well on television. He appeared again shortly afterwards, this time conducting his own music, and afterwards received an encouraging letter from the producer, Philip Bate:

> Everybody thought your appearance enhanced the programme. Believe me, you did not look in any way unduly diffident, and your modesty about your compositions was very charming.[44]

Although Malcolm's socialist conscience caused him some distress as the trappings of his growing fame came his way, he nonetheless enjoyed them. Broadly smiling and quick in cheery repartee, he easily slipped into the business of being a public figure. His work led him to dine out more and more, usually without Sheila who had their two young children to look after. Drinking and eating much more than was good for him, he began to put on weight. In 1951, when conducting his First Symphony, he was still slim. A photograph in the Cheltenham programme shows him with short, well-groomed hair, lips pursed

---

[41] Malcolm, as was his wont, had recently had an argument with his publisher, when Michael Diack happened to attend the concert where the *Divertimento* was being played and was amazed at the response it was creating from the audience. The critic Felix Aprahamian was openly laughing at each new musical joke. After the concert, therefore, he asked Malcolm if he could publish it. A long association and friendship resulted.

[42] He wrote the 67-minute score in just two weeks.

[43] 31 May 1952

[44] 12 June 1952 (BBC Written Archives)

*Malcolm on holiday at Southbourne in 1951 with Sheila, Robert (in pram), niece Gill, Katherine and Lizzie Witts*

quizzically, eyes alert and challenging, a cross between Gregory Peck and Ivor Novello.

A year later he looked distinctly chubby. But a large physical persona seemed to chime in with the public perception of jovial Malcolm Arnold, so he was happy to oblige. Fortunately for him the media of the time were more involved in building up celebrities than taking them to pieces. He was a beneficiary from the lack of bedroom journalism.

His family in Northampton watched in awe and delight as he became steadily more famous. His relationship with Pappy had slightly improved thanks to Sheila's influence. On visits to Craigmore Malcolm would delight his young nephews and nieces. Ruth's two little children, Jenny and Penny, thought him the ideal uncle, full of fun and games, a constant source of peals of laughter. But when Malcolm visited Ruth's chaotic home, it was clear that his worldly success had opened up between them a gulf. Malcolm's shiny new car looked as if it was showing off, parked beside Ruth's battered Riley. There were not many cars those days in Milton Street, let alone shiny ones. Malcolm sensed that Ruth's marriage was no longer working, that money was as short as ever, and he did his best to cheer her up, but he didn't stay long. If only 'Uncle Malc' could visit more often, thought the two girls, he could make such a difference to their mother.

It was genuinely hard for Malcolm with his great workload to maintain close family contact. And he did have his own growing family to consider. He and Sheila were discussing a possible move, the small flat no longer really being appropriate, now that he was becoming something of a public figure. Sheila was only too keen to leave St Margaret's with its mixed memories, and they eventually found a new home in Richmond. 19 Denbigh Gardens was the epitome of middle-class suburban prosperity, the very bourgeois ideal which his Suite of 1940 had decried, a quiet road of detached houses in friendly red brick, just around the corner from Richmond Park and conveniently close to a number of the big film studios.

Malcolm took an inordinate pride in the house, and his friends sometimes struggled to understand why. He rarely let on that it marked the start of a new beginning. It was everything which Sheila and the children needed, and that was important to him, especially after all the emotional damage of his breakdown two years earlier. It was a token of his earnest to Sheila, Katherine and Robert. An expression of his determination to be the kind of husband he had once promised, as he and Sheila sat on a damp bench in St James's Park, their future before them. In Richmond, he fully believed, he could contribute to the family more meaningfully, be a father figure who counted, a mature and tranquil presence. No longer the *enfant terrible*.

# 7
# The Midas Touch
## Richmond, 1953-56

MALCOLM'S INTENTION at the time of the move, to shed the role of *enfant terrible*, was not easily fulfilled. On a personal level, try as he might, he would find it unachievable, for he would never lose the capacity for saying and doing the most inappropriate, unexpected and embarrassing things; it was part of his nature, charm and tragedy. Nor as a composer would he ever entirely lose a childlike delight in shock tactics; it was part of his temperament, a consequence of his determination to listen to his own inner voice, and a trusty weapon in the constant battle for clarity of expression.

Nonetheless, his desire to prove himself worthy of his wife and family motivated and sustained a remarkable feat of creativity in these early years in Richmond. It was a period in Malcolm's professional life when he could do little wrong, and he responded with naïve and unconcealed delight to the adulation of the public. His was the Midas touch, his work suddenly seeming to be everywhere – in the concert hall and cinema, on television, radio and stage – the output vast, its scope divergently extensive. Ignoring the artificial boundaries which, he believed, needlessly compartmentalised music and limited its appeal, Malcolm continued to encourage his listeners to share his joys and sorrows, loves and hates, hopes and fears, and in so engaging a manner that he drew to classical music fresh audiences, eager to enjoy a new medium to which they now felt able to relate. It was a significant achievement and it all emanated from 19 Denbigh Gardens.

There Malcolm had a small study on the first floor at the front of the house, looking out onto a line of trees which protected an overgrown garden beyond. The walls and ceiling were yellowed by the billowing cigar smoke which was a necessary part of the writing ritual. The room was bare but for his desk and a piano, which was rarely used. He wrote directly into full score in ink, with a penknife to hand, in case, like a medieval monk, he had to scrape away an error, but he hardly ever did so, because the music was assembled within his mind before he even began to bar the manuscript paper. It was just a question of putting it down accurately.

Sheila loyally did her best to help, providing meals and keeping the children quietly in the background. Once he had begun, Malcolm might write for days and nights, sleeping only a little:

> If he was writing, he would switch off completely from all other contacts. He just concentrated. There was too much in his head to sleep properly. He'd come down for a meal or I'd take a tray up to his room. It varied, depending on what he was doing. But there were occasions when he would just sit there and leave the food. The music was going round and round in his head.[2]

'Mum cooked three good meals a day,' remembers Katherine, 'two with potatoes! She saw her role as providing a nest for a genius.' Vegetarian dishes still prevailed. 'Life in Denbigh Gardens would revolve around grated carrots,' remembers Robert with amusement. 'Good healthy stuff, but not necessarily to Dad's taste!' It encouraged him to eat away from home, and his absences away from Denbigh Gardens meant that his relationship with his children, though a loving one, was never totally secure. Nor did he always communicate well with them, as Katherine remembers:

> Dad was once left to look after Robert and me. We played up and wouldn't get out of the bath! He smacked us, and that was a big shock to us because we knew he strongly disapproved of smacking! All his life he would cause problems for himself by not saying what he was really thinking. Instead of telling us, on this occasion, what he wanted, he just kept quiet. And then there was this big explosion![3]

He naturally expected his children to be musical. When Katherine was about five, just starting school at the nearby Old Vicarage, he wrote a short violin piece for her, *Katherine Walking and Running*. She had been having violin lessons from a friend of her mother's but was still at an elementary stage, so Malcolm wrote the piece for two violins with a simple part for Katherine and a more challenging one for her teacher, Sheila or himself. It was the ideal kind of teaching aid, helping the young pupil along and enhancing her sense of achievement, but it seems not to have achieved its purpose. Katherine has no memories of ever playing the piece, and her short time as a violinist she remembers as fairly undistinguished:

> My mum was keen on the idea that to be a violinist you must start at four, and I think I did. It was not a success, however, and ended one Saturday morning when Robert and I were playing with toy cars together at the entrance to the house in Denbigh Gardens and I refused to break off to go to my lesson. That was the end of the violin for me! I was about six!

Ironically, while breaking down compartmentalisation in music, Malcolm was unable to to do the same in his private life, his family having to take its turn within his crowded schedule. He always greatly enjoyed his time with his

[1] Sheila, August 2003
[2] December 2003

*Robert, Sheila, Katherine and Malcolm, Denbigh Gardens, 1954*

children, but treated them a little like electric lights, to be switched on and off as convenient.

Sheila did her best to compensate and, at the same time, to protect her children from their father's alcoholism. With a steely determination, supported by Granny Nicholson, she declared 19 Denbigh Gardens to be an alcohol-free zone. There might be an occasional bottle of cider in the pantry, but that would be all. This was a non-negotiable situation and one which Malcolm respected. If he returned to the house late at night and found himself with a bottle in his hand, he would do his best to conceal it behind the boiler or some other, equally inappropriate, hiding-place. In the early years Sheila's dictat did, in fact, work out quite well. While Malcolm was engaged on his music, he was entirely absorbed and needed no stimulant stronger than coffee. But it created a double life for Malcolm, which would eventually fracture the marriage.

Sheila in retrospect regrets there was so much writing for films, believing that these pressures increased Malcolm's need to drink:

> In films you can't write down exactly what you're thinking. You have to fit in with the timing and the scenario. That's appalling. It cramps your creativity. Malcolm responded by doing a few hours' work and then going off drinking, to get release from the frustration.

Looking back, some fifty years later, Sheila prefers to see the alcoholism rather than the mental illness as the root of his problems, and is still deeply saddened by the damage it steadily inflicted.

> His ear was a terrific gift. It was so awful to see him destroying it. When a work was completed he might sleep for several days. Suddenly he would appear in his dressing gown before going off on a spree with those awful drunks and spongers. Nobody could stop him.

All the hurts and frustrations still rankle.

> How can you look after someone who keeps coming in at two or three in the morning blind drunk, and then is laid out all day?

But she did look after him for quite a while and with considerable success in the earlier years, as the Second Symphony testifies. On her encouragement, not long after the move to Denbigh Gardens, Malcolm called a temporary halt to the film work, to begin the symphony, for which there was, as yet, no commission. The Second Symphony is a far more balanced and less turbulent work than its predecessor. It shows the *enfant terrible* on his very best behaviour, giving us a view of what it meant to be living in Denbigh Gardens in the winter of 1952/53, with a wife wishing him to be a properly adjusted husband and father, the kind who might give talks to local music societies without raising eyebrows, sober, faithful, and no longer a figure of mistrust to Granny Nicholson.

The tranquil first movement, an *allegretto*, shows Malcolm's new intent. The first subject, offered at once in three attractively different sets of orchestral colouring, takes us straight into the heart of the English countryside, and the second subject, carefully reached by a short bridge passage,[3] is an even more extended expression of rustic bliss. Malcolm thereafter ensures that the development section does not in any way damage the atmosphere. As he explores one phrase after another, in the manner of Sibelius, birds can be heard fluttering overhead and we are secure and comfortable in a green and pleasant land. The recapitulation asserts the values of the countryside in a triumphant *fortissimo*, and a movement remarkable for the consistency of its benign viewpoint ends softly and without any unnecessary fuss. 'Look!' Malcolm seems to be saying to Sheila. 'No more mood swings or aggression! Just gentle rustic pleasures in glorious Richmond Park!'

A short scherzo (*Vivace*) follows, and although there is constant interplay between major and minor, an impish optimism prevails throughout, the movement ending assertively in the major. All along Malcolm shows obvious delight in displaying his mastery of the orchestra, but, for all the high spirits and special effects, for all the rustic vulgarity of the main tune, everything is essentially under tight control. There is no hint of mania.

---

[3] Based on parallel thirds to enhance the pastoral atmosphere

Following the cheerful opening two movements, the sorrowful third movement, *lento*, comes as something of a shock. Yet for all the depth of its distress the movement lacks any overt displays of anger or signs of emotional mayhem. The interval of a third dominates and, by superimposing thirds on top of each other, Malcolm creates some heavily dissonant harmony, but the tone is more of resignation than protest. The climax of the movement is the entrance of a sombre funeral cortège, Malcolm here paying quiet homage to the third movement of Mahler's First Symphony.[4] But the emotional content in Malcolm's slow movement is deeper than Mahler's, for whereas the Austrian was simply mourning the desertion of the blue-eyed Johanna Richter, Malcolm's loss was an amalgam of all the things that had gone irretrievably wrong in his life, from the death of Philip to the mad attack on Sheila. And as the cortège of woe passes away, and a solo horn eventually brings the movement to its disconsolate conclusion, Malcolm is left alone with his burden of unexpiated grief.

After this long and poignant slow movement the balance of the symphony is restored by the final *Allegro*, dominated by one of Malcolm's jolliest tunes, orchestrated in a variety of scintillating ways. Here is the much-loved Malcolm of the *English Dances*, at his happiest, secure again in his marriage to Sheila, delighting in his children and buoyed up by his new-found standing in the musical world. Although the tune is soon contrasted with new material – a stern fugal passage followed by some macabre high jinks – Malcolm is careful to accentuate its positive, rather than negative, potential. In an exhilarating E flat major coda, he shows how clever and happy he is by combining the movement's two principal ideas in a triumphal conclusion.

It is a fine symphony, with a constant flow of invention in its four highly contrasted movements. If a 'masterwork' is 'a piece in which one can hardly imagine a passage or a note changed for the better',[5] then Malcolm's Second Symphony has strong claims to be just such a work.

All along, everything about the Second Symphony was auspicious. This time there was no two year wait before performance. One day, while it was being written, the telephone rang. It was Charles Groves, who had succeeded Rudolph Schwarz as conductor of the Bournemouth orchestra. Was there any possibility, enquired Groves nervously, that Malcolm might be able to provide a small piece for the orchestra's Diamond Jubilee that summer? 'Would you like the symphony I'm writing?' replied Malcolm. Groves gratefully accepted it, sight unseen.

Finished in early February 1953, the Second Symphony proved a great success in Bournemouth that May. It was soon broadcast, given its London première at the Festival Hall (where Malcolm conducted the LPO), and featured

---

[4] Malcolm's four movements correspond to those in Mahler's First Symphony, the first movement of which was initially headed *Wie ein Naturlaut* – 'like the sounds of nature'.

[5] Hugo Cole, *Malcolm Arnold*, p.55

in the Proms, Malcolm this time conducting the BBC Symphony Orchestra.[6] Since then it has been played all over the world and regularly recorded, remaining one of the most popular of the nine symphonies.[7] As usual, there was a marked discrepancy between the public reaction and that of the critics. When Malcolm conducted the work at the Festival Hall, the audience laughed in delight at the end of the Scherzo and roared out its approval at the end. But in critical circles, tunes and optimism were swiftly going out of fashion, as atonalism began to make ground in the musical establishment. *The Times* greeted it cautiously. A piece of such bold and bright instrumental colours, said the critic, was a 'welcome and agreeable' addition to the repertoire, but should such a 'workaday subject' really be called a symphony 'in the absence of any apparent inevitability in the sequence of four movements'?

The carping of an esoteric minority was not enough to stop the work's progress. It was clearly too good not to survive, and soon it enjoyed premières in Switzerland, Canada, America, South Africa and Australia. The Second Symphony, Sheila's greatest triumph, established Malcolm's international reputation.

However, the success of works like the Second Symphony drew Malcolm further from the family at Richmond. When, for example, he went to Grenoble for the symphony's European première, it was in the company of his publisher friend, Michael Diack. Sheila stayed at home looking after the children, while Malcolm got up to considerable mischief, carried away by his symphony's highly enthusiastic reception:

> Oeuvre haute en couleurs, riche par ses modulations, par ses belles mélodies, par ses rythmes ... oeuvre plaisante aussi à lire, où y trouve la luminosité des partitions de Saint-Saëns; toujours agréable à entendre; oeuvre qu'on pourrait qualifier de classique, s'il n'y avait en plus un esprit nouveau, une recherche personelle et moderne dans l'orchestration digne d'un Mahler ou d'un Berlioz ...[8]

Malcolm had a wonderful time in Grenoble. There is a photograph of him looking plump and radiant on the conductor's rostrum, turning back from the wildly enthusiastic audience to congratulate the players, arms outstretched like a Messiah, a Cheshire cat grin spreading roguishly across his face:

> Le compositeur anglais, acclamé par le public, se retourne vers l'orchestre pour lui faire partager son triomphe.

---

[6] It was performed at the Winter Gardens, Bournemouth (Bournemouth Municipal Orchestra) on 25 May 1953; the first broadcast was on 9 February 1954 (BBC Scottish Orchestra/Alexander Gibson); Malcolm conducted the LPO on its first London performance (Royal Festival Hall, 3 June 1954); and Malcolm conducted the BBC SO at its introduction to the Proms on 8 August 1956.

[7] When asked in a radio interview celebrating his eightieth birthday which of the nine symphonies was his personal favourite, Malcolm gave the Second as his answer.

[8] *Le Dauphiné Libéré*, 5 March 1954

Many fine works followed the Second Symphony. Of particular interest is the Second Violin Sonata, which showed Malcolm exploring the virtues of atonality. Malcolm had studied serialism carefully and sometimes voiced admiration for Webern and various English followers of the Darmstadt school,[9] particularly Humphrey Searle and Elizabeth Lutyens. In the first of the four thematically linked sections of this sonata, the violin sings a meandering melody of Mahlerian intensity, while the piano grumpily refuses to play along, casting constant doubt on the tonality. Harmonic ambiguities persist through both the violent scherzo and the following wistful waltz, only finally to be resolved in the last bars of the work. Ironically the Sonata had been commissioned by the Hungarian violinist, Suzanne Rozsa, because she liked 'the light and cheery' nature of his music: 'I was a little disappointed when I found it wasn't written in this style at all.'[10] She had met Malcolm through her father-in-law,[11] a cellist in the LPO, and took to him at once. 'He was always so nice as a person.' To her surprise Malcolm charged her nothing for the Sonata. The first performance at the Festival Hall[12] happened to fall on his thirty-second birthday, he told her. So what better present could he have than hearing her play his music?

In 1954 Malcolm wrote three more concertos: for Richard Adeney, the first of two flute concertos;[13] for Larry Adler, the Harmonica Concerto;[14] and for Denis Vaughan (and the Festival Hall organ), an Organ Concerto.[15] Each is in the traditional three movement form and lasts a little under twelve minutes. The brevity of Malcolm's concertos has led to their being undervalued. These three works are typical in showing Malcolm's uncanny ability to comment in depth on both the character of the dedicatee and the instrument itself. All three have particularly beautiful slow movements, the *Andante* of the Concerto for Flute and Strings capable of holding its own in any list of 'A Hundred Best Tunes'. Few composers would have dared to write a slow movement of such simplicity, Malcolm displaying an optimism that was rare in European art of the period.

The *Sinfonietta No 1*, which Malcolm dedicated to the Boyd Neel Orchestra and scored for a Mozartian chamber orchestra of strings with pairs of oboes and horns, is unashamedly melodious and good humoured, including a chaconne of

---

[9] The geographical centre for a new style of composition developed by Stockhausen, Boulez, Nono, Maderna and others, where the music was excessively concerned with intellectual and cerebral methods and obsessed with impenetrable systems.

[10] December 2003

[11] Sam Lovett, father of the Amadeus Quartet's Martin Lovett

[12] Recital Room, 21 October, 1953. Paul Hamburger was the pianist.

[13] The first performance was given by Richard Adeney and the Boyd Neel Orchestra (conducted by John Hollingsworth) at the Victoria and Albert Museum, 11 April 1954.

[14] Commissioned by the BBC Proms for their Diamond Jubilee season and first performed on 26 June 1954, Malcolm himself conducting.

[15] The first performance was given in the Festival Hall, 11 December 1954. This Concerto gave Pappy, an organist himself, particular joy, and he would tell of the hours Malcolm spent practising on the organ of St Matthew's Church, Northampton.

great beauty as the central slow movement. Equally fine in its different way is the *John Clare Cantata* for choir and piano duet.[16] Commissioned by William Glock for one of his Summer Schools at Dartington Hall, Devon, where Malcolm was from time to time a cheerful and inspiring presence, it is a highly engaging and often beautiful work, hinting of Benjamin Britten.

Malcolm's versatility was remarkable. In the same year as the *Cantata* came the humorous *Tam O'Shanter*, which was to prove an enduring success. Robert Burns's poem about the late night adventures of a hard-drinking Scot provided Malcolm with an ideal scenario for a musical romp, which attracted good notices at its première in the Proms.[17]

> Britain's brightest, breeziest composer at thirty-three is still busy proving that modern music is not all dog-biscuit and sour apples. This tall, plump man almost exploded into last night's Promenade Concert. Taking over the conductor's baton from Basil Cameron, he drove the Royal Philharmonic Orchestra through the jolliest, noisiest musical ride of the year ... It set the orchestra laughing, sardine-packed Promenaders dancing, and the whole Albert Hall audience in a ferment of delight.

*The Times* agreed:

> No-one in music today has a more uninhibited sense of humour than Malcolm Arnold with which to savour the drunken Tam's relish in the sight of the old witch dancing in her too short skirt. Everything is there, the Scottish background (bagpipe drones and Scottish snap rhythms), the drunken Tam (trombone glissandos), his ride home through the stormy night, the witches' revels at Kirk Alloway, their furious pursuit of him, culminating in the loss of his poor nag's tail and the inevitable moral of the story.

The applause at the end lasted four minutes and proved something of a frustration for the BBC announcer, eager to introduce the next item of the live broadcast:

> ... and that, ladies and gentlemen, was the first performance of *Tam O'Shanter* by Malcolm Arnold conducted here in the Royal Albert Hall by the composer himself ...
>
> And here once again coming back onto the platform is Malcolm Arnold ... and he brings the Royal Philharmonic Orchestra to their feet to acknowledge this tumultuous applause ... the audience seems determined Malcolm Arnold should come back once again ... and here he comes now ... The second work will be *The Last Sleep of the Virgin* by Massenet ... but no, the audience demands that Malcolm Arnold comes back once again ... and he's shaking the leader of the orchestra by the hand ... And now a word perhaps about *The Last Sleep of the Virgin*. Massenet, a French composer, is, I think it is true to say, chiefly renowned for his opera, but the piece we're about to hear comes from *La Vierge*, which is a sacred legend which he wrote in 1888 ... Malcolm Arnold is taking another bow ... and now we're waiting for the appearance

---

[16] The cantata has settings of six of Clare's poems on the seasons. Malcolm used words by John Clare again in 1956 for his *Song of Praise*, commissioned by Ruth Railton for the Jubilee of Wycombe Abbey School.

[17] *The Yorkshire Post*, 16 August 1955. The work was dedicated to his new publisher, Michael Diack.

of Basil Cameron … but it's not Basil Cameron that appears, it's Malcolm Arnold once again …[18]

It was so successful a work, said *The Times*, it should have a place in the first or last nights of the Proms 'for years to come'. Alas, for prophecy! In the next fifty years, despite its being played all over the world to great acclaim, it would only manage two more Proms performances.[19]

It was earlier on in this period of great success that Malcolm started a productive association with the Sadler's Wells Ballet[20] at Covent Garden. It came about by chance, Humphrey Searle finding himself unable to meet a commission for a Coronation ballet and suggesting Malcolm instead. Malcolm was just beginning to be recognised by the establishment – it was only in April 1953 that the BBC put his name on the list of those whose work did not have to be vetted by their Reading Panel – and so he relished the opportunity of writing for the Coronation alongside eminent figures like Vaughan Williams, Walton and Britten.[21] *Homage to the Queen*, choreographed by Frederick Ashton and danced with a cast headed by Margot Fonteyn and Michael Somes, proved every much a triumph at its première on the night of the Queen's Coronation as Britten's *Gloriana*, four days later, proved a disaster.

The run-up to its first performance was marked by an extraordinary correspondence, as Malcolm, usurping the job of his agent, tried to extract some sense from Covent Garden's General Administrator, David Webster. In a highly interesting exchange of letters[22] Malcolm shows himself more than capable of dealing with the unbusiness-like (or slippery) Webster. On 9 April, for example, less than two months before the first performance of the ballet, Malcolm was writing, determined to receive a clarification of the terms of the commission:

> Please forgive me for troubling you but I have been working on a ballet for the last eight weeks which is now complete and only remains to be orchestrated, and have not yet had an official letter commissioning this work. As it will take all of my time for the next six weeks to orchestrate this ballet I would be most grateful to receive a letter setting out the customary terms of agreement over a work like this, which lasts forty minutes,[23] so that I can arrange other work accordingly.

A holding letter was sent by Webster's secretary, as he was abroad, with £50 sent on account. It was hardly business-like and smacked of sharp practice.

---

[18] A transcript of the actual broadcast.

[19] 1964 (LPO) and 1988 (National Youth Orchestra of Scotland)

[20] Three years later, in 1956, it became the Royal Ballet.

[21] Vaughan Williams caught the mood of the Coronation year with his Seventh Symphony, the *Sinfonia Antarctica*, a reworking of the film score with which he had embellished the heroism of John Mills's Captain Scott. Walton wrote the *Orb and Sceptre* march and Britten the opera *Gloriana*.

[22] Reproduced by courtesy of the Royal Opera House, Covent Garden

[23] The final score was to last fifty minutes. Malcolm's fourteen weeks of work is no doubt deliberately pitched on the high side.

Malcolm gave Webster the benefit of the doubt, waiting for a few weeks. Eventually however (on 15 May, now only two and a half weeks before the Coronation) he decided he had better set out his terms, Webster still having failed to do so:

> Thank you very much for the fifty pounds on account. 'Homage to the Queen' with the additions made in rehearsal will last for at least fifty minutes. I suggest £250 to be a reasonable commissioning fee for this work. The ballet is complete and half of it is scored ... Paterson's [24] will negotiate the performing right fee, but the question of the commissioning fee is my affair ...

The request for £250 (about a quarter of a good annual income in 1953) jolted Webster (19 May) into action:

> I have never paid more than £150 for a commission fee for a ballet and I would not normally be prepared to do so. Mr Diack tells me, however, that you have turned down several film jobs in order to complete this work for us and in the circumstances I am prepared to arrange for a fee of £200. I would be grateful if you would realise that this is an arrangement that I would not be prepared to make again and would like it not to be regarded as a precedent.

Malcolm accepted the reduced fee (23 May), but hardly with good grace. He could write just as tart a letter as Webster:

> Thank you for your letter. As this ballet is for the Coronation I will not argue about the money and will accept your offer of £200. The work is complete and I would be glad to have the balance at your earliest convenience. Please do not think that there is any likelihood of your having to make such an arrangement again, because it is only because of the National circumstances that I would work for such an absurdly low figure.

Malcolm, it seems, quite enjoyed his jousts with Webster. He also found very appealing the backstage atmosphere of a great ballet company, loving the glamour and camaraderie of stage life. He was more than happy to identify himself closely with the rehearsal process as Frederick Ashton began creating the steps.

There was not much story in the forty-minute ballet Ashton had in mind as the centre-piece of his Coronation triple bill. As the title suggested it was an opportunity to show off the company in a series of *divertissements* honouring the new Queen. Initially Ashton had the idea of splitting the piece historically, with four ballerinas representing the ages of the first Elizabeth, Anne, Victoria and the second Elizabeth, and it was on such an outline that Malcolm wrote his music. Ashton then changed the identities of his four main ballerinas (Margot Fonteyn, Violetta Elvin, Beryl Grey and Nadia Nerina) to the Queens of the four elements, Air, Water, Fire and Earth, which is why the music is less elemental than it

---

[24] Malcolm had by this time changed his publishers from Lengnick to Paterson, run by Michael Diack. Michael's son, Jim, later took over Paterson after many years as first horn in the BBC Welsh Orchestra.

otherwise might have been. The ballet ended with an apotheosis in which the first Elizabeth presented a sceptre and orb to the second.

With his experience of writing film music to precise timings Malcolm had no trouble meeting the suggested requirements, which, Ashton was at pains to point out, were merely an 'indication' which could be 'departed from at will'. It was exactly the kind of business-like commission which Malcolm enjoyed. The opening sequence, for example, could hardly be more precise:

> Distant fanfare developing into loud fanfare as curtain rises.
> Entrée of entire company. (March Allegro e Maestoso 2 min.
> developing into Adagio 2 and a half mins developing into coda Allegro Vivo half min)
> 1st entrée (Elizabethan) 6 girls 1 min' [25]

Malcolm produced a wonderfully virile opening march for the entrance of the company, and excelled himself with the *pas de deux* for Air (Fonteyn and Somes) and Water (Elvin and Hart). He seemed to know intuitively what would work, and when changes were needed he effected them rapidly, as Anya Linden remembered:

> Fred loved the way the music came so quickly and easily out of Malcolm. He was a heavy, lovely, jovial man and would stand by the piano to watch us, twinkling and laughing. If Fred didn't like a particular passage, he'd happily write something else. [26]

Alexander Grant, who danced the Spirit of Fire, agrees.

> Ashton was thrilled to have a composer who was so willing to do exactly what he asked. He was amazed at the pace he worked. He had never worked with a composer who produced so quickly. [27]

Malcolm's score enjoyed a host of complimentary reviews. Douglas Churchill of the *Dancing Times* thought it possessed 'a superb suitability for dancing, it has charm of melodic invention, strong flowing rhythms'. Above all, he delighted in 'the unfailing variety and brilliant colouring of the orchestration'.

Malcolm and Frederick Ashton quickly became friends, sharing a common interest in literature and art. There was a great deal of laughter too. One evening Malcolm persuaded the young and handsome Richard Adeney to come with him on a late night visit to Ashton's London home. Adeney agreed, little realising what Malcolm intended. After several knocks on the door, Ashton appeared, appropriately elegant in an exquisite dressing-gown. 'Ah, Fred!' exclaimed Malcolm delightedly. 'Look! I've brought you a present! Here's Richard!'

The gala night on the evening of Coronation Day [28] was a glittering affair, Oliver Messel's glamorous new costumes and set designs for Malcolm's ballet

---

[25] David Vaughan: *Frederick Ashton and his Ballets* (Dance Books [2nd ed.] 1999) p.451

[26] Julie Kavanagh: *Secret Muses* (Faber & Faber, 1996) p.408

[27] December 2003

[28] There were two other items in the 'Homage' triple bill: William Walton's *Façade* and Act Two of *Swan Lake*, Robert Helpmann returning to Covent Garden to partner Margot Fonteyn two years after he had left the company.

colourfully matched in the stalls and stalls-circle by all manner of chic 1950s evening gowns. The piece was aptly named. As a prelude, just before it began, the audience listened to speeches by Winston Churchill and the Queen, broadcast live from Buckingham Palace. There was just the right atmosphere for the outrageous piece of sycophancy with which Ashton ended the ballet:

> After dancing in a misty avenue of candelabra-trees, lit with scores of lights, the company lined up in rows and faced a far off vista. Out of the distance appeared a glorious vision of Elizabeth I. Gliding in stately fashion towards her went Elizabeth II trailing a richly brocaded royal train and offering the Tudor Queen a sheaf of flowers.[29]

Ninette de Valois, the director of the company, was delighted. It did Malcolm no harm at all when the word got round that 'Madam' had declared him the best composer for dance since Tchaikowsky. So successful was the ballet that it was revived for several years afterwards.

Just over a year later Malcolm was commissioned to provide another score for Ashton, this time for a one-act ballet on Tasso's story of *Rinaldo and Armida*. Armida was a frozen-hearted sorceress who lured men into her mysterious magic garden. When they fell in love with her, they perished. If she were ever to fall in love herself, however, she would die. Enter the handsome Rinaldo ...

The all-important atmosphere which such a slender storyline demanded was beautifully created by the set designs of Peter Rice. Everything except for Armida's red rose was black, white or grey. Slender trees stood silhouetted in a mysterious moonlit garden. Mist rose from the frozen ground. Black leaves fell gently from the boughs, and, in an elegant rotunda, sat Armida, her long white dress adorned with the ubiquitous black leaves.

There were just four dancers and, at the heart of the ballet, were three *pas de deux*, in which the relationship between the impetuous young warrior and implacable enchantress slowly changed. Malcolm himself conducted the first few performances.[30] He was in his element, the centre of attention, playing his own music to packed houses in one of the most beautiful opera houses in the world, with the enchanting Svetlana Beriosova just a few feet away from him and, when it was all over and he'd taken his bow onstage, any number of pretty members of the *corps de ballet* to chat up afterwards.

It is surprising that Malcolm's short score for *Rinaldo and Armida* languishes at present in obscurity.[31] It has hardly been heard since the ballet was dropped from the company's repertory after 1959. Nor was its cause helped when the respected ballet historian David Vaughan made it the scapegoat for the ballet's ultimate failure. Vaughan wrote of 'a score of no great distinction by Malcolm

---

[29] *The Star*

[30] Later performances were conducted by Fistoulari.

[31] It was published by Faber Music in 1984. In 2001 a recording was eventually made, albeit by an excellent Danish student orchestra.

Arnold'. The ballet, he continued, might well have grown in stature with greater familiarity 'except that one essential ingredient was certainly lacking, a score that might have inspired Ashton to a poetic handling of the subject…' It sounded, he wrote, 'like film music'. One only has to listen to it once to realise how mistaken Vaughan was.[32] The five-minute *Andante con moto* of the final *pas de deux* may well be the finest piece of British ballet music ever written. The whole score is a fine one by any reckoning[33] and was widely praised by the critics. *The Times* called it a neo-romantic tone poem which finely expressed the vehemence and sinister undercurrent of Armida's sorcery. *The Dancing Times* was equally impressed:[34]

> Malcolm Arnold's score first stresses the garden's cold mystery, where only the wind seems to have a life of its own. Gentle, then boisterous, it blows the lovers to their fate, but having joined them in a kiss, it cruelly bursts into the fatal storm. Arnold's development of his melodies is masterly in giving both rhythm and emotional content to the dance movement.[35]

The problem with *Rinaldo and Armida* lay with Ashton's choreography. Cyril Beaumont in the *Sunday Times*, while praising Malcolm's 'colourful score', blamed Ashton for faulty plot construction and many reviewers commented on the lack of choreographic invention. There was also another problem. Instead of using the regular leading partnership of Fonteyn and Somes, Ashton had opted instead to partner Somes with the tall Lithuanian, Svetlana Beriosova, a lovely dancer with an abstracted air which suited the ice-cold temptress Armida. But there was less chemistry between Beriosova and Somes than there would have been with Fonteyn. Michael Somes, however, loved everything about the ballet and always spoke highly of it in later years.[36]

Nearly a month after the first performance Malcolm had to chase up David Webster, Covent Garden's General Administrator, who was again being tardy in his administration of financial matters:

> I realise the fees for 'Rinaldo and Armida' must have slipped your memory, and have worked out a minimum figure, which although nominal, I am willing to accept. £100 commissioning fee and £5 guineas[37] per performances. I hope this will be acceptable to the Royal Opera House, and if there are any points to discuss I shall be pleased to call and see you any day this week.

Webster hastily agreed.

---

[32] Something which David Vaughan later acknowledged (Jackson: *The Life and Music of Sir Malcolm Arnold,* p.70)

[33] There was just one momentary fall from grace when for some not too obvious reason Malcolm seems to have briefly admitted the Rushden Town Brass Band into the violent storm while Rinaldo was making good his escape.

[34] 7 January 1955

[35] February 1955

[36] Wendy Ellis, November 2003

[37] For the fifteen performances on the American tour at the end of 1955 Malcolm received a useful cheque of £78 15s 0d.

The commissioning fee was far from being a nominal sum at that time, but Malcolm would probably have participated for much less, because he so much enjoyed being a part of the company. Anne Heaton, who danced Sibylla (Armida's sorceress companion) on the American tour, remembers Malcolm in great spirits in rehearsals at Baron's Court. There was one incident in particular in which he, for once, was a peripheral figure:

> We were all in the studio at Hammersmith. It was the early stages and Fred was still choreographing it. Fred was working just with Svetlana [Beriosova]. Michael Somes and I were one side of the room. I had been having a bit of trouble with Michael – he was upset about my going out with my future husband, John – and this quiet voice in my ear was going on and on and on, and I was getting more and more fed up. Eventually I got so fed up that I sloshed Michael over the face with such a whack it stopped the rehearsal dead! Hilda Gaunt, a divine old pianist, whom Malcolm loved and who would have played for you for ever provided there was a bottle of Guinness on top of the piano, got up and strode across the room to remonstrate with me. 'Anna, you never do that again! You never hit a man across the face!' 'Well I just have!' I replied. Fred was looking distinctly nonplussed but there, on the opposite side of the room, was Malcolm in absolute hysterics. He was laughing so much he eventually had to leave the room. It totally saved a difficult situation.[38]

Anne Heaton and her future husband, John Field, who had both danced in *Homage to the Queen,* became close friends with Malcolm, introducing him to a former dancer, David Paltenghi, then a film director and choreographer.[39] Malcolm and David Paltenghi shared two big interests: drinking and womanising. Paltenghi had enjoyed matinée idol good looks, and though by the mid-fifties the excessive drinking had made him plump, he was still a charismatic character. Anne Heaton stresses the strength of the friendship:

> Malcolm, David and my husband John were the hugest of friends. Like blood brothers! When they got together it was wonderful, the high spirits and repartee! John used to call David 'Plonk' and Malcolm 'Dad'. He had a nickname for everyone. We had a lot of meals out. It was always a laugh a minute with Malcolm.

After a night out, Malcolm would sometimes ring up in the early morning and ask if he could come to the Heaton flat in Lancaster Gate for a clean-up.

> In the end I gave him his own razor and everything else he needed. He used to appear, have a shave and breakfast. It became quite a thing. David would sometimes be with him.

As with many who met Malcolm at this period of his life, Anne Heaton was not aware of Malcolm's dark side.

---

[38] September 2003
[39] Malcolm and he got to know each other very well when Paltenghi was choreographing the film *You Know What Sailors Are* to Malcolm's music.

John might have noticed it when the boys were out together, but I never did. My dearest memory of him is his lovely sense of humour, giggling and being very happy with us. I can't remember any time when it was different. I shall always think of him with a lot of love.

Malcolm's involvement with the Royal Ballet widened shortly afterwards when Ashton's future successor, Kenneth MacMillan, then a promising twenty-six year-old,[40] was persuaded by Ninette de Valois that he should be moving away from his recent preoccupation with jazz and ragtime to something 'classical'. She suggested Malcolm's two sets of *English Dances*. MacMillan, liking the idea, used the *English Dances* for *Solitaire*, which also included two items Malcolm wrote specially for him, a Sarabande and Polka. In June 1956 the Sadler's Wells Theatre Ballet[41] gave *Solitaire* its first performance and, nearly fifty years on, it remains in the repertoire of both Royal Ballet companies.

MacMillan introduced sex and psychology to ballet. A troubled spirit who was to experience both alcoholism and breakdown, MacMillan did not hear the *English Dances*, as many would have done, as a jolly romp. He wrote instead about a young girl and her mixed relationships with those around her. Desmond Heeley's abstract set of steel scaffolding against an ice-ground background gave the work an added ambivalence. The girl seems to be happy. Much of the time she and her friends have tremendous fun. And yet ... is it all in her imagination? Does she in real life lack the friends who are milling around? Amid the gaiety we can sometimes feel the tenderness of a deep loneliness, as the girl responds to the other dancers performing with, around or in opposition to her. MacMillan uses the music deftly. He 'picks up ideas from the composer's keen colour sense'.[42] More than this, as he explores Malcolm's music in visual terms, he unerringly discovers the hidden depths, the anxieties and sadnesses welling up beneath all the surface glitter. *Solitaire* is not just a hugely entertaining ballet; it is an insight into the psyche of its composer.

Malcolm and Kenneth MacMillan worked well together, responding sympathetically to each other's inner disquietude, yet Malcolm also found the outward exuberance of Robert Helpmann equally to his taste, a reflection of Malcolm's dual-sided personality. In his almost childlike delight at being actively involved in the theatre, Malcolm had forgotten all his homophobia and delighted in Helpmann's camp, outrageous sense of fun. Helpmann's facility with slick one-liners – 'Centre stage, dear, is where I am' – and constant determination to shock was everything to which Malcolm aspired. So when Helpmann approached him to write the incidental music to his production of *The Tempest* at

---

[40] *Solitaire* formed part of the first ever all-MacMillan evening, put on by the company.
[41] Now known as the Birmingham Royal Ballet. At the time Ninette de Valois ran two companies, the Sadler's Wells Theatre Ballet, which had a brief to tour, and the Sadler's Wells Ballet, based at Covent Garden and shortly to be renamed the Royal Ballet.
[42] *The Times*, 8 June 1956

the Old Vic,[43] Malcolm quickly agreed, pushing aside for the moment all his other commitments.

Helpmann's fine cast included Michael Hordern as Prospero, Richard Burton as Caliban and Claire Bloom as Miranda. Amongst Malcolm's thirty-five pieces of incidental music were four songs for Robert Hardy's Ariel and one for Fay Compton's Juno. Robert Hardy remembers enjoying the songs:

> I wished at the time I had a purer voice. I could sing them better at this end of the game. Alas, I can't remember them any longer. But Malcolm did come up on stage on one occasion with Bobby Helpmann and Michael Benthall. I'm not sure if he heard the songs that day – pray God he didn't – though he did take me through them at the piano once early on, before handing over to the musical director. He seemed a comfortable man, comfortably covered. A rural man and something of a surprise as a composer, notwithstanding Vaughan Williams.[44]

With his dance background Helpmann encouraged Hardy to produce an unusually balletic Ariel, all pirouettes, bird movements and poses. He also gave Ariel virtually no costume, just a thong and some spangles, and this unfortunately drew more attention from the critics than Malcolm's songs.

> The critic of *The Times* sent a message to Bobby that 'Unless Mr Hardy is better dressed *The Times* will not review it'. Bobby replied 'Of course we'll put him in a new costume' and then did absolutely nothing about it. Indeed, at the end of the masque he insisted that I should bow to Ceres, arse-end on to the audience.

The critics duly had the last word. Philip Hope-Wallace,[45] while praising the 'highly agreeable music' deplored Ariel, 'all too clearly seen as a near-nude in jaundiced yellow constrained to take up and hold poses with the anxiety of young persons in non-stop Parisian revues'. Ivor Brown, putting songs before thongs, declared simply

> The music is a delightful change from the harsh discordance that is so often and so wrongly imposed on the poet's harmonies nowadays.[46]

That Malcolm could so easily produce exactly what was wanted was impressive, yet he was never again to write incidental music for the professional stage. Briefly, however, he flirted with revue. When William Blezard was organising the music at the Fortune Theatre for Joyce Grenfell's new show, Malcolm contributed a quick piece, *Paddy's Nightmare*.[47]

Malcolm's forays on the stage were essentially diversions. His main preoccupation continued to be films. In the first four years in Richmond, he wrote

---

[43] Opening on 13 April 1954, it was part of the Old Vic's famous five-year First Folio project, involving all thirty-six of Shakespeare's plays. Gordon Jacob wrote scores for two of the other plays that season.

[44] June 2003

[45] *Manchester Guardian*. He also wrote in *Time & Tide*.

[46] *The Observer*

[47] 2 June 1954: *Joyce Grenfell Requests the Pleasure*

thirty scores, mostly for important feature films. In 1953, for example, these included *The Captain's Paradise*, in which Alec Guinness jauntily sails between his two wives, Celia Johnson and Yvonne de Carlo;[48] *Albert RN,* a stirring war adventure directed by Lewis Gilbert; *You Know What Sailors Are*, a farce starring Donald Sinden;[49] and *Hobson's Choice*, another collaboration with David Lean and starring Charles Laughton and John Mills, for which he produced what became his own favourite score; and *Devil on Horseback*, a drama with a horse-racing background.

By 1954 Malcolm was well enough established to be giving a talk in the Festival Hall on 'The Serious Composer's Approach to Film Music'.[50] Predictably he had few insights. Working intuitively, he struggled to articulate his processes of composition, confining himself to only two major suggestions: to use music as sparingly as possible and to observe Peter Brook's dictum that film scores consist of quarter-ear music:

> Its impact must be immediate, on the fraction of the ear that is listening to it. Practically all film scores are built on a single theme or figure. You don't often get the opportunity to write a long tune … There must be a very short phrase which can be caught immediately by the ear that is only 'quarter-listening'.[51]

It was advice he often put into practice. For example, in Carol Reed's *Trapeze*, an Anglo-American blockbuster made in Cinemascope, which grossed record box office receipts in 1956, he produced exactly just such a piece of 'quarter-ear music'. It is heard underneath the main credits, strongly dramatic, yet romantic too, capturing the twin attractions of the film, the drama of high-wire acrobatics and the triangular romance between Burt Lancaster, Gina Lollobrigida and Tony Curtis.

Yet it was Malcolm's instinct for capturing mood and atmosphere which made him such a valued film composer. As he had learnt in Rome many years before, it was grainy realism which most mattered, fitting the right sound to the right situation. For *Trapeze*, where all the action was set in a circus in Paris, he adopted his usual eclectic approach, offering the director, Carol Reed, a wide range of popular tunes: a beguiling dance tune ('Lola's theme'); an old-fashioned fox-trot; a piece of jazz ('Juke Box'), the kind of thing extemporised in the Craigmore cellar, with solos for clarinet, saxophone, piano and trumpet; a cheerful tune, featuring an accordion, to express all things French ('Tino's arrival in Paris'); and any amount of vulgar circus music, including an irresistibly comic

---

[48] The scenes with Yvonne de Carlo allow Malcolm to indulge in some lurid dance music in which he naturally gives the trumpet the leading role. Malcolm, it seems, could easily have outdone bandleaders like Joe Loss or Ted Heath.

[49] Malcolm wrote the particularly idiomatic and witty clarinet part for his friend Jack Thurston, now published for clarinet and piano under the title 'Scherzetto'.

[50] 11 March, Recital Room

[51] Lecture given to the British Institute of Recorded Sound, 17 January 1962 (*Recorded Sound*, 18)

'Elephants' Waltz' led by a tuba and embellished with appropriately entertaining harmonies.

But for authenticity in such a circus situation, Malcolm needed sounds with which the audience would quickly identify. He therefore brought in two marches by Sousa, to capture the glamour of the circus parade, Julius Fucik's *Entry of the Gladiators*, to give the trapeze act a big build-up, and a Chopin Nocturne, played fast on an old piano during the Circus dancers' rehearsals. Key dramatic moments involve 'the triple', a somersault few trapeze artists attempt. The film shows how Lancaster was seriously injured in the past when attempting the feat; how Curtis persuades Lancaster to teach him it; how they practise it, with Lancaster as Curtis's catcher; and how eventually they achieve it. Malcolm's inspiration was not just to give 'the triple' a musical motif, but to give it the very opposite of what we might expect. Instead of something nerve-tinglingly dramatic, he uses a brass band arrangement of *The Blue Danube*. Placid, cheerful and inexorably repetitive, the familiar waltz assumes a surreal, nightmare quality. As soon was we hear it, we know what lies ahead of us.

Films like *Trapeze*, together with continued television appearances, helped to make Malcolm a celebrity. By the mid-1950s he was a household name and often interviewed. He was learning to cope better with the media and usually came over most engagingly:

> Malcolm Arnold wears his success lightly and with a smile. He himself is as free from pomposity as his music. He has an infectious way of enjoying life and this élan is in much of his music. He is a most amusing companion and when he catapults into a genial gathering of friends the temperature always rises and the fun increases. A serious and concentrated worker, he knows when and how to relax, and I can personally recall happy occasions when gloom and introspection, had they dared to show their faces, would have been unceremoniously kicked out through the door.
>
> He has a strongly made physique, a big and friendly face with a welcoming smile, and now a waistline about which he certainly does not look as if he worries! On the rostrum he generates tremendous energy, and seems to enjoy that experience too. In an age where there is much that is anaemic, tentative and morbidly introspective his gusto is refreshing ...[52]

This was only a part of the picture. Interviewers either chose to ignore or did not see the other, less attractive side of his character. But even in this early, highly successful period of his life it was there. John Amis remembers the intermittent difficulties in their friendship:

> He used to get pugnacious when drunk. Even as a young man he could suddenly turn a bit nasty. There is a dual nature in him. He can be verbally cruel. He can suddenly turn the conversation and be really nasty. He would be terrific fun and very generous and then – oomph! – on comes the black! The changes of mood didn't seem to be

---

[52] *London Musical Events*, August 1955

triggered by anything. Suddenly, out of nowhere, he'd create ragged holes in his friendships.[53]

Fortunately, he tended to make two new friends for every one lost. His gregarious instincts were well met in the mid-1950s when a rendezvous for musicians from all over the world was opened up in South Audley Street, Mayfair, the International Music Association (IMA) of which Malcolm was a founder-member. It had been started by a rich American lady, Mrs Hubbard, in the hope (so it was said) that it would provide a safe haven for her errant son. Heavily subsidised, it offered some of the cheapest but best meals in London and quickly numbered over a thousand members, including celebrities such as Heifetz and Rubinstein. Malcolm found it of great use professionally. Meetings at the club, for example, helped cement his relationship with the current controller of Music at the BBC, Richard Howgill,[54] and it was at an IMA chamber concert that Malcolm's Piano Trio was first performed, with Howgill's daughter Pauline, to whom it was dedicated, playing the piano.[55]

The IMA also offered Malcolm a place to relax, a bolt-hole from Richmond, somewhere to eat, drink and be merry, outwitting the kill-joy licensing laws of the day. He was extremely popular at the club, and there were many, like Joseph Horovitz (another founder-member), who found him 'generous, charming and witty'.[56] However, from time to time he seriously overdid the charm and generosity. Two major symptoms of the manic-depressive illness were evident at the IMA: reckless negligence with money and an enhanced and equally reckless sexual drive. Neville Marriner remembers parties at the IMA, funded by Malcolm, which would last 'for two or three days or until the money ran out'.[57] John Amis, the club's first secretary, similarly remembers gross over-indulgence:

> On one occasion, and it was typical, he got through an enormous meal – three or four dozen oysters, a couple of carpet bag steaks, puddings, cheese and with it all several bottles of wine – before ending up on the floor having sex with a waitress.[58]

The effect of this kind of behaviour on those of somewhat more discriminating taste was considerable. If William Glock, the club's second secretary,

---

[53] May 2003

[54] Howgill (1895-1975) was in charge of BBC Music in important years for Malcolm, 1952-1959.

[55] With Sylvia Cleaver and Norman Jones, 30 April 1956. The *Musical Times* was surprisingly critical: 'Mr Arnold's lack of caution is often one of his most valuable attributes, but slap-happiness, especially in the sphere of chamber music, does not lead to satisfying results. The *Andante*, more rewardingly, offered Mr Arnold's own vein of delicate sentiment ... and both this movement and the first bore witness to an original mind labouring in an uncongenial context.' Fifty years on, the deeply felt Piano Trio seems to have worn rather better than this critic predicted.

[56] November 2003

[57] November 2003

[58] May 2003

happened to be entertaining Igor and Vera Stravinsky at the club, or Jean-Louis Barrault and Pierre Boulez, the last thing he wanted in the far corner of the dining room was a Malcolm Arnold binge. Malcolm's outlandish behaviour won him many fair-weather friends, but harmed him enormously in the eyes of important members of the musical establishment. He would pay dearly for it.

Malcolm's lifestyle was becoming more and more spendthrift. Everything had to be done on a grand scale. If he hired a car, for example, it would have to be something very *de luxe*. Thea King remembers Malcolm arriving to pick up her husband, Jack Thurston, from their home in a hired Rolls Royce. Malcolm and his friends then used the hired Rolls for a day's drinking, eventually 'arriving home slaughtered'. All through his life Malcolm would insist not just on the best restaurants, when out with friends and colleagues, but also on paying the bill. Bill Rainer remembered being invited out to fish and chips. 'We finished up at Wheeler's, top floor.' Malcolm had his own private table there. Bill Rainer would often accompany Malcolm with other musicians to one of the brighter West End venues, the Panama Club, where Malcolm would order vast quantities of food and drink, make 'funny squiggles' on the table-cloth, and when the waiter produced an inflated bill, cross out half the items, fling down a number of notes and sweep out.[59] 'Generous' is the adjective most commonly used of Malcolm by those who knew him. But Sheila would have used another word. She did not see much of this generosity.

The marriage was under considerable pressure by 1955. Sheila gamely came out on parade, suitably dressed up, at the premières and first nights, maintaining the appearance of marital harmony, but she hated these events. Anne Heaton was surprised by how much Sheila worried for the future:

> She said to me one day, 'I just wished he'd stayed in the orchestra'. I think she was afraid of looking after a famous person. She felt she wasn't right for the job. She couldn't keep up with him.

There was also a further anxiety for her. Sheila knew Malcolm's weaknesses and fully understood what lurked behind the jovial exterior. Robert was now five, Katherine seven. *They* had to be her priorities. She would support Malcolm all she could. She still loved him, but it was the children who had to come first. Determined that they would grow up with her values, not Malcolm's, she braced herself for a battle of wills.

She was particularly insistent that the family should take a long summer holiday together. While the children had been very small they had visited seaside resorts where there was a good promenade for the pram. In 1954, however, Sheila organised four weeks on the remote Scottish island of Soay, just south of Skye. From 1955 onwards there would be an annual pilgrimage to

---

[59] Letter to Malcolm, 16 June 1984

Cornwall, reconnecting them to the earliest, happiest days of the marriage. For Malcolm these summer holidays were not just a period of recovery from over-indulgence but also a realisation of how much he enjoyed simple family pleasures, the very things he so carelessly and so often put in jeopardy. For Sheila the holidays were all-important, a chance for the children to have their father to themselves for a change, away from all the pressures of the music business. She usually invited Granny Nicholson, under whose eagle eye Malcolm would behave himself. Sheila also often invited her sister's three children. It was all part of her campaign for family solidarity. As far as she was concerned, the marriage was tenable only as long as Malcolm committed himself to the summer holiday.

The choice of Soay, in 1954, was unusual. It is a beautiful island, but wet, boggy and exposed, the beaches all boulders and pebbles, with no sand apart from a coarse, reddish gravel. There were only half a dozen houses on the island, overlooking the curving bay of Camus na Gall, the anchorage on the east of the island, where they stayed. The journey there was arduous: the overnight sleeper to Mallaig, followed by a steamer making irregular progress in swollen seas. After two highly uncomfortable hours they rounded the Point of Sleat and there before them, lying low, was the tiny Soay, difficult to pick against the dark back-drop of Skye's Cuillin hills rising sheer out of the water. The island had no anchorage so a perilous transfer took place from steamer to skiff. Katherine remembers climbing down the side of the ferry into a little boat in enormous seas:

> But we made it, and away we went in the little rowing-boat, bobbing up and down in a really horrendous sea! We were all sick! The au pair chose to be sick in a fisherman's teapot!

Malcolm was the one who had decided on Soay, having come across a book by Gavin Maxwell, *Harpoon at a Venture*, describing how Maxwell had bought the little island at the end of the war and later attempted to start a shark-fishing business. By the time of Malcolm and Sheila's visit Maxwell had been five years gone, but his derelict base was near their house, including the rusted remains of a steam locomotive he had shipped there, an incongruous contrast to the wild, natural beauty of Soay.

Katherine remembers the holiday with great affection:

> We all had a wonderful time. We were there a month. A boat came in once a fortnight, delivering food that we had to order. The house we rented was fairly primitive. There was only an Elsan.[60] Dad had to dig for us. The au pair watched! She was the kind of person who painted her nails all the time! She had quite an easy time, as my mother is the sort of person who would clean the grate before the au pair came in to light the fire![61]

---

[60] A portable lavatory
[61] May 2003

There may not have been a pub within miles, but Malcolm was in the highest of spirits throughout the holiday:

> Dad must have been as he was when he first married. He was wonderful. We would go for walks together, since I was a little bigger than Robert, and there were days when we went right round the island. On one occasion we found water lilies in the lake. Dad climbed out on a tree to get me one. We carried it home in triumph and put it in a vase – only for some goats to come into the house, climb up the stairs and eat the water lily. It became one of Dad's favourite stories …

It was this single family visit north of the border which fired his imagination for the *Scottish Dances*.[62] Although they were written three years later, they undoubtedly contain something of Malcolm's unalloyed Soay happiness.[63] And on the cover of Paterson's original score there is a photograph of Malcolm and the little Robert, looking out from Soay across the waters to the majesty of Skye.

Though the summer holidays afforded some respite from the unrelenting work and play of the 1950s, there was little time for his wider family. It was something of a shock for Malcolm, therefore, to learn in 1955 that his mother was ill. She had last been down to London earlier that year to see a performance of *Homage to the Queen* at Covent Garden but apart from that Malcolm had seen very little of her recently. By that summer she was seriously ill. Summoned by Ruth to Northampton, Malcolm learnt the worst. Nan was dying of cancer. The visit was a traumatic one, with Pappy crying at her bedside and a constant stream of visitors formally coming in to take their leave of her. In a state of shock, Malcolm put aside all his work until, on 21 October 1955, his thirty-fourth birthday, Nan died.

For a time guilt and grief consumed him. Pappy had the consolation of his faith to support him. Malcolm only had drink, and for several months he could do little work. He had loved his mother dearly, but with a love he had always found difficult to express. She had indulged him, encouraged him, and been an unswerving source of support, and, like most sons, he had taken her devotion for granted, anxious not to be too much in her debt. And there had always been Ruth and Lizzie who had mothered him with more overt affection. He had always felt guilty on his infrequent visits to Craigmore that he found things easier with Lizzie. Fun without formality, and no strings attached. He had even tried to persuade Lizzie to come and join him at Richmond. He remembered how distressed his mother had looked at the time.

Somehow, even when Nan reached seventy earlier that year, he had imagined her a fixture at Craigmore, as unmoveable as the corner cabinet holding all those dolls, or the rocking chair, in the front room. Pappy too would always be in his high-backed chair beside the brass-topped table, reading his *Radio Times*.

---

[62] Completed February 1957

[63] The third dance, however, which takes a song attributed to Robert Burns as its starting-point, was written earlier, for his 1949 documentary *The Beautiful County of Ayr*.

*Ruth's view of her father, 1939, with later comment*

He remembered their pleasure when in Coronation Year he had conducted the LPO at Northampton's New Theatre, an event which Pappy helped organise. Such devotion to music now, such a change of heart since his son had joined the

LPO. And Nan had not been slow to tease him about it. 'I'd better put a placard round your neck with the words MY SON'S IN THE LPO!' Pappy was never one for half measures. He had acted as concert guarantor for the orchestra's visits for years, and now Northampton even had an organisation called The Friends of the London Philharmonic.

Malcolm remembered how proud they and all the family had been as he conducted the new Suite he'd created from his Coronation ballet.[64] Not that the visit had been without its problems. He had flared up with Pappy on discovering reporters at the doorstep of Craigmore. There he was, wishing to sit down quietly and complete the orchestra parts for his new Suite – and there was Pappy, selfishly besieging him with reporters, purely for his own self-glorification. As a result he had only managed to get the hand-written parts to the orchestra with time for ten minutes' rehearsal before the afternoon concert! He smiled at the thought of the newspaper cutting Nan had sent him afterwards. 'Malcolm Arnold conducted broadly and unconventionally.' Little Jenny, Ruth's daughter, had put it differently at the reception Pappy had organised afterwards. 'Uncle Malc, your arms were flapping so much I thought you were going to fly!' But at least his efforts had succeeded. Miraculously the Suite hadn't fallen apart.

As he stood in the graveyard, unlistening and inconsolable, staring at the massed array of flowers and hating every single one of them, his thoughts turned to composition. He would write a symphony. He could hear something of a *Lento* already. Bleakly sad. More Sibelius than Mahler. But like neither really. Just as bleakly sad as a Northampton graveyard in late October, with a few, dry handfuls of meaningless earth being flung on his mother's coffin.

---

[64] Malcolm turned *Homage to the Queen* (Op 42) into a seventeen-minute Suite (Op 42a).

# 8
# The Hoffnung Years
## Comedy, Tragedy and an Oscar, 1956-59

M ALCOLM WAS much in evidence at the bar of the IMA Club in the immediate aftermath of Nan's death, depressed and frustrated, the new symphony nothing but a series of unresolved ideas. He forced himself to keep working on his latest film score, but the usual flair had temporarily deserted him. He was working by rote, effectively enough to the outside world, but with a heaviness of spirit that precluded real inspiration.

Malcolm's life, however, was revitalised by a sudden new friendship. One afternoon at the IMA Club he was introduced to a plump little man, balding, with a pair of circular horn-rimmed spectacles perched on his nose. Gerard Hoffnung, an elderly-looking twenty-nine, was one of life's natural comedians, someone who loved to be the centre of attention, delighted in good food and wine, and, above all, was a keen amateur musician, playing the tuba and ocarina. Already well-known as a cartoonist, raconteur and radio and television personality, he had recently been enjoying great success with his books of musical cartoons. *The Maestro* made gentle, surreal fun of the foibles of conductors, *The Hoffnung Symphony Orchestra* of instruments and instrumentalists. The humour was simple and direct: a cymbals player with a bandaged nose, for example, and a timpanist tuning his drums with a stethoscope. In 1956 came *The Hoffnung Music Festival*, the cartoons ranging from John Barbirolli on the podium, earnestly sharpening his baton in a pencil-sharpener, to a group playing the *Trout Quintet*, fishing lines leading from their instruments to a pool inside the grand piano.

Gerard was currently interested in the idea of staging an actual *Hoffnung Music Festival*, a zany and irreverent concert in the establishment's heartland, the Royal Festival Hall. Malcolm was at once enthusiastic and he and Gerard were soon discussing the project with others over a long lunch at Wheeler's. New works would be needed, they decided, written in the spirit of the cartoons, and Malcolm at once volunteered to contribute.

Shortly afterwards, he was thumbing through *The Hoffnung Music Festival* with Gerard, seeking inspiration. He paused at a cartoon of a *Vacuum Quartet in A Flat.* 'How about my writing a piece for four vacuum cleaners?' Gerard's eyes twinkled. 'Brilliant! But how about three vacuum cleaners and a floor polisher, together with an organ and the biggest symphony orchestra ever assembled?' 'Trouble is,' said Malcolm, 'How do we know what notes they play?' 'That's easy! We go down to Hoover's showroom in Regent Street!'[1] Not long afterwards Malcolm was being photographed by the press, wielding a tuning fork in the Hoover showrooms. Armed with the knowledge that the vacuum cleaners played in B flat and the floor polisher in G, he hurried back to Richmond to write a work involving his four unusual soloists.

The Hoffnung Music Festival, which duly took place at the Festival Hall on 13 November 1956, was full of fun. More surprises were put into Haydn's *Surprise* Symphony; Dennis Brain played Leopold Mozart's *Concerto for Hose-pipe*; Humphrey Searle's *Lochinvar* featured an alpenhorn, a rattle machine, an air-raid siren and police whistles; Gordon Jacob wrote a work for two piccolos, heckelphone, two contra-bass clarinets, two contra-bassoons, serpent, contra-bass serpent, harmonium, hurdy-gurdy and a sub contra-bass tuba (three times the size of Gerard Hoffnung, who played it). But the best of all the contributions was the one which started the evening off, the *Grand, Grand Overture*, in which Malcolm's anarchical imagination gives perfect musical expression to Gerard's surreal imagery.

Dedicated to President Hoover, the *Grand, Grand Overture* is a comic masterpiece, with its vacuum cleaners and floor-polisher (finally silenced by rifle fire), and a whole series of other musical jokes including an ending which threatens never to end. The overture also contains a fine tune, happy and uncomplicated, but so emotional that when the organisers first heard it they were 'caught up in a surge of joy and tears'.[2] Sam Wanamaker, the show's director, has written of the way this exhilarating, madcap music set the Festival going, removing all doubts and inspiring the students and volunteers of the nervous Hoffnung Symphony Orchestra:

> The first full rehearsal with Lawrence Leonard's Morley College Orchestra[3] was approached with a kind of controlled horror over the hoax we were about to perpetrate on an unsuspecting public. There was no turning back. Here we were, by now hundreds of people involved, driven by Gerard's enthusiasm, and yet I had a premonition that it would all end in a terrifying shambles of amateur high jinks.[4]

One hundred and thirty players sat nervously, waiting for Malcolm and staring at the newly copied parts of his overture with considerable misgivings. But as soon as he bounced onto the podium, exuding massive, seventeen-stone confidence, the atmosphere changed. The orchestra readied itself. Gerard Hoffnung at the tuba and Dennis Brain at the organ grinned broadly at Malcolm,

---

[1] As described by Malcolm in the BBC television *Omnibus* programme, 1991
[2] John Amis: *Amiscellany*, p.115
[3] Hoffnung had been playing the tuba for some years in the Morley College Orchestra which the highly popular and hard-drinking Lawrence Leonard conducted.
[4] Annetta Hoffnung: *Hoffnung* (Gordon Fraser, 1988), p.136

*The cartoon which inspired the Grand, Grand Overture: 'Vacuum Quartet in A flat'*

who winked cheerfully back, took up his baton and with a cheerful 'Let's have a bash, shall we?' gave a characteristically energetic down beat. 'The impact of sound,' wrote Wanamaker, 'fairly lifted us all out of our seats. From time to time bursts of laughter from the non-playing members of the orchestra greeted each audacious musical joke, nearly halting the wild flow as Malcolm flayed the air relentlessly.'

The overture later surprised and thrilled the audience of three thousand, setting the Hoffnung Festival off on the best possible of starts.[5] Ballerina Anne Heaton was in the front row:

> There was an amazing atmosphere. Electric! Malcolm was enjoying himself enormously as he conducted the overture and from time to time would look our way and grin!

Sheila enjoyed the night too, as a soloist on one of the vacuum-cleaners, glad to feel part of things.[6] She was fond of Gerard and Annetta Hoffnung, but not at

[5] To add to the excitement the BBC were televising the first half of the concert live and EMI recorded it all, their LP subsequently becoming a best-seller, the recording still available fifty years on.

[6] Jean Stewart (a viola player to whom Vaughan Williams had dedicated his string quartet) and violinist Olive Zorian (John Amis' former wife) were the others, while Norman Del Mar's wife, Pauline, was on the floor polisher.

all sure, deep down, that Malcolm's best professional interests were being served by this diversion from serious composition. As usual she put on her best smile and hoped for better days, her Yorkshire upbringing ensuring that at the end of the concert she claimed the polisher, which did useful service on the parquet floors of 19 Denbigh Gardens.

The evening was a huge success:

> At the close, all the principals including the well-beloved Yvonne Arnaud, Malcolm Arnold, Norman Del Mar[7] and Francis Baines[8] trooped on for a great reception. Then Hoffnung, author of the whole idea of this gay night, came on to storms of applause.[9]

What had started out as an evening of ephemeral fun became overnight an institution and there were overwhelming demands for future concerts.

The crazy world of Gerard Hoffnung may seem only gently satiric today, but in 1956 it was ahead of its time. In the days before the Swinging Sixties and the aggressive satire of David Frost's *That Was The Week That Was*, the humour seemed thrillingly iconoclastic. John Amis's programme notes for the *Grand, Grand Overture* gave a taste of things to come:

> … The handling of the heavy brass in the recapitulation is exemplary and the masterly use of the tam-tam (Arnold specially differentiates between the gong and the tam-tam, a typical example of his discerning ear) recalls a phrase in an early poem by Kingsley Amis about 'the malignant hand of opacity'. The penultimate peroration is a veritable paean of praise, but even so the listener is scarcely prepared for the quietness of the closing passages where the affirmation of the bassoons' undulations, although here their utterance is no longer laconic, but, having gone through a spiritual metamorphosis, a polemic re-orientation, affords something like catharsis in order to reduce the whole of the exordium to an unequivocal, single unison …

The satire of the Hoffnung concerts played its part in delineating the growing divide between the general public with its preference for traditional classical music and an emerging avant-garde, catering for an intellectual minority and questioning the need for music to have public appeal. In 1958 Milton Babbitt famously wrote:

> The composer would do himself and his music an immediate and eventual service by total, resolute, and voluntary withdrawal from his public world to one of private performance and electronic media, with its very real elimination of the public and social aspects of musical composition.[10]

This was the era of works like Karlheinz Stockhausen's *Kontra-Punkte*, effected by a serially organised interplay between horizontal and vertical lines,

---

[7] Horn player and great friend of Dennis Brain, he went on to become a distinguished conductor. He worked regularly at Morley College at the time.
[8] For a time professor at the RCM specialising in 'early' instruments. Baines (brother of the instrument historian Anthony Baines) himself played the hurdy-gurdy.
[9] Percy Cater, *Daily Mail*, 14 November 1956
[10] 'Who Cares If You Listen?', *High Fidelity*, New York, 1958

*The composer at work in Denbigh Gardens, 1958*

and Olivier Messiaen's *Le Réveil des Oiseaux* in which the music was derived entirely from birdsong. Stockhausen's *Der Gesang der Jünglinge*, for boy soprano and electronic tape, was performed through a five-channel stereophonic system, while John Cage's electronic *Concerto for Piano and Orchestra* could either be performed in whole or part and by any number of performers.[11] Pierre Boulez's *Poesie Pour Pouvoir* was written for two orchestras and nine loud-speakers, one of which had to be suspended from the ceiling and rotated, and Stockhausen's *Gruppen* had three orchestras surrounding the audience and playing independently. Even more unusual was Nam June Paik's *Homage à John Cage*, which featured the composer sitting at the keyboard and throwing eggs at a mirror, rosary beads at the audience and attacking and ultimately destroying the piano with scissors.

It was all wonderful material for Hoffnung satire. A later sketch, for example, *Punkt Contrapunkt*,[12] featured Gerard Hoffnung as Dr Klaus Domgraf-Fassbaender and John Amis as Professor von der Vogelweide, ridiculing Stockhausen and the Darmstadt School. Malcolm loved *Punkt Contrapunkt,* not just for the blows struck at Darmstadt but for its whole anarchical premise. Both men, for all their worldly success, were essentially outsiders, Gerard Hoffnung, despite his public school background, being a Jewish refugee from Nazi

---

[11] An example of aleatoric music where at least part of the performance is left to chance

[12] A play on Stockhausen's *Kontra-Punkte* and the Aldous Huxley novel *Point Counter Point.*

Germany. Both enjoyed madcap humour at the expense of an over-serious musical establishment. With good reason Malcolm was now described as 'the nearest lunatic creative artist to Gerard that could be imagined'.[13]

Sheila and Annetta Hoffnung, as wives of ebullient eccentrics, had much in common and the two families became close. In 1958 the Hoffnungs, who were renting a holiday home at Middleton-on-sea, invited the Arnolds down for a picnic. 'Bring some strawberries, if you like!' said Annetta. Malcolm rose to the challenge and arrived not just with a punnett or two but with whole armfuls of them. Annetta smiles at the memory:[14]

> We seemed to have strawberries everywhere! It was typical Malcolm! He could never do things by halves!

Bad weather confined that particular picnic to indoors, but both Malcolm and Gerard later braved wind and rain to plunge joyfully into the waves. They were soon happily floating on their backs, cigars in mouth, bobbing up and down like smoking steamers.

Sheila and Malcolm also developed a circle of friends in Richmond, mostly connected either with the Barnes Music Club or the Richmond Community Centre. Sheila's friend 'Bunny' Swann[15] had started a string orchestra at the Centre, in which Sheila played, and which Christopher Finzi, son of Gerald and husband of Hilary du Pré, often conducted. 'We had a really good orchestra at Richmond,' remembers Sheila. 'Malcolm would come and conduct sometimes. He quite liked amateur orchestras. He could tell them what to do!'[16]

Malcolm's homing instinct for the Richmond pubs was too much of a good thing for some of his friends. There is a story of William Walton's publisher, Alan Frank, taking cover behind the counter of a butcher's shop at the sight of Malcolm coming up Richmond High Street towards him. But Malcolm spotted this evasive action and followed him into the shop, where he was confronted by a flustered butcher. 'Come on, Alan,' boomed Malcolm. 'We're going to the pub for a pint! I know you're behind there – and you know it makes sense!'

Sheila's support at the first Hoffnung Festival belied the problems in the marriage. Katherine remembers being sent away in 1956 to a Quaker boarding school, St Christopher's, Letchworth, as a tactical move:

> The idea was to see if Mum could cope better with Dad, if she had more time for him. But, in the event, it made little difference. I went for one summer term and was desperately homesick and sent frantic letters home! Dad was distressed, responded to

---

[13] William Mann's notes to the Hoffnung LP booklet (1974). Mann himself was involved in the Festivals. He wrote the libretto for 'Tales of Hoffnung' where excerpts from over forty operas were ridiculously juxtaposed. As music critic of *The Times* (from 1948 to 1982) he was not always Malcolm's strongest supporter.

[14] May 2003

[15] Step-mother of the pianist and composer Donald Swann

[16] August 2003

the letters and organised an interview at St Paul's. He was very pleased when they took me – I was the only one starting at the time – and I was grateful to him. He was, in fact, something of a softee about us.

Malcolm was delighted with St Paul's and would sometimes join Sheila in supporting Katherine at functions like Carol Services; and he also maintained some contact with Robert's Prep School, King's House, close to Denbigh Gardens. On one occasion, says Robert, his father donated an elaborate chair 'for the headmaster to sit on', a huge green affair with a gold 'portcullis' back, which had come from a film set representing the House of Lord's.

*A publicity photograph taken in Denbigh Gardens for the first Hoffnung Music Festival. Malcolm practises with a shotgun. Sheila and Pauline Del Mar play vacuum and floor polisher.*

*On holiday with Gerard Hoffnung, 1959*

This was the period when the family summer holidays were augmented by a few days together on the south coast after Christmas. They would usually stay at the Farringford Hotel, the former home of Alfred Tennyson, at Freshwater on the Isle of Wight.[17] Malcolm was at his best there, leading the family on long walks over the hills behind the hotel onto the Afton Downs, where, he informed them with glee, Tennyson had once composed 'The Charge of the Light Brigade'.

Each summer they would spend much of August in Cornwall. After holidays at farmhouses at St Issey and Wadebridge, they went regularly to the Padstow area, always renting the same house, The Bryn, looking out over the quiet, rocky beach of Newtrain. Malcolm tended not to bring work down to Cornwall, and even when he did, he sometimes found the lure of the rock pools, sand and sea too great. 'I'll simply put "Repeat"!' he cried to Katherine on one occasion, 'and that will mean we can all go down to the beach straight away!'

In May 1957 Malcolm and Sheila went without the family to the Prague Spring Festival as guests of the Union of Czechoslovak Composers. Humphrey Searle[18] and his wife were also there:

Czechoslovakia was very Stalinist at that time, as was reflected in the modern Czech music we heard in the Festival, mostly enormous heroic symphonies based on the principle of 'social realism'. Malcolm and I tended to opt out of performances of such

---

[17] Robert also remembers an Easter family holiday at Balmer Lawn Hotel, Brockenhurst, with walks and pony rides in the New Forest.

[18] The previous year Malcolm had repaid Humphrey Searle for getting him the commission of the Coronation ballet, by recommending him to Muir Matheson for feature films. Malcolm was enormously impressed with the score Searle had written for Kenneth MacMillan's *Noctambules* at Covent Garden.

works – there were plenty of other events in the Festival, including an enchanting production of Dvořák's *Rusalka*.[19]

The British party managed to evade their hosts from time to time to see the real Prague, often in the company of the genial Polish composer Kazimierz Serocki. In cafés and bars the locals were eager to talk about the West and tell them the true nature of conditions in their country. For Malcolm it was something of a setback to his left-wing ideals. When they attended a Congress on the 'Problems of Modern Music' and Dmitri Kabalevsky in the main address put forward the official Soviet view about the need for 'social realism' and 'music for the people', Malcolm's response was somewhat confused and it was left to Humphrey Searle to reply spiritedly that the British Government felt no need to compel composers to write in any one style. The highlight of the visit for Malcolm was the opportunity to get to know Shostakovich. 'I had a fairly happy time in Prague,' he was to write many years later, 'and became very friendly with Shostakovich and his wife.'[20]

It was strange for Katherine and Robert as they grew up to discover that their father was famous. 'I was about eight,' Katherine says, 'When I noticed one day at the Festival Hall that there were people wanting Dad's autograph, and I realised that he was important, admired by more than just me.' Robert was sometimes aware of the tension before concerts:

> Dad studied the scores for days before. He was quite big and he had this tail-coat which used to come back wringing with sweat, just as if it had been dumped in the river. I was fascinated by his batons, which were very beautifully crafted, with a turned mahogany handle. He used to have them hand-made because he liked very light ones and he would therefore get through several a year![21]

The children grew up expecting their father to be absent for long periods and thinking little of it. For Sheila, Malcolm's absences on binges caused great tension:

> It was terribly difficult to keep my temper with him. But I had to. I had to remain calm for the children.

She dreaded his drunken returns to the house.

> It's a terrible thing to frighten small children. You can't do anything worse to them.

Annetta Hoffnung still remembers the strain Malcolm's alcoholism inflicted on Sheila and, indeed, all his relationships.[22]

> Gerard was a dear friend of Malcolm's, immensely fond of him and a tremendous admirer of his work, but it was quite a fraught relationship, because Malcolm drank so much. When he was drunk he behaved atrociously. Sometimes Gerard would go

---

[19] Humphrey Searle: *Quadrille with a Raven* (unpublished)
[20] Letter to Edward Arnold, 27 November 1978
[21] Years later Robert, when working up at Skye, made them himself for his father.
[22] May 2003

out and have a meal with Malcolm specifically to see if he could help. Unlike Malcolm, Gerard was quite conservative in his attitudes. He was very concerned at Malcolm's drinking. On two occasions he went down to the IMA and rescued Malcolm from the club when he was absolutely paralytic and took him back to a nursing home[23] to recover. Gerard was a well-organised person, able to cope with that sort of thing. But he would always come back very upset when Malcolm had been in a bad way.

Although Sheila would never discuss it with anybody, it was clear to Annetta that Malcolm's problems extended beyond the alcohol:

> Sheila was a lovely person but had an impossible time. It seemed to me as if Malcolm couldn't bear to be too close to anybody. He couldn't cope with affection. He seemed unhappy, perhaps, with the idea of inter-dependence. It brought out a destructive instinct.[24]

Gerard's creative energies were a useful challenge to Malcolm, who, despite his problems, managed to keep writing prolifically. But he continued to struggle to be taken seriously, his Hoffnungian exploits helping to confirm him as a musical clown. And within months of the vacuum cleaners and floor polisher he was producing a wonderfully absurd *Toy Symphony* for the Musicians' Benevolent Fund at a much publicised banquet at the Savoy Hotel. Malcolm's witty three-movement work, written in similar style to his St Trinian's music, was scored for twelve toy instruments (including a whistle 'played' by Gerard), a string quartet and piano (played by his friend Joseph Cooper).[25] Malcolm conducted with relish.

All his life Malcolm would look upon music as a unifying bond and music-making as the ultimate act of friendship. Although these were concepts which, because of his mercurial temperament, were sometimes more to be honoured in the breach than the observance, they were sincerely, indeed passionately held. In 1957 several lively works represented this spirit. A delightful Oboe Quartet written for Leon Goossens's sixtieth birthday; a Horn Concerto, Malcolm's second, but the first for Dennis Brain; and a fine March for the hundredth birthday of the Royal Military School of Music, at nearby Kneller Hall.[26] Keith Llewellyn, then a clarinettist in the Kneller Hall band, remembers the occasion:

> I noticed Malcolm on this large grass patch talking to the Queen – they stood there chatting together for ages. Although the Duke of Cambridge was the founder of

---

[23] The Hoffnungs were living in Hampstead Garden Suburb, not too far from the Greenway Nursing Home in Belsize Park, where Malcolm would sometimes dry out.

[24] May 2003

[25] Also playing the toy instruments were Sir Thomas Armstrong, Eric Coates, Astra Desmond, George Baker, Edric Cundell, Lt Col David McBain and Eileen Joyce.

[26] The College supplied precious help in the Hoffnung Concerts in the course of which Malcolm became friendly with Lt Colonel David McBain, to whom *HRH The Duke of Cambridge* is dedicated.

Kneller Hall, we all believed that Malcolm had actually written the *Duke of Cambridge* march for the pub of that name which stood outside the gates![27]

Dennis Brain first played the new Horn Concerto at the Cheltenham Festival in 1957[28] with Malcolm conducting the Hallé Orchestra. Malcolm and Dennis Brain had known each other since their days as students in London and been friends since concerts with the London Baroque Ensemble in 1949.[29] Brain did not conform to the traditional figure of the extrovert, hard-drinking brass player. He was reserved and shy, but shared Malcolm's quick-wittedness and enthusiasm for music-making. Although Malcolm's previous Horn Concerto had been written for Charles Gregory, it was Dennis Brain who gave it its first broadcast performance.

The Second Horn Concerto, written specifically to exploit Dennis Brain's virtuoso technique,[30] is a challenging work, demanding accurate control in the highest register, superb legato, and agile, rapid playing. Brain rose magnificently to the challenge in the Cheltenham performance. Tragically, he was never to play the concerto again, for six weeks later, returning in the early morning from the Edinburgh Festival, he mysteriously lost control of his TR2[31] on the Barnet Bypass. It overturned and crashed into a tree, killing him instantly. He was thirty-six, just a few months older than Malcolm.

Malcolm's status as a 'light' composer was enhanced by the success of his *Four Scottish Dances*, commissioned for the BBC Light Music Festival and given their première at the Festival Hall in June 1957, with Malcolm himself conducting the BBC Concert Orchestra. In these dances Malcolm was giving the public what they most expected of him, tunefulness and gaiety, an idealised expression of Highland life. The final bars of the first dance contain a Hoffnungian joke, and the use of a gruff bassoon towards the end of the second dance cannot fail to raise smiles. And although the lyrical *Allegretto* encourages us to drink in and ponder the beauty of the Scottish landscape, the work effectively fulfils its commission as an entertainment for a Light Music Festival.

---

[27] Keith Llewellyn went on to become secretary of The Malcolm Arnold Society in 1994.

[28] Malcolm also conducted a performance of the popular *Tam O'Shanter*. In the two years since its first performance the work had enjoyed, at home and abroad, nearly sixty performances.

[29] 'Malcolm Arnold once arranged a Hocquet by Guillaume de Machaut for trumpet, horn and trombone, which he and Dennis played many times together and also broadcast for the BBC. They were both so struck by the humour of the piece that they had to stand back to back in the studio to avoid breaking into laughter.' Stephen Pettitt: *Dennis Brain* (Robert Hale, 1989)

[30] The work was written in just ten days the previous December – a quite remarkable achievement.

[31] It is thought that he fell asleep at the wheel. Richard Adeney, however, who owned a similar car, had serious problems with the engine's rear mountings and believes such a breakage could well have caused Dennis Brain's car to somersault.

It was now two years since Nan had died, and the Third Symphony was still unwritten. But shortly after completing the *Scottish Dances*, Malcolm received a commission from the Royal Liverpool Philharmonic Society, whose current manager, Gerald McDonald, was a strong admirer of his work. The Society had been waiting patiently for William Walton's Second Symphony, and when this again failed to materialise[32] they turned to Malcolm for a symphony. He settled down to the challenge on his return from Czechoslovakia, which may well be why it is full of echoes of Shostakovich.

A many-stranded memorial to his mother, the Third Symphony states its position clearly with the opening bars of the first movement: sorrow is in the air, the harmonic direction uncertain, and melody fragmentary. The first subject, which prominently features the interval of a fourth, has an elasticity which allows shifting moods and varying degrees of resignation and distress. If Malcolm is arranging his memories of Nan at Fairview and Craigmore, and it seems likely this is case, they are uneasy ones, and the unease is heightened as the brooding first subject gives way to a chattering motif, first announced by the winds. Malcolm was always to say that second subjects should be feminine. When, therefore, the oboe[33] introduces as second subject a lovely melody, fragile and poignant, we are being introduced to Nan herself, whose later life was beset by her family's problems. Nan's melody, accordingly, suffers interruptions which become more and more insistent, the interruptions expressed by that all-important interval of a fourth. This recurring interval could well reflect Malcolm's unease at the part he played in his mother's growing anxieties.

The movement undergoes a major change[34] on the unexpected introduction of a disturbing scherzo (*vivace*), with ideas fragmented and the dissonant interval of the seventh dominating. Nan's secure and affluent little world has been undermined. But there is nothing Malcolm can do about it at this late stage, and the movement ends abruptly with a quiet restatement of a fragment of the first subject, as if he suddenly cannot bear to give it more thought.[35] It has been an emotionally-charged first movement, full of dramatic development as it has fluctuated between regret and despair. The stage is set for one of Malcolm's big slow movements.

Dark and brooding, its tone colour reminiscent of Shostakovich, the *Lento* is

---

[32] Commissioned in November 1955, Walton's Second Symphony was finally given its first performance by the RLPO in 1960.

[33] Bar 97

[34] At Letter Q

[35] Colin Mason of the *Manchester Guardian* was one of the few critics to realise that Malcolm was boldly condensing two movements into one: 'When the movement is almost complete, the composer turns abruptly into a brief but intensely developed scherzo, based on the same material, before ending the movement with a few bars recalling the themes as they were originally presented. This is an innovation in the way of condensing or combining symphonic movements, and although it could be hardly repeated or copied in another work, it is successful here.'

a tightly structured set of variations, based on a passacaglia.[36] There is a deeply yearning and troubled nature to the melodic writing, the tensions set up never fully resolved. We are far removed from the sweet sadness of the *Allegretto* of the *Four Scottish Dances*, the sadness much more bitter, the harmonies teetering on the brink of dissonance, the structure of the movement encouraging elegiac, dreamlike repetition. As one variation bleakly succeeds another, we realise there is no hope at all. Nan is dying. We are in the Craigmore front parlour on Malcolm's leave-taking visit, Pappy weeping inconsolably beside her, respectful friends paying last, embarrassed calls, Malcolm watching, unable to cope with the reality, puzzled and uncomprehending, wishing that this was a scene he could leave on the cutting room floor. The music changes mood. There is a brief announcement on the brass, and drums roll. Nan has died, but Malcolm is no longer with her, but back in Richmond, looking out at the rows of poplars and seeing beyond them not the usual overgrown garden but the whole ghastly ritual of the laying out of the dead, with the grief-stricken family responding in their individual ways. But the mood changes as the scene fades and the movement reaches its climax, the music swelling into noisy, passionate denials, the brass complaining, all restraint gone, nothing but anger, torment and the recurring, unanswerable question of Why? Why? Why? The *Lento* has travelled a long way in its fourteen minutes.

The unexpected follows, just as it did for 'the triple' in *Trapeze*. Instead of a movement bringing healing, dignity or hope, comes a light-hearted *Allegro con brio*, full of selfish fun, with the interval of a fourth again very prominent. Malcolm is getting on with life, applying his tuning fork to vacuum cleaners, chatting up the girls, chasing his friends into butcher's shops. But it all becomes too much for him, and the more he tries to forget, the more he remembers. The frenetic geniality won't work. Thoughts of Nan's death and his own mortality cannot be shaken off, and at the end of a memorably mad finale, all instruments blazing, restraint thrown to the winds, he finally collapses centre-stage, like Pagliacci, as the curtain falls.

The Third Symphony, like so much of Malcolm's music, is deeply personal. In attempting to come to terms with Nan's death, he sublimates his grief and guilt, making it bearable. So he was able to enjoy the first performance given by John Pritchard and the Royal Liverpool Philharmonic Orchestra at the Festival Hall[37] and at the manic conclusion, greeted by a solitary boo and a crescendo of cheering, Malcolm sped down from the stalls to the stage, beaming and waving, to shake hands with John Pritchard and his leader, Peter Mountain, and acknowledge the applause.[38]

---

[36] A movement that is constructed on a repeated bass line or chord sequence. In this case it is a chord sequence.

[37] 2 December 1957

[38] John Pritchard later signed Malcolm's programme: 'For Malcolm. In thanks and excitement!!'

It was hard for the critics to know what to make of it. Malcolm was the composer who wrote them tunes and made them laugh in an ever-increasingly gloomy world. What was he up to? Was this the real Malcolm Arnold? The shrewder critics answered in the affirmative. Colin Mason gave various reasons why this was the first new symphony since Shostakovich's Tenth which he positively wanted to hear again:

> The chief of these reasons is the abundance and virile lyrical quality of Arnold's tunes, out of which, like Shostakovich, he shapes a sustained and original symphonic form ...[39]

Felix Aprahamian was similarly positive:

> Once again the marvellous fluency of the orchestral writing reveals Arnold's ability to think orchestrally rather than merely orchestrate. There are the usual flamboyancy and clarity of texture and also, in the first two movements, a greater continuity than before.[40]

These critics, however, were the exceptions. On the whole the response was bemused and negative. Leading the hostility was Peter Heyworth of *The Observer*.[41] Heyworth was to attack Malcolm relentlessly, for as a well-known exponent of traditional tonality, engaged in large-scale works, Malcolm was an important impediment to the new avant-garde on whose behalf Heyworth was fighting.

Peter Heyworth was a typical Darmstadt missionary. Erudite and well-educated, though without any specific musical training, he espoused with passion the cause of atonality in general and Pierre Boulez in particular, fighting hard to emancipate British music (and particularly the BBC) from what he saw as Euroscepticism. The programming of contemporary music in the BBC, he rightly felt, had been unadventurous in the post-war years, with Schoenberg, Webern and Stravinsky all undervalued in the 1950s. Younger talents – Messiaen, Boulez, Berio, Nono, Dallapiccola, Carter, Tippett, Gerhard, Lutoslawski, Henze and Ligeti – were rarely heard in performances which did them justice. Heyworth's frustration was understandable, but led to some highly subjective musical criticism.

Malcolm, like all those who favoured traditional tonality, had to be ridiculed and removed for the new music to come through. Peter Heyworth's review of the Third Symphony gives an indication of the urbane skill with which Darmstadt missionaries went about their business. He was careful to avoid any feeling of confrontation. The tactic was to give (a little) with one hand, and take away (a lot) with the other, making charges of bias hard to prove:

---

[39] *The Spectator*, 6 December 1957
[40] *Sunday Times*, 8 December 1957
[41] Peter Heyworth (1921-1991), music critic of *The Observer* (1955-1987), *The New York Times* (European correspondent, 1960-1975) and biographer of Otto Klemperer

Mr Arnold sets out with one great advantage: he is blessed with a melodic fertility that many composers with a larger reputation might well envy. And to this he adds an imaginative flair for orchestral colour that is here particularly evident in his handling of the woodwind.

But a symphony is a symphony, and not just a matter of good tunes and bright colours. This is not just a question of pious respect for an historic form; nor, I need hardly add, of believing that a symphony must be solemn. It is because extended movements must have some firm structure if they are to hold attention on repeated hearing. Mr Arnold is enormously engaging. His problem is to retain the interest and sympathy he has engaged and it is one that he has not fully met in this symphony.[42]

Many would disagree about retention of interest and sympathy. Malcolm's adventurous approach to symphonic form often led to charges of lack of structure, but the first movement is clearly a near relative of sonata form, and in his melodic development – fragmenting, reshaping and recolouring – Malcolm is strongly influenced by Sibelius.

It was understandable that critics should find the second movement puzzling. But Peter Heyworth preferred to poke gentle fun at it rather than puzzle it out:

The second movement, a set of variations, opens on a grave note. But instead of the deep emotional waters this suggests, we soon find ourselves floating, agreeably enough, in some shallow cranny after the tide has gone out. I could not find much continuity or purpose about the movement.

It is doubtful if he tried.

His criticism of the third movement, which, at seven minutes, he found too long, relied on generalisations, which he did not attempt to substantiate, presumably because, had he done so, he would have failed:

After this Mr Arnold tries to take us by storm in a Shostakovich-like finale, full of fireworks and high jinks, much of it entertainingly done. Somehow it doesn't quite work. For one thing, it is too long, for another, the material, though genial, is a bit slick; and finally, and most important, there is a lack of that point, pungency and precision that raises mere good humour to hilarity or wit.

The polish of Peter Heyworth's prose and his dry sense of humour helped make him a formidable adversary. So too his homosexuality. Malcolm's two bitterest critics, Peter Heyworth and Desmond Shawe-Taylor, were part of a cultured and sophisticated circle of gay music critics living in severely homophobic times. To them Malcolm was a dangerous alien species, a loud, coarse heterosexual; in their eyes he would have few redeeming features. He might fling his money around, but he was gauche, brash and definitely not a gentleman.

Other attacks came from stupidity rather than missionary zeal. The *Daily Express* somehow managed to run the heading of THIS DONKEY SYMPHONY HAS FIRECRACKER PEP, shortened in its Manchester edition to THE

---

[42] *Observer*, 8 December 1957

HEE-HAW SYMPHONY IS A HIT. Its critic (a reputable writer, having an off day) had apparently identified donkey sounds in the first movement ...

Malcolm had little time in the aftermath of the symphony's première to worry overmuch about donkey noises or, indeed, shallow crannies after the tide had gone out. It had made a good impression in important places and the next year Malcolm recorded the work with the LPO and also conducted it at the Proms.[43] 'Fortunate is the composer,' enthused the writer of the Albert Hall programme notes, 'Who, in these cerebral and dodecaphonic days, can write music that sounds fresh and spontaneous.'[44] Unfortunately the symphony had been included as the last part of the programme on a Proms night which was traditionally all-Beethoven. 'I had to wait a considerable time between each movement,' Malcolm later wrote, 'As people rushed madly, almost under my nose, for the exits.'[45]

A year later, in 1959, Malcolm and the LSO gave the symphony another airing at the Royal Festival Hall. The more percipient critics, like John Warrack, began to realise there was more to Malcolm than just 'a flair for engrossing turns of phrase and felicities of scoring'. Although stating he was still baffled by the work, Warrack glimpsed something of the real Malcolm Arnold:

> When the surface is most brilliant there is the clear suggestion of melancholy depths. Even the breeziness of the finale has a chill in it.[46]

Public performances in more recent years have been irregular. But the symphony's merits have continued to be appreciated through records and CDs.[47] It is a fine work, awaiting wider discovery.

There was to be a pause before the next symphony. Malcolm might shrug off the criticisms, but they undoubtedly hurt him, inhibiting further symphonic thoughts. His film scores, by contrast, had never been more successful, and in 1958 he concentrated almost entirely on the cinema. Apart from the huge financial rewards there were two further incentives for taking this direction.

The first was the acquisition two years before of a secretary, Dorothy Payne, whose background in films lightened his load considerably. Daughter of a university don and married to a salesman in the jewellery business, Dorothy was the kind of intelligent, no-nonsense career woman Malcolm needed. She was working at Pinewood when she met him. Politely but firmly putting him in his place when he made the usual advances, she delightedly accepted the suggestion she work exclusively for him, and no-one could have been more loyal or helpful

---

[43] 1 August 1958. This was Richard Howgill's last Proms season as Controller, BBC Music. In his last seven seasons (1952-58) he included at least one major Arnold work, including two symphonies and two concertos.

[44] Promenade Concert programme, 1 August 1958

[45] 'Finding the Money', *Sunday Times*, 2 November 1958

[46] *Daily Telegraph*, 2 August 1958

[47] 'This is an impressive work,' wrote Peter Pirie defiantly in 1979, at a time when the symphony had largely been forgotten. (*The English Musical Renaissance*, p.208, Gollancz)

over the next few busy years. Dorothy brought a much-needed sense of order to his working life, for he never seemed to keep an agent very long before a row developed, and, in particular, her inside knowledge of the film industry helped him meet the most demanding of schedules. In her first three years with him he produced scores for fifteen major feature films, mostly for big Anglo-American companies, paying enormous fees.[48] He in his turn brought her life a glamour and sense of fun, for which she was always grateful. She resolutely ignored Malcolm's dark side, until, after a time, it seemed utterly unimportant to her:

> If there was a film on, I would work everyday from 9.00 in the morning to 9.00 at night. I would find out from the directors where they wanted the music. I would then take all the measurements for it – a foot of film is two-thirds of a second – and produce for Malcolm a long list of all these timings with detailed comments about what was on screen. What the actors said, where they said it, and where they moved. There was an enormous amount of typing.[49]

David Lean's *The Bridge on the River Kwai* was one of Dorothy's earliest films, and, in March 1958, it won Malcolm an Oscar for best film score. A letter Malcolm received from David Lean in February, shortly after the film's release, anticipated the Hollywood triumph which was to come.[50] Filled with the warm glow of total success, Lean describes Malcolm's score as 'simply <u>brilliant</u>'. He had started watching the completed film, he wrote, in a terrible state of nerves.

> But each time you came in and took over the thing with your music, I sat back in admiration not only of you but of my own work! God, what a gift you have, dear Malcolm! What <u>size</u>. What <u>sensitivity</u>. What <u>guts</u>. You don't miss a bloody thing.

Lean picks out several scenes where the music particularly embellished the action.

> I liked the kite scene very much – the sheer attack of the music saved that awful dummy shot of Holden falling into the river.

Then there was the big moment when Alec Guinness led his soldiers into the new camp, from which they would build the bridge:

> That march in was OK from my point of view, but you gave it that something which I couldn't say in pictures. I admire so much your full-bloodied swagger – that's the nearest I can get to describing what I mean. No sterile little highbrow 'effects' – just, <u>boom</u>!

Lean found most moving of all the sequence immediately after Alec Guinness's Captain Nicholson had outfaced the camp commandant and won the first, all-important battle of wills:

> You don't miss a bloody point ... The way you sneak in the march theme when old Nicholson wins and starts to do up that button on his tunic is sort of miraculous and

---

[48] Around £10,000 (perhaps £250,000-£300,000 in today's figures) on each film
[49] April 2003
[50] 4 February 1958. Lean was writing from Hotel Fourteen, New York.

fills me with the sort of wonder in the same way as I had it at your Coronation Ballet. What an eye you have, coupled to that talent of yours! A dramatic eye too. You know all the rules (by instinct, I'm sure) of a good story teller. The way the music built up from the above mentioned moment – all sorts of undercurrents, question marks, suppressed excitements – and then – boom!! – out it all spills, falling over itself, fulfilling itself, building and building and laughing and crying and proud as unpompous Punch!

Most interesting of all are Lean's observations on something which Sam Spiegel, as producer, insisted on Malcolm including, a theme to illustrate Guinness's growing obsession on completing the bridge, regardless of other ramifications. It was something which had caused a row between Malcolm and Spiegel – 'He told me all about your walking out on him. I don't blame you.' – but in which he had to acquiesce.

Sam is reluctantly very pleased with the score … He was not that pleased with what he calls 'the obsession theme'. He's a silly sod. It was his one little idea to have this theme and I think you did the best anyone could have done under the circumstances – but the pictures weren't directed that way. I have tried to explain this to him but he doesn't allow himself to see his own shortcomings. If one has a musical idea such as this it has to be introduced via the pictures on the screen and not painted on over a dialogue scene. If I had thought of this idea as a musical linkup I would have taken a close-up of Alec when the virus started to infect him – and leave you with it. It works in the end, of course, but you must have had a hell of a lot of head-scratching over the introduction of it.

Lean, who had worked with Malcolm before, on *The Sound Barrier* and *Hobson's Choice,* and had a home not far from Richmond, knew Malcolm shared his fascination about the kind of big money the cinema could generate:

The film is a wild success here. You can't get into a theatre unless you pay almost double prices via the ticket agency racket. Same in Boston. In Paris they have been taking £20,000 per week out of three cinemas! Same sort of business in Japan. Yesterday somebody told me it should gross about 20 million dollars worldwide!

One of the lesser beneficiaries out of all this success would be the widow of Kenneth Alford, composer of the tune *Colonel Bogey*,[51] which Malcolm had successfully grafted into his score. He had used it because of its connections with both world wars but reckoned virtually any tune with period flavour would have been equally successful. David Lean agreed. *Colonel Bogey*'s success, he believed, owed everything to Malcolm:

Colonel Bogey may be good in its own little way but now the whole of bloody New York is whistling it. I can get it any time on the radio. Cab drivers whistle it. All the record shops on Broadway are playing it into the street. Everyone asks about it, and the record sales will go to the million! That's what your swagger has done for it – and

---

[51] Alford, who died in 1945, directed the Royal Marines Plymouth Band. He wrote eighteen marches.

it was there for years un-noticed before your particular wand touched it. Bloody marvellous, my old Malcolm.

The letter contained a postscript. Malcolm was in with an excellent chance, Lean wrote, of an Oscar. He could almost bank on a nomination 'which would get you a nice little plaque'. But he should hope for more. In the event Malcolm's Oscar was just one of seven won by *Kwai*.

Malcolm was so busy with film work[52] at the time of the award ceremony that Lean had to collect his Oscar for him at the RKO Theatre, Los Angeles. It later arrived in England by air. 'A telegram from America said the Oscar was being sent to London Airport,' Malcolm remembered,[53] 'And we had to drive in and out of planes to get it. The Airport said "What is an Oscar? We've never heard of it!"' Like Lean, Malcolm was showered with film offers. 'Afterwards I was sold every bloody war movie that there was!'

He was too busy for much celebration, though he found time to buy a shiny new car, and an 'Oscar Lunch' was given in his honour at Shepperton Studios during a hard-working day on Carol Reed's *The Key*.

Dorothy's arrival in 1956 had coincided with the breakthrough of Malcolm being allowed to conduct all his own scores. In the past Malcolm had occasionally done the conducting – notably in *Stolen Face* and *Wings of Danger* (both 1952) and *The Belles of St Trinian's* (1955) – but usually Muir Matheson or John Hollingsworth did so. Not only did conducting mean more money, but also the chance to select whichever musicians he wanted, the pay being so attractive that he could have the pick of the London players.

Most of the players at these sessions admired him greatly. Bram Wiggins, for example, always found him 'very precise and very professional'.

> There was never any sign of drink or anything other than a genial effectiveness. The man was a genius with a 'blotting-paper' brain.[54]

His speed of working awed everyone.

> He saw the documentary film of the Queen's visit to New Zealand on a Wednesday and we recorded the soundtrack the next Friday.

Lunch breaks tended to be jovial. Dorothy Payne was often present:

> Malcolm chose the musicians he wanted and so there was a very friendly atmosphere. He was kind and funny, and a large number of them would lunch together in the pub. These would be lively, amusing sessions. Some players would down considerable amounts, yet, come two o'clock, everyone played quite beautifully. The drinking did

---

[52] The final stages of *The Key* were going very badly in March 1958. Carol Reed had given up on it and Carl Foreman, brought in to finish things, wanted fresh sections of music.
[53] Paul Tonks: 'Oscar Winners' (British Academy of Composers and Song-writers: *The Works*), 1999
[54] April 2003

not seem to affect a thing adversely at all. It was always remarkable how little Malcolm had to rehearse the orchestras before making the recordings.[55]

However much he might be on his best behaviour at recording sessions, his mischievousness was never quelled. Bram Wiggins and Denis Egan both have stories of Malcolm passing to them at the very last minute fiendishly difficult trumpet parts, over which they spent many an anxious moment, quietly practising extremely difficult passages, only to discover Malcolm grinning broadly at them from the control room, as they discovered that, when synchronised with the film, these demanding parts were totally obscured by the sound of cannons or tanks.

Orchestral players are notoriously critical of their conductors. They can be very unforgiving.[56] Malcolm and his players, however, always enjoyed a mutual respect. 'You knew what you were doing with him,' commented one player. 'There was no going round in fancy circles as with Boult!'

Because Malcolm was so swift at sorting out sudden emergencies in recording sessions, the players did wonder whether he kept a stack of composed phrases, to use when appropriate. This would certainly explain a comment by his film composer friend Bernard Hermann, who, getting into difficulties one day while making a recording, suddenly stopped the orchestra. 'Let's cut out the next few bars,' he declared with a smile, 'and then we can send them to Malcolm Arnold!'

In 1958 Malcolm produced an hour's splendid music for Mark Robson's epic, *The Inn of the Sixth Happiness*, for which he subsequently won an Ivor Novello Award. Dorothy's diary gives an interesting timetable of involvement. They visited Elstree together for a first sighting of the uncompleted film in April, when Malcolm acquired a copy of Alan Burgess's book[57] on which the true-life story is based. Four months later, in August, they returned to see a much altered film, lasting three hours – twenty minutes longer than the final version. Although precise timings could not yet be taken, Malcolm now needed to begin thinking seriously about the music. He had already decided to use a children's song for the climax of the film, the escape of the children over the mountains, and he now played several different nursery rhymes to the film's star, Ingrid Bergman, including one he had been taught by Lizzie Witts at the age of three, *Knick Knack, Paddy Wack*. It was the one Ingrid Bergman chose.[58] In mid-September

---

[55] April 2003

[56] When one nervous conductor got into difficulties with the LSO at the start of an overture, for example, the distinguished clarinettist Jack Brymer called out cheerfully: 'Don't worry! We'll start it off and you catch up when you can!'

[57] *The Small Woman*, telling the story of Gladys Aylward, the British missionary in China.

[58] Malcolm with his catholic musical tastes had always been good at blending existing music within his own. He had enjoyed great success the previous year by writing a march in counterpoint to Kenneth Alford's *Colonel Bogey* of 1914 and, back at the start of it all, he had given Badger Green's Major just the right Edwardian ballad, *Drake Goes West*, to sing badly in a village concert.

Malcolm and Dorothy watched a third version, but, infuriatingly for them, the director was still undecided as to where he wanted all the music. Eventually, after he had made up his mind, Dorothy spent a frantic fortnight working out precise measurements (with an accompanying scenario of the action) from which Malcolm made his score. He now had just ten days for this before the first of the five days set aside for the recordings. A project which had begun in April was finally completed mid-October.

Malcolm worked extremely hard throughout 1958. In addition to *The Inn of the Sixth Happiness* he had many other projects going on at the same time. He completed work on another epic film, *The Key*;[59] for the Jacques Orchestra he wrote the delightfully sunny *Sinfonietta No 2*, all grace and unhurried charm in the first movement, bucolic good humour in the last, and a central *Lento* of haunting wistfulness with occasional glimpses of Ingrid Bergman; then there was a short work for percussionist James Blades[60] and a significant contribution to Gerard Hoffnung's forthcoming *Interplanetary Music Festival* at the Festival Hall. Malcolm also found time to conduct his own *Commonwealth Christmas Overture*;[61] he appeared on TV in *Words and Music*[62] as well as several children's shows with Joseph Cooper and Gerard Hoffnung;[63] he was also on radio with Gerard Hoffnung in 'The Lion and the Parrot House'.[64]

Such enormously heavy demands naturally drew Malcolm constantly away from Richmond. So too did the camaraderie of London Club life. The sudden closure of the IMA had been amply compensated, in 1956, by Malcolm's election to membership of the Savile Club. This all-male enclave offered not just food and drink of admirable quality and quantity, but a cultured ambience and ready, unde-manding friendship. Business too could be combined, occasionally, with pleasure.

The Savile Club also helped Malcolm to develop further his friendship (begun at the IMA) with the current Controller of the BBC Music, Richard Howgill. Outwardly austere and extremely sensitive, Howgill would never be one of Malcolm's cronies at the bar. He was, however, quietly devoted to the cause of British music. William Alwyn's Third Symphony was commissioned by Howgill at the Savile, and it is highly probable that several of Malcolm's works

---

[59] The score subsequently coming out on a Columbia label long-playing record. Columbia also issued LPs of the music for *Kwai* and *Trapeze*.

[60] *Concert Piece* for percussion and piano: one of the first works in this genre and an opportunity for Malcolm to be unashamedly witty.

[61] A BBC commission celebrating the 25th anniversary of the Christmas broadcast by a British monarch. In addition to large symphonic forces Malcolm adds three guitars, marimba and an Afro-Cuban percussion group. He wrote of the work, 'I have purposely designed it so that the whole idea will be easily grasped by people listening after a large Christmas dinner, with children all around the room.'

[62] 14 August

[63] Joseph Cooper, pianist and TV personality, was a great friend who lived nearby.

[64] 16 May 1958

for the BBC,[65] including the Fourth Symphony, were commissioned within its grand Victorian setting. William Alwyn was later to make a moving tribute to Howgill:

> A whole generation of us – Edmund Rubbra, Alan Rawsthorne, William Wordsworth, Malcolm Arnold, to name but a few – owe much to his championship during his period in office …[66]

Situated in Brook Street, the club had always enjoyed a strong musical connection. Elgar, Delius, Stanford and Parry had belonged, and Walton, Bliss, Vaughan Williams and Adrian Boult were current members. In addition to musicians, there were many actors and writers and, most importantly for Malcolm, the cinema was also strongly represented.[67]

It was Sidney Gilliat[68] who had put Malcolm up for membership. Gilliat, with his long-time associate Frank Launder, was already an important figure in the British film industry. He was shortly to join the board of British Lion and become Chairman of Shepperton Studios. Malcolm held Gilliat, several years his senior, in considerable esteem. In varying capacities, as script-writer, director and producer, Gilliat had been involved in many of the best British films of the past twenty years.

In 1956 he and Malcolm were working together on a sequel to *The Belles of St Trinian's*, that glorious saga of schoolgirl anarchy which Gilliat and Launder[69] had created from Ronald Searle's cartoons. The new film, *Blue Murder at St Trinian's*, would feature the St Trinian's School Song, Gilliat writing lyrics to the main theme[70] from Malcolm's first St Trinian's score. 'Maidens of St Trinians,' it started, 'Gird your armour on! Grab the nearest weapon! Never mind which one!' Malcolm delightedly pointed out to Gilliat that he had written this tune originally as a parody of the kind of revivalist hymn which his father used to play at Methodist Services.[71] Fortunately, Pappy never knew that he had inspired the St Trinian's School Song.

Malcolm was also working, with Gilliat as his librettist, on a one-act opera for six voices, based on a short story by Saki. *The Open Window* was commissioned by the BBC and televised in December 1956, the popular Australian

---

[65] *The Commonwealth Christmas Overture* and James Blades's *Concert Piece* among them.

[66] *The Times*, 31 May 1975

[67] Friends and acquaintances in the film business included Muir Matheson, Bernard Hermann, Michael Powell, Ronald Neame and Sidney Gilliat.

[68] Malcolm had first worked with Gilliat on *The Story of Gilbert and Sullivan* (1953), and had also written the score for Gilliat's *The Constant Husband* (1954).

[69] With Launder he had written several of the most notable films made during the war: Hitchcock's *The Lady Vanishes* (1939), Carol Reed's *Night Train to Munich* (1941) and *The Young Mr Pitt* (1943).

[70] Scored with typical wit for piano and school percussion band

[71] Malcolm confirmed this in the 1960s to Avril Arnold (his nephew Robin's wife). The basic theme, he said, was a 'Come to Jesus' hymn.

soprano June Bronhill playing the heroine, a young girl with a gift for story-telling. She produces out of a perfectly normal shooting party, returning from a day's sport, a ghost story so vivid it proves far too much for a bank clerk, in the country to recover from a nervous breakdown. Perhaps Malcolm found the subject of breakdowns off-putting. At all events the score, on the whole, disappointed. The BBC scheduled the opera after the late news. It has yet to resurface.

Malcolm's generosity at the Savile quickly became legendary. Taxi-drivers outside the club would be astonished to be given tips of £50, even sometimes, according to an eye witness, as much as £100. Doorkeepers and barmen enjoyed similarly extraordinary handouts. The drinks at the bar were, more often than not, on Malcolm. It soon became known that when Malcolm was celebrating, at the completion of his latest work, the festivities could last several days. At the Savile it was the boisterous side of Malcolm's nature which was most often on show. William Alwyn with erroneous confidence wrote of 'Arnold, the complete extro-vert to whom life is a glorious adventure and composition a delight and a joke'. He was 'broad, exuberant and indefatigable' in energy. Malcolm, said Alwyn, 'swept into my life like a tornado'.

Malcolm's breadth of friends at the Savile was extremely wide. One of the most popular comedians of the 1950s, Jimmy Edwards of the handlebar mous-tache, was a drinking crony, and even the glum J B Priestley was a friend. On one occasion Malcolm found himself alone at the bar with Priestley. The mood was solemn. ''Ere, Malcolm,' said Priestley. 'Why does everyone in this place go around calling me Jolly Jack?' 'Well, Jack, since you ask,' replied Malcolm, 'it's because you're such a gloomy old sod!' There was a pregnant pause. Priestley thought about this for a moment, eyes glistening. 'Thank you, Malcolm,' he said at last. 'Thank you for telling me that. Why did none of the other boogers tell me?'[72]

Malcolm was always making new friends. After judging a competition at the Festival Hall for Brass Band music, he approached the winner, the young composer David Ellis. 'What are you doing now?' asked Malcolm. 'I'm going back to Manchester by train.' Malcolm looked at his watch. 'You've got hours left! Come and have a drink with Ronald Binge[73] and me!' They drove off in his car to the Savile, where they joined up with Compton Mackenzie, whose large bottle of Scotch they drank in record time. Eventually David Ellis realised he was in danger of missing the last train. 'I'll take you in the car,' said Malcolm help-fully. They drove at great speed, going up at least one major street the wrong way, but still arrived at Euston just after the train had left. 'Never mind! You'd

---

[72] Garrett Anderson: *Hang your Halo in the Hall* (London, 1993) p.95
[73] Best known for his *Elizabethan Serenade* and *The Water Mill*. He also 'invented' the cascading strings sound for Mantovani.

better come back to the club!' said Malcolm. 'We've still got a lot to talk about!'[74]

Malcolm was always ready to help the young. Although he never had either the patience or time to do much teaching, all his life he delighted in conducting school and college orchestras. Back in the late 1940s he had helped Ruth Railton found the National Youth Orchestra. Now, in 1958, despite his burgeoning film music commitments, he conducted the NYO in concerts at Leicester and Birmingham.

The programmes included performances of his Second Symphony, which since its première five years earlier had continued to be played, including recent performances in Moscow, Leningrad and Chicago. That the young orchestra could cope with it spoke volumes for its high standard. A critic in Birmingham Town Hall noted:

> Mr Arnold's Second Symphony continually demands real instrumental virtuosity from all departments, ensemble and solo, and it got it. I doubt if Mr Arnold himself has ever heard it played better ...[75]

There was the same programme of Arnold, Beethoven, Tchaikovsky and Bach at the de Montfort Hall, Leicester, and Malcolm again extracted exciting music from his young players:

> Mr Arnold's readings were suitably matched by the youthful personality of the orchestra and straightforwardness was the guiding principle. It would be wrong to infer from this, however, that the concert yielded no more than brash and superficial excellence. The *Leonora No 3* developed an inner strength that thrilled the hearer. 'Romeo and Juliet' glowed with intense passion and Bach's Concerto in D Minor for two violins and orchestra was played with considerable musical understanding.[76]

Two of the pieces played were to have far-reaching consequences. So inspired was Malcolm by the unusual format of Bach's Double Violin Concerto that, within four years, he was to appropriate it himself, his Double Concerto for Yehudi Menuhin proving a glorious twentieth-century successor to its 18th-century inspiration. And then there was *Leonora No 3*, Beethoven's third attempt to write a satisfactory overture for *Fidelio*. Three years hence Malcolm would write *Leonora No 4* for the Hoffnung Astronautical Music Festival of 1961.

Malcolm's contribution to the *Hoffnung Interplanetary Festival* of 1958, *United Nations*, was splendidly satirical and extremely noisy. It began with a lush parody of the kind of 'English' tune Elgar made famous. Shortly afterwards, while the orchestra kept on playing, six bands appeared from six different entrances in the Festival Hall auditorium, each playing a different tune. One band, led by two sousaphones, offered 'Yankee Doodle Dandy'; another, a theme

---

[74] As related by David Ellis, August 2003
[75] *Birmingham Post*, 6 January 1958
[76] *Leicester Mercury*, 6 January 1958

from Tchaikovsky's *Pathétique*. There was much marching and countermarching and utter pandemonium. Chabrier's *Spanish Rhapsody* seemed to be fighting with 'The British Grenadiers'. Eventually the bands all marched out, leaving a limp Malcolm conducting a string quartet. The *Daily Mail's* Percy Cater was as supportive as ever:

> I shall bring an action! Nice goings on at the Royal Festival Hall, the home of music as they say! It is no part of my contract to be deafened by six military bands. Two of them had a traffic jam in the gangway by my seat ... I don't suppose so much sound has ever been assembled under one roof!

This second Hoffnung concert proved so popular that two repeat performances were quickly arranged.

Malcolm was wearing himself out. To an alarming degree the chaos and confusion of *United Nations* reflected his own life. Since the Third Symphony of December 1957 he had lost his way as a serious composer. But if 1958 was bad, 1959 was in many ways much worse, the year in which he virtually ground to a halt. But it was redeemed by one composition of great merit, a Guitar Concerto for Julian Bream.

Malcolm had already written Julian Bream a *Serenade* [77] and, ever since, the guitarist had been pressing him for another work.

> I'm ashamed to admit that, when I commissioned it, I only offered him the sum of £50, and I think he decided to write it because he realised that my offering even such a piddling sum showed I was really serious: in those days I wasn't at all well off, and 50 quid was a princely sum for me to shell out. [78]

They were already old friends and drinking partners, who loved nothing better than to play jazz together, so the Bream cheque was quickly returned. It was not long before Bream had contacted Benjamin Britten over the possibility of including the new work in a concert at Aldeburgh with the Melos Ensemble. Britten wrote enthusiastically to Malcolm:

> Julian Bream has told us of the exciting news that you are writing a concerto for him and eight instruments. [79] Do you think that the work would be ready, and would you be inclined to let us do the first performance of it at this coming Aldeburgh Festival in June? Julian may have mentioned this to you as a possibility as he will be playing here, and certainly likes the idea of launching the work here. I can hardly say how happy and honoured we should be if you were to agree to this.

---

[77] The *Serenade* for Guitar and Strings Op 50, first performed by Bream with the Richmond Community String Orchestra, conducted by Malcolm in the summer of 1955.

[78] Tony Palmer: *Julian Bream, A Life on the Road* (F Watts, 1983), p.81

[79] The work was initially performed with clarinet, flute, horn and single strings, but later adapted for chamber orchestra.

*With Julian Bream at the time of the Guitar Concerto, playing the Thomas Goff clavichord*

The proposed date will be June 25th, and if you felt inclined to conduct it, our pleasure would be doubly great.[80]

The commission was a brave one. No major British concerto had ever been written for the guitar. It was something of a Spanish monopoly. Bream, however, was extremely optimistic. The guitar is a romantic instrument and Malcolm, he believed, was harmonically a romantic composer. His qualities of wit, directness and easy melody were ideal for the instrument. As they put the finishing touches to it together in Denbigh Gardens in early 1959, Julian Bream was delighted, all his hopes fully realised. Although the work is probably best known for the glorious second subject in the opening *Allegro* movement, referred to by Bream as 'my meringue', all three quasi neo-classical movements are equally appealing. The central *Lento* is the core of the work; a dark and deeply moving movement inspired by and dedicated to the memory of the legendary jazz guitarist Django

---

[80] 15 December 1958 (letter by courtesy of the Britten-Pears Library). The concert took place on 25 June 1959.

Reinhardt, whose music Malcolm had known from the age of five through sister Ruth's record collection.

Richard Adeney played the flute in the Aldeburgh première of the Guitar Concerto. At the reception afterwards he was disappointed in Peter Pears's reaction: 'Really a little vulgar, I thought.'[81] The words were spoken, says Richard Adeney, with disdain, 'as though talking about something dirty and smelly'. Malcolm was out of his natural habitat at Aldeburgh. For all his huge admiration of Britten, there was little common ground between them. Britten too suffered from depression at times, his confidence vulnerable to the slightest criticism, but his form of protection was the reverse of Malcolm's, withdrawing from, rather than seeking, the noise of the crowd.

Britten would certainly have found the celebrations after the first recording of the concerto not at all to his taste. Malcolm, Richard Adeney and the rest of the Melos Ensemble had stumbled out of the Decca studios into an old pub close by, in West End Lane. Spirits rose swiftly as Malcolm, having made the discovery that there was some champagne hidden away in the basement, bought the whole stock. Corks began popping merrily, as Richard Adeney reported:

> Everyone was given as much as he or she wanted. The news spread, the pub filled and we all admired Malcolm for his generosity. 'Oy,' said a local bloke, 'Is it always like this 'ere on a Sa'urday?'[82]

Life in the grandiose surroundings of the Savile Club only served, in 1959, to move Malcolm further away from the realities of life. Even with the assistance of the redoubtable Dorothy Payne he found it increasingly difficult to turn out film scores at will. In 1959, with a struggle, he completed just one, for an Irish drama, *The Boy and the Bridge*, directed by the lively Kevin McClory.[83] Like most of those in the film industry, even if they were not Irishmen, McClory liked a drink. He and Malcolm enjoyed some good times, as Dorothy Payne noted in her diary:

> Picked up Malcolm, who had been partying with Kevin McClory. Couldn't get him home and spent all day seeking out champagne at Twickenham with Malcolm, Kevin and Kevin's exceptionally pleasant secretary, Betty.[84]

The situation at Richmond was also steadily worsening. By 1959 Malcolm had met Susan, a merry widow, who liked the bright lights and began to think it would be fun to share them with Malcolm. He was as publicly careless in this new relationship as he was with various good-time girls and hookers, some of whom occasionally, and most insensitively, he brought to Denbigh Gardens.

---

[81] Richard Adeney, *Flute*

[82] *Ibid.*

[83] Later to make a name with James Bond, as the co-writer/producer of *Thunderball* and executive producer of *Never Say Never Again*

[84] 13 November 1958

As the marriage came under impossible strain, it seemed it was only music which held things, ever so fragilely, together. Sheila's string orchestra, based at the Richmond Community Centre, had lost its conductor and Malcolm was persuaded to take his place that winter. Christopher Finzi, who was closely involved at this time and later took over as conductor from Malcolm, remembers the situation between Malcolm and Sheila, the orchestra's leader, as extremely tense. The front door of 19 Denbigh Gardens would be ostentatiously jammed open by the Oscar. Malcolm would be drinking mugfuls of Black Velvet. He would rail quite violently in front of Sheila and their friends, often on the subject of women. Sheila's tactic was to grit her teeth and say nothing, but this only seemed to infuriate him further.[85]

It is surprising that Sheila was able to play a note. Yet in one concert she and her friends 'Bunny' Swann and Betty Hey were soloists in Handel's Concerto Grosso No 6 and the local critic was most impressed. In the *Allegro* 'Mrs Arnold gave a brilliant exposition of the solo violin part'. Perhaps by way of a peace offering, Malcolm brought the well-known contralto Pamela Bowden to Richmond on another occasion, for the première of his setting of *Five Songs by William Blake*. Sheila was again commended for her playing in Purcell's *Pavane*. As a further peace offering in this turbulent year of 1959 Malcolm wrote for the family *Four Pieces for Chamber Ensemble*, with violin parts for Sheila and himself, a flute part for Katherine and a recorder part for Robert. The four movements (Prelude, Waltz, Chorale and Carillon) carefully accommodated the abilities of the four players.

There was also a surprisingly successful family holiday at the ski resort of Saas Fee, a quaint Alpine village near Zermatt, with narrow, cobbled streets and the kind of chalets for ever associated with toy musical boxes. They walked rather than skied, enjoying spectacular views, and Robert remembers 'getting hooked on glaciers and high peaks'.[86] For a nine-year-old there was the added thrill of strawberry cake, souvenir shops with wooden model marmots, toy rucksacks, and that holy of holies, the Swiss Army penknife.

On holiday Malcolm had been in good spirits but on his return to London he sank into a depression which made work temporarily impossible. Several commitments were causing him great anxiety. He had agreed earlier in the year to write a score for a new John Cranko ballet at Covent Garden, *Sweeney Todd*,[87] but, although he had written some of it, time was fast running out. He was only thankful that he had recently, and reluctantly, turned down another Covent Garden offer, to rework old music by Hérold for Ashton's *La Fille Mal Gardée*. Films were also a problem. At the last minute he had agreed to write some extra

[85] Christopher Finzi, December 2003
[86] January 2004
[87] His friend John Field had taken over the touring company, now based at the Royal Opera House, and had organised the commission.

*Malcolm and Robert on holiday at Saas Fee, August 1959*

music for *Solomon and Sheba*[88] and he had made an ill-judged commitment to *Suddenly, Last Summer*, another high-budget Anglo-American venture, Sam Spiegel's bold bid to turn Tennessee Williams' steamy play into a blockbuster movie. He no longer wanted to have anything to do with it, its subject of insanity being intolerable. As he struggled in his confusion to work out whether it was to Sheila or Susan he should now turn, he was dimly aware of a mounting mania.

*Suddenly, Last Summer* had its own inner tensions. Its glamorous stars, who had made their grumbling but well-paid way to Shepperton, where Oliver Messel had recreated sub-tropical New Orleans, were mostly in emotional disarray. Elizabeth Taylor, in shock at her husband's death, was seeking comfort with crooner Eddie Fisher, who had accordingly jilted Debbie Reynolds. Montgomery Clift was on the road to self-destruction with drink and drugs, staggering about

---

[88] Mario Nascimbene, having completed the score, was not available for some extra scenes.

on the set in a terrible state, struggling to memorise the shortest line. Albert Dekker is said to have had problems of his own which were to result in him hanging himself while indulging in sexual fantasies, while an unhappy Katharine Hepburn engaged in a fierce battle of wills with director Joseph Mankiewicz.[89] But somehow, by coaxing and cajoling his recalcitrant cast, Mankiewicz had enough of Tennessee Williams' play in the can by September 1959 to begin cutting and thinking of adding the music.

Malcolm turned up with Dorothy at the Columbia Pictures headquarters in Wardour Street, Soho, for a first showing. Mankiewicz was the most scrupulous of directors in researching the background to his films. For *Suddenly, Last Summer* he had found out from Tennessee Williams exactly the kind of lunatic asylum he had in mind. He demanded a neuro-surgeon on hand to act in a consultative capacity, spent time at the Manhattan State Hospital and pored over the photographic files of the National Association for Mental Health. The Lion View State Asylum, where much of the film was set, was accordingly authentic in all its horrendous detail, and Malcolm was aghast.

The following day he was better and in apparent high spirits as he drove Dorothy in his new Alvis to the Dorchester, where Spiegel was staying, to discuss the music with him and Mankiewicz. 'He'll be in his dressing gown,' he warned Dorothy, 'and he'll come rushing out, saying he was on the telephone all morning to America!' No sooner were they ushered into Spiegel's lavishly furnished apartment than out the little man rushed, duly saying he'd just been phoning America. 'His dressing gown,' added Dorothy, 'was of beautiful silk!'[90]

Two days later they returned to Wardour Street for another showing of the film, which Malcolm watched in obvious discomfort. The heroine, Elizabeth Taylor, was in a mental asylum. Katharine Hepburn, her aunt, was pressing the doctor, Montgomery Clift, to give her niece a frontal lobotomy, an operation involving removal of part of the brain to alleviate severe schizophrenia. During the film the true reasons for Elizabeth Taylor's seeming 'madness' were revealed and, at its dénouement, she escaped to live happily ever after with the good doctor, and Katharine Hepburn, instead, slipped into total madness.

Malcolm left quickly at the end of the showing, taking refuge with Dorothy in the Quo Vadis restaurant. Dorothy chattered on about this and that, aware that Mankiewicz's strong imagery of the Lion View State Asylum was the only thing on Malcolm's mind. That it was proving something he couldn't drink away was unsurprising. The opening sequence was harrowing: a close-up of the high brick wall surrounding the institution, as damaged and unloved as the patients within; a pan to the name of the institution; a cut to the women's ward and a pan across the haunted faces of many inmates; a cut to an operating theatre where a twitchy Montgomery Clift performed a lobotomy. When Dorothy left the Quo Vadis to

[89] Natasha Fraser-Cavassoni: *Sam Spiegel* (Little, Brown 2003), pp.201-214
[90] *Ibid.*

type out her notes on the film, Malcolm carried on drinking. It didn't help. He was violently ill afterwards.

Against Dorothy's advice he visited Shepperton a few days later to take a closer look at the opening reels. The sadly deranged inhabitants of Mankiewicz's lunatic asylum appalled him even more. So too Montgomery's wild-eyed Dr Cukrowicz, surveying his huge array of scalpels. 'Now you're going to watch an operation never performed before,' enthused Albert Dekker's Hospital Manager to an array of eager watchers. 'A lobotomy on a woman suffering from acute schizophrenic withdrawal!' Dr Cukrowicz meanwhile was fumbling around as he made measurements on the patient's head …

Malcolm fled from Shepperton in anguish and found himself in Richmond, but he wasn't sure that he shouldn't have been at Susan's, and, when Sheila suggested he calm himself down, he took offence at her effrontery and made his point the only way he could think of, which was as strongly as possible, with a certain amount of determination that this time he would be treated with respect and not as if he were mad, unless, maybe, if he really were mad, he couldn't demand respect, a thought so frightening that, on another word from Sheila, he lashed out in anger. Sheila, for the second time in her life, fled away, slammed a door, and summoned help. Only two months before, as a family, they had been admiring the beauty of Zermatt, and Malcolm could not have been more gentle or considerate. Now he was raving, in a strait jacket, on his way to the nearest mental hospital, where he was calmed down by electric shock treatment and returned home, three days later, with a massive headache, no memory, and timid as a mouse. He lay upstairs in bed, hardly aware of who he was, and it was while he was in this comatose state that Sheila took the phone-call from Annetta Hoffnung with the tragic news that Gerard had died.

Taken ill at home shortly before lunch, Gerard had died in hospital two hours later of a cerebral haemorrhage.[91] He was thirty-four. Only the last Christmas, Malcolm had given him the ultimate gift of friendship, an original score.[92] Just a few weeks earlier, the Hoffnungs had joined them at their Cornwall holiday home. Gerard had been his usual extrovert self at Newtrain Bay, raising smiles all around the beach with boyish pranks. He had played his favourite trick of floating on his back, smoking a cigar. He had done his usual gleeful duck-diving in the waves, on one occasion surfacing crowned with red seaweed.

Two days later Malcolm, locked in his own silent thoughts and still utterly cowed, went into Greenway Nursing Home to convalesce. Dorothy, meanwhile, was busy protecting his interests. Of course he would be all right for the new film, she assured Richard Attenborough. *Sweeney Todd* was coming along nicely, she informed John Cranko. And, as luck would have it, there was Buxton Orr, the

---

[91] On 28 September 1959
[92] The Second Horn Concerto, played by Dennis Brain at its Cheltenham Festival première the previous year.

composer, living close to her in Belsize Park, who, of course, was only too delighted to take over the score of *Suddenly, Last Summer*.[93] When the time came, she would ensure that Malcolm's name came first on the credits.

Sheila had somehow managed to maintain an air of calm at Denbigh Gardens. Katherine and Robert were not aware that anything special was amiss. Father was sick, that was all, and taking a rest in a nursing home. Granny was staying with them again, and that was always a blessing when their mother was tired. Their worlds were still intact.

Malcolm's was more confused, though he was glad of the peace of Greenway. He felt and looked awful, remembering very little. There had been a lot of music, he was sure of that. An Oscar for a door-stop and a Symphony for Nan. And something good for Dennis Brain. But quite exactly what he wasn't sure. And then there had been Gerard, who one day, as he often joked, would be making plans to conduct Debussy's *La Mer* in a tank of seawater pumped up from the coast from a pipeline of a thousand tubas ... Gerard, the inspiration, Gerard the magnificent, Gerard alias Doctor Klauss Domgraf-Fassbaender.

As usual he had any number of thoughts he wanted to share with Gerard. But for some reason he couldn't think of a single one of them ...

---

[94] Buxton Orr (1924-97) was an avant-garde composer who taught at the Guildhall School of Music and Drama. Apart from orchestrating Malcolm's sombre and entirely appropriate title music, Orr added little to the film of note. The climax of the drama – the pursuit of Sebastian by street urchins and his ritualistic killing, as they played their home-made instruments – might well have elicited something special from Malcolm. Orr struggled with it.

# 9
# A Symphony for the BBC
## ... and Other Mid-life Crises, 1959-60

MALCOLM WAS LUCKY. His memory quickly returned and his creative abilities were not impaired by the many applications of electro-convulsive therapy he endured on this and subsequent occasions. ECT, which is coming back into medical favour today as alternative drug therapies begin to be questioned, has always been highly controversial. There is something inherently alarming in passing electricity, strong enough to power a light-bulb, through the brain to induce convulsions, even in the cause of lessening violent or suicidal behaviour.[1] To treat violence with violence seems inherently wrong, particularly when there would seem to be no real understanding of how it works, even when (as in the case of Vladimir Horowitz[2]) there are beneficial outcomes.

Robert strongly believes that his father's experiences with ECT were a personal affront:

> ECT has similarities to John Cleese thrashing his car with a branch, or fixing a TV by bashing the cabinet with a fist. Both methods *sometimes* work! Violence can be effective on a mechanical device. But a human being is not a mechanical device and the violence of ECT is an assault on a person by another person. Any therapeutic effect has to be measured against the patient's reaction to the assault, which may either provoke violent outrage or else break the spirit, so the patient will do exactly as the doctors or family want in order to avoid more ECT. In my father's case I think both reactions have occurred, violent indignation as well as fear and acquiescence. It is not very effective therapy, in my opinion.[3]

Around the time of Malcolm's first bout of treatment several other well-known personalities had been less fortunate. Ernest Hemingway's suicide in 1961 and Sylvia Plath's in 1963 came after (or despite) ECT. Paul Robeson

---

[1] Shortly after Malcolm's first spell of treatment, public disquiet was aroused by Ken Kesey's novel *One Flew Over the Cuckoo's Nest*, in which the protagonist is taken to the 'shock room' in a hospital's Disturbed Ward to suffer ECT. At the end of the book he has been lobotomised and, minus part of his brain, becomes a total vegetable. The 1975 film of the novel led to a series of legal actions for abuse of patients by ECT.

[2] The pianist's manic-depressive state had led to a twelve-year absence from the concert platform. But, treated by ECT, Horowitz eventually made a triumphant return, his prodigious memory as good as ever.

[3] February 2004

underwent massive ECT, following a suicide attempt in 1961, and afterwards was unable to resume either as a singer or a political activist.[4] Vivien Leigh's manic-depressive illness and alcoholism were regularly treated by ECT in the early 1960s, causing her much pain but little obvious benefit.[5]

In 1959, without the use of general anaesthetics or any muscle-paralysing drugs, the pain could be enormous and broken bones possible. During treatment there was no continuous supply of oxygen to the brain, and a different, stronger form of electricity was used compared to today's brief pulse current. Patients usually suffered retrograde amnesia.

Malcolm's memory loss proved mercifully mild. The effects on his music could have been far-reaching, but there is little evidence that this was so. If anything, there would seem a greater, rather than lesser, creativity emerging from this period of mental turmoil. In the breakdown's immediate wake came two symphonies (his Fourth and Fifth) remarkable for their strongly idiosyncratic, almost revolutionary content, so far outside contemporary musical fashion as to create strong controversy.

Greenway Nursing Home, where Malcolm was convalescing, was run by Dr Lincoln Williams, a distinguished psychiatrist specialising in alcoholism.[6] Malcolm had first been put in touch with Dr Williams by a friend, the writer John Pudney,[7] whose own alcoholism had been cured by Dr Williams. But Pudney's problems were not related to a manic-depressive condition. His was an altogether easier case.

Dr Williams' usual treatment involved a three-week stay, but Malcolm rarely remained that long. During the first days of this convalescence Malcolm was encouraged to stay in bed as he underwent Aversion Therapy, a direct assault upon the addiction. This took the form of getting Malcolm to drink first wine and then sea water until he was sick. Unfortunately all it gave him was an aversion to sea water. The following days he was given massive doses of vitamins and daily sessions of psychotherapy, but was otherwise a free agent. Dorothy Payne, whose Belsize Square flat was conveniently close to the nursing home, noted in her diary that Malcolm called in to see her on his first full day there, which hardly suggests that he was taking the aversion therapy seriously. Later in the week he visited Dorothy again, this time with Sheila and Katherine. Visiting Dorothy was

---

[4] Robeson's case has been complicated by allegations of foul play by the CIA. It has been suggested that the doctors treating Robeson were 'CIA contractors'. (St Clair & Coburn: *Nature & Politics*, Volume 3, 1999).

[5] She died in 1967 and controversy seems to surround a possible misdiagnosis of her condition.

[6] 11-13 Fellows Road, Belsize Park, South Hampstead. It closed in the early 1980s. Dr Williams (1900-69) was an important pioneer in the treatment of alcoholics, operating from his main nursing home at The Hall, Harrow Weald.

[7] John Pudney (1909-1977) found fame with his poem 'Johnnie Head in the Air', featured in the popular war movie *The Way to the Stars*. In 1958 there had been talk of Malcolm writing a ballet score to a poem of Pudney's, but film commitments intervened.

perhaps his way of avoiding some straight talking with Sheila as to his plans and hopes for the future.

Malcolm did not return to Denbigh Gardens after leaving Greenway, but remained instead in London. 'Malcolm seems to have left Sheila,' wrote Dorothy in her diary. This was true, up to a point. Sheila herself, however, may well have felt she needed some breathing space to reconsider the relationship. A temporary parting was probably by mutual consent.

Malcolm celebrated his release from the nursing home[8] with a morning's shopping, driven around by Dorothy in her AC two-seater[9] to buy presents for all the nurses. It would keep them sweet, if he were to return. He also bought armfuls of flowers for his friends Diane and Philip Jones, at whose flat in Emperor's Gate, Kensington, he was to stay for the next two months.[10] In the afternoon he made a diversion to Richmond, to collect a few belongings, returning, according to Dorothy, 'in a terrible state'. Sheila had 'given him a piece of her mind' but 'he was better by the evening'. Diane Jones recalls:

> Malcolm had been planning to live in a hotel, but he would have run riot there, with all the money at his disposal! Phil and I always looked after him as best we could when he had problems. So we offered him our spare room.[11]

It was a brave gesture of friendship, for he was in a volatile state.

Philip Jones was a highly successful, self-employed music copyist.[12] Malcolm had first burst into his life in 1944, in uniform, when Philip was working for ENSA and Malcolm wanted neat parts quickly copied for the Quintet being performed at the National Gallery. They had met again after the war, when Philip was employed at Lengnick, Malcolm's first publishers, the friendship developing in tandem with their careers. Philip Jones, like Dorothy Payne, helped bring order into Malcolm's disordered life. Their assistance was particularly crucial in film work, Philip being Malcolm's 'fixer' at the recording sessions, organising all the *ad hoc* orchestras in addition to copying out their parts.[13] Diane Jones was always much involved in her husband's work. 'They were much kinder to Malcolm than I was,' declares Dorothy. 'I always went home and left him if he was getting tight. They both drank with him patiently. They were wonderful friends for him. Di looked after Malcolm as well as anyone could.'[14]

---

[8] 13 October 1959

[9] The spirited Dorothy owned an AC Aceca at a time when young married women tended not to drive sports cars.

[10] Flat 4, 29 Emperor's Gate

[11] September 2003

[12] Philip Jones (1903-1986) worked for some distinguished clients, including Vaughan Williams, Arthur Bliss, Richard Rodney Bennett, Richard Addinsell, Maurice Jarre, Dimitri Tiomkin and Benjamin Frankel.

[13] Philip Jones's speed of copying was as legendary as his neatness. 'He could produce a page of full score in next to no time,' says Bram Wiggins in some awe. (April 2003)

[14] October 2003

Diane was the kind of effervescent personality who might attract wolf-whistles even on a dull Monday morning in the Cromwell Road. Like Dorothy, she had to make it very clear to Malcolm early on exactly where their relationship would, and would not, lead:

> If Malcolm had been drinking with a woman all evening, he thought it natural to go to bed with her, but I doubt if he took the fact that he had been to bed with someone seriously. He was surprised when he didn't sleep with someone. He was quite surprised when I told him it wasn't going to happen with me.

Diane had soon discovered, however, that Malcolm was not easily put off. With Falstaffian cunning he would ring her up at times when he knew Philip was away and she had needed all the resourcefulness of one of Shakespeare's Merry Wives. 'I know a good restaurant in Barnes,' Malcolm would say. 'Let's go there for lunch.' 'I know the one you mean!' Diane would reply. 'Joseph Cooper likes it too. Let's ring him up!' 'Well,' Malcolm would counter, 'We don't *have* to lunch in *Barnes* ...' Seldom taking no for an answer, this latter-day Falstaff could so easily have ended up floating down to Richmond in a laundry basket.

Malcolm's stay at Emperor's Gate began with an incident Diane Jones would not easily forget:

> On the first night, he went up to the spare room and laid out a whole line of pills on the top of the mantelpiece. 'I think I'm going to commit suicide!' he said. My face must have been a picture. He smiled, but there was no laughter in his eyes. 'Don't worry! I won't do it in your place. It wouldn't be fair!' [15]

Malcolm's moods were swinging sharply. One meal he shared with Philip and Diane at Kettner's had started in appalling gloom. He had come back from a meeting in total despair, yet, only minutes later, he was the life and soul of the party:

> On the whole we had hilarious times! He behaved very well really, much better than we feared! After film sessions we'd often go to Wheeler's and then on to the Windmill or some slightly decadent night club! He never seemed to mind how rough they were. On one occasion Philip and I were with him and his latest bimbo when a fight broke out, one gang against another. Malcolm was out cold at the time so the waiters came and stood around us protectively. On another occasion the Chief of Police most alarmingly came in to case the joint.

At the Panama Club a dancer called Paula, whose flat on the Embankment was being subsidised by Malcolm, always gave them a specially warm welcome. Malcolm's lavish behaviour ensured great popularity. On his arrival the Panama band would strike up the main theme from *The Inn of the Sixth Happiness* or 'Chop Suey Polka' from *The Key*.

One of the advantages of Emperor's Gate was that Malcolm could pursue more comfortably his involvement with Susan, with whom, for a while, he was

---

[15] September 2003

besotted. A rich widow in her thirties, living in fashionable Wimpole Street, she was in many ways the antithesis of Sheila. Made up like a film star with hair restyled every day, she was a fashion-conscious socialite, whose address book included at least one well-known Duke. Sheila, by contrast, wore little make-up, only dressed up when the need arose and was quite content with a homely meal at the kitchen table.

Malcolm had been conducting the affair with his usual lack of finesse. He would urge Sheila to buy things from the fashionable boutique which Susan ran as a sideline. When Robert's prep school, King's House, put on a play, Malcolm brought Susan down to see it. Malcolm also marked his thirty-eighth birthday with a short break in Canterbury with Susan, after which she told Dorothy that she was 'optimistic' about the whole outcome. In this she was to be disappointed. Although Malcolm dutifully commuted between Emperor's Gate and Wimpole Street for a time, his mind was mostly juggling with the overdue ballet, *Sweeney Todd*, and a 'nativity masque', *Song of Simeon*. And one morning Diane Jones answered a knock at the door at Emperor's Gate to find, to her surprise, a dispirited Sheila. They chatted on the doorstep for a while about the current situation, before walking back together to the Tube station. Diane, who supported Sheila more than Susan, offered encouragement:[16]

> I told her he would come back to her, if she asked him. He was ready. He'd had enough of the current complications.[17]

Sheila, however, bided her time. It hardly seemed propitious as Malcolm was now looking for flats in the area and still spending excessive time in Wimpole Street. But the affair with Susan did not prosper long. Malcolm's passion waned, as Diane had prophesied:

> That's Malcolm! He can be terribly enthusiastic, go absolutely overboard about something, and then it suddenly all collapses.[18]

Susan was soon on the telephone in tears. There had been a fearful argument, she said, ending in Malcolm's abrupt departure. He had gone off 'on the razzle', but she didn't know where. He turned up eventually at Emperor's Gate, sheepish but defiant. He would never, he said, make it up with her. But he did. Days later, however, there was startling news on the grape-vine. Malcolm had decamped and was back in Richmond.[19]

For a few days that December Malcolm's spirits seemed to have been restored by Sheila's decision to have him back. When Dorothy called in at Richmond, she

---

[16] Despite the current situation Sheila had maintained friendship with both Philip and Diane. After her divorce from Malcolm, Philip fixed up film sessions for her, though, of course, never for one of Malcolm's.

[17] September 2003

[18] September 2003

[19] He returned on 23 November. He had twelve days to put the finishing touches to *Song of Simeon*.

found him 'still in his pyjamas but in a very good mood'. And the next day, when she tried to see him at Shepperton to sort out some final details on *Suddenly, Last Summer*, she could not do so because, at 5.00 pm, he was still enjoying a highly social lunch. For a while there was no news of Susan. The title of the latest film, *The Angry Silence,* seemed most apt. But the silence proved effective, for Malcolm made a brief return to Wimpole Street before thinking better of it. It was understandable that the 1959 Christmas lacked the customary seasonal good cheer. 'He is obviously having a trying time at home with plenty of rows,' wrote Dorothy, staunchest of allies. He was also 'in a sorry mood, having had an accident with his new Alvis'. Fortunately only his pride was injured, and there was enough of that to spare, for John Cranko's uproarious ballet, *Sweeney Todd*, had just had its première,[20] and the public's response to Malcolm's score was overwhelmingly favourable.

The critics, as usual, were divided. When the ballet, full of glorious Victorian melodrama, later reached London, knives were sharpened with demon barber alacrity. 'Brash and vulgar!' cried Clement Crisp in outrage.[21] 'As common-place as the dancing!' declared Noël Goodwin.[22] Richard Buckle, with a blithe disregard of the facts, rebuked the music for 'no grasp of the period' and a lack of 'essential satirical bite'.[23] Fortunately there were some critics, like Ernest Bradbury of the *Yorkshire Post*, whose sensibilities were not offended by the broad idiom of the Music Hall:

> Arnold matches the late Victorian set, the antics of the comic policemen, and the arch-ness of the courting couples with appropriate music – the shrieks of Sweeney's victims, trombone jokes, thumps on the drum, bird-whistles and all.[24]

Malcolm's cheerful insouciance, which so uplifts the story of the demon barber, is also to be found in his Nativity Masque for mimes, soloists, mixed chorus and orchestra, *The Song of Simeon*, which mingles the serious and the comic as naturally as a medieval mystery play. 'Lord, now lettest thy servant depart in peace' could not be set with more tenderness, 'Bring worship to the Son of man' more emotionally engaging, 'Behold the handmaid of the Lord' more holy. And yet Malcolm also contrives to have a certain amount of fun along the way.

Written as a charity fund-raiser for a single matinée performance[25] at the Drury Lane Theatre and conducted by Malcolm, it enjoyed the collaboration of

---

[20] 11 December 1959 at Stratford-upon-Avon. The music's merits are well captured in the *Sweeney Todd Suite*, which David Ellis produced, in association with Malcolm, in 1984.

[21] *Financial Times*, 17 August 1960

[22] *Daily Express*, 17 August 1960

[23] *Ballet Today*

[24] 27 October 1960

[25] 5 January 1960. The masque formed the first half of the programme, the second being a series of variety turns including Peter Sellers and Dickie Henderson. It says much for the accessibility of *Song of Simeon* that the two halves made a coherent whole.

some remarkable talents. The director was Colin Graham, who staged most of Britten's operas and some of the Hoffnung Festivals, the choreographer John Cranko, fresh from *Sweeney Todd*. Malcolm's librettist was the poet Christopher Hassall, who had worked with Walton on *Troilus and Cressida* but perhaps was best known as Ivor Novello's lyricist. Hassall was a popular visitor to Denbigh Gardens at this period, though, it seemed to Robert, he and Malcolm spent less time discussing the masque than the lavish bar they talked of opening in Cyprus. The enjoyable time they had together comes out in some comical lyrics. The song of the innkeeper and his wife, for example, seems to fall somewhere between Lionel Bart and W S Gilbert:

> Tho' a hostel somewhat gloomy,
> Our accommodation's roomy,
> And I ask you, sir, to do me
> The courtesy to hear me.
> We've completed our expanding;
> In the corridors they're standing
> And they're sleeping on the landing
> (Only fitfully I fear me) ...

Malcolm's impish response falls somewhere between Bart and Sullivan.

*Song of Simeon* is a real *jeu d'ésprit*. A charity matinée, crowded with celebrities and graced by Princess Margaret, was just the kind of event to make Malcolm forget all about his Bolshevik ideals and make sure that the party atmosphere was all the better for his contribution. Although it works well in concert form and does not need the elaborate staging it was given at Drury Lane, the hybrid[26] *Song of Simeon* seems likely to remain in its current obscurity, despite its many charms.

Immediately afterwards Malcolm diversified still further, turning from a stage oratorio to a television musical, *Parasol*, a project initiated by the young Ned Sherrin and his collaborator, Caryl Brahms. Sherrin remembers clearly how it came about:[27]

> Caryl was a big admirer of Malcolm's. Caryl knew her ballet and she and Arnold Haskell[28] believed Malcolm's ballet music was the best there was. We had both been impressed by his one-act TV opera, *The Open Window*. The idea was clinched over some drunken lunches at Wheeler's – lots of champagne and oysters – including one where Bert Feldman's nubile secretary was tossed from one lap to another. We wrote the words first and Malcolm set them to music. Malcolm made the words sit on the

---

[26] Henry Raynor of *The Times* enjoyed Malcolm's eclectic approach:
'Arnold's music is direct in utterance; the hymn, sung by full chorus at the discovery of the Adoration, is perfectly of the tradition of Victorian Christmas Carols; the innkeeper and his wife sing a duet which would hardly sound out of place in one of the Savoy operas; and the shepherds retail their experiences to a sort of students' song.'

[27] July 2003

[28] A leading authority of ballet, Haskell was also a member of the Savile Club.

music; we had to do very little accommodating. He'd simply play us his tunes and we'd cry 'Lovely! Lovely!'

*Parasol* was adapted from Arthur Schnitzler's *Anatol*, seven one-act plays chronicling the affairs of a melancholy playboy in the 1890s. Schnitzler, a friend of Freud and author of *La Ronde*, explored the relationship between the sexes in a daring way which scandalised Viennese society at the turn of the last century. Malcolm warmed at once to the sexual undercurrents of the piece, quickly assimilated the period flavour and wrote some excellent music, which the critics much enjoyed:

> It is hardly fair to ask a English composer to write half-a-dozen waltzes in succession, but that is the task set Mr Arnold in Parasol. It says much for Mr Arnold that he not only wrote them with considerable variety of mood but also captured in their lilt the atmosphere of the Viennese never-never-land of wine, women and song ...[29]

Malcolm was at once at ease in the world of light operetta, but the musical, lasting just under the hour, is the wrong length to attract interest and consequently still awaits a professional stage production. Ned Sherrin is nostalgic:

> I'd love to have the chance to work on the words again. Had Caryl and I written it five years later, when we were more experienced, it would have been much better! We were heavily into *My Fair Lady* at the time – saw ourselves as the new Alan Jay Lerner, though Malcolm had probably never heard of Loewe. We were also into Sondheim, but, alas, we didn't have Sondheim's facility for words.

Malcolm had little time to worry too much about *Parasol*'s fate. There was a highly important commission from the BBC to meet, a symphony, which dated back over a year.[30] He could no longer put off the confrontation that this would mean with Peter Heyworth and other Darmstadt missionaries. For this renewal of hostilities he had been paid rather less than for the TV musical – the BBC gave him a handsome commissioning fee of £600 for *Parasol* and £150 for his Fourth Symphony – but he would be fulfilling an obligation to his loyal friend, Richard Howgill, who had commissioned the work for the BBC as one of his final acts before retirement as Controller of Music.

The BBC had been very good to Malcolm in the 1950s, playing a considerable part in fostering his career.[31] The new symphony was doubly important in that he could no longer be totally sure of the BBC's continuing support. Although Malcolm counted the new Controller as a friend, William Glock's affiliations

---

[29] William Mann, *The Times*, 21 March 1960

[30] The commissioning fee was mentioned in a letter of February 1959

[31] Perhaps the culmination of this decade of goodwill was Malcolm's appearance on *Desert Island Discs*. His choice of music was totally selfless: Elgar's *Introduction and Allegro for Strings*; Purcell's *Fantasy Upon One Note*; Sibelius' Fourth Symphony; Holst's 'This I Have Done For My Own True Love'; Berlioz's *Symphonie Fantastique*; Stravinsky's *Symphony of Psalms*; Muggsy Spanier & his Ragtime Band playing 'Dippermouth Blues'; and Tom Lehrer's 'Fight Fiercely Harvard'. His book was the *Oxford Book of English Verse*; his luxury, some green Havana cigars.

with the modernist camp were well known. Glock's stated intention was to bring the Corporation in line with developments elsewhere in the world. 'Glock block' would be applied to the careers of those British composers whom the new Controller did not admire. Malcolm was relieved, therefore, that there had been no last-minute 'block' applied to his Fourth Symphony.[32]

The new work, to be performed by the BBC Symphony Orchestra at the Royal Festival Hall in November 1960, was scheduled for completion in July. So Malcolm tried to clear his desk and mind at Denbigh Gardens after the New Year, but distractions kept appearing. The first, a particularly well-groomed one, tall, slim and with soulful brown eyes, surfaced early in January 1960. Susan was back from the Swiss ski slopes, and her New Year's resolution was to forgive Malcolm everything. Her first phone-call found Malcolm friendly; the second, distant; and the third, drunk. It was not an auspicious new beginning. But Malcolm was setting off for three weeks to New York,[33] where a march for military band, commissioned as part of a British Trade Fair celebration, was to be played[34] and Susan joined him there. In the event Malcolm had such a good time in America he even toyed with the idea of an apartment in New York. His wide musical tastes found full expression, his visit including meetings with two men he much admired, Aaron Copland and jazz trumpeter Dizzy Gillespie.[35]

Susan's very public holiday with Malcolm was an affront to Sheila, who in exasperation spoke her mind forcefully just before his departure. Dorothy, who was only hearing Malcolm's side of the argument, was shocked.

> She told him he hadn't written anything good for the past three years and, further-more, that he was insane. This upset him terribly, as he has always been afraid his mind isn't quite right.[36]

And Dorothy noted that on his return the sparks were still flying:

> He appears to have had his usual row with Sheila. I wouldn't say she seemed pleased to see him.[37]

Probably not. But, like Agamemnon and the many thousands of unfaithful husbands who came after him, Malcolm could hardly have expected a red carpet …

---

[32] Although it is said that Malcolm suffered badly at the hands of Glock's modernist crusade, in terms of performances at the Proms this is not so. Eleven of his works were heard in Glock's thirteen seasons.

[33] He was in New York from 23 January to mid-February.

[34] The march *Overseas*, for military band, is full of appropriate splendour and majesty. Its trio is particularly memorable in its fine and arresting melodic and harmonic writing.

[35] Malcolm was outraged with the New York audience which was eating and chatting as Gillespie played.

[36] 20 January 1960

[37] 16 February 1960

Sheila's criticism of the music, if reported accurately, was exaggerated. In the past three years Malcolm had written the Third Symphony and the Guitar Concerto, along with several lesser but wholly delightful works, like the *Second Sinfonietta* and the Oboe Quartet. *Sweeney Todd* and *Song of Simeon* are, of their own genres, extremely good. Nevertheless, his output for the concert hall had dwindled markedly, the cinema and stage becoming his chief preoccupation. In that time too he had suffered one fit of madness, had several spells under medical care and been highly erratic at many other times. Sheila's shock tactics, therefore, had a certain amount of truth to them and were certainly worth a try.

They only served, however, to drive Malcolm back to Wimpole Street. But Susan, distressed at his liaison with Paula at the Panama Club, was using her influence to try to get the latter closed and the former deported, and Malcolm responded by going 'on the rampage'. Dorothy was shocked when he turned up 'tight as a tick' at 9.30 in the morning to make a recording at the Associated British Picture Corporation studios.[38]

> As Phil couldn't tell, presumably nobody else did, and he gradually sobered up. I gave him a talking to when he was sober enough.

Sheila, meanwhile, aware that time was now short for the new symphony, was still trying hard to get common sense to prevail. There was talk of a family holiday in the Canary Islands, but it had to be put off when Katherine caught measles.[39] So Malcolm flew off instead with a new girlfriend for an illicit weekend on an island off Malta. His luck, however, was out. He discovered Eugene Goossens, whom he much respected, staying at the same hotel and, with his protesting girlfriend in tow, he returned to London by the next plane. Sheila now took the drastic step of discussing the situation with the jilted Susan over dinner. Malcolm's best interests were carefully explored and a plan of action agreed. Susan would gracefully retire from the fray, while Sheila would remind Malcolm of his duties as a father and of his important, unfinished commission. The place to complete the Fourth Symphony was to be Denbigh Gardens, measles and all.

It was now Easter and its spirit seems to have had a calming influence. The siren voices of distraction were no longer singing, or, at least, if Malcolm could hear them as he worked away in his Richmond study, he simply consigned them straight into his manuscript. There was a place for sirens of all kinds, including Susan, in the third movement.

But there were somewhat wider issues he wished to explore in his new symphony. Racial problems, for example. His visit to New York had sharpened his awareness of these. So too had *West Side Story,* the Bernstein-Sondheim musical, which had been running in London since 1958, conducted by his good

---

[38] Elstree, 12 April 1960

[39] Sheila did not favour prophylactic medicines. The body, she believed, was designed to cope by itself naturally and built up its own immunity.

friend Lawrence Leonard. He loved the Bernstein score and would regularly visit Her Majesty's Theatre to hear it. The more he saw the show – and he had recently taken Sheila and the children to share his pleasure – the more the tragedy of the Puerto Rican outsiders upset him. As an outsider himself he had always identified with underdogs. Outsiders mocked and oppressed could perhaps be the subject for a symphony?

At last coherent ideas were presenting themselves. His cold, hard winter was over. The sun shone encouragingly on the rows of poplars across the road, but he hardly saw them. He had little time for gazing out of the window, for now he felt a quickening of the pulse and an excitement in the air, as the symphony began fast unravelling itself in his head. It was simply a question of steadying himself, and getting it all down in orderly sequence. Now that he had started, confidence was no problem. He would write as *he* wanted, and not be bullied by current orthodoxies. Yet with a good tilt at the critics while he was at it. There would be much for them to ponder in all four movements!

By early June the last page was blotted and forty minutes of music lay in a neat pile before him. Delightedly he added the date[40] to the last page. There would now be over four months to wait before he conducted the first performance, but there was no question of him revisiting anything he had written. Once he had handed over the manuscript to Philip Jones that was always that. He never tampered with a completed work.

Malcolm had seen his Fourth Symphony as an opportunity to make a national statement, not just about social injustices which currently concerned him, but also about music itself. It was a call to arms against the dreariness and pomposity of modernism, a merry shot across the bows of the Glocks and Heyworths, an example of how the tonal tradition of the European mainstream could still produce work doubly as exciting as anything concocted by the most eccentric of the avant-garde. His was a symphony, which, as he would state in his programme notes, set out to arouse emotion and 'to be as direct as possible at first hearing'. If music did not add something to the listener's emotional life, he declared, it was worthless. In his view excessive chromaticism was 'the most devastating dead end in the music of the last sixty years'.

He had one over-riding intention: not to be boring. This had meant considering a new approach to all development sections, something he had long pondered. Back in 1956 he had written:

> If one is really honest, in listening to music of all periods there are times when one's mind is inclined to wander. This will happen even when listening to accepted classical masterpieces and to a greater extent when listening to contemporary works. To put it crudely, the mind wanders during the sections that occur between recognisable themes …[41]

---

[40] 9 June 1960
[41] 'I Think of Music in Terms of Sound', *Music and Musicians*, July 1956

Although he was to write in the programme that the first movement followed traditional sonata form, this was a deliberate red rag for the critics (and most of them were to put their heads down and charge). For included with two strong and well developed ideas was a serenely attractive melody which reappeared several times, always in exactly the same shape, simply wearing different orchestral clothing. Its very inclusion was as arresting as its deliberate lack of development. What was Malcolm trying to say?

Characteristically, he never gave much of an answer. Even in a pre-performance interview with Charles Reid of the *Daily Mail,* ominously headed 'Tonight It's Bongo Night', he impishly highlighted the controversial melody, but side-stepped any meaningful discussion:

> Malcolm Arnold, a massive, beaming boy of 39, sucked on his cigar stub, wreathing himself in smoke. Sitting down at my piano he played the second subject of the first movement of his new symphony. The subject turned out to be a long (30-bars) tune, sweet as candy-floss but with a touch of winking impudence in the unique Arnold manner.
>
> 'Many people,' I said, 'will hate that tune. It's not the kind one *expects* in a symphony. It sounds as though written for a soubrette with a sunshade on an Edwardian pier.' Arnold opened his arms in a wide, welcoming gesture. 'That,' he said, 'is exactly what I had in mind. What's wrong with a bit of Edwardian nostalgia? The comfort you get from this tune of mine is the comfort you get from the thought of Macmillan and pre-1914 autumns in Streatham and Blackheath and stately gentlemen in striped bathing costumes.'[42]

Malcolm may have ignored the point at issue, the inclusion of such a tune in a symphony, but at least he had let slip one small clue as to its possible meaning.

The Conservative Prime Minister Harold Macmillan, comfortingly avuncular with his vaguely Edwardian aura, was at the height of his popularity in 1960. Known affectionately as 'SuperMac', he had just won an election and, in so doing, had coined the immortal words 'Most of our people have never had it so good'. Malcolm, of course, loathed everything about Macmillan's catch-phrase. He sympathised with those who were not having it so good. And in 1960 this especially meant the 250,000 black minority in the country. There was, in particular, a community of 7,000 West Indians around London's Notting Hill, who were being subjected to systematic violence and abuse from rioting white gangs, encouraged by bone-headed neo-fascist leaders like Colin Jordan. The first Notting Hill Caribbean Carnival had just taken place, instigated by the black community out of self-defence, and so too the first racist murder of a West Indian, which the police force unfortunately failed to solve. In mentioning the 'comfort' which Charles Reid might get from the thought of Macmillan, therefore, Malcolm was getting close to the real feelings which generated much of the

---

[42] *Daily Mail*, 2 November 1960. Reid was the biographer of Barbirolli, Beecham and Sargent.

work. And his mention of 'stately gentlemen in striped bathing costumes' was not quite as affectionately intended as Charles Reid might have supposed. Pappy had once owned one such costume and, for all Malcolm knew, was still making a daily exhibition of himself at the Northampton Municipal Pool. The serenely attractive melody, it seems, represents a false kind of comfort, yearnings for an ideal past and present, which inhibit real hopes for happiness.

Several years later, in 1971, Malcolm would admit that the Notting Hill race riots had been much in his mind at the time of the Fourth Symphony. But in 1960 he was not going to do the listeners' thinking for them. He might mention in the programme notes that he was including 'percussion instruments which have been used for years in West Indian and South American popular music', but he would give no hint as to why. Malcolm challenges his listeners to think for themselves.

In the first movement, there are three main interacting ideas. The first is distinctly pastoral and we are reminded at first of Olde England and Vaughan Williams in rustic vein; of the days before the world became unsettled; Juliet before she met Romeo; Maria before she met Tony; life before The Bomb and Cuban missile crises; Malcolm before he met his demons: Fairview on a sunny afternoon with Pappy on the tennis courts and Nan playing Mendelssohn in the music room. Or a stroll across Northampton Racecourse, hand in hand with darling Lizzie Witts, and not a hint of a shoe factory in that verdant landscape, not a scent of its sweaty, underpaid work force. And yet, for all the apparent peace and tranquillity, the occasional comment from bongos, harp, celesta, marimba, and tom-toms suggests that something untoward is possibly not very far away.

The second idea is violent and alien. Featuring strongly are Malcolm's percussive instruments from the West Indies and South America (Notting Hill and Puerto Rico). We are face to face with the violent imbecilities of Colin Jordan's National Socialist Party and Bernardo's Sharks, looking and hoping for trouble. This angry, dissonant section (its loud, staccato percussive chords closely allied to Bernstein's *West Side Story*[43]) reminds us, more widely, that Malcolm's world in 1960 was a dangerous, abrasive place. London, for all its glamour, was a flawed city, its soul scarred not just by social divisions, but by demolition-happy property development, racketeering and corruption.

Malcolm deftly develops both these strangely conflicting sections, the pastoral and the violent. But rising out of them emerges a third idea, the serenely attractive melody, Charles Reid's 'candy-floss' tune, Malcolm's crowd-pleaser, ensuring no listeners to the broadcast concert would change station mid-symphony. The tune seems the distillation of every romantic sweet-nothing ever

---

[43] There are in fact a number of striking resemblances between the Fourth Symphony and *West Side Story*, notably in melodic flavour, harmony and rhythm. *The Rumble* (the closing number of Act One), for example, has interesting similarities with sections of the symphony's first movement.

played in Palm Courts and Odeons up and down the country. It is Romeo and Juliet's idyll before the death of Tybalt. It is Maria's *Tonight*. It is Audrey Hepburn and Cary Grant, high up on a giant, flickering screen. It is even the comforting thought of SuperMac. But, alas, it is just a dream, nothing much more than our own wishful thinking. Malcolm gives us several hints that this lushly scored melody is, in fact, too good to be true. The quiet accompaniment, for example, is in the wrong rhythm[44] and the tune never quite completes itself, taking only 31 bars instead of the expected 32. We are being offered, Malcolm tells us, a fantasy. As the movement progresses, the conflict deepens. Only the unreal world remains unaltered, ensnaring, mocking and, ultimately, deluding.

The first movement provides a highly dramatic and thought-provoking opening to the symphony, and its ending is brilliantly cinematic. Just as screen lovers so often walk misty-eyed into the sunset at the final dissolve, so here too a sense of happily-ever-after pervades the tranquillity. The final chord is as melting as an Audrey Hepburn smile.

In the short second movement, a *Scherzo*, which Hugo Cole has suggested has inspirational affiliation with Berlioz's *Queen Mab* and Holst's *Mercury*,[45] Malcolm plays mischievous avant-garde games. Using a simple A-B-A construction, with a trio in the middle, Malcolm turns the scherzo, when it returns, neatly backwards, thereby effecting the kind of palindrome serialists ardently admire. The tuneful trio also runs backwards from its centre. As regards its effect on the audience, Malcolm leaves just one simple comment in the programme notes: 'This movement is not intended to arouse emotions that are pleasant.'

The *Andantino* third movement is a *tour de force* of sustained orchestral writing. As in the first movement we are again given three themes, only this time they are shorter and closely interrelated. With great skill Malcolm spins out his gossamer-thin melodies, weaving us a magic carpet for a strange, almost psychedelic journey, perhaps of the inner psyche. A sensuous peace reigns for all but one surprising, painful moment. Quite where we are being taken it is difficult to tell. Christopher Palmer[46] thought perhaps he was in a Turkish bath or opium den. Paul Jackson[47] sensed relaxation on some Caribbean island, feeling the sun and listening to the sea lapping the golden sand. Just as easily we might be with Maria and Tony in a moment of tranquillity before onset of the tragedy. We are certainly far removed from the humdrum monotony of daily living. And, as in the first movement, Malcolm employs his full range of exotica – marimba, bongos and tom-toms – while celesta and harp add touches of Hollywood glitter. Hugo Cole for once is uncomfortable and on the defensive:

---

[44] A disturbing 3+2+3 rather than the expected 3+3+2
[45] Cole: *Malcolm Arnold*, p.108
[46] Chandos CD: Arnold Symphonies 3 and 4
[47] Jackson: *The Life and Music of Sir Malcolm Arnold*, p.103

Arnold is as well aware as any composer of the dangers of schmaltz or cliché. He is also courageous enough to admit them into his music when the context demands it.[48]

The context of an idealised happiness, snatched in the face of impending disaster, is certainly cinematic enough for schmaltz and cliché. This is an *Andantino* of voluptuous Sirens. Susan, Paula and all Malcolm's other favoured *femmes fatales* have inspired a languorous and relaxing interlude before the symphony's tumultuous climax.

The final movement, *Con fuoco*, returns us to the debate of the opening *Allegro*, but with a clinching, manic ferocity which sweeps us along, breathless, to a startling conclusion. It all begins conventionally enough, though in a strongly dramatic manner, as, again, three groups of material are explored: a cheerful, disquietingly original rondo motif, an eerie, highly cinematic interlude, and some familiarly percussive violence. These by themselves would have been enough to have made an exciting conclusion. But Malcolm suddenly[49] applies as violent a shock to proceedings as a sudden application of ECT. The listener is convulsed as a wildly violent and strongly dissonant march is introduced by a bizarrely grotesque rendition of what sounds like a combination of 'Oh When the Saints' and 'Alexander's Ragtime Band'. An allusion to the yobbish camaraderie of Colin Jordan's ragtime band of fascist thugs is clearly intentional, and probably likewise to all the bullying authoritarianism of racially prejudiced Britain. But human nature can triumph over the slings and arrows of an outrageous State, some time, some place, somewhere. And the carnival-loving Caribbeans of the earlier rondo theme come bouncing back, bravely singing their revivalist songs, to take on and conquer all the thuggery thrown at them. Bernstein's staccato chord sequences are in the heart of things in this movement too. Maria, even in death, triumphs in the spirit. Like the finale of Bernstein's *West Side Story*, Malcolm's last movement overwhelms the audience. In both works the conclusion is tragic, yet not pessimistic. A quiet, firm hope emerges from the destructive violence.

Malcolm's Fourth Symphony is a work of vast scope and ambition. Its composition had been emotionally draining and Malcolm unwound in his usual rumbustuous way. Fortunately, however, the August holiday near Padstow was at hand. Malcolm was delighted to disport himself with the children once more among the rock pools of their own, unspoilt Newtrain Bay. For the twelve-year-old Katherine it seemed as if nothing had changed:[50]

> Just having Dad along with us was wonderful. He threw himself into everything we did – swimming, surfing, walking on the cliffs and rock-pooling. It was a glorious summer for me. I had brought a friend along, and there was also our lovely West Highland terrier, Lucy. Dad was always popular down in Cornwall – so funny and very friendly with everyone.

---

[48] Cole: *Malcolm Arnold*, p.110
[49] At letter R
[50] January 2004

Back in London again, Malcolm felt equally expansive. He had no immediate deadlines to meet, so there was time for a little fun. One lunch party at Shepperton developed into a 48-hour frolic. He emerged hung over and depressed. A few days later, however, he met up with Bruce Montgomery at Pinewood, who had already been 'on the bat'[51] six days and, to Dorothy's eyes, 'was looking distinctly shaky'. Montgomery, who wrote much of the music for the Dirk Bogarde *Doctor* films as well as many *Carry On*s, would accompany Malcolm regularly to Soho's Windmill Theatre, famous for its non-stop entertainment and provocative nude tableaux. Montgomery was a scholarly man – he wrote novels under a pseudonym[52] – and a chronic alcoholic.

Malcolm now joined Montgomery on his bat, disappearing for the next couple of nights. When he re-emerged at Richmond, just in time for some recording sessions on *The Pure Hell of St Trinian's*, Dorothy found him 'looking well, considering'. But he was in an uncharacteristically foul mood when recording the music.

A rehearsal for an amateur performance of the Fourth Symphony at Maida Vale in mid-October began another bat. After lunch at Braganza's (close to Wheeler's in Frith Street) and fun at an Italian club 'with a rather glamorous owner called Mario', Malcolm left Dorothy to join Lawrence Leonard at Morley College, where he was rehearsing Malcolm's new symphony with the students. Somehow, however, Lawrence and Malcolm only managed to reach their homes late morning the next day, just in time to go out to Wheeler's for a reinvigorating lunch. All in all, in the forty-eight hours following the Maida Vale rehearsal Malcolm managed just two hours' sleep. Two days later he was back in Greenway, hung over and in the depths of depression. The first professional performance of the Fourth Symphony was only a fortnight away.

There had been another row at Richmond, perhaps something worse. 'He seemed gloomy and at present determined not to go home,' wrote Dorothy after a Greenway visit.[53] She felt Malcolm's relationship with Sheila had deteriorated badly.

> Saw MA in afternoon with Phil and Di. He was very cheerful, but phoned in the evening right down in the depths again because Sheila had been round.

Dorothy found him even more distressed the next day, complaining that Sheila had again told him he was mad. He was probably misrepresenting her badly. Malcolm was so fearful of the madness he sensed within himself and his potential to be destructive that, when Sheila tried to discuss these problems with him, he could not bring himself to do so, and, in talking later to Dorothy, simply

---

[51] Dorothy's term for a drinking binge

[52] Edmund Crispin. An exact contemporary of Malcolm's, Bruce Montgomery died in 1978. At the time of the 'bat' he had just finished working on *Carry On Constable*.

[53] 17 October 1960

misinterpreted Sheila's wish to help. In his disturbed state he could believe white was black.

It was hard for Sheila to know how to proceed. There was no way of reaching Malcolm when he was in a deep depression. Nor could she win in her battle with his alcoholism, whether she condoned or criticised. As Dr Lincoln Williams explained, an alcoholic's wife had a dual role. She was both mother and wife:

> The alcoholic is often a very dependent person. Part of him likes the mothering and the other part fiercely resents the dependence. How can he play the dual role of husband and son? How can she be both mother and wife? And so the marriage is turned into a civil war or breaks down completely.[54]

Sheila's quiet, determined desire to look after her children and keep the home functioning as normally as possible, paradoxically, only made matters worse, for, as Dr Williams told her, the more a wife accepted the responsibility of running the family, the more irresponsible and resentful an alcoholic became.

After just a week in Greenway Malcolm returned to Richmond, and Sheila braced herself to cope as best she could. In the days before the symphony's première Malcolm had no opportunity for rest. There was a new film score, *No Love for Johnnie*, waiting to be written. There was also a highly emotional anniversary to attend.

It was now a year since Gerard Hoffnung's death, and Annetta and his friends had decided to stage a *Hoffnung Vintage Festival*, using a mixture of old and new items. Malcolm's presence was as important to its success as his creative input. And despite the première of his Fourth Symphony only two days later, he supported the concert with passion, contributing two new pieces: a Fanfare for thirty-six trumpets which 'made a thrilling effect simply through the sound of group on brazen group stationed throughout the hall'[55] and a suite of short pieces representing some of the animals which Saint-Saëns had carelessly omitted from his Carnival. Malcolm's *Carnival of Animals* included a flock of sheep, 'a delightfully placid, pastoral canon, wandering on undisturbed by the most violent of irruptions',[56] some totally silent bats, elephants desperately trying to be elegant (with Delibes' famous pizzicato grotesquely transferred to deep brass) and, most interesting of all, cows. The latter cavorted, un-cow-like, to a strip-tease number (which Malcolm had used only the month before for his latest, not yet released St Trinian's romp). Seemingly Malcolm's cows were the two-legged variety.

The *Vintage Festival* delighted a packed hall and gave notice that the Hoffnung brand of mischievousness would endure, even without Gerard's own

---

[54] *To Each his Memories* (Regency Press, 1969), pp.121-122
[55] Andrew Porter, *Financial Times*, 1 November 1960
[56] *Ibid.*

electrifying presence. The highly-charged atmosphere of the occasion was well captured by Percy Cater:

> We laughed and cheered, albeit with sadness in our hearts, at the boisterous fun of those abundant friends of Gerard who, because he was so much in their minds carried on the joy which he conferred on the London concert scene.
>
> This show, representing a decision that these concerts, proving the gay propensities of serious musicians, shall go on, was a good show, a noisy show. Over most of the hits Gerard's influence still presided.
>
> Two features I found touching. Gerard's five-year-old son, Benedict, at his first evening concert, watched from a box with grandparents the jollity which his father had inspired. And at the close Annetta Hoffnung, Gerard's charming young widow, was conducted to the platform and, adding to the pluck she had shown by playing in the orchestra, made a speech thanking all the performers.[57]

The concert ended with Malcolm conducting his *United Nations Overture* of 1958. Andrew Porter's review [58] makes particularly interesting reading in view of the Fourth Symphony's conclusion, when a military band comes in unannounced and attempts to take over proceedings:

> There was nothing funny about the final item, Malcolm Arnold's *United Nations Overture*, a sober and chilling composition.
>
> There is a characteristically Arnold theme radiating goodwill and generosity, but it peters out in futile exchanges. National anthems compete; and then one military band after another enters the hall, marching and countermarching through the audience. The terror which the sound of a military band can strike is well-known from Beethoven's, Berlioz' and Shostakovich's music; and these bands, producing insane confusion, though each of them is strictly true to its own ideals, have a shattering effect. There is an enormous, explosive climax and the ash drifts down on desolation.
>
> Very quietly, the 'goodwill' theme returns – an alternative; but again it degenerates into the futile patter... Arnold has made his point. This is a deeply impressive composition which, if the forces can be mustered, deserves to be heard in a serious context.

The next day Malcolm was back at the Festival Hall to conduct a rehearsal of the Fourth Symphony. Photographs of this occasion suggest that, apart from his increased girth and pronounced double chin, there was little outward sign of all his social and domestic problems. In the *Sunday Times*, for example, he was shown in rehearsal sharing a joke with the percussionists. He is wearing an immaculate new suit; his striped Club tie is tightly drawn at the neck; his curly dark hair – with as yet no trace of grey – is neatly in place. Malcolm all his life had an instinct for the right moment to be professional and put on a good performance. The alternative life-style always amused him.

---

[57] *Daily Mail*, 1 November 1960
[58] *Financial Times*, 1 November 1960. Porter was its music critic from 1952-72, before moving to the *New Yorker*.

The rehearsal was a great success. The orchestra[59] enjoyed themselves hugely. Dorothy was equally excited on the day of the concert:[60] 'Great day! Everybody there.' That included Sheila, who loyally attended. Despite Malcolm's insufferable behaviour she was still maintaining, as best she could, the semblance of a stable marriage. It must have been hard for her, psychologically, to enjoy the music and unfortunately, with typical Yorkshire bluntness, she repeated her view that his work had deteriorated over the past three years.

The critics agreed with her pessimism almost to a man. They were understandably confused in that only two days earlier, in the very same concert hall, they had been listening to Malcolm's musical jokes. Nonetheless, the contrast between the tumultuously enthusiastic reception given to the symphony by the Festival Hall audience and its acerbic rejection by the critics is very marked. Malcolm's symphony was totally written off. The 'candy-floss' tune in the first movement, as Charles Reid had forecast, came in for particularly heavy punishment. 'A ballroom dance tune,' complained Martin Cooper, 'that would have captivated Tchaikovsky'[61] (who was distinctly suspect in some quarters in 1960 because of his melodic gift). Andrew Porter[62] attributed it to a more modern source, 'Edmundo Ros or Victor Sylvester'.'Never an inhibited man,' wrote Desmond Shawe-Taylor, 'Arnold has here shed the last rags of taste and discrimination.'[63]

Malcolm's serialist ploy of a second movement completely eluded all the critics, though Peter Heyworth[64] at least disliked it the least of all four movements. Martin Cooper thought it 'a damp squib', while John Dalzell thought it mainly memorable for the drummer's stick 'which broke and sailed majestically into the air'.[65]

The *Andantino* provoked predictable scorn. Cooper felt 'the cheap romantic eloquence' was not only 'deplorable in itself but destructive of the whole work'. 'A complete failure,' agreed Heyworth. 'Its material is undistinguished and here again a lack of momentum is not disguised by resort to the facile climaxes of routine film music.' 'A piece of inflated sentimentality,' wrote Mosco Carner, 'in a somewhat Delian vein.'[66] John Amis bravely pronounced it 'highly effective in a way' before quietly admitting it was 'film music slush' suffering from a 'low level of musical thought'.[67] Shawe-Taylor also found the level of invention low throughout the work, but 'in the languorous waltzes of the *Andantino* distressingly so'.

---

[59] Included in the trumpets was Malcolm's former flatmate from his student days, Wesley Woodage.

[60] 2 November 1960

[61] *Daily Telegraph*, 3 November 1960

[62] *Financial Times*

[63] *Sunday Times*, 6 November 1960

[64] 'Symphony For Fun', *Observer*, 6 November 1960

[65] *West London Press*, 18 November 1960

[66] *Time and Tide*, 12 November 1960

[67] *The Scotsman*

The fourth movement was, to Heyworth, 'a conventional and noisy apo-theosis' to what, overall, he had found 'a slapdash symphony'. 'Such was the concluding uproar,' confirmed Shawe-Taylor, 'that the performance seemed wrongly dated: it was the very thing for Guy Fawkes night.'

Overall there was something of the distasteful malevolence of an inept school teacher getting his own back in a report on a cheeky pupil. 'An extraordinary piece of musical exhibitionism,' declared Rollo Myers,[68] 'a monstrous parody of everything that music ought not to be ... cheap sensationalism' 'I call it a rag bag,' muttered Arthur Jacobs, 'and decline to take it seriously.'[69] ' Directness of speech is splendid,' purred Heyworth, 'but it does not necessarily consist of saying the first thing that comes into one's head.' Adrian Gaster toed the party line dutifully: 'His music does not convince us that it has anything of vital importance to communicate. It is predominantly light-hearted.'[70] And seventy-year-old Neville Cardus, of whom better things might have been expected, applied the most unkindest cut of all: 'The symphony had probably been left over from the Hoffnung concert given the night before.'[71] Cooper also used the same cheap jibe. Malcolm, he said, had donned the motley of a clown and presented a confection of 'popular entertainment and the cinema, the Salvation Army and Tales from Hoffnung'.

There was one voice crying sensibly in all this wilderness, and it came from *The Times*. William Mann was himself involved in the Hoffnung concerts, so he knew Malcolm well. Perhaps that gave him an insight into his serious music. At all events, he listened to the Fourth Symphony with more sensitivity than the braying host and gave his readers a much closer idea of what it had to offer:

> It is a noisy symphony, but behind the façade of rumbustuous extraversion the music is disturbed ...
>
> In earlier symphonies Arnold seemed indebted to Sibelius, but here the ghost of Prokofiev stalks more frequently, particularly through the regretful, languishing waltzes of the slow movement – present doubt, innocent and hardly articulate but goaded into self-expression through the bitter-sweet voice of a hollow, vanished past. The scherzo floats insubstantially and horror-struck through a procession of nightmare, familiar fragments of a theme and texture pitilessly distorted... The inspir-ation, though not the influence, of Mahler is discernible here, and in the finale too, which swaggers off into a cluster of fugues and is brought up short by a terrifying mob at whose centre a brass band is evoking vague memories of 'Alexander's Ragtime

[68] *The Listener*, 10 November 1960

[69] *Reynolds*, 13 November 1960. Jacobs had greeted the Third Symphony very differently: 'Banishing that musical clowning that upset his previous symphonies the 36-year old composer had found a new way to combine tenderly expressive melodies with his love of explosive surprises. I welcome this bold, clear music.' (*Evening Standard*, 3 December 1957). Clearly he thought Malcolm in the Fourth Symphony was back to musical clowning.

[70] *John O'London's*

[71] *The Guardian*, 4 November 1960

Band'. The dénouement is, as in many post-Mahlerian symphonies, all brute force and optimism ...[72]

Malcolm would at least have found encouragement here.

Several of his friends were outraged at what had happened, Lawrence Leonard writing an entertaining and heartfelt riposte in the *Daily Telegraph*.[73] The BBC certainly supported their commission loyally. A few days after the concert Malcolm recorded the work with the BBC Symphony Orchestra and it was subsequently broadcast on the Third Programme.

The day of the broadcast had not started auspiciously. Dorothy had driven Malcolm from Richmond to the Maida Vale studios in the early morning.

> We found nothing could be done until the afternoon. So MA had a row with the BBC and I drove him home. We came back in the afternoon for the recording which went well.[74]

Colin Bradbury, the orchestra's principal clarinet, remembers how much they had all enjoyed playing the work and how startled they were when, at the end of the recording, Malcolm announced 'And that, ladies and gentlemen, is my farewell to the Third Programme!' before sweeping off the podium.

Among those listening to the broadcast was the veteran composer Havergal Brian, who wrote to a friend of Malcolm's,

> I was amazed at the inventiveness, urge and power, and the originality of his orchestral painting. Of the four movements the first and last made the greatest impression, though the whimsical fantasy of the second and third have greatest individuality.
>
> His letting loose a hurricane of sound reminded me of Shostakovich, yet it was all his own, and so different from that sort of thing done by Richard Strauss. Evidently the English musical stock is ascending and leaving the academics far behind.[75]

Malcolm expected criticism, wilfully invited it, and almost seemed to need it as a spur to further creativity. Even his gloomy forecast at Maida Vale of future ostracism by the BBC was delivered with a wide grin. And when Dorothy called in at Richmond the day after the concert, she found Malcolm in buoyant mood, still on the highest of highs. 'MA didn't seem at all put out by a couple of bad write-ups of 4th Symphony,' she wrote. 'Times are good.'[76]

---

[72] 3 November 1960

[73] His letter (22 November 1960) mocks the critics' didactic response to performances of Malcolm's Fourth and Peter Racine Fricker's Third Symphony. Fricker was strongly preoccupied with form and strict counterpoint and much influenced by Schoenberg: 'From a careful comparison of these reviews it has at last proved possible to envisage the perfect symphony, which perhaps someone one day will write. The scoring should not be so utilitarian as Fricker's nor so brilliant as Arnold's. It should go easy on the contrapuntal devices, yet not state its tunes undecorated. The gestures must be big, but not too big; the romanticism romantic, but not romantically romantic. It should neither be academic nor commercial, and the composer should avoid the dangers of living on film music or teaching. Indeed, there appears to be no reason why he should live at all ...'

[74] 11 November 1960

[75] Letter to Bryan Fairfax

[76] 3 November 1960

He had written the symphony in a strongly confrontational frame of mind, doing his uttermost, it seems, to open himself up to accusations of a shocking lack of taste. Having included within it certain features which were bound to cause mystification, at best, and outrage, at worst, he had made no effort at all to mitigate the coming storm by carefully explaining his point of view. His programme notes, for example, though full of little digs against the modernists, explained the symphony in only the baldest of ways, commenting merely on a few technicalities and offering no illuminating overview, let alone a justification of its most controversial features. Of the 'candy-floss' melody he wrote:

> The second subject is in the major scale, and is accompanied by a rhythmic figure in 8/8 time where the quavers are divided into 3+2+3.

Of *Alexander's Ragtime Band* and all that followed in the finale there was no mention. This was sheer bloodymindedness and an expression of his confrontational, self-destructive nature.

It also expressed his growing conviction that his symphonies were never going to be properly understood or fairly assessed. The critics who had dismissed his Fourth Symphony were both progressives and conservatives. His brand of experimentation within traditional tonality left him acceptable to neither. Neville Cardus's scorn was significant: Cardus, a conservative who could not abide Hindemith, Berg or Webern, let alone Messiaen, Gerhard or Boulez, and who likened works by Varèse, Antheil and Jolivet to 'a concert for a breakdown gang and furniture remover',[77] might have been expected to offer a more balanced view of Malcolm's symphonies than the Darmstadt missionaries and other progressives. But Cardus was too steeped in the music which he himself had championed – Mahler, Bruckner, Richard Strauss, Elgar and Delius – to appreciate contemporary innovation even when it was, like Malcolm's, within the European mainstream. Instead he was happy to write insultingly of the Fourth Symphony that it was 'thirty minutes too long'.

This utter rejection by the conservative Cardus showed Malcolm how much of an outsider he had become. In the passionate gang warfare of 1960s musical criticism he was to be mown down by both sides. In his calmer moments, of which there were still a few, Malcolm understood this, and was somewhat amused by it. What did it matter anyway? He had nearly reached forty. He had already lived ten years longer than intended. Gerard had died at thirty-four, Dennis Brain at thirty-six. He by contrast had lived long enough to meet the BBC's commission of a Fourth Symphony, which Neville Cardus in his wisdom thought thirty minutes too long. He was, up to a point, lucky.

---

[77] Christopher Brookes: *Neville Cardus: His Own Man* (Methuen, 1985), pp.139 and 213-14

# 10
# The People's Champion
## In the Age of Piotr Zak, 1961-63

THE MORE MALCOLM thought about the critics, the more he resented what seemed to him the abuse of their privileged and powerful position. He had been given an overwhelmingly warm ovation at the Festival Hall at the end of the Fourth Symphony and after the concert he had been buoyed up by the many expressions of goodwill and gratitude. All around him there had been a sea of faces lit with enthusiasm, proof that his music was communicating in a meaningful way. The public's response was as positive as the critics' was negative. And more and more, in his elevated moods, Malcolm saw himself as the public's champion, a popular composer with a mandate to oppose the idiocies of the progressives and, at the same time, the unwillingness of the conservatives to accept responsible development of traditional forms. So when a commission for a new symphony suddenly came his way from the Cheltenham Festival Committee, he saw it as a providential opportunity for making another musical statement on behalf of the silent majority of intelligent music lovers, a duty not to be shirked. On 3 July 1961 he would have another chance to rally the right-minded.

He had not yet had time to begin to marshal his thoughts on the symphony, when, in early January 1961, he learnt appalling news. His eldest brother, Aubrey, and sister-in-law, Wyn, had committed suicide.[1] It was hard to believe. Aubrey, fifty-two and recently out of work, had hired a car and driven with Wyn into the Salcey Forest, south of Northampton, with their pet dog and cat on the back seat. The next morning a gamekeeper had discovered all four of them dead, with a pipe leading into the car from the exhaust.

Malcolm had always taken Aubrey's success in the shoe trade for granted. Now, as he reflected on the tragedy, he realised that there had been a series of debilitating disappointments. The first had come as Aubrey had returned from war, basking in glory as a Lieutenant-Colonel. He had expected to run his grandfather's business, A & W Arnold, but various loopholes in Grandfather William's muddled will had disinherited him. So instead he had joined Pappy and Uncle Mat at Arnold Brothers, where for a time they prospered. Aubrey had been able

---

[1] 8 January 1961

to indulge his taste in antiques – maps, silver, copper, prints and paintings – and on one famous occasion he and Pappy had acquired a large set of 1760 Sèvres plate and a service of nineteenth-century Crown Derby, about three hundred pieces, which they had generously shared around the family.[2] But by the time Pappy and Uncle Mat had retired and Aubrey was running Arnold Brothers with his two cousins, cheap Italian shoes were threatening the firm's existence. Malcolm remembered his surprise on learning that Aubrey had had to bring in help from outside the family, eventually surrendering his majority shareholding. Finally, a few months ago, Aubrey had become involved in an argument with those now controlling the business and had resigned.[3] But even then it had not occurred to Malcolm to ask his eldest brother, always so calm and correct, whether he had any financial problems.

The carefully organised suicide pact came as a terrible shock to the whole family. His niece Penny still expresses incredulity:[4]

> Aubrey was so confident and sure of himself. Aunt Wyn always seemed so happy and smiling, whenever we saw her, and though we thought that Aubrey might have a dark side to his character, we never expected it with Wyn. The family was shaken rigid with the news of their deaths.

Their son, Robin, believes his father's elaborate sense of honour precluded him from coping with wholesale redundancies in the family's work-force. His cousin Edwin, similarly distressed by this, also attempted suicide:[5]

> My father was a man of great integrity, but never one to let emotions show. His public school education had inculcated an exaggerated sense of honour and 'the stiff upper lip' mentality.[6]

Winifred Arnold, Malcolm's sister-in-law, had enjoyed a carefree dancing career which had taken her to pre-war Berlin, like Sally Bowles, and left her with a pretty daughter. She had brought great warmth into Aubrey's staid life, but her own hidden problems were so severe she had attempted suicide more than once before. By the early 1950s Robin started discovering bottles of gin around the home and it slowly dawned on him that his mother was an alcoholic. Sometimes, he says, his father had to rush back from business meetings to take

---

[2] Malcolm, like Clifford and Ruth, quickly sold his share, and later was too 'embarrassed' to tell Robin, Aubrey's son, why he had done so. He did not need the money.

[3] On his father's death Robin inherited the 40% of shares in Arnold Brothers. He tried hard to acquire from the other shareholders an extra 11% so that he could clinch a rescue deal with Norvic, but met with resistance. The business collapsed a few years later, the banks realising their assets and the final loss being the large sum (in the 1960s) of £17,000.

[4] October 2003

[5] He survived and later acquired a modest job designing shoes. The third family member to be pushed out of Arnold Brothers, Uncle Mat's son Ron, fared better, going into another company on the production side.

[6] July 2003

care of her. Marriage to the solid Aubrey had helped stabilise Wyn but it ultimately destabilised him.

The tragedy inevitably reached the national newspapers, several mentioning that 'Mr William Aubrey Arnold was a brother of Malcolm Arnold, composer of *Bridge on the River Kwai*'.[7] Dorothy was surprised by how calm Malcolm was. It seemed not to have affected him at all, but inwardly he was as distraught as the rest of the family. He may not have loved Aubrey, or even liked him very much, but there was always a deep, residual respect. Leaving everything, Malcolm drove up to Northampton where he comforted the distraught Pappy and shared his grief and guilt with Ruth and Clifford, who had both thought Aubrey strait-laced. Robin remains very grateful for all Malcolm's help at this period.

> He was deeply concerned for me and my half-sister, Toni, attending the Coroner's Court and making sure we had all the legal aid we needed. He could not have been more supportive. 'Regard me as a father,' he said. 'I will provide you with whatever you need. Money? A house? You name it!'[8]

Robin, newly married and impecunious, preferred to fend for himself[9] but was grateful for all the moral support. He remembers one telling moment, shortly after Aubrey's death, when he and Malcolm were having a drink at the White Elephant Club. Robin had been expressing his perplexity that his father had given no hint of suicidal tendencies. 'You can never hope to get to know anyone else's inner person,' said Malcolm, puffing on his cigar reflectively. 'No matter how well you think you know someone, there will always be the last five per cent of their inner person which is barred to you. That's about as close to anyone's soul as you will ever get.' Robin replied that maybe it would be a good thing if people *did* release that last five per cent, at which Malcolm removed the cigar from his mouth, leant over the table and looked Robin straight in the eyes. 'Bloody well *don't* is my advice!'[10]

But this advice did not extend to his music, as the new symphony would show. In the weeks after the funeral Malcolm's thoughts moved from Aubrey's untimely death to those of three particularly dear friends: Gerard Hoffnung, Dennis Brain and Jack Thurston. In February there was a further blow, the death of David Paltenghi, who, at forty-one, was just two years older than Malcolm. The Fifth Symphony was beginning to take shape in his mind as an emotional response to these bereavements. He was later to write that the work was 'filled with memories of friends of mine who died young'. He excluded any mention of Aubrey, not wanting to comment publicly on his brother's suicide.

---

[7] *Daily Sketch*, 10 Jan 1961
[8] July 2003
[9] Malcolm had been supporting Pappy and Lizzie Witts with money and there may well have been other recipients of his rather unwilling charity. 'We were on our beam ends,' writes Robin, 'But we said "If ever we need help, we'll ask". We made sure we didn't. There was too much family tapping into him at the time.'
[10] As recalled by Robin, April 2004

In March 1961, with his thoughts still in flux, he was pleased to be invited down to Cheltenham to speak at the Festival Society's Annual General Meeting.[11] It was an opportunity to mount a first attack on the progressive critics:

> I think the language of modern music has got too vast. Its vocabulary has got too complicated for the ordinary listener to understand. It is now in a state of complete chaos! There are absolutely no conventions at all! There is nothing for people to hang on to any more! As far as I am concerned, I want what I write to be comprehensible, so that I can share my ideas and emotions with other people. What is the point of talking at all if nobody understands you?

This had been a positive beginning. There were so many encouraging smiles around the room that he plunged on decisively.

> To me, Britten and Shostakovich are more contemporary and fresh than a great deal of those composers who write in a more 'advanced' and experimental style. These experimental composers seem to find the putting together of music cleverly their main justification. But Beethoven was not a great composer just because he did that – which he most certainly did. He was great because he really said something.

Some applause followed. Cheltenham might still focus on contemporary music in its Festival, but, whereas in 1951, at the time of Malcolm's First Symphony, the Festival represented the most radical musical thinking of the day, so much had happened in the past decade that the Cheltenham outlook was now derided by progressives as hopelessly reactionary. Malcolm was preaching to the converted:

> Music must never become just a mathematical, intellectual exercise. A composer should think in terms of sound not programme notes. Some of these modern composers might just as well stand up on the rostrum and recite their programme notes for all the satisfactory noise they produce![12]

The words boomed round the room confidently, as more applause followed, and Malcolm embarked on a long coda about his own career, and when he finally brought things to a close with resounding praise for the courage and hard work of the Festival Committee, he received a rapturous reception.

In 1961 the progressive lobby in favour of electronic and aleatoric music had not yet won the day, and it was not only in conservative Cheltenham that there was staunch resistance. There were even concerns in William Glock's forward-looking BBC Music Department. Hans Keller, for example, although one of Glock's first appointments and an earnest advocate of the twentieth century, was so frustrated by the sheer fatuity of many avant-garde pieces, not least some incomprehensible Stockhausen, that he perpetrated a remarkable hoax. Having gathered together a few percussion instruments, he made a ten-minute recording

---

[11] Held at the Carlton Hotel, Cheltenham
[12] 'Language of Modern Music in "Complete Chaos"', *Gloucestershire Echo*, 24 March 1961

of himself and two friends hitting them at random, thereby creating an 'avant-garde work' of his own.

> I wanted to broadcast senseless noise in order to prove that, nowadays, we have reached a stage where even musicians can't decide whether something is music or not.[13]

Keller's 'senseless noise' was broadcast in an otherwise genuine chamber concert of contemporary music.[14] The composer was said to be a certain 'Piotr Zak', to whom Keller gave some splendidly bogus credentials. The two soloists, it was alleged, had come to England specially to give this performance. Shortly afterwards, to Keller's great delight, Jeremy Noble's review in *The Times* took the structure of Zak's work seriously. Noble disliked the work, but declared that he had grasped its broad outline. It was an embarrassing moment for the progressive critics, and Keller loudly protested that such a collection of meaning-less sounds could never have been mistaken for music in Mozart's day. But Piotr Zak was speedily forgotten. He was a horrible embarrassment to the musical establishment, which quickly closed ranks. Too many professional reputations were at stake to allow doubts about music's new élite.

Encouraged by his friendly reception at Cheltenham, Malcolm had returned to Richmond to write his symphony. But the euphoria soon evaporated, and the symphony was completed in a chaotic two months[15] during which, most unusually, he did not enjoy a period of calm, free of drink and all other distractions. Instead, he was also involved on a new film score,[16] the pressure of which led to some heavy drinking. The reason for the chaos was the break-up of his marriage. He used Richmond for periods of writing, but was looking for alternative pleasures outside the home at the same time. Sheila had done her best to salvage the marriage for the sake of the children. She and Malcolm had attended a Mahler concert at St Pancras Town Hall at the end of February.[17] But to all intents and purposes the marriage was over, and, a month later, at a showing of some cartoon films featuring the music of his friend Francis Chagrin,[18] Malcolm was accompanied by Annetta Hoffnung, Gerard's attractive young widow. It was an important friendship.

---

[13] Full details are given by Alison Garnham: *Hans Keller and the BBC* (Ashgate, 2003), pp.122-125

[14] Third Programme, 5 June 1961. Keller organised a discussion programme, 'The Strange Case of Piotr Zak', on 13 August 1961

[15] The date of completion on the manuscript is 7 May 1960, but 1961 must have been intended as David Paltenghi, commemorated in the work, did not die until February 1961. Dorothy Payne's diary suggests that work carried on beyond 7 May right up to the trial run it was given at Walthamstow on 26 May.

[16] *On the Fiddle*

[17] Bryan Fairfax's amateur Wind Music Society

[18] Nicholas Chagrin, the composer's son, had been one of the mimes in *Song of Simeon.*

Just as Malcolm had been generous and supportive to his nephew Robin on the death of Aubrey, so too he had looked after Annetta:

> I saw quite a lot of Malcolm after Gerard died. Very kindly he kept an eye on us. He was lovely with my children. And of course he really spoilt them! [19]

Malcolm's support included help in keeping the Hoffnung concerts alive. Actively involved in *The Hoffnung Vintage Music Festival* of 1960, he was now masterminding a new venture, *The Hoffnung Astronautical Music Festival*, to be put on at the Festival Hall later that year. He and Annetta had been busy working on this together, soliciting help from the Hoffnung fraternity. [20]

He was in too much mental turmoil in April to complete the symphony he had begun in March. He was particularly distressed to realise that, as the marriage faltered, so too did his relationship with Katherine and Robert, both of whom he adored. Robin saw much of his uncle at this period, and witnessed this distress:

> One of his absolutely constant themes was his absolute devotion to Katherine and Robert. He spoke to me constantly about them. Their welfare was always at the very forefront of his mind. But I sometimes wonder if he was able to articulate properly this deep love he had for them. I suspect he sometimes struggled to do so. But I can't exaggerate how much he loved them. [21]

He coped with the emotional turbulence within him in his customary way. Dorothy's diary has references to 'on the rampage' and 'on the razzle' at the very time he should have been completing the symphony. She also notes him 'very taken with a nice girl called Bernadette' at Shepperton Studios. Drink was a refuge every time Malcolm called in at Richmond to work on a score and came face to face with his betrayal of Sheila. 'MA must have been tight when I arrived at Richmond,' Dorothy wrote in late April, 'to behave in such a peculiar way.' Just over a week later, with the symphony still unfinished, Dorothy visited Richmond to find him 'tight and peculiar, as of late'. He had refused to do any work with her, but instead made her drive him round Richmond Park before adjourning to a pub. Shortly after this, it seems, in his emotional and physical exhaustion at the completion of the symphony, Malcolm had another brief psychotic outburst, followed by a stay in the psychiatric ward of Springfield Hospital and recuperation at Greenway. [22] He emerged 'in good form' two days before the symphony's first rehearsal, only to discover it was far too late to get Philip Jones to copy out the orchestra parts. So he rang up Christopher Finzi and several other musical friends in Richmond, and with their frantic, last-minute help just met his rehearsal deadline.

---

[19] April 2003

[20] In particular with Francis Baines, Humphrey Searle, William Mann, John Amis, Francis Chagrin, Lawrence Leonard, John Dankworth and Joseph Horovitz

[21] April 2004

[22] There is strong circumstantial evidence of this.

*On a visit to Prague*

Malcolm had written the symphony primarily for Gerard and Annetta, so it was appropriate that, in early July 1961, he took Annetta, her two children and a good friend, violinist Olive Zorian, with him down to Cheltenham for the symphony's première. For a few days the crises of the past few months were forgotten. Malcolm was on superb form, looked plump and well, laughed a great deal and was always immaculately groomed. Few could have guessed the inner torment which had created the Fifth Symphony. And when he came to conduct the new work, the Hallé Orchestra played it magnificently. There was a triumphant five-minute standing ovation, the kind of reaction which had not been seen at Cheltenham for a decade.

Malcolm's emotional 'memorial' to his friends has continued over the years to be popular with audiences, remaining, with the Second, the most widely played of his symphonies. 'It's got the two things I stand for,' he once said.

'Simplicity and melody.'[23] This was the battleground between him and the critics, whose combative instincts were aroused by both.

A solo oboe opens the symphony enigmatically, its five notes symbolising Malcolm's five symphonies. The first four notes represent the final tonality of the each of the previous four symphonies (D, E flat, B flat and F), while the last note is that with which the new symphony ends (E).[24] This was not a coincidence but wholly intentional, as Malcolm himself pointed out in a later interview.[25] And the exact nature of these intentions soon becomes clear.

The first movement (*Tempestuoso*) contains two sets of subject groups, the solo oboe introducing the first, which, most surprisingly, uses serial techniques, the very style embraced by the progressives and which Malcolm largely ignored. He is beginning his symphony, therefore, with a statement to his critics: 'I have now written five symphonies. And I will show you that, had I wanted to, I could have written all five of them in the style you make such a fuss about, but which I don't particularly like.' And off he goes, dabbling in serialism as he progresses through the movement.

Serialism is not the most obvious way of writing music when the avowed intention is to communicate easily with the general public. Malcolm's gifts, however, allow him to progress from the manufactured but highly meaningful oboe theme into a sombre first section, which sets the scene well for the rest of the movement. In a work which laments the premature deaths of friends and family, the eerie sounds of the first subject could not be more appropriate. Death is waiting in the wings, and in the first subject we can hear him. Malcolm's choice of instruments also helps promote this atmosphere. The enigmatic oboe solo is followed, after a series of chords in the strings, by celesta and harp, two instruments so often associated with heavenly sounds, reinforcing Malcolm's preoccupation with death.

For the second subject group, introduced by timpani and brass, Malcolm reverts to his usual diatonic style, the use of tubular bells and glockenspiel together with the other heavenly instruments giving it a strong memorial flavour. The tubular bells are also highly significant in that the notes they play, GB, celebrate Gerard Hoffnung.[26] And the first three notes of the actual second subject material, introduced most sweetly on harp and celesta, are GAH, Gerard and Annetta Hoffnung. Ciphers[27] like this were a device which Malcolm used extensively enough in his later works for there to be no doubt that this is an intentional tribute to the Hoffnungs. During the course of the movement there are clear references to Jack Thurston (a long clarinet solo) and Dennis Brain (many

---

[23] To Antony Hopkins, 1986

[24] He had decided, therefore, where he was going in the final movement even before he started writing the first.

[25] *Notes from Norfolk*, Anglia TV, 1990

[26] B natural is H in German notation.

[27] First pointed out by Paul Jackson (*The Life and Music of Sir Malcolm Arnold*)

horn solos) while a boisterous drunken waltz is a tribute to the light-footed, heavy-drinking David Paltenghi. Gerard's tuba is busy throughout.

There is much melody in this movement, and simplicity too, but it is an artistic rather than a naïve simplicity. Nothing could be more simple than the hushed way in which the movement ends, yet the simplicity possesses a profundity, clinching, as it does, the whole argument of the first movement. Nor does the simplicity bring with it any feeling of barrenness. The use of solo instruments and hushed strings produces extraordinarily delicate tone colours. And even in this passage of supreme calm Malcolm keeps us alert by offering subtle contrasts. Beneath the heavenly music of harp and celesta is Gerard's tuba, grunting quietly in the background, before the movement, marked *tempestuoso*, dies away into thin air, *niente*. It is an example of Hans Keller's comment that 'Arnold's profundity manifests itself in pseudo-shallowness, which is his historical inversion of pseudo-depth.'[28] In other words, the apparent artlessness of Malcolm's writing is, in fact, his artful response to the over-complex music being championed by many critics in 1961: pseudo-depth.

Simplicity and melody abound in the second movement. Malcolm was to write many memorable melodies but none, perhaps, is quite so striking as that which opens and closes this movement. This Mahlerian melody begins with Annetta's initials – AH (musically AB), an attribution which is unquestionable, as Malcolm told Annetta herself, while at Cheltenham, that she had inspired this main theme. The inclusion of the living as well as the dead might seem at first something of an irrelevance to Malcolm's thinking. But the passionate, even idealised nature of the music shows that Annetta's presence is as the grieving widow, who with her young children has to face up to a new life without the much loved Gerard. It is the *pity* of it all which Malcolm is expressing so eloquently in this melody. It is Virgil's *Sunt lacrimae rerum*: 'There are certain things about the human condition which are inevitably and shockingly sad.'

In offering so romantic a theme Malcolm was making a trenchant statement to the critics who had strongly attacked his 'popular' melody in the Fourth Symphony. Antony Hopkins, in assessing the symphony twenty-five years later and defending Malcolm's right to use such a melody, was scornful of such attacks:

> What is regarded as forgivable or even totally loveable in Mahler seems open to condemnation in Arnold's music ...[29]

But this is to ignore the difference between what Malcolm is doing here and what Mahler might have done in similar circumstances. With Mahler both the 'Annetta theme' itself and the soft *legato* melody which Malcolm places next to it would have undergone some far-reaching transformations. Malcolm, by contrast, prefers pure repetition, note for note, without any transposition or

---

[28] *Musical Events*, January 1958
[29] *Talking about Music*, BBC Radio 4, October 1986

development. As with the 'popular' tune in the first movement of the Fourth Symphony, he wishes to make a direct statement, uncluttered by any kind of melodic or harmonic transformation. Here, in the Fifth Symphony, Malcolm is using the 'Annetta theme' to underline the point that it is the bereaved who suffer most in the tragedies of untimely death. These 'set pieces' act as stable points of reference within his symphonies, unaffected by all that is going on around them. It is a bold, innovatory device, making his work more immediately appealing and coherent to the listener. It is another example of Malcolm's profundity manifesting itself in pseudo-shallowness.[30]

The *Andante*'s very simple structure offers a sombre central section sandwiched between the attention-catching romantic tunes. This central section also subdivides into A-B-A, the outer sections of which are passages of eerie quiet. The second of these eerie passages[31] offers another good example of the kind of simplicity Malcolm was championing. With great dexterity he manages to construct something deeply meaningful out of the very barest of musical materials. Antony Hopkins commented:

> Look at the score, and it appears absolute trash! A rumble on the drums and sustained chords passed from the wind to the strings to the brass and back again. Nothing seems to be happening that could be of any interest to the listener except for a little da-da-da-dee-da on a horn or a trombone. And yet, when you hear the actual sounds, the wonderful play of tone colour, it's totally original, without resorting to any of the ultra-sophisticated, weird and wonderful devices which are becoming so fashionable nowadays. There's simplicity for you![32]

Malcolm's 'simplicity' is entirely illusory in the *Con fuoco* third movement, a fiery scherzo full of very complex rhythmic play, the kind of intricacies with which Malcolm had experimented in his early works, like the second movement of the Wind Quintet, now coming to full maturity. 'Five-unit rhythms and ostinatos are thrown across the beat,' explained Hugo Cole. 'Lumbering canons for bass instruments call up visions of jostling elephants desperately hurrying to catch their trains. There are extreme, Berliozian contrasts of dynamic, abrupt shifts of tonality, daring juggling acts with massive blocks of orchestral masonry.'[33]

The scherzo starts in an atmosphere of fierce anxiety and ends in catastrophe and recrimination, a reminder of the extreme bitterness with which Malcolm

---

[30] Malcolm believed that the current suspicion of popular melody ran counter to music's traditions. 'The composer should not be frightened of … using the language of popular music and learning from it,' he once said. 'Too many composers of today restrict their language unduly and ignore fields that have always been part of a composer's experience.' (Festival of Recorded Music, Blackpool, March 1963)

[31] From bar 93 to 110

[32] *Talking about Music*, BBC Radio 4, October 1986

[33] Cole p.118

responded to Gerard's death.[34] But, in the central section, a fascinating struggle is taking place between the forces of jollity and disaster. Here, perhaps, Malcolm is with his great drinking partner, David Paltenghi, having yet another self-destructive good time, as, in one long passage the spirits are temporarily lifted where the melody is fragmented and flavoured by the occasional jazzy syncopation. But even as the two friends dance the nights away in revelry, death is stalking them, sometimes coming out of the shadows to interrupt them with a reminder of his presence, always threatening.

In a final movement of extraordinary power, *Risoluto*, Malcolm begins with a surprise, a perky military march scored for piccolos and drums, which quickly undergoes attack and is soon in the kind of chaos Malcolm's *United Nations* bands caused in the Hoffnung concert three years earlier. In a highly dramatic opening, the march is eventually overtaken by a searingly romantic melody in the strings, which, impassioned as it is, still struggles to evade the all-enveloping side-drums and soon gives way again to the military struggle. This is not Gerard Hoffnung's world at all, nor are there any clues relating the military theme to Jack Thurston, Dennis Brain or David Paltenghi. So who is marching at the head of this parade, so confidently and so secure, oblivious of all the chaos in which he will shortly be enveloped? It is Aubrey, of all Malcolm's recent bereavements the most tragic, debarred by the circumstances of his death from mention in the concert programme, Aubrey, the war hero, with his stiff upper lip and high sense of honour, brightly leading his work-force on the march to Salcey Forest, all ninety-five per cent of him.

Malcolm loves surprises and he has not finished with us yet. By carefully graduated stages,[35] he leads us, via passages of foul menace and savagery, away from all the old material of the *Risoluto* on an exciting mystery tour. The musical temperature rises, grotesque parodies of earlier motifs fly around, until, in a magnificent climax, the 'Annetta theme' comes in with all the magnificence which Malcolm and Hollywood can between them muster. As soaring strings introduce the hauntingly sad melody one last time, before entrusting it to majestic brass, we are thankful for some respite after all the grief and bitterness we have shared, 'Annetta's theme' no longer reminding us of bereavement so much as the beauty left in the world.

But there is one final surprise, at the very end of the symphony, when the mood abruptly changes. We had seemed to be heading for a finale in fine Shostakovich style, a paean of praise and glory, triumph in the face of adversity and so forth. But not a bit of it. From a concluding, triumphant chord of D Major Malcolm takes us swiftly to a tragic E minor. The cellos (Aubrey's instrument)

---

[34] Annetta Hoffnung particularly stresses Malcolm's bitterness at the time of Gerard's death. In addition to grief he felt resentment. (January 2004)

[35] From bars 152 to 240

and double basses hold the note ever so softly, and the bells chime out Gerard's initials. It is a breathtakingly enigmatic ending.[36]

The five-minute standing ovation at the Cheltenham Town Hall was well deserved. Malcolm had written a fine symphony, a vindication in sound of everything he had said to the Festival Committee last March. And he had also thrown down the gauntlet to the critics, who quickly picked it up. Peter Heyworth led off for the progressives:[37] 'Mr Arnold stands revealed as tub-thumper.' He has 'thrown the last shreds of discretion to the winds', and his symphony is 'tedious to listen to ...'

Among conservatives, Percy Cater[38] found it 'a lightweight production not in Arnold's best style', Noël Goodwin[39] 'a succession of platitudes ...' and Arthur Jacobs[40] grumpily declared: 'This anti-symphony seems to flirt with serious musical dialogue only as background furniture for farce.' In the *Sunday Times* Desmond Shawe-Taylor was on good form:

> The new work, which was greeted with rapture and much stamping of stoutly shod feet, seems to aim at going one better than the notorious 'pop tune' symphony of last year.
>
> Constant oom-pah backgrounds and a similar but still more banal and more remorselessly plugged hit-tune convey the impression that Arnold has begun to make a revivalist's platform out of his cultivation of 'the common touch'...

In marked contrast to all these disappointments there were perceptive thoughts from *The Guardian*'s R L Henderson, who wrote of the symphony's 'two opposing centres, one of a sweet, sentimental nostalgia and the other a gritty, almost cynical defiance'.[41] In the first movement 'the vague, bell-like fantasy of the initial bars prepares the way for a disturbing contrast between quiet woodwind chorales, easy flowing melodies, and violent dissonant climaxes of taut, broken rhythms.' Henderson was giving the music a chance to speak, rather than pre-judging it. 'If the long lyrical melodies with their blues inflexions,' he wrote of the *Andante*, 'seem to establish a more confident tone, even this is shattered for a brief space by new rhetorical outbursts.' He thought 'the short, brilliantly scored' scherzo took a further step towards the world of popular music, 'but popular music seen through a distorted mirror'. Of the conclusion,

---

[36] It has been a subject of much debate. Donald Mitchell, believing that Malcolm's best music stems from the basic tension between truth and beauty, sees this as a moment when truth wins over beauty. Ross Pople, by contrast, believes that Malcolm, at the last, suddenly gives up on the world: 'It has let him down. He's given it the finest music possible. It won't, he knows, be properly appreciated, and suddenly he says, "Oh stuff it! Let's all go down to the pub!"' (February 2004)

[37] *Observer*, 9 July 1961

[38] *Daily Mail*, 4 July 1961

[39] *Daily Express*, 5 July 1961

[40] *Financial Times*, 4 July 1961

[41] 5 July 1961

Henderson shrewdly suggested 'the quality of negation rather than true affirmation'. His summing-up was calm and fair:

> In this new symphony Arnold displays yet again his seemingly inexhaustible melodic invention and imaginative resource. The orchestra responded to the composer's own direction with a persuasive vigour and conviction, their finely disciplined and sensitive playing giving just the right emphasis to each change of mood and idea.

But peer pressure can be hard to resist. Just a week later, Henderson wrote again of the concert, this time after he had had the chance to assimilate everyone else's reviews. In 'Cheltenham is Losing its Way' for the *Sunday Telegraph,* last week's 'lyrical melodies' in the second movement had become this week's themes of 'almost unbelievable banality'. On the whole, however, he still got more out of the music than most, and at least he had actually listened to all four movements, whereas several of his colleagues were spotted on the telephone to Fleet Street while the symphony was still being played.[42]

Of all the criticisms, the one which hurt most was an unsigned piece in *The Times*, which, after a tilt at 'the disparity between its modest ends and inflated means' and 'the disparity of style and merit as between one section and the next' and an inevitable reference to 'banality', ended:

> His orchestration and a number of deft transitions still reveal a genuine musical talent, but as a whole this new symphony suggests a creative personality in an advanced stage of disintegration.

The writer was Jeremy Noble,[43] the very same critic who a year before had heard the random noises recorded by Keller in the name of Piotr Zak and had told his readers that he was getting to grips with their structure. Yet again Malcolm's friends rose to his defence, firing off outraged letters to the newspaper, but the damage was done. Thirty years later the comment still caused distress in the Arnold household. Jeremy Noble, in fact, had no knowledge of Malcolm's mental problems. The wording was pure bad luck:

> Had I known, of course I would have rephrased that comment. The disintegration, as I intended it, was a musical one. There were too many contrasts in the piece for my liking, too many styles, too many switches between the banal and the inventive.[44]

It was a problem some critics were to have with the work for many years. Meanwhile odd sounds, perpetrated in the name of modernism, were sometimes being given a somewhat more generous hearing.

Jeremy Noble saw Malcolm 'red-faced at the bar' of the Savile Club shortly afterwards, but wisely gave him a wide berth. The Savile for the moment was Malcolm's main base as he absent-mindedly severed ties with Richmond. He left himself no time to take thought for what was happening to him and those around

---

[42] 'A Black Mark for Putting a Tune in a Symphony', *Richmond Times*, 8 July 1961
[43] Assistant Music Critic 1960-63
[44] January 2004

him, whom he was hurting and whom he was pleasing. It was helter-skelter every day. Not that he could have easily imposed proper working patterns on his life, for commissions presented themselves in too quixotic a fashion. He was earning huge sums from films, but spending as fast as he received, living in extreme luxury, and thereby being forced to accept more work than was wise simply to maintain his current lifestyle. After the Fourth Symphony he had left himself just ten days to write a score for *No Love for Johnnie.* After the Fifth he rushed to complete *Whistle Down the Wind.*

Malcolm's qualities of simplicity and melody served this score well. The film's producer, Richard Attenborough, a friend and neighbour for some years, who was himself to be heard whistling the tune in the opening credits, has nothing but praise for their collaboration:

> Malcolm would come along to the sessions having thought really deeply about the music – he truly understood how integral the music can be.[45]

The director, Bryan Forbes, was less impressed:

> I always thought he sentimentalised *Whistle Down the Wind* – I made a much harder film which, by his music, he made softer.[46]

Malcolm, aware of this criticism, has said that when he first saw the film he thought it too stark and dour, and deliberately set out to lighten the tone. The result was to set up an interesting tension between the story and music, which mostly works to the film's advantage. The most difficult decision for Bryan Forbes was whether or not to use the main theme as the captured Alan Bates was led away by the police, watched by all the children. He feared the gentle, happy melody might make the moment ridiculous. In the event it enhances it, its innocence encouraging us to see things from the children's point of view. But it was a close call. Hayley Mills herself greatly admires the score:

> The music for *Whistle* is just classic – so brilliant that it did an enormous amount to impress the film onto the consciousness of the audience for a long time – it really was the heart of the movie. It caught the spirit of the film – of those children, their faith, their innocence; a kind of pathos – Malcolm's music had such heart and love.[47]

The delicate piccolo on the soundtrack was played by Richard Adeney, who had left the LPO to follow a successful career as a soloist. It was now over twenty years since he and Malcolm had been fellow students at the RCM and the long friendship had cooled:

> Knowing I was gay, Malcolm used to make sexual advances on me when he was drunk, which I had to repel. I don't know whether they were ironic or sincere, but they were certainly embarrassing. If he had simply been mischievous, I could have coped. But he was cruel. He made cruel jokes towards me. He was, I am afraid, one of those

---

[45] May 2004
[46] August 2003
[47] December 2003

people who would put a joke before kindness. He never stopped to think about the hurt the joke might cause if it would make others laugh. So I quietly withdrew from a friendship which had once been extremely strong.[48]

Malcolm hardly noticed. He was too intent on meeting and impressing interesting new people and getting the very most out of his life. As he rushed around London in the summer of 1961, one hand as often as not clutching the latest score, the other the latest girl, he was aware of a dangerous fragmentation of routine and wondering if he might be helped by buying a retreat in the country. Quite with whom, if anyone, he was planning to retreat, is not known. But when the time came for the family to go down to The Bryn, for the usual Cornish holiday in August, he failed to materialise. He may well have been still working on a film score, but he did not manage to contact Sheila, who had to take the children down by herself.

As far as Sheila was concerned, the marriage was over. Malcolm might pursue his own life as selfishly as he liked for the rest of the year, but the summer holiday had always before been sacrosanct, the token of his commitment to her and the children. The sticking point had been reached. This time there would be no question of him coming back. Years later Sheila could talk of the break-up dispassionately, yet not without regret.

> He finally left us in the summer of 1961. I knew he wouldn't be able to look after himself, but I had two children and my responsibility was that they should turn out into good human beings. How could they, with somebody like *that* around?[49]

At some stage in August, however, Malcolm was overcome with remorse. He rushed down to Cornwall, and signed in at a local hotel. How best, he wondered, might he reinstate himself within the family he had so carelessly repudiated? He roamed the familiar beaches, sandy Trevone and rocky Newtrain, pondering a plan of action. He thought that, on the whole, it might be best if, in the first instance, he spoke to Katherine. He would bide his time …

It was an enormous shock for Katherine, as she walked along the beach by herself on the way to the shops, suddenly to be confronted by her father. At thirteen, Katherine understood something of what her mother was going through, hard though Sheila had tried to hide things from her children. Her father's conduct was as hurtful as it was perplexing. At the sudden sight of him she burst into tears, and he followed suit. They stood on the beach together, crying. Katherine was too overwhelmed with conflicting emotions to be able to utter the words needed to take him back with her to the Bryn. 'I think I must go and see my mother,' was all she managed. So they went their separate ways, and shortly afterwards Malcolm checked out of his hotel and took the next train to London.

---

[48] April 2003
[49] July 2003

It was only later, that September, at the start of a new school term, that the marriage break-up was explained to the children. 'I remember being very shocked on being told that Dad was not coming home,' recalls Robert. 'To me it was sudden and unexpected as I had not realised anything was wrong. We had accepted all his absences as being quite normal. I can remember there was fog the morning she told me.'[50] He cried on the way to school.

Malcolm quickly settled in a flat in Knightsbridge,[51] where he was to be based for the next two and a half months. That summer there was, for a change, no writing. There was too much else swimming in his mind. His future relationship with his children was a preoccupation, now that divorce was under discussion. Above all, he was keen to make up for the holiday his absence had just ruined. He would take Katherine and Robert to the south of France.

A ten-day trip to Banyuls-sur-mer, a resort near Perpignan, began inauspiciously with a cool reception from Sheila at Richmond, which was hardly surprising in the circumstances, and a seriously delayed flight because of fog. Katherine too was not sure, initially, that she had much to say to her father. After an uncertain beginning, however, the holiday picked up. Malcolm had had the good sense to avoid for once the most luxurious hotel on offer in favour of something more intimate. It was 'very French' and just across a quiet road from the sandy beach. For Robert, over forty years on, there were many happy memories:

> Learning to snorkel; interesting tanks in an aquarium at the marine research station; Catalan dancing in the square in starlit evenings; sitting in cane chairs on the sea front drinking hot chocolate; swimming in the deep blue water and taking pedalos out into the bay.[52]

One memorable excursion involved crossing the border to Port Bou in Spain in a decrepit taxi, the kind of Citroën saloon which in its better days Simenon's Maigret might have used. They quickly gave it the name 'boom boom!', because every so often it cried 'boom boom!' and broke down.

> The friendly taxi-driver had a big joke with Dad about 'petit contraband', which he showed us after he had successfully negotiated the customs on the way back: bottles of absinthe, cleverly wrapped up in rags …

That autumn Malcolm moved from his Knightsbridge flat to one in Buckland Crescent, Swiss Cottage, conveniently close to his secretary, Dorothy, not far from Annetta and very near to Greenway. Dorothy, who had found the flat for Malcolm and bought things for it, was helping him as best she could, sometimes doing his shopping. His new bachelor life-style, however, seems not to have been particularly conducive to work. 'Went round to Buckland Crescent several

---

[50] January 2004
[51] Hans House, Hans Crescent
[52] January 2004. His father, he remembers, was so taken with Catalan music that he bought an LP.

times,' Dorothy noted, 'but paper on step with milk.' The next day there was similar frustration: 'Still no work from MA, who is on the bat.'[53]

Part of Malcolm's autumn was spent in preparation for the *Hoffnung Astronautical Music Festival*. But it was not all hard work. Annetta still has vivid memories of the fun of it all:

> We would go to places like The Ivy and Wheeler's. He loved the artistic ambience of both places. We would occasionally see Lucien Freud and Francis Bacon at the latter. It was a place people went to again and again. Malcolm used to give enormous tips at the end of meals, simply because the money was in his pocket. The waiters loved it, but it was almost out of control.[54]

When it came to negotiations about the impending concert, Annetta discovered that Malcolm was not always the ideal collaborator. The Wigmore Street offices of Harold Holt and Ian Hunter, for example, seemed to bring out his most mischievous streak:

> He was outrageous. He helped himself to things on their desks! Papers, elastic bands, whatever was to hand … Anything he could do to make it a mess …! He could be so destructive!

Sometimes Malcolm's more outrageous behaviour had a direct correlation to something in his personal life that he would keep very private, not even sharing it with his closest friends. He learnt, for example, in the autumn of 1961, only months after Aubrey's suicide, that his 46-year-old brother Clifford was dying of cancer. Malcolm had been as close to Clifford as he was distant from Aubrey. Clifford had been the charmer of the family, handsome and highly personable, Lizzie Witts' acknowledged favourite when they were all children.[55] It was hard to absorb that so much vitality was about to be extinguished so early.

Clifford died on the last day of November 1961, two days after the Hoffnung concert. Malcolm mentioned neither his illness nor his death to Dorothy, and at the Hoffnung Festival he concealed all grief about his dying brother. But while he laughed and joked, inspiring his fellow contributors with his own loud enthusiasm, half of him was back in Northampton. He saw the miniature steam railway Clifford had built in his back garden, on which he loved to take bone-shaking journeys; and all the Buddhas and other oriental exotica which Clifford had brought back from his sea adventures to turn his home into an Aladdin's cave; the grand old Bentley – had it really been owned by a maharajah? – in which he, Clifford and Doll, Ruth and Wag had delighted local hostelries in their, triumphal, regal progress; fun too with Clifford and his wild friend Alec, telling

---

[53] 27 October 1961. Malcolm had moved into Buckland Crescent on 18 October.

[54] April 2003

[55] Lizzie Witts remained devoted to Clifford's cause. She had helped bring up the elder daughter Gill (who many years later, tragically, was to commit suicide) and, having been begged by the dying Clifford to look after his baby daughter, she did that very conscientiously, bravely coping with the many problems.

*Rehearsing the Grand Concerto Gastronomique with Tutte Lemkow*

each other outrageous stories while the girls went riding across the fields near Billing village. It was all a long, long way from the Festival Hall.

Malcolm had worked hard to make the *Astronautical Music Festival* the great success it proved to be.[56] Among his many triumphs as organiser, Malcolm had persuaded William Walton, now a great friend, to participate; it was a short and sweet contribution, as Annetta wrote:

I remember particularly how Sir William Walton teased the audience by conducting, after elaborate foreplay, a brief excerpt from *Belshazzar's Feast* – in fact it was just

---

[56] Although this was the last Festival Hall concert, Hoffnung concerts have continued to be staged all round the world.

the shouted word 'SLAIN!' echoing dramatically round the hall. It was a brief performance but it brought the house down.[57]

Malcolm himself wrote two new items for the Astronautical concert: The *Leonora Overture No 4*, in which he subjected Beethoven's original to unlikely counterpoints, bizarre melodic transformations, sneering trumpets, unexpected interruptions and mistimed fanfares. And the *Grand Concerto Gastronomique* for eater, waiter, food and large orchestra, later ennobled as Opus 76. The 'eater' was 20-stone theatre impresario Henry Sherek, whose presence, commented Noël Goodwin, added weight to the occasion.[58] As soloist Sherek had to consume a six-course meal in fifteen minutes: from oysters (*cantabile*) and brown Windsor soup (*presto*), through roast beef (*nobilmente*) and Peach Melba (*dolce*), right down to coffee and brandy (*spirituoso*). The *Sunday Telegraph*'s critic, T S Ferguson, applauded Malcolm's gastronomical score as 'perfectly good light music for the gramophone, even without the comic business'. By contrast, the *Daily Telegraph*'s Martin Cooper, who was not enjoying his evening, thought it 'singularly inept and unfunny'.[59] It was a minority view.

There was thick snow on the ground on 2 January 1962 when Malcolm left for a nine-day visit to Delhi to research Indian music for a film about the death of Ghandi, *Nine Hours to Rama*. While he was there, meeting many Indian musicians and, in particular, friends of Yehudi Menuhin, he started planning his only major concert work of the year, a Double Violin Concerto, commissioned by Menuhin for the Bath Festival. Ghandi and Menuhin, both of whom Malcolm admired greatly for their compassion and humanity, briefly became intertwined in his mind, the Concerto initially having something of the Indian idiom of *Nine Hours to Rama*. Back home, however, rethinking the concerto, he scrapped these early ideas. He decided instead that, like the Fifth Symphony, the Double Concerto would be commemorative, the two solo violins leading Malcolm to thoughts of his two brothers who had died the previous year.[60]

The Double Violin Concerto lacks many of Malcolm's more usual traits. There are no abrupt modulations, changes of mood or catchy tunes. A sustained nostalgia underpins all three movements. Like the famous Bach Double Concerto, it is full of serious contrapuntal dialogue between string orchestra and soloists. The dialogue flows in a severely neo-classical way. If the opening *Allegro risoluto* movement is as uncompromising as Aubrey, and the final *Vivace*

---

[57] Annetta Hoffnung: *Gerard Hoffnung*, p.166

[58] *Daily Express*, 29 November 1961

[59] 'Joke Concert has its Painful Sides', 29 November 1961

[60] Malcolm has never publicly acknowledged this, but when Paul Jackson put the idea to him some years ago Malcolm 'agreed that I wasn't out of line with my thoughts' (February 2004). It is possible that the *Divertimento No 2* of October 1961 also reflects Clifford. It was based on a work Malcolm had written for the NYO, Malcolm replacing the tango of the middle movement with an expressive nocturne based on a falling minor third. The latter could well reflect his feelings about his dying brother.

redolent of the cheerful Clifford, it is the spirit of the punctilious elder brother which dominates throughout. Even the serenely spacious central *Andantino*, while scaling the heights of beauty, plunges back to earth. At one point a reverie of happiness, perhaps of the gentler age of their childhoods, is interrupted by an uncomprehending ghostliness which hints at Aubrey's tragedy.

It is a fine work. When Malcolm himself conducted its première at the Bath Guildhall with Menuhin and his protégé, Albert Lysy, as soloists,[61] the audience's enthusiasm was met with an encore of the entire concerto. Malcolm's attitude to death informs it. This is no cloying, sentimental adieu, but under everything is a sense of ironic anger. He was the one brother who had proclaimed that he would kill himself by thirty; yet, in the end, the staid, reliable Aubrey had beaten him to it. He was the heavy drinker, smoker and eater, who risked his life in a self-indulgence he could not control; yet Clifford had turned out to be the one who first paid the price. Yehudi Menuhin, who knew nothing of all this, nonetheless sensed that all was not as it seemed on the surface. He was struck by a mocking tone in the work and felt that Malcolm was 'hiding something from his depths'.[62]

Despite this huge success at the Bath Festival (which Malcolm attended with Annetta and Dorothy), film work was his chief preoccupation in 1962. The Double Violin Concerto, indeed, had been composed between recordings for two important Twentieth-Century Fox movies, *The Inspector* and *The Lion*.[63] *Nine Hours to Rama* followed. But in April he severed friendly relations with Sam Spiegel when he turned down an invitation to write for *Lawrence of Arabia*. Spiegel, having first rejected an unpromising score by Richard Rodgers, unsuccessfully wooed the unlikely combination of Britten and Khachaturian, before inviting the colourful trio of Walton (an opening march), Khachaturian (desert music) and Malcolm (the remainder of the score). William Walton and Malcolm turned up together to watch a screening, both the worse for drink. 'It was the dullest film I have ever seen.' Malcolm declared to Dorothy afterwards. 'Just people on camels, and camels with people, and people with camels … an interminable camel travelogue!' There was also a parting of the ways with Bryan Forbes, over *The L-Shaped Room*, Forbes wanting a simple piano score and Malcolm feeling this was a slight on his reputation as an orchestrator. Forbes opted for Brahms instead.

Malcolm was also kept busy in 1962 by his role as Chairman of the Guild of Composers, a post he treated as a signal honour, surprising many by his attention to detail. His presence inevitably lightened the tone in the Guild's St James's

---

[61] With the Bath Festival Orchestra, 12 June 1962
[62] Jackson: *The Life and Music of Sir Malcolm Arnold*, p.119
[63] *The Inspector* was recorded 21-23 February 1962, the Double Concerto completed on 25 April, and *The Lion* recorded on 24-28 May. A month later the concerto was given its première (17 June 1962).

*With Yehudi Menuhin, 1962*

Square headquarters and, as such, was warmly welcomed by the Secretary, Topsy Levan:

> The atmosphere always changed when Malcolm entered the building. Everything at once got brighter. His grin and laughter cheered everyone up![64]

He showed remarkable restraint on occasions. David Wright, for example, has written vividly of the way artistic temperament within the Guild could cause tempers to fray:

> Although Malcolm was often incensed at remarks made at the meetings by other composers and would often go red in the face, he would say nothing. The worst offender at such meetings was Britten, who would take over meetings and say what a brilliant composer he was and that he was the only great British composer. He would complain about the failure of the BBC to perform his work and how awful his publishers Boosey and Hawkes were who used to print works by Stravinsky before his. After one such outburst of Britten's megalomania, Alan Bush led a revolt in the

---

[64] May 2004

meeting saying 'Ben, your music is arid and replete with homosexuality, perversions and sadism. No one else in this room wants to fondle choirboys!'

Malcolm's hypertension disappeared in a moment. The redness in his face reverted to a normal colour and he was heard to say 'Well said, Alan!'[65]

Malcolm's restraint was all the more impressive as in 1962 his private life was in considerable disarray. On 21 June the divorce finally came through and he spent anxious days fearing that news of his adultery would be broadcast in the papers. Thereafter he seemed intent on celebrating his new status as a dashing divorcee. Girl-friends abounded. Dorothy arrived at the Buckland Crescent flat for work one morning to find him in bed with a new acquisition, Linda. She took the day off. For quite a period a Mrs Richardson was hot in Malcolm's pursuit. And he was seen guiltily lurking from time to time at the Gondola Club with a friend's wife. He would go missing for days on end, sometimes to emerge, 'as bright as a daisy' and sometimes 'in the depth'. 'He is not looking well and is on edge,' wrote Dorothy of him in July. 'I am worried how things will pan out.' Meanwhile there was 'the party of all parties at the Briganza' with Linda and half the orchestra from *Nine Hours to Rama*. Several people passed out, but Malcolm kept inviting others in.

Annetta Hoffnung promised Malcolm greater stability, but he seemed to withdraw away from the friendship, now that he was free to marry. Their relationship ended almost by default. He would fail to get in touch. On one occasion he even forgot to turn up for a dinner she had organised.

> I realise now just how mixed up he was. He was a very loveable person, so colourful, such company! He had great presence. For such a big man he moved with remarkable grace, almost on tip-toe. But there was a streak of cruelty in him. He would take against someone and make all sorts of jokes and remarks. He would go on and on at them. Often his targets were quite grand people…
>
> He was impossible really. So perhaps it was as well that he just went off. There was no argument, no actual crisis. The children were very young when he suddenly disappeared out of their lives and at first they missed him enormously. I would guess Malcolm must find certain things in his life quite hard to live with. He must have felt guilty sometimes at the way he would shy away from relationships …[66]

Like so many friends, Annetta was alarmed at the excessive drinking.

> He had to give a lecture once at Sussex University. And he went down there so absolutely stoned, he told me afterwards, that he could not remember either going or coming back. He only knows he was there because he had a letter thanking him for the interesting talk! No doubt it was very interesting! He couldn't remember what he had said!

---

[65] David C F Wright writes that this was told him by Adrian Cruft, Edmund Rubbra, Humphrey Searle, Alan Bush and Alan Rawsthorne on separate occasions (March 2004)
[66] April 2003

As the year progressed, work was coming more and more a bad second to pleasure. He turned down a possible commission from the BBC for a set of variations on the theme from *The Archers*, even though Adrian Boult would conduct and the fee was a hundred guineas:

I am sorry to say that I haven't time to accept any more work this year, but thank you for asking me.[67]

Though this was not entirely true, it was hardly a commission which would have redeemed his reputation with the critics. Dorothy, meanwhile, found herself with an increasing number of days off. In late summer 1962 her diary chronicles a growing chaos:

Went round to MA. Flat tidy but both bedroom doors closed and a pair of yellow shoes in the sitting-room, so I left a note and did not investigate. MA phoned up later and said it was Michael Ayrton!

Towards the end of September Malcolm gave up his flat at Swiss Cottage, having at last acquired a home in the country. 'Canbury', situated in the village of Thursley near Godalming, was a square, detached house of red brick, built in the 1930s on the edge of the village not far from the pub. It had a small but attractive back garden which opened onto Thursley Common. Robert, who spent several weekends there, remembers the Common as 'a magical, wooded place':

Dad told me that Joseph Conrad's brother, still using his Polish name, lived in a hut somewhere in the wood, and that he had met him.[68]

It was not long before Malcolm was making his presence felt at the local bars, with Dorothy chronicling further excitements:

Went to Thursley in afternoon and found MA in remarkably good spirits except that a girl from the Godalming Hotel was threatening to move in with him. She phoned while I was there and I answered so I don't think she was surprised when he put her off. She has a mum in Oxford, so I told him he had no need to feel responsible for her.[69]

Enjoying a whole series of treats himself, from time to time he thoughtfully provided treats for his children. Robert remembers being taken by Dorothy in her open-topped AC to the Television Centre, 'where we met Dad and I was introduced to Dixon of Dock Green'. On another occasion, travelling through London in a taxi with his father, Robert was once highly impressed when they interrupted their journey outside a theatre, and he was taken backstage to be introduced to the star, John Mills. 'He seemed very friendly, not at all put out by our sudden appearance.'

---

[67] 30 May 1962 (letter courtesy of BBC Written Archive Centre, Caversham)
[68] February 2004
[69] 18 February 1963

Katherine remembers visits with her father to London Zoo and Whipsnade, and it was as a result of one of these that she wrote a poem, *Peacock in the Zoo*. Perhaps she subconsciously had thoughts of her father as the peacock, a great public attraction, but sometimes a little wilful:

> Everyone goes to see the peacock.
> They wait for him to fan out his tail,
> As he wanders looking for food,
> Dull and drab behind the fence.
> To annoy the crowds standing by,
> He drags his tail feathers
> And will not deign to reveal their latent splendour.

However, seeing the need to entertain, the peacock puts on his usual splendid show:

> The crowd feels bored and disappears.
> The peacock advances and fans out his tail,
> Flaunting it, swaying his whispering feathers,
> He struts with his head held high
> Around his pen, until the crowd reappear again …

Although perhaps it is rather more effective as prose than poetry, Malcolm seized upon the poem delightedly and set it to music. Having produced a lilting arrangement for piano and unison voices, he then persuaded Michael Diack to publish it. As treats go it was a charming and expensive one, and a token of his great pride in Katherine's successes at school. In finding his children treats Malcolm tended to use *his* world. He found it more difficult to step into theirs.

Both Katherine and Robert were taken from time to time to exciting restaurants. Robin, slowly coming to terms with his parents's tragic suicide, was similarly treated to the high life. His wife, Avril, remembers that on one occasion, after she had praised the cream on her strawberries, Malcolm immediately ordered a champagne bucket full of it. Visits to Wheeler's would often begin with the Italian doorman melodramatically stopping the traffic for Malcolm and his party, and then dancing before them as they crossed the road. There were many riotous evenings there. Robin also remembers 'fabulous food' at the White Elephant Club in Belgravia 'and beautiful waitresses.' It was a stunning place, he said, with its mirrors all round the dining room, but Malcolm would electrify it. 'It was partly his sense of humour, his ability to pull everyone's legs, whatever class or position.'

Malcolm seemed to know all the actresses of the day, many of whom he had dated. Through Malcolm Robin met several film directors, on one occasion being entertained by Joseph Mankiewicz in his suite at the Savoy Hotel. When Mankiewitz called for pine wood on his open fire rather than beech or oak, he was teased mercilessly by Malcolm. Robin remembers his uncle at this period as 'a gargantuan, charismatic figure'. He conversed with everybody, from high to low, and everything revolved around him.

He was in less elevated mood and feeling resentful when the winter of 1962-63 brought the worst snow in the south of England for the last eighty years. The roads were treacherous and there were regular power failures, and, instead of going to the film studios, Malcolm sulked in bed at Thursley claiming his Alvis wouldn't start. He had virtually done no work for six months, and a score was required for Philip Leacock's *Tamahine* in six weeks. Dorothy gingerly headed her AC down to Thursley. Most of the side-roads were single file only, and the journey was precarious. Malcolm refused to talk about work but took her out to his local hotel for 'delicious roast beef with champagne'. She returned home in a more confident mood. The end of January arrived, however, with the cold and snow still around, and the score still unwritten. Fifteen days from the scheduled first recording of a score for which Malcolm had not yet written a note, he telephoned Dorothy to say he had no water, his car wouldn't start and he couldn't get to the running of the film.[70] Two days later the impasse continued. It was too cold to get out of bed to go to the studios, he told her. With just ten days left Dorothy deployed all her considerable powers of persuasion in one final effort to overcome what was, in effect, a form of writer's block. To her delight he moved into Philip and Diane's flat and asked to see the film. But Dorothy feared it was all too late:

> Very worried as to whether MA can complete *Tamahine*. He sounded gloomy on the telephone, but not too bad when I saw him. He drove into a snowdrift and was got out by four stalwarts from the cutting-room. Most relieved that he has started. Everyone in the cutting-room very friendly to him.[71]

By staying up late and eating and drinking little, Malcolm finished the score with hours to spare. On the first day's recording session, against all the odds, he was 'in tremendous fettle'. Three days later, with the recordings complete, he celebrated by taking a large party for a long lunch at the Grosvenor.

Having surmounted his problems, Malcolm turned his attention to a commission which he had long put off, a one-act ballet for Robert Helpmann. It was nine years since they had worked together on the Old Vic *Tempest* and Helpmann, returning to choreograph at Covent Garden for the first time after a long absence, wanted a dramatic score on the Greek legend of Elektra.[72] A story of murder, revenge and madness fitted Malcolm's mood of the moment perfectly. Comfortably esconced with Philip and Diane, he wrote a score fittingly powerful for the less-than-totally-sympathetic mother-killer and father-avenger, Elektra.

---

[70] 24 January 1963
[71] 28 January 1963
[72] Malcolm finished orchestrating the score at Thursley on 13 March 1963, just ten days before the first performance.

Helpmann, who in a previous Covent Garden ballet had put the ham back in *Hamlet*, was entertaining equally lurid visions himself. The resultant, sexually explicit, musically manic, entertainment sent the audiences home in delirious delight[73] and the critics sourly seeking acid for their inkwells. Clive Barnes was typical:

> Helpmann's Elektra is an insult to the intelligence! [He has] taken one of the great classic themes and transmuted it into a vehicle for melodrama and petty eroticism ... Clytemnestra (Monica Mason) and Aegisthus (Derek Rencher) enter and indulge in a *pas de deux* which will not look unfamiliar to students of the *Kama Sutra*.

Noël Goodwin deplored 'the most empty-headed agglomeration of sound I have ever heard in a long way'. His splendidly trenchant review conjures up a great deal of what so delighted the audience:

> Even the precise handling of orchestral sound that is one of Arnold's strong virtues is missing in this score. In its place is a mélange of woodwinds and strings with great dollops of brass and percussion poured liberally over the top like ketchup. It is a moot point whether the eye tires sooner of the grotesque contortions on stage that pass for choreography or the ear of the wailing chromatics, vamping rhythms and thunderclap drums which pass muster for music. Elektra herself is endowed with a dementia in 6-8 time that would scarcely illuminate a knockabout farce and the Clytemnestra-Aegisthus relationship (if that is the word) is greeted by ribald 'raspberries' from the trumpets and trombones ...

Not long after *Elektra*, towards the end of April 1963, Malcolm visited Russia for three weeks, as a representative of the Guild of Composers, which organised annual reciprocal visits at this period with the Union of Soviet Composers. In 1962 Malcolm had, as Chairman, led the official welcome to a Russian delegation, which included Rodion Shedrin.[74] This was at the height of the Cold War, and the Russians were initially taken aback by the warmth of their reception, but by the time of his own visit in 1963 Malcolm had made several good friends in Russian musical circles.

In Moscow Malcolm and his party were greeted by Tikhon Khrennikov, Chief Secretary of the Union of Soviet Composers, looking sinister in his tinted spectacles, and all the more so for his known involvement in engineering the downfall of Shostakovich in 1948. At one early reception in Moscow the six-man British delegation was unexpectedly called upon to produce an impromptu musical offering. Ignoring the proffered piano, Malcolm gathered his anxious party around, whispered a few instructions, and then delighted his hosts by a

---

[73] The ballet lasted fourteen minutes, but the applause even longer. The twenty-three first night curtain calls mainly reflected Helpmann's popular return to Covent Garden. But the athletic nature of the choreography must have impressed. There is a photograph of Nadia Nerina (Elektra) sent flying horizontally twelve feet in the air by three Furies with another three Furies anxiously waiting to catch her. Film of the ballet is said to survive in the National Film Theatre archive.

[74] A signed presentation copy of Shedrin's first piano sonata was a much prized possession.

rendition, in the style of an unaccompanied part-song, of 'Three Blind Mice'. The Russian hosts watched Malcolm conduct this strange performance in stony-faced bemusement, until, one after the other, they collapsed in laughter. The applause was out of all proportion to the (somewhat uneven) quality of the singing. Though history books remain silent on the subject, it was probably the very first glimmer of *glasnost*.

Malcolm was a guest at the May Day Parade in Red Square in addition to attending many concerts and discussions. There were several long harangues about the need for music to show a militant party spirit, civic ardour and optimism. Brooding introspection was looked upon with disfavour by the Union of Soviet Composers, though, as Rhodion Shedrin had demonstrated in his second and third piano concertos, aleotoric techniques were allowable. A Western book on serialism, translated into Russian, had just been published.

From Moscow they travelled, carefully chaperoned, to Leningrad, Armenia (where they met Edvard Mirzoyan at Yerevan) and Tbilisi (for discussion with Georgian Composer-in-Chief, Alexey Machavariani). For Malcolm the highlight was to renew his acquaintance with Shostakovich, about whom he would speak, unreliably, in later years.

> I knew him very well. He used to be ashamed of having written so many symphonies. I asked him how many. He looked round as if he was going to be shot and whispered 'Fourteen'. Stalin hadn't liked them at all and Shostakovich was ashamed.[75]

Although Stalin had been dead ten years by the time of the visit and publicly denounced by Krushchev as a mass-murderer, Shostakovich, he said, was still looked upon with a certain distrust by his Soviet masters. When he had visited Shostakovich at his home, he had drawn the curtains, talked in whispers and constantly looked around him for fear of being overheard. Eventually they completed their conversation in the lavatory, where he was more relaxed.[76] Shostakovich always used to pretend to Westerners that he could not speak English, declared Malcolm, whereas in reality he could:

> When I got him alone, I said 'Look, my Russian is terribly bad … Your English is better, and we'll talk all night long [in English]. We're kindred souls in a very rough, barbaric world …' If we were stuck in English or Russian, we'd talk in Italian …[77]

Malcolm made many friends in the course of the visit and kept in touch with his interpreter-guide for some years afterwards. He also managed to pass secretly through the customs a Russian icon, 'painted rather beautifully and in a metal frame'. Clearly Malcolm's capitalist inclinations overcame his communist sensitivities at this juncture.

---

[75] Interviewed by Peter Paul Nash, Radio Norfolk, 1991
[76] As related to Robin Arnold
[77] Nash interview

But despite the beautiful icon Malcolm quickly sank into a depression on his return. Perhaps his capitalist way of life now distressed him. At all events he lectured Dorothy earnestly on the merits of the USSR, and, to anyone who would listen, he offered a homily on the superiority of Moscow over London. Robert remembers a fragment:

> Take soap! Here we have a hundred brands, each competing meretriciously with the other, wasting money on useless advertisement. In Moscow, on the other hand, you just buy one brand of soap. 'Soap' is the simple description on the outside of the packet. Soap is what you get! You don't get perplexed by a load of frills!

Malcolm's return to bachelor life wasn't without its difficulties. He found it impossible to look after himself *and* write music. Philip and Diane kindly put him up at Emperor's Gate as each new compositional crisis arose, and he employed a good housekeeper at Thursley, but there was no substitute for Sheila's three good meals a day, twice with potatoes, with one's washing regularly reappearing, fully ironed, unbidden, as if by magic.

With some of these considerations possibly in mind, two days after his return from Russia he wrote Sheila an extraordinary letter.[78] He was in some confusion, for he sent it to The Bryn, not Richmond, but he wrote with passion, for he sent it Express Delivery. Nearly a year had elapsed since the divorce and Sheila was very taken aback at what she read:

> Dear Sheila,
>
> I am deeply ashamed of the way I have treated you and sorry that whenever I try to talk to you about it, I give you the impression of arrogance and complacency. The last two years have been a terrible nightmare for me and I would like the chance to spend the rest of my life with you. I find life very difficult to cope with as you know, because I have had no discipline or education in my early life and a completely unstable family background. My experience over the past two years will be some guarantee that I would not repeat my past mistakes.
>
> Please think seriously about this,
> With love,
> Malcolm

It was very touching in its simplicity, a sincere expression of his feelings, at least at the time of writing. But Sheila knew that the only guarantee she could rely on was that 'past mistakes' would be repeated, probably with interest. 'I didn't answer it,' she says quietly, forty years later. 'I didn't want to get involved in an exchange of letters which could lead nowhere. I knew he couldn't look after himself, but I had two children and was responsible beyond all else to fashion two reasonable human beings! How can you do that with someone not interested in family life?'[79]

---

[78] 17 May 1963
[79] August 2003

Malcolm was not used to his will being crossed. The greater the rebuff, the more his sense of outrage. Sheila could at least have had the courtesy to answer his letter. He had apologised, humbled himself, even given guarantees. What more did she want? Two months later he was still feeling misused and misunderstood, so he went down to Denbigh Gardens to reason things out. Next day Dorothy found him crestfallen: 'MA came round very depressed about row with Sheila and Katherine.' [80]

Katherine remembers the visit:

> Dad had arranged to come and take Mum out for lunch. They started to talk about where they would go, and quickly Dad became exasperated and said he wouldn't go after all. This went on for a bit in the hall. I was sitting on the stairs and I felt for my mother. She had taken this risk of seeing him again and was now being rejected. It seemed to me that he was tormenting her, and I told him he was perverse. Dad cried out 'Who told her that?' He'd misheard me and thought I'd said 'perverted'... They didn't go out to lunch, of course. [81]

At least Malcolm could briefly take his mind off his woes with a film he much enjoyed, Ronald Neame's version of Enid Bagnold's *The Chalk Garden*. At the same time, however, he started fulfilling an appalling commitment of fifteen television films for MGM, a series called *Espionage* (with such unpromising titles as *The Dragon Slayer* and *A Tiny Drop of Poison*), which elicited from Dorothy awestruck comments about his professionalism:

> Forty minutes of music in one session! The last of it without rehearsal to picture. How does Malcolm do it? All most successful and everybody pleased ...[82]

He was squandering his talents on such well-paid but second-rate projects. He had written nothing else in the six months since *Elektra*. In the eighteen months since the Double Violin Concerto, apart from a little film work, he had produced just a couple of suites for youth groups.[83] He was losing touch with his calling. Britain's most promising young symphonist of the 1950s had almost disappeared from public view.[84] Two years ago he had been the people's champion, the persuasive voice of sanity in an ever increasingly mad musical world, his Fifth Symphony's five-minute ovation at Cheltenham a vindication of his whole career and philosophy. Now it was becoming clear that the review in *The Times* which had hurt so much by suggesting 'a creative personality in an advanced stage of disintegration' was not so wide of the mark after all. Jeremy Noble had identified

---

[80] 29 July 1963
[81] March 2003
[82] 29 August 1963, on the recording of the soundtrack for *Covenant with Death*.
[83] The highly popular *Little Suite No 2* (for the Farnham Festival) and *Little Suite No 1 for Brass Band* (for the National Youth Brass Band of Scotland)
[84] In 1963 Malcolm's name is hard to find in the popular monthly magazine *Music and Musicians*.

within the Fifth Symphony the self-destructive forces of Malcolm's inner person which had wrecked his marriage and brought his career to a point of stagnation.

Fortunately both his personal and professional lives were to find a sudden, fresh direction from a most unexpected source, the advent of a new girl-friend. Like many others of this period, the new girl-friend saw Malcolm as a highly eligible divorcee, rich, famous and very fascinating, but, unlike the others, she gloriously succeeded where they had all failed. In November 1963, six months after Malcolm had written to Sheila, asking if he could spend the rest of his life with her, she married him. Her name was Isobel Gray.

# 11
# Dances and Lifeboats
## The Cornish Rhapsody, 1964-67

THERE ARE two different versions of Malcolm's and Isobel's first meeting in the summer of 1963. In one they are both stranded on the same platform at King's Cross Station. They catch each other's eye and, eventually, the same late train. Since Isobel is travelling up to Scotland, to see her family, and Malcolm to a far northern city, to conduct, they have plenty of time to get acquainted. They discover they have a mutual friend, the artist and writer Michael Ayrton. He and Malcolm, exact contemporaries, have shared many a hard-drinking evening at the Savile Club; he and Isobel were briefly lovers, but have now split up.[1]

In the other account they are in a TV studio. Isobel is walking down a corridor, visiting former colleagues at the BBC, when she almost collides head-on with a portly forty-one-year old in white tie and tails, red-faced from conducting on a live TV show. They catch each other's eye, apologise for their narrowly averted collision, and carry on down the corridor, both in the same direction. They discover they have a mutual friend …

Dorothy Payne's diary gives the first definite date in the whirlwind affair. On 16 September, during a visit to Phil and Diane Jones's Emperor's Gate flat, where Malcolm was staying, Dorothy was told he was thinking of marrying 'a school teacher, Isobel Gray'. Less than a month later, on 11 October, Malcolm and Isobel moved into a flat in Hans House, Knightsbridge. And although several friends were warning him not to make a hasty decision, by late October he had decided to ignore their advice and re-marry. Isobel had told him she was pregnant, though this turned out to be a false alarm. 'I've got my foot caught in the door!' Malcolm declared sheepishly in the bar of the Three Horseshoes, Thursley. 'Well, I'm not a shit! I'll have to marry her, won't I!'[2]

The more Malcolm's friends heard about Isobel, the more suitable she sounded. Twenty-nine years-old, tall, dark and pretty, she was strong-willed and vivacious. Brought up on Scotland's south-west coast, the daughter of a sheep

---

[1] Justine Hopkins' biography, *Michael Ayrton*, is dedicated 'To the Ayrton women; a truly remarkable regiment …' Michael Ayrton, a fellow member of the Savile Club, was a particular friend around this time, inscribing his *The Testament of Daedalus* 'For Malcolm with love from Michael, October 1962'.

[2] Tim Holford and Robin Arnold, April 2004

farmer, she had been educated at a Quaker boarding school, Overstone, outside Northampton and, by a strange coincidence, close to where Aubrey and Wyn were living. Isobel was one of Overstone's more lively pupils, even as a twelve-year-old showing a healthy disrespect for petty officialdom, and causing her headmistress to complain to her parents on at least one occasion:

> I am sorry to say that Isobel has been breaking rules and being very greedy over food. She and three other children have actually removed part of the floor in their sitting room and have hidden food underneath – jam tarts, lemonade etc …[3]

The same streak of cheerful independence was observable when Isobel later went up to St Andrew's University to read Modern Languages. There was the occasion, for example, when her father, David Inglis Gray, drove across to Givan Station to pick her up at the end of one term. The train drew in, the steam and smoke all cleared, but Inglis, to his irritation, could see no sign of Isobel. Just a girl with hair dyed an outrageous red. 'Hallo, dad!' smiled Isobel.

The Gray family had made money in shipbuilding, so Isobel's parents were comfortably off, her childhood spent in a large house outside Ballantrae, overlooking the river Stinchar and the rolling Ayrshire countryside.[4] When her parents retired from farming, they moved inland to the quiet market town of Newton Stewart. Isobel loved the Scottish lowlands but as a student regretted the lack of lively company there. On graduation, therefore, she travelled south, taking up a job in London in the Education Department of the BBC. There her social life escalated promisingly, and it was not long before she was romantically involved with Jack de Manio, the radio presenter, who was about to begin his long association with the *Today* programme. The fact that he was nearly twenty years her senior did not matter. He exuded wit and glamour. It was not to be a long friendship, however, and after a sudden parting of the ways Isobel abruptly left the BBC to train as a teacher.

She and Malcolm found they had much in common. Isobel was bright and well-read, capable of solving the *Times* crossword in fifteen minutes. Above all, she matched Malcolm's ebullience. 'She was always ready for a joke,' comments her cousin, Jill Smallshaw. 'She would always be the first person to pull your leg!'[5]

They also shared a love of nature. Malcolm since boyhood had been an expert on spiders and was fascinated by nature all his life. Isobel was an expert on butterflies and birds' eggs and could name virtually every flower and tree. As a girl she had spent hours with her grandmother in her manse in the heart of the Ayrshire countryside and she retained a love of nature all her life.

---

[3] Letter from Helen Wix to Isobel's mother, 10 March 1946
[4] Davaar House. Ballantrae was not as grand as the use of its name by Robert Louis Stevenson has suggested, but just a small fishing village.
[5] August 2003

They both had suffered in their younger days from an over-strict father. On the occasion of Isobel's dyed red hair, for example, her father didn't speak a word to her on the journey home nor, indeed, for some time afterwards. He insisted on regular church attendance on Sundays and he did not allow Isobel to cross her legs at meals, nor to drink water, as it was 'bad for the digestion'. Inglis had served as a Captain in the Home Guard and on one occasion shot himself by accident, causing a scar on his face and some 'selective' deafness. 'He could hear when he wanted to!' comments his niece Jill.

Isobel's mother, Ruby, pursued a similarly strong moral code. Her father had been a Minister and one of her brothers was Headmaster of George Watson's Academy, Edinburgh. Inglis and Ruby were a staid couple for a daughter with a strong taste for fun, Isobel finding communication easier with her uncle and aunt,[6] to whom she brought the first tentative news of Malcolm. Jill remembers:

> There was certainly some family disquiet over the hasty wedding. Isobel came up to Cambridge one weekend to see us. She was unusually quiet all day. Later that evening, in the garden, she suddenly said, 'I've met somebody who I know is going to be the right person for me. You won't have heard of him, but he's in the musical world. His name is Malcolm Arnold.'

Her uncle smilingly went indoors and returned with some of Malcolm's LPs. It seemed a good omen.

On 2 November 1963 Malcolm and Isobel were married quietly at the Guildford Registry Office. Although Malcolm had carefully sought Katherine and Robert's approval, there were no family or close friends present, the witnesses being the Thursley housekeeper and a Polish lady who frequented the Three Horseshoes. Two days before the wedding, Malcolm had written, a little defensively, to Isobel's parents:

> Dear Mr and Mrs Gray,
>
> I am very sorry it has not been possible to meet you before I marry Isobel on Saturday. We will come to Scotland at the earliest possible moment so that I may meet you.
>
> You may feel that this is all very hurried and unsatisfactory but I can only promise you that I will do everything in my power to give Isobel the happiness that such a wonderful person deserves.
>
> Yours Sincerely,
>
> Malcolm Arnold.[7]

There was no time for a honeymoon. At the end of the weekend Malcolm returned to London, where he was now renting a flat in Queensway, Bayswater, close to where he and Sheila had lived in the early years of their marriage. He was still working on the interminable *Espionage* series and was also involved as a presenter and conductor in a new series of the popular television arts

---

[6] Jill Smallshaw's parents.
[7] 31 October 1963. The Grays were living at Linloggan Cottage, Newton Stewart.

programme *Gala Performance*. From the introduction given in the *Radio Times* the show would seem to be based around Malcolm's own philosophy:

> 'Why treat good music as sacred? Why not enjoy it? Let's knock out the pomposity and have fun.' So says Richard Attenborough and the sentiment is echoed by two friends – Malcolm Arnold and Julian Bream. Together the three form a resident team talking about the music and introducing the stars in Gala Performance – starting tonight this series will have the world's greatest artists and singers, dancers, pianists and other instrumentalists bringing you the best loved classics.[8]

In the first, live programme[9] Malcolm conducted the Philharmonia Orchestra as Margot Fonteyn and Rudolf Nureyev danced excerpts from *Swan Lake* and Khachaturian's *Gayaneh*. Joan Hammond sang an aria and György Cziffra played some Chopin, while Julian Bream and Malcolm combined on the last movement of the Guitar Concerto. The programme went out on the BBC's single channel at peak viewing time, sandwiched between *The Lucy Show* and *Maigret*. Opera and ballet were strongly represented throughout the series, the next programme featuring Geraint Evans, followed by Galina Samsova dancing excerpts from *Cinderella*.

Towards the end of November Malcolm and Isobel made a 24-hour visit to Scotland to meet her parents. All went well, Malcolm's letter of thanks suggesting he had successfully circumvented every social hazard:

> Dear Mr and Mrs Gray,
>
> Thank you very much for your kindness and generosity. It was wonderful to meet you in such friendly and enjoyable circumstances.
>
> We had a very good flight back and managed to get a taxi straight away, arriving home before six o'clock.
>
> As I know you realise, I love Isobel more than anybody I have ever met and will do everything I can to make her happy.
>
> Thank you again,
> With love,
> from
> Malcolm

Isobel was well versed in the artistic temperament but even she was taken aback in her first year of marriage at Thursley by the pace of Malcolm's life and the obsessional extremes of work and play. When writing music, he shut himself away in a special extension he had had built onto the side of the house, a completely self-sufficient area with bed and bathroom, and a hatch through which food could be passed without comment, to frustrate his garrulous house-keeper, Mrs Winter. When not writing, he was down at The Three Horseshoes all the hours it was open, offering champagne to all-comers and, from time to time, impressive trumpet solos. He was a Thursley legend. On New Year's Eve,

---

[8] 14 November 1963
[9] 19 November 1963

exasperated by lack of numbers in the pub, he went round the village attracting attention on his trumpet and exhorting support of the Three Horseshoes. On coming out of solitary confinement at the end of a film score, he traditionally put on a pair of funny spectacles, climbed onto the bottom of a lamp post outside the house and blew a fanfare to announce the beginning of revels, even if it were the middle of the night. One summer's day he threw a party at a time when paper clothes were the latest novelty. All the ladies were given paper swimsuits, which, at his insistence and with some misgivings, they donned. They were right to be anxious. No sooner had the last paper swimsuit been put on than Malcolm rushed to the sprinkler, directed it at his unfortunate guests and guffawed in delight as the paper quickly disintegrated.

The first months of marriage represented Isobel's best opportunity of establishing a proper footing for family life, and although she herself enjoyed much of the fun and was not disposed to criticise, she did her best to counter Malcolm's excesses. It was not easy. Sheila, who had failed before her in this, at least was his contemporary, whereas Malcolm was twelve years older than Isobel and set in his ways.

It didn't help that Malcolm was often away on film commitments[10] and was at other times anxious to take her away, sharing his love of foreign travel and grand hotels. In February they enjoyed a late honeymoon in Tangiers and, in May, two weeks in Paris.[11] They also visited Scotland, where Isobel shared with her parents the good news that she was pregnant. But the most important holiday of all, just a month before the birth of the baby, was one spent in Cornwall.

Isobel had grown to dislike Thursley, realising that there were too many bad influences and traditions. London likewise was full of seductive watering-holes and fair-weather friends. With the baby soon due, it was distressing when Malcolm, after disappearing for two days, rang her up to say he'd mislaid the Fiat, which she later heard from the police was causing an obstruction in Soho. So that June, when down in Cornwall, Isobel seized her opportunity, persuading Malcolm that, as he loved Cornwall so much, they should move there.

Shortly afterwards, in mid-July, the baby was born and named Edward Isaak.[12] 'Much nicer than most newborn babies' was Dorothy's comment, after her first visit, and 'Baby most presentable' after her second. A month later Dorothy discovered that their plans for Cornwall were well advanced:

---

[10] In February 1964 Malcolm was recording the soundtrack of *The Thin Red Line*. By then he had virtually completed his commitment to the *Espionage* TV series.

[11] In Paris Isobel had a chance to use her French, but it was a little rusty, and they were taken by taxi on their arrival not to their hotel but the British Embassy. Malcolm dined out on the story.

[12] Malcolm invited Katherine and Robert to help with names. Katherine chose Edward after Edward Bear and Robert chose Isaak after Isaak Walton.

> Went to Thursley. Found MA moody. I don't think he is really pleased about the move
> to Cornwall.[13]

There was some stress at Thursley in those final months of 1964, with Malcolm's
moodiness continuing. But Katherine has happy memories of a visit there to see
her new half-brother.

> I was curious about the strange situation, but Isobel was so generous and kind to us
> and Mum had explained to us carefully why she couldn't continue with Dad, that I
> accepted that their marriage was over. I also always felt my relationship with Dad was
> special and would survive anything. I suspect now I was not alone in thinking this, for
> he had this very wonderful ability to make people feel they were special. He could be
> very seductive. He was my Dad and the best Dad there was, and I believed it! So visits
> to the new family at Thursley were good, really.[14]

Having briefly seen and admired the baby, Katherine was ushered downstairs and
stayed there most of the day with her father and Isobel. The baby was left upstairs
by himself, only visited at four-hourly intervals to be fed. Unlike most newborn
children, little Edward was not the family's focal point.

This was partly because Malcolm, with his fears of inadequacy and need to
be liked, was very possessive, demanding to be the centre of Isobel's attention;
but he was also working again, having restarted just before Edward was born.[15]
In the weeks immediately after the birth, he completed two important commissions: the Five Pieces for Violin and Piano, for Yehudi Menuhin, and his *Third
Sinfonietta*, for the New Philharmonia Orchestra. Menuhin, who had the greatest
admiration and affection for Malcolm, had asked some time previously for a set
of encore pieces, and a month before Edward's birth had sent a gentle reminder:

> I haven't forgotten about you: I hope you haven't forgotten about me …

The two had subsequently joined forces at the Victoria and Albert Museum for
the first London performance of the Double Concerto,[16] and three weeks after
Edward's birth the Five Pieces were completed. Although Menuhin courteously
called them 'charming,'[17] they proved an oddly amorphous collection.

They begin with a dissonant Prelude, erroneously marked *Con energico*. ('It
is either *con energia* or *energico*,' corrected Menuhin cautiously, 'or, if you like,

---

[13] 18 August 1964

[14] March 2004

[15] Two short, bright works: ten minutes of cheerful *Water Music* for the National Trust (to be
played in the open air to celebrate the opening of a canal at Stratford-upon-Avon) and a two-
minute *Sunshine Overture* (now lost) for ballerina Beryl Grey and her charity, the Sunshine
Home for Blind Babies.

[16] 17 June 1964. Arthur Bliss and Michael Tippett also conducted their own work at this
concert.

[17] On receipt. After playing them in public for the first time he wrote to Malcolm: 'The Five
Pieces were a great success and both Ivor Newton and I enjoyed playing them.' (26 July
1965)

*molto energico, energia* being the noun and *energico* the adjective.')[18] There followed an *Aubade*, based on an Indian raga of no obvious melodic merit, a strange, ghostly Waltz, and a Ballad taken directly from the final *pas de deux* of *Rinaldo and Armida*. Other-worldly and strongly cinematic, the languid melody sounds very well on the violin and proves the highlight of the work, but the borrowing suggests Malcolm was short of time or inspiration. The final piece, *Moto Perpetuo*, dedicated to the saxophonist and heroin-addict, Charlie Parker, is bright and breezy, a fine opportunity for virtuosity, but it bears no obvious kinship with its four companions. The Five Pieces[19] serve their purpose as crowd-pleasers but lack an overall coherence. For once Malcolm failed to communicate.

The *Third Sinfonietta*, completed at Thursley on 1 September 1964 and virtually the last music of any kind Malcolm was to write for nearly a year,[20] is far more sombre than the first two *Sinfonietta*s, it never quite managing to shake off its initial expression of anxious regret. The opening *Allegro Vivace* has a haunted, graveyard feel, with all manner of gremlins appearing as the nightmare proceeds. The second movement, *Vivace*, tries to have fun, but the merriment is splintered into fragments and in the end solemnity wins. The *Andante* is hushed, plaintive and full of regret. At one stage one of Malcolm's 'big' romantic tunes nearly makes an appearance, but it gets interrupted and though the strings eventually throw off their inhibitions and sing out their feelings, the bitter-sweet atmosphere remains, the movement ending quietly, in deep uncertainty. In the final *Allegro* (*con energico,* as Menuhin will have noted) a sardonic march frames a weird passage of confusion and melodic fragmentation. There are slight hints of the cheeky *Beckus*, but if the Dandipratt is around, he is older, wiser and decidedly world-weary.

The advent of a new wife and child hardly seemed to be the moment for such gloomy introspection. In the *Third Sinfonietta* Malcolm is looking backwards at the recent past, purging his soul of the chaotic, selfish last two years before the advent of Isobel, briefly showing us something of his real self, that inner five per cent.

His public image remained falsely glossy. There is no sign of the writer of the *Third Sinfonietta* in a contemporary pen portrait:

---

[18] In a letter of 9 July 1965 Menuhin tells of the coming first performance of the Five Pieces at Bamburgh Castle, Northumberland. 'I don't suppose there's any chance of your coming up – it is not a very great occasion, but it would always serve as a good excuse to be together again (you might even conduct them if you like ...)'

[19] Completed at Thursley on 8 August.

[20] Hugo Cole persuaded him to write a short duo for two cellos for his book *Playing the Cello* (completed 5 January 1965), and he wrote short solo fantasies for bassoon, clarinet, horn, flute and oboe for the City of Birmingham Symphony Orchestra's International Wind Competition of May 1966. These are not works on which he would have expended much time. The theme he wrote for a John Player's cigarettes advert, sometimes attributed to 1965, was in fact written three years earlier.

Malcolm Arnold is 42. Large, plump and jolly, he is always laughing, always bubbling over with humour and high spirits. He is the sort of person who might stand next to you at a football match, or wash his car next door on a Sunday morning.[21]

It was only half the picture. In this unsettled period before the move to Cornwall Malcolm even managed to wreck his long friendship with Philip and Diane Jones. They had been having dinner at Bertorelli's after a hard day in the recording studio, Malcolm in quixotic mood, confiding to his friends, out of Isobel's earshot, that he regretted getting married, yet spending much of the dinner holding her hand under the table, seemingly seraphically happy. Diane Jones, always anxious not to take advantage of Malcolm's generosity, had quietly suggested to Philip that they should settle the bill that evening. Malcolm overheard and took immediate offence. He later rang them up to express, insultingly, how insulted he was. The next day Malcolm's temper had still not abated. A further abusive phone-call followed, but, even though he apologised afterwards, and would ring them up occasionally from Cornwall, the friendship never revived.[22] It was particularly sad as Philip and Diane had done much to support and protect him.[23]

There was a less dramatic parting with another great ally, Dorothy Payne, Malcolm's secretary over the past eight years, who ceased working for him on his move to Cornwall.[24] Isobel had secretarial skills herself, and Dorothy's role had steadily diminished during 1964. In late September she wrote:

> Drove to Thursley for last time, and drove MA on to Punch Bowl where he had oysters and I had smoked salmon.

In December he was still occasionally turning up on her doorstep with a batch of letters. The last diary entry smacks of anti-climax:

> Waited all morning for Malcolm, who finally phoned that he was not coming.

Dorothy gradually lost touch, although each Christmas for several years she received a large hamper from Fortnum and Mason. Her devotion to him had been unwavering.

Malcolm and Isobel moved to Cornwall in early January 1965, fourteen months into their marriage.[25] Primrose Cottage, which they had bought from the

---

[21] *Music Magazine*, May 1964

[22] Ironically, when Philip finally retired, he and Diane themselves moved down to Cornwall, but Malcolm and Isobel had just moved away.

[23] But for their intervention, for example, John Freeman would have interviewed Malcolm in his live television show, *Face to Face*. His unscripted interviews were famous for their mercilessly searching questions. He had reduced the television celebrity Gilbert Harding to tears and could have made a public spectacle of Malcolm just as easily.

[24] She and her husband moved to Sussex shortly afterwards, later opening a Donkey Sanctuary near Eastbourne.

[25] A change-of-address card states 'as from 23 February 1965', but letters were being written to and from Primrose Cottage by the beginning of that month. A move in several phases, therefore, seems to have taken place with January a likely conjecture for the first move.

writer James Turner[26] and where they were to live for the next seven years, was just outside the village of St Merryn, two and a half miles from Padstow. Built in the 1650s, as three small homes for farm labourers, Primrose Cottage stands by itself, at right angles to a narrow, winding lane, its façade of white-washed pebble-dash nestling unobtrusively in green rolling hills, the sea just out of sight half a mile away.

Their new home was so remotely situated that it has been suggested the move to Cornwall was made to hide Edward's autism. This cannot have been the case. Edward was only seven months old at the time, his autism not yet obvious.[27] And the family did not hide away. In 1965, for example, Malcolm took both Isobel and Edward all the way to Aldeburgh. A friend remembers Malcolm's pride in his new family:

> It was a good time for Malcolm. He had emerged from a period of much uncertainty. There was new hope. He loved Edward dearly. Really loved him. When the family came across to Aldeburgh you could see the marriage was working well; there was much optimism.[28]

Primrose Cottage is only a mile away from Newtrain Bay where Malcolm and Sheila had holidayed for so many summers. Isobel shrewdly saw the importance of Malcolm re-establing links with that part of the past which had given him most happiness. He felt keenly the loss of Katherine and Robert, still with Sheila in Denbigh Gardens. By living near to the Bryn, he would, in a way, still be near to them. And also to Sheila. Like a Berlioz *idée fixe*, Sheila, or part of her, would be with him the rest of his life. However hard Isobel might work over the next few years for his happiness, she would always be competing with the ideal woman of his romantic imagination, pure rather than sexual, intelligent but undemanding, always warmly approving and utterly supportive. For the moment the ideal centred on the Sheila of his college years, the English rose, handing out political pamphlets with him with virginal sweetness. He loved Isobel, up to a point, and appreciated her qualities, but she was too modern and liberated ever to begin to approach this ideal of perfect womanhood.

Both at once agreed, however, on the good sense of their move, liking the simplicity of life at St Merryn, an unremarkable cluster of houses and shops where two minor roads happened to cross, and loving the quaint charm of its busy next-door neighbour, Padstow. The Farmer's Arms, sited anonymously within the cluster, was already the hub of the village before Malcolm's arrival

---

[26] His interests included gardening, ghosts, the countryside and martyrdom. His first volume of autobiography, *Seven Gardens for Catherine*, told of his experiences as a gardener, writer and poet. (1968)

[27] Dorothy's diaries show clearly that by August 1964, a month after Edward's birth, the decision was taken to move to Cornwall. And they were in the Padstow area, finalising the move, in late September. (Malcolm's copy of John Betjeman's *A Shell Guide to Cornwall* is inscribed 'Padstow, 29 September 1964'.)

[28] Martin Kingsbury, formerly Assistant Director, Faber Music, July 2003

spread its fame even further. Isobel's hopes that Malcolm would lead a more sober existence away from London and the Home Counties were quickly dashed. Today, over thirty years since they left the area, Malcolm is still vividly remembered by many of the older members of the community:

> There were plenty of big sessions in The Farmer's Arms. He was great friends with the landlord, Derek Cripps, who was also a farmer. He used to put money behind the bar – £60 or £70, which was a lot of money in those days.

> Isobel sometimes came out and drank with him. Not often, though.

> He liked nothing better than to get people to sing. Sometimes he'd go from one pub to another, starting a song in each.

> When word got out – and it used to spread like lightning – 'Malcolm's out!' – people would come rushing out of Padstow and all over the place to join in. He loved having a lot of followers.

> He liked the pretty girls, know what I mean? He had his favourites. But mostly they knew how to handle him. There wasn't any trouble.

> He could be aggressive and loud – embarrassing. He did have that side of him. But he was a lovely person, really. He knocked over one of the petrol pumps at the St Merryn garage one evening. 'Awfully sorry,' he said. 'I've knocked over your pump. Here's a cheque for a new one!'

> He used to drive in first gear only when he was worse for wear. One night it took him three hours to get back from Padstow.

Malcolm soon became well-known in Padstow itself, a familiar figure in most of the pubs and better restaurants. He loved the sights and sounds of the sea; the wit and wisdom of fishermen in smoky bars; the cries of the boatyards, the smell of the lobster pots; the seafood shops with their laden counters of skate, turbot and Dover sole; the view across the wind-swept Camel estuary to John Betjeman's Rock; the bobbing boats in the harbour, winking up at the rows of slate-hung houses in delight at the swelling tide. When he fell off the Padstow quayside one day and broke his arm, he took it in very good heart.

For all his joy in Cornwall, however, Malcolm was to have long absences away. Very soon after the wedding Dorothy had commented with surprise on how little Malcolm seemed to stay at home, and this was to continue throughout the marriage. At the beginning of 1965, for example, he embarked on a typically elaborate odyssey: a week in Manchester, conducting the BBC Northern Symphony orchestra; a TV interview[29] in London; a concert at Croydon, conducting the New Philharmonia; and a discussion at the Savile Club with representatives of the newly-founded publishing house, Faber Music.

---

[29] A contribution to *In Search of Constant Lambert*, recorded at Hornsey Town Hall, for which he was paid 25 guineas.

The move to Faber came after a disagreement with Michael Diack, his friend and publisher for the past twelve years at Paterson.[30] Faber Music, formed to publish the work of Benjamin Britten after his parting with Boosey & Hawkes, were in the process of enlarging their list, and Donald Mitchell, the firm's Managing Director and long an admirer of Malcolm's work, saw him as an important acquisition:

> We had an extremely agreeable lunch in posh surroundings – we consumed quite a few glasses of something or other – Malcolm insisted on being the host, so one's glass did not remain unfilled for long.[31]

The lunch went on most of the afternoon, with Malcolm 'big-hearted and big-spirited', and the stories flowed:

> He was immensely proud of all his forebears, not least the great William Hawes. His reticence about his immediate family was in marked contrast to his expansiveness about those further removed.[32]

Later Donald Mitchell walked somewhat dazedly with Malcolm through Soho.

> We'd been looking at the score of the Double Concerto. His agreement to come to Faber was signed and sealed on the back of the score. We wrote it and signed it in the street!

Donald Mitchell was to become an important steadying influence, one of the few people to whom Malcolm would always listen with care. Though younger than Malcolm, he at once took on the role of the wise elder brother. Contacting Malcolm the next day, he employed a calm, authoritative tone:

> I am going to have a close look at the double violin concerto and shall be writing again to you about it within the next few days. Meanwhile I should be very grateful if you could think about the piano reduction and perhaps let me know how soon we might be able to have this from you …
>
> We shall meet again soon to discuss the future in rather less elating though I hope no less amiable circumstances …

Malcolm, back in St Merryn, promised to do the piano reduction 'when I have finished the work I have on hand at the moment'.[33]

In reality he had little work in hand, other than preliminary thoughts on a new, sixth symphony, for which he had no commission. He was focused on the possibility of doing more conducting, not just of his own works but the full classical repertoire. In this he had initially been helped by Paul Huband, Head of Music at BBC North in Manchester, but it was his successor, David Ellis, who was instrumental in starting off Malcolm's wider conducting brief, which lasted

---

[30] Of Malcolm's more recent work Diack had published the Little Suite No 2, the *Third Sinfonietta*, the *Water Music* and the Five Pieces, but he seems to have jibbed at the Double Violin Concerto, thinking it unlikely to attract many performances.

[31] August 2003. The meeting took place on 2 February 1965.

[32] July 2003

[33] 11 February 1965

throughout his years in Cornwall. Every year Malcolm would make a couple of week-long visits to Manchester, as David Ellis remembers:

> He would usually do one public concert, and, if possible, I would also organise one studio broadcast before an invited audience, just to get him used to the public again. He loved coming to Manchester and staying in the Midland Hotel! [34] They adored him too! As soon as they knew he was coming the staff were galvanized into action. Partly, of course, because he was a very generous guest. When the week was over, he'd be bundled in the overnight train, the Manchester-Penzance sleeper. They looked after him as well on the train as they did at the Midland. [35]

Malcolm's experience as an orchestral player was very helpful as he developed his conducting career. David Ellis thought him more concerned with practicalities than niceties.

> The orchestra knew they couldn't play any tricks on him, because in his time he'd played them all himself. He was extremely professional and essentially undemanding. He'd listen to them and then say, 'Yes, that sounds good. Just tweak it a bit at bar so and so.' Or 'Keep your eye on me at Figure 27. OK. Lunch!' He would always be a welcome visitor, because he was reliable. He never went on overlong and they knew they would have a good time musically and socially.

Malcolm had assimilated much of the conductor's art as a student playing under Constant Lambert. David Ellis saw the similarities between them:

> When Lambert set a tempo, that *was* the tempo, and you knew exactly where you were going. There was nothing airy-fairy about it. And although he set the tempo firmly he was still very flexible with the interpretation. Malcolm conducted along those lines. He also hugely admired the undemonstrative Jascha Horenstein. I once said to Horenstein, 'Jascha, whenever you come to Manchester, you always make the orchestra sound different. Yet you don't *do* anything! You just stand there!' Jascha coughed modestly. 'Ah well,' he said. 'It's all in the tempo.' That's what the orchestra *most* needs. They can then concentrate on making a nice sound. And Malcolm knew that.

Another conductor Malcolm had admired when a player was Hans Knappertsbusch, one of the elder statesmen of German music after the war, especially respected for his interpretations of Wagner and Richard Strauss. After his death in November 1965 Malcolm wrote a tribute in *The Times*:

> Some time between 1945 and 1948 Professor Knappertsbusch came to London to record with the London Philharmonic Orchestra, during which time I was its principal trumpet. He had the unique gift of being able to convey the most subtle inflections to his players by the movement of his hands, and he was able to obtain the finest performances possible, although rarely speaking a word at rehearsal.
>
> Over a period of a fortnight, recording seven hours a day, the excellent results he achieved with what seemed so little fuss, and with such a human approach to his players, were a revelation …[36]

---

[34] Now the Crowne Plaza Midland Hotel
[35] August, 2003
[36] 4 November 1965

Malcolm would have been attracted by both the brevity of the Knappertsbusch rehearsals and his strong sense of humour. He would tell with delight of the time Knappertsbusch was at Bayreuth, conducting with Karajan. There were just two lavatories at the end of a long corridor backstage and Karajan's PA, it is said, put up a notice on one: 'For the exclusive use of Herr Karajan'. An hour later a notice appeared on the other one, written by Knappertsbusch: 'For all the other arseholes.'[37]

Although Malcolm admired the undemonstrative approach of conductors like Knappertsbusch, he was not of that school himself. William Mann likened him to 'an impatient tic-tac man on a racecourse' and a rock'n'roll guitarist with thrusting pelvis.[38] The excitement of the occasion to which William Mann was referring, the première of the *Third Sinfonietta*, may have elicited an extra bounce. It was an early example of Malcolm's widening conducting role. In addition to the *Sinfonietta* and two other works of his own, *Beckus the Dandipratt* and the First Flute Concerto,[39] he conducted Berlioz's *Symphonie Fantastique* and, in memory of Winston Churchill who had just died, Walton's *Spitfire Prelude and Fugue*. The Berlioz was 'magnificently successful' and the applause 'prolonged'. In the Walton 'the audience stood, unbidden, and listened to a scintillating performance'.[40]

Malcolm needed the applause. Fortified by it, he was able to cope with the musical establishment's ever increasing cynicism towards him. The critics were having more and more fun at his expense. The *Daily Telegraph*, for example, wrote sneeringly of the admirable *Third Sinfonietta*:

> Even where he has a striking melodic idea Arnold is apt to keep on at it so persistently that, brief as his movements always are, they seem longer in proportion to their subject matter than Bruckner at his most expansive.

William Mann, a former friend, described the final movement of the *Third Sinfonietta* as 'the *locus classicus* of sound without musical content'.[41] William Walton, who knew all about critical malevolence, tried to be supportive:

> I was pleased and proud to [hear] about your conducting the Spitfire music and that it made such an impression ... I was furious to read what the damn fool of a critic said about your new piece. They are really insufferable – all of them ... [42]

---

[37] John Amis, April 2003

[38] *The Times*, 1 February 1965. The concert was at the Fairfield Hall, Croydon.

[39] The soloist, Gareth Morris, was a central figure in the administration of the orchestra.

[40] *Croydon Advertiser*, 5 February 1965

[41] 1 February 1965. Critics of the period struggled with Malcolm's abrupt mood changes. The material in the short final movement (of A-B-A construction) is tautly, if unconventionally, argued. The sardonic march comes to a sudden halt, as if by an explosion, the central section offering only fragments of melody, fluttering around in the air like debris. When the march reappears, it has become slower, harsher and vulnerable. To deny the movement 'musical content' is to say black is white.

[42] 20 February 1965. Hayes (ed.): *The Selected Letters of William Walton* (Faber & Faber, 2002), p.351

Not *all* of them. *The Guardian*'s Hugo Cole wrote perceptively of a more mature Malcolm now emerging, less concerned at attracting the listener's approval:

> The new Sinfonietta suggests that Arnold is perhaps tiring of his allotted role of enter-
> tainer: the entertainer must always work with at least one ear sharply tuned to his
> particular audience; he must carry the listener with him at all costs, even at the price
> of labouring the obvious. This is the line Arnold has taken in his 'public' works
> (Beethoven did the same in his symphonies.)
>
> The Sinfonietta is, I think, less concerned with audience reaction; although
> the tone of voice is still easy and conversational, its themes tend to be fragmented,
> there are none of the rambling, easy-going tunes of the popular works; the range of
> dissonance is wider, and developments are more likely to follow unconventional
> routes. At a first hearing the two quick movements seemed to understay their welcome
> – as though various inhibitory processes were at work. What is certain is that the
> music is not functioning on the usual Arnoldian timescale ...[43]

In 1965 Malcolm conducted an entire Promenade Concert for the first time. It was a long programme: in addition to the *Scottish Dances*[44] there were Berlioz's *Roman Carnival* overture, Grieg's Piano Concerto, Ravel's *Rapsodie Espagnole*, Debussy's *Prélude à l'Après-midi d'un Faune* and Tchaikovsky's Third Symphony. And it was a huge success, receiving excellent notices:

> The great surprise of the season was the emergence of Malcolm Arnold as a
> conductor. In a colourful and expressive programme he recreated with admittedly
> rather uncomfortable gestures the sheer physical delights of orchestral sound, and
> offered a pleasure and impact which reminded one of the now legendary Beecham
> Popular concerts.

The Prommers would not let Malcolm or the London Symphony Orchestra off the platform at the end.

> This reception was justly earned, for the orchestral playing was of the highest
> standard throughout the evening, and Arnold's interpretations were pungent as well as
> subtle.[45]

Malcolm, unfortunately, was carried away with all the applause and did his relationship with the BBC little good when he demanded more money, 100 guineas, for this appearance. Memos written in high dudgeon scurried around Broadcasting House. The decisive one declared:

> Glock agrees with extreme reluctance. Perhaps you would get in touch with Arnold
> and say that we agree to pay the 100 guineas which he demands providing it is made
> up in the way I have indicated below:

---

[43] 1 February 1965
[44] Receiving their second Proms performance. This popular work, however, was not to be heard again in the next forty seasons.
[45] The first comments are from *The Strad*, October 1965, the second from the *Glasgow Herald*.

|                      |               |
|---------------------:|:--------------|
| Basic fee:           | £60           |
| Sound relay:         | £30           |
| Fare:                | £6 14s 0d     |
| 3 nights' subsistence: | £8 14s 0d   |
| Total:               | £105 8s 0d    |

By contrast, Malcolm was happy to be paid only modestly to participate in the European Summer School for Young Musicians, held in 1965 in the Vienna Woods, because Katherine was going to be there. Each year the organiser, John Davies, Professor of the Clarinet the Royal Academy of Music, invited a famous composer to join his staff.[46] He began to realise there were going to be problems with Malcolm as early as their first meeting, which took place, at Malcolm's insistence, at one of his favourite hotels, the Gore, not far from the Albert Hall. They met for lunch. Malcolm, after a couple of quick straight whiskies, drank a bottle of red and a bottle of white wine during the meal and, as they took effect, became loud-mouthed and overbearing. Afterwards they retired to an elegant, crowded sitting room, where Malcolm, having loudly insisted 'I'll be mother!', succeeded in pouring most of the contents of a tea-pot over their table. 'Oh! Bugger it!' he yelled, stopping nearby conversations. John Davies found the whole meeting something of a trial, never having before experienced such an extrovert and unmanageable personality: 'I suspect he had always got his own way. It certainly showed!'[47]

The course took place at a famous concert hall, the Theatre of Wien at Modling, south of Vienna. Katherine loved the beauty of her surroundings but was uncomfortable to find herself in an orchestra including high-quality players like Simon Rattle and Julian Lloyd Webber. It had always been taken for granted by her parents that she was musical. After rejecting the violin, and a not altogether happy experience with the piano, she had graduated from the recorder to the flute, on which she achieved more competence than confidence, as she recalls:

> I was simply muddling through, hoping it wouldn't be discovered that I couldn't really play the challenging passages. I really didn't know what I was doing! But people expected great things of me! I sang in school choirs and liked that. But the flute, to be honest, was a miserable experience. But I dared not let on! The result of all this pressure was that for periods afterwards I found I just couldn't listen to music![48]

The course included a visit on a hot summer's day to Esterháza, where Haydn lived as Kapellmeister to his patrons, the Princes Esterházy. Malcolm, who had long felt a special affinity for Haydn, delighted in going around the sights with Katherine. And, strangely, he felt he knew the place intimately:

---

[46] Other professors on the ESSYM courses included Sydney Harrison, John Gardner, Wesley Woodage, Amaryllis Fleming, Gareth Morris and Rodney Slatford.
[47] April 2003
[48] August 2003

I'd never been there before, and yet I seemed to know it. I said to my daughter 'This is his theatre!' And it was! She said 'How do you know, dad?' [49]

There were many less happy days, however, for Malcolm found the local wines very much to his taste. 'There was hardly a moment when he wasn't drunk,' comments John Davies, 'and when he was sober, he was very edgy and not at all easy.' [50] Julian Lloyd Webber agrees: 'He was always drunk on the course, and went out drinking much more than the students. But he was surprisingly frisky (if unfit) in the mornings.' [51] There were many moments of extreme embarrassment for Katherine.

> I had a close friend on the course with me and Dad kept proposing to her and making a big thing of it. Whether he thought he was being funny in doing this, I don't know. But it shook me to see what absurd things he could do.

Julian Lloyd Webber remembers him upsetting Katherine by going up to other students and saying 'Do you fancy my daughter?'

> He would then tell Katherine what they had said and she, desperately embarrassed, would run off.

The course was to culminate in a concert where Malcolm would conduct Dvořák's Eighth Symphony and his own Second. To publicise this event, John Davies had persuaded the local television company to film the final rehearsal, which took place in the open air, in the park beside the concert hall. Around mid-day everyone was ready, except Malcolm of whom there was no sign. Messages were carried swiftly to the Two Ravens Inn, where he was thought to be relaxing. Eventually, after a long wait, he emerged, clearly the worse for drink.

With the cameras rolling, he succeeded in starting off well, but unfortunately became too enthusiastic on one upbeat and toppled off the rostrum and on to his back. Legend has it that he carried on conducting with his feet, though in fact a member of the television crew took over for the rest of the filming. Malcolm was later locked in his room, but tried hard to smash it open. John Davies meanwhile spent a long time persuading the television company not to include any of the incident in their broadcast. Poor Katherine was mortified. The next day she tearfully declined to leave her room.

The sadness of the whole episode was accentuated by Malcolm's wonderful support of the students when he was not incapacitated, as Julian Lloyd Webber remembers:

> He was very kind to me on the course, giving me great encouragement. He even allowed me to play through the Saint-Saëns Cello Concerto, the first time I had ever played solo with an orchestra. We all loved the slow movement of his Second

---

[49] Interviewed by Peter Paul Nash, Radio Norfolk, 1991
[50] April 2003
[51] July 2003

Symphony. It stands well against Shostakovich. As young players we struggled to understand some of the strange juxtapositions of different moods, the almost schizophrenic quality that is often there in his music.

The heavy drinking in Austria occurred eight months after the move to Cornwall, a period in which Malcolm had written no music at all. Isobel had organised for him an attractive study at the far end of the top floor of Primrose Cottage, its three windows looking out over the garden and pleasant fields. But he was in too exalted a frame of mind to settle down to writing, until, eventually, the quiet charm of John Mills coaxed him back to work. *Sky West and Crooked*, the story of a mentally retarded girl who runs away to the gypsies, did not particularly appeal to Malcolm, but ever since *Whistle Down The Wind* he had become devoted to the Mills family, and not only was John producing and directing, but the screenplay was written by his wife, Mary Hayley Bell, and Hayley herself was starring. When he completed a fine score in October 1965, Mary Hayley Bell sent him by way of celebration her latest book, *Far Morning*, an allegory on major human questions: birth, death, suffering, compassion and eternity. It was more an act of love than a thank-you, Mary realising that Malcolm's problems stemmed from an inner disquiet. Helped over his block by the warmth of the Mills family, Malcolm quickly completed three more films,[52] thereby re-establishing his precarious finances.

Two weeks after completing *Sky West and Crooked* Malcolm was in a pub with some of the crew of the Padstow lifeboat when they were called out on an emergency. The subsequent rescue of two fishermen from a stricken, rudderless vessel, shipping water in mountainous seas, left a deep impression on Malcolm. It was a three-hour operation carried out in a force eleven storm and thick November mists, for which the coxswain, Gordon Elliott, was later awarded a silver medal for gallantry.[53] Malcolm promised him a piece of music, but nothing immediately materialised.

Isobel was disappointed that Malcolm was struggling to write music in Cornwall, but kept these feelings to herself. Unlike Sheila, she made no effort to discourage the drinking, trying to keep up with it rather than fight it. 'It was probably a slightly more successful approach,' comments Robert, 'though it was all relative. But it did lead to her getting through quite a lot of cook's sherry down in Cornwall, while the cigarette consumption must have been up to around 50-a-day.'

A very enthusiastic gardener, Isobel made much of the small, secluded cottage garden. There was a flourishing greenhouse and Edward was bought his own playhouse, swing, paddling pool and any number of outdoor toys. Plans were already afoot for building over the detached double garage to create an

---

[52] *The Heroes of Telemark*, *The Great St Trinian's Train Robbery* and another film starring John Mills, *Africa – Texas Style*.

[53] *Lifeboat Story* (1967). The rescue took place on 25 November 1965.

extra guest bedroom. Perhaps partly out of self-defence – for Malcolm would behave a little better when guests were around – family and friends were warmly encouraged to come and stay.

Isobel tried hard to encourage Katherine and Robert to holiday with them, knowing how much Malcolm rejoiced at their visits. 'Isobel had been immediately kind to me from the very first meeting,' remembers Robert. By now he had won a scholarship to St Paul's and would stay at the Cottage with his friends in his school summer holidays whenever he could. 'I would go by train and Dad would meet me at Bodmin…' Robert as a young boy had nursed ambitions to be a lighthouse keeper and loved the sea. He would regularly go fishing at Padstow with one of his father's friends, Tom Morrissey, 'a lovely man who was also a folk singer and marine artist, and very witty'. As it was important to catch the early tide Malcolm would drive Robert across to Padstow at the crack of dawn and would return mid-afternoon to meet the incoming fishing boat.

> Every single day I stayed there with him, Dad would chauffeur me without ever complaining! He enjoyed seeing the boats and the early morning activity, but how he recovered the rest of the day after that I cannot imagine! He was often greeted on the quay by yells of 'What's up, Malcolm, shat the bed?' and such like, in a strong Cornish accent.[54]

Intent on identifying himself as much as possible with the local community, Malcolm bought a beautiful 14ft clinker dinghy with a three-sided sail and an outboard motor. It was kept on a moored ring at Padstow harbour and looked after by an old man who worked on the quayside. Malcolm would use it occasionally to go bass fishing with friends in the estuary. For Robert it offered further holiday pleasures:

> I used to use the boat for sailing and sometimes mackerel fishing and plankton trawling. Back in the cottage afterwards I would use his music writing desk to examine the catch.

On one occasion an expedition in the dinghy with his father almost ended in tragedy:

> We went out together towards the island at the mouth of the River Camel. The tide was falling, there were offshore winds, and we were caught out by the conditions. It was entirely my misjudgement, as Dad did not take much notice of practical details! We got carried out and were having to bail out all the time with heavy seas breaking over us, and the engine spluttering. Dad was fairly annoyed, not with me so much as with having lost overboard one of his smart new Italian slip-on shoes which he had been using as a bailer. We had already lost our proper bailer. Eventually we ended up in a bay about two miles down the estuary.

Safely back on shore but soaked to the skin, they had to walk ingloriously back along the cliff path to Padstow, Malcolm squelching along in his one remaining shoe.

---

[54] February 2004

We got told off by various lifeboatmen and fishermen for our dangerous stupidity in going out on a falling tide. The lifeboat crew arranged to tow the dinghy back to the harbour.

Malcolm always took a great delight in being with the young, and continued to keep a fatherly eye on Robin, Aubrey's son. He, his wife Avril and their two babies all stayed in the cottage over Christmas 1965. Arriving on Isobel's birthday they stayed up all night to celebrate, drinking port.

It was an enjoyable Christmas. Malcolm showed them round the cottage and vicinity with great pride, pointing out the various Michael Ayrton paintings and bronzes, sharing his collection of books on Cornwall and playing for them on his prized possession, a clavichord specially made for him by Thomas Goff, a reconstruction of the soft-timbred eighteenth-century keyboard which Bach and Handel used. He took them to the Blue Lobster, a favourite restaurant just outside Padstow, which named a dish after him.[55] They also went out to the Pendogget Arms, for lobster lunches, on the road to Tintagel. Eating and drinking had pride of place that Christmas:

> Isobel was a most wonderful cook. We went to any manner of bibulous parties with their friends. The fishermen loved him. It was drinks all round, all the time! There seemed to be no-one that he didn't know, and walking through Padstow with him was an experience in itself![56]

This first year in Cornwall had been an exhilarating experience for Malcolm. For perhaps the first time in his married life he had found a community in which he felt he belonged. And although he had written little music, there had been considerable local musical involvement: 'I am now aggressively, chauvinistically Cornish,' he declared typically in one interview and, as good as his word, he interested himself in the Cornwall Youth Band, the Cornwall Symphony Orchestra, the Cornwall Rural Music School and the East Cornwall Bach Festival.

In 1966 he made an important friendship. He was in Newquay, emerging from The Sailor's Arms, when across the road he noticed an art gallery above a bakery. Inside he found a series of paintings depicting Mussourgsky's *Pictures at an Exhibition*. Having enthusiastically identified every one, he asked to be put in touch with the artist and in this way met Tony Giles.

Tony was in his early forties, worked for the council as a draughtsman and was a prolific painter, specialising in semi-abstract landscapes.[57] He lived with his partner and future second wife, Hilary, in St Agnes. It was not long before visits to and from 'Tony and Hil' became important features of the Cornish years. Malcolm and Tony relished each other's company and would sit for hours

---

[55] Lobster à la Malcolm Arnold (a whole lobster in curry sauce)
[56] Robin Arnold, July 2003
[57] Tony Giles (1924-1994)

contentedly chatting about Cornwall, music and painting. Tony's delight in the Cornish landscape, as Hilary remembers, was infectious:

> Tony was a great enthusiast. He had intended to paint seascapes and harbours when he came to Cornwall. But when he saw the interior, the mines and the clay hills, he was totally taken aback. He became fascinated by the mark man had made on the landscape. Not just the mining, but viaducts and trains. There is a passion in his painting. He tilts his horizons, devises crazy patterns, comes up with a highly individual off-beat compositions. He specialises in convoluted landscapes, deserted tin mines and branch lines.[58]

Malcolm had at this stage begun to think of a set of dances, so he and Tony were now both trying to find in their respective mediums a personal response to the landscape and people around them. The *Cornish Dances*, completed on 26 May 1966 and subsequently dedicated to Isobel,[59] strike a much deeper note than their English and Scottish counterparts. Carefully contrasted in tempo and texture, they are more a miniature tone poem than a set of dances, an act of homage to a people with whom he felt strong affiliations. His subsequent programme note is an indication of this:

> The Cornish people have a highly developed sense of humour. Many are sea-faring folk, and it's a land of male-voice choirs, brass bands, Methodism, May Days, and Sankey and Moody hymns. The Cornish, despite, or even because of, their great sense of independence, have been ruthlessly exploited. The deserted engine-houses of the tin and copper mines bear silent witness to this, and these ruins radiate a strange and sad beauty.
>
> I hope some of these things are present in this music, which is Cornish through the eyes of a 'furrener'.

The first movement, *Vivace*, sings of the sea. Piers Burton-Page has pointed out that this sea-going song of Malcolm's own invention copies the Cornish trick of repetition on a single note: 'The tune as a whole is a fine and strong one, with a rhythmic hiccough at the end, and each time it comes round it lurches into a new and often hilariously unexpected key ...'[60] There is an insouciance about it which also suggests the confidence which the Cornish air gave Malcolm, the swagger and panache, 'the sense of community more so than I've ever known'.[61] This is the movement of a man who can 'breeze into his local before midday, amiably abuse the landlord for not stocking a hangover cure, buy drinks all round, then hammer out the end of Walton's First Symphony on an out-of-tune upright, shouting the percussion parts he can't play, followed by sweltering chunks of *Tosca*'.[62]

---

[58] August 2003
[59] He had the score beautifully leather-bound and suitably inscribed.
[60] Burton-Page: *Philharmonic Concerto*, pp.93-94
[61] Christopher Ford, *The Guardian*, 17 April 1971
[62] *Ibid.*

*On the Padstow
quay, 1968*

The second dance, *Andantino,* is most obviously the fruit of his discussions with Tony Giles, the ghostliness of the melody and orchestration – with tubular bells, harp and percussion to the fore – suggesting deserted tin mines, not so much as interesting archaeological remains in themselves as symbols of all the sufferings of the exploited individuals who once worked there and are now but hovering ghosts.

The third movement, *Con moto e sempre senza parodia*, seemingly represents the kind of revivalist hymn which would have been sung with fervour in many a Cornish Methodist chapel. Some find the melody, escalating from quiet reflection to brazen protestation, very moving; others refuse to take the composer's instructions seriously, and think him merely mocking Cornish revivalism. But the instruction 'without parody' (*senza parodia*) is unambiguous, and Malcolm in his notes has mentioned Methodism, brass bands and Sankey and Moody. He knew all about Methodism from Pappy, and here, like a dutiful son, he would seem to be saluting it.

The final movement, *Allegro ma non troppo*, is a picture of Padstow on May Day. By 1966 Malcolm was a devotee of the Obby Oss ritual, a celebration of the First of May dating back to an ancient fertility rite of the fourteenth century. 'We used to meet Malcolm sometimes on Padstow Obby Oss Day,' remembers Hilary Giles. 'It starts at midnight outside the Golden Lion, one of Malcolm's favourite pubs, with lots of singing, accompanied by accordions, triangles and drums.' Malcolm loved it, couldn't indeed believe his luck. It was a combination of all he held most dear. 'There are two "horses",' continues Hilary, 'one blue, one red. One is the charity horse, one the drinking horse, so you can guess which Malcolm supported! The "horses" are the key features in hugely long processions which would weave down the narrow streets sloping to the harbour.'

Padstow decked out with flowers and greenery in May looked unbelievably beautiful and Primrose Cottage was always crammed with visitors invited down to share the Obby Oss pleasures. It was a social highlight in Malcolm's year.

The *Cornish Dances* were Malcolm's tribute to his new home. And yet, all is not be totally what it seems. The main tune of the ghostly second dance, for example, was taken from *Sky West and Crooked*. Malcolm may be down in Cornwall, but there is nothing to prevent him paying a sly tribute to Hayley Mills and her family. The second *Cornish Dance* is not just a reminiscence of ghostly tin mines, but contains his own private tribute to another precious *idée fixe*.

The third dance likewise has ambiguities. Malcolm's revivalist hymn is indeed of the kind dear to Pappy. The tambourines are there. And even the final 'amen'. But there is more to it than that. In the early months of 1966, just as he began his *Cornish Dances*, Malcolm learnt that Ruth was dying. First there had been Philip. Then Aubrey and Clifford. And now Ruth. Nan too had gone and left him with just Pappy. Philip the first at twenty-one, Ruth the last at fifty-seven. Now only he was left, ironically, with Pappy. He could imagine the old man, listening to his revivalist hymns in some God-forsaken chapel, gritting his teeth in his grief.

Ruth's life, he knew, had been a sad travesty of her potential. The marriage with Wag had been as catastrophic as Nan had predicted. The two had nothing in common but their confining poverty. Ruth's spirit soared towards the arts, her efforts in this world towards sexual and racial minorities, the desperate and the downtrodden. Wag thought her mad and cared only for his mugs of beer in the evenings and a few coarse women on the side. In her last years Ruth's spirits struggled. Mentally she grew frailer.

When Ruth's cancer was diagnosed, her daughter, Penny, wrote to Malcolm, urging him to pay a visit, but this was something he could not face. All he could think of was to sit down at his desk and write her a hymn: Pappy's kind of hymn. Unlike Pappy, she might not nurse conventional belief, but she believed in the supernatural. He, an atheist from boyhood, would write for Ruth a hymn in Pappy's style. The irony of it pleased him. But it would be with sincere emotion. No mockery, *senza parodia*. It would be his tribute from Cornwall to his dying sister. And, most importantly, it would be his secret; no-one else would ever know. Friends might wonder, audiences might smile, but every time he conducted the work, only he would remember Ruth, how much she had once meant to him, and how she had suffered.

The *Dances* were completed just seven weeks before Ruth's death.[63] She died at St Crispin's Hospital, her mind unable to cope with the illness. 'Mum was desperately disappointed that Malcolm didn't visit her,' writes Penny, 'when she became more and more ill. Out of all the members of the family it was Malcolm to whom she was closest and the fact that he didn't come really affected her.'

Malcolm did not come down for the funeral, though he did send a large bouquet. Years later, however, he still remembered the pain he felt over Ruth: 'Her death nearly destroyed me. I nearly went mad. I didn't know what to do.'[64]

Only four weeks later he had to steel himself to conduct the *Cornish Dances* at their première in the Proms. The *Northampton Chronicle and Echo* proudly proclaimed:[65]

> One of the season's triumphs! The work received an ovation lasting several minutes during which the Prommers stamped their approval vociferously demanding an encore, which was unfortunately not forthcoming.[66]

Donald Mitchell, listening in to the concert on the radio, sent Malcolm a congratulatory letter shortly afterwards:

> I really feel that anything I say about your Four Cornish Dances would be super-fluous, after the ovation they received at the Albert Hall on Saturday night. What a glorious roar of approval! It almost wrecked our radio at Barcombe, but even had it done so we would have thought it a worthy sacrifice … They are a stunning set of dances …[67]

There was a sense of unreality at this moment of success. He had paid his tribute to Ruth. The audience had chuckled, as he knew they would. What more could he do?

He had thought of putting some poems to music. Like 'Beauty Haunts the Woods' all those years ago. But the poems reproached him. They were too painful to skim, let alone ponder. In one of her last stays at St Crispin's, for example, Ruth had written 'The Ladies in the Corridor'. It reminded him only too well that while he had been basking in the glory of the Bath Festival, making music with Yehudi Menuhin and enjoying the applause for his Double Violin Concerto, Ruth had been

---

[63] 16 July 1966
[64] Paul Jackson: *The Life and Music of Sir Malcolm Arnold*, p.122
[65] The major critics, on the whole, looked the other way. Having pilloried Malcolm, they now ignored him. Malcolm, they felt, was on the whole no longer a threat.
[66] 15 August 1966
[67] 15 August 1966

in St Crispin's, forgotten by her only surviving brother, in mental distress herself yet movingly compassionate towards others: [68]

> Today, yesterday, tomorrow? – never!
> Release will come, like the quickening
> Sound of Gabriel's horn – or during
> The dreary chanting of hymns –
> False relics of a long-dead martyr!
>
> Forget the weary body for a moment;
> The idle ridicule of the 'normal' fools,
> Who do not know that they are more
> Pathetic than these lost souls –
> Their day will come, and agonising
> Will be their awakening.
>
> Suddenly, another mortal frame
> Drops sighing to the ground –
> To be swept aside by the undertakers –
> No more value, really
> Than a lost leaf of Autumn,
> Or a shell from a mouldy nut.
>
> Children gathering conkers
> Are happy in a brief afternoon of ecstasy,
> Kicking the leaves along in bundles,
> Like the ladies are treated in the corridor –
> Or sitting in stuffy rooms,
> Unaware that they are 'God's people' –
> Intricate, broken-down machines,
> Each one a miracle of conception,
> Even tho' the blood, bones, muscles and nerves
> Are worn out and useless
> Eternally torn two ways -
> Between good and evil.
>
> That also is my martyrdom.

There was only one thing to do: throw himself into his work. There had been plenty of conducting that summer, notably two Promenade Concerts in August, both with the London Philharmonic, whose ranks included old friends like Wrayburn Glasspool, Johnny Kuchmy and Sidney Ellison. These had been triumphant evenings in which he had conducted not just his own works, but Mendelssohn's Fourth Symphony, Brahms' Third and Dvořák's Eighth, not to mention work by Rossini, Bach, Grieg, de Falla and Bizet.

Then there was the idea from BBC (West) that the opening of the Severn Bridge should be marked with three English and three Welsh composers

---

[68] Taking the title from T S Eliot's *Sweeney Erect*

contributing variations on a Welsh folk tune. A visitor to Primrose Cottage remembers Malcolm taking a phone-call from the BBC in which he was asked what instrumentation he was considering and, as he replied, he scribbled the instruments down on the sitting-room wall, so that he would not forget. In the event, as no Welsh folk tune could be agreed, Malcolm himself produced the theme and the jazzy first variation, and he did so in a matter of days.[69]

That autumn Malcolm took Katherine up to Durham University for her first day as a student there, reading Geography. He was delighted that Katherine was prospering so well academically and did his best to support her, occasionally making the long journey to Durham and trying to develop a good relationship with the University's Professor of Music, Arthur Hutchings. Having learnt that his old friend Rudolf Schwarz was intending to conduct the Northern Sinfonia in Durham Cathedral in Katherine's first term, Malcolm volunteered to conduct a work of his own in the programme. His choice was the Flute Concerto, Katherine's instrument.

Back at home, Malcolm worked with Tony Giles on a project dear to both of them, the creation of an Arts Centre for Cornwall. Presenting prizes in St Austell at the Cornwall Rural Music School's open day, Malcolm suggested the School's need for its own headquarters should be met within this new arts centre. A site had been identified, he said, an open cast mine near St Agnes. Malcolm did his best for the project, bringing Lord Goodman down to inspect the site, but it all came to nothing. So Malcolm and Tony Giles pursued an alternative site, this time out on the cliffs at Wheal Kitty. Tony Giles produced an expensive campaign book, and Malcolm not only involved Lord Goodman again but wrote an introduction to the book, including his own setting of *The Obby Orse Song*. But the idea was ahead of its time and perished.

There were other distractions. His relationship with the Proms was understandably a major concern, so he was greatly alarmed at a letter from one of William Glock's assistants, offering him rather less conducting for 1967 than 1966. He replied hotly to the snub:

> Are you asking me to conduct my 2 Violin Concerto and that only? And is that the only date I am to be offered at the Proms this year? In other words, have I been dropped as a conductor for this year's Promenade Concerts? Your letter implies this, but I would like it made clear to me if this is so. I realise I have no right to know why I have been sacked, but one always likes to know whether one has been sacked or not![70]

---

[69] Malcolm received confirmation of the commission from a letter written on 7 October. He returned his contribution on 17 October. Writing with him for England were Michael Tippett and Nicholas Maw. Wales was represented by Alun Hoddinott, Daniel Jones and Grace Williams. Adrian Boult conducted the first performance, in Swansea on 11 January 1967.
[70] Letter of 27 January 1967 (courtesy of BBC Written Archive, Caversham) responding to letter from Christopher Samuelson asking whether he would conduct the Double Violin Concerto next August.

Malcolm's letter was speedily passed up the line to William Glock himself, who did not offer Malcolm the kind of response he was expecting:

> I do understand about not wanting to conduct an isolated work, but I would like you to know that it is entirely a matter of circumstance or accident that you have not been invited to conduct one or two Proms this year, as you were in 1966. No criticism whatever is involved and I hope there will be an opportunity in 1968 for you to take part.[71]

Malcolm was taken aback to see that even the single work had now been taken from him, and he wrote back hurriedly, trying to retrieve the situation:

> Dear William,
>
> I am afraid you have been misinformed. I said on the telephone to your concerts assistant that to be asked to conduct a single work, when I had conducted that same work within the context of two Promenade Concerts last year, was deeply insulting and damaging to my musical reputation. I never at any time suggested that I would be unwilling to conduct my work at the Proms. I do hope this will be made clear in the records.
>
> With best wishes,
> Yours,
> Malcolm

But it was not enough to retrieve the situation. The Double Concerto was removed from the 1967 season. Nor was it to appear again in the Proms that century.

The more rebuffs, real and imagined, which Malcolm received from the musical establishment, the more he turned in upon himself at St Merryn. He often saw himself these days as a specifically Cornish composer. Returning one night in February to Primrose Cottage, he paused at the door to listen again to the familiar foghorn from Trevose Head. He had heard it many times since coming to live here. But tonight it was more insistent, calling out to him. He left his key in the door unturned, and listened. It was somewhere between middle C and D he thought. Probably nearer D? He had always promised Gordon Elliott that one day he would commemorate the great rescue of 1965 with something for the local brass bands, on which Gordon was so keen. It was to be called *The Joseph Hiram Chadwick*, after Gordon's lifeboat, but he had never got much beyond the title, which he had always found forbidding. Tonight, however? There was certainly the germ of an idea. He listened again. He knew all about the old Victorian lighthouse on Trevose Head with its eight new 'Supertyphon' horns sounding on foggy nights two mournful blasts every thirty seconds, loud enough to be heard five miles out to sea as well as inside Primrose Cottage. Perhaps at last he could write a piece commemorating the bravery of Gordon and his crew: Philip and Arthur May; Ernest and Horrie Murt; George Pinch and Arthur Permewan? He finally turned the key. Isobel was waiting up for him, but he

---

[71] 7 February 1967

declined the proffered food and went upstairs to his study. *The Padstow Lifeboat* was already forming in his mind.

The short, four-minute March, which Malcolm wrote over the next three days, tells of the lifeboat's gallant mission in 1965 to the stricken *Deo Gratias*. First comes the lighthouse foghorn, loud and dissonant, as the *Joseph Hiram Chadwick* slips its moorings. Soon the plucky little boat is cheekily steaming out to those in peril, the foghorn still audible until it disappears. A second, counter melody enters, when it seems the boat is no longer in touch with dry land. This noble tune reflects the courage of Gordon and his crew as well as the self-sacrifice of generations before them. And Malcolm so identifies with the gallant crew that he cannot resist joining them on their enterprise, for we now hear a solo trumpet playing in exuberant counterpoint to the noble theme. In the centre of the march comes the actual rescue. The sea, wonderfully evoked in sound, rages in fury as Gordon manoeuvres the lifeboat's bow against the fishing vessel's starboard quarter. Arthur and Phil haul the fishermen aboard moments before heavy waves roll the *Deo Gratias* under the lifeboat's bow, which crashes through her bulwark. Triumphant, the *Joseph Hiram Chadwick* makes for port, soon coming back within range of the Trevose foghorn. Finally, as it nears the harbour, it slows down, allowing Malcolm to participate in a jubilant homecoming. In the last bars of the march, he flies gleefully around the boat, a trumpeting Ariel, before swooping down to dry land, eager to be the first one in the bar, lining up the drinks.

Though light-heartedness predominates, *The Padstow Lifeboat* is all the more effective for the underlying sense of menace which Malcolm achieves, boldly juxtaposing the foghorn's D against the home key of A flat. The Trevose Head lighthouse, standing staunchly above sheer, grey cliffs of granite, had many tragic associations.

Not long afterwards Malcolm gave the march a resounding first performance as he conducted the joint bands of the Black Dyke Mills and the British Motor Corporation at a broadcast concert at the Festival Hall, part of the BBC International Festival of Light Music.[72] He had enormous Hoffnungian fun at the same concert conducting the Black Dyke Mills Band while Harry Mortimer conducted the BMC in Ronald Binge's *Duel for Conductors*, but the more success he had in the light music field, the less seriously he was taken as a composer. There was a commission by the BBC at this time for songs for a children's television play, *The Turtle Drum*, which he fulfilled with aplomb, but frustrations began to grow. He would have preferred a commission for a new symphony. Why couldn't a Cornish Composer be taken seriously? He didn't only have to write for brass bands, did he? He was still being sidelined and it upset him.

[72] 10 June 1967

Thinking this over, Malcolm decided to take the initiative, shut himself away in his study and began to grapple with the Sixth Symphony, completing it in late July. There had been much personal upheaval in the seven years between the Fifth and Sixth Symphonies. Paradoxically, though the Fifth was written when his first marriage was disintegrating and the Sixth in the stability of a new one, his mood was now darker and more introspective. The Sixth is, for the most part, a disturbing and unsettling work, but it also shows a growing resourcefulness in the use of material and contains some of his most compelling music.

Unusually, before beginning the symphony Malcolm sketched a few thoughts in words and music on a single side of manuscript paper. These reveal two disparate influences, Charlie 'Bird' Parker and Hector Berlioz. Of the first movement Malcolm wrote: 'The Bird. Free improvisation!!!' Of the second and third: 'Funeral March' and 'March Trionfale', references to Berlioz's *Grande Symphonie funèbre et triomphale*. There was one further comment: '2nd movement add Berlioz perc.'

There were many reasons why Malcolm should be intrigued by Charlie Parker, in addition to the impetuous, humorous fantasies he wove with his alto saxophone.[73] 'The Bird' had flown too high and had severe drink and drugs problems. And there had been mental instability which led to a period of institutionalization and several suicide attempts. In 1955 Charlie Parker finally destroyed himself at the age of thirty-five. One of Malcolm's favourite Parker records contains the ballad 'Lover Man', to face the recording of which Parker is said to have needed a quart of whisky, which took away his sanity for a while. But the tender melodies he improvises in 'Lover Man' are of a delicate beauty. 'The innate artistry of Parker,' writes Mike Butcher, 'enabled him to express the confusion in his mind not as confusion but as a dramatic message. The notes he blows through his alto tell you more about his condition then than any words of his ever could have done.'[74] That is also true of Malcolm's work.

The first movement, marked *Energico*, contains, as Malcolm explained in his programme note, 'many phrases of the type used by Charlie Parker, whose brilliant imagination coloured the whole of jazz in the 1940s'. It is one of Malcolm's most intelligently and tightly argued movements, virtually everything in this elaborately free 'improvisation' stemming from the first four notes.[75] Malcolm did less than justice to it in his programme note. Having mentioned Parker, he might have helpfully explained how the first subject contains a series of

---

[73] Parker belonged to the age of 'bop' or 'bebop'. 'Technically, bebop was characterized by fast tempos, complex harmonies, intricate melodies, and rhythm sections that laid down a steady beat only on the bass. Bebop tunes were often labyrinthine, full of surprising twists and turns.' (David Rosenthal, *Hard Bop*, Oxford, 1992)

[74] Mike Butcher, Vogue Records, *Charlie Parker Plays*, EPV 1011, sleeve notes.

[75] These introduce the major/minor dichotomy. Harmonically the four notes constitute a chord containing both a major and minor third, traditionally (if somewhat simplistically) denoting happy/sad. And there is to be no resolution – throughout they battle for supremacy.

Parker-like phrases, excitingly translated from saxophone to symphony orchestra. First the woodwind, next the strings, later a single piccolo all take on the mantle of *The Bird* with wonderful dexterity. Malcolm also ignores all mention of the fascinating second subject, a melody of intense yearning, not unlike the main theme in the first movement of the *Third Sinfonietta*.

As the movement unfolds Malcolm develops his melodic and rhythmic thoughts in a more strongly organic manner than in his previous symphonies, manipulating classical form into something better suited to his needs. There is no development section as such, because the music is continually developing from the start. The orchestral colours are often unusually dark, provoking an atmosphere of unremitting disquiet. The melodic ideas[76] range from terse to tender, savage to soulful, until the movement culminates in a harsh crescendo and ends as it began, with scurrying passages in the woodwinds.

The references to Charlie Parker (previously honoured in one of the Five Pieces for Violin of 1964) and to the *Third Sinfonietta* (of the same year) are significant. Malcolm, it seems, is taking as his starting point the early years of his second marriage and the birth of Edward, a period of great hope, which now, three years later, was turning sour. He and Isobel had started having arguments. Isobel's best friend was banned from staying at Primrose Cottage because she had taken her side in too spirited a way. Hilary Giles, when visiting, was shocked that plates would sometimes be flying through the air in the heat of battle.

> It was a very stormy relationship. If I were Isobel I would have murdered him! He could be awful to her and say the most dreadful things, and that was when we were there. We always wondered what went on when they were on their own.

Robin Arnold, who enjoyed good times with Malcolm and was grateful for them, was nonetheless awestruck by the volume of drink, which fuelled the aggression.

> It was certainly damned heavy. Excessive. Many pints of beer, then whisky, then brandy.

Primrose Cottage was a confined space around which Malcolm's huge presence would reverberate. Little Edward was quietly breathing it all in, getting more anxious and frightened. About the time of the writing of the Sixth Symphony Edward was taken to London to be seen by Professor Michael Rutter, one of the leading experts in children's mental health. He it was who told Malcolm and Isobel that Edward was autistic. 'It was a terrible trip for Dad,' remembers Katherine. 'He couldn't cope with that day at all. It was all too much for him.'

So it isn't too fanciful to hear some of this turmoil within the first movement of the symphony and to remember Diane Jones's enduring memory of Malcolm, clutching Isobel's hand under the table at Bertorelli's only minutes after confiding that he really had rather not have married again.

---

[76] All of which grow from the introductory germ, the major/minor third, either in their own shape or in their accompaniments.

The second movement, written with Berlioz[77] in mind, is marked *Lento – Allegretto – Lento*. In a highly arresting opening our attention is caught by a long, shrill B natural unison, which commandingly ushers us forward to enter Malcolm's landscape of grief. A ghostly, sighing threnody[78] dominates. We are down in the Land of the Dead with Odysseus, or sharing with Malcolm the anguish of depression. We feel trapped and entombed. In a marriage which needn't have happened? With an autistic son? By thoughts of our own folly and senseless self-destructive nature? It is a full 44 bars into the movement before a side-drum and tenor drum remind us of 'Berlioz's percussion' and introduce us to a funeral march, with its despairing melodic lines made up of falling semitones and accented long notes that seem to pile on top of each other, like so many stabs of pain.[79]

But it does not last long, and with the abrupt arrival of the central *Allegretto*, there is startling change of mood with sexy syncopation and pizzicato *ostinato*. We seem unexpectedly to have put on a pair of psychedelic Sixties spectacles and joined a *dance macabre*. Berlioz is there, but as it were, in a Yellow Submarine, with Malcolm gleefully inside having the time of his life, challenging musical boundaries and being impishly provocative. The *dance macabre*, after a fierce climax, fades and drums lead us back to the *marche funèbre*, only this time it is far too solemn and emotionally charged to be merely a funeral. This is Malcolm's *Symphonie Fantastique* with his very own *Marche au Supplice*, and Malcolm's unnerving march to the scaffold quite outdoes Berlioz. Hushed and awful, the nightmare march makes its inexorable progress, threatening drum rolls in the background all the while. And in the final *coup de théâtre,* instead of heightening the sound (in the Berlioz tradition) as we approach the guillotine, Malcolm reduces everything to a whisper, so that, undistracted, we may focus on the gleaming, silent blade. Then comes that screaming B natural, the same shrill note which began the movement, building from *pianissimo* to *fortissimo* as more and

---

[77] Isobel had recently given him a copy of Berlioz's letters, edited by Humphrey Searle, which would have brought back vividly his favourite composer, the purity of whose orchestrations he tried so hard to follow, and whose own troubled life resonated with his own. The quotation from Victor Hugo at the front of the *Symphonie Fantastique* was very dear to Malcolm: 'All I have suffered, all I have attempted … The loves, the labours, the bereavements of my youth.' Intense personal experience motivated the writing of both. But whereas Berlioz gave his listeners hints at the inner meanings, Malcolm did everything in his power to cover them up.

[78] It is emotionally even more highly charged in its later return when Malcolm halves the note values.

[79] It is hard to equate what we are hearing with Malcolm's joking commentary: 'The movement is elegiac in character, and pays tribute in passing to a style of pop music which will be dead by the time the work is performed, which might justify the whole movement being somewhat funereal.' Malcolm is baiting the critics with the reference to pop music, as well as joking about the delays he has had to get the work performed. In so doing he was perplexing everyone and damaging his own cause.

*On the beach in Cornwall with Edward and Isobel, c.1971*

more instruments gradually join in[80] until, at the end of the shrillness, down comes the blade, rasping and rapid, and this utterly intriguing movement ends with somebody's head tumbling off.[81]

The second movement is as mystifying as it is dramatic. Malcolm, we may safely assume, sees himself as the hero being led to the scaffold, for he always had to be the centre of attention, but we can only surmise as to who or what has

---

[80] Offering us an exact, if much condensed, version of Berg's Wozzeck killing his Marie with a knife.

[81] At the time he was writing the Symphony Malcolm had on his desk Litolff's *Maximilian Robespierre Overture*, which he was planning to conduct with the BBC Northern Orchestra in September. This work also ends with the guillotine: 'The suspense reaches a high pitch until the crash and thud of falling blade cuts across the score and the rolling of the head into the basket completes the stunning effect.' (*The Liverpool Weekly News*, commenting on Malcolm's performance of the overture at Widnes, 28 September 1967.)

been responsible for his sudden demise. The critics and the musical establishment? Constricting family life? The burden of the past? A combination of all three? It is a strange, moving and vivid psychedelic nightmare.

The idea of Berlioz's *March Triomphale* may have been the starting point for the third and last movement, marked *Con fuoco*, but the triumph expressed is Cornish rather than French. The strongly tonal and highly energetic rondo theme, which dominates this movement, includes the Cornish device of repetition of a single note which Malcolm had used before in the first of the *Cornish Dances*. The contrast to what has gone before is so striking that even Hugo Cole was moved to remark that 'Its crude ebullience may well distress the sensitive'. This is Malcolm, escaping from his gremlins, down in the Farmer's Arms. But Malcolm's happiness can never be total. The three episodes which intervene between the four statements of the rondo are tonally ambiguous, referring back both melodically and rhythmically to the first movement. There is not much *fuoco* in these. The wild fun of the Farmer's Arms is being thrown into relief by Malcolm's most recent domestic woes.

Malcolm's Sixth Symphony sits very much in the mould of Beethoven's Eighth and Shostakovich's Ninth in that it is very different from the two symphonies that lie either side of it, their expansive scope and argument being replaced by something a little more succinct, immediate and personal. For all its moments of savagery and *Angst* Malcolm's Sixth is an intimate work, full of subtle nuances and hidden meanings. His only Cornish symphony, it expresses little of the world around him but a great deal of the inner man. Its fusion of musical structure, orchestral sonority and symbolic narrative is handled with expert skill throughout.

In the aftermath of its completion, Malcolm relaxed in his customary manner. Down at the Golden Lion, Padstow, he found the usual crowd of ready listeners, as the champagne flowed. He was frustrated, he explained to a group of fishermen, that he had finished a symphony for which as yet he had no outlet. It was a worry, driving him to drink. He needed to hear it live to find out how effective it really was!

After a drink or two, however, the anxieties passed and soon, indeed, he was in the best of moods. The première would happen in its own good time. He still had friends enough in high places. It was good to be in Cornwall, where he could write the kind of music he wanted. In the past year there'd been the Sixth Symphony, the *Dances* and the *Lifeboat*. That was a useful beginning.

Just for the moment, too, he was on good terms with his wife. Had he really thrown a plate at her the other day? It was hard to believe. Isobel was such a good sort, always so keen to do the best by him. She didn't nag him when he went out on a bat. She understood and would sometimes join in. It was also good to have a wife who could pick him up in her Mini from the Padstow pubs at the first call of a telephone. Apart from anything else, it saved wear and tear on the Mille Cinquecento, the precious Fiat which had seen a few Cornish ditches in its time.

A few hours later Isobel was driving him once more up the hill and out of Padstow, with a neighbour, whom he'd just drunk under the table, soporific on the back seat.[82] As they climbed high above the little fishing port, the estuary came into view in all its calm, self-effacing splendour. The sun, too, was obliging, choosing in its setting splendour to light up the horizon. Round the coast, at Trevose Head, where the new lifeboat station was being built, the sea would be raging, fighting its eternal battle with rock and cliff. But here, every second, the Mini was opening up a golden vista of beauty and tranquillity. It somehow seemed symbolic. 'There *will* be peace in our time,' said Malcolm suddenly. 'Peace and music! Naught shall go ill!' Isobel flashed him a grin. 'Jack shall have his Jill?' Instead of replying Malcolm lit a cigar and settled himself more comfortably in the front passenger seat. 'Fancy a night out, Iso?' he queried, as the gallant, well-laden little car made its way along the bumpy road to St Merryn.

---

[82] George Greenfield, August 2003

*Cornwall, 1970*

# 12
# Bard of the Gorsedd

## The Later Cornish Years, 1968-72

MALCOLM did not have to wait long before the Sixth Symphony was taken up by David Ellis at BBC Manchester and a first performance by the BBC Northern Symphony Orchestra was provisionally agreed. All BBC regional centres had to clear their programming with headquarters in London, although this was usually a formality and David Ellis rarely experienced problems.

> I never found William Glock behaving in the dictatorial way that is now popular gossip. He was open-minded. He never turned down a programme our orchestra planners or conductors wanted.[1]

Nonetheless Glock's senior assistants were less than enthusiastic about the project. David's request went first to the CAOC (Chief Assistant, Orchestra and Choral), Hans Keller (the creator of Piotr Zak), who passed it on to the CAMP (Chief Assistant, Music Programmes).

'I should be very pleased for the first performance of this work to be included in a BBC NSO Music Programme broadcast,' replied the CAMP to the CAOC, 'subject to the score not revealing any of the, to my mind, lamentable attempts of Osric trying to play Laertes (to put it no higher), which the Fifth Symphony revealed.'[2] Keller had brought a messianic belief in Schoenberg and serialism to the BBC and was not sympathetic to Malcolm's conviction that the western symphonic tradition still had potential for development. His reply to the CAMP was accordingly grudging:

> I have now seen the score. It's better than his last symphony – though I still wouldn't describe it as good. But I propose that we go ahead.[3]

To have done otherwise would have been to have compromised Glock's policy of complete support for regional wishes. These grudging responses illustrate the problems Malcolm now faced in the all-powerful BBC Music Department, and things would only get worse shortly, when the arrival of Pierre Boulez as Chief Conductor of the BBC Symphony Orchestra would raise the Darmstadt profile within Broadcasting House itself.[4]

---

[1] August 2003
[2] John Manduell, 31 August 1967 (BBC Written Archive Centre)
[3] 4 September 1967 (BBC Written Archive Centre)
[4] The appointment was announced in January 1969.

Although Malcolm was pleased at the prospect of a first performance of the Sixth Symphony, he inevitably felt a sense of anticlimax after the prestigious premières of the Third and Fourth at the Festival Hall and the Fifth at the Cheltenham Festival. In a letter to Donald Mitchell he did his best to gloss over the situation:

> Manchester BBC are very anxious to arrange a public first performance, and I prefer that it should be done in Manchester, because I have performed my 1st, 2nd, 4th and 5th Symphonies either with the Hallé or the BBC Northern in Manchester, whereas the only two works of mine in the past with premières that have been performed in London are the Cornish Dances and the Two Violin Concerto.[5]

Donald Mitchell knew how inaccurate[6] this statement was, and understood the reasons for it. It must have been a considerable blow to Malcolm's self-esteem to have lost the support of the BBC in London and the LPO, both of whom were firm allies in the 1950s. That Malcolm was upset at this down-swing in his fortunes is evident from his garbled attack on contemporary tastes in the concert programme:

> Although in the present day, there is only one type of music allowed to call itself modern (and this type of music can all be fairly accurately described by the term 'Post-Wagnerian Chamber Music') I can accept and be interested in many types of music, some of which seems to me modern, because it looks towards the future. A future as it concerns human beings, and not a vision of people transplanting organs in space...

The BBC Northern's schedule eventually led to the première taking place in Sheffield on 28 June 1968 as part of Sheffield University's Arts Festival. Malcolm was amused to be conducting in the City Hall, where, twenty-seven years before, he had first met Sheila. Despite an attractive programme,[7] however, there were more empty brown leatherette seats than full ones, and the première would have been a very modest affair indeed, had the performance not been recorded and subsequently broadcast. Yet Malcolm, in the best of spirits, hardly noticed the empty seats and inspired the orchestra, which knew his music[8] and liked him, to play particularly well.

Only William Mann of the major critics seems to have been present. He began his review by expressing regret that so 'fluent and exuberantly inventive a composer' should have been silent so long, before giving a short and insulting resumé of his career:

---

[5] 5 September 1967

[6] Not only were the Third and Fourth Symphonies first played at the Festival Hall but the First and Second were given London performances by Malcolm and the LPO shortly after their premières. The Double Violin Concerto had its first performance in Bath, not London.

[7] It also included Beethoven's *Prometheus Overture*, Rachmaninov's *Rhapsody on a Theme of Paganini* and Tchaikovsky's Second Symphony.

[8] Only the previous year, with Malcolm conducting, they had given the first broadcast of the Fifth Symphony and they had already played his Second and Fourth Symphonies.

Ever since *Beckus the Dandipratt* in the 1940s, Arnold has kept his creative colours nailed to the mast of music as entertainment. He revolted against the shenanigans of progressive composers since, say Bartók, and by the time of his Second Symphony (1951)[9] he was diving gamely from the springboard of music-hall and military bands. Then, when modern pop music rose from its sick bed and became progressive and vital, he found inspiration there.

This travesty of a summary demonstrates the serious problems now facing Malcolm. Too often he had played the clown, disdaining to talk or write seriously about the innovations he was bringing in his music and thereby making the current denigration of his serious work comparatively easy. Lone voices still spoke up on his behalf. Stewart Deas wrote encouragingly in *Country Life*:

> Here is a composer who certainly does not believe in esoteric musical language. He is a man with a heart and he speaks from it. One thing is certain about his work: it is always magnificently written. Arnold is a great craftsman and that is the beginning of strength and the only sure foundation of inspiration. His inspiration comes from many sources often popular in origin...[10]

In the same article Deas put William Mann into context:

> Mr Mann takes the view that 'those of us who relish the latest Stockhausen and Xenakis[11] will love and understand Bach and Mozart more deeply and more immediately'... There must be less devious ways of approaching the classics. Are we really to believe that because of today's near chaos we are better equipped than our fathers and grandfathers to appreciate Mozart and Bach?

A month later all the problems over the Sixth Symphony were forgotten. Padstow was *en fête* for the visit of the Duke of Kent to celebrate a new lifeboat and station. As he arrived early for the morning ceremony, which would allow the lifeboat to catch the tide inside the harbour, the little town twinkled delightedly in the July sunshine.[12] Grandstands for over four hundred local grandees had been erected on the North Quay, and the curving quayside was colourfully lined with onlookers. Isobel, resplendent in an elegant, all-yellow two-piece suit, and Malcolm, smartly suited as always, were among those lined up to meet the Duke, before a service of dedication and the naming of the boat. Later, when the new vessel moved around the quay to a position where the Duke could board her for

---

[9] The date was, in fact, 1953

[10] 11 July 1968. But Deas, a distinguished Professor of Music at Sheffield University, could be easily discounted, as he was involved in the Sheffield Arts Festival.

[11] The latest compositions of the Romanian Iannis Xenakis, an exact contemporary of Malcolm's, included *Terretekorth*, an orchestral piece in which the players sat among the audience, making sounds 'similar to flames' with small drums and policemen's whistles. In 1965, on the death of Varèse, Xenakis was famously moved to declare, 'Away with the scale, away with themes, away with melody, to the devil with so-called "musical" music!' Stockhausen, seven years younger than Malcolm, had recently produced *Hymnen*, scored for electronic accordion and various taped noises, including wheezing and shrieking.

[12] 19 July 1968

a closer inspection, Malcolm conducted the St Dennis Band in a rousing rendition of the *Padstow Lifeboat*. It was a moment he would always treasure.

A few weeks later he was having equally good fun in Truro Cathedral,
conducting two amateur symphony orchestras, two brass bands and over two
hundred singers from eleven local choirs in a concert honouring the sixtieth
anniversary of the death of an obscure local composer, Thomas Merritt. This
enterprise, which occupied Malcolm, on and off, for twelve months,[13] sheds
significant light on his current state of mind.

The Thomas Merritt affair began in the garden of Tony Giles' house in
St Agnes, where the two friends were chatting about one of their preoccupations,
the rise and fall of the Cornish tin mining industry. Malcolm had read widely
around the subject, including two recent Christmas presents from Isobel, *The
Cornish Miner* and *Old Cornish Mines*.

'There was an interesting tin miner, who lived not too far away from here,'
said Tony, 'also something of a composer. I don't suppose you've ever heard of
Thomas Merritt?'

Shortly afterwards they were visiting his graveyard at the village of Illogan
and the ruined engine house and stack of the Carn Brea tin and copper mine,
where Merritt had worked from the age of eleven.

In the 1890s Merritt had been organist and choirmaster in a small Methodist
chapel, where he had composed many carols, several of which are still sung in
Cornwall. Malcolm, his interest aroused, set about discovering what other music
Merritt had written, excitedly unearthing several anthems and a march. The new
material gave him the idea of putting on a concert, and, never being one for half-
measures, he decided the venue should be Truro Cathedral, not far from Merritt's
village. He himself would write a tribute to this talented lost composer, and he
would involve the BBC!

He immediately contacted William Glock, shortly to retire as the BBC's
Controller of Music. Glock hurriedly passed the idea down to his CAMP and
HMSW (Head of Music, South & West).

'Have listened to a couple of Merritt carols,' wrote the CAMP to the HMSW,
'and am not very impressed.'[14] The HMSW meanwhile was mulling over some
Merritt sent by Malcolm.

'My own opinion of the enclosed music,' replied the HMSW to the CAMP,
'is that it's rather meagre Victoriana and frankly best forgotten; but perhaps you
are more generously disposed?'[15]

These were reasonable reactions, for Merritt possessed limited merits. His
exhumation seemed odd and the proposed tribute absurdly grandiose with
Hoffnungian overtones. Malcolm had decided there would be one vast orchestra,
together with two brass bands, playing in different galleries in the cathedral. At

---

[13] November 1967 to November 1968.
[14] John Manduell, 19 December 1967
[15] Philip Moore, 1 January 1968

times the three groups would be playing separately and at times together (or, as near together, as Malcolm, conducting, could get them.) Malcolm was also promising an orchestral version of the *Cornish Dances* enhanced with the addition of the two brass bands. Nonetheless the CAMP generously confirmed that the BBC would record the whole of the concert on 16 March and then broadcast part of it on 17 April, the anniversary of Merritt's death.

For the next few weeks Malcolm was extremely busy orchestrating Merritt's anthems and taking particular pleasure in the March he had discovered, written in honour of Edward VII's Coronation. The concert itself was a huge local success. The cathedral was packed and everyone had a good time. In the euphoria of the occasion it was probably not noticed that Malcolm's own original contribution, *Salute to Thomas Merritt*, was disappointing. Maybe inside the Cathedral, with the brass bands and orchestra playing in three different areas, the effect was novel, but the dreary, four-minute fanfare is among his poorest works. Nor indeed did Merritt's carols, anthems and march bear much relation to Malcolm's hyperbole ('some of the most vigorous and joyous music it has been my pleasure to hear').

But the Thomas Merritt affair was not over. Malcolm had managed to interest South & West Television and a further concert at Truro was mooted, Malcolm clinching the deal by wining and dining his new friends from the West in a manner probably not seen since Lucullus. They were sent reeling back to Plymouth, any misgivings they might have been harbouring totally erased from their befuddled brains. A letter of thanks survives:

> Tom and I are most grateful to you for a splendid day yesterday. I only wish I could recall what happened between the end of lunch and the *Magic Roundabout*. Did I promise you a £500 fee or something?

Both concerts gave great pleasure to participants and audiences alike, but Malcolm's involvement was hardly the most productive use of his time. During the thirteen months on which he worked on behalf of Thomas Merritt he himself produced nothing other than the effective but slight *Anniversary Overture*.[16] He was being driven by outside forces, reacting in this parochialism against the dominant London musical establishment. Despite regular visits to the capital (where the elegant Gore Hotel had become something like a second home), he felt more and more of an outsider there, so he immersed himself obsessively in Cornish life, exaggerating his role as 'a people's composer'.

In late 1968 he had the encouragement of being the subject of a first television documentary, Herbert Chappell's *A Portrait of Malcolm Arnold*, made for the BBC *Omnibus* series and based on interviews with John Amis in Cornwall, which were linked with extracts from his music, specially recorded by Malcolm

---

[16] Written for the twenty-first anniversary of the founding of the Hong Kong Philharmonic Society, and originally entitled *Hong Kong Festival Overture*, it was given its first performance in Hong Kong on 8 December 1968.

with the LSO.[17] Initially Chappell had encountered much resistance to the idea in the BBC television hierarchy, where his view that Malcolm was 'one of the most grossly underrated composers of our day'[18] was not shared. The suggested programme, he was told, would be 'rather lightweight'. Might he not consider a documentary on Edmund Rubbra? 'I do not find this alternative immediately appealing,' replied Chappell with asperity. And he quickly returned to the attack, upset that England's recent win in the football World Cup seemed to have undermined cultural values:

> I don't know whether the fault lies with me, the innumerable programme ideas I have submitted in the past year and which have got nowhere, or whether the BBC is intent on letting music programmes crumble away completely, but I understand that Paul Fox has turned down the Malcolm Arnold idea and, quite honestly, I can think of nothing else that might appeal to him apart from 'Nobby Stiles conducts Beethoven's Fifth'...[19]

Most tellingly, Herbert Chappell quoted an off-the-record remark from 'a distinguished music critic who asked to remain anonymous':

> Had Malcolm been born a few hundred years ago and been christened Vivaldi or Haydn, we'd all be raving about his melodic genius, his good humour, and his instinctive flair for orchestral colour.

*A Portrait of Malcolm Arnold* did much to remind the general public of the genial composer of many popular works, the interviews setting him evocatively within his Cornish landscape. In the course of the film Malcolm stressed his pleasure in his new role and could not resist a few criticisms of musical life in London, 'where you get a lot of highly specialised professionals giving the thousandth performance of the same works'. Music, he believed, was 'what people do for themselves'. A composer's job was to encourage music-making in the community. That was why he enjoyed writing music for children and amateurs.

It was an understandable position to adopt as an outsider whose work was either being ignored or ridiculed. And from the security of the West Country Malcolm could sally forth to take on the establishment, whenever the mood took him:

> It's terribly unlikely that what we call 'contemporary' music will be listened to in a differently angled society...[20]

---

[17] There were extracts from *The Bridge on the River Kwai* and *Whistle Down the Wind*; *Tam O'Shanter* and *Peterloo*; the *Cornish Dances*; the Guitar Concerto with Julian Bream; and the conclusion of the Sixth Symphony. It was first transmitted on 2 March 1969.
[18] Memo to Norman Swallow (HMP.Tel.), 20 August 1968 (BBC Written Archive)
[19] Memo to Walter Todds (MPO.Tel.), 2 September 1968
[20] *The Listener*, 14 October 1971

It is a symptom of the times that we tend to take a vast and complicated machinery in order to crack a nut…. My view of music is that it should endeavour to express what it has to say in the simplest-sounding way possible …[21]

Schoenberg was a great musical thinker but a *bad* composer. The *Orchestra Variations* are dreadful … I have never found it necessary to listen to anything of Stockhausen's more than once. I really don't admire *Gruppen* … [22]

When asked about his treatment by the critics and musical establishment, Malcolm was usually tactful, declaring himself delighted that his music was played at all. Just occasionally, however, he let the wounds show. *The Guardian*'s Christopher Ford managed to ease through his defences and elicit an explosion:

I'll tell you how bitter I am – only as bitter as a man who wants to stand up and walk down the street and doesn't want people shouting offensive, patronising remarks after him. The critics have got to live, but for Christ's sake why don't they let me live too? [23]

There is also one very telling moment in Herbert Chappell's film, during most of which Malcolm exudes quiet bonhomie. Fat and double-chinned, he seems reassuringly avuncular, smiling a great deal and gesticulating warmly like an Italian. The face is almost cherubic, the voice soft and caressing. But there is a change when John Amis provocatively reminds him that some of the critics treat him 'as a musical buffoon'. His hands cease to gesticulate comfortably. The voice becomes more clipped.

Well, you see, people should always realise however intellectual any art form is, and particularly music, the very basis of it is exhibitionist. The very basis of music, or any artistic endeavour, is exhibitionism, and once you've realised this, people won't worry whether people are introverted or extrovert because you know that this is a bit of high class exhibitionism.

The words are imprecise, almost to the point of incomprehension, but the flashing eyes show just how much hurt motivates them. At the end of the outburst, with composure regained, he raises his eyebrows to John Amis as if to say 'Sorry about that, but if you will ask such bloody questions…!'

Thomas Merritt, therefore, offered Malcolm a refuge. But he was more than that. As a boy forced to go down the mines every day, Merritt was also a symbolic victim of man's inhumanity to man. In rehabilitating his reputation Malcolm was honouring a martyr of capitalist exploitation. Merritt's strong Methodist background would have been less appealing. But, as the third movement of the *Cornish Dances* showed, Malcolm seems at last to have come to terms with Pappy's Methodism (if not Pappy himself). He still saw himself as an atheist – 'religious thought,' he told an interviewer sternly, 'has led to some of

---

[21] *Ibid.*
[22] *The Guardian*, 17 April 1971
[23] *Ibid.*

the most awful situations in the world' – but non-conformist religion was part of the Cornish heritage and, as such, had attractions.

Not long after the concert at Truro Cathedral Malcolm had a big success at the Festival Hall with the one concert work, the *Peterloo Overture*, which he had managed to write between the Sixth Symphony and Thomas Merritt. He had struggled initially to make a start on the project, commissioned by the TUC for its Centenary celebrations, and had been helped by a letter of encouragement from Donald Mitchell. 'Thank you for your tremendous encouragement,' he replied. 'I shall approach the work I have to do with new heart and I appreciate your remarks greatly.' [24]

The *Peterloo Overture* tells of the demonstration of 1819 when many thousands of working people took to St Peter's Fields, Manchester, to listen to a Radical speaker protesting against low wages and appalling working conditions in the cotton mills. They also were protesting against the suppression of political rights, most notably the right to organise themselves in trade unions. This was an attractive theme to Malcolm and in portraying the nobility of the socialist cause he produced one of his finest melodies, an Elgarian salute to a pastoral utopia; its simple beauty stirs the emotions, radiating the love and peace which Malcolm so struggled to achieve in his own life.

This melody precedes and follows a loud and dissonant central section depicting the Manchester Yeomanry charging in to break up the demonstration, killing and wounding many in the process. It is the kind of manic military uproar which came easily to Malcolm. 'It will make the 1812 Overture sound like a string quartet,' prophesied the TUC's Vic Feather. [25]

The overture's wildly enthusiastic reception at the Festival Hall was repeated that summer in the Proms, [26] when Vic Feather and his TUC colleagues were again present. He wrote to Malcolm afterwards:

> We were all delighted with Saturday evening, and particularly with the tumultuous reception so justifiably given to the performance... [27] We are immensely proud of your composition to commemorate our Centenary and feel we have been responsible, through you, in giving something to the world of music.

By the late 1960s the Proms were a focus for the bad feelings between the general public, who on the whole liked traditional tonality, and the influential

---

[24] 5 September 1967

[25] Assistant General Secretary. *The Sun*, 3 February 1969

[26] At this concert on 3 August 1968, Malcolm also conducted Elgar's overture *Froissart*; Mozart's Flute Concerto (K313); Strauss' *Till Eulenspiegel*; Rachmaninov's Second Piano Concerto and Britten's *Variations and Fugue on a theme of Purcell*. The BBC Symphony Orchestra that evening contained many old friends in the brass and woodwind, among them Wesley Woodage, Philip Jones, William Waterhouse, Sidney Sutcliffe, Alan Civil, Colin Bradbury and Jack Brymer.

[27] *Peterloo*, despite this 'tumultuous' first appearance in 1967, did not again appear in the Proms that century.

lobbies within the BBC and London concert management which were anxious to promote both serialism and the avant-garde. A surprising commission from the BBC projected Malcolm briefly into the middle of this dispute. Asked to provide a work for the husband and wife team of Phyllis Sellick and Cyril Smith, to be included in the single Prom of 1969 which he would be conducting,[28] Malcolm produced a real crowd-pleaser, his *Concerto for Phyllis and Cyril*,[29] with a meltingly romantic slow movement and a brilliantly witty and uplifting finale, its style unashamedly popular. His programme note was particularly brief and pointed:

> It is in three movements and is written for normal symphony orchestra seated in the normal way. While not attempting to plumb the depths of the great truths of life and death, I hope the concerto will sound brilliant and give some pleasure.

Whereas at a previous concert large numbers of the audience had noisily walked out during Peter Maxwell Davies' *Worldes Blis*, protesting against what they considered the boring, tuneless music being inflicted on them, Malcolm's work received a five-minute ovation and the third movement was reprised. Significantly, it proved his last serious BBC commission.[30]

This pleasing success was soon followed by the excitement of a ceremony two weeks later in which he became a Bard of the Cornish Gorsedd. The ancient Gorsedd, which had been re-established in the 1920s, had aims which were very close to his heart: 'to maintain the Celtic spirit of Cornwall and give expression to such spirit; to encourage the study of Cornish literature, art and music; to link Cornwall with other Celtic countries; and to promote a spirit of peace and co-operation among those who work for Cornwall.' The honour of becoming a Bard of the Gorsedd was a real one, the previous year's new bards including A L Rowse and Barbara Hepworth.

A cheerful family party, therefore, drove down to Liskeard one sunny September morning for the investiture ceremony.[31] After changing into his striking, tailor-made bardic robes at the County Secondary School, Malcolm processed, a flowing apparition of bright blue from head to toe, to a bardic circle on the high ground at Castle Park. The ceremony was an impressive sight, watched by a crowd of nearly two thousand. One hundred and ten former bards had assembled, and, much to Malcolm's delight, all the ceremony was in

[28] 16 August 1969. Malcolm conducted all the programme apart from Bliss's Concerto for 2 Pianos which Bliss himself conducted. The all-English programme contained Purcell's Suite from *Abdelazer*, Elgar's *Enigma Variations*, Delius' *Dance Rhapsody No 1* and Walton's *Façade*.
[29] Now known as the Concerto for Two Pianos (3 hands). Cyril Smith had only the use of his right hand since a stroke twelve years earlier.
[30] The final commission – the *Fantasy for Audience and Orchestra* for the last night of the 1970 Proms – hardly furthered Malcolm's reputation as a serious composer.
[31] Details from *Cornish Guardian*, 11 September 1969

*The Bard of the Gorsedd, 1969*

Cornish.[32] Malcolm enjoyed it all, but particularly the sounding of the Horn of the Nation (Corn Gwlas) to the four points of the compass and a flower dance by local dance school pupils to the music of a harp. Malcolm was one of thirteen bards initiated, but even with his hood on was plumply recognisable. He took the Cornish name 'Tromba', trumpet, because as he confided to reporters, 'I still have a trumpet, and play occasionally at dead of night in my cottage near Padstow'. A fairly bibulous celebratory lunch followed. 'We sat in a field under a brilliant sun,' Katherine recalled, 'Dad still in bardic blue, all of us getting hotter and merrier. Fortunately Dad hadn't brought his trumpet along, so there were no extra soundings to the four points of the compass!'

Malcolm took his new honour extremely seriously, regularly wearing the bardic tie when in London. He liked the bright blue robes as well; he would take them out to Ischia, he said, to show Willie Walton.

A visit to the Waltons at Ischia had become a regular occurrence at this period, a holiday which was occasionally shared by Katherine and Robert and their friends. Malcolm would fly to Naples and then take a helicopter across to the island, at one end of which the Waltons had built their own lovely home, La Mortella, high above the village of San Felice. They had also created a series of holiday cottages in their subtropical garden, ideal for their guests. Robert has happy memories of one such visit:

[32] The welcome by the Mayor and the address by the Great Bard were also in English for those who, unlike Malcolm, had not studied Cornish.

We'd have wonderfully leisurely times, sitting on terraces in the sun with amazing views of the sea below us. We used to borrow two Fiat 500s and drive them all over the place, up the mountains and down to the beaches. Teenage girls from the village would cook simple but amazingly good 'handmade' meals. A big, grand bowl of *gnocchi* in tomato sauce and a glass of wine. Very Italian.

Dad used to write while he was at Ischia, but he and William Walton would often sit together in the garden, talking and laughing, their conversation usually peppered with risqué jokes.[33]

Robert found Walton engagingly funny.

He used to whisper to me little asides. He loved taking the mickey! He hated pomposity!

It was one of the many attitudes he shared with Malcolm.

One morning Walton gave Robert a detailed tour of La Mortella, pointing out with pride the various artefacts and furnishings: carpets woven for them in Sardinia; majolica stoves handmade in Bolzano; inlaid marble tables from Taormina. And on the walls were a whole series of fascinating paintings at which he would wave his stick in enthusiasm as he explained them.

Eventually we got back to the big hallway. 'Yes,' said Walton reflectively, 'This *is* a nice house, isn't it! But I tell you what...' – and here he looked cautiously around him – 'it's a bit of a *prison*!'

Katherine remembers her father basking in the welcoming atmosphere and endearing himself to the beautiful girls who cleaned the guest houses. Other remembered images are of Lady Walton, expertly warning off stray cats from her gardens with an air rifle, and Edward, mesmerised in the kitchen as he kept watch on the waste disposal unit which, for some reason, would hurl half lemons up into the air with a delightful gurgling noise.

Little Edward was not the most obvious guest to have in a house full of precious antiques, but he was very welcome at La Mortella. After one holiday in which Malcolm and Isobel had expressed their worries about him, Lady Walton wrote back urging a further visit:

Edward was no trouble at all. He is so much brighter than any of us. I wish you didn't have to worry about him. I am sure no harm will come to him. Please bring him back![34]

It was a token of the great warmth between the two families at this time.

The return to England from Ischia was always depressing for Malcolm. 'Italy a great success,' he wrote to Donald Mitchell on one occasion, 'and am sad to be back in an aggressive police state.'[35] Walton from time to time came over to England, when the two would usually meet up over dinners where the wine was

---

[33] August 2003
[34] 29 September 1969
[35] 15 April 1968

plentiful. Each supported the other's concerts if possible and Walton dedicated a new work, his *Five Bagatelles for Guitar*, to Malcolm.

Walton's return to the cinema in 1969 was also something of a joint venture. *The Battle of Britain* had more input from Malcolm than has been credited, but the business of helping out his friend went back much further, if Malcolm is to believed.[36] Walton was now in his mid-sixties, had not written a film score for many years, and contacted Malcolm at the start of the project:

> Would you by any good chance be willing to conduct the sessions ... I should feel much more confident with you about if things should go wrong.[37]

By January 1969, with time beginning to run out, help with conducting had turned to help with composition. Malcolm had answered an SOS and was duly sent the start of two sections of a scherzo. 'I think they should be fairly loud,' added Walton, 'as I imagine there are a lot of background airplane noises to overcome. On the other hand it is probably better the other way round.'[38] Walton himself found he had nothing much to offer. 'No sign of a tune!' he wrote to Malcolm. 'Every time I think of one I find I've written it before.' Building on various scraps sent from Ischia, Malcolm soon helped Walton produce the requisite twenty minutes of music: a German waltz to accompany shots of pre-war Berlin; a blitz sequence, with Walton's Wagnerian allusions to Siegfried's horn-call; a scherzo for the dog-fights; and a stirring march for the finale in Malcolm's most exuberant style.

By April they were both in the Denham studios, recording the score. Edward Greenfield of *The Guardian* called in just as the dog-fight scherzo was being recorded:

> In the studio a whole wall opposite the conductor takes the widescreen projection of the film, with the timing in seconds flickering along on one side like an Olympic bobsleigh transmission. Arnold, a beacon of sweat, whips up the orchestra furiously ... First time through Arnold overruns by thirteen seconds: 'My God! I've got to get a move on!' And get a move on he does, so that on the third go it is the other way round. 'I was so excited I got to the Heinkel too soon!' The fourth take is perfectly timed. Arnold comes to the Heinkels at exactly the right moment, and crashes the last German into the sea on the right chord precisely. We watch the playback in colour and Arnold asks with a hint of modest uncertainty 'That was the best one, wasn't it?'

The final sequence, wrote Greenfield, was 'a grand superdambusting march' for which Malcolm encouraged Walton to take over the baton, whispering in his ear 'a piece of cake!' As Walton entered the studio to applause from the orchestra, a technician in the control room turned to Malcolm with a smile: 'Got your assistant on, Malcolm?' Walton was soon attacking the 'grand superdambusting march' with relish, with Greenfield exulting in the control room:

---

[36] In an interview with Sam Edenborough for Oxford University Radio (1996) he claimed, for example, to have helped Walton with his Coronation March, *Orb and Sceptre*.

[37] 8 September 1968. Malcolm Hayes (ed.): *The Selected Letters of William Walton,* p.383-4

[38] January 1969, *ibid.* p.385

*William Walton and Malcolm during the recording session for* Battle of Britain

> A grand patriotic tune, to out-hope and out-glory anything that Sir William has yet written, whether for films or coronations. We hug ourselves at the barefacedness of it, Arnold laughing in admiration.

When Greenfield gently suggested to Walton that the March began a little like Elgar's Second Symphony, Walton turned to Malcolm and gave him 'a pointed look'.

But the March never became the popular hit it promised to be. For United Artists rejected the score on the grounds that there was not enough music to make an accompanying LP. Malcolm was outraged. 'The music is Walton at his very best,' he cried. 'It would be lunacy to reject it!' Walton was equally upset. 'It's a bloody cheek. All these Americans want is more money.'[39] A well-known writer of light music, Ron Goodwin, was called in to produce a new score, and Laurence Olivier, who played Air-Vice-Marshal Dowding in the film, threatened to have his name taken from the credits unless the 'Walton' score were reinstated. A compromise allowed the dog-fight scherzo to stay in, and some prints of the film also retain the Elgarian march in the closing credits. (The Walton-Arnold recordings were miraculously preserved and have recently been issued on DVD.)

It is said that this rebuff turned Malcolm away from films for good. Perhaps it did, but his involvement had already slowed notably. Apart from a little flurry of four films written in 1965-66 and *The Reckoning* (released in 1969) he had kept away from the film studios during his Cornish years. He had one final commitment to fulfil, an all-star *David Copperfield* for which he wrote a very moving score in late 1969.

---

[39] The LP could make them an extra £40,000.

*Malcolm and Deep Purple, September 1969. Jon Lord is second from the left*

There were still many new projects. That year, for example, he collaborated with Jon Lord and the Deep Purple rock band in a concert at the Albert Hall, in which he conducted Jon Lord's *Concerto for Rock Group and Orchestra*[40] and also gave his Sixth Symphony its London première in front of four and a half thousand Deep Purple fans.

With his shoulder-length hair and hungry expression Jon Lord might have looked like the Sundance Kid, but he was a highly articulate, trained musician. With progressive rock flourishing at the burgeoning universities, popular music was rapidly becoming more intellectually respectable, and a huge cultural shift was in progress, threatening to marginalise classical music. Malcolm, believing in inclusivity, relished the chance to work with an emerging rock group like Deep Purple.[41] He yearned to help bridge the gap, showing the New the virtues of the Old, not minding if he might be mocked.

His involvement, however, came about by chance. He had business interests[42] at Feldman in Soho, where Ben Nesbitt, Deep Purple's publisher, worked. Jon

---

[40] 24 September 1969. There were three items on the programme: Deep Purple also played a set.

[41] Deep Purple at the time of the concert consisted of Jon Lord (keyboard), Ritchie Blackmore (lead guitar), Roger Glover (bass guitar), Ian Paice (drums) and Ian Gillan (vocals).

[42] He marketed his brass band music via Feldman, via his own Henrees Music.

Lord had mentioned to Nesbitt that Malcolm would be the ideal conductor. Nesbitt sang out on the phone shortly afterwards:

> Hallo Malcolm! I've got a lunatic in my office who wants you to conduct his work for orchestra and rock group. He's got the Royal Philharmonic Orchestra and Albert Hall booked, and he's just started writing the piece!

When Malcolm was next in London, Jon was invited to meet him to show him his work.

> My insides turned to jelly. One of the first records I ever bought was Boult's superb recording of the *English Dances* on Ace of Clubs.[43]

So the young rock star turned up at the Gore Hotel with the first ten pages of his score. He had never written for an orchestra before, but had bought a book on orchestration as a guideline.

> There was Malcolm, this lovely man, a great, heavy-set, jocular fellow, and he said, 'Ye-e-es, Deep Purple! Marvellous stuff! Let's have a look, then!' I tremblingly handed him my dog-eared pages, the first minute and a half of music. It all went quiet in the room. He looked through it, making encouraging grunts, and then said 'Oh, yes, this will work very well indeed. This will be fine. Fabulous stuff, in fact! Well done, young man!' Then he stood me lunch ... He gave me the confidence I needed to get it down on paper without too much self-examination ...

Neither the orchestra nor the group were uniformly enthusiastic about the project, and the first introductory meeting between the two was extremely tense. Real, live, long-haired rock stars were something of a novelty in orchestral music circles, and one or two amused wolf-whistles hardly eased the situation. The first of the two rehearsal sessions was even worse. Malcolm had deliberately let the orchestra and band play the piece through, mistakes and all. The copyists, under pressure, had put in many wrong notes, and each mistake received a bigger reaction from the orchestra, the atmosphere quickly degenerating into open hostility. Jon Lord dejectedly left at the first break. Malcolm came bustling after him.

'Hey, where are you going? Sit down! I told you the first rehearsal would be fucking awful!'

'Yes, but my God...!'

'Don't worry! I know they're playing like bloody drains, but we'll change all that! Come on!'

Malcolm, on resumption, harangued the orchestra and quelled the worst dissidents with several choice expletives. At lunch he headed out of the Albert Hall with the lead singer, Ian Gillan, disappearing into one of his favourite Italian restaurants. Jon Lord marked their return with awe:

> Malcolm was drinking very heavily although you couldn't tell. He really could put it away. In fact, he utterly destroyed Ian Gillan, who was also a bit of a legendary

---

[43] Jon Lord, July 2003

drinker. He brought him back in pieces, an absolute dripping wreck, yet he himself was absolutely *compos mentis* and took a rehearsal all afternoon.

At the climax of this rehearsal a viola player[44] stormed off the platform, crying that she had not joined the orchestra to play alongside 'second-rate Beatles'. Malcolm told her not to be silly and winked in the direction of a somewhat glazed Gillan. 'She's just paid you,' he hissed, 'quite a bloody compliment!'

Even the rehearsal on the day of the actual concert was no better. Malcolm grew increasingly annoyed at 'the continued haughty disinterest of the orchestra'[45] and he suddenly stopped halfway through the first movement. The RPO were confronted with eighteen stone of outrage.

> I don't know what you think you are doing. You are supposed to be the finest orchestra in Britain, and you're playing like a bunch of fairies.[46] Quite frankly, with the way it's going, you are not fit to be on the stage with these people, so pick yourselves up and let's hear some bollocks![47]

Deep Purple looked on in fascination, half expecting the orchestra to pack up their instruments and walk out. Jon Lord was hugely impressed:

> It became clear that every one of them – even the violas – really loved him! So the RPO forgave him the outburst and began really playing. By the end of that rehearsal there were even a few smiles on the faces of the band. They began to realise that it wasn't going to be quite the disaster it had appeared earlier. Had it been a lesser man in charge, not just a lesser conductor, it would have been an utter débâcle …

For the rest of that rehearsal Malcolm kept everything extremely light-hearted. If a wrong note was played, he'd correct with a 'Is that note really on the instrument, dear chap?' or 'Are we certain that note actually exists?' At one break the principal cellist was complaining to Lord that a passage was unplayable at the speed he wanted it. Malcolm came up just as Lord was apologising.

'Don't apologise, dear chap. It's what you heard in your head. That's important. Now, what's the problem?'

The cellist explained and suggested removing a note.

'Why don't you leave that one in and take this one out,' queried Malcolm.

'Oh yes!' said the cellist in much relief. Malcolm's tiny alteration not only solved the problem properly, but improved the passage.

---

[44] Three of the RPO's viola section were female. Otherwise it was an all-male orchestra at the time.

[45] Vincent Budd: *The Gemini Man* (Gnosis Press, 2003). The book gives a fascinating insight into Jon Lord's several forays into classical music.

[46] Not the actual word used, which was stronger

[47] Ian Gillan: *Ian Gillan: The Autobiography of Deep Purple's Lead Singer* (Blake, 1998) p.83

He was equally soothing with the band. Drummer Ian Paice might be one of the best in the business but he found it hard to understand that whereas rock musicians play at the top of the beat orchestral musicians play at the bottom.

'Why can't they just come in on the bloody beat?'

'There's ninety of them,' replied Jon Lord. 'It's the way orchestras have to play.'

'Well, it's bloody stupid!'

'You're right!' interrupted Malcolm. 'It really *is* bloody stupid. But unfortunately it's the way things are!'

The performance, which was filmed and shown on the BBC's *Omnibus* as 'The Best of Both Worlds', went very well. Katherine was in the packed Albert Hall, having booked a whole row for her college friends.

> I remember it as great fun, and yet at the same time of being aware that Dad was being pretty outrageous, so there was some anxiety too. When I was little I always had anxieties that Dad would fall off the podium while conducting. At the Deep Purple concert it was, I suppose, an adult form of that anxiety.

Disc jockey Alan Freeman, writing in the *Melody Maker*, emphasised the hugely emotional atmosphere:

> The orchestra played like mad, the group played like demons and Malcolm Arnold (God bless him!!) conducted the orchestra like a man possessed!!! At times he looked rather like an older Elvis Presley. I nearly went out of my mind with excitement ...[48]

At the end, the enormous audience rose to their feet, screaming applause, clapping, shouting, whistling and stamping their feet. There were streamers flying, flags waving, joss sticks being lit and utter pandemonium. Jon Lord thrust a quart mug into Malcolm's hand and filled it with champagne. It was, wrote Alan Freeman, swiftly drained.

> The orchestra looked stunned, the group looked disbelieving and Malcolm Arnold looked ecstatic – like a man who has lost a shilling and found a fiver!!!! I did not count the number of times the group and Malcolm Arnold left the stage and had to come back again. It must have been seven or eight, because I was on my feet as everyone else was for nearly fifteen minutes ... Eventually they had to come back and play half of the last movement again ...'

The great success of the Concerto project cemented a friendship between Malcolm and Jon Lord and they kept in touch for some time, Jon always remaining grateful for Malcolm's devoted help:

> Malcolm helped shape the whole work. He cast a very benign eye over it and understood totally what I wanted to do with the piece.

No-one else, he believes, could have begun to have done such a professional job:

---

[48] 10 October 1969

If you watch the DVD of that night, you can see that it's held together only by the intent strength coming from the podium and the absolute confidence the band and orchestra both had in him that he'd get them through it.

When Jon Lord was involved in a similar project for the BBC's *South Bank Summer* the next year, he asked Malcolm to join him. Lord's *Gemini Suite* took collaboration between rock group[49] and symphony orchestra a stage further and was a much more sophisticated composition, in effect a series of six short concertos, each of the group's six electronic instruments being featured with the orchestra in turn.

> We had a lot of fun with the *Gemini Suite*! Malcolm was never anything if not fun. He was always ebullient. 'Come on!' he'd say. 'Don't worry! Everything will be fine!' We only had five hours' rehearsal. The fact it got played at all was again down to that mighty man on the podium.[50]

Some time later Malcolm was asked to conduct a recording of the *Gemini Suite*. He turned up with the full London Symphony Orchestra at the Abbey Road studios to find that he was expected to record just the orchestra parts, the tapes of which would then be taken to the rock musicians in a different studio. Always a stickler for correct procedures, at first Malcolm bridled. 'This is not right, Jon, this is just not fucking right!' Eventually, however, he saw the sense of it and backed down. From then on, as Jon Lord recalls, he was magnificent.

> The orchestra were bemused to begin with. There were certain parts of pure accompaniment which was very boring without the band. So I played the piano with them to rehearse it, which was a terrifying experience, but Malcolm again got me through it, just by encouragement. I could tell by the way the orchestra responded to what I asked them to do that they adored Malcolm. 'Adored' is a strong word, but they really would appear to have done anything for him.[51]

Malcolm's involvement with Deep Purple, for all its excellent aspirations, was damaging to him in the short term. Yet, ironically, as Malcolm's reputation continued to sink in critical esteem, official honours started coming his way. In 1969[52] he and Isobel were guests at an informal lunch at Buckingham Palace, together with the round-the-world yachtsman, Robin Knox-Johnston, and the Director-General of the BBC, Charles Curran. Malcolm found the invitation perplexing:

---

[49] The two concerts caused ructions within Deep Purple. Ritchie Blackmore and Ian Gillan (who had been given the leading role in Andrew Lloyd Webber's pioneering recording of *Jesus Christ Superstar*) did not participate in the studio recording, replaced by Albert Lee (guitar), Tony Ashton and Yvonne Elliman (vocals).

[50] The concert took place at the Festival Hall on 17 September 1970. The first half of the programme consisted of Malcolm's *Anniversary Overture* and Gershwin's *Rhapsody in Blue*.

[51] Vincent Budd (*The Gemini Man*) was told by Malcolm in 1997 that the LSO caused him less trouble than the RPO and the increased rehearsal time (two whole days) was another bonus. He was paid the not inconsiderable sum of £1,500 to make the recording.

[52] 9 July

During the meal, the chap next to me, as puzzled as I was at being there, leaned across and whispered 'Have you done anything important in the last twenty years?' 'Not a thing,' I said. 'Neither have I,' he said, and we both looked relieved.[53]

Later that November, he was invited to give the toast of St Cecilia at the annual St Cecilia Festival Dinner at the Savoy Hotel, in the presence of the Queen Mother and Prince Philip.[54] In the New Year's honours list of 1970 he was made a CBE. And a few months later he drove down to Exeter for investiture as an Honorary Doctor of Music at the University.[55] Malcolm spread the word that henceforth he was to be known as Dr Malcolm Arnold CBE.

Pappy, back in Northampton, was delighted to read of Malcolm's various honours. But his relationship with Malcolm remained distressingly poor. One small incident in 1971, when he was nearly eighty-five, was typical. Pappy had just come across eight early piano pieces, birthday presents from Malcolm to Nan, and wrote to Faber enquiring whether they might care to publish them. Donald Mitchell, sensing a possible upset, sent tactful enquiries down to Cornwall only to receive a short, sharp blast:

> I am shocked at my father's letter, and have asked him to return this music to me immediately, as he should have done immediately after my mother's death.[56]

Pappy's subsequent letter to Faber could not have been sadder.

> I fail to understand why he should say 'Nothing has upset me more'. He told me to pack up all the music that 'legally' belonged to him and send it off without delay which was done yesterday…

He added a pathetic PS: 'I have not seen Malcolm for eleven months'. Encouraged by a kind reply, Pappy wrote to Faber again.

> I agree with all you have said but I fail to see what I've done to cause Malcolm to insult me. Surely he ought to be thankful that his early music has been kept in a safe for over 30 years. Until a few weeks ago I had no idea that this music was in my home. All along I've been too proud of my clever son ever to intentionally hurt him. Besides, for many years he has been very kind financially.[57]

Whatever hurts Pappy may have caused in the past would seem to have been repaid with interest. Having lost his wife, his daughter and three sons, the old man longed for some affection from his sole surviving offspring. But just as in

---

[53] *Daily Mirror*, 24 September 1969

[54] 'The most difficult thing about conducting,' he said in his speech, 'is getting the dates.' His *Toy Symphony* was again part of the post-dinner entertainment. Among the players of the toy instruments this time were Dr W S Lloyd Webber (father of Andrew and Julian), then Principal of the London College of Music, and Robert Ponsonby, William Glock's successor at the BBC.

[55] 2 July 1970. 'No musician of our times,' said Professor Clayton at the ceremony, 'has more enhanced the gaiety of the nations.'

[56] 10 May 1971

[57] 24 May 1971

his younger days he had never understood Malcolm and the turbulence within him, so now in old age he quite failed to come to terms with Malcolm's emotional problems, the difficulty he always had in accepting strong affection, the inner fears of loss of independence, the asthmatic's need to breathe. The more intense the old man's desire for reconciliation, the further apart he and his son grew.

Robert remembers that on visits to his grandfather around this time he found him as charmingly eccentric as ever:

> He would tell everyone his age, whenever he could. And how many lengths he'd done in the local baths, which he'd visit weekly, even in his eighties. He still kept a leather-bound copy of the *Radio Times* and would go through it, marking anything that related to Dad. He would play Dad's music on the piano too, which could be alarming. Scrabble was his favourite, all-consuming pastime so I made him a board out of blocks of wood …[58]

Robert remembers times when his father attempted to be friendly with Pappy, but former unkindnesses were not easily undone, and the relationship remained difficult:

> Pappy in old age used to ring me up and say 'Why doesn't Malcolm speak to me any more?' He would be crying on the phone, particularly on one occasion when Dad had stopped his money. I rang up Dad and said 'Hey, what's going on? Your dad's been on the phone!' And I think I persuaded him to start paying again the weekly sum which helped him through …

By this time Robert had left St Paul's and gone up to Cambridge to read anthropology, a subject which Katherine at Durham was now also studying. Robert's departure to university in 1968 was the moment for Sheila to move from Denbigh Gardens to a smaller house in nearby East Sheen. It had taken her some while to come to terms with the break-up of her marriage, about which she felt so strongly that in the immediate aftermath she had sent off their double bed to Thursley. Sheila herself spent the year after the divorce laid up with a slipped disc, the condition thought to be largely psychosomatic, for, although the last years of the marriage had been a battle, she was nonetheless devastated at its outcome. She never remarried, devoting herself instead to teaching the violin. She had given up her own promising career as an instrumentalist to safeguard her children's best interests and accordingly she always expected from them the highest of achievements. It could not have been easy for Katherine and Robert at times to accommodate conflicting parental attitudes, the one demanding, the other indulging. But without the former they might well have floundered.

In their university years both Katherine and Robert found their father very good company. His celebrity lent him understandable fascination and, when they went down to Cornwall, there was always Isobel to act as the patient intermediary, absorbing the problems much as Sheila had done. Malcolm continued

---

[58] August 2003

*Katherine as a student
at Durham University*

to encourage their music-making as a matter of course. He celebrated Robert's interest in the guitar by writing a short piece for him and Katherine.[59] It is an attractive little work, its chief melody a distant cousin of *Whistle Down the Wind*. Malcolm took Robert to Newquay on one visit to buy him a Spanish guitar. They spent an entire morning in the music shop, Malcolm engrossed in chatter with the assistants and having a delightful time with some of the trumpets.

During Katherine's time at Durham University a new College, Trevelyan, was built and she was one of its first students. At the official opening,[60] at which Lord Butler was chief guest, Malcolm conducted *The Trevelyan Suite*, a work in three short movements written for the occasion. He scored it for ten players, all studying at Trevelyan: 3 flutes, 2 oboes, 2 clarinets, 2 horns and a cello. As the loving father he intermittently tried hard to be, he wrote a special part for Katherine. The Suite was a great success, though it nearly ended in disaster. The performers were stationed on a balcony overlooking an enclosed courtyard and one of the clarinettists remembers that Malcolm, 'a bit tipsy', at one point nearly toppled over the low balustrade and down on top of the listeners.[61]

That summer term Malcolm also came up to Durham for a second time with Rudolf Schwarz and the Northern Sinfonia, who were still including the Flute Concerto in their repertoire, and stayed at the County Hotel where Katherine and her friends came to uproarious dinners. Malcolm marked Katherine's twenty-first

[59] 1966. The *Fantasy for Flute and Guitar* has recently been published by Queen's Temple Publications.
[60] 12 March 1968
[61] Edward Kay, March 2004

birthday with the score of *The Trevelyan Suite*, beautifully bound in green leather, as well as a Michael Ayrton painting and a big celebration in the Gore Hotel.

> He could not have been kinder. We only had good times with Dad at this stage. There were marvellous meals out and shopping expeditions![62]

But Malcolm was possessive. When boy friends came on the scene they did not always find him easy. Adrian Harris, for example, whom Katherine was later to marry, was taken aback at being called 'a jumped-up, middle-class accountant', finding Malcolm at that period 'a bit bloody terrifying!'[63] He also remembers incurring Malcolm's wrath when he mislaid his prized key-ring, a gift from Dorothy with Fiat in platinum in the centre. It also took time coming to terms with the various bizarre outcomes of Malcolm's erratic driving. On one occasion Malcolm hit a kerb so hard that a front wheel became detached, but he persevered, three-wheeling in unruffled calm, until stopped by the police. On another occasion, there was great alarm at Primrose Cottage when a message came through that Malcolm, on his way back from Newquay after a heavy drinking session with a fisherman friend, had crashed into a ditch. At the time it was causing Malcolm great alarm too, for he was vaguely aware, as he sat slumped in his marooned car, of blood seeping all over him. Death was always something of a preoccupation, and this, he thought, must be it. But he waited patiently and nothing further seemed to happen, and there was no pain at all, which was odd, so eventually he and the equally bloody fisherman emerged, very shakily and cautiously, from the stricken vehicle. It was at this point that he became aware of the large quantities of tomato juice, which he had loaded in the back seat with the vodka, now leaking all over the car.

Malcolm was not a father on whose presence his children could totally rely. He was not around when advice was sometimes needed, nor was his advice always objectively given. Robert, for example, was dissuaded at the age of twenty-one from becoming a painter:

> He said 'If you want to live as an artist, you have to sell things. You'd do better to sell something of higher value and more practical than a painting – like a washing-machine!' He was very bitter and disillusioned at the time about the music business. 'The problem with being an artist,' he said, 'is that the British media only allow one type of artist to exist, just as they only allow one type of composer or sculptor.' He was really angry about what he called 'the cult of celebrity'. He thought it was total-ly wrong that the media should impose their own single way of doing things. His atti-tude was that lots of people do creative things and they all deserved an audience.[64]

Robert remains grateful for the advice given at this time. But he had talent in abundance as an artist, as he was able to show later in life when he developed it

---

[62] February 2004
[63] July 2003
[64] August, 2003

full-time; it must have been a disappointment that his artistic father did not feel confident enough to back his own artistic endeavours.

Family holidays during the Cornwall period tended to be intermittent, usually relating in some way to Malcolm's work. Thus in 1970 Isobel and Edward accompanied him to Canada, where he taught at the Shawnigan Lake International Summer School and Festival of Music, held in the attractive lakeside setting of a private school in British Columbia. Ruggiero Ricci and Janos Starker were also involved and the Vancouver Symphony Orchestra played many of Malcolm's works in the course of the three weeks. But Edward was never easy to take abroad and when Malcolm returned to Shawnigan Lake the following summer he went alone.

Edward was now seven, a delightful and beautiful child, but detached and lonely. As he grew older he became obsessional about certain things. Gates and lifts were particular interests and he could mimic the sounds of gates with great accuracy. He would sit for hours watching the washing go round in the washing-machine. While Malcolm was away in Canada, Katherine kept Isobel and

*Primrose Cottage, St Merryn*

*Isobel with a Michael Ayrton sculpture behind*

*Isobel, her mother and Edward*

*Isobel, Edward and Malcolm, Primrose Cottage*

Edward company at St Merryn, writing her M.Phil thesis and determinedly helping Edward with his speech. After weeks of encouragement Edward began using the first person instead of the third when talking of himself.

Edward's problems put different, but equally great, pressures on both Malcolm and Isobel. Yet in the early 1970s Malcolm could still exert much of his old charm when he wanted to do so. He had that precious quality of making other people feel special. Indeed it was what kept Isobel going, even though Malcolm was often more careless of her than others. 'Isobel would say things which led to terrible rows,' says Katherine, 'yet when a stranger said the same thing and I was waiting for the row, it very rarely happened.' [65]

To the outside world Malcolm still presented an extrovert façade. Inside Primrose Cottage he was often troubled. Fear was replacing laughter, and problems were escalating on all sides. Katherine remembers 'an increased feeling of being embattled, trying not to let people know how bad things really were, especially as regards the drinking...' [66] Isobel was a willing party to the concealment of the truth. When Malcolm was too ill to work or convalescing in hospital, Isobel disguised the fact in her capacity as his 'secretary'. She firmly put visitors off in such circumstances.[67] If in the morning she bore scars from an argument the night before, she would always have good excuses ready. She was intensely loyal. But the strain was telling all round.

Malcolm's behaviour was becoming less and less predictable. Hilary and Tony Giles, for example, had unexpectedly met him when he was staying by himself at the Queen's Hotel, Penzance. Always trying to repay some of his hospitality, Hilary invited him up to have Sunday lunch with them.

> I got all the food ready only for Malcolm to turn up late and very drunk, a half-full bottle of vodka in his hand. How he drove up from Penzance we'll never know. He sat down in a chair for a bit, very comatose, and then we all had to go to the St Agnes Head Hotel for a pre-lunch drink, an occasion with Malcolm at his worst, shouting out 'Drinks all round!' and making us all want to cringe in the corner! [68]

In the later stages of his time in St Merryn he was less popular locally. 'He certainly wasn't universally loved,' says Hilary, citing an occasion when, after he had driven into a hedge, someone phoned the police to ensure he was caught while still drunk. 'It was a humiliation for him, though there was, of course, no breathalyser then.'

---

[65] March 2004

[66] February 2004

[67] 'We were going on holiday in the West country,' writes Robin, 'and rang up Isobel, asking whether we might pop in if we made it to Padstow. She was, at best, unenthusiastic. Malcolm, she said, wasn't available to speak to. She followed this up very quickly with a rather formal letter insisting that we did not call. She said Malcolm wasn't available.' (April 2004)

[68] September 2003

Jon Lord too had received an invitation to travel down with his wife to stay, but when Malcolm came to the door of Primrose Cottage he gave them both a very strange look.

> 'What are *you* doing here?' he asked. Obviously he wasn't having a great day so instead of saying 'You invited us,' I just said 'We were passing!' 'Hmm. Well, it's not a very good time.' So we went away! Although it was a bit of a shock, I wasn't total-ly surprised because I'd seen that mercurial change of character before. Even though he was terribly nice to me, I was always slightly intimidated by him. There's a side to him that can generate anger very quickly.[69]

Up in Manchester David Ellis began to notice a gradual deterioration:

> He was essentially a very warm person. So when he was depressed and drunk and started being rude, he felt bad about himself. He was frustrated that he couldn't do anything about it. He knew he wasn't being what he wanted to be, and the realisation of that just made him worse![70]

While Malcolm was working, David Ellis always found him sober and professional. But as soon as the music was finished, he became depressed and started drinking. It was not unusual for him to consume as many as five or six bottles with a meal, during which he would become maudlin and start talking about the sadnesses of his life. But the stories he gave David Ellis and his wife were not so much the truth as his own, more comfortable fantasy:

> He could never forgive himself for leaving his first wife. But he felt he had to. He felt he was morally bound to look after the child he was going to have with Isobel. He didn't really want to leave his first wife. He must have been in a terrible dilemma!

After the non-sparkling wines he would turn to champagne, always a signal for a downward spiral of his spirits. And at the end of the meal there would be brandy – 'And it wasn't your local brandy!' says David. 'It was as if he wanted to self-destruct.'

There was particularly heavy drinking on the evening which preceded a half-hearted suicide bid. A morning rehearsal in the Milton Hall, Manchester, had gone so well that Malcolm was able to complete the recorded broadcast by midday. David Ellis was delighted.

'Well, Malcolm, you can have the rest of the day off! You might as well catch an earlier train!'

They walked back to the Midland Hotel together.

'Coming in for a glass of sherry?' asked Malcolm.

'No. I can't.'

'You haven't got anything to do. You were scheduled for recording all after-noon. Come on! Just one!'

'No, I can't, Malcolm.'

---

[69] July 2003
[70] August 2003

'Well, come and sit with me in the French Restaurant and have a quiet chat while I drink.'

David gave in. A long bibulous lunch merged into an early bibulous dinner, and Pat Ellis had to come across to the Midland to pay for the meal and settle Malcolm's hotel bill, as he was in no condition to do either. Later that night he was carried onto the Manchester-Penzance sleeper. The next day David and his wife were shocked to hear on the News that Malcolm had been taken to Truro Hospital with a suspected drug overdose. They rang up Primrose Cottage. 'It's all been a mistake,' Isobel told them. 'I'd had enough of Malcolm coming home drunk. I couldn't wake him, so I called an ambulance and had him taken to hospital. Do you want to speak to him?' A distinctly croaky Malcolm came on the phone. 'There's nothing at all wrong with me,' he said, crossly. 'This embarrassment has all been my bloody wife's fault!' Waking up in hospital, he said, he'd put a dressing gown on over his pyjamas, walked out of the hospital and caught a taxi back to St Merryn.

Robin was one of a number of other relatives and friends who rang up in alarm at the news. He was told a different story: that Malcolm had taken a double dose of sleeping tablets accidentally.

It would have been out of character for Isobel to take the action she said she had. Year after year, foolishly or courageously, she went along with the whole horror of the manic depression and alcoholism. The sleeping tablets were probably not taken in an overdose accidentally, for, as Malcolm himself said, years later:

> I tried to commit suicide on many occasions, even in Cornwall, which was the height of my happiness.[71]

Malcolm wrote just one major work in 1970[72] and it very much reflects the darkness of his life at this period. In the *Concerto for 28 Players*, completed just two months after the Truro Hospital incident, Malcolm has ostracised his melodic muse. Instead he has turned, a little half-heartedly, to the twelve-note system of Schoenberg and to the dry sonorities and angular melodies of Stravinsky. Devotees of serialism also found it perplexing, for Malcolm, in his confused state of mind, did not seem to have the confidence to maintain the serialism. And so, from time to time, diatonic melodies flutter gloomily around. The solo violin melody in the first movement and the almost perky, diatonically-inclined march in the third sound out of place.

The work was commissioned by the English Chamber Orchestra, which was essentially Benjamin Britten's Aldeburgh Festival Orchestra. The

---

[71] BBC *Omnibus*, October 1991

[72] 1970 also saw the BBC commission a *Fantasy for Audience and Orchestra* for the last night of the Proms. Malcolm much enjoyed the challenge, adding an extra beat to the traditional sailors' hornpipe (making 5-in-a bar!) and including the popular hymn 'On the road to Freedom, we shall not be moved'.

commission[73] was an important one, with a première at the Queen Elizabeth Hall where Malcolm had been asked to conduct the whole evening's programme. Malcolm seems to have decided, for once, that he would ingratiate himself with the London critics by writing a work to their taste. Unfortunately his Concerto allows only limited individual virtuosity, whereas the ECO had been looking for a work which would showed off the talents of all twenty-eight of its players.

The perplexity this uncharacteristic work caused was nothing to the unease generated by his programme notes, scornfully attacking current avant-garde enthusiasms. He took as his starting point the current fad for introducing the element of chance into a composition:

> In these days of aleatoric music, it is necessary to say that the piece is composed. Aleatoric music is based on a profound ignorance of the performance of music. All musical performances, and particularly the best, have a chance and improvisatory quality about them. The subtleties that can be changed from performance to perform- ance in the way of phrasing, nuance, and dynamics are infinite, and such an infantile idea as music by chance could only exist because so many people think of music as something on a record player, and not a live performance.
>
> The players in this piece, particularly of the wind, all play in what we accept as the conventional manner, that is, well. I have not resorted to any of the split notes or squawks, which have even had books written about them recently, because they are the sounds a player produces during his first week of playing the instrument, and it is insulting, and also wasteful, to ask artists who have spent their lives trying to avoid.

The tirade moved on to attack the avant-garde for splitting an orchestra up into various sections away from each other, to achieve surround-sound effects, and ended with a heartfelt, but not particularly relevant, comment on war:

> In the music I have written over the past thirty years, I have often noticed that there are passages which could be described as a send-up of martial music. This may be because in the forty-nine years of my life there has not been a day where there has not been some country at war.

The comments are in keeping with so much that went on in 1970. For example, he announced bad-temperedly in the press that he had decided to limit severely his work as a conductor:

> I don't think I can exist on the commercial roundabout. Conducting today consists largely of packing and travelling by aeroplane, train and car. You have to earn so much in such a short time that you can only give a superficial view of it, and that does not interest me. I'd rather go fishing....
>
> I had a lot of experience playing under many great conductors. I wanted to put their sort of ideas into practice. But all that is wanted nowadays is that you keep them together at roughly the same tempi.

---

[73] Via the Peter Stuyvesant Foundation

He was dropping nearly all of his commitments, he said, including a conducting tour of Japan, Australia and New Zealand. It would seem likely that the announcement, coming out in a year beset by depression, had a medical background to it. But it was all something of a muddle. At the very same time that he was 'rigorously cutting back' his agent[74] was trying to get a bigger conducting fee out of the BBC:

> I think the time has come to look at the fee Malcolm Arnold is paid when he conducts for you, particularly as his activity in this field looks like increasing …

The concert-going public was the loser. Malcolm could galvanize an orchestra to exciting, unpredictable feats. One performance of Elgar's First Symphony[75] finished ten minutes quicker than the norm. Whatever the reason, it delighted at least one critic:

> I doubt whether there are any living conductors who could have equalled Arnold's breadth of interpretation…. Great Elgar conductors are rare. In Arnold we have one of the finest I have heard.[76]

On another occasion Malcolm 'made the National Anthem sound like part of an unknown Respighian tone poem'.[77]

This surrender of his ambitions as a conductor coincided with a decision to leave Cornwall and move to Ireland. Malcolm had visited Ireland quite recently to research *The Reckoning* and Katherine was now working there and sending back glowing reports. The decision in favour of Ireland was taken in 1971, a few months before Malcolm's fiftieth birthday and nearly a year before the actual move. Malcolm paid a preliminary visit that January. 'I hope the Irish trip is worthwhile,' William Walton had written to him. It clearly was, for by July Walton was declaring, 'I am so glad that you have definitely decided to go to Ireland'.[78]

By 1971 Malcolm's finances were in a mess. *David Copperfield*, his last film, had been completed in 1969, so for two years he had not received the huge cheques which used to come automatically with the latest film contracts. He had tried to start a new, profitable career as a conductor, to allow him escape from the tedium of yet more film scores, but, with the hostility of the BBC now assured for the long term, it looked as if he was never going to achieve more than fringe status and he had never been keen on playing bit parts. He still had large royalties coming his way from his many films, but, as his accountant kept telling him, without the occasional big cheque to support them he needed to make cuts in

---

[74] Jack Phipps of Pears-Phipps
[75] At the Camden Festival with the Royal Philharmonic Orchestra, the Odeon, Swiss Cottage, March 1967
[76] Denby Richards, *Music & Musicians*, May 1967
[77] Neil Tierney, *Daily Telegraph* (Manchester edition), 18 November 1968. Malcolm was conducting the BBC Northern Symphony Orchestra at Liverpool.
[78] 24 July

expenditure. It was unthinkable that he should no longer be able to live in his customary style, so he had to go to Ireland, where he would enjoy important tax benefits.

But he kept putting it off. He had too much to lose in leaving Cornwall. He was a celebrity, the composer of the *Cornish Dances* and *Padstow Lifeboat*, a Bard of the Gorsedd and known in most pubs from Tintagel to Bude. That was important to him; a compensation for the loss of his critical reputation. And life was comfortable at St Merryn in a way it had never been before. It may have militated against the flow of music, but he was getting older, with longer periods of tiredness and depression, increasing sleeplessness and reasons to be anxious about his state of mind. On the whole, in the six years since the move from Thursley, he had not done too badly. One symphony, two concertos, two overtures, a set of dances, two works for brass band, six films and various bits and pieces. It hardly compared to the vast productivity of his younger years, but everything was harder for him now. He knew his brain had slowed.

In the early months of 1971 he wrote one final Cornish work, a Viola Concerto. He had been wanting to write for the viola for some time, for the two composers he particularly idolized, Berlioz and Walton, had each written a fine work for the instrument. He was delighted, therefore, to be commissioned by Rudolf Schwarz[79] to write a concerto for the Northern Sinfonia and its principal viola player, Roger Best.

The delight shows through. After the uncertainties of the previous year Malcolm has again found himself. The concerto contains some wonderfully expressive melodies, much tightly written diatonic argument, and a mastery of orchestration which allows the viola the full range of its register (which even Walton could not manage) without it ever being in danger, as the viola so often is, of being drowned. The concerto's heart is its slow movement, its principal melody full of regret, an elegy for all the happiness he has known in Cornwall. Elsewhere the work is confident in tone, the first movement lyrically positive and the last containing a fast, folk-like theme which conjures up smiling rustics on a summer's day. Yet this *Allegro vivace* is curiously short. It is as if Malcolm cannot bear to think that this is the finale of his time in Cornwall, and so he cuts it off abruptly, letting a sterner, demanding theme, with which the folksy main tune is contrasted, win the day. The fun is in the past. So too the security of St Merryn. The future is again uncertain.

Malcolm was to spend another, final year in Cornwall, after the completion of the Viola Concerto in March 1971, but his last year was as unproductive musically as his first. The resentment of being forced to move spilled over into all aspects of his life. In June, when asked to write an article for *The Guardian*, he gave unfortunate vent to his pent-up fury with the critics:[80]

---

[79] Via a grant from Northern Arts
[80] 'Don't Shoot the Pianist', *The Guardian*, 3 June 1971

> There is no possible justification for the arrogant, high-minded way in which British music critics treat musicians.

From their arrogance he moved to their ignorance:

> Our music critics, with two notable exceptions, are people who are unable to perform or compose, and have not enough musical knowledge to be able to give elementary music lessons.

Next came their lack of impartiality:

> Certain artists who are either 'in' or 'out' will get the same criticisms regardless of what they do.

No wonder, then, that the critics were an object of ridicule:

> I should be sorry in some ways to see any alteration in our music criticism, because the astounding gaffes that are made every day are a source of constant amusement to all musicians.

And his peroration was short and sweet:

> Let us say down, down, down with the music critics before they make our music the arid and joyless music of the concentration camp.

The critics noted his comments and waited. As Malcolm's fiftieth birthday approached, they happily ignored the concerts put on by the four BBC regional orchestras,[81] but the Northern Sinfonia, which had given the première of the Viola Concerto in Carlisle, asked Malcolm to conduct a 'birthday' concert at the Queen Elizabeth Hall, which included the Viola Concerto and several other of his works.[82] The critics swooped down on him. The glorious Viola Concerto was ripped to pieces – it was far too melodious for the 1970s – and the other, earlier works were similarly dispatched. Max Harrison was typical in the relish with which he set about the *Sinfonietta No 2* of 1958:

> It would be agreeable to write a more positive review of Malcolm Arnold's fiftieth birthday concert and to report a larger audience. But, alas, the nondescript quality of his compositions defies the greatest initial goodwill.
>
> The three movements of Mr Arnold's *Sinfonietta No 2*, for example, are like pieces of cloth snipped at random from the same bolt, competently woven – there is a pleasing delicacy to the *Allegro non troppo*'s flue [sic] and horn writing – yet their shape arises from no inner necessity. And the 'eloquence' of the lento is a matter of such conventional gestures. Involuntarily one asks, does Mr Arnold never stop to think, to reject the stereotypes which come all too readily to anyone's mind? The finale poses the same question or rather answers it in a most depressing fashion.[83]

---

[81] The BBC orchestras in Manchester, Glasgow, Cardiff and Belfast all honoured his fiftieth birthday.

[82] There was a party afterwards, in which William Walton gave Malcolm a bound copy of the *Five Bagatelles*, and which several other composer friends, notably Humphrey Searle, attended.

[83] *The Times*, 16 October 1971. Max Harrison contributed to *The Times* for many years. Ironically, he was a great expert on jazz and the biographer of Charlie Parker.

Malcolm, who could hardly blame anyone but himself for the outcry, was glad to get away from London and down to Cornwall for his actual birthday. He would spend it, he told a local reporter, working on a seventh symphony and dining in the evening on local lobsters and Helford oysters. There was, in fact, a big family party at the Blue Lobster, which had a restaurant on the first floor where he could order his Lobster à la Malcolm Arnold. Katherine was back from Ireland for the celebrations, which the devoted Isobel ran with aplomb. Isobel understood that, for all his love of grand occasions, Malcolm was at heart someone of simple tastes. Her birthday present was typical of this understanding, a biography of the popular bandleader of the 1940s, Lew Stone.

On their last Christmas in Cornwall Malcolm invited down John Gardner and his entire family to stay. Malcolm needed people around him all the time. A quiet family Christmas for three was unthinkable. He and John Gardner were old friends, who twenty years previously had both had their First Symphonies performed at the Cheltenham Festival. John Gardner has strong recollections of Malcolm's idiosyncrasies at that time:

> He would nearly always dress very formally with a dark-blue suit and tie; he would insist on steady, day-long drinking, but there was always a break for tea at four o'clock. He was neurotically tidy – everything had to be put away in its place at the end of the day. He used the Oscar as a doorstop to his dining-room. And I remember him staggering some visiting friends of mine when, in the middle of Boxing Day lunch, he took his shoe and sock off to show where he'd shot his foot.[84]

The Christmas holiday gave Malcolm a short respite from the financial problems which were besetting him more and more as he delayed his flight to Ireland. But, as he told his accountant, he could hardly move until after the festivities for William Walton's seventieth birthday, for which he was contributing a brief tribute, *Popular Birthday*, to the series of pieces written in Walton's honour.[85] Photographs of Malcolm with William Walton at the Festival Hall show him plump and smartly dressed, looking younger than his years. He showered Walton with lavish entertainment during his short stay in London, and Walton was so moved that he left a case of wine for Malcolm at the Gore Hotel. When Malcolm's muddled life-style led to the gift going astray, Walton wrote to him a few weeks later in terms which underline their close relationship:

> Dining at the Gore the other night, I asked about my letter which should have reached you with the vino – but no sign of it – perhaps it's in the boot of your car! However this is more or less what it said as it was a spontaneous burst of thanks from the heart.
> 'Dear Malcolm,
> 'This is a small token of my affection & esteem & regard & thanks for your help & support both practical & moral, for I was often at the point of cancelling before we started as I was feeling very low about everything etc etc'

---

[84] April 2004
[85] Named after Walton's *Popular Song* (from *Façade*) and including a quotation from the Walton work

I can't remember the rest of it but it was in a similar strain & I just want you to know in writing how I feel about it all ...[86]

Malcolm and Isobel both attended the party at 10, Downing Street, given to William Walton by the Prime Minister, Edward Heath, the chief guest being the Queen Mother. It was a glittering affair with nearly sixty guests, all friends of the Waltons. Unfortunately Malcolm had been told by William Walton that he intended to be carried out of the party drunk (in the event he stayed comparatively sober) and Malcolm, wrongly sensing the spirit of the occasion, was drunk as the party began and got drunker as it proceeded. Early on he was violently rude to Bryan Forbes, reviving a disagreement they had had years before over *The L-Shaped Room*. During the meal, in which the guests sat round both sides of tables in a horseshoe formation, with the Queen Mother flanked by Walton and Heath at the top, Malcolm got louder and louder. Richard Rodney Bennett, whom he had known and helped as a young composer, was sitting opposite him. Benjamin Britten was two places to his right and ostentatiously ignoring all comments flying his way. Malcolm noticed, bided his time and eventually took action. Leaning across an astonished Lady Armstrong, he seized Britten by the lapels. 'You know, Ben,' he said, 'this Richard Rodney Bennett is a fucking good composer – better than you!' 'It was,' says Bennett, 'the most embarrassing moment of my life.'[87] Britten, who disliked uncouthness, had been getting more and more upset as Malcolm had continued to make loud and wild pronouncements on all things musical. Breaking the protocol that no-one moved before the chief royal guest, he abruptly left the table and made a swift, dramatic exit.[88]

By contrast, only two weeks later, Malcolm was beautifully behaved when he and Isobel went to Windsor Castle for a reception given by the Queen and Prince Philip in honour of the Queen of the Netherlands. The invitation probably stemmed from growing interest in who might one day succeed Sir Arthur Bliss as Master of the Queen's Musick. At the time of the invitation Malcolm had been a contender, but his behaviour at Downing Street had hardly helped his chances. It was a lengthy reception, beginning in the late evening and including both supper and breakfast. The highlight for Malcolm was a display of twenty-five exhibits from the Windsor Castle Library, each chosen with the guests in mind. For Malcolm three items had been selected: an account book, showing Handel drawing pay as music master to King George II's daughter; a programme of music by Handel drawn up by George III; and an original Mozart score. Malcolm was deeply moved by all three and was still on his best behaviour by breakfast time.

It was time to face the move. The accountants were very insistent, and he had run out of excuses for further delay. But now that his bags were being packed,

[86] 2 May 1972. Hayes (ed): *The Selected Letters of William Walton*, p.402
[87] January 2004
[88] Britten seems to have got over his upset quite quickly. Only four months later Walton reported to Malcolm 'Ben incidentally extremely aimnable [sic] about you'. (Hayes (ed): *The Selected Letters of William Walton*, p.405)

there was optimism at the opportunities of a new beginning. Katherine was still writing of the fun she was having in Ireland. And hadn't Dr Johnson said 'The Irish are a fair people'? He had, of course, qualified it in the next breath: 'They never speak well of one another!' But Malcolm liked that. It promised some good bar-room debate. Now was the right time to say goodbye to the Farmer's Arms, the Blue Lobster and Golden Lion. It would be odd, of course, not hearing the foghorn from Trevose Head on misty nights. And he would miss those chats with Tony Giles as they walked along the dramatic cliff-top at St Agnes Head, and the wisdom of dear Tom Morrissey down in Padstow harbour. But a new location might bring new inspiration, and that, certainly, would not go amiss. He had said his goodbyes to Cornwall in his Viola Concerto. There should be no more sadness. The Bard of the Gorsedd would still be under a Celtic sky.

# 13
# The Dubliner

## Camelot in Monkstown, 1972-75

THE CATALYST in Malcolm's long-delayed move to Dublin was the urgent insistence of his accountant that he should be there by the start of the new tax year. As the beginning of April approached, chaos and confusion had briefly reigned in Primrose Cottage, but somehow Malcolm reached Ireland in time. Isobel and the seven-year-old Edward, however, stayed behind for another three months, Edward's welfare being the one topic on which Isobel would now make a stand. He was well settled at school, no plans had been made for him as yet in Dublin, and Isobel insisted he see out the school year in Cornwall. Malcolm's intention of staying at the expensive Gresham Hotel was another good reason for their coming over later, his bank account being temporarily so overdrawn that Isobel was helping finance both the move and the new house for which Malcolm would be searching.

Katherine, who was working for the Committee for Research into the Irish Language, had shortly returned from Galway to Dublin with her fellow researcher Claire Devlin, when news came through of Malcolm's impending arrival. She quickly gathered around her a small group of friends as a welcoming party at Dublin Airport. Betty Hilliard was one of their number:

> It was unstated, but we were a kind of buffer. It worked very well, for he took to us all immediately. He loved young people. And the buffer worked two ways. He also liked having us around.[1]

Despite his overdraft Malcolm took a suite of rooms in the Gresham Hotel, where, he was pleased to learn, Caruso and Melba had once stayed, and, more recently, Prince Rainier and Princess Grace of Monaco, Elizabeth Taylor and Richard Burton, and the whole of President Kennedy's retinue.[2] But Malcolm was even more impressed that in the Easter Rising of 1916 the Gresham had miraculously survived the British shelling of O'Connell Street; that during the Anglo-Irish war Michael Collins, while boldly dining there with four other IRA officers, had eluded capture by the British; and that, in the following Civil War, after the hotel had been shelled by the Free State Army, Cathal Brugha had

---

[1] August 2003
[2] Ulick O'Connor: *The Gresham Hotel, 1865-1965*

bravely dashed out of the front entrance of the burning building to be gunned down in the street. In 1972 the troubles in Northern Ireland were at their peak and Malcolm took a great interest in Irish History, quickly identifying with the Republican cause. 'I am ashamed to be British!' he would declare with passion. But when drunk and belligerent, he could disconcertingly swop sides and proclaim unswerving allegiance to Queen and Country.

Malcolm now concentrated on treating Katherine and her friends to the good life. All the best restaurants, clubs and pubs were visited, and there were forays into rock'n'roll, for Claire's brother was a highly successful pop star.[3] Once, thirty years before, Malcolm had played pied piper in London. Now he had another youthful band to lead around the night life of a big city, and this time his wallet was bursting with notes.[4] For Katherine it was something of a mixed blessing. It was good to be closer to her father than she had been for many years, but it was at the price of his gate-crashing her party, monopolising her friends, and causing embarrassment with his excesses:

> In a way Dad did mess it up, though not completely and not without my going along with it. It was both fun and yet, at the same time, difficult.[5]

Malcolm enjoyed engaging Katherine's group in stimulating discussions. Politics dominated – he was still reading up on Lenin and Marx – but literature came a close second, his latest interests including James Joyce,[6] Samuel Beckett and Brendan Behan. He was excited to learn that Claire's brother-in-law was Seamus Heaney, who had just completed *Wintering Out* and settled in a cottage in Wicklow. Malcolm's love of poetry had never been stronger.

Betty Hilliard, like all of Katherine's Irish friends, found Malcolm a personality of absorbing interest:

> He was a very generous person, but he didn't know how to draw the boundaries, which made his life difficult. He didn't have enough of a shell around him. He was a bit like an egg without a shell! Katherine was very good with him, for he was not always easy, swinging between exuberance and depression, and sometimes showing a destructive streak. I think she would sometimes get angry, but never in his presence.

Claire Devlin agrees:

> Katherine was the adult figure, father to the man. Very kind to him, sensible and grounded, yet quite exotic too!

---

[3] Barry Devlin, bass guitarist of The Horslips. Formed in 1972, the Horslips packed out venues like Dublin's National Stadium.

[4] Because his income from film royalties was so considerable, the bank never questioned his intermittent need for large overdrafts.

[5] March 2004

[6] He had begun studying Joyce some time before. He expatiates knowledgably on him in an article in *The Listener* six months before departure: 'The work of James Joyce, particularly the end of *Ulysses*, gets very close to music, when words are used not for their precise qualities but to express an overall mood or emotion. I find it most significant that Joyce as a young man had ambitions to be a professional musician.'

Malcolm had this childlike curiosity about everything. There was this thirst for life, but no contentment. He didn't know how to get it. I felt that if he were to get contentment, he would lose his genius. The price of his genius seemed his lack of contentment. In all the generosity and all the fun I never saw contentment. I don't think he was even searching for it. It was as if he had given up the search. He was reaching out to other people to know what they were doing, but nobody could reach out to him. There was a cut-off point. You couldn't get through. The central part of him was untouchable. It seemed to me that the price of his music was torture.[7]

At the end of June 1972 Isobel and Edward rejoined Malcolm, staying briefly at the Gresham Hotel before moving into Meadowcroft, a house in Monkstown village, south of Dublin, high up on a hill not far from the port of Dun Laoghaire. Meadowcroft was an attractive semi-detached Georgian building, its impressive red brick façade standing well back from The Hill, a quiet road which curved down into the centre of Monkstown. It was not particularly large – there were just three bedrooms on the first floor and a study for Malcolm – but it had considerable period charm, its front door approached by stone steps and flanked by Doric pillars, its basement making an ideal self-contained flat for guests.

One of the greatest attractions in Monkstown was a zany little pub called Goggins. Famous once as a James Joyce watering hole and claiming an acquaintance with Bernard Shaw, it was run in the 1970s by the colourful Joe Keegan, whose bohemian customers crowded into the single, narrow downstairs bar, ignoring the one above. Goggins' charm was in its utter unpretentiousness, its dim Edwardian mirrors attempting an illusion of space which its low ceiling, yellowed by smoke, defeated. The furniture was of timeless dark wood, the room's main ornament a battered upright piano nestling beside the front entrance. In recent times it has been extended by the acquisition of what was once an adjacent boutique, but in the 1970s it had just a single, unprepossessing frontage, belying the fact that it was the hub of the close-knit, artistic Monkstown community and from time to time attracted many of Dublin's more distinguished writers and artists. Those who remember the Goggins of Malcolm's time describe it affectionately as 'Camelot', a brief and fabled moment in Monkstown folklore, with 'drinkards' for knights, a smoky bar-room as the round table, and good fellowship the holy grail. 'We had a few bob at last,' comments one survivor. 'The staid restrictions had started to disappear and boys and girls were doing what they should be doing.'

Johnny Doyle, a diminutive ex-jockey who sits hunched up at the bar most lunchtimes, finds it quieter these days. 'In the 1970s you had to be a little exotic to fit in here! They were a pretty racy lot. And a lot of fun!'

'It was an absolute panic while it lasted,' comments another old local soberly, surveying with approval his third dram of lunchtime Irish. 'Camelot they called it, be Jaysus!'

---

[7] August 2003

The names of all the chivalrous knights of Camelot and their ladies still resonate around Goggins. Framed photographs are quietly brought out with pride from secret places. Names trip off the tongue: Patrick Jammet, of Jammet's restaurant, for the best French food in Dublin; Rodney Ging, gardener and jazz buff; Victor Connelly, dentist and wine connoisseur; Anna Connelly, of the *Thro' the Looking Glass* antique shop; Lucinda O'Sullivan, writer on all things Irish and owner of a second-hand clothes shop; Brendan O'Sullivan, actor; Tony O'Riordan, writer and broadcaster; Monica Sheridan, television cookery expert, author of *Monica's Kitchen*; Michael O'Herlihy, director of many feature films, also responsible for television episodes of *Star Trek* and *M\*A\*S\*H*, as well as being a sculptor, businessman, jockey, and brother of actor Dan O'Herlihy; Mick Harkin, deep sea diver. And perhaps above all in memory, Goggins's own Arthur and Guinevere, John and Deirdre Ryan, Malcolm's two greatest friends.

John Ryan, four years younger than Malcolm, was a painter, editor of *The Dublin Magazine* and broadcaster. His current radio programme, *Sunday Morning Miscellany*, featured all the leading Irish artists and writers of the period. He had previously been a set designer, publisher and licensee, having famously bought the well-known Bailey restaurant and pub when he had gone to an auction intent only on acquiring a toaster. John Ryan had been part of the Dublin literary scene since, as a young man, he had founded and edited *Envoy*, a review of literature and art, which lasted two chequered years. This, together with the running of the Bailey, had brought him in close touch with a fiery group who revitalised post-war Irish literature: Brendan Behan, Patrick Kavanagh, 'Pope' O'Mahony, Gainor Crist and Flann O'Brien.

John's reputation brought many Dubliners to Goggins in Malcolm's time: Alan Simpson, for example, who not only had run the Abbey Theatre for a while but founded the Pike Theatre in a Dublin mews, where Beckett's *Waiting For Godot* and Behan's *The Quare Fellow* both had their first performances in Ireland; artist Tom Harem; and Professor Thomas Flanagan, who came over to Ireland each summer from America, and was planning the first of his great Irish historical novels during Malcolm's time in Dubin. John Ryan attracted writers and artists from all over Dublin to Monkstown. Everyone in Dublin seemed to know him.

He was the greatest of raconteurs, and he and Malcolm would trade stories by the hour. 'They were like homing pigeons, John and Malcolm,' remembers Deirdre.[8] Malcolm, indeed, had met his match in John Ryan, not only for anecdotal skill but also for alcohol, Ryan drinking a good three bottles of spirits a day. Inspired by his new friend, Malcolm read up voraciously on mid-century bohemian Dublin, and soon became an authority on the works of the hard-drinking Flann O'Brien, whose humour he adored. John Ryan at the time of

---

[8] August 2003

Malcolm's arrival was writing a book of reminiscences of mid-century Dublin,[9] and included a whole chapter on O'Brien.[10]

Deirdre Ryan, John's young second wife, owned the boutique, *Designs On You*, next door to Goggins:

> Shortly after arriving in Monkstown Malcolm came in with Isobel, intent on buying her something grand, fixing upon one of my most expensive dresses. I liked Isobel right away. Very ladylike and attractive. She was a good person, and that's what she radiated.

Intelligent and highly articulate, a striking red-head with the kind of pre-Raphaelite beauty which inspired Rossetti, Deirdre was Malcolm's ideal of Irish perfection and soon became his new *idée fixe,* a little more accessible than Sheila, who continued, however, to assert herself in his imagination and to whom he had just sent his love on her birthday. Deirdre found Malcolm charismatic but lonely, and did her best to cheer him up:

> We'd have lunches in the Bailey, which would usually be very indulgent affairs for he was very rich. Lunching with Malcolm was a long drawn-out business. It might start at 1.00 and end at 6.00. He was always very sober, that's the funny thing. Lunch times were always very pleasant times.

Malcolm, she says, introduced a new cult to Goggins, champagne:

> He was a complete champagne man. We weren't used to drinking champagne all day. He'd come into the shop and say 'Come in for some champagne!' Then inside the door of Goggins he'd clap his hands and call 'Champagne time!' Some people at the counter would say 'Oh Jaysus! Here he comes again!' for you really couldn't keep up with him.
>
> There was a thing called the Holy Hour when the pubs all closed from half past two to half past three. So we all piled out of Goggins at the beginning of Holy Hour and went to the Restaurant Na Mara, down by the harbour, where we had amazing lunches and terrific fun. Everyone was in clover!

Goggins had many great characters, and there were several older ladies in whom Malcolm took a keen interest. He would often sit beside Eileen Braid, a former violinist with the RTE Orchestra, a highly proper spinster, who none-theless was a Goggins regular and played the piano there with considerable dedication. Rodney Ging was often not far away:

---

[9] *Remembering How We Stood* (Gill & Macmillan, 1975)

[10] It ended, very typically, with a conversation John had with Paddy Kavanagh in the aftermath of O'Brien's funeral:

> 'Do you know the last thing he said?' Paddy asked me coming out of the church.
> 'I don't,' I replied.
> 'When he was lying in bed in the hospital, some fella brought him in a naggin of gin and a baby tonic. He filled Flann's glass with the contents of the gin, adding about half a thimbleful of tonic. "Almighty God," Flann gasped, "Are you trying to drown it entirely?"' (*Remembering How We Stood*, p.143)

*In the garden at Meadowcroft, 1974*

> Malcolm was very kind to Eileen. He would be feeding her drink after drink and, as
> he himself drank, so his language became more colourful in his encouragements of
> her efforts at the piano.[11]

Malcolm was also very friendly with the elegant Beatrice Coogan, author of a
recent best-selling historical novel, *The Big Wind*, a labour-of-love for thirteen
years.[12] Good-looking in an Irish way with her red-blonde hair, and seemingly
always dressed in pale purple, Beatrice Coogan would talk literature with
Malcolm for hour after hour. They found O'Casey one of their many shared
interests; Beatrice was currently writing about him, while Malcolm had first
come across the O'Caseys in 1953 when he had made arrangements of Irish folk
songs for a production of *Purple Dust* in Glasgow. Inspired by Beatrice Coogan,
he read all six volumes of Sean O'Casey's autobiography.

---

[11] August 2003

[12] *The Big Wind* (1969) was later reissued as *The Flower of The Storm*.

While Malcolm was settling in at Goggins, Isobel was helping Edward adjust to the move, delighted with his start at the Benin Casa School at Rathmines, which at least allowed her some respite in the mornings. 'He was a sweet, gorgeous looking little boy,' remembers Deirdre Ryan, 'but there was no peace with him. He needed attention and the cumulative need could be hard to take.'

Deirdre felt Malcolm showed great affection to Edward but struggled with his demands: 'He was often adorable with him. But then, at a certain point, he would be able to take no more and would say "Edward, out!" It was highly difficult for them all.'

Malcolm's twinfold reaction to Edward reflected a nature which often exhibited two contrasting sides. In entertaining, for example, he would either be elaborately formal or hilariously the reverse. 'He enjoyed being posh,' says Deirdre.[13] Dinner parties at Meadowcroft often began somewhat tentatively in the atmosphere of deep formality which Malcolm encouraged. But then, when things warmed up, there would be a swing from one extreme to another. There seemed little central ground:

> On one occasion, Malcolm, at the head of the table, was way past gone, and he stood up and pulled his trousers down, to huge applause and merriment, because he was wearing Union Jack underpants!

The atmosphere at the Ryans was more consistently relaxed. Rodney Ging on one occasion made some very mild criticism of one of Malcolm's works being played on the gramophone. Malcolm was suddenly at his shoulder, glowering. 'Well, fuck you, Rodney!' John Ryan had to jump in quickly, to separate the two. Another time Rodney brought along a very pretty American actress, whom Malcolm speedily appropriated. Rodney, to get his own back, began chatting up Isobel. As his hand strayed to her knee Malcolm exploded in jealousy and this time John Ryan could not stop the fight in the course of which a valuable Chippendale chair was smashed.

Malcolm's sudden swings of mood, which were now becoming more pronounced, soon became accepted in Camelot. Deirdre never felt totally at ease:

> Unpredictable. That was the word for Malcolm. I was always thinking in ten minutes all hell could break loose! But he could switch in the same sentence! If a waiter or someone displeased him, the eyes would go dark chocolate brown. There'd be no light in them. He would shout, or rather, bark. He could get very grand and demanding at a certain time of day. It was an awful shock because, generally speaking, he was particularly nice to anyone in service. Especially at the Restaurant Na Mara.

---

[13] Isobel had accordingly ensured that the interior decoration and furnishings reflected this side of Malcolm. 'Everything,' says Deirdre, 'was perfection with Isobel. 'Beautiful curtains, linen, glassware…'

When the depressions came, the attempts to combat them with drink only made things worse. On one evening, quite early in the Irish period, Deirdre was present at a dinner party Malcolm and Isobel were giving:

> And he was desperate to her. He was desperate to all of us! It was really awkward. He just lost it, and it was so embarrassing for Isobel. If I'd had a row, I'd be shouting back, but not Isobel. She was a lady. She just took it.

Music, as ever, kept depression at bay. Although nothing was produced during his three months at the Gresham, not long after they had settled into Meadowcroft Malcolm began to write again. For certain periods, it was noted in Camelot, he would disappear completely. The spongers slipped away disconsolate; the friends waited with interest.

He had three good commissions. The National Schools Brass Band Association had asked for a work to celebrate their twenty-first year. A nation-wide competition was organised to encourage children to write poems on freedom, from which Malcolm selected texts for a twenty-minute *Song of Freedom* for sopranos, altos and brass band. It was a highly effective work.

Shortly afterwards he was asked by the Croydon Arts Festival for an overture to celebrate the tenth anniversary of the opening of the Fairfield Halls. The Concert Hall had been built on the Fair Field, an open space for five and a half centuries, which had once held a trading fair and later was turned into a pleasure ground, until suppressed in 1866, because of riotous behaviour. For his inspiration Malcolm used an engraving of the riotous pleasure ground, as it was in 1833. 'I am completing an overture, which is turning out well,' he wrote to Donald Mitchell in his usual self-deprecating way, 'call[ed] 'THE FAIR FIELD' and is merely a fairground piece... I will send it to you when I have finished it, if you should be interested ...'[14] On receiving a copy of the manuscript Donald Mitchell was duly impressed, and, as often, used the euphoria of the moment to sow further ideas:

> I am delighted with the new Overture – it's a lovely piece, and full of marvellous tunes, as usual. I think the dedicatee ought to be very pleased with this tribute... One day, Malcolm, what about a set of Irish Dances? Has the idea occurred to you? And might it be a possibility?[15]

'Lovely' pieces 'full of marvellous tunes' was what Malcolm had given with prodigality over the years and what was still expected of him. But *The Fair Field*, which Malcolm dedicated to William Walton, was more than this. Although Malcolm modestly declared in his programme note that he had 'attempted to create the atmosphere of a pastoral fair field, with overtones of a fun fair', superficial glitter conceals a more sombre interior. The ending, in particular, gives a glimpse of the kind of writing which was to be such a part of the

---

[14] 2 October 1972
[15] 1 November 1972.

devastating Seventh Symphony, and reflects the current uncertainties in his life. He and Isobel were just emerging from a period of extreme difficulty, Malcolm inscribing Isobel's copy of the Overture 'For Isobel, with a new found love'.[16]

The third commission came from Richard Adeney, who had enjoyed great success for many years with Malcolm's First Flute Concerto and now asked about the possibility of a Second. Malcolm set to work at once, drank nothing stronger than Perrier water and refused every offer of payment. By the beginning of December 1972 the concerto was complete, a fine, thoughtful work, very different in mood from its predecessor of 1954, the usual lyricism muted except in the highly attractive final movement. The opening *Allegro* contains some dramatic mood swings and includes a Shostakovich-like fanfare motif described by Hugo Cole as 'the gesture of one who whistles to keep up his spirits'.[17] A sense of impending disaster hangs over the entire piece. Richard Adeney was delighted with it:

> As always with his concertos written for specific soloists, Malcolm kept in close contact throughout the writing. I found this really helpful, but it was probably helpful to both of us. For instance the scherzo movement ends with a difficult top E *altissimo*, a suggestion of mine which at first surprised him.[18]

William Walton was as pleased with his Overture as Richard Adeney with his Concerto. Malcolm's friendship with William Walton had never been so strong, and that December, as soon as he had finished the Flute Concerto, Malcolm went alone to Ischia to stay with the Waltons. He was back there in mid-January, having quickly written *A Flourish for Orchestra*, a commission from the City of Bristol celebrating the 500th anniversary of their Charter.[19]

At Ischia, Malcolm lived in San Felice, an old converted cottage on the Waltons' land where they themselves had lived while La Mortella was being built. It was a planned two-month stay in which he would make a start on the Seventh Symphony. He was again intending to use ciphers and had several pages of preliminary sketches with the names of Katherine, Robert and Edward worked out in cipher form, together with Isobel and Sheila.[20] The Seventh Symphony, he had decided, would be about his family, with the emphasis on the children. It was his way of trying to re-establish some semblance of coherence in relationships which were becoming looser and looser.

---

[16] 26 October 1972

[17] Cole: *Malcolm Arnold* p. 147

[18] April 2003

[19] Rudolf Schwarz conducted its première at Bristol in September 1973. Malcolm had accepted the commission, he told Donald Mitchell, because he had often been asked by conductors – 'particularly Tausky when he was with the B.B.C. Concert Orchestra' – for four minute pieces which were not necessarily overtures. 'There is a shortage of such pieces, and I think it might do well, as they say.' (12 January 1973)

[20] As if creating a code, Malcolm assigns each letter of the alphabet a note and then creates his musical equivalent of all those names he intends to include. Other composers, like Schumann and Berg (in his *Lyric Suite*), had also used ciphers to generate musical ideas.

As he sat alone in the cottage in front of his sketches, Malcolm regretted not having achieved a closer relationship with his two eldest children. He was sorry that Katherine's contract in Ireland had come to an end the previous September, just five months after his arrival, when they were having such a good time. Back in England, she was now about to go out to Peru to do some anthropological research. It seemed a long way away; a dynamic idea, but dangerous. Robert too had taken it into his head to fly away to distant parts. He should perhaps have seen more of Robert at Cambridge. It was good he had persuaded him, when he was wavering, to hold firm and finish his degree. But that apart, in retrospect, he hadn't perhaps been quite the support he might have been. He had made a couple of visits to Cambridge during Robert's time there; he could distinctly remember good food at the Blue Boar; and a shopping spree somewhere; but perhaps that was Ischia. He had probably drifted slightly away from Robert, proud though he was of him. Quite unintentionally, just without thinking. But when Robert had visited Cornwall, to say goodbye before departing on post-graduate research to Papua New Guinea, he had been supportive then, hadn't he? 'Always remember,' he had said firmly, 'that there will be a home for you at St Merryn.' Well, St Merryn or Monkstown, it was all the same, wasn't it? And Isobel would have sent a change-of-address card...?

With a frown of anxiety, Malcolm brought himself back from thoughts of Peru and Papua New Guinea to the empty manuscript sheet in front of him. Much of the first movement, which was to explore his relationship with Katherine, was now in his head. The ideas which had come to him on the plane on the journey out were definitely workable. He had thought them through carefully, and now it was all in his head.

Isobel, in Monkstown, received encouraging letters that things were going well. 'Malcolm is basking in Ischian sunshine,' she wrote to Donald Mitchell, 'working well and very pleased to get your letter.'[21] But she had no idea when Malcolm planned to return, and the strains of life in Meadowcroft seem to be telling on her. On Malcolm's behalf, for example, she wrote to another member of staff at Faber[22] calling herself 'Isobel Gray, secretary to Dr Arnold', a fiction which, had she only thought about it, would have been quickly recognised as such. It was in keeping with what was becoming a life of deception. And she sounds oddly peremptory in tone:

> Incidentally, I think perhaps you should know that Mr Arnold is in fact a Mus.D. and a C.B.E. as well.

There was a strict routine at La Mortella. Every midday Malcolm and William Walton met up for a chat and a beer. Once a week they all dined together. It was

---

[21] 26 January 1973. The Faber letter to Malcolm had told the good news that the new Flute Concerto would be given its première at Aldeburgh. Martin Kingsbury, the senior editor, was offering to write the programme notes, since one of Malcolm's jocular efforts would hardly impress Benjamin Britten.
[22] Julian Elloway, 19 February 1973

at one of these dinners that an eruption occurred which would have done credit to Vesuvius, just across the bay. Malcolm had been chatting the previous day to the Taits, who lived nearby and were good friends of the Waltons. Gudrun Tait was in charge of the letting of the Waltons' holiday properties and Malcolm was renting San Felice through her. Unfortunately her husband had spent much of the dinner criticising Susana Walton, and Malcolm, 'emboldened by a lot of wine',[23] now began repeating these complaints. With an expletive decorating nearly every noun, he declared hotly that Susana was ruining La Mortella by charging too much for the holiday houses, that Susana was being so tough with the young domestics that these lovely young people simply wouldn't stay, that Susana … William angrily interrupted.

> You have stayed with us often enough, Malcolm, to bloody well know how well Susana has built up the property and how well she runs it! Apologise this instant!

Malcolm preferred to storm away from the table. He arose early the next morning, threw his belongings in the back of William Walton's prized vintage Bentley, and drove across the island to the port, leaving the car stranded across some tram lines. A crowd was just beginning to gather around it as he boarded the ferry.

The next morning the Waltons held a conference and decided to delay going down to San Felice till lunchtime. It was something of a surprise when they found he'd gone, and a distinct shock to learn from a note that he'd taken the car. They managed to contact him at Naples Airport, but could not persuade him to return. William Walton, deeply upset, next tried ringing Meadowcroft, but nobody answered. Eventually he resorted to a letter:

> True, we had a bit of a mix-up the night before but what is a fallout between friends? I find it tragic that your mind has been poisoned against the unfortunate Su who has always gone out of her way to be kind to you & help you, & is most sad and distressed about it.
>
> So as you still have a long time on your house, till mid-March, I think you might think about coming back to finish off at least one movement of your Symphony. It distresses me to think that anything that has happened here should have stopped you composing further. As for mine it is in an even more paralytic state!…[24]

Further letters from Walton mention various articles of clothing and the stocks of drink that Malcolm had in his haste left behind him. They are full of the desire for speedy reconciliation.

> What marvellous progress about your Symph. I wish I could say the same for mine. It was obviously the psychological moment for you to leave. I doubt if you could have picked up the threads of the music if you had stayed here.[25]

---

[23] Susana Walton: *Behind The Façade* (OUP, 1988) p.220
[24] 24 February 1973. Hayes (ed.): *The Selected Letters of William Walton* p.408
[25] 5 March 1973. Hayes (ed): *The Selected Letters of William Walton* p.409

Susana Walton, who had deliberately kept quiet during the argument, has always felt that Malcolm resented her closeness with her husband. She would certainly not be the first to find this. Hilary Giles, for example, often found Malcolm difficult, not liking at all the fact that she had a mind of her own which she was prepared to express.

> He liked women to agree with him. I would tease him that he wasn't really Cornish and he would rise to it! He was more friendly with Tony than with me. I don't think he really liked women very much.

It was a point of view that Deirdre Ryan, whom he very much liked, was to share.

> He was very fond of women, and yet he hated them! He liked certain women, but was more a man's man. He wasn't a misogynist, but he liked women in their proper place.

And there was one in Meadowcroft, where Malcolm had returned by late February. He was soon writing to Donald Mitchell, covering up about the row in Ischia and probably believing every word:

> As you see I am here three weeks earlier than I intended, because in the five weeks I was in Ischia, I was able to plan what I want to do in detail in the 7th Symphony and the first movement is almost completed. It will be in three movements and I honestly find it much better to work here. It all goes well.

He was hoping to have the symphony ready by April. In the event it took another five months. There were too many distractions.

He was still conducting his own works whenever the opportunity arose. In the months when the Seventh Symphony awaited completion he packed his batons and crossed the Irish Sea on several occasions. In June 1973, for example, he was in Glasgow, conducting a programme of British music with the Scottish National Orchestra which included his Fifth Symphony and Concerto for Piano Duet (with Richard Rodney Bennett and Susan Bradshaw as soloists).[26] The orchestra radiated Malcolm's enthusiasm, said a local reporter, 'and this quickly spread to the audience.'[27] Throughout this visit he exuded high spirits and was full of good stories when interviewed:

> Did you ever hear about the lady composer who was conducting her own music in Canterbury Cathedral? It's true, I promise! Workmen were hammering somewhere underneath the place – and she pointed to one of those great big stone coffins in the cathedral. 'It's coming from there,' she said to the verger. 'Surely not,' the verger smiled. 'He's been lying there for centuries.' Whereupon a voice from the orchestra yelled 'Yes, but he's wanting out now!'[28]

---

[26] He conducted in the same programme Elgar's *Enigma Variations* and Alexander Mackenzie's *Britannia Overture*.

[27] *Glasgow Herald*, 2 July 1973

[28] Interview by Neville Garden, Glasgow, June 1973

The next day he travelled down to Snape Maltings for the première of the Second Flute Concerto. 'Softened Prokofiev,' suggested Stanley Sadie in *The Times*, 'with a Gallic hint of bitter-sweetness.'[29]

Two weeks later he was back in England, this time in Bath, conducting the English Chamber Orchestra in the Pump Room in a programme broadcast by the BBC. Mozart's Symphony 29 and Divertimento in D accompanied his own *Sinfonietta No 1* and a further performance of the new Flute Concerto. The *Birmingham Post* was wholly laudatory:

> Malcolm Arnold's flamboyant technique and amusing little speech to the audience did as much as the interval wine and cheese to ensure a mood of informality.[30]

Katherine, who had not yet gone off to Peru, came down for the concert with boy-friend Anthony King. Afterwards Malcolm, still dressed in his concert clothes, delightedly entertained them both to dinner in his hotel. At one stage he put a napkin over his sleeve and acted out the part of wine waiter. 'Does the wine have a good nose, mademoiselle?' he asked Katherine solicitously.

A trip to England at the end of April had been typically hectic. After conducting *The Fair Field* at Croydon, he had gone down to Padstow to have a good time with old friends at the May Day celebrations. He had then returned to Harlow to conduct the first performance of *Song of Freedom*.[31] It was while he was staying at the Gore Hotel on this excursion that he met a young lady who was to embellish his years in Ireland significantly, Irene Duffy.

Irene was one of three Irish girls who happened to be dining at the Gore Hotel the same evening as Malcolm. They had been sent over to England to study Elizabethan and Georgian banquets, prior to a launch of a similar enterprise at Castleton House, a well-known Palladian mansion close to Dublin. Malcolm, sitting in a corner of the dining room and captivated by the Dublin brogue and smiling Irish eyes, asked the restaurant manager to invite them to join him. It was a meeting Irene Duffy was not to forget:

> We were in our twenties, so we were 'game' to join this distinguished man who had, I think, about nine empty bottles of champagne on his table … Great fun ensued … We were enchanted by him and stayed up for long hours that night talking and having fun and drinking more champagne.[32]

The next day he went back to Dublin, but they kept in touch and, some weeks later, the three girls met up with him in Goggins:

> He invited the three of us to lunch – in a rather impromptu style, as it turned out – the invitation came as a surprise to Isobel, as I think he called her from the pub to say he

[29] 30 June 1973

[30] 16 July 1973

[31] Netteswell School Band and Choir, Harlow Sports Centre 12 May 1973

[32] February 2004

was bringing us up to Meadowcroft. Isobel coped very well and a very enjoyable lunch was had by all. Conversation was sober and light and all passed off well.'

Irene, daughter of an Irish policeman, had a degree in English and Gaelic, was a qualified teacher and had become, by the time she met Malcolm, an RTE television announcer. With her classical high cheekbones and dark beauty, Irene complemented Deirdre's colleen charm. Malcolm now had two Irish goddesses to worship.

The impromptu lunch was followed by further occasional meetings, sometimes with Isobel and sometimes *à deux*.

> We got to know each other quite well and grew to enjoy one another's company in a big way… Hours would pass by over a meal or listening to music or just sitting in one of his elegant rooms or in a gracious hotel. Malcolm was extraordinarily well read and had opinions – real ones – on a vast range of topics. He spoke honestly, with conviction and passion. He was even then a man who had suffered (giving him huge insights into the human condition) but who had also experienced intense joy. These experiences gave colour and intensity to his conversation.

Like Robert Graves who later in life became obsessed with his young muses, Malcolm's devotion to his Irish goddesses fired his creativity and, though his personal problems increased severely, he was more productive in Ireland than Cornwall. Malcolm's relationship with his goddesses, like that of Graves with his muses, was never a sexual one. Malcolm and Irene would simply hold hands, link arms, or lightly kiss each other on the cheek when meeting or saying goodnight. A cynic might add that by this time Malcolm's huge input of alcohol would almost certainly have had damaging effects on his sexual performance.

Deirdre Ryan believes him both sexually and socially insecure:

> He was not a tactile man. The sexual bravado was very much a front to compensate for what he felt inwardly were his own inadequacies. His loud sexual innuendo was all show. His loud shouts of 'knickers!' for example. It was all a front. He was essentially a very nervous man. On entering a room he would always be edgy. He wasn't a composed or still person. Even when he was on good form he was still awkward and shy, being boisterous as a cover for the shyness. And he could make you feel awkward too, sometimes. Awkward for him. I used to feel awkward with him on occasion, because his moods were different from everyone else's that I have ever met.

A further stay at the Gore Hotel was again highly productive, Malcolm meeting another researcher for the Castleton House Georgian dinners, Niamh O'Kelly.[33] Malcolm was fascinated to discover that Niamh was not only in charge of the musical side of the Castleton project, but was a singer, working towards taking up her place at the Royal College of Music. Later, when back in

---

[33] Niamh O'Kelly went on to a musical career. In 1979 she won the Golden Voice award to study in Germany and for thirteen years she was the Director of Music to the American Army in Germany. As a composer she has had particular success, with a number of published choral works.

Ireland, Malcolm went to a Castleton House banquet, where he was impressed by Niamh's voice, discovered she still was keen to earn money for College, and suggested she might give Isobel some help with Edward for two to three months that summer.

Niamh began her new job at the beginning of August, when Malcolm was completing the final movement of the Seventh Symphony.[34] On her first day at Meadowcroft she arrived to find that Isobel and Edward had baked a cake on the top of which Edward had written OULART in icing. Asked why he had chosen this word, he replied it was a nice-sounding island in the Pacific. It also happened to be the name of Niamh's house. It occurred to Niamh that Edward had a psychic streak, for he was sometimes able to say who was phoning as soon as the telephone rang. On her first day of work Malcolm made much of how gifted Edward was, but for the next two months he more or less ignored him, seemingly unable to face up to the problems. Niamh did not find Edward easy. When out for a walk with him she would sometimes find herself suddenly kicked for no reason.

Niamh's earliest weeks were the easiest ones, when Malcolm was still working on his symphony, spending whole days shut away in his study on the first floor, which contained a large table with piles of manuscript paper and a small Japanese upright piano. Malcolm, she discovered to her surprise, felt uncertain about himself as a composer. There was a lack of confidence about him as he went about his work.

> It was as if by this time he had had too many criticisms, particularly those which said he was only good at writing for films. He was really weighed down by it.

He never talked to her about the symphony, but he did share his love of the Dublin-born tenor John McCormack, playing her the favourite track from his well-worn McCormack LP, Mozart's *Il Mio Tesoro*. 'I want to write a song for you,' he said to her one day. 'Choose one of your favourite poems.' The next day Niamh offered him John Donne's *The Good Morrow* and *Woman's Constancy*, but heard nothing more about them. Six months later, however, when she was a student at the RCM, she received through the post the two songs, dedicated to her.[35]

Malcolm completed the Seventh Symphony early that September, after which Niamh watched helplessly as things at Meadowcroft deteriorated.

---

[34] So much was going on that the Seventh Symphony still needed completion in August. A promised conducting session in Harrogate, therefore, had to be cancelled, even though Grimethorpe Colliery Band was to play (and the sixty-strong choir of St Aidan's School to sing) *The Song of Freedom*.

[35] The settings are characterful and effective. Malcolm had also completed 33 bars of a third song, *The Dreame*. The songs were first performed by Ian and Jennifer Partridge on 23 June 1977 at Bristol University.

He would drink a bottle of vodka in the bath. He was lovely when he was sober, so interesting and well-read, but that really was extremely rare.

Isobel had stopped drinking but was on large doses of valium which caused giddiness and falls. Her relationship with Malcolm, Niamh felt, teetered on the brink of violence. The smallest thing seemed to annoy him.

> Isobel just wouldn't stand up to Malcolm. I hated the fact she always made excuses! And though she seemed to have the money to extricate herself from her impossible position, she just surrendered to it helplessly, saying she was trapped.
>
> On one occasion she sustained a black eye and some bruising and finally admitted to me that he had thrown her down the stairs.[36]

The offer of well-paid work had been a very kind one and Niamh was grateful, but it was a relief to head for London and her new studies.

There was delight at Faber when Malcolm wrote that the symphony was finished, had 'turned out well', and he was looking forward to Martin Kingsbury's visit to collect the manuscript.

> I will fetch you at the airport or ferry, if you let me know the date, time and flight. I hope you will manage to stay a day or two so that I can show you some of this beautiful city and countryside.[37]

Martin was met at the airport by Malcolm and the taxi driver who had become his personal chauffeur, Sam Kelly, a loquacious and knowledgeable Dubliner. Together they adjourned straight away to the airport restaurant. It was, says Martin Kingsbury, 'the booziest of lunches with innumerable bottles of wine. He scattered huge tips like confetti'.[38] When they eventually reached Meadowcroft, Malcolm went straight to bed, Isobel gallantly entertaining Martin Kingsbury in his absence. 'She was charming and lovely, but couldn't cope with him.' Malcolm's interpretation of showing his guest 'the beautiful city' was to take him on an almighty pub crawl.

> Eventually at the end of the weekend he bowled me into a taxi, clutching the new symphony. He briefly said to me, 'This symphony describes my children.' That was all he would say about it.

As he flew back to London and began to gather himself together again, Martin Kingsbury felt alarm at what he had witnessed. Malcolm's generosity was an impulse run riot; his relationship with Isobel seemed fundamentally flawed; unpleasant jokes and immodest talk about their sexual performance had been hugely embarrassing. As for Edward, he looked terrified whenever Malcolm embarked on a drunken tirade. Malcolm professed to be very fond of him, and no doubt in his own way he was. But it was noticeable how much mother and son kept close together, as if for mutual protection. It was not a comfortable topic on

---

[36] March 2004
[37] 10 September 1973
[38] July 2003

which to ponder. Martin turned back to the precious manuscript. Deadly serious and highly arresting, the symphony blazed before him, as he turned the pages.

Malcolm most unusually was soon explaining to the press the inspiration behind his new work:

> Composer Malcolm Arnold, talking of his Seventh Symphony admits that it is, in a way, a family affair. 'Each of the three movements,' he says, 'in the very loosest way, is a musical portrait.' The portraits are of his children Katherine, aged 25, and Robert, 23. Both are anthropologists. The third portrait is nine-year-old Edward. That promises to be a lively movement.[39]

The portraits are certainly painted 'in the very loosest way'. The style is neither realistic nor impressionistic, but something much more esoteric. The abstract-expressionist canvases of Jackson Pollock spring to mind.

The first movement, Katherine's *Allegro energico*, is long and turbulent, its first subject group based on musical ciphers,[40] formed from the names of all three children, Sheila and Isobel, and expressing the conflicting demands Malcolm feels as a father and husband. We first meet Katherine by herself in the second subject, an expansive melody of great beauty and poignancy, first played by violas and cellos.[41] This theme, however, is subjected to much distress and upheaval, suggesting that, though he loves her deeply, he is aware that things have not always gone the way they should. Of all the various other melodic elements introduced early, one of the most striking is a coarse 'oom-pah' figure, which could be straight from the musical *Cabaret*. Does Malcolm see himself, in deep self-criticism, as nothing more than a grotesque Master of Family Ceremonies? Certainly the brutality that underlines the tawdry glitz of *Cabaret* is more and more to the fore as the movement relentlessly develops, not least in an extraordinary section of jazzy ragtime, full of despair and mockery.

A machine-gun-like semiquaver motif leads the music forward to ever more aggressive discussion before a plunge into a quiet, if unreal, wilderness, where Katherine's theme, gently presented, at last introduces relief, beauty and hope, until swept away by Malcolm's grotesque oompah clowning. There are parallels in this wilderness with the more psychedelic moments of the Sixth Symphony. Back, inevitably, comes all the aggression, a period of deep distress, solace eventually arriving in an anguished version of the Katherine theme in the strings, followed by a quiet, moving reverie, led initially by a flute. For a while we again cling to the hope that everything is going to be all right after all. After such chaos and confusion can there really be happiness? Alas, it would seem not. In the recapitulation the atmosphere darkens further. Tensions build, dissonance reigns,

---

[39] *Evening News*, 1 May 1974
[40] Jackson: *The Life and Music of Sir Malcolm Arnold* p.156
[41] Based on emotionally charged falling semitones and sevenths, richly harmonised with throbbing seventh chords in the strings

and we are finally left with a huge, devastating unison F,[42] over which a cowbell is struck three times.

The cowbell, with its Mahlerian associations, poses a mystery of its own. One of a number of colourful extra percussion used in the symphony, it is struck at the end of each movement. Malcolm is typically dismissive and brief in his programme notes, but he does inform us that the cowbell symbolises 'hope', adding with a despondent smile 'and if it is only a cowbell, at least that is something'. Hope may indeed have been intended, but, in the mood Malcolm has reached by the end of the movement, the three sounds the cowbell makes over that unison F smack more of desperate cries for help.

Much of Katherine's movement had been written in Ischia before the row with the Waltons, when the sun was shining on San Felice and ripening the grapes. Robert and Edward's movements, by contrast, were written in the chaos of Meadowcroft as witnessed by Niamh. We may expect the work, therefore, to become bleaker. And it does.

The *Andante*, Robert's movement, is a particular shock in its serial coldness. So many of Malcolm's slow movements are of great beauty, but in this 'portrait' he has opted for the sombre hues of Schoenberg as he expresses himself on the relationship between a father and his son. There is an intense darkness, a sustained solemnity. The opening sighing chords preface a long, solo journey by trombone over a bleak and hopeless landscape. Violas, plaintive and unaccompanied, lead to one of the most eerie passages in all Malcolm's music. Long, overlapping dissonant chords in the brass accompany a knocking-at-the-door motif – four even notes – played at rhythmically irregular intervals by an assortment of percussion instruments. The effect is utterly menacing. Like Macbeth, we are confronted by the immutability of mortality. 'Wake Duncan with thy knocking! I would thou couldst!' Life meanwhile goes on, after a fashion, and in due course the journeying trombone returns, leading to a climax of unbearable anguish. And then the cowbells toll again. Hope? Hardly. The ending is uncompromisingly stark. A low F sharp[43] played by the low strings, going on and on into eternity.

By the time Malcolm had written this movement Robert had returned from Papua New Guinea. He had had some eventful travels, including illness and hospitalisation in Goroka and a highly adventurous tour around Malaysia and Thailand with his girlfriend Anne. After a long period away he would have enjoyed a tranquil return, but it was not to be. Stopping at Kabul, on the flight home, he consumed some ice cream and carrot juice in the street market and thought nothing more about it. Back in England, however, he began to feel unwell, struck down by a mystery bug. The doctors of the isolation hospital to

---

[42] The keynote of the work.

[43] A conflicting semitone above the work's keynote.

which he was taken were utterly defeated by it. He became weaker and weaker, his weight eventually dwindling to seven stone.

He did eventually pull through, but further illness followed, requiring yet more hospitalisation. Malcolm, who had earlier considered flying out to Papua New Guinea, had the doctors there encouraged him to do so,[44] now failed to get involved or offer any sustained support. As at his sister Ruth's time of need, he withdrew into himself, unable to cope. For his part, Robert remains remarkably non-judgemental about it. 'He was certainly mainly unhelpful to me at the time,' he observes quietly.[45]

Robert and Katherine both see in their movements of the Seventh Symphony more a reflection of their father than themselves and Robert indeed queries an over-reaction to the work's austere and desolate character.

> I do not see the symphony as such a dark thing. I probably share a sad view of the world with my father, and so it seems a fair way to see things. He was very torn by the horribleness of the world and that children never ask to be born and so there was something very sad and tragic, just being a child or a parent. That is to say the musical sadness or distress is more like his distress at having caused these three lives to start against what may not necessarily be their best interests.[46]

It has been suggested that the tam-tams used in the second movement are making a reference to his time in Papua New Guinea. Robert disagrees:

> The tam-tams are nothing like the instruments used there. And Dad never made any enquiries about the native music. The Papua New Guinea highlanders do a menacing and dramatic dance in a long row, fully painted and feathered, flexing their knees and banging monotonously on their 'kundu' drums. It becomes mesmerising and very powerful, a slightly untuned or flat note endlessly repeated. I could imagine it being used like the Trevose foghorn. But it wasn't.

The second movement gave Malcolm an opportunity to express unsettling, latent emotions. Robert's period of illness had provoked thoughts on mortality, which led, inevitably, to Pappy. He hadn't asked Pappy to beget him. What right had he to bring him into the world? He still loathed the old man's idolatry just as once he had loathed the bullying. He had tried to shut the garrulous old fellow up by telling him he would retire from music after this symphony, but he had simply gone rushing off to the press as usual: 'Malcolm says he'll retire this year,

[44] 'I received a letter from Robert's doctor this morning,' Malcolm wrote to Katherine, 'who is a lecturer in psychiatry at the University, also at the Goroka Base Hospital, where Robert has been. He is an extremely nice and helpful person and he told me that Robert is out of hospital and staying with friends in Port Morresby … I told Dr Beckett I would go to New Guinea if he thought it necessary and he said it was not.' But Malcolm did not let his worries get him down too much. The letter (5 May 1973) also enclosed a Wine Society brochure: 'I hope the enclosures will interest you. The Wine Society's Claret and White Burgundy are wonderful wines, fit for anybody.'
[45] March 2004
[46] March 2004

*Pappy in later life*

but if you've got music in your soul, how can you?'[47] At eighty-eight, however, he wouldn't live much longer. Everybody died; generation after generation. But generations sometimes became muddled. Pappy had ceded his place to Aubrey. And now there were three generations, Pappy, he and Robert, forming an orderly queue, with no more jostling for position. Yet, as those bugs from Kabul had so nearly proved, death was always fractious and unreliable.

Edward's *Allegro*, the shortest movement for the youngest child, is livelier. The opening theme, persistent and striding with its repetitive dotted rhythmic figure, is unerringly evocative of a constantly noisy, attention-seeking child. This is one side of Edward, the active little boy in whom Malcolm often expressed great pride in his letters:

> Edward has been marvellously good. Helping, doing his homework and even learn-ing to play the piano in short bursts. Yesterday he had a holiday and we went to Bray by train (great and continuous excitement!). We had lunch at the Starlight Hotel, which he explored from top to bottom five times, naturally including all the lifts.[48]

> Edward is very well and back at school. He is thoroughly enjoying T S Eliot's *Cats* and reads it continuously, laughing aloud. Another recent entertainment for him are wine catalogues, the descriptions he finds hilariously funny and I must say I do as well. He sniffed a glass of wine the other day and said 'Will improve with age'. He has all the jargon at his finger tips![49]

But the other, less active side of Edward is missing from the *Allegro*. At Meadowcroft Edward was often withdrawn, overawed with life as he saw it and

---

[47] 18 May 1974

[48] Letter to Katherine, 18 September 1973

[49] Letter to Katherine, 16 January 1974

unwilling to venture too much. The music fails to capture all those long periods when Edward would sit quietly, watching some repetitive movement which fascinated him, or, with infinite care and patience, piecing together the most complicated of models. Repetition delighted him. We can see it in a little poem he wrote in Meadowcroft at the time of the Seventh Symphony. The poem also disturbingly expresses how choking Edward found the physical and emotional violence of Meadowcroft:[50]

> Weeds, weeds,
> Here and there.
> Weeds, weeds
> Everywhere.
> Hundreds of weeds,
> Thousands of weeds,
> Millions and billions and billions of weeds.
>
> Weeds are enemies.
> I choke your plants.
> I am your enemy
> And I reproduce myself to do more damage.
> And I creep under the ground choking all your plants.
> You have to pull me up
> To stop me doing damage.
>
> I am your enemy,
> Creeping to more flowers.
> And choking is my theme.
> I choke your plants.
> I am your enemy.

This nightmare vision of an escalating damage which can only be countered by violent eradication does not come out fully in the opening material of the *Allegro*, arriving instead later in the movement. In the meantime Malcolm introduces new ideas: a Celtic harp appears with some Irish music distorted by an accompaniment which doesn't quite fit, whereupon Malcolm cheerfully brings in a traditional folk group, creating a convincing pastiche of Edward's favourite Irish band, The Chieftains. Edward's devotion to The Chieftains was a precious interest shared with his father, but this happy reverie is soon broken by the return of the opening 'Edward' theme, this time much more aggressive and building to a massively violent climax. Here at last Malcolm seems to be coming to terms with the unintentional damage on Edward of his own destructive urges, the destructive weeds inside Meadowcroft, multiplying into their millions and choking any flowering of emotional maturity. As the *Allegro* reaches its conclusion, no resolution is offered, no reconciliation, simply violence and frustration, until the cowbell makes its final appearance – again

---

[50] 2 February 1975

three blows – followed by an extraordinary short coda: just two enormous, defiant chords of the tonic F major and three short orchestral hammer blows on a unison F. These are not chords of hope and optimism. The artist is declaring his own stark message to his three sitters. 'Take your father as he is. I can be no other.'

The most surprising thing of all about the Seventh Symphony is that Malcolm should have chosen to tell the world that it was a 'portrait' of his children. All his career he had subscribed to the view that music should be left to make its own message. The change of heart would have been more understandable if the music had warmly endorsed his love for all three. But it does not. It is a work which, by its very substance, expresses turmoil rather than harmony.[51] If he wished to explore his failings as a parent or, alternatively, the decisions of Katherine and Robert to find some meaning to life in distant lands, he might have done so more privately. Going public in such a private matter – not least in offering a musical portrait of the autistic Edward – was an indication that by the 1970s he was often in a confused state of mind. The so-called 'portraits' are the work of an artist in great personal distress, who has superimposed on the faces of those he loves most  his own inner fears and anxieties.

In the euphoria of completing the symphony he was probably vaguely aware that Katherine and Robert might be taken aback by the apocalyptic nature of it all, and he did think to send a letter from Meadowcroft, explaining what he had done:

> My Dear Katherine,
>
>   Yesterday I finished my Seventh Symphony, which has turned out well. It is dedicated to you, Robert and Edward. It is in three movements and each movement is an expression of what sort of person I think you each are, in that order. I hope you will not be insulted. The first performance is at the Festival Hall in May next year.[52]

The rest of the letter, however, is extremely buoyant:

> The weather is marvellous and we are weighted down by vegetables and tomatoes, as are all the neighbours. The garden has been a remarkable success, and I have never seen things grow like it anywhere. It is also full of butterflies, Peacocks, Red Admirals and a host of tortoiseshells. It is quite incredible.

He ends with a cheerful reference to William Walton and Benjamin Britten:

> The huge jungle plant with yellow flowers that looks as if it is going to take over the whole greenhouse is from seeds you sent from Peru. I believe it should bear luscious

---

[51] So often in his music Malcolm allows an interval or melodic shape to form the organic germ of a movement. 'Looking over my scores,' he once wrote, 'I am amazed at the way in which a whole section has taken its musical texture from a few basic intervals.' In the Seventh Symphony he calls upon the most conflicting of intervals, the tri-tone, the second and seventh. These dissonant and harsh intervals form the basis of the entire work.
[52] 10 September 1973

fruit, but all the flowers have turned out to be male! I wrote and told William that it must be the variety PERUVIUS ALDERGHUS![53]

> Love to you both,
> Dad

In a matter of days after completing the Seventh Symphony Malcolm was in Mount Carmel Hospice, drying out. The Dublin pattern of excessive drink followed by hospitalisation followed by more excessive drinking was now established. By the autumn of 1973 the periods of mental torment were also perceptibly lengthening. The highs were just as deliciously high as ever, but the lows significantly lower. Isobel was later to sum it up succinctly:

> When he was up, he was 100%. If he was going to be friendly, amiable, jolly, happy, wonderful, he was absolutely that, and nobody, *nobody*, could have been nicer or more generous. But, if he was sad or if he was depressed, it absolutely ate him up and there was nothing left of him but blackness, miserableness and total moodiness, and nothing could get him out of it.[54]

Just such a mood followed the completion of the Seventh Symphony when Isobel endured an especially scathing attack. In his black moods he was particularly good at seeking out and exploiting other people's weakest points. Always on the defensive, Isobel sometimes took to lying to try to ward off verbal attack. It became part of her lifestyle. So Malcolm seized hold of this, homing in on what he saw as her biggest lie of all, the fact she had never told him that she had once had an abortion. She'd slept around like a whore, he told her! He knew all about Jack de Manio, Michael Ayrton and all the others! If only she'd told him about the abortion, he needn't have married her! He only married her because he thought she couldn't face one! From there he rushed off onto an entirely different tack and accused her of being a lesbian. But then, he said, all women were lesbians…

On one particularly bleak October day Malcolm drew a whole series of obscene pictures of Isobel and posted them round the house. It was the very worst kind of lavatory humour, the product of a seriously sick mind. Under attacks like these Isobel was becoming dazed, absorbing the worst he could offer and thereby only stoking the fires of his cruelty. But even when his anger became so violent that they would brawl together – in one such brawl he smashed one of their marble-topped tables – she would afterwards maintain a dog-like loyalty. It was if she sensed that in these periods of insanity he was the greater sufferer, aware of the appalling nature of his behaviour, hugely angry because of it, and utterly frustrated that he was unable to climb out of the slippery-sided pit of depression into which he had suddenly fallen.

---

[53] This seems to be a reference to Aldeburgh. 'Aldeburghus' might have been clearer.
[54] Kriss Russman's 1991 BBC TV *Omnibus* programme.

But instead of destroying the drawings she kept them, a first silent token of resistance. If she ever needed to prove what few would believe, they might come in useful. It would never be easy to stand up against him. The famous could always rely on a ready sympathy. No-one would easily disbelieve his public façade of bright gaiety. Isobel no longer knew what to think or where to go, but she would keep safe the drawings …

To the outside world there was little that was obviously wrong other than the compulsive drinking. At exactly the same period that Isobel was suffering this latest trauma, David Ellis was enjoying wonderful support from Malcolm. Although Malcolm no longer conducted the BBC Northern at Manchester, the two had kept in touch, often discussing the musical world for long periods on the phone. In one such conversation Malcolm had learnt that David's First Symphony was about to have its première in Liverpool. A matter of hours later, in the middle of rehearsals, Malcolm walked in, unannounced.

'What are you doing in Liverpool? gasped David Ellis..

'I wasn't going to miss your symphony,' replied Malcolm.

He had come across from Dublin on the overnight boat. After attending the concert and subsequent party, he spent the night at his favourite hotel, the Adelphi, and went back to Ireland the next day.

> He'd given up two of the precious ninety days he was allowed outside Ireland by the taxman, just for my concert. That was Malcolm! [55]

Malcolm was operating two different codes of conduct, men generally being much better treated than women. Deirdre Ryan understood Malcolm's inconsistent treatment of the two sexes:

> He really liked me, so I was very lucky. I wouldn't have wanted to be on the wrong side if him. I wouldn't have liked to be Isobel. He could cut women down to size very quickly if annoyed in any way. He had this command. He wouldn't be like that with men.

The goddesses possessed a strength of character, however, that, allied to their beauty, gave them a psychological advantage. Irene Duffy, for example, only once experienced Malcolm's worst side and she dealt with it so competently that it never recurred.

> Malcolm had just returned from London and had had some difficulty with the airport police. He was very upset when I met him for dinner that night in Snaffles. He must have had some drinks during the day and continued to drink during dinner, getting more gregarious as the evening progressed. Up to that night he had never turned his anger on me, but he started into it in the restaurant. I decided I wouldn't take any public abuse. I slipped to the Ladies Room, told the manager I was leaving and asked him to make sure Malcolm was safely delivered home by taxi. Basically, I had to let him know that he couldn't turn on me like that. It was the one and only time he did.

---

[55] David Ellis, August 2003

Malcolm's visits to England became ever more expensive retreats from reality. Niamh, in her first term at the RCM, spent one hilarious evening with him. They had met up at Wheeler's, where Malcolm ordered twelve oysters each, but Niamh, not an oyster lover, ended up eating bread while Malcolm downed all twenty-four, before he cheerfully led her off to Ronnie Scott's jazz club. Much less happy was small dinner party at the Connaught to which Niamh was invited. Malcolm brought along Isobel, who, in the course of the evening, confided *sotto voce* to Niamh that her patience was near breaking point. Niamh found it an awful evening. Malcolm, sitting next to Niamh, was constantly rude and making advances. Eventually in exasperation she stuck a fork in his leg. Later, as discussion around the table grew ever more outrageous, Malcolm began insulting the Irish, offending Niamh, a strong republican and the only Irish person present. She stormed out, vowing she would never set eyes on him again.

> I had witnessed how offensive he could be to Isobel and I certainly was not going to permit him to treat me in such a manner.[56]

When the score of the John Donne songs unexpectedly arrived some months later, they bore a plaintive note, but no apology:

> Dear Niamh, where are you these days? Love, Malcolm.

Malcolm was no longer in a state where regular composition was possible, but occasional commissions came along which he managed to honour. One important one, completed in 1974, had begun its life in Cornwall. The telephone had rung at Primrose Cottage. 'Malcolm. Benny Goodman here!' 'Sod off!' replied Malcolm hanging up the phone, only too used to friends playing jokes of this kind. But the phone rang again. 'Please don't hang up, Malcolm, this *is* Benny!' 'Well, if you're who you claim to be,' replied Malcolm with less than total logic, 'give me your number and I'll ring you back.'[57] Goodman, it transpired, wanted a new clarinet concerto and Malcolm happily agreed to write it.

Three years had passed and Goodman was thrilled when, in April 1974, he heard from Malcolm that it was finally being written. 'I can't wait to get it,' he wrote excitedly from New York.[58] A month later he crossed over to Dublin to collect the score. Malcolm booked him a room in the Gresham Hotel and, on the morning of his expected arrival, acquired the key from the hotel manager and propped the score on a chest of drawers with a big bouquet of flowers on one side and a litre of Jack Daniels on the other. Four o'clock that afternoon the phone rang. 'Malcolm, this is Benny. I may be a bit stoned but I think your concerto is just great.'[59]

---

[56] April 2004

[57] Goodman's sister-in-law was, in fact, a close neighbour of Malcolm's, so the phone-call was probably not quite so unexpected as Malcolm, in retelling the story, liked to claim.

[58] 30 April 1974

[59] The story of the Goodman concerto was related by Malcolm to Stan Hibbert and published in *The Gramophone* in 1996.

Because the concerto ends with Malcolm blowing raspberries cheekily in an outrageously popular rag,[60] and because performances always send audiences away in the best of spirits, the darker side of the work can be overlooked. There are some wonderfully lyrical passages, which, superficially, suggest that things are back to normal. But they are not. For all the tender beauty in the slow movement[61] and, most unexpectedly, in the middle of the Finale, the despair and anger which so characterised the Seventh Symphony permeate this concerto too.[62] The extremes of emotion Malcolm was experiencing in his life are there in the music. The rag, for all the raspberry-blowing, is a very manic form of happiness.[63] And it is this unease, lying behind the seeming certainties, which makes it such a fascinating work.

Shortly afterwards Malcolm crossed to London to conduct at the Festival Hall the first performance of the Seventh Symphony.[64] This upturn in his fortunes stemmed from the further support of Gerald McDonald, now General Manager of the New Philharmonia Orchestra, which had commissioned the symphony.[65] The hall was half-empty, but those who were there were carried away by the music, and Malcolm, 'as breezy as ever',[66] received a standing ovation. Many of the major critics stayed away. William Mann was there for *The Times*, but the work was altogether too much for him. Writing 'as an old admirer of Malcolm Arnold's cheerful, extrovert music', he found the Seventh 'verbose and unprofitable'. Another old friend, Felix Aprahamian, also struggled to come to terms with it, mesmerised like many a colleague by the cowbell:

> This master of telling orchestration has miscalculated the connotations of a cow-bell struck with a hard stick. His 'symbol of hope', far removed from Mahler's evocation of mountain heights, sounds more like a summons to the communal feeding trough.[67]

As ever, there was encouragement from Faber, a telegram speedily sent after the concert to the Gore Hotel:

> Heartfelt congratulations on your magnificent Seventh. Warmest greetings. Donald Mitchell.

And there was again solid support from Edward Greenfield of *The Guardian*:

---

[60] The rag, he declared smilingly, was 'pre-Goodman' in style. It also includes a passage that clearly pays homage to the typical Sousa March style.

[61] The beautiful theme of the slow movement first appeared as the love theme in *The Sound Barrier* (1952).

[62] Like the Seventh Symphony the work also includes excursions into serial writing.

[63] The deceptively jolly 'rag' theme is in fact a close relation of the much more *Angst*-ridden first subject from the first movement. Malcolm has simply transformed its rhythmic shape.

[64] 5 May 1974

[65] McDonald tried hard to get the work recorded by EMI at the same time, but failed. He had also been involved in the commissioning of the Third Symphony, when working at Liverpool, and the Sixth, when in Manchester.

[66] Felix Aprahamian, *Sunday Times,* 12 May 1974

[67] *Ibid.*

> Malcolm Arnold is nothing if not a man of big gestures… Even when he is putting his tongue out at the world (figuratively, of course) he does it with cheerful panache. His latest symphony represents his biggest musical gesture yet, a massive piece of three movements, each of almost Mahlerian proportions.[68]

Praising the orchestration as 'never less than memorable, colourful and apt' and delighting to discover 'a flowering of inspiration' in each, testing movement, Greenfield declared how much he was looking forward to hearing it again, to fathom it deeper.

> At first hearing the very scale is disconcerting, let alone the unaccustomed tone of voice.

It is a monumental work, possessing in the scope and compulsion of its arguments a craggy grandeur. Unsurprisingly in recent years its reputation has steadily grown. Piers Burton-Page is a passionate advocate:

> The symphony is the diametric opposite of everything that the composer's public image leads one to believe. It is also one of his greatest works and one of the finest symphonies the twentieth century has produced; properly played, it can be overwhelming in performance. It must be heard in the flesh; loudspeakers tame the huge, elemental forces it unleashes into shadows of themselves. It embraces chaos, disorder, unreason, of the kind Vaughan Williams confronted in his Fourth and Sixth Symphonies. It therefore makes not the least attempt to be ingratiating. Nowhere is a melody spun out for its own sake; instead it will always be geared to the symphony's uncompromising logic.[69]

None of the three children was present at the première, Katherine returning from a visit to Peru just too late. She was getting married, and, in opting for the quietest of ceremonies at a registry office, she was following her parents' example, but she was also avoiding the embarrassments which Malcolm might bring to a wedding reception. Katherine was a modern and broad-minded young lady with a streak of unconventionality in her, yet she found it hard to cope with her father's social gaffes and cavalier treatment of women.

Aware of his possessiveness, she knew that breaking the news of the marriage was not going to be easy, and seized a late opportunity when Malcolm was visiting London with Irene. Katherine struggled to accept this seeming betrayal of Isobel, so simply gave her news and made good a quick escape. Irene has a strong memory of the occasion:

> We were dining in Soho in Wheeler's when Katherine came up to the restaurant towards the end of the meal. She didn't want to eat anything, but finally had a starter course of potted shrimps. She had come to tell Malcolm that she was going off to marry Tony, her boyfriend ... It was all very friendly – Malcolm adored Katherine and always introduced her as 'Katherine spelt with a K'. But he did not seem at all keen on this wedding, wondering out loud to me after she had left why she would want to

---

[68] 6 May 1974
[69] Burton-Page: *Philharmonic Concerto* p.110-111

marry a man who had already had two children – but of course he was not a man to forbid anything, not remotely …

Had Malcolm reflected a while, he would have realised that Katherine, in marrying a divorced man with children, was only doing what Isobel herself had done when she had married him. He might also have understood what an important moment of stability in her life this was. After one final trip to Peru she was to settle down with Anthony King in Highgate, and was soon working in a children's home in Islington.

Anthony King remembers Malcolm as 'totally delighted' with the marriage. This is borne out by the birthday present from her father that July: the original score of the Second Flute Concerto[70] – *her* instrument again and a reminder of happy visits to Durham – beautifully bound in leather and lovingly inscribed. That summer Katherine and Anthony King joined Malcolm, Isobel and Edward on a holiday on the west coast of Ireland at Leenane. Malcolm had many good days there, reverting to the ebullient figure he had once been on the sands of Cornwall. 'Come on in!' he shouted to them all, as they sheltered from the rain and he rushed into the waves. 'It's glorious!' Anthony King found his father-in-law tremendous fun throughout the holiday. 'He was a wonderful mimic – did a wonderful Winston Churchill!'

Malcolm by now was only writing intermittently. Almost a year went by between the completion of the Clarinet Concerto (in April 1974) and his next important work, the *Fantasy on a Theme of John Field* for piano and orchestra[71] (in March 1975). There are several reasons which attracted Malcolm to using a nocturne by the Irish composer and pianist, John Field.[72] He was a Dubliner by birth; also an alcoholic who went through a long period of public neglect later on in his career. But, above all, it was a reconnection with Nan, who was coming more and more into Malcolm's thoughts as the twentieth anniversary of her death approached. She had loved the Field nocturnes, and as a little boy on her instruction he had learnt one by heart. The Fantasy was written without commission, purely because he felt the need. He wrote enthusiastically to William Walton:

> I have become wildly interested in music again, and have finished a new piano concerto in one movement.[73]

'Wildly' is the key word, for it is a wildly impassioned work in which the orchestra frequently assaults the piano, offering shattering rebukes to its beauty.

---

[70] The score is dated 8 December 1972

[71] The only completed work in this period was the *Fantasy for Brass Band*, a test piece for the 1974 National Brass Band Championships which was played 17 times at the Albert Hall on 5 October. Malcolm did not attend. It is a highly accomplished work, nearly ten minutes long, full of changing moods. It contains both delightfully sunny and tragically sad melodies, all inimitably scored. It was dedicated to Tony Giles.

[72] John Field (1782-1837) is largely remembered as the first composer to write nocturnes.

[73] Quoted by Paul Jackson, *The Life and Music of Sir Malcolm Arnold*, p.164

*With Terence Emery and David Drew outside the Carlton Tower Hotel, 1975*

Totally in accord with the violence of the Seventh Symphony,[74] the *Field Fantasy* nonetheless ends in an extraordinary affirmation of hope, when, in one of Malcolm's most spectacularly romantic inventions, he presents the theme in a triumphant mix of Tchaikovsky and Rachmaninoff at their most passionate. It is genius of a kind, but close to madness.[75]

Immediately after completing the Fantasy Malcolm was involved in an exciting ballet project, *The Three Musketeers*, which unfortunately never came to fruition. He was approached in the first instance by Ninette de Valois, who asked him to get in touch with one her soloists at Covent Garden, David Drew. Margot Fonteyn, two years older than Malcolm but still involved with the company, was also making encouraging noises in the background. David Drew, a promising choreographer, told Malcolm he had been working for some time with designer Terry Emery on an idea for a three-act ballet on Dumas' story. The designs were already well advanced and they were now looking for a composer. It was still a speculative venture, he emphasised. He had not yet approached Kenneth MacMillan at Covent Garden about it.

---

[74] As in the Seventh Symphony, Malcolm generates some of the melodic material through the use of ciphers. John Field, Dublin, Saint Petersburg and Naples (cities Field lived in or visited) all appear.

[75] The work was sent to John Lill who organised, and played in, the first performance, at the Festival Hall in 1977. Disappointingly the critics all stayed away. 'I don't regard the work as a masterpiece,' writes John Lill, 'despite the dedication to me! Sections of it are expertly written with exemplary orchestration yet I never feel the work has architectural strength, consisting of a series of enjoyable sections rather than an inevitable unfolding of variation form.' (April 2004)

All Malcolm's old love of dance resurfaced and he responded enthusiastically. He would be staying at the Carlton Tower Hotel on 23 March, he told David Drew. He had already made enquiries about hiring the ballroom, which he knew from experience would be suitable, as when he was staying there he sometimes played the piano at tea dances. 'I will be bringing at least eight themes to play,' he wrote. 'I think it goes well and hope you do.'[76] Thoughts of a return to Covent Garden revitalised him. A three-act ballet there would see him re-established in the thick of things. It would be like *Homage* all over again. Even Margot would still be around! The meeting with David Drew could not come quickly enough:

> If you like the flavour of what I have done, I will write the entire ballet (I hope) while you are away, so that we have a basic structure, keeping to your timing as strictly as I possibly can. When you return we can then knock it finally into shape and I will orchestrate it.
>
> I am working on a piano sonata at the moment and the ballet will be welcome work and keep me out of mischief during the summer months no doubt ...[77]

David Drew and Terry Emery, a music hall turn in themselves with their bubbling repartee, arrived at the Carlton Towers in Cadogan Place at 11.00 in the morning. They found Malcolm seated at a piano in the ballroom surrounded by a large enough supply of champagne to last out the Siege of Ladysmith:

> He was enormously welcoming, insisting we joined him in a drink. He already seemed to have got through quite a lot![78]

They drank from great silver schooners, regularly replenished over the next three and a half hours.

Such was Malcolm's enthusiasm for the project that David was again at great pains to spell out to him that it was purely a speculative venture. 'I'm not worried,' Malcolm replied with equanimity. 'The money doesn't matter. You could even do it at St Pancras Town Hall, for all I care.' Impressed by the detailed expertise of Terry Emery's set and costume designs, he pointed to his few sheets of sketches with a grin. 'I feel like a charlatan! I've only done a few sketches[79] – nothing by comparison!' But it was all in his head. He excitedly sat down at the piano and David switched on an open-reel tape recorder:

> He worked through the story. – 'well, I had this sort of dreamy theme in mind' – and he played it – 'and how about this one?' – and off he went – it was bloody marvellous! By the time he'd finished all the material was there!

---

[76] 21 March 1975

[77] 21 March 1975. Nothing came of the piano sonata. 'Sonata' might just possibly be a slip of the pen for 'concerto', the *John Field Fantasy* having been completed just four days before. Alternatively, the *Fantasy* may have sown seeds for a further piano sonata.

[78] David Drew, September 2003

[79] Thirteen brief ideas, the manuscript now held by the Royal College of Music.

Terry Emery was equally impressed:

> All the difficulties in the piece just disappeared. Galloping horses, for instance, he
> solved by music. Also that highly complicated and important incident with the little
> box with diamond studs in it. Highly problematic for a ballet? But not with Malcolm!
> He had an immediate solution, which would clearly work! He improvised his way
> though, not writing anything down. There was a marvellous moment when he came
> to the 'dance of intrigue' – all the court would be there – Richelieu, the Queen,
> D'Artagnan and so on – dancing on a chessboard floor – and Malcolm produced for
> it something just right – 'it's a passacaglia,' he told us. I couldn't believe how such
> superbly appropriate music could just flow out of him. Mind you, we were drinking
> top quality champagne![80]

There was a great rapport between all three. They loved each other's jokes.
'At this stage in proceedings,' said David, with a serious glance at his synopsis,
'Richelieu comes on and a titter runs through the crowd.' What kind of costume
would you like for him?' asked Terry. 'Better still. Let's have three of them, all
running through the crowd.' 'And this,' said Malcolm, improvising with gusto,
'will be the Dance of the Three Titters!' Eventually, still exchanging jokes and in
a state of great euphoria, the three stumbled out of the ballroom, David to his
horror suddenly realising he was dancing in a performance of *Sleeping Beauty*
that night.

> It was not my custom to drink much, and never before a performance! But here I was
> arriving back home around four o'clock absolutely paralytic. My wife did everything
> she could to sober me up but it was a lost cause. There was no way I was going to
> manage a series of double *tours en air* with five other lads in the Prologue, so I got
> hold of them before it began and we simplified the choreography!

Unfortunately, in his current muddled state Malcolm forgot that the project
had yet to be presented to the Covent Garden hierarchy and instead contacted the
General Administrator, John Tooley, to say how delighted he was to be doing the
ballet and perhaps they could now discuss terms. Tooley and MacMillan were
furious at David Drew's seeming high-handedness. Any possibility of *The Three
Musketeers* appearing at Covent Garden had vanished!

David, however, saved the project by contacting Robert Helpmann, then
Artistic Director of the Australian Ballet. Helpmann was at once extremely keen
to mount the piece, particularly with a score from Malcolm. When Malcolm
threw a tantrum mid-summer over what he considered an unclear synopsis,

---

[80] September, 2003. Terry Emery, theatre designer, artist and teacher, married to the dancer
Mavis Osborn, died shortly after this interview. His outstanding set and costume designs for
*The Three Musketeers* still await professional use.

[81] 'How nice to hear from you,' Malcolm wrote to Helpmann on 7 July. 'I am sure that
David Drew could make a great success if we ever got a scenario. I enclose a letter I wrote
to him which seems clear enough to me, and if he is able to do what I asked, I would willingly reconsider the decision. As it is, we have talked around it and through it, which I am

Helpmann soon smoothed his ruffled feathers.[81] But still, tantalisingly, the score itself did not get written.

One reason was Malcolm's restless desire to be travelling. In London again in early June, he was in what he described to Katherine as his 'usual state of exhaustion'. Katherine was anxious about him – he had suddenly aged, his hair thinning and greying, his face more lined – and she did her best on these visits to meet him at the airport and help as much as she could. But there was nothing to be done about the gremlins in his mind. On the journey back from London, he told her, he had re-read Evelyn's Waugh's *The Ordeal of Gilbert Pinfold*, 'which just matched my mood'.[82] It is the story of a famous fifty-year-old novelist, fat and heavy-drinking, who is out of tune with modern life and sets off on a cruise to foreign parts to try to escape growing hallucinations and paranoia.

All his creative energies were now focused on a second String Quartet, suggested by Hugh Maguire, the leader of the Allegri Quartet, and completed at Meadowcroft in the middle of August. Malcolm and Hugh Maguire had been colleagues in the LPO, and they would often share a pint or two when Hugh was visiting Dublin to play at Castleton House in the annual 'Festival of Great Irish Houses'.

> We would meet at Ryan's on the Liffey, sitting in one of the dozen 'snugs', discussing and planning the quartet. Malcolm specifically asked me whether I would like the work to have an Irish flavour.[83]

The Quartet proved as strong and unusual as the works immediately preceding it, sharing many of the dark emotions of the Seventh Symphony. Much of it makes hard listening, expressing deep disquiet of mind, but the arguments are tight and taut and its several idiosyncrasies totally engaging. There is both anger and conflict in the first movement (*Allegro*) as well as a startling conclusion in which Malcolm presents an earlier troubled theme in a tenderly romantic manner, only to have it fade away alarmingly into nothingness. The second movement begins with an extended and impassioned cadenza for first violin (*Maestoso con molto rubato*) leading to a wild Celtic dance. The other three instruments, however, do not join in – rather, they argue and bark aggressively at the protagonist. There is a bleak, nervous calm about the long, catharctic *Andante*, and the final movement brings back tensions and conflict which, at the end, the glorious and seemingly confident melody in D major never quite resolves.

Whereas the First String Quartet was written in studiously conventional style, the much later Second brings to its serious thoughts refreshing originality, as Hugo Cole pointed out:

---

afraid brought me to a total standstill of confusion. I am delighted your ballet company is such a success, and may it go on for ever and ever ...'
[82] 7 June 1975

Taking a leaf out of Shostakovich's book (Shostakovich himself having taken a leaf out of Beethoven's), Arnold treats the quartet as a group bound by no precedents, able to go anywhere, do anything. He finds room for cadenzas, for long solos, for cliché accompaniment figures, for 'empty' passages which have dramatic rather than strictly musical justification, for primitive simplicities as well as sophisticated and ingenious patterning of sounds.[84]

Together with the Seventh Symphony the Second Quartet represents the height of Malcolm's achievements in Ireland, comparing favourably with the very best quartets of Britten, Simpson and Shostakovich.[85] The awful crises in Malcolm's life at this juncture seem to have inspired him.

They had also resulted in Isobel resorting to flight on several occasions, hiding out with Edward at the Dublin home of Katherine's friend, Betty Hilliard.

> I do remember once Isobel having a bruise of her forehead. She had to get out. There was a certain amount of cloak and dagger going on. We lived in an old house in Rathmines at one stage, which wasn't in good condition at the time and Edward would go charging round crying obsessively 'Pink walls! Brown carpet! And spiders!' There was a certain amount of fun in all the fraught drama …

Isobel's flights were obliquely referred to by Malcolm in his letters to William Walton. 'Our domestic difficulties have got over a very rough patch indeed,' he had written at the time of the *John Field Fantasy*, 'and are better now than when we were married.' Alas, it was only wishful thinking.

Robert and Katherine both visited Meadowcroft independently in 1975 and were shocked at the deteriorating situation. Their memories of Meadowcroft have been fashioned from this traumatic period, their perception of it radically different from that of others not locked into the family crisis. Irene Duffy, Deirdre Ryan and Niamh O'Kelly, for example, all remember it as 'a wonderful, beautiful house'. Irene Duffy stresses how proud of it Malcolm was. For Katherine and Robert, however, it was never 'home' like Primrose Cottage, and they were always emotionally on edge there. Meadowcroft for all its expensive furnishings, its Chinese carpets, G Plan furniture, marble-topped side tables and twelve-branch chandelier had an ugliness and darkness about it. To Katherine it had been ill-omened from the beginning.

> It had been lived in by one elderly man and his valet. There had been a fire in the house and part of it had to be rebuilt. The garden was empty, such a contrast to Primrose Cottage where Isobel had created a pretty and productive set of little gardens going down to the stream. The Meadowcroft garden was dominated by the ugly wall of a school run by the Christian Brothers who, according to Dad, were notoriously hard task-masters to their pupils. It upset Dad. He went on and on about it.[86]

---

[83] April 2004

*Meadowcroft,
Monkstown*

But if there was fear on the far side of the ugly wall, it was matched by the fear lurking in every nook of Meadowcroft. Katherine and Robert could not but sense it and be anxious.

During the daytimes there would be the doughty housekeeper, Mrs Brennan, to act as a restraining influence., as well as the gardener, the brother of Malcolm's taxi-driving chauffeur. The concerned Dr Benson would also call in with some frequency. It was in the unprotected evenings, after a day's drinking, when things were at their most dangerous. Isobel and Edward would spend hours together in the little kitchen at the back of the house, Isobel smoking incessantly and drinking again, and Edward either very noisy or very withdrawn. All the help that he was getting at school was being negated by the home nightmare which he could not but witness. What could a ten-year-old make of occasions when both his parents were lying around the house unconscious? Or the sight, one evening, of his father with a knife at his mother's head? His Irish traumas were appalling, and had the tragic effect of heightening his fears and, through fear, aggression. The Second String Quartet, with the harshness and scurry of its first movement, sums up something of the turmoil of Meadowcroft in 1975, just as the beautiful tune, sad as a misty Irish evening, which breaks out, after several attempts, at the end of the same movement, can only reflect the latent love in Malcolm's heart for Isobel, the awareness of something awful happening despite his very best intentions. But the more he hated himself for what was going on, the more constricted he felt, and the less able to break out from the oppressive gloom which fired the anger. At least, on occasion, he could find some release in his music. Isobel and Edward had no respite.

[84] Cole: *Malcolm Arnold,* pp.194-95
[85] Burton-Page: *Philharmonic Concerto,* pp.121-22
[86] July 2003

The lively inhabitants of Camelot caught only occasional glimpses of the tragedy of Meadowcroft. There was so much concealment and Malcolm, on his good days, still radiated optimism. Isobel was rarely seen around Camelot – she had stopped her occasional visits to Goggins – but word was out that all was not totally well. Anna Connelly, who owned a nearby antique-shop, was aware of the problems but struggled like everyone else to know how to help:

> She looked weary, emotionally drained. A lovely person, but so tense, especially when Malcolm would bring us up from Goggins to continue a 'batter'. I did see signs of bruising on her face. She was having a hard time.[87]

Father Cyril Barratt, an engaging Irish priest on the fringe of Camelot, agrees:

> I admired her enormously for putting up with dear Malcolm. She was as restrained and compassionate and long-suffering as any human being could be.[88]

Malcolm had been on a 'batter' after the String Quartet. He already had a new commission, a cantata, *The Return of Odysseus*, but he could not face it. Nor could he face turning his sketches of *The Three Musketeers* into a full-length ballet, despite the encouragement of David Drew and Robert Helpmann. Turning David Drew down, he sounds strangely indecisive. He knew at the moment he had no music in him, even though to make a comeback in the world of dance would have been a tremendous boost to his morale.

> I think your notes are excellent and provide a solid structure to what can be a very good ballet.
>
> Only one snag for me is that I have a vast choral work to finish in the next few months and could only work on the ballet intermittently. This would delay the ballet.
>
> To make sure that it is produced while we are all still alive it might be better to get somebody else to compose it. I would suggest John Addison, an excellent composer who composed a very successful ballet called 'Carte Blanche' which is on record. If you try various people it will not affect my working on the ballet should you fail to get another composer.[89]

The comment 'while we are still alive' was not simply a joke. A month later, in October 1975, while Isobel and Edward were away, in hiding, Malcolm made another suicide attempt. It has been suggested that this was triggered by the appointment of Malcolm Williamson as Master of the Queen's Musick, but it was also the twentieth anniversary of his mother's death. Whatever the immediate crisis, Malcolm swallowed every pill he could find in Meadowcroft and washed them down with a bottle of Metaxa brandy.[90] This time he was doubly determined. This time he really would succeed.

He happened to take the pills, however, on the publication day of John Ryan's book, *Remembering How We Stood*. Deirdre Ryan, knowing that Malcolm was

---

[87] August 2003
[88] April, 2003
[89] 4 September 1975
[90] Kriss Russman's *Omnibus* programme, 1991

very low in spirits, decided to take a copy round to him. John Ryan had dedicated the book to Deirdre and fondly inscribed Malcolm's copy. He would be sure to love it. Particularly John's humorous chapter on Distilled Damnation. 'Most of the Dubliners I knew then,' began John, 'had an alcohol problem: *they couldn't get enough of it.*' John had a fund of jokes on alcohol. Malcolm had heard most of them, but would love them just as much in print. She paused at the garden gate of Meadowcroft, solid and secure in its red brick, its sense of well-being enhanced by the long, tidy front garden. She struggled for the wording of that other old joke which was often heard in Goggins.

'Which is the more correct?' Yes, that's how it started. 'Which is the more correct? In Dublin the best Irish is drunk. Or, in Dublin the best Irish are drunk?' She smiled as she rang the bell. There was no reply. She rang again. Silence. She rang a third time, loud and long. Some instinct made her peer through the letter box. And there on the floor, stretched out like a corpse, lay Malcolm, deeply unconscious.[91]

---

[91] Father Cyril Barratt gave an alternative version of this incident in Tony Palmer's documentary film of 2004, in which Malcolm managed to open the door before collapsing. Deirdre Ryan is clear that this did not happen.

# 14
# Irish Tribulations
## Monkstown and Dun Laoghaire, 1975-77

DEIRDRE RYAN'S LUCKY ARRIVAL saved Malcolm's life. Left only a
little longer, he would have died. Instead, he was swiftly taken by ambulance to Meath Hospital in central Dublin where he made a slow recovery. It was
a grimly significant destination for it was here that another friend of John Ryan's,
Brendan Behan, had died a few years earlier. 'I only drink on two occasions,'
Behan had declared famously. 'When I'm thirsty and when I'm not.'

It was Malcolm's custom in later life to turn his various crises into well-
polished, humorous stories, and the suicide bid of 1975 proved no exception. He
enjoyed in particular the drama in 'the Dublin hospital built by Dean Swift' when
he first regained consciousness: 'I am dead, I thought. This is heaven, but where
the hell am I?' At that moment, with a bevy of nuns swimming before his eyes ,
he finally focused on the beautiful, if anxious, face of Deirdre Ryan. It confirmed
his best thoughts! He really *was* in heaven![1]

Malcolm's persuasive story-telling has led to Deirdre Ryan becoming a latter-
day Florence Nightingale, looking after Malcolm and nursing him back to health,
whereas it was the faithful Isobel, returning at once on news of the attempted
suicide, who organised Malcolm's move from Meath to St Edmundsbury, a
private clinic. Situated four miles down the River Liffey at Lucan,
St Edmundsbury was a branch of St Patrick's, Dublin's leading psychiatric
hospital.[2] At Lucan Malcolm came under the care of Dr Moore, a leading
psychiatrist adept at handling the many famous alcoholics who sought
St Edmundsbury's help.

After the initial euphoria of his heavenly reawakening Malcolm's spirits
slumped. This had not been just a cry for help, but a determined bid to end an
existence he struggled to understand or approve. Self-pity was involved. How
dare Isobel remove his son from the house and go absent without leave? But it
was mixed with self-loathing. How had he, an apostle of non-violence, become

[1] The story is told to Kriss Russman in the *Omnibus* feature of 1991.
[2] St Patrick's, built with a bequest by Jonathan Swift (who himself went mad at the end of
his life), would more accurately have been called 'the hospital founded by Dean Swift',
although Meath Hospital was built on Jonathan Swift's old garden and where he was said to
have kept his horses.

a party to aggression? Why was he no longer true to himself? And why was he destroying his talents? Writing was now a terrible struggle, and all the critics ever did was sneer at him, so hadn't he better end the whole charade? To discover that he had not done so angered him. Even a visit from the adored Irene found him despondent. 'He was in a quiet but sort of sad mood,' she recalls.[3]

In an attempt to understand his own problems Malcolm read widely. His present interest was the novelist Malcolm Lowry,[4] whose alcoholism (related to his manic-depressive illness) had led to his suicide.[5] Malcolm was so enthusiastic about the semi-autobiographical *Under The Volcano*, with its theme of self-destruction, that for his fifty-fourth birthday, spent in hospital, Katherine gave him *Lunar Caustic*, the sequel. Malcolm was intrigued by certain similarities of background between himself and Lowry. Both had an autocratic father, came from bourgeois Methodist stock and were the youngest of four brothers. Lowry's second wife also did secretarial work for him and picked up the pieces at the end of binges. There that particular parallel ended. Margerie Lowry, distinctly less sympathetic than Isobel, was at one stage planning to have her difficult husband lobotomised …

Failing to learn anything from his study of Lowry, Malcolm was back at Meadowcroft sooner than advisable, unable to face work and drinking as heavily as ever. David Drew had again been in touch over *The Three Musketeers*, explaining that Robert Helpmann was parting from the Australian Ballet but still keen to take the project on elsewhere. Malcolm responded cautiously:

> I'm sorry I've taken so long to reply, but I have been away. It is very difficult for me at the moment to be tied to any definite date with the ballet, but of course I'm still interested in it.[6]

Interest was not enough. A score was needed and, without it, the project now died.[7]

Robert, having just returned from a second period in Papua New Guinea, paid a less than easy visit to Meadowcroft around this time, after which Malcolm apologised for his rudeness.

> I can only say that (as you may have gathered) I was very pissed, in fact so much so that I remember very little of your entire visit …[8]

It was deeply discouraging. There seemed no possible eventual outcome other than catastrophe.

---

[3] March 2004

[4] 1909-57

[5] There are theories, however, suggesting he was murdered by his second wife.

[6] 18 November 1975

[7] It finally died when Helpmann's successor at the Australian Ballet, claiming it was pure coincidence, brought out *The Three Musketeers* with a score and set designs by his own team.

[8] 29 November 1975

Robert continued the struggle to find a meaningful adult relationship with his father. He cites as a small but significant example of his difficulties a time they were together in Goggins:

> I'd gone over to Ireland specially to see him, we'd gone down to the pub, and I was determined to buy him a pint! That's what you do, isn't it, when you grow up, you buy your dad a pint? But he absolutely refused. He just wouldn't let me! I was shoved out of the way, crushed into a kind of humiliation![9]

Malcolm always needed to play the liberal host. Paying for others gave him confidence. When others paid, he felt irritation or anger instead of gratitude, believing in some strange way that he had been undermined.

There were other quirks of temperament which stemmed from an inner lack of confidence. His inclination to search out and exploit other people's weak points extended well beyond Isobel to the majority of those he knew. Robert had found it happening to his own friends.

> Things would start well. We'd go out for a meal and that would be really nice. He'd choose a pleasant restaurant and be friendly and interested in all of us. But then, after a few drinks, he'd started picking on each of my friends' weakest points. He could absolutely devastate and humiliate people who weren't up to it.

Robert had brought his future wife, Anne, on an earlier visit and was alarmed when his father began this same tactic on her:

> I thought to myself. 'Hang on! We've made a huge effort to come over here to see him, and all he's doing is getting at Anne.' He was really hurting her.

It was becoming clear to Robert, as it had already to Katherine, that the situation of Isobel and Edward at Meadowcroft was no longer tenable:

> I have a strong memory of staying quite a long time there with Dad being really horrible to Isobel, really horrible.

Malcolm was drinking whisky or brandy from 8.00 in the morning and was more or less perpetually drunk and aggressive. He could be so violent in his anger that Katherine feared he might one day kill Isobel. It was difficult to know how best to help, as interference could easily make matters worse. Opportunities for calm, open discussion were negligible. But both Katherine and Robert quietly assured Isobel of their support and encouraged her to come to London with Edward. Isobel, however, for all her distress, was fearful of change.

In mid-November a new crisis arose when Malcolm heard talk of Isobel's interest in leaving Ireland and attempted to procure a court injunction against her doing so. He failed, and in the ensuing arguments he conceded the possibility of Edward going to school in London in the next academic year and having treatment at the Tavistock Clinic. Malcolm also agreed to an exploratory visit and wrote to Katherine outlining the situation:

---

[9] August 2003

My dear Katherine,

Without the aid of too much alcohol, things have sorted themselves out, as always.

We are coming to London on Wednesday December 10th and shall be at the Connaught until Saturday December 13th. I have decided firmly in this time of crisis[10] that when the worst comes to the worst, I shall cut down on the basic necessities and keep only the luxuries.

On Thursday and Friday we have interviews, or assessments of Edward I think they are called, and on Friday also we have an interview at the school you told us about. It would be marvellous if you and Tony could come and have dinner with us on any or all of the evenings. We have a sitting room so we shall be away from the bombs![11]

Edward will definitely be coming to school in London next year and Isobel will be coming with him. We are going to keep Meadowcroft indefinitely. Whatever happens it will be a useful place for all of us. They will come back here for the holidays except when we go to Italy or somewhere.[12]

Isobel was lucky to have Katherine's support in London. Katherine herself had just started studying child psychotherapy at the Tavistock Clinic, so she was in a good position to help organise interviews for Edward there. The school she had mentioned was one for children with difficulties, close to the Clinic.

Malcolm was exploring the possibility of staying in London with Isobel and Edward, at least part of the time, and had been discussing this with Kimble, his accountant, as he outlined to Katherine:

I put the following ideas forward because Kimble suggested them. I do it without having much of an opinion of them, but I think I should tell you all of them.

Kimble, of course, does not know the detailed picture, also my total dislike of burdening my children with my problems. However, he suggested that you might enlarge or do something to your home so that Isobel and I stay there for the term. Obviously if this was a possibility I would pay your mortgage, rates and all the household bills (electricity etc). But he thought that a better idea might be to buy (us, that is) a larger house in your name that would be your property without any ties whatever. It is, of course, just an idea that might be useful to Tony and you if you thought it might work. It would be for a few years only ...

These suggestions are unlikely to be Kimble's. Malcolm, having discovered that he could not, like some fabled eastern potentate, invoke the law to keep his wife under restraint, might now have been deluding himself that he could create a family ménage where all might yet be well. And the shocked and desperate Isobel, clinging to the faint hope of saving the marriage, might have encouraged the suggestion. Perhaps she thought there could be safety in numbers, while the Tavistock Clinic close by could offer Malcolm support, and the Greenway

---

[10] OPEC had raised crude oil prices in 1975, triggering an international recession.
[11] The IRA was currently targeting London restaurants. There had been fatalities in a Chelsea restaurant just days before.
[12] 26 November 1975

Clinic and psychiatric ward of the Royal Free Hospital would both be on hand for emergencies.

For Katherine, trying to establish her own life with Anthony, the idea of living each day with her father's problems was not attractive, but for Isobel's sake she did not immediately reject the idea. And although the letter concluded as positively as it began, she sensed from the PS that there was more fantasy than fact in the 'Kimble' suggestions:

> The weather is marvellous here and I shall spend Christmas writing 'The Return of Odysseus' for which my friend Patric Dickinson has written the most wonderful libretto.
>
> With love to you both from all of us and looking forward to seeing you both,
> Love,
> Dad
> PS Separation is still a possibility but not yet awhile.

Philip Pfaff, Malcolm's teacher over thirty years ago in Northampton, had been instrumental in arranging the commission of *The Return of Odysseus*, a cantata for chorus and orchestra, from the Schools' Music Association. The librettist, Patric Dickinson, was a member of the Savile Club, a delightfully eccentric poet with a passion for golf, who had made his mark with translations of Virgil and Aristophanes. Malcolm did indeed make a start on this project over Christmas, but there was too much else on his mind for proper progress.

By the Christmas of 1975 Malcolm was in a highly volatile state, which, in Robert's observation, made him 'extremely horrible' one moment and also 'very charming and considerate' the next. When the charming and the considerate Malcolm held sway, Edward's every need was indeed of great importance,[13] and Isobel's resolve to leave was weakened.

Around Camelot the drinks continued to flow, but it was now well-known that in Malcolm's case drink and chivalry were largely incompatible. Father Cyril Barratt remembers embarrassing moments at the Restaurant Na Mara bar:

> He used to get very drunk there. He would make approaches to young ladies under such circumstances. Very unsuccessfully. Indeed, I've no recollection of his ever being successful. But that didn't stop him from trying![14]

Father Cyril had never met anyone of quite such quixotic moods as Malcolm.

> The changes would often be absolutely instantaneous and totally inexplicable. He could be quite aggressive with it. On occasions he was very ferocious with me. It upset me. But what carried me through was that I knew deep down he had an affection for me, so I put up with it.

---

[13] A few months earlier, for example, Malcolm had been contemplating a move to Italy, to Santa Margherita, near Rapallo, which had impressed him on earlier holidays. He felt that the way the Italians brought up their children was kinder than in England and that Edward might therefore benefit.

[14] April 2003

Malcolm was very fond of 'The Reverend Father', as he always called him, and on his good days they would have wide-ranging intellectual discussions. Father Cyril was head of Warwick University's Philosophy Department for many years, a subject in which Malcolm could more than hold his own.

> I always felt very cautious in Malcolm's presence. But even when you were being very cautious he could turn on you for that! You would say something, upset him, and then just chat on, cautiously leaving Malcolm out. But when you tried to bring him back in, he would turn on you, lean close, smile and be very challenging indeed! It was as if he were playing games with you.

By January Isobel's situation had become worse, Malcolm no longer relishing the idea of a move to London and resenting a further interview which Isobel had organised with Katherine's help at the Tavistock for February. The situation was in danger of slipping out of his control, and he became paranoid about it, suspicions of Isobel's 'duplicity' fuelling his anger. He insisted that he should make all the arrangements. 'Isobel is ringing you tonight,' he wrote to Katherine, 'because she has heard from the Tavistock Clinic.'[15] Two days later he wrote again:

> Isobel would like to stay at the hotel near the Tavistock when she comes with Edward, and we would very much like its name and address and number if it would not be a trouble to you.

Katherine made sure that she gave it to Isobel and not her father, for violence had broken out again at Meadowcroft. And she urged her not to wait for the appointment in mid-February but to come with Edward to safety in London straight away.

The escape from Meadowcroft, when it happened, proved remarkably easy. Malcolm was out of the house when Isobel, on the spur of the moment, phoned for a taxi and hurriedly packed two suitcases. She left no note, for she could think of nothing to say appropriate to a situation which demanded secrecy. With Edward close beside her, she walked down the front garden, shut the gate on Meadowcroft for the last time and waited nervously on the pavement outside. The Hill was quiet. There was no sign of Malcolm. Shortly afterwards a taxi drew up and in next to no time they were on an Aer Lingus flight to London.

From Heathrow they made their way to the Post House Hotel, Haverstock Hill, where Katherine had booked accommodation for them. As the flight had progressed, the more and more fearful of reprisals Isobel had become, so she told the hotel receptionist not to put telephone calls from Ireland through, for Malcolm was sure to guess where they were. One call, however, was put through in error. Isobel answered, but not a word was spoken. She merely heard the sound of breathing at the other end of the line. Malcolm now knew where they were.

---

[15] 19 January 1976

Isobel was in no condition to organise the next phase of her life, so Katherine helped her cope, arranging Edward's enrolment in his new school and regular sessions at the Tavistock. They began to look for flats nearby, eventually finding one in Belsize Park Gardens, a road of dignified, white-stuccoed Victorian houses.[16] 72d was tiny and on the top of four floors, but it offered a security which neither Isobel or Edward had known for several years. The worst of their ordeal was over.

Alone in Meadowcroft, Malcolm might well have tried to kill himself but for the intervention of friends. One of them, a dark, pretty girl called Dymphna, who worked part-time for Aer Lingus in the Pavilion Centre at Dublin Airport, understood much of what had been happening at Meadowcroft. She was Malcolm's newest goddess, shrewd enough to appreciate the benefits of his patronage, but deeply religious and able to understand Isobel's embattled position. The two had become friendly, and Dymphna had often helped her with Edward, with whom she had an easy rapport. Dymphna knew that the answer to Malcolm's current crisis lay in his music, and as she exerted a considerable influence over him it was not long before he was back at work on the unfinished cantata.

Dickinson's *The Return of Odysseus* offered Malcolm an interesting new challenge, although some of the versification was of a kind which could well have brought out Malcolm's baser musical instincts:

> Circe was a great enchantress, a witch of powerful eye.
> She turned Odysseus's mates to pigs and shut them in a sty.[17]

But Malcolm resisted all thoughts of parody, preferring to take very seriously the story of the devotion of Penelope to a husband from whom she had been parted for twenty years. He saw the faithful Penelope as a vivid contrast to the fickle Isobel, and she fired his imagination.

*The Return of Odysseus* is very different from most compositions of the Meadowcroft period in that the work begins softly and ends with an Olympian serenity. In between there is plenty of drama in the lively handling of Odysseus's wanderings and the final defeat of the suitors, but there is absolutely nothing manic in the whole, thirty-minute work. Like all his later works the Cantata does contain many sombre and highly chromatic touches, but the dissonance is under tight control and never allowed to dominate. The dexterity with which he develops themes is a reminder of less troubled days. A mischievous sense of humour is in evidence, though never obtrusively so. In the spoken cries of shock when the suitors meet their death at the hands of the 'dirty old beggar' we have a sly tribute to William Walton's 'Slain!' in *Belshazzar's Feast*. The jazzy negro spiritual of 'Odysseus he went down to hell' salutes Michael Tippett's *A Child of Our Time*, and there are even some touches of Benjamin Britten in the melodic

---

[16] 72 was only a few houses away from where Michael Ayrton and his parents had lived, so Isobel may have known the area well.
[17] Faber Music Ltd, London 1976

writing. *The Return of Odysseus* was completed on 30 March 1976, less than two months after Isobel had left. Yet, in focussing on Penelope, the faithful wife, Malcolm has seemingly expunged all painful thoughts of Isobel and Edward from his mind and music.

The Cantata rebuts the assertion, sometimes made, that Malcolm had problems in setting words effectively to music. Written to be sung by young voices, *The Return of Odysseus* works admirably for any age. It may not be particularly challenging – it was written for schools – but it is still terrific fun to sing.

Only a few days after completing the Cantata, Malcolm was back in London, to participate in the BBC Radio 3 series *The Composer Conducts*, in which he was giving his Seventh Symphony its first broadcast in a programme which also included *The Fair Field*[18] and the Concerto for Two Violins. The concert was an encouraging sign that there was still some sympathy to his music within the BBC, but in his poor physical and mental state he struggled with the six hours of rehearsal. The performance he gave of the Seventh Symphony, however, with its poignant final movement inspired by the son he had now lost, was quite over-whelming in its drawn-out intensity, and critics with open minds, like Edward Greenfield and Colin Mason, were highly moved by it. Malcolm himself was always very proud of the symphony and had been eager that his children should be there, giving Robert six months' advance notice.[19]

During this stay in London Malcolm contacted Isobel, suggesting that she and Edward returned to Ireland for a few days. Isobel could prevaricate no more. She saw the separation, she told him, as final. She had fought her way through twelve highly difficult years, always supporting as best as she could, never disloyal whatever the affronts or the assaults. Despite her own fragile mental state she might herself have soldiered on, because she loved him, had the effect on Edward not been quite so catastrophic. Edward's future had to come first. As far as she was concerned the separation was absolute.

Malcolm felt utterly humiliated. Fortunately he had the means at hand to give expression to his pent-up fury, an exciting commission from his old orchestra. Bernard Haitink was taking the LPO over to America that November. 1976 was Bicentennial Year, and a new piece celebrating the anniversary of the American War of Independence was required.

The resultant *Philharmonic Concerto* is, in the words of Piers Burton-Page, 'a fifteen minute firework display'. But it has little to do with the Bicentenary, despite Malcolm's unusually long programme note to that effect:

---

[18] This performance was subsequently released on the BBC's double CD celebrating his 75th birthday in 1996. Payment for such broadcast concerts was comparatively modest. He was paid £30 for the day's rehearsal, £60 for the broadcast and £120 for the recording.

[19] 'On April 10 next year I am conducting the BBC Symphony Orchestra at Maida Vale studios in a programme of my music including the 7th Symphony, there will be an invited audience and I hope you can make it. I can get as many tickets as you would like. 7.00 pm.'

The middle of the eighteenth century seems to me to have been one of the most stimulating and interesting times in human history. The music, literature and the arts in general, particularly that of architecture, flourished with unsurpassed splendour. What, however, has such great significance for us in the present day are the great eighteenth century struggles for freedom amongst subject peoples. These of course found their peak with the American War of Independence of 1776. This piece has no quotations from war songs. It celebrates this great event with as much brilliance as I am able to muster, in what to me is the glorious sound of a symphony orchestra.[20]

Paid to write a celebration of a historical event, Malcolm is sheepishly covering his tracks as best he can. From time to time there are snatches of fanfares which suggest that military triumph was somewhere at the back of Malcolm's mind, but the piece, which takes its tone from the first *fortissimo* chord of dismay, speaks more of the beaten English oppressors than the conquering Americans. If it treats of 'this great event' at all, it does so bizarrely, with Malcolm himself the leading soldier, his foot bleeding, taking the worst that the enemy can hurl at him. There is much serial writing in the first movement and the main theme is in the form of a palindrome, the mechanical territory of the avant-garde which he had long despised. The effect of this odd sop to modernism is predictable. When the main theme starts running backwards, it becomes tuneless and dull. Malcolm's intentions at this point are difficult to fathom.

The second movement is powerfully emotional, but the emotions are more suitable to a husband recently turned away by his wife than the triumph (or even the cost) of the American Dream. The finale is utterly manic, Malcolm sounding as if he is having drunken fun in one of the seedier pubs of Dun Laoghaire. It is hard to picture a great struggle for freedom or fine eighteenth-century architecture.

The whole work is indeed a firework display, as the large orchestra is violently flung around this way and that, each instrumental group having its turn to leap about like jumping crackers. But it is not a pretty firework display. It is a violent, brash, deafening one, with a sad intermission in the middle where the display stops, the organisers go off to look for a new box of matches and the children wander round on the damp grass hoping to find the hot sausages which someone has forgotten to bring. It is, overall, a very odd creation and – odder still – the critics really loved it.

Malcolm had other diversions to keep him from brooding on recent events. Shortly after the completion of the *Philharmonic Concerto* Hugh Maguire's Allegri Quartet gave the first performance of the Second String Quartet at Castleton House, a delightful but obscure setting for the première of an important work. Hugh Maguire had accordingly asked Peter Pears if he might play it at a forthcoming concert at the Aldeburgh Festival, which Malcolm attended, staying as usual at the White Lion.

---

[20] Programme note to the first performance, Festival Hall, 31 October 1976.

This was a particularly important occasion for Faber Music, who, as Benjamin Britten's publishers, had tried hard but without much previous success to persuade him to put on more of Malcolm's music at Aldeburgh. A successful launch of Malcolm's new Quartet at the concert to be given jointly by the Allegri Quartet and the Tuckwell Wind Quintet (who were playing Mozart, Ligeti and Spohr[21]) might just possibly start off a productive new relationship between Malcolm and Benjamin Britten. Unfortunately Malcolm, who was never at ease in the atmosphere of Aldeburgh, had sampled the cellars of the White Lion too much beforehand. The performance went well, Pears telling Hugh Maguire, 'Yes, I quite liked that'. But there was a terrible moment shortly afterwards when Britten and Pears came up to give Malcolm their congratulations, and Malcolm's fierce homophobia surfaced. After a few, uneasy pleasantries, as Britten and Pears started to move away, Malcolm turned brusquely to his neighbour, James Burnett,[22] and said in ringing tones, 'I say, Jimmy! Will I bugger you tonight? Or will you bugger me?'[23]

It was a catastrophic remark. Britten was ill at the time, with just six months to live. Peter Pears was understandably alienated. Faber's hopes for Malcolm at Aldeburgh had been dashed.

After the concert Malcolm made his way to London for an appointment with his solicitors. Although Meadowcroft was being sold, he still held out hopes that the marriage could be retrieved, and instructed his solicitors to write to Isobel. She was somewhat shocked to receive their bland overtures:

> We understand that like all marriages there have been ups and downs, good periods and bad periods. So far as your husband is concerned, he would have liked the marriage to continue. He has still not accepted that the marriage has irretrievably broken down. It has caused him very great distress and concern that your departure from Dublin in February, with his consent, has been turned by you in what you say is a 'permanent' separation. He understands you now feel the marriage is over, but should you have any second thoughts about this, he would be very happy to see whether the relationship could be put on a firm footing, as he still feels very deep affection for you and believes that together you could effect a mutually satisfying relationship.[24]

To have received such comments from Malcolm himself would have been difficult enough. To receive them from a third party only reminded Isobel of the

---

[21] Whereas the Aldeburgh programme offered copious notes on Mozart's Fantasia in F minor, Ligeti's Ten Pieces for Wind Quintet, and Spohr's Nonet, Malcolm insisted on the barest of help: 'The first movement is mostly tutti; the others each feature one particular instrument: the first violin in the second movement, the cello in the third and the viola in the fourth. The second movement is strongly Irish in character, a tribute to the work's dedicatee and the country where the composer now lives.'

[22] Music producer at the BBC Transcription Service

[23] Martin Kingsbury tells the story.

[24] 18 June 1976

extent to which he would shy away from taking responsibility in time of any difficulties. If he could not express those feelings himself to her in person, he was unlikely to make good his promise of a 'mutually satisfying relationship'. And it was hardly fair to equate his drunken aggression with 'the ups and downs' of 'all marriages'.

The rest of the letter centred around the difficult matter of Malcolm's access to Edward. Malcolm could never accept that Edward needed the reassurance of Isobel's presence. He suggested, therefore, via his solicitors, that it would be reasonable for Edward to spend time with him in Ireland in the holidays. He was sure that Edward needed him every bit as much as his mother. Had he not, only recently in Suffolk, received a delightful little letter? [25]

> Dear Dad,
>
> Thank you for the postcard. I'd like to go for a drive in your car. We went to Hampstead Heath ponds and I had a picnic and I made sandwiches. On occasion we go to Parliament Hill Fields or Primrose Hill Park.
>
> Look forward to seeing you,
> Edward

Malcolm was back in Dublin when, a few days later, Edward celebrated his twelfth birthday and sent him a charming thank-you letter:

> Dear Dad,
>
> Thank you for the telegram you sent me. The watch is very nice and the second hand is a good idea. Katherine brought me a Magpie record-breaking kite. I flew it on Primrose Hill. There was not enough wind to fly it. The stamps you sent me are very nice. Katherine and Tony came to my party.
>
> Love from Edward

For a time, having access to Edward became the most important thing on Malcolm's mind. The more he thought about it, the more he suspected that Isobel was taking his son away from him. Anger at Isobel increased in parallel with regret for Edward. Preparing to move into a small flat on the outskirts of Dun Laoghaire, Malcolm systematically stripped all vestiges of Isobel from his life. As soon as Meadowcroft was sold, he sent off all its furniture and furnishings to auction. Everything – even the HMV stereo player, the Chinese carpets of questionable taste and the much-admired twelve-branch crystal chandelier – went under the hammer. In his desire to break off all continuity with his old life he happily parted with his cellar of fine vintage clarets and ports and many other high-class French and Italian wines.

At the same time, in the spirit of excess which characterised the climax of the *John Field Fantasy*, he divested himself of the majority of his personal belongings, sending several crates of them, without a word of warning, to Katherine at

---

[25] 14 June 1976
[26] 17 July 1976

her Highgate home. The briefest of explanations eventually followed. He wrote to Robert on a postcard: [26]

> All the books, pictures, sculptures etc. are for you and Katherine, to share and keep or sell if you like! Dad.

It was as if they had been contaminated by Isobel's 'treachery' and had to be discarded. He would none of them. Isobel no longer existed.[27]

The flat at 4 de Vesci Terrace, which was only ten minutes away from Monkstown, had been found for him by friends, Niall and Monica Sheridan. Set on a steep hill, rising up from the main Dun Laoghaire-Dublin road, de Vesci Terrace has considerable period charm. The Georgian terrace of white-stuccoed houses, with their raised entrances embellished with little porticoes and small front gardens protected by high hedges, faces onto a narrow strip of public garden and feels genuinely secluded from the hubbub of the busy port. A newly-married couple lived on the lower two floors, allowing Malcolm entrance to a self-contained top-floor flat through their hall.

Despite its attractions, after Meadowcroft the flat was something of a come-down. Yet Malcolm seems at first hardly to have noticed this. A glorious new life, he felt, was opening up, uncluttered by material possessions and Isobel. He was to be single again. At last he was able to concentrate on being a composer! He wrote of his new situation to William Walton with great enthusiasm:

> Having been through the worst time I have ever had in my life I have emerged fresh in spirit, drinking far less and enjoying it so much more.
>
> Isobel prefers to stay in London throughout Edward's holidays and I prefer Dublin permanently. Edward has a room at both places and lives where he pleases. I am delighted that he prefers here mostly.[28]

This was not true. Edward was unable to travel without Isobel and did not visit by himself that summer. The diminished drinking was another delusion, Malcolm now consuming more rather than less; and his claims for the flat were also slightly exaggerated:

> My housekeeper stays on, and this two-bedroomed, two-bathroomed flat in a beau-tiful Georgian terrace with wonderful views of the sea, gardens and the Wicklow mountains suits me well. I have not looked forward to each day so much for twenty years and over …

The house faces towards Monkstown, at right angles to the sea, which is visible but some distance away. The Wicklow mountains are too distant to be seen; there is a view, instead, of the Dublin mountains. The main bedroom was *en suite*, but the second so small that he had to install bunk beds to accommodate two guests.

---

[27] Edward and the address of the Belsize Park flat were included in Malcolm's diary for 1977. But of Isobel there was no mention.

[28] 12 August 1976. The letter is quoted by Paul Jackson, *The Life and Music of Sir Malcolm Arnold,* p.172.

Malcolm's short period at De Vesci Terrace began surprisingly well, with Mrs McQuade[29] on hand to tidy up and cook lunch if he had visitors. Robert remembers sitting at a beautiful antique table, while he was plied with drinks all afternoon. Sometimes Malcolm himself attempted bold culinary efforts. Robert was regaled with one such success:

> Claire came to lunch yesterday, and I tried some virtuoso cooking, which to my surprise came off. Then we went to the RTE studios to see a private performance of a TV film we missed the week before. Such is the advantage of being friendly with Niall Sheridan,[30] a TV producer who lives three doors away.[31]

Irene Duffy remembers Malcolm enjoying himself when cooking her dinner once at de Vesci Terrace, 'chicken with a lot of garlic and excellent vegetables'. By this time he had created a new cellar, for there was 'as always, excellent wine to drink'. On another occasion they went to the theatre with the Sheridans, to whose house they returned afterwards, Malcolm producing a memorable burgundy for the meal prepared by Monica, the TV cook. It was, says Irene, her own 'first real appreciation of a good burgundy'.

Malcolm still visited Goggins, but his best days were, as ever, in the company of his young goddesses. One of his happier diversions around this time was helping Irene learn to drive. He proved a remarkably calm instructor. On one occasion, driving Malcolm's Fiat quite early on in her endeavours, Irene very nearly had a head-on collision with a car coming very fast round a corner of a narrow country road. She pulled up in some shock and alarm. 'You need not worry, my dear girl,' replied the unruffled Malcolm indulgently. 'There is no problem. The car is fully insured!'

By this time Malcolm had found a fourth goddess, another Deirdre, married to one of Dublin's most famous dance band leaders. 'She was wonderful with him,' remembers Deirdre Ryan. 'She had a great Dublin sense of humour and was very often part of the Na Mara lunches.'

Malcolm was to be most distressed when, after he had left Dublin, he heard news of her suicide. Overwhelmed with personal upsets, the second Deirdre had walked into the sea and was never seen again. Deirdre Ryan still harbours the faintest of hopes:

> She's never been found, and my husband, John, who was a yachtsman, reckoned she would have been found three miles down the coast. I sometimes wonder: Did Malcolm give her a load of money and she went somewhere? What she did was so unlike her. She has, however, now been declared officially dead …

---

[29] She had taken over from Mrs Brennan in Meadowcroft, and was as capable and admired as her predecessor.

[30] Niall Sheridan as a young man had met James Joyce and was very knowledgeable about his work. He was also a published poet and had written on Flann O'Brien.

[31] 28 March 1977

Malcolm's sex-less obsession with his goddesses caused amusement in Camelot. Nonetheless the goddesses continued to be important influences in bolstering his fragile sense of well-being. Dymphna was particularly helpful in this period, trying to interest Malcolm in the religio-scientific thinking of Pierre Teilhard de Chardin, a Jesuit priest[32] who had distressed the Pope by recon-structing the most basic Christian doctrines from the perspective of science. Malcolm read several books on the subject and for a while found comfort in them. To someone who often saw nothing in the world to justify living, Teilhard's belief that the divine was everywhere in the world was attractive as well as startling:

> We imagined the divine as distant and inaccessible, whereas in fact we live steeped in its burning layers ... This world, which we were wont to treat with the boredom and disrespect with which we habitually regard places with no sacred association for us, is in truth a holy place ...[33]

Malcolm had always been interested in religious debate, but this was the nearest he ever came to some form of belief. For a time he would embarrass family and friends by talking about it with huge enthusiasm. Teilhard's view of the material world as a source of mystical illumination was quite hard to take amid day-to-day conversation. But Malcolm was very moved by Teilhard's visionary language, with its descriptions of the world 'taking on light and fire' until it came to envelop him in 'one mass of luminosity glowing from within':

> The purple flush of matter fading imperceptibly into the gold of the spirit, to be lost finally in the incandescence of a personal universe.

Dymphna only achieved a temporary conversion. Malcolm was to leave the Jesuit priest behind him when he left Ireland. But he was grateful to Dymphna for this spiritual and intellectual excursion. The second of his *Irish Dances* would eventually commemorate her helpfulness to him.

After his first two months in de Vesci Terrace Malcolm, feeling the need for change, spent most of October in London. He was planning several parties in this period, one, as he told William Walton, 'for a very few select friends, my progeny and concubines and one or two delightful Irish birds'.[34] There was also a Gala Concert[35] to conduct at St John's, Smith Square, to which he was much looking forward, as it included Benny Goodman and the European première of the Second Clarinet Concerto. Goodman had played the concerto successfully in America for the past two years, though, as he wrote in a letter to Malcolm, the première with the Denver Orchestra had had its problems:

[32] 1881-1955
[33] From Pierre Teilhard de Chardin's *The Divine Milieu*, as quoted by Charles P Henderson in *God and Science*, Chapter 5
[34] Jackson: *The Life and Music of Sir Malcolm Arnold*, p.172
[35] 11 October 1976

We played outdoors in a place called Red Rocks which under good conditions is quite good but if the winds are blowing, which was the case that evening, the music sort of gets lost …[36]

By contrast the baroque church of St John's offered superb acoustics. It was, however, in need of restoration and the concert, attended by Princess Margaret as Patron of the Friends of the Church, was a fund-raising venture, supported by the BBC who were recording and broadcasting Goodman's performances of both Mozart's Concerto and Malcolm's. The orchestra, the Park Lane Group, was led by Suzanne Rozsa, the dedicatée of Malcolm's Second Violin Sonata.

The church was packed for the concert, with Princess Margaret and the former Prime Minister Edward Heath in the front row. Malcolm was delighted that Katherine and her husband were present as well as William Walton and many friends. Unfortunately Goodman himself, then sixty-seven, was not really on top form and was ill at ease with the Mozart, even though Malcolm helped all he could by taking it at an exaggeratedly slow pace. The audience were also unsettled by the regular clicking of the soloist's teeth. Goodman was a little happier with Malcolm's concerto, as Alan Blyth noted in *The Times*:

> The work exploits his more usual style, especially in a free and easy first movement cadenza and a ragtime finale. In both of these Goodman cast off the cares that seemed to oppress him during the rest of the evening.[37]

Despite Goodman's cautious playing and dry tone, Blyth wrote glowingly of the concerto's slow movement, 'a mood piece with menacing undertones displayed in dissolving harmonies and a languid diatonic melody'.

In contrast to the nervous Goodman, Malcolm was obviously enjoying himself hugely, and seldom can the National Anthem have been given such rousing treatment. Just before the Mozart concerto a glass of water was placed ceremoniously on a chair between soloist and conductor. Edward Heath turned round to Pamela Weston,[38] sitting behind him. 'Bet you that's not just water!' he whispered loudly. Malcolm, sensing the audience's interest in the glass, made big play with it between the movements, taking a careful sip, turning to the audience and winking knowingly.

Freed of the worry of keeping Benny Goodman in tow, Malcolm was able to conduct the rest of the concert without restraint, winning the approval of *The Times*:

> Dr Arnold's conducting was more apt in Delius' *First Cuckoo* and *Summer Night on the River*, both of which served to show how mellifluous the St John's acoustics can sound, given a medium sized orchestra.

---

[36] 2 October 1974
[37] 13 October 1976. The cadenza was Goodman's.
[38] Clarinettist and writer

Malcolm also conducted his own *Serenade for Small Orchestra,* written at a troubled time 26 years earlier. Its studied elegance perfectly matched the lovely Queen Anne church.

After the last piece on the official programme Goodman played some informal jazz with a few friends. A party followed, down in the crypt, with Malcolm on piano running through his Sophie Tucker repertoire. Constantly overweight and being told to diet, Malcolm felt a certain rapport for the similarly plump 'Last of the Red Hot Mommas', whose songs included 'I Don't Want To Be Thin!' and 'Nobody Loves a Fat Girl, But Oh How a Fat Girl can Love'. Princess Margaret, enjoying the party even more than the concert, was one of the last to leave.

For these happy, riotous few weeks in London Malcolm was based at the Savile Club. Irene, whom he showed off proudly in the club on one occasion, was most impressed with it. He also took her to Wheeler's, where they met his friend and former publisher, Michael Diack, who was trying to woo Malcolm back to Paterson. Irene found it 'all very civilised' and was impressed by Malcolm's 'skill, subtlety and high levels of diplomacy'. At Wheeler's Malcolm introduced Irene to Francis Bacon, a good friend, 'who had a very pale skin and looked as if he had been sitting on the bar stool for days drinking'.

Malcolm was one of the great characters of the Savile at this period. One evening a club tribute to William Alwyn had been organised. Malcolm was in the chair for the occasion, with Benjamin Luxon singing. However he fell asleep on duty and began snoring, so he was quietly removed to the bar, where he was left, still asleep. The performance restarted but not for long. Smoke had dramatically started billowing out from one of the back rooms and the fire brigade was called. Quickly the firemen ran their hoses into the building, past a sleeping Malcolm, put out the fire, and, just as speedily and noisily, ran their hoses out of the building. Malcolm dozed on.

A comatose Malcolm was safer than a hyperactive one, as Gavin Henderson once discovered. Chatting to Malcolm in his capacity as chief executive of the New Philharmonia Orchestra, he reminded Malcolm that William Alwyn had recently invested some of his considerable film income in subsidising the recording of a complete edition of his symphonies. Malcolm's own symphonies at the time were not properly represented on record, only the lighter music being widely available. They had reached the top of the Savile staircase when Gavin Henderson made his fateful suggestion: 'Malcolm, what about us recording all the symphonies?'

'What do you mean?'

'Well, we could get Lyrita or EMI to do it. You put up the money and in that way you make sure there's a complete edition of your works!'

The Savile Club had rarely heard such an explosion, as, with one sturdy push, Malcolm sent Gavin Henderson tumbling down the stairs.

'Are you suggesting that I should *pay* for my music to be performed? How *dare* you!'

'No, no!' cried Henderson, still rolling, 'This is you being wise! Instead of bunging a £100 tip to taxi drivers and that sort of thing, you invest in your own work!'

At the bottom of the stairs Gavin Henderson picked himself up, dusted himself down, and restarted the debate, pointing out that now was the time to consolidate the commission of the Seventh with a recording of all the symphonies with the New Philharmonia.

> The orchestra would welcome you as conductor. It's what everyone is doing in these days of no sponsorship! It's what the Delius Trust did. And the Vaughan Williams and Frank Bridge Trusts. Look at them all! The recordings are there for ever! You should do the same![39]

But Malcolm refused to listen. He preferred to squander his money on other things.

Malcolm also did himself enormous damage by making absurdly critical remarks of his fellow musicians through bitterness at his own neglect. In 1977 there was just a single work of his, *Beckus*, at the Proms.[40] For the two previous years there had been nothing, and future prospects were poor.[41] He had a huge body of impressive work behind him, but nobody in Britain seemed to notice. 'The only catalogue of my works,' he wrote morosely, 'seems to have been done by a musician in Poland.'[42] In the 1960s he had been cautious, on the whole, not to let the hurt show. Now, with a persecution mania that the whole musical establishment was plotting against him, he was often very waspish. 'Elgar's Cello Concerto is the most effective laxative I know,' he was heard to say. Arnold Bax 'was a cure for insomnia'. Bernard Hermann's use of strings in the film *Psycho* 'put the string music of both Elgar and Britten to shame', both of whose orchestrations were 'turgidly thick':

> They make the mistake of doubling the middle of the orchestra and making music sound like a fly struggling to survive in treacle. It is the extreme parts of the orchestra which need reinforcing, if any do. There are some shocking orchestrations in Britten when he writes notes for instruments which are beyond the range and, for example, expects the side drum to blend with the strings. Crazy![43]

When sober, Malcolm admired Elgar and Britten. Drunk and disorientated, he could turn on those he most admired.

---

[39] Gavin Henderson, November 2003

[40] *Beckus the Dandipratt* played by The Royal Liverpool Philharmonic under Sir Charles Groves on 23 July

[41] There would be nothing in the next three years.

[42] In a letter to Dr Stewart Craggs, who was compiling a bio-bibliography of William Walton (12 January 1976).

[43] The quotations come from David C F Wright

His birthday occurred during this long stay in London, the highlight being a card from Edward:

> 55th Birthday today. It's a special day for you, dad. Happy Birthday with love from Edward.

The next few desultory months back at Dublin were to be marked with similar brief messages from Edward, all of which gave him much pleasure. There was a delightful letter, for example, in which Edward sent him the numbers of all the trains he'd spotted on platform 2 of Paddington Station. It was a considerable number. All kinds of transport interested Edward.

> Dear dad, having a nice time in London. This is from Heathrow Terminal.

And in the autumn Edward sent him a poem, 'Autumn', in which, despite the season, he managed to include wasps, with which species he had long associated his father.[44]

The loss of Isobel had a highly deleterious effect on Malcolm's professional life. The *Philharmonic Concerto* had somehow, miraculously been written in May. The rest of 1976 had yielded absolutely nothing. Projects were begun and abandoned. There had been much talk of a set of *Irish Dances*, but none had yet been written. He had ideas for an eighth symphony and there was a commission from the Welsh Arts Council for a flute sonata for James Galway, but he found it difficult to get started. The flute, in the past, had been so inspirational. The Sonatina, still a favourite work of his, had seemed to write itself back in 1948. The two concertos similarly. But though this latest commission was reaching its deadline, he preferred to drink, only getting as far as working out musical ciphers for 'James Galway' and 'Belfast'.

He binged his way through his solitary Christmas and ended up in a deep depression in St Edmundsbury, Lucan, where he was destined to spend a third of 1977. His gloom was partially lifted by a letter which arrived at his bedside in early January. It was largely, wonderfully inconsequential. Malcolm read and re-read it:

> Dear Dad,
>
> I am sorry that you are in hospital. Hope you are better in time for your recording in London on 12th January. I will see you in London. I hope the staves on the letter heading will cheer you up. I got lots of Christmas cards. Martin Tucker sent me some stamps. I will come to your flat in the summer. I am not sure how long I will be staying in your flat …
>
> We went to Euston in the car. It was frosty in London. Stephanie Grant came up for tea yesterday. We had tea with Katherine last week. I cleaned the furniture in the flat. I made gingerbread on Friday. I have a hyacinth bulb on my desk.
>
> Love from Edward and Isobel.[45]

---

[44] '… hedgehogs getting sadder, wasps getting madder, the spider makes its ladder …'
[45] 4 January 1977

Isobel! He had blotted out her name for six months. And here she was, sending him her *love*. Isobel, whom he had appallingly mistreated. *Love* from Edward and Isobel! The more he thought about it, the more he hated himself. He had thrown away so much.

A few days later, and there *were* Edward and Isobel, standing at the door of his room, smiling awkwardly at him. Armfuls of flowers! Cascades of tears! His depression slipped off him. He walked around the hospital proudly, as if he owned it, showing them the views and laughing at the jokes which surprisingly came to him again so easily. Edward, introverted and shy initially, clutching at Isobel, began to venture a little towards him. It was a very good visit.

Malcolm now decided that he could still salvage the Flute Sonata. He would meet Jim Galway on the 16th, show him what he'd done and talk through the rest. There might still be time. Ignoring the ciphers he had been playing with earlier, he settled down with confidence to a new first movement, and, on January 22nd, less than three weeks after that first letter from Edward, the Sonata was triumphantly finished, full of the love and joy which had come rushing to fill an aching void. In its fragile simplicity the Flute Sonata could not be more different than vast-sounding *Philharmonic Concerto*. But it says so much more.

In all three movements Malcolm provides his virtuoso soloist with opportunities for brilliant technical display and sumptuous melody. The opening *Allegro* places the soloist centre stage. And although Malcolm makes virtually no use of the resonant and seductive low register, the melodic writing is nonetheless highly engaging. Here is Malcolm by turns serious, vulnerable, charming, and even trying somehow to find some of that old wit. The *Andantino* begins with a long unfolding melody over a simple piano accompaniment redolent of Satie's *Gymnopédie*. It is a melody of considerable beauty and yearning simplicity. Casting around for a melody to express his new-found gratitude to Isobel, he had re-worked 'Constance's Sad Dance', one of the sketches he made for David Drew's *The Three Musketeers*.[46] The third movement, *Maestoso con molto ritmico*, is a bright but fevered rag, which in rhythmic and melodic shape shares much with the seemingly joyous finale of the Second Clarinet Concerto. But the more intensely he strives in his desire to have fun, the more *maestoso* he remains, unable to hide the deep disquiet and instability that is now plaguing him.[47] With its three shrewdly complementary movements, the Sonata explores deeply-felt

---

[46] The dance remains intact and, at the bottom of the page of manuscript paper, he has also sketched what was to become the four-bar piano introduction.

[47] For the first performance, two months later, Malcolm for once wrote a serious and non-confrontational programme note, declaring that, unlike many works for the flute which were solely vehicles for instrumental virtuosity, his was a piece where 'the musical element' was more to the fore. 'Although this is a virtuoso work with a particular virtuoso in mind, as are all my solo pieces, it endeavours to be as interesting musically as I can possibly make it.' He added, almost apologetically, 'I hope I have succeeded in this without being dull'.

emotions with great artistry and, as such, will surely one day find its way into the mainstream flute repertoire.

The Flute Sonata represented a very brief period of euphoria. Within a day or two of its completion Malcolm was back in hospital feeling suicidal. This was to be the pattern for 1977, lucidity alternating with confusion. Isobel, weighed down by a guilt of her own false imagining, anxiously paid another visit with Edward to St Edmundsbury at the end of January, both writing letters on their return. Malcolm wrote back to his son gratefully:

> My dear Edward,
>
> Your letter has just arrived. I like your drawing of the ship and am very sorry it was so rough for you both. It was the roughest day for years so no wonder you were sick! Monica and Niall Sheridan came yesterday and livened the place up a lot. Also Mrs McQuade came and brought some flowers which was nice of her. The flowers you brought still look lovely and fresh and are always admired.
>
> It was lovely to see you and Mum and hope it will not be long before I see you again.[48] Many thanks for drawing and letter and please thank Mum for her letter.
>
> With love
> From Dad

In March he was briefly back in De Vesci Terrace, drinking heavily. Writing to Robert, he at least sounded cheerful:

> My dear Robert,
>
> Thank you for your letter. I am glad to know that things are well. Anne sounded delighted with the kitchen, which is very good.
>
> We alternate our weather at the moment here, between warm sunny weather and blistering north-easterly gales. A large number of people have 'flu because of this. The rest of us suffer merely from alcohol poisoning!...[49]

Around this time there was a visit from Jon Lord, over in Dublin on promotional business for Deep Purple. Malcolm delightedly led him off on a pub crawl and after several hours they ended up at a disreputable club on the banks of the Liffey. Jon Lord remembers every single detail:

> I went to the bar to get some drinks, and when I got back with them I discovered Malcolm in a fierce conversation with a group of tough Irishmen. He was smiling sweetly at them and telling them that they were the best people on God's earth, but they didn't understand how good they were, and they ought to be better than they were because they were the best people on God's earth. It wasn't going down too well. 'The trouble with you bastards,' smiled Malcolm ingratiatingly, 'is that you let yourselves down.'
>
> 'Oi don't know what the fuck you're talking about,' said one of the tough Irishmen. 'But nobody calls me a bloody bastard!'

---

[48] Isobel and Edward were later to pay visits to see him at de Vesci Terrace. Isobel, much to Malcolm's delight, also left Edward there for a few days with his father.
[49] 28 March 1977

'No no!' said Malcolm, still smiling sweetly but sinking further into trouble. 'You don't understand. I like you lot. You're the best bloody people on God's earth, you just don't understand how good you are. You let yourselves down …'

'Oive had enough of this! Yer come outsoide, yer great fat barrel of lard!'

'No, no, you don't understand …'

Jon Lord hastily intervened, urgently explaining that Malcolm was over the limit and hadn't a clue what he was saying. He put a hand on his shoulder to direct him to the door.

> At this Malcolm swung round on me, suddenly stern, quite a different person. 'I can handle myself, boy!' But somehow I managed to talk him outside and thereby saved the greatest living British composer from a serious brawl on the banks of the Liffey![50]

Malcolm continued to make regular forays across the Irish Channel. He flew to London in March for two days to conduct the BBC Symphony Orchestra before going on to the Cardiff Festival, where James Galway gave the Flute Sonata its first performance.[51] In April he was on a nine-day spree in London, calling in to see Isobel and Edward, replenishing stocks of snuff and cigars, attending concerts, buying presents for his friends ('snuff box for Jim, moustache wax for Dick') and dining with Katherine and Anthony. The visit culminated with the arrival of Irene for the first performance of *The Return of Odysseus*.

> Malcolm invited me to London for it and had me stay in the Carlton Towers Hotel.[52] He was also staying there. It was a lovely experience. We had dinner (just the two of us) at the hotel's wonderful restaurant the night before the performance. The whole evening was enchanting and he was in wonderful form.

The next day Malcolm and Irene took a taxi to the Royal Albert Hall where David Willcocks was conducting the orchestra of the Royal College of Music and the massed choirs of the Schools' Music Association.[53] They went by themselves, Irene resplendent in royal blue and brown velvet. Malcolm's mood had suddenly become less expansive.

> I don't remember meeting many people and I don't think Malcolm wanted to get involved. I think I was surprised that we did not make much contact with others. Malcolm's attendance was low key and quiet.

Even with Irene on hand as inspiration, he was entering another depressive phase. Patric Dickinson, his librettist, had been expecting him at the various functions laid on at the Albert Hall and did not realise he had even attended the concert:

---

[50] July 2003

[51] With Anthony Goldstone (piano) at The New Hall, Cardiff, 19 March 1977

[52] Malcolm was a well-known and popular guest in the hotel restaurant with a good understanding with the French waiters. Anthony King remembers a dinner there with Katherine and her father when there was continual banter: 'Garçon, pardon! Three more bottles, s'il vous plaît!' 'Mais oui!' '*May* we? Of *course* we may!'

[53] 24 April 1977

We were *so* disappointed not to see you. I'm so sorry for I'm sure whatever did [happen] must have been something awful. You can't imagine how many messages of best will came from our box. Whatever was wrong I *do* hope is righted by now.

Hearing Odysseus simply made me long to do something more with you. Cross the Jordan & besiege Jericho?

Do drop me a line, soon. I hate not seeing you. Keep well. There's nothing *like* work! I battle on ...[54]

Unfortunately his collaboration with Patric Dickinson, which could have produced so much, started too late. Further hospitalisation followed this visit, but he was back in London in May at the Queen Elizabeth Hall for the London Mozart Players' series, *The Composer Conducts*. Malcolm was the fourth of five composers[55] given the opportunity of choosing a programme of their own work and that of others. Each work was to be introduced by an explanation as to why it had been chosen. Malcolm began with Rossini's overture *La Cambiale di Matrimonio* as a salute to Thomas Beecham, under whom he had played the work with the LPO. He followed this with William Boyce's Fifth Symphony, edited by Constant Lambert, to whom he paid a fulsome tribute. And, in contradiction to the drunken criticisms he sometimes made of Elgar, his third choice was the *Introduction and Allegro for Strings*, which, he declared, was 'sublime'. In the second half of the programme he chose two Cornish works, the Viola Concerto – 'I usually get behind in this, but I'll try not to tonight!' – and the *Concerto for 28 Players*.[56] The reasons for the choice of these Cornish works he did not divulge to the audience. Derelict musically and emotionally adrift in Ireland, he looked back to the days of Primrose Cottage with great nostalgia.

The concert seemed to pass off well enough. He did not fall off the podium, there were no harangues, and, although his comments were far briefer than the organisers might have hoped, at least he created a good rapport with his audience as he spoke on his old theme of music 'as an act of friendship'.[57] The critical response was inevitably muted, summed up perhaps by Meirion Bowen:

> Malcolm Arnold's occasional flirtations with musical modernity rarely hide the fact that he is writing primarily for the man on the Clapham Omnibus.[58]

Malcolm's conducting was its usual idiosyncratic self. His response to the Elgar, wrote Meirion Bowen, 'suggested more the roast beef of Old England than the sensitivity of a late-romantic artist. Certainly I have rarely heard the work so broadly phrased, with tempi often slowing nearly to a halt.' As his concentration struggled in the second half of the programme, his handling of his own works

---

[54] Letter from Patric Dickinson, 5 May 1977
[55] Among the other composers featured were Walton and William Mathias.
[56] 'Patently one of his most cogent scores,' declared Nicholas Kenyon in the *Daily Telegraph*, 12 May 1977.
[57] 'With Malcolm Arnold it goes without saying,' wrote Joan Chissell in *The Times*, 'that it was a friendly occasion.'
[58] *The Guardian*, 12 May 1977

became disappointingly perfunctory. Joan Chissell thought that he could have drawn much more from the orchestra:

> In the communal concerto, Arnold was too much the time-beater, too little concerned with dynamic gradations and countless other subtleties of characterisation. There was much more in this work than his players were encouraged to tell us.[59]

Had she known his current problems she would have marvelled at what he achieved. Just to get through the concert required an act of considerable will-power.

A similar determination was needed for the second and last work he was to write at de Vesci Terrace, a set of variations on a theme of Ruth Gipps, an old friend and supporter. In their College days he and Ruth had been spirited rivals, particularly over the Cobbett Prize. Her career as a composer had fallen away after a promising start, partly because she too had turned her back on the avant-garde and written firmly within the diatonic tradition. As founder and conductor of two very fine amateur orchestras,[60] she had strongly identified herself with twentieth-century British composers, always playing as much of Malcolm's music as she could.[61] Malcolm in his turn made use of her orchestras in trying out new works. She once told a mutual friend,

> Malcolm is a very cheeky and witty person! I've always found him tremendously loyal. When George Weldon wanted me to be the choir director of the City of Birmingham Symphony Orchestra a certain musician fought ruthlessly against me and acquired the position for himself by foul means, stating that no woman should ever be in charge of a choir or orchestra! He also spread the malicious falsehood that I was having an affair with Weldon and he would tell my husband.
>
> Malcolm was outraged on my behalf and gave the new choral conductor a right grilling in front of choir and orchestra. This was followed by a spontaneous and highly enthusiastic round of applause![62]

Ruth 'Widdy' Gipps was important to Malcolm as a link between the beginning of his career and what he was coming to think was probably the end. Having decided it was a fitting moment to commemorate her, he found an easy starting-point. He always associated 'Widdy' with the pastoral theme she had used in her *Coronation Procession*.[63] It had an attractive purity, a sense of past happiness in a much less hostile world, and, as such, would lend itself to a set of variations, full of nostalgia for his student days.

---

[59] *The Times*, 12 May 1977

[60] The London Chanticleer Orchestra and The London Repertoire Orchestra of which Malcolm was President.

[61] On 11 December 1982 Ruth wrote to Malcolm, 'I have done so much of your music now that I wonder if the last movement of my Fifth Symphony has a section influenced by Arnold …'

[62] Ruth Gipps' comments supplied by David C F Wright, March 2004. She died in 1999.

[63] It had first been heard on BBC television as the music for a serial *The Silver Bowl*. Shortly afterwards she incorporated it in the middle section of *Coronation Procession*, written in 1953 but never performed publicly in England.

The work begins arrestingly. Instead of going straight into Ruth's theme Malcolm gives it a stirring, atonal introduction. Because 'Widdy' was so hostile to twelve-note music, this has sometimes been taken as a joke at her expense,[64] but it could just as well be Malcolm reminding himself of the harsh, dissonant, modern world of 1977. The Ruth Gipps theme which follows, introduced by that purest of instruments, the oboe, takes him back to calmer times, the secure milieu of the Royal College, where they were two of the outstanding students in their generation. The war might have been raging outside, but within the College they were supreme, the world of music at their feet, just waiting to be conquered.

The first variation, *vivace*, seems to summarise these feelings. Perhaps Malcolm is remembering how amused Ruth was when he jazzed up the trumpet part at the end of a Mozart piano concerto when practising for a College concert, out of protest against six boring weeks of rehearsals, and then, as a dare, did the same thing in the actual concert, despite stares of outrage from George Dyson.[65] The second variation, *Alla marcia*, is largely bleak and atonal, seeming to reflect the war, with Malcolm surveying the carnage of millions and the débâcle of his own National Service. But he also places 'Widdy' within this ghastly period, for, at Letter J, he brings in the cipher of 'Ruth Gipps', the oboe lyrically spelling out her name.[66] The third and fourth variations both include this cipher, the *Lento* exploring a deep sadness and suggesting that once upon a time, perhaps, he was romantically involved with 'Widdy', the *Vivace* expressing her bold, forthright character. The fifth variation, a slow sombre Waltz, led by a plaintive flute, has much that is idyllic but concludes in harsh dissonance. A falling-out? The final variation, *Maestoso*, has a solemn opening, with unison strings, expansive wind chords and militaristic timpani, making way for a solo oboe which re-introduces Ruth's pastoral theme, softly and gently. Order has been restored, hysteria calmed and good memories abound. We are back in the hopeful 1940s as the work ends *fortissimo* with a stout, almost regal affirmation that all is well, 'Widdy' confidently striding forwards to likely peacetime triumphs, which, in the event, just eluded her. Malcolm's idealised finale, however, ignores any hints of failure.

Malcolm's real world, by contrast, continued to disintegrate. The immediate aftermath of the completion of *Variations for Orchestra on a Theme of Ruth Gipps*[67] in June 1977 was characterised by even greater swings between hope and despair than usual. Further stays in hospital that summer were mitigated by

---

[64] Hugo Cole (p.211) has suggested that the introductory first chord, built up note by note, consisting of all twelve tones of the scale, was written as a 'quiet joke'.

[65] Ruth described the incident in a letter to Alan Poulton (20 May 1984). The concerto in question was No 20 in D minor, K466, the concert taking place in July 1939. 'Dyson was a bad man to cross and one admired a student who dared do such a thing.'

[66] As in his 'codes' for the Seventh Symphony, Malcolm numbers all the letters of the alphabet, then assigns numbers to each of the notes in a chromatic scale. By cross-referencing he then spells out musically Ruth's name.

[67] Completed on 22 June 1977, the *Variations* were given their première by Ruth Gipps herself with her Chanticleer Orchestra on 22 February 1978.

delightful days out in young female company, sometimes at his latest discovery, the fine restaurant at Killiney Castle, which also offered a swimming pool and sauna.

His friendship with Irene was still a stabilising influence. They continued to meet on an irregular basis and enjoyed long talks, Malcolm finding a tranquillity in her company that otherwise eluded him.

> He liked to go to Killiney Beach from time to time and I remember walking it with him on one occasion. He was childlike in his joy, happy, happy, happy…
>
> I was so fortunate to be able to sit for hours and listen to him. I learned so much. To me he was the finest of fine English gentlemen. His manners were impeccable. And he had vast resources of insights, knowledge and compassion. I thought him – and think him still – a truly great man.

He especially liked to sit beside the wine-dark sea at Dun Laoghaire, at his favourite seafood restaurant, the expensive and select Na Mara, to which so many parties from Camelot had in the past diverted in 'the Holy Hour'.

> Malcolm loved it. He never ate that much in restaurants when I knew him. A starter course; then he would fiddle around with the main course; and of course wine, the best; He particularly liked Gaelic coffee and he described it in rhapsodic terms as a winning combination of flavours. They made particularly good Gaelic coffee at Restaurant Na Mara.

By the time they had reached the Gaelic coffee, the talk would usually be soft and romantic:

> After Isobel departed from Malcolm's life he did speak to me on many occasions about the possibility of us being together – even married. I have to admit that at times it seemed that it might be possible, but always at the back of my mind lay the fear that I would not be able to manage Malcolm on a day to day basis, as I knew very little about handling somebody who might continue to take a lot of alcohol …

If she had any doubts over this decision, these disappeared with the appalling drama of another suicide attempt that September. The weeks which led up to it are confused. In the middle of August Malcolm spent two weeks in hospital drying out. He was in better form by the time Katherine and her husband arrived to stay for a few days. They both remember the pleasure Malcolm took in cooking – fish, steak and scallops were all on his menus – and, although there were horrific tales of him waving his arms around when lying drunk in the road to warn approaching cars, they nursed no more than their usual anxieties when they left at the end of August.

Malcolm, however, had not told them of an imminent two-week holiday at his favourite Italian seaside resort of Santa Margherita, presumably because he knew talk of his latest girl-friends would pain Katherine. Quite who accompanied Malcolm to Santa Margherita is not known. It could have been Dymphna, or a girl called Sally who had recently entered his life and been dined at the exclusive Mirabeau, a sign that she was highly favoured.

Something happened at Santa Margherita that upset Malcolm very greatly. He returned by Aer Lingus from Italy, with or without his companion, on 16 September.[68] For the four next days he did nothing worth entering in his diary, which presumably meant that he was drinking On the evening of 22 September he met Irene for dinner. The next day he stayed in his flat. He had again decided to drink himself to death.

Katherine was in the habit of phoning her father every so often to check that all was well. She had tried to get through for some time but without success and began to get anxious. On 24 September, with Malcolm lying on the floor of his flat in a deep coma, she rang up the housekeeper:

> Mrs McQuade, I'm sorry to bother you, but I have a feeling that all may not be well at de Vesci Terrace.

---

[68] Sheila's birthday. The 22nd was Robert's.

# 15
# Madness

## The Belsize Park Nightmare, 1977-79

INFORMED THAT HER FATHER was deeply unconscious and could well die, Katherine left her work[1] and headed for Ireland. She found Malcolm still in a coma.

> It seemed important to talk to him, hold his hand and touch him gently in the hope that something would reach him. To let him know he was not alone, that someone was there who loved him. As I sat there beside him, all the loneliness and sadness of his recent life rose up in stark relief.[2]

Prior to this crisis Malcolm had strongly resisted the suggestion from both Katherine and Isobel that he should move to London, where they could more easily keep an eye on him.

> Looking back, I think he has always been afraid of damaging the people he is close to, so he maintains a distance. But it adds to the difficulties of those trying to help.

The next day Katherine found him conscious but suffering from an attack of delirium tremens.

> He was hallucinating, picking imaginary insects off the wall and putting them into his mouth as well as talking to people who were not there.

Katherine tried to help him through this nightmare as best she could, though it was clear that he was not aware of her presence.

> The doctors were now confident that he would survive, but as yet not committing themselves on whether there would be brain damage. On my third day at the hospital the delirium had left him and, though weak and exhausted, he had improved enough to recognise me.

When in later years Malcolm came to talk of this suicide attempt, he would emphasise his feelings of loneliness as he lay in hospital, seemingly deserted by everyone. But these were imaginary feelings, generated by the manic-depressive illness. Katherine soon paid a long return visit, Isobel joined her, and Robert also

---

[1] Completing her training as a child psychotherapist, Katherine was counselling at a school which had been the subject of a public scandal for the mistreatment of the children under its Trotskyite regime.

[2] September 2003

*A birthday greeting from Pappy in the form of an old photograph of the five children,
which Malcolm tore up. 21 October 1977*

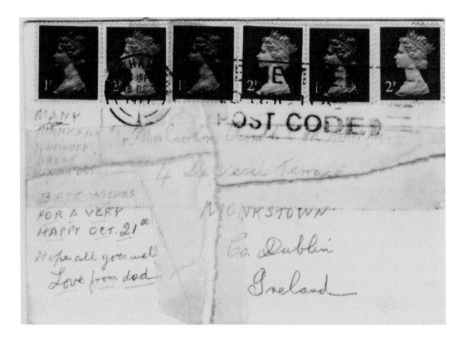

visited shortly before going to live in Skye. Arrangements were soon made on Malcolm's behalf for a period of convalescence at St Edmundsbury, again under Dr Moore.[3] All this family concern, however, never managed to establish itself in Malcolm's mind, as Katherine points out:

> He remembers no-one being at the hospital. He seems to prefer a worse picture of what happened to him. He prefers to feel abandoned when, in fact, it is usually he, if anyone, who does the abandoning.[4]

In October 1977, just weeks after the latest crisis, Robert and Anne left Cambridge for Scotland. It was not an act of abandonment but, rather, a necessary career move. Since returning from abroad Robert had been discovering that the only outlets for anthropology were academic ones, which did not particularly attract him; the spirit for adventure which had taken him out to remote places was not being met in suburban Cambridge. Ten years earlier he had met an imaginative inventor, who had left London for Skye where he had established a company making electronic measuring devices, Robert sometimes going up in the university vacations to help out. The wild, unspoilt nature of Skye strongly attracted him. So when in 1977 his inventor friend, helped by support from the Highlands and Islands Development Board, expanded his business and offered him a full-time job, Robert accepted.

> I get accused sometimes of running away from London and my family, but I was just doing what was right for me! It looked like – and proved – a good idea![5]

Malcolm was not short of useful advice. Donald Mitchell, his publisher for the past twelve years, did his best to make a positive intervention, writing in strong terms:

> It seems to me that the time has come, Malcolm dear, when you must try to take a grip on the present unacceptable situation and see if something can't be done to resolve the problem in the future. Your family and your friends cannot stand by and see you destroy yourself, for that is what is happening at the moment. You know how profoundly devoted to you I am and how deeply I respect your genius – and I use that word advisedly. Forgive me for lecturing you, but you have no right to go on abusing your great gift in this reckless way, which causes such pain to those who love and admire you.[6]

Malcolm's problems were unfortunately too deep-rooted for him to be able suddenly to 'take a grip'. Endogenous depression, which grows from within and needs no external stimulus, motivated the urge to self-destruction and could not be assuaged by words, however well-chosen and heartfelt.

---

[3] Malcolm spent nearly a month in the Meath, leaving on his birthday, 21 October 1977, for St Edmundsbury, where he was to spend another month.

[4] September 2003

[5] August 2003

[6] 10 October 1977

It seems from Donald Mitchell's following comments that the family had concealed the full nature of Malcolm's hospitalisation:

> I do beg you to get the best possible advice and if necessary contemplate the idea of a spell of treatment. It is my view that the best facilities are to be found here, rather than in Eire, and I would hope that you would think seriously about a visit to the UK and seek the best expert advice that can be found.

The suggestion to return to London was sensible, Malcolm's damaging lifestyle in Dublin having become so habitual it would not be easy to break. But Donald Mitchell's most telling argument concerned Malcolm's dissipation of his talents:

> Things cannot be allowed to go on just as in the past. You have a wonderful creative talent which must at all costs be preserved. There are still many fine works which you have to write. I am sure you know that to be the truth and that the moment has come when you cannot afford to take further risks. Please, please do take these words seriously and accept the advice that is offered. You and your music mean too much to us all for writing in any other way to you except plainly and directly.

Two weeks later, when he was capable of writing, Malcolm replied.

> My dear Donald,
>
> Thank you very much for your extremely kind and generous letter, which I appreciate very much. I am at a convalescent home in Ireland despite Katherine's more than determined attempts to get me to go to London. She did not give up to the very last second! I am not sure what I will do, but I will be in London shortly for some time.[7]

Malcolm enjoyed his good days in Dublin too much to let go of Ireland without a struggle. His network of goddesses could not be lightly surrendered. When Irene visited Malcolm at St Edmundsbury, she found him, as nearly always, in a 'jolly' mood.

A month after the suicide bid Dr Moore wrote to Isobel about Malcolm's future. He knew nothing of the traumas Isobel had suffered at Meadowcroft or he might have felt less comfortable in his suggestions:

> I am sorry to see that by the tone of your letter you are pessimistic about the prospect of establishing a happy and stable relationship with your husband. May I reiterate the advice I gave you when we met recently that in these matters it is wise to hasten slowly and not come to any final judgements or make irrevocable decisions too hastily.[8]

Malcolm, he said, was 'in very good spirits of late' and had appreciated Isobel's telephone calls and letters. He had indicated that he would like to spend some time in London 'near' Isobel which, Dr Moore was pleased to see, represented a distinct change of outlook:

---

[7] 27 October 1977
[8] 7 November 1977

Please do not think I am trying to put pressure on you to re-establish a relationship with your husband, but from long experience in these matters I know that sometimes what appears quite unlikely can come to pass.

With Malcolm shortly coming to London, it was important to find him the right hotel. Isobel was in an increasing state of indecision, so the thirteen-year-old Edward took it upon himself to lend her a hand, writing to St Edmundsbury with a short, holding statement:

Dear Dad,

I hope you are well.

I am trying to find you a place to stay in London, for the Carlton Towers charges so much.

We saw a bonfire and there were lots of bangs going on.[9]

A week later Isobel heard again from Dr Moore. Malcolm was making very satisfactory progress, was sleeping well without medication and taking a good interest in the educational programme put on for alcoholics.

I am glad to say he has begun to work again, finds he can concentrate and seems optimistic about his ability to cope with some commissions he has been offered.[10]

The biggest commission at this period was a Symphony for Brass from the trumpet virtuoso, Philip Jones, whose own Ensemble had often played Malcolm's fine Brass Quintet of 1961. He had asked Malcolm on many occasions for another piece in the same mould, and Malcolm had at last agreed to write a four-movement work for his fiftieth birthday. But Dr Moore was being too optimistic about the return to composition, for whatever Malcolm wrote at St Edmundsbury came to nothing. Important works like the *Symphony for Brass*, the Eighth Symphony and the *Irish Dances* were all begun after his return to London.

Dr Moore's well-intentioned bridge-building included plans for Christmas which caused Isobel some apprehension.

He has spoken to me about visiting you in London in the near future and I think this is a very good plan. We agreed that if all goes well in the meantime he might leave here at the beginning of December and spend a few weeks in London. I wonder if it would be possible for you and your son to come back with him for Christmas in Dublin? He is quite adamant that he intends to go on living in Ireland, and I think it would make him very happy if he felt that you both could spend a few weeks here with him at Christmas. Perhaps you would think this over and let me know.

In planning to stay on in Ireland Malcolm was ignoring everyone's advice, and, on release from care, he was likely to be just as headstrong in his personal behaviour as in the past. So Isobel held out against Christmas in Dublin. Let him spend it, she urged, in London, where he could continue the psychiatric

---

[9] 7 November 1977
[10] 18 November 1977

treatment. He was already booked in at the Swiss Cottage Hotel[11] from 1 December, only two minutes' walk from her flat and close to the Tavistock Clinic; regular sessions with two leading psychiatrists were also being organised.[12] Malcolm conceded defeat. The euphoria which had encouraged him to be combative had passed and another depressive phase followed. At the end of November he rang up David Ellis to tell him of his imminent departure.

> I said 'Oh, great!' but he said 'No! I've just got to regroup.' He sounded terribly depressed. Not that that was anything new in the last couple of years. He was always depressed when he was not writing or otherwise working.[13]

But he was in a reasonable mental state when he arrived in London. After three weeks, just before Christmas, he moved from the Swiss Cottage Hotel into a small rented flat in nearby Lindfield Gardens.[14] Two days earlier Katherine had taken him to a poignant reunion lunch at Sheila's East Sheen house. On Christmas Day Katherine and Anthony entertained Sheila and Malcolm at their Highgate home, and they all went over to Sheila's for Boxing Day. Malcolm behaved impeccably throughout, clearly still nursing much affection for Sheila, who was cautiously sympathetic.

At the start of 1978 he continued to see much of his family, lunching with Katherine and Anthony on New Year's Day and with Isobel and Edward on the 2nd. The next week he entertained Katherine and Anthony at the Pilgrim's Restaurant, lunched with Robert and Anne in London and at Isobel's with Edward, Katherine and Anthony. He was no longer, however, in good spirits, for he had become fixated on the idea of living again with Isobel and anything less than that was unsatisfactory. In several letters of this period he uses her address and it seems he may even have moved into her flat, against her wishes, for a few days.

On the suggestion of Dr Wedeles he kept a notebook, and though his thoughts are not expressed clearly and he soon gave up, two entries in January 1978 give an interesting insight into his state of mind:

> Awoke not depressed and thought about the situation with clarity and reality. It all seemed possible until I lapsed into a daydream, answering my own questions and arriving at doubt.
>
> Cause of all this depression was inaction, caused by recognition that the situation is hopeless … This thought totally stymies action on my part (an excuse?). It has to be because there is no alternative except escape. And why not?'[15]

His second entry is less vague but equally negative:

---

[11] Room 42. The hotel is in Adamson Street. It was also very close to the Greenway clinic in Fellowes Road.
[12] Dr Claude Wedeles and Dr Donald Meltzer
[13] David Ellis, August 2003
[14] Flat 7, 12 Lindfield Gardens
[15] 14 January 1978

LONDON IMPOSSIBLE
>   Sacrifices I have to make and life in the future are impossible for me.
>
>   Helpers (?) are mistaken in not taking any notice, or understanding I have a point of view.
>
>   What I required was rest and tranquillity not nightmarish upheaval making the whole situation worse.[16]

The 'sacrifices' refer to the biggest point at issue, his sudden change in lifestyle. The new flat was smaller and less stylish than that at de Vesci Terrace. There was an absence of expensive restaurants in the immediate area of Belsize Park as well as old drinking cronies and young goddesses. Used to a grander lifestyle, he felt so constricted and irked that he was noting, a week later, 'suicide still a possibility'. The moves to hotel and temporary flat certainly represented a considerable upheaval, but it is unlikely he would have discovered 'rest and tranquillity' in Dublin.

The psychiatrist and analyst Dr Meltzer, whom Malcolm saw at this period, told Katherine that her father had not yet made up his mind whether to live or die. The problem was his anxiety at the need to make changes in his lifestyle. It was a situation well-known to psychiatrists:

> The patient realises only he can set right. He feels he must change himself, and he is terrified of change; death seems a far preferable alternative. In the face of such unlimited potential and freedom, the patient yearns to retreat into oblivion. He is hovering between self-creation and self-destruction ...[17]

For the moment, however, Malcolm's depression temporarily lifted. In his notebook's final entry he wrote more generously of his 'helpers', Isobel and Katherine:

> Value of relationship between [us] makes all difficulties worthwhile. Both of them consciously trying to surmount them because of the value and nature of their relationship to each other.

Malcolm's improved outlook was related to the commission of a new symphony, which came by surprise from America. Peter Kermani ran a foundation[18] in memory of his father, Rustam K Kermani, an important benefactor of the Albany Symphony Orchestra, the only professional orchestra in New York State. Founded in 1931, the ASO has always enjoyed a lively interest in commissioning new scores[19] and Peter Kermani had written in February 1978 to Malcolm, asking him if he might write them a symphony and suggesting that he might consider including a setting of poems by John Ashberry inside the work, which, he hoped, might be dedicated to the memory of his father.

---

[16] 15 January 1978

[17] Albert Rothenberg: *Creativity and Madness* (Johns Hopkins University Press, 1990), p.68

[18] The Foundation had already commissioned works by other British composers including Edmund Rubbra and George Lloyd.

[19] Charles Wuorinen, Tobias Picker, Lester Trimble and Francis Thorne are among those commissioned.

Malcolm replied (from 72d Belsize Park Gardens) very positively:

> I shall be delighted to compose my Eighth Symphony for the Albany Symphony
> Orchestra. I have in mind, and have had for some time, a spring-like work, very much
> in the character of my Second Symphony, although, of course, by no means exactly
> the same. My thoughts seem to coincide with yours on this score. $5000 would be a
> very acceptable fee for this ...[20]

He showed considerable tact in evading the setting of poems:

> I do not wish to write a choral work at the moment, although I agree entirely with you
> about the time being right for such a work. (The time is always right for such a work
> really)...
>
>    I am very much enjoying the poems of John Ashberry.[21] They appeal to me a lot
> and I would very much like to keep the copy you sent me, if this is alright...'

He also rejected the idea of a memorial dedication:

> Although I would very much like to make this gesture in gratitude to your father, over
> the past fifteen years my work has been over-burdened with thoughts of death, and I
> feel the need to get entirely away from this. Hence my ideas on my Eighth Symphony
> being a symphony somewhat of re-birth. Any dedication in the form of an in
> memoriam would go quite against the idea I have in mind.

Heartened by the encouragement from Albany, Malcolm began to feel that he
might, after all, be able to write the *Symphony for Brass*, of which Philip Jones
was now despairing. Jones and his wife Ursula, after many patient reminders,
had invited Malcolm to their home and played him records of the Ensemble to
show its scope and to try to get him going. Although he had expressed interest in
the recording of Elgar Howarth's arrangement of *Pictures at an Exhibition*,
Ursula remembers him being 'very sad'[22] for most of the visit. It looked as if the
commission would not be met, but then came Peter Kermani's letter, and
Malcolm sat down at his desk in Lindfield Gardens and started writing Philip
Jones' symphony. It was nearly eight months since he had completed his last
work, the *Ruth Gipps Variations*.

The *Symphony for Brass Instruments*[23] turned out to be a gloomy work, full
of serial dissonance, dark and murky melodic invention and written as if
Malcolm's sole aim was to upset the Man on the Clapham Omnibus. But he was
clearly intrigued by the timbral possibilities of the ten brass instruments. The
long first movement, though extremely sombre, is cogently presented and not
without attractions, but there is no respite in the following movement, a so-called
*Allegretto grazioso*, which is lugubrious rather than graceful. There is much

---

[20] 21 February 1978

[21] An experimental poet (b. 1927) associated with the New York School, a group much
influenced by Jackson Pollock and abstract art. Ned Rorem used some of his verses in
*The Nantucket Songs*.

[22] October 2003

[23] Completed on 9 March 1978

two-part writing here – a forewarning of things to come in his works of the 1980s. Nor is there respite in the third movement, *Andante con moto*, which starts off with anguished, dramatic chords more suitable for a horror movie and has at its core some ponderous statements, like so many ghostly fanfares for the dead. The final *Allegro con brio* displays initial vitality only to lose it later, though the double fugue shows Malcolm still adept at working with complex compositional devices. As an *Allegro con brio* it sounds strangely woe-begone.

The *Symphony for Brass* in some ways gives a clearer indication of Malcolm's depressed state than the entries in the notebook for Dr Wedeles. The sounds he hears are distorted ones, the harsh outpourings of a mind which cannot come to terms any more with basic concepts like fun and beauty. His world is stripped of colour; he sees only black and grey. The work, for all its lack of outward attractiveness, has nonetheless found considerable critical favour. It places such awesome technical demands on all ten instrumentalists, even the tuba, that it has been dubbed 'one of the Everests of brass literature'.[24] Howard Snell, who conducted it at its first performance at the 1979 Cheltenham Festival, still thinks it 'an important work, if spare and abstract'.[25]

During the period of composition Malcolm unusually had not shut himself away from the outside world. That February he had seen Isobel and Edward for lunch each Sunday and gone round to their flat every day of Edward's half-term. He had also met Katherine for regular meals and had paid another visit to Sheila at East Sheen. He was anxious, it seems, about the possible repercussions of isolation, for he had also been meeting regularly with his analyst. His family for its part was doing all it could to keep him on an even emotional keel, even though it was a losing battle.

Two weeks after completing the *Symphony For Brass* Malcolm voluntarily went into Greenway, the Belsize Park clinic he knew well from the past. There, shortly after his arrival, he experienced a psychotic episode which resulted in his being transferred, under restraint, to the psychiatric ward of the Royal Free Hospital. 'Abducted by four ambulance men' was how he described the experience in his diary. The details of what led up to his 'abduction' are not known, but its occurrence would have been as devastating for him as for those around him. Being mildly manic was something with which Malcolm had learnt to cope. He might be confused or ecstatic, but, like most manic-depressives, he steadily developed mechanisms of self-control that limited the problems and allowed work and leisure to proceed. A psychotic episode, on the other hand, was very different.

There would have been a steady building up of tension over several days, an increasing knowledge that something was going seriously wrong, an ever mounting worry that what he said and what he did were barely in control. And

[24] Burton-Page: *Philharmonic Concerto*, p.132
[25] April 2004

then the moment of implosion, when his thoughts began to race so fast his mind surrendered to the jumble of fragmentary ideas, images and sentences rushing by; unable to respond to instinct urging slowing down, he watched in panic-stricken fear as actions and intentions ceased to synchronize, and the realisation hit him that however fast he ran, however loud he screamed, however much he cried for help, there were to be no solutions, no helpers, no understanding of a world grown unfamiliar, dark and fearful.[26]

Malcolm had long lived with the dread of going mad. The heavy drinking to which he had always cheerfully admitted was a useful form of camouflage. He had had his first mental breakdown in the 1940s; so for over thirty years he had been trying to cope with this inner fear.

He was to spend two months in the Royal Free, where he was given large doses of anti-psychotic drugs. Like other sufferers, he faced a regime of 'endless days of endlessly terrifying drugs – thorazine, lithium, valium and barbiturates'. Gradually his mind was 'reined in, slowed down and put on hold'. But it would be a long time before he could claim his mind as his own again, and even longer till he trusted it.[27]

Malcolm, coming back to normality under the care of a leading psychiatrist, Dr Hailstone, listed in his diary his most pressing requirements. On one day it was 'more Badedas' and on another '10 Mannikins and lighter fuel'. His thoughts soon turned to how he might escape the clutches of his fascist nurses – 'Ask Nazis how many days' – as well as the construction of the commissioned symphony. In his muddled state he was not sure whether it would be his eighth or ninth but he boldly outlined the three movements:

> I Tranquil 12 note 3/4
> II Scherzo
> III Dignity

For the moment that was as far as his mind would take him and nothing further came of it. The monotony of hospital life was his chief preoccupation and instead of music he carefully wrote down the precise timings of Breakfast, Coffee Break, Lunch, Tea and Supper as well as his intake, four times daily, of medication.

Three weeks after admission Malcolm was 'really not well at all', according to the faithful Isobel, and, two weeks later, 'never the same two days running'. Physically he was fine but 'nothing seems to put him to sleep'.[28] Only a week later, however,[29] the sleepless Malcolm discharged himself against advice after

---

[26] Kay Redfield Jamison, in *An Unquiet Mind* (Alfred Knopf, 1995), p.82, gives a first-hand account of the frightening nature of a psychotic episode.

[27] Kay Jamison: *An Unquiet Mind*

[28] Letter to Martin Kingsbury, 26 April 1978

[29] 7 May 1978. Four days later he officially moved into 26 Holmefield Court.

two months in the hospital. It was a serious error of judgement, but there were no mechanisms in place in the care system to counter his foolhardy wishes. Disregarding the pills he had been urged to take, he now addressed what he saw as the real need of the moment, Isobel. She had been enormously helpful in his purchase of the flat of his own, into which he now moved. Holmefield Court in Belsize Grove, built in the 1930s, was conveniently close to the shops on Haverstock Hill and even more conveniently close to Isobel. He simply had to walk one minute down his road, turn left at Belsize Park Gardens, and there she was! And there he too quite soon would be, he had no doubt. His little ground floor flat, with its pleasant outlook onto a communal back garden, was in his mind only a temporary resting-place.

Isobel had largely organised both the acquisition of the flat and the subsequent move, because he was in too confused a state to do so himself. But the more she helped, the more advantage he tried to take of her, as Katherine explains:

> Isobel would have died for him! She felt Dad's best chance was if she kept in some kind of contact with him. But as soon as he arrived he kept overdoing things. He would insist on moving in on her. He invaded her space. He didn't respect it. There would always be one person for whom he had an obsession, a clinging need, and at the moment it was Isobel. When Isobel invited him for a meal, because he was fixated on her, he would never want to leave. He'd stay in her flat saying 'Let's try and work this out' and she couldn't get him out. On occasions she had to call the police! But she always thought she ought to try again, and so the saga went on.[30]

Eventually the situation came to a dramatic climax, when, not long after Malcolm had moved into Holmefield Court, he and Isobel had an enormous row on the subject of his expectations. Isobel was so alarmed that she decided to put her situation to him in writing. A rough draft survives:

> Dear Malcolm,
>
> All this is very disturbing – you seem to be dismissing everyone who wants to help you – the pills from Dr Hailstone, me and now Dr Wedeles. This leaves you pretty much on your own, and though I think it's a good idea to try to run one's own life, you seem to be overdoing it fairly drastically and this isn't the moment.
>
> You seem to think we should simply go on from where we left off – which was a disaster. I don't see any possibility in building up a new relationship on the remnants of what was for both of us an unsuccessful marriage. I think we have to start entirely afresh, with ourselves as well as each other, if we're going to have any kind of genuine relationship, whatever it is.
>
> If you keep on saying we're the same people, we're not much good for each other. If we're changed, we need to find out how …[31]

---

[30] September, 2003
[31] 17 May 1978

This sensible letter was not well received, for Malcolm could see no need for a reassessment of their relationship. He was paying her bills and that, he felt, gave him certain conjugal rights. He replied intemperately:

Dear Isobel,

I have received your extraordinary and smug letter, but of course cannot thank you for it; because of its smug and unbelievably complacent air. Have you never done anything wrong in your life?

The menopause and your age can explain your superior and condescending attitude towards me but cannot excuse it.

Please try harder to show your goodwill and try harder not to kick me when I am down, as you have been doing with monotonous regularity for the past three years. Why continue this practise [sic] with such unabated vigour, as your letter so clearly shows you still do...

Love to Edward,

Yours with great disappointment

Malcolm

Isobel would never return fire with fire and her draft reply is remarkable for its restraint. But she was firm in her resolve, which no doubt Katherine helped strengthen, that she should not expose Edward to further distress:

Dear Malcolm,

Yes – I'm a bit disappointed too, because I'd hoped we could carry on in simply friendly terms but basically independent of each other. This obviously isn't going to work because you can't stand it and I do see it was rather an unrealistic scheme anyway.

I did say when you came over from Dublin in December that I didn't envisage our living together again at any rate for the present, but we could see how things went, and you know that as time goes on it gets clearer and clearer that all the resentments we've felt about each other are still there and exactly the same as they always have been, and unless we sort ourselves out considerably they always will be.

I know you want the key of this flat because you think you have a right to it, and the whole business of your rights is alarming because you seem to think they're the only important thing and I think they're irrelevant and destructive of any direct relationship between us. Then we are both angry and it's useless and impossible to ask you round here at all, because of the same sarcasm and innuendo and dragging Edward into it. You can't stop being sarcastic and it ends up exactly as it was in Meadowcroft. It was as much your sarcasm and innuendo as the violence that made that unbearable and made me want to go back [to England] ... [32]

Malcolm was in no state to make a calm and reasoned response. Instead he exploded into righteous indignation and swung violently round from an obsessive desire for the restoration of conjugal rights to an obsessive hatred, based on what he saw as her betrayal. It was a return to the situation immediately after the sale of Meadowcroft. Isobel, utterly distressed, finally gave up, and a month later,

[32] 19 May 1978

in June 1978,[33] she told him she would be asking for a divorce on the basis of the two years of separation. She could have sued on far more damaging grounds.

The impending divorce only heightened Malcolm's manic approach to the summer of 1978. He acquired new drinking companions and briefly became a legend of generosity in all his new locals. On Haverstock Hill he breakfasted late at Kukuruz, an Austrian coffee shop, and lunched long at a Spanish restaurant, La Baita. He was an even greater habitué of Peachey's Wine Bar up the hill next to the little cinema. His tips were more prodigious than ever and, though there may be no connection, he made several new girlfriends (of varying ages) at these establishments. He continued to be outraged with Isobel and he associated Katherine and Anthony with her 'betrayal', ostentatiously ignoring them and not even answering their anxious phone-calls.

For a time his greatest friend was the trumpet player John 'Jumbo' Wilbraham, who lived locally. Although over twenty years younger than Malcolm, he had much more in common than just his size. John Wilbraham was the outstanding classical trumpet player of his generation and a great story teller, who drank extremely hard and loved Cuban cigars. Like Malcolm he lacked all musical snobbery, happy to be a session player on the Beatles' *Magical Mystery Tour* and play the theme for television's *Brideshead Revisited*. The two would often start the day in the Belsize Tavern at 11.00, sometimes discussing the possibility of a trumpet concerto which, in the past, Malcolm had always avoided writing, despite many requests. 'I'll bloody well write one for you,' he told Wilbraham, but though the intention was there, the concentration was lacking. It remained largely in his head and was something of a blur.

Sensing perhaps the shadows closing in on him, Malcolm paid a surprise visit that summer[34] to Pappy in Northampton, where Lizzie Witts provided lunch for the three of them. Five years earlier, with Malcolm providing the funds, Pappy had left Craigmore, moving into a specially built bungalow at the bottom of its garden, where the garages had stood.[35] Old age had finally caught up with Pappy,[36] who at ninety-two could move only with the use of a Zimmer frame. But his mind was as active as ever, and his gratitude for Malcolm's financial aid very

---

[33] On 13 June 1978 her solicitors wrote: 'We act on behalf of your wife Isobel Arnold who has instructed us that she wishes to petition for divorce on the basis that you have lived separate and apart for two years and on the basis of your consent. Your wife would envisage the custody of Edward being granted to her on divorce.' It was finally lodged on August 25.

[34] 29 May 1978, just nine days after Pappy's ninety-second birthday

[35] Restawyle, Homestead Way

[36] 'Pappy had virtually no resources apart from the house and his old age pension,' writes Robin. 'He had spent a great deal of money after Nan's death on taking elderly women on cruises (he liked P&O and Cunard), his love of luxury no doubt being an influence on Malcolm. He believed in spending. He sold anything and everything – furniture, silver, paintings, Nan's cottage at Capel Garmon. In the end there was nothing, so he called on Malcolm for funds, using the fact that Lizzie needed to be kept on by the family. Malcolm turned up trumps and made him a monthly allowance.' (April 2004)

sincere. Sheila had kept in touch with him and he followed the exploits of Katherine and Robert with great interest. 'A midday meal awaits you here any time you feel like coming,' he had written to Katherine the last Christmas. Lizzie Witts, now eighty-eight herself and in her seventy-second year of service, continued her devoted administrations, living in the bungalow with Pappy. 'If I had my time all over again,' she had told a local newspaper, 'I would spend it with the same family.'[37] Lizzie had made Pappy's final years dignified and comfortable, allowing him to play host to the end.[38] Delight at Malcolm's visit more than compensated for anxieties that he seemed so withdrawn and tired.

In July Malcolm spent a fortnight in Dublin, which did nothing for his emotional stability. He stayed initially at Jury's before moving on to the Royal Marine Hotel, Dun Laoghaire. Drinking heavily and ill on several occasions, he twice was taken to St Gabriel's Hospital. He also saw various doctors and even called in on Dr Moore.

Somehow he managed to remember Edward's fourteenth birthday, marking the occasion with a somewhat perfunctory communication, which suggests the stresses under which he was living. Edward was his latest fixation, the battle-field on which he would fight the treacherous Isobel. That he wrote so little says a great deal:

> My dear Edward,
>    I am leaving Jury's tomorrow and will not be in London for some weeks. So I enclose an Irish pound note in place of a card for your birthday on Tuesday.
>    Many Happy Returns,
>    Love from Dad XXX
>    PS Dublin is beautiful and everybody sends their love.
>    Many Happy Returns of Tuesday July 18th
>    Love from Dad X

For much of the Irish visit he was very depressed. Even when he telephoned Irene he was not his usual urbane self:

> I received a telephone call from him, and he seemed in a bad state. He wanted me to visit. I couldn't as I felt I would have been unable to help him – but I subsequently regretted not having gone down and reached out in whatever way I could. I still feel sad about that.[39]

So the chief focus of this final Dublin foray was Dymphna, with whom Malcolm, aided by his long-standing chauffeur Sam Kelly, tried to recreate some

---

[37] 1971

[38] The previous Christmas she and Pappy had entertained his daughter-in-law, Clifford's widow, Doll, and his less than easy grand-daughter, Sally Anne.

[39] Later that year Irene Duffy was to get married. She telephoned Malcolm with the news: 'His quick retort was "You could have been Lady Arnold and are going to opt to be Mrs Lynch!" He was amusing and serious about it at the same time … He had always talked a lot about getting a knighthood …'

romantic dinners of the past. He revisited many of his favourite haunts: Snaffles, Roundwood and, on three successive evenings, the Restaurant Na Mara. In his depressed state Malcolm would not, however, have been easy company and at some stage on this holiday Dymphna, in his eyes, 'jilted' him. It was a traumatic moment, later to be included in the Eighth Symphony.

He arrived home to learn that Isobel had taken Edward up to her parents in Scotland. So he sent Edward a series of postcards in which he purported to be looking after their (or, as he asserted, *his*) flat in Belsize Park Gardens with the aid of Karen, who lived on the floor below:

Having a lovely time with Karen looking after my flat.

Lovely time in London looking after the flat.

Paddy has been to empty the rubbish, as he always does. He also minds the flat when I am away. Mr Harry Shaw also looks after it to see that nobody breaks in.

It was all too much. Edward away! Isobel treacherous! Katherine her ally! Dymphna deserting! Belsize Park the usual nightmare! He began to express his mounting frustrations physically. Windows in Holmefield Court were smashed. Nights became unruly. Verbal abuse became intolerable and, on 12 August 1978, a psychotic Malcolm was arrested by the police, seen by doctors and quickly sectioned. Three months after coming out of the Royal Free he was back in its psychiatric unit.

He was to stay a patient there for nearly four months, so that in all he spent nearly half of 1978 in the Royal Free Hospital, where he underwent more electro-convulsive therapy.

The treatment in Nicol Ward is very violent at times, very different from St Edmundsbury in Lucan. That was quieter and kinder. No rough stuff there![40]

For a month he had been so ill that he even wrote no postcards to Edward. By mid-September, however, he was much recovered and wanting to make some excursions into town. He wrote crossly to Edward of his frustrations:

I am tired of waiting for my clothes. I still only have my hospital pyjamas and yellow dressing gown. Not very comfortable or elegant. However, I have my own sandals.[41]

His first forays down Haverstock Hill to his flat were therefore made in his sandals and yellow dressing gown. Arnold legend has it that he bribed workers in the hospital to allow these daily forays, dutifully returning in the evening for his supper. The authorities, we are told, grew so alarmed at his proclivity for escape that eventually they moved him up to a surgical ward on the fifteenth floor, but the bribes got bigger and the escapes continued. It all sounds in character. Whether these regular trips to the flat were made with or without official approval, they were extremely important in that they allowed the writing

---

[40] Letter to Edward, 14 September 1978
[41] 14 September 1978

of the Eighth Symphony. Malcolm noted in his diary: 'September 16: Started Symphony No 8 in D Major'. Nearly two months later, on November 11, came the proud entry: 'Finished Symphony No 8, Opus 121.'[42]

That Malcolm started to write his Eighth Symphony only a month after a psychotic episode and while still an in-patient in a psychiatric ward is remarkable. There had been six months of total musical silence since the sombre *Symphony for Brass*, and at least one suicide bid and two serious bursts of madness since his last orchestral work. It seems likely that the shock impact of the electro-convulsive therapy kick-started the creative process in his brain.

For the first month he worked quietly in Holmefield Court. In the difficult process of getting started he withdrew from the outside world, not even writing to Edward. His starting-point was a piano score from one of his last films, *The Reckoning* of 1969, which contained a folksy Irish march, 'Ireland's Enemy', which he initially intended to adapt for use in the second of the three movements. Surviving sketches show that he toyed with a larger orchestra and a first movement marked *Vivace irato*, the anger expressed by terrific dissonance. Later, however, he rethought the whole thing, using the 'Crazy march' (as he called 'Ireland's Enemy' in his sketches) as a focal point in the first movement and composing new themes for the slow movement.

A month on, with the first movement completed, his confidence began to grow. To the outside world he was still very sick. 'Sadly, Malcolm Arnold is still in hospital under medical supervision,' wrote his publisher to EMI, who were enquiring whether he might conduct a recording of his own work in 1979, 'and as yet there is no indication of what his prospects for the next few months might be.'[43] Around the same period, Isobel wrote to Martin Kingsbury:

> These are several overdue letters to Malcolm which I kept in the hope that I could take them to him myself – however, he's still declining visitors … Malcolm is still in hospital, but apparently spending the day in his flat. I haven't seen him or his doctor (who also seems to decline visitors, but I'm still trying) for about a month so I don't really know how Malcolm is – obviously much better than he was a month ago but I doubt very much if he's able to cope very well with everything yet.[44]

He was coping very well, however, with the symphony, his spirits so high that the writing of the second and third movements were accompanied by regular cards to Edward. He had, after all, to get his priorities right. Much more important than any symphony was the campaign to ingratiate himself with Edward at the expense of Isobel:

---

[42] It was published as Op.121, but that was the number he had already given to the Flute Sonata. It subsequently became Op.124.
[43] 18 October 1978
[44] 19 October 1978

My dear Edward,
It is another warm sunny day like being in Ischia. Look forward to seeing you when Mum allows us to meet. Love from Dad X *(October 12)*

Yet another cold morning. BRRRRRR! *(October 16)*

Here is a showman's engine, run by steam. Do you remember them at Derrick Cripps' in Cornwall? *(October 19)*

Thank you very much for your birthday present of beautiful flowers they look lovely in my room. I have them on the window-sill and the plant on the table. You were a day too soon. *(October 20)*

Thank you for your long and very informative letter. So glad everything is going so well. You were a day too soon for my Birthday. It is October 21 1978 but thank you all the same. *(October 20)*

The Eighth Symphony was also delightfully interrupted by a telephone call from Sheila, wishing him well on his birthday. He was very touched when she followed this up with a birthday present. His reply, on the back of a change of address card, was somewhat vague:

Dear Sheila,
    Thank you very much for the biscuits and the beautiful roses which are lasting well despite the central heating. I very much appreciate your offer of help, even though I am 57 not 58 as I thought.
    Love from
    Malcolm

Meanwhile his postcards to Edward continued:

Thank you very much for the Castellas, I am enjoying them while I am writing my Eighth Symphony. *(October 21)*

I made a mistake over the 5 Wills Castellas for my 57th Birthday. Mr Harry Shaw put them through my letter box. *(October 24)*

My garden is beautiful in the sunshine we have in the afternoon at the moment. *(October 25)*

Robert and Anne came to see me yesterday, Wednesday October 25 1978, on their way to Scotland. I work at home and eat and sleep at the hospital. Have finished the second movement of my Eighth Symphony today. *(October 26)*

I have begun the last movement of my Symphony No 8 Opus 121. It is in three movements: I Allegro II Andantino III Vivace *(October 29)*

I am on the third and last movement of my 8th Symphony. It is going well. *(October 30)*

It is lovely and sunny now and the last movement is vivace and very lively indeed. *(October 31)*

There is quite a nip in the air this morning. Here are some stamps for your letters. *(November 4)*

The police are getting the squatters out in no 40 opposite here. *(November 6)*

I am working hard at my 8th symphony. Soon have it finished. *(November 6)*

It was completed ten days later, and shortly afterwards Martin Kingsbury arrived to collect the manuscript. He recalls:

> The two-roomed flat was in a state of chaos and squalor. Though unshaven, Malcolm was nevertheless smartly dressed. In his lucid moments he was still genial, but the mood swings were now violent.

Martin had brought a bottle of champagne with him and they toasted the new symphony together, though, as with the collection of the Seventh, Malcolm was not at all disposed to talk about the new work.

> As soon as he had delivered a work, he lost interest in it. He had completed it and now it was up to the publishers to take it over. As usual, the manuscript was clearly written, and exuded a real sense of flow.[45]

There was excitement at Faber when they examined the score in detail. It was clearly a symphony of great originality. Malcolm had re-found his muse.

It would be hard to realise from Malcolm's few terse, inconsequential comments to Edward, that he was engaged in a major work, a symphony of deep emotion, highly distinctive in its language and beautifully proportioned. Utterly different from the 'spring-like work' he had promised Peter Kermani eight months earlier, it has long been misunderstood, even Hugo Cole somehow managing to describe it as 'light-hearted'.[46] It is not without its light-hearted moments, but it offers so much more as it makes its considered commentary on Malcolm's beleagured existence.

The Eighth begins where the *Symphony for Brass* left off, with strident trumpets and trombones much to the fore,[47] setting the troubled scene, though the pounding of the timpani at once announces that this is going to be a work of much greater dramatic vigour than its predecessor. For some forty-four bars loud martial conflict rages, a battle in which order (represented by the home key of D major) is constantly under attack from disorder (the persistent and alien G sharp), a battle that will endure, on and off, throughout the movement.

The introduction of the second subject is a typically well-handled surprise: all the anguish suddenly subsides and in struts a jaunty Irish marching tune, the theme from *The Reckoning*, introduced on the piccolo in the home key of D Major, with a simple chordal accompaniment on the winds and a walking pizzicato bass line played by the cellos. It is a surreal moment. We ask ourselves if we are dreaming. Can Malcolm really be introducing something so light-hearted? But we begin to realise that there is another element. Behind this seemingly naïve statement there lurks continuously that G sharp (now notated as A flat) played by

---

[45] July 2003
[46] Cole: *Malcolm Arnold*, p.186
[47] A scowling augmented fourth, the so-called 'devil in music', starts things off, setting up the battle between order and disorder.

the rest of the strings, the one note which causes the most disharmony. The first statement of the simple marching tune goes on to end in unexpected violence.

The movement develops with the continuing battle between order and disorder joined by an aggressive twelve-note motif and ever more disquieting versions of the theme from *The Reckoning*, which remind us of Malcolm's description of it as 'a crazy march'.

Disorder threatens to win the day when, almost against expectations, the piccolo returns with the Irish tune, this time without the bitter A flat in the background. Hugo Cole rejoices. 'Its treatment seems to illustrate the incorruptibility of innocence,' he cries.[48] But he ignores the movement's extraordinary last moments, when harp and tam-tam enigmatically undercut the message of hope.

This challenging first movement inevitably leaves us wondering what exactly Malcolm had in mind, if it was not Hugo Cole's vision of incorruptible innocence, when he introduced the theme from *The Reckoning*. Piers Burton-Page hypothesises it as a political statement, low-key support for Irish republicanism, and Paul Jackson, delving into the plot of *The Reckoning* in which the hero's father dies, suggests it is Malcolm's reaction to the death of Pappy (though in fact Pappy was still alive at the time of the symphony's completion). Fortunately, for once, Malcolm has left us some clues. On a copy of the published piano arrangement of *The Reckoning* he itemised four things under the heading of First Movement: 'End of Dymphna (jilted)', 'I.R.A.', 'Sweet Ireland', and 'Lousy accountants'. 'Sweet Ireland' represents the ideal to which he sailed in 1972 and found for a while in the camaraderie of Camelot and the beauty of his Irish goddesses. But his five Irish years, alas, had ended in utter disarray. His final disaster had been the row that summer with Dymphna, which symbolised everything that had gone wrong recently in his personal life. Then there were his 'lousy accountants', with whom he had had a blazing row. His finances were in chaos and he blamed it all on them. Finally there was the troubled Irish political scene. He sympathised with the ideals of the IRA but their methods grieved him.

The theme from *The Reckoning*, therefore, seems to represent a summation of his Irish aspirations and disappointments, the innocent jauntiness of the melody encapsulating his aspirations and the sourness of the harmonies his disappointments. It is indeed a 'crazy march', for he subjects the simple tune to all manner of indignities, the very thing which he believed that he himself had experienced. There was no particular significance in the fact the theme was taken from *The Reckoning*. It just happened to be the best Irish tune he had written which could reflect his years at Meadowcroft and de Vesci Terrace.

In the slow movement all anger is spent, resignation rules and an unearthly beauty is sustained throughout. In the creation of this sombre, ethereal world of highly original sonorities there is a strong emphasis on low-pitched instruments, with solos for bassoon, horn and tuba, yet, at the other end of the range, there is

---

[48] Cole: *Malcolm Arnold*, p.182

(as so often) a starring role for the oboe, while the harp, glockenspiel and vibraphone all play parts of significance. There is still dissonance, promoting an underlying feeling of bitterness but never threatening the intense lyricism which characterises the movement. The contrast with the conflict and drama of the first movement is very marked. The spirit of Shostakovich is also apparent – both in the melodic and harmonic writing – complementing a Mahlerian intensity of feeling, yet the sum total of the *Andantino*'s parts is quintessential Malcolm Arnold.

For Malcolm, sitting at his desk in the little ground floor flat at the back of Holmefield Court, the slow movement is both a further retrospective look at the Irish period, with all its joys and sorrows, and a gaze forwards to a future of much uncertainty. As the conclusion approaches there is an arresting climax, where, as Hugo Cole puts it, 'chromatic brass figures are projected against a glittering web of G major harmony spun by harp, glockenspiel and vibraphone.'[49] This is the one occasion of drama, the one time when the *Andantino*'s ethereal beauty is threatened by stronger, deadlier forces, but it is only a passing moment and very soon the chromatic, threatening brass has been silenced, the glittering web remains intact, and it is surely still there, glittering away in the heavens, as the movement draws to a most peaceful and harmonious close. If Malcolm is pondering on the fragility of his current mental state, the deep uncertainties now surrounding his own future and the ever-present, beckoning figure of Death, he is doing so with the calm acceptance that what will be will be.

The concluding movement, *Vivace*, contains a rondo of tremendous inner energy which Malcolm presents in brilliantly different orchestral colours on four separate occasions. This is Beckus, dusting himself down after his latest contretemps and getting on with his life, just as cheekily as ever. But, as always with Beckus, there is also something a little unsettling about him, the rondo possessing a feverish intensity and side-stepping in all manner of chromatically unexpected directions.

There is additional interest in the last movement. Between each of the ambiguous rondo's appearances come three different episodes, each highly contrasted. If the rondo represents Malcolm facing up bravely to a new life, these episodes could be reflections on important aspects of his recent past. Edward, the current fixation, is the most obvious contender for inclusion, and he could well be there in the third episode, a simple tune, repeated no less than eight times in some very spare, two-part writing.[50] It has the fascination of a dripping tap, from which one cannot pull one's gaze, or the taking down of train numbers, relentlessly hour after hour, from the platform of Paddington Station. The first episode is desperately sad and dramatic, with its sighing falling semitones, the second more ethereal, a wistful dialogue initially between first and second violins and

---

[49] Cole: *Malcolm Arnold*, p.185
[50] The kind of writing which was to become such a feature of the Ninth Symphony. There are long dialogues in the wind and then the brass sections.

*A page of sketches for the third movement of the Eighth Symphony*

later between violas and cellos. The first might be a thought of the lost Sheila and Isobel, the second of the lost goddesses, but Malcolm has characteristically left the field wide open for surmise.

This Symphony, so full of surprises and enigmas, ends in fitting ambiguity. For nearly two months Malcolm had daily made his way to Holmefield Court to write what was to be his last major work for many years. It had required a huge effort of concentration. The final statement of the rondo he orchestrated with a particularly bold flourish, but how to bring the work to a close? He was a master of strong, dramatic conclusions, but here, instead, he opted to end with a couple of rudely abrupt chords, as if suddenly he had had enough of it all. He had given the Albany Symphony Orchestra its moneysworth. 'That's that!' he seems to be saying. Or is it something cruder, a cheery rejoinder to all his critics and foes?

In early December, only a few weeks after the completion of the Symphony, Malcolm left the Royal Free. Edward was still the perplexed recipient of a plethora of postcards:

> I am having an avocado bath, lavatory and sink in my flat and staying at the Savile Club while it is being done *(December 4)*

> I have ordered a surprise hamper for you for Christmas. I would like to buy you something big for Christmas! *(December 4)*

> What about getting you some clothes from Simpson's in Piccadilly? *(December 6)*

Then, on December 14, instead of the usual enticement came a piece of family news:

> Pappy (my father) died last night aged 94 years old! Happy Christmas to you!

Pappy was, in fact, ninety-two. Apart from a loss of mobility in his last year he had kept extremely fit, swimming regularly and taking a Turkish bath on his birthday right up to the age of ninety-one. On his ninetieth birthday, when he swam four lengths, he attributed his good health to being a non-smoker and non-drinker all his life. 'Life is very pleasant,' he had told reporters, 'and I am going to cling on to it for as long as I can!' Even in his old age he was the antithesis of his son.

Katherine and Anthony drove Malcolm to Pappy's funeral, which took place at the Mount Pleasant Baptist Church, Northampton. Throughout the day Malcolm was completely cut off from the whole experience. He was wearing a smart new Crombie overcoat – he was still very precise about wearing the right thing to the right occasion – but he was in a different world from everyone else. As they walked along to the church from the car, Katherine turned to Sheila.

'He looks so lonely. Why not go and talk to him!' Sheila went over to him, but found Malcolm unapproachable. Katherine was similarly unsuccessful in attempts at normal conversation:

> He'd had enough. Even at his father's funeral he referred to him as 'the bastard'! I don't remember any family gathering after the burial. If there was one, we didn't go.

I was in a kind of daze that day! Walking with him, watching, wondering what would happen next. Just as when I was a child and feared he would fall off the podium![51]

Death was still very much on Malcolm's mind when he was invited to partic-ipate on a live BBC radio show. It was one of those early morning programmes which are intended to lift the spirits as everyone prepares for another day's work. The subject was humour. All the other participants had been appropriately cheerful and humorous and eventually they turned to Malcolm, who had been up half the previous night, carousing. 'You've got to realise this,' he lectured them inconsequentially, 'We're all going to die!' He rambled on incoherently for a while as sounds in the background suggested that efforts were being made to ease him away from the microphone. He was, however, not to be moved. It was his last appearance on a breakfast chat show.

Now that he was writing no more music, Malcolm was able to give his full attention to his fixation over Edward's needs, which he believed Isobel was not meeting. He would hang around Belsize Park Avenue spying up at their windows and he tried several cunning ploys of gaining admittance, which helped drive Isobel towards a breakdown and encouraged Edward to take it upon himself to consult their solicitors. He itemised one crisis:

My father has been pressing the entry-phone continuously.

He posed as a doctor, saying that I was ill and that we weren't answering the bell.

He went up to the landlady's flat and got the front door Yale key.

He went upstairs, knocked three times and said that he was a German policeman.

We told him that we wouldn't let him in and that we would phone the police.

Then I phoned Katherine, but when we phoned the police, the phone didn't work. We thought he had cut the wire.

We banged on the floor to attract Karen's attention.

She came out on the stairs and my father called her a German lesbian and was shouting abuse.

So Karen went to a phone box and phoned us and then the police came in ten minutes.

My father was polite and went away with them.

Then he rang and said he was going to Ischia and had the key.

The police were phoned and then they got the key and returned it to Mrs Brewster.

If this happened on Sunday, could you grant an injunction against him and add it to the divorce?'

The solicitors went to work and in due course, around the time the divorce came through in February 1979, an injunction was served on Malcolm restraining him from all contact with Isobel and Edward. Malcolm responded by visiting the Chinese Supermarket in Haverstock Hill each week to stock up with

---

[51] December 2003

picture postcards, with which he then bombarded Edward.[52] These constantly denigrated Isobel and occasionally Katherine and her husband:

> Here is another seaside scene. The donkey's name is Iso!

> I saw Iso Gray in Belsize Park Gardens yesterday. Isn't she getting fat and bloated!!!!

> Iso (the old punk rocker)' [On a blank postcard he had drawn a nude female, with hair askew and a cigarette dropping ash.]

> Iso Gray looks fat and bloated. She should get a job cleaning the home of Mr Tony King and Mrs Tony King!

> Here is one of the entrances to Piccadilly tube station. A place to avoid at all costs. It is where the old punk rockers go!!!

> I hope you are not working too hard and Ms Iso Gray (Mistress of the Arts St Andrew's)[53] is being kind to you.

> This is Richmond where I brought up Robert (well) and Mrs Tony King (badly!!!)[54]

Isobel herself received a few cards, which were specifically aimed at a recent friendship she had made:

> Dear Gray,
>> When are you starting in the antique business? *(March 11)*

And

> Gray,
>> How is your antique business with your friend? *(March 14)*[55]

Isobel could have been forgiven for trying to block Malcolm totally from her mind. Instead, alarmed to hear that Malcolm had been injured in a fight, she wrote anxiously to his GP, Dr Cyril Gill. The reply was hardly reassuring:

> Yes! I know about the stitches! He says he was hit by a beer bottle and I did not ask further, but when I saw him he was not too bad. I am sorry you are still being alarmed in this way.[56]

Malcolm's life was totally out of control, so it was not surprising that 1979 proved a barren year for composition. Conducting had also ceased. His last conducting engagement had been back in 1977, so when an opportunity unexpectedly came his way to make some recordings that Easter he wrote proudly several times to Edward on the subject.

---

[52] He sent twenty-one cards between 30 January and 17 March 1979.

[53] As someone who had no formal secondary education he always felt unease at Isobel's degree and so, when he was ill, he would take her to task for it.

[54] In fact the postcard is of the Serpentine, London.

[55] The envelope was addressed to 'Ms Iso Gray (antique dealer)' and is marked on the back: 'Dr Malcolm Arnold, CBE, Hon. RAM, London, UK.'

[56] 5 March 1979

I shall be going next week to Bournemouth to record an LP and then the following week at the Southampton Guildhall for another LP. The first is me conducting the Bournemouth Symphony Orchestra (the full orchestra) and the second LP is me conducting the Bournemouth Sinfonietta (the smaller orchestra, larger than a chamber orchestra). Sorry you will not be able to be with me, but as it is Easter you will of course be having a jolly time with Granpa and Iso Gray MA. *(March 21)*

He was in no condition to undertake such work, but the opportunity of beginning a major recording deal with EMI was not something to pass over lightly, offering just the boost his work needed. It seemed to his publishers to be a risk worth taking. So at the beginning of April Malcolm, accompanied by Faber's Delma Tomlin, travelled down by train to Bournemouth, where they were met by the BSO's driver and taken to the Norfolk Hotel. That evening in the company of a few Bournemouth friends he sat down to dinner in the hotel's elegant restaurant. As the meal progressed and the drink started to tell, he began looking around him with some displeasure. How dull and conventional everyone looked! How ghastly polite it all was! He stood up, determined to bring a little life to the occasion. 'You old hags, this place is boring!' he shouted, and then marched to the grand piano, climbed on its lid, took down his trousers and pants and danced to the hotel's piped background music.[57] As the startled diners struggled hard to resume forgotten conversations, he was coaxed down from the piano, given his clothes and taken hurriedly to his room. In the middle of the night, however, he returned downstairs, broke a few windows, flung some furniture around and set off the fire-alarm. It was enjoyable while it lasted, but eventually outraged officialdom prevailed.[58]

The next morning Malcolm was waiting meekly in the hotel lobby with his bags all packed. 'I shall need another hotel,' he explained quietly to Keith Whitmore, the manager of the BSO who had arrived to take him down to the Winter Gardens for the first of two days of rehearsals. 'There was a little bother last night! But first of all, I must have a drink!' Keith Whitmore did his best to suggest that this was not a good idea. There was a heavy schedule ahead, he pointed out, with the First Symphony to rehearse, and quite a number of other pieces. But when Malcolm insisted, they found an appropriate bar, where he downed several glasses of a mixture of whisky and water. 'I find this gets the best effect,' he explained.

Malcolm's behaviour at the rehearsal was highly charged and several times he had to be calmed by the leader of the BSO, Brendan O'Brien,[59] who had once met him in Ireland.[60] 'He was not in the best of shape at the Bournemouth

---

[57] The story comes from eye-witnesses.

[58] Delma Tomlin remembers him thinking it 'terrifically funny'. She phoned Faber next morning and Julian Elloway was dispatched to lend her support. (April 2004)

[59] Brendan O'Brien also played under him during his years as a London orchestral musician.

[60] He called in at Goggins and found a very generous and friendly Malcolm there. 'We hardly spoke about music. I discovered Malcolm had a love for Flann O'Brien. Malcolm knew his books intimately and was amazed I hadn't read them …' (April 2004)

rehearsals,' he explains mildly. 'He was drunk a lot of the time,' declares trumpet player Barry Latchem, 'And he was sometimes rather brusque with the Orchestra.'[61]

The two days of rehearsals were scheduled to be followed by two days of recording from which an LP would be made of the First Symphony, supported by *Beckus*, *The Fair Field* and the Sarabande and Polka from *Solitaire*. Malcolm stumbled through the first day's recording. It helped that the orchestra liked him, respected him as a conductor, realised he was ill and did its best to compensate. Brendan O'Brien's assessment is typical:

> He was a very nice guy, very unusual. Despite the joviality, I always felt that there was quite a deal of uneasiness in his make-up. He was tremendously talented, a better conductor than most. He found it very easy, he was unaffected and spontaneous. A very clear conductor, with a big and less than very subtle beat. He had a swashbuckling air and there was a shrug and raising of the shoulders – as if he didn't quite care. But if things weren't going as he wished, he usually wouldn't be bothered. You could sense a smouldering impatience, but that was all. He'd just leave it. What was happening this time at Bournemouth was not the real Malcolm.[62]

During a break in the first day's recording, horn player Ian Lowes went round to Malcolm's dressing room for a friendly chat. He had been up at Durham with Katherine and played in the *Trevelyan Suite*: 'You won't remember me, but ten years or so ago I played with your daughter in the piece you wrote and conducted at the opening of Trevelyan College!' Malcolm stared at him blankly. 'I don't have a daughter.' Ian Lowes smiled at the joke. 'I knew Katherine well at Durham. What's she doing these days?' But there was no reciprocating smile on Malcolm's face, just the same blank stare, and the reply: 'You are wrong, quite wrong. I don't have a family at all!' Ian Lowes gave up the unequal struggle.

That evening Keith Whitmore took Malcolm out for a meal. At first he seemed his usual jovial self. There was sweetcorn on the menu. 'We won't have that,' joked Malcolm. 'We've been playing it all day!' But a wedding celebration going on in the restaurant interested Malcolm. He went across and butted in, oblivious to the obvious annoyance this caused, insisting on buying the party more champagne and drinking large quantities of theirs. With some difficulty Keith prized him away and back to their table. The embarrassments had only just begun. Later on in the meal Malcolm removed his jacket and then his shirt. Faced with Malcolm's bare upper torso, Keith Whitmore opted for a speedy departure, promising the waiter he would return and settle up later. Shortly after they left the restaurant, Malcolm, fully dressed again, suddenly started running away without a word of warning. Keith Whitmore followed, but it was a fruitless chase and he gave it up. Malcolm disappeared out of sight, still running. He turned up, much later, at the hotel, but offered no explanation. How could he explain that he

---

[61] April 2004
[62] April 2004

needed to run to try to tire out his racing brain, but the more he ran, the faster
it raced?

On the morning of the second day's recording Keith Whitmore turned up at
the hotel to collect Malcolm only to find him in the process of being taken away
by the police. Malcolm had gone berserk during the night, causing considerable
damage and confusion. An elderly lady was going round in great distress,
regaling everyone with her story.

> I had been woken up by a great deal of noise and then my door opened. A naked man
> tip-toed across the room, kissed me and ran out.

It was Malcolm.

With the conductor locked away, the second day's recording was cancelled.
'I still feel bad about not going to see him,' says Brendan O'Brien. 'It's on my
conscience! But I just thought he would find it too embarrassing.' In the end EMI
salvaged enough from the first day's work for an LP, albeit a little short on
playing time and without the *Fair Field*. The performances are, in all the circumstances, remarkably good.

Martin Kingsbury, who had come down to assess the situation, visited the
police station.

> Malcolm was in a cell by himself. No-one was taking an interest in him, but then
> nobody could have coped with him. I have never had such an unpleasant encounter in
> my entire life. He was utterly vicious and obsessed by the need to get out, so he could
> have a drink.[63]

A doctor was called, at Martin's request. Malcolm was immediately sectioned
and taken away to St Ann's Psychiatric Hospital, which Martin visited shortly
afterwards.

> On my arrival the sister briefed me in her office. Her account of Malcolm's condition
> was not encouraging. As I spoke in reply, she suddenly lifted her hand. 'Hush,' she
> said, 'windows have ears.' And there outside the open window was Malcolm, eaves-
> dropping and grimacing grotesquely. He was led back to his room.

Malcolm of course missed the rehearsals planned for the Bournemouth
Sinfonietta for the second LP and so the leader of the orchestra, the Australian
Ronald Thomas, took over the conducting for the *Third Sinfonietta* and the
*Serenade for Small Orchestra*. Malcolm was driven back to London and further
medical care.

EMI were none too pleased. The previous year they had made a first recording
of the two Flute Concertos with the Philharmonia under Neville Dilkes only
for Malcolm to take exception to their soloist and threaten legal action. An
important part of the Southampton recording sessions, therefore, was to make a
new version of the concertos, under Malcolm, with the soloist of his choice,
Richard Adeney. Now with all the latest crises they needed an extra day's

---

[63] July 2003

recording under Ronald Thomas, costing £1,000. EMI's enthusiastic support of Malcolm's music had been undermined. Any future Arnold projects, they declared, would be very carefully vetted. The Horn Concertos (with Alan Civil) and Clarinet Concertos (with Jack Brymer), planned for the autumn, would not now go ahead. In due course the Sinfonietta's LP did come out, and Richard Adeney's superb, definitive performances of both Concertos must have been some justification for all the fuss that Malcolm had made on his behalf.

Malcolm spent nearly a month in the Royal Free Hospital following the recording débâcle, but somehow, against all his best interests, managed to obtain release in early May. There were accordingly three last months of mayhem that summer. These began with a bizarre return to Southampton and Bournemouth, where, in a determined bid to prove that nothing had gone wrong, he even stayed at the same hotels. Edward was sent a postcard with a photo of the Civic Centre, Southampton, with the proud message 'Both my flute concertos were recorded in the Civic Hall pictured overleaf'. A card of the Royal Hotel, in all its art deco glory, was also sent[64] to 'MS Isobel Arnold, Ms Katherine Arnold, T King (Con Man) and Edward Izaak Arnold':

> Dear People,
>
> An excellent place to rest the mind from the rigours of every-day work. Like music for instance.
>
> Malcolm Arnold

In Southampton, having forgotten where he had left his car, he alerted the police to its theft.

Shortly afterwards a card featuring one of Malcolm's more obscene drawings of Isobel was sent to Edward,[65] the start of a new campaign of hostility caused by the application which had just been made by Katherine's husband, after family consultation, for Malcolm's affairs to be put under the jurisdiction of the Court of Protection. Katherine had visited Malcolm to discuss it with him on 28 May, the formal application being submitted the next day. Two months on, just as the application was about to be granted, Isobel called in on Malcolm to try to explain its advantages.[66]

The Court of Protection was an office of the Lord Chancellor's Department, existing for the purpose of protecting and managing the financial affairs and property of people who, because of mental disorder, are unable to manage these for themselves. The application had been supported by Malcolm's local doctor, Cyril Gill:

> The patient suffers from recurrent hypomanic attacks, with unpredictable behaviour. On occasions he has been in a state of sustained psychotic excitement, which has

[64] 19 May 1979
[65] 30 May 1979
[66] 26 July 1979

needed detention in hospital under section. His behaviour is undoubtedly aggravated by alcoholic excess.

Bringing in the Court of Protection was a helpful move, even if it only offered financial controls and did not take responsibility for Malcolm's day-to-day care. The financial chaos caused by the parting from his accountants had been exacerbated by excessive spending, a characteristic of hypomania. A young lady living in the same block of flats, whom he often took out to meals, was said to have been given £13,000. Katherine, on a visit to his flat one day was presented with a Rowlandson print. 'Take it!' said Malcolm. 'I don't want it any more!' She gently suggested he keep it, but, on her next visit, it had gone.

Katherine and Isobel were surely right in having recourse to the Court of Protection. The move not only brought some order into his chaos, it also offered hope that if his spending was limited, so too might be his drinking. Malcolm, however, in his confusion could only focus on his diminished flow of funds and in his outrage at this affront he knew exactly whom to blame.

He should have been under care, but, resisting the idea fiercely, he continued to roam London at his own and other people's peril. The state welfare system, no doubt anxious not to usurp individual liberties, had totally failed him. Isobel and Katherine, who from time to time had tried to help clean his flat after the walkout of his domestic help, were now forbidden entrance. Malcolm refused to come to the door or answer the telephone. He had always taken personal hygiene to extreme lengths, but now the situation was reversed and he sank into a degrading squalor which included sleeping on urine-soaked mattresses. In a humorous attempt to brighten up the gloomy mess he had decorated some of his pictures with ladies' knickers.

Throughout the distressing events of 1979 Malcolm did not entirely give up thoughts of composition. In July 1979 the Northern Ballet Theatre asked whether he might write a thirty-minute score for a ballet based on the works of Helen Bradley, to be performed a year hence at Sadler's Wells. In August 1979 Julian Elloway of Faber replied to them that this would not be possible because he was already working on a ballet project of his own:

> He is particularly concerned at present with the idea of a ballet based on George IV and Mrs Fitzherbert. He has already three main schemes planned – an opening duet for the two, a divertissement in the Pavilion and the death of the King.

Nothing seems to have survived either by way of synopsis or musical sketches of this project, so we cannot even be sure that it was the third King George rather than the fourth whose death Malcolm was including. George III undoubtedly came into the ballet because two of Malcolm's main interests at this time, according to Julian Elloway,[67] were 'loony celebrities, including poets and royalty, and sex'. A Regency ballet might have worked well, for in addition to

---

[67] April 2004

insanity and adultery it touched on other themes on which Malcolm had strong views: religion, drinking and fashion. It sounds like another good idea which, like *The Three Musketeers*, just came at the wrong time.

Malcolm's mind was now very troubled and perverse. The experiences of his next door neighbours were particularly harrowing. The Coates were a quiet, elderly couple, yet, for a long period, had their lives made into a misery by Malcolm. Their front door was only six inches apart from Malcolm's and he would put garbage or burning papers through their letter box, leave rubbish outside their front door, play the piano loudly in the early hours and even appear naked in the corridor. Only after a binge-drinking session would there be peace and quiet for a while, but this would usually be interrupted when the police arrived to break the door down and take him to a hospital or clinic, a fairly regular occurrence. The old couple were grateful for the efforts which Isobel and Katherine made to try to alleviate the problems.

Malcolm became known as an eccentric, slightly menacing figure around Haverstock Hill, the local drunk, no longer an ebullient presence flinging his cash generously in all directions. The once fastidious gourmet was now resorting to chicken and chips from the take-away. He couldn't sleep. He was awake at 4.00 every morning. In late August he gathered together his scattered resources for a visit from Mr Graham Preston, Clerk of the Supreme Court, from whom he planned to extract new funds. It was not a good visit. The future before him looked more and more bleak. There was very little to do any more. Music had always been an antidote to depression. So, as Katherine points out, once the writing stopped, he was looking into a void:

> Dad didn't really have any hobbies. It was either music or nothing. He had his family, from time to time, and he had his books, but essentially it was music or nothing. And there must have been a lot of anxiety with the music. As children we picked up something of the atmosphere! My fears about his falling from the podium were expressions of his greater fears. Composing and conducting was a very anxious-making profession. There you are, standing up in front of everyone, so successful … and yet! You know that some people are watching and waiting for you to fall. And then you get the critics baying at your heels! So when the music stopped …[68]

That slippery podium had done what it had always threatened. He had finally fallen off. The fears continued to multiply in his mind now that the euphoria had all evaporated. He could no longer cope, and realised that he was going mad – an asylum beckoned. It was not a prospect to savour. Once, at Di Jones' lovely flat, he had measured out the tablets along the mantelpiece, and then failed to take them. On subsequent occasions he had botched the job. Pray God this time he got it right. He realised now that he had damagingly hurt those whom he most loved. He, an apostle of the underdog, had bullied and harassed and hurt beyond measure. He would do so no longer. He hoped that Katherine would be all right

---

[68] September 2003

with the baby she was expecting, but another generation was not a prospect to bring him leaping back from the abyss. He preferred to make the jump. What a curious, squalid final resting-place after so much in life that had been exquisite and first-class. Christ! he kept on thinking, as he settled himself more comfortably, how he hated this fucking flat!

He would not have cared, had he been conscious several hours later, that the police, in gaining entrance, broke down the front door rather more roughly than usual. Its splintered remains, lying oddly far away from the empty hinges, quaintly mirrored Malcolm's inert body, the most obvious object in the jumbled, rank interior. He had been saved, yet again, by the loyal vigilance of Isobel and Katherine. But saved for what?

He was soon back in the psychiatric unit of the Royal Free Hospital, as a physical presence at least. He had several visitors in the next twenty-four hours, but didn't see or hear any of them. There was a little pile of cards and letters beside his bed, but they had been opened by other hands. One sheet in particular would have much moved him, had he been able to read it:

Dearest Father,
> I love you such a lot,
> I shall love you until I die.
> I hope you will get better as soon as possible.
> I will keep sending you letters until you are better.
> Please don't reply to this letter.
> Yours Sincerely,
> Edward Arnold

# 16
# The Lost Years
## Northampton, 1979-84

THREE WEEKS LATER, in September 1979, Malcolm had recovered sufficiently to decide that the all-too familiar surroundings of the Royal Free Hospital were not for him. In discharging himself Malcolm unwittingly precipitated another crisis, for he was quite incapable of looking after himself. Neither Katherine, now seven months pregnant, nor Isobel could cope with the situation, but a temporary solution was found when an old friend, the composer Geoffrey Bush,[1] looked after him for a few days and then found him a vacancy at St Cecilia's, the Musicians' Benevolent Fund's Home, at Westgate-on-Sea, Kent. This was a well-intentioned move, but a musicians' rest home was not the right place for someone who was mentally disturbed.

From Westgate-on-Sea Malcolm wrote to Isobel in a shaky hand a strangely facetious note:

> Please make up the bed and do the two lights either side! Back in three weeks (I think!)[2]

In the event he proved too much of a handful to last even three weeks at St Cecilia's, and although the matron there patiently explained to him that he needed specialised care, Malcolm continued to fight against a return to a psychiatric ward. He therefore wrote to Katherine, expressing a preference for a short stay in Belsize Park:

> My dear Katherine,
>     I would like to go to Greenway for two weeks from October 19th. Please arrange this. I shall be very grateful to you for this.
>     Love, Dad

A week later he travelled up by taxi to the clinic where so many times in the past he had dried out. Fortunately after just one day there his former GP, Dr Gill, finally persuaded him of his real need. They discussed the possibilities and, with the Court of Protection's sanction, chose St Andrew's, Northampton, described at the time as 'the leading private mental hospital in the country, pioneering the

---

[1] Geoffrey Bush (1920-98), like Malcolm, had been Chairman of the Composers' Guild of Great Britain and a visitor to Russia under its auspices (1964).
[2] 1 October 1979

self-help approach to psychiatry'.[3] He was moved to St Andrew's three days before his 58th birthday.[4]

Malcolm knew the hospital well, for it was on the Billing Road just around the corner from where he was born. He had always feared he would end up there. He was assured, however, that he would not need to stay too long, perhaps three months at the most, and shortly after arrival wrote brief notes to both Isobel and Katherine which indicate that the hostility he nursed for them at the height of his derangement had quite vanished. The note to Katherine was short but affectionate:

> Am eventually in Northampton 'loony bin' being dried out. It is a fearsome process. Love to Anthony. Love Dad XXX

For Isobel there were some simplistic travel instructions:

> I am in Northampton, as you see, at the loony bin, being dried out. Please would you forward the letters other than the ones you can answer yourself. You could come and bring Edward this weekend or next weekend. It is straight along the M1 and easy to find.
> Love from Malcolm
> XXX
> PS Please tell Edward I took his pizza out to eat as the taxi came to take me to Euston and the drying-out station!
> Love Dad XXXXX

Isobel came as bidden and afterwards reported on the visit to Julian Elloway:

> Edward and I went to see Malcolm last Saturday – he was extremely pleasant and friendly (quite perturbing, really) and looks incredibly well. He is quite convinced that drink is his only problem, that he's stopped for ever and everything will be fine for ever, which ain't so, and some of him knows that. It is pathetic and sad.[5]

Isobel, however, was cheered by the setting of St Andrew's, which even on a grey day in November was impressively grand. Founded in 1838 in the centre of Northampton specifically as an asylum for the mentally disturbed, St Andrew's is set in one hundred and ten acres, like a country house, approached down a curving drive, its wide, stone façade looking out over well-kept lawns. Close by is a Gothic chapel, designed by Gilbert Scott, and beyond, stretching down towards the Nene Valley, is a park dotted with buildings old and new, giving it something of the atmosphere of a university campus.

Malcolm was placed in a short-stay unit, the newly-opened Isham House. 'Most of the names on patients' doors seemed to be either Arabic or members of the House of Lords,' commented Faber's Julian Elloway.[6] Overlooking the golf

---

[3] *Northampton Independent*, August 1983. A private hospital for over 100 years, St Andrew's currently caters largely for NHS patients on psychiatry.

[4] He arrived at St Andrew's on 18 October 1979, having been at St Cecilia's from 29 September.

[5] 8 November 1979

[6] 23 December 1979 (letter to Ruzena Wood, one of Malcolm's well-wishers)

*Malcolm with his grandson Sebastian outside St Andrew's, 1981,*
*after he had come through the traumas of 1980*

*St Andrew's Hospital, Northampton*

course, Isham House exemplified the hospital's belief in the therapeutic value of a good view and it was not long before Malcolm's horrors at Holmefield Court began to recede. 'He is in a pleasant, quiet private house,' wrote Julian Elloway to Patric Dickinson, 'and is pulling through very well.'[7] Patric Dickinson had written verses for a possible sequel to *The Return of Odysseus*, called *Jericho*, which Elloway had left with Malcolm. 'He was absolutely delighted, and intends to start work straight after Christmas.'

Malcolm was diagnosed by the consultants at St Andrew's as suffering from two specific disorders, alcoholism and schizophrenia. 'It was evident on testing that he had quite gross schizophrenic thought disorder,' wrote Dr Curson to Katherine, 'and this particular phenomenon tends not to occur in manic-depressive psychosis.'[8] Modern experts might disagree. The two conditions tend to overlap and can be hard to tell apart, both in fact presenting 'thought disorder', abnormal, idiosyncratic speech which is difficult for others to follow. Many features of Malcolm's illness suggest manic-depressive illness rather than schizophrenia: periods of good recovery, episodes of intense artistic activity, an above-average interest in sex, as well as the alternating periods of optimism and of despondency.

Having outlined his diagnosis, Dr Curson moved on to the treatment prescribed. Malcolm had been given, he told Katherine, two injections of the anti-psychotic drug, Fluphenazine Decanoate, 'of a relatively low dose' and had shown no adverse side-effects.[9] He would be given one more injection and then tested to see if there had been any changes in the thought disorder. As regards the drinking problem, St Andrew's had recently set up a special unit to deal with alcoholism, putting emphasis on behavioural and educational aspects of the problem. Malcolm's diary in the early weeks was full of references to this programme. Each day was different, yet there was a dogged purposefulness about it all: '9.00 Relaxation, 10.45 Coffee, 2.00 Film, 4.00 Discussion Group.' He was also constantly involved in 'Physical Activities' and 'Social Skills' as well as the occasional, not wholly expected 'Prayer Meeting'.

Malcolm's positive approach to all this won quick official approval. 'He has exhibited a remarkable degree of insight,' wrote Dr Curson to Katherine, 'and I have no reason to doubt his sincere motivation in wishing to change.' Two months later Dr Curson gave Katherine even more encouraging news: 'He is committed to total abstention from alcohol for life.'[10] There were now, he continued, no psychiatric indications for keeping him in hospital over a prolonged period. It was better for him to be released. With the help of his GP or a local clinic Malcolm could be given regular injections of the anti-psychotic

---

[7] 26 November 1979

[8] 12 November 1979

[9] The commonest side effect of anti-psychotic drugs like Fluphenazine Decanoate (brand name Modecate) is persistent, restless physical movement.

[10] 10 January 1980

drug, Modecate, as 'a long-term follow-up'. Katherine instinctively felt that this was over-optimistic, knowing what an unreliable out-patient Malcolm usually was, but her anxieties were silenced by the doctor's strong support for a policy of trial-and-error:

> If Malcolm finds it impossible to survive in the community, then I think we will have to seriously consider long-term in-patient care. I believe your father is aware of this and not totally opposed to the idea.

There were, consequently, hasty deliberations as to where he should live. The Court of Protection applied unavailingly to the Musicians' Benevolent Fund, and, in the end, Katherine, who was nursing a two-month-old baby, booked her father in at the Swiss Cottage Hotel, where he had stayed on his return from Ireland.[11] A Victorian building, beautifully restored and brimful with paintings, antiques and tapestries, it had an ambience he liked, being quiet but stylish. It was, as its brochures proudly proclaim, 'a little piece of England where the pace is a little gentler and the quality of service a little higher'. It was also a little piece of England which was a little closer to Isobel and Edward, in fact, just around the corner from Belsize Park Gardens. The Court of Protection would pay the hotel bills ('but on no account was alcoholic drink to be included') and give Malcolm £40 a week pocket money.[12] He had regular appointments to see Dr Curson at his Harley Street practice and he would come under the care again of Dr Gill. All in all, it represented a generous attempt by all concerned to give Malcolm a fresh start. Above all, with his money now rationed, the destructive binges of the past could not easily recur.

Just before the move Malcolm was interviewed by Michael Oliver for his Music Weekly programme on BBC Radio 3. Julian Elloway, who accompanied Malcolm down to London and sat alongside him in the studio, remembers him 'in extremely good form' throughout the long day. Michael Oliver, who had gone to the studio in some dread, was mightily relieved and agreeably surprised by some interesting responses.[13] Malcolm, for example, expressed a long-held admiration for Webern.[14] He replied to questions quickly and, although he had written nothing for over a year, he used the present tense throughout, as if he were still active. There were just occasional moments when an inner melancholy could be sensed. Asked which aspect of his job he found most difficult – 'Is it the waiting for ideas?' – Malcolm briefly bared his soul:

---

[11] He moved from St Andrew's to the Swiss Cottage Hotel on 12 January 1980.

[12] Drink was temporarily no problem. Prior to a lunch with a group from Faber Music in late 1979 at a restaurant outside Northampton, Malcolm had written to Julian Elloway 'I would love to go out on Thursday December 20th when you will all get drunk except me!'

[13] The recorded programme was broadcast on 20 January 1980.

[14] 'I admire [him] enormously for the clarity of his writing. I've always tried to write with as much clarity as that but with greater simplicity harmonically.'

Yes, I think that *is* the worst time, for you are buoyed up when you're creating something, and the times you're not can be very depressing and flat and boring. One is only interested in life when one is working, I find!

In addition he also declared 'the loneliest place in the world is to be in a room with a desk and a piece of manuscript paper'. Writing was 'a completely lonely occupation' and, had he been able to earn a living conducting, he would have composed much less.

There are brief hints, even in this edited interview, that his brain was not as sharp as it had been. He spoke unconvincingly when trying to use the Fifth Symphony as an example of a new phase in his work:

> That was a time when I went back to using serial techniques as well as tonal techniques. I use all techniques. I take what I fancy from all the various techniques of writing in order to make it as simple as possible – that is a serial work but if I had said in a long programme note at the time, it would have been damned. It was damned anyway, but it wasn't because of that reason …!

On the whole, however, the interview bears out the doctors' optimistic view of things. And for a while Malcolm began well enough at the hotel, with Isobel doing her very best to make sure he had regular company. She was also around to solve any small crises:

> My dear Isobel,
> Here is £4 for the shoes. I am most grateful to you for getting them mended for me.
> Love to Edward XXX
> Love from Malcolm [15]

But it was not enough. The stark truth was that Malcolm could no longer cope in the outside world. His stay of nearly three months at the Swiss Cottage Hotel ended in another psychotic episode with him setting fire to his rooms. He needed the security of institutional care. He went back to St Andrew's as a voluntary patient,[16] initially to Isham House, but when it became clear that there was a serious thought disorder, he was moved, in May 1980, into Thornton Ward, within the main building, where he was to be based for nearly two years. A Court of Protection case worker wrote to Isobel:

> I confirm that Malcolm has been moved to a long-stay ward at St Andrew's, and has apparently settled down there. Whether or not he does remain there we shall have to wait and see but at least we know he is receiving proper medication and treatment and if he endeavours to do anything silly, then there is medical staff available and on the spot.[17]

Thornton Ward, though hardly as elegant as the Swiss Cottage Hotel, nonetheless has a certain distinction and Victorian amplitude. Its corridors, then as now, are wide and well-carpeted, with high, moulded ceilings and walls faced

---

[15] 3 March 1980.

[16] He was back by 5 April 1980.

[17] 6 May 1980

with mahogany, the institutional regularity offset by unusual rest areas, with open fireplaces, plush seating and high, leaded windows. It is an open ward. Malcolm was at no time detained at St Andrew's under the Mental Health Act, so when he felt well enough, he was at liberty to walk in the grounds or even go into town. Close to his ward was the Great Hall, approached up a fine staircase, a splendid setting for dances and concerts, with a grand piano at which Malcolm would spend time, improvising jazz and playing the dance tunes of his younger days. One favourite, often repeated, was 'These Foolish Things' to which one of the social workers would sometimes sing along.

The piano-playing, however, occurred later in his stay. For much of the rest of 1980 he was suicidally gloomy, too depressed to do very much at all. For a time both he and Katherine hoped he could be moved to The Priory, Roehampton, nearer to family and friends, but negotiations petered out confusingly. These discussions involved a contentious issue, whether or not Malcolm might benefit from psychotherapy. Katherine, who had first-hand experience of its value from her own training at the Tavistock, suggested it to both St Andrew's and The Priory. Both sets of specialists, however, rejected the idea and the Court of Protection came strongly down on side of the doctors in the cause of limiting expense.[18]

Thwarted in his desire to move to The Priory, Malcolm turned his thoughts to the possibility of a return to Belsize Park:

My Dear Katherine,

Though naturally disappointed about The Priory I have been thinking about all the trouble you have taken on my behalf, and as I do not want to stay at St Andrew's for ever, it is very comfortable for the time being.

I think I must make the effort at trying to live at Holmefield Court. It is cramped but better than nothing, and I feel I can manage without giving all my money away like I have in the past.

Please help me to get back to Holmefield Court and away from St Andrew's.

With love to you all,

Love, Dad XXX[19]

From a further letter, written four days later, Malcolm would seem to think that Katherine now had this unworkable scenario in hand:

My dear Katherine,

I am looking forward to getting back to the flat, despite past experiences. I will go to any analyst you can find. So far I have not discovered one. Perhaps your doctor would know of one willing to take me on. I am really anxious to get better.

Love to you all,

Dad XXX

[18] Katherine's suggestion has since been vindicated. Today psychotherapy is looked upon as a helpful aid to the treatment of manic-depressive illness and it is widely agreed that psychotherapy in conjunction with medication reduces the risk of relapse. It also permits the use of lower levels of lithium or anticonvulsants, minimising very serious, possibly irreversible side effects.

[19] 13 July 1980

Isobel, visiting St Andrew's at this time, found Malcolm 'still thinking about coming back to his flat'[20] even though he displayed not the slightest interest in the large collection of mail she had brought him. 'Nobody else thinks it a good idea,' she commented. But, a few days later, Malcolm had changed his plans:

> My dear Katherine,
>     I am most anxious to get to The Priory under the care of Doctor David Thomas who I find most sympathetic.
>     Love from Dad to you all, XXXX[21]

Further discussions with the Court of Protection did follow, but Malcolm stayed on at St Andrew's. With his immediate future settled, the Court finally took the decision to sell the Holmefield Court flat and it asked Katherine and Isobel to organise the final clean-up and dispersal and storage of his belongings. It was now two years since the divorce, but Isobel loyally helped out, just as she continued to visit St Andrew's once a month, often with Edward, though she herself was only coping with the pressures in her life with help from the Tavistock. Her little top floor flat was intolerably constricting now that Edward was nearly sixteen and her situation there, as she told the Court of Protection, was becoming 'desperate'. Her financial problems were exacerbated by all manner of unexpected extras, like damage caused unintentionally in the flat by Edward and the ongoing saga of her elderly Mini:

> This year already it's needed a new exhaust, a new carburettor, a repair to the radiator, and an uninsured Greek has bashed in the boot.

Malcolm by the terms of the divorce supported Isobel and Edward together to the extent of £5,500 a year and it was a great relief for her when this was raised to £11,000.[22]

1980 was a totally lost year, with Malcolm deeply depressed and under strong medication. Most of those visiting him came away from St Andrew's gloomily. Robin Arnold had first visited his uncle shortly after the return from the Swiss Cottage Hotel:

> It was around 7.00pm and seemed dark and so very quiet that everyone must have been sedated just beforehand. The nurses all went around with torches. As we walked with Malcolm and his carer along a dark corridor to his room, another patient came along, his face lit by his carer's torch and looking like Vincent Price. To come

---

[20] Letter to Julian Elloway, 27 July 1980

[21] 8 August 1980

[22] Malcolm's finances were in a mess because of his tax debt. He had paid no tax since 1977-78 and had debts of around £50,000. His income from royalties in 1980, a year when his professional fortunes were at their lowest, was an encouraging £47,000. By the terms of the divorce he was paying Sheila just £1,000 a year; he was currently supporting Katherine, Robert and Lizzie Witts by £500 each a year. St Andrew's was costing around £10,000 a year, with the Court of Protection allowing him 'pocket money' of £60 a week (to include a rented colour television). It only needed changing fashions to bring a revival of interest in the full range of his music for him swiftly to become rich again.

suddenly into this strange world was quite scary. We were left with Malcolm in his little room. He was calm and, though heavily sedated, he was still of this world with insight into his condition. 'I don't know why I'm here!' he said. Then he smiled. 'Oh yes, I do. I tried to kill myself!'[23]

Robin and his wife Avril on the whole were encouraged by this visit, thinking Malcolm not much worse mentally than in happier days. He was sadder, but talked about family matters sensibly. 'He didn't know what to do next and we went away asking ourselves in what way we might help.' Robin made the next visit alone, and was surprised at the difference.

> The room was unkempt and there were cigarette burns on both bed cover and curtains. Malcolm was extremely agitated. He only wanted to get down to the pub for a few beers and I had a great difficulty in extricating myself.

A third visit was even worse. At one moment Malcolm, encouraged perhaps by the presence of Avril, leapt dramatically out of bed and pranced around naked. He then urgently suggested they all escaped by climbing out of the window. It was clear he was drinking again. He talked a great deal about his pub visiting and hospital workers, whom, he said, he paid to bring in drink. Their visit ended precipitately. 'Come on now,' he cried, putting on some clothes hurriedly, 'Let's go off and have a few beers at the pub!' When Robin defensively made an excuse, Malcolm suddenly lost all interest in his nephew. 'Oh, well, goodbye then!' he said, as he climbed back into bed.

Robin has remained very struck by the alteration in Malcolm between the first and subsequent visits:

> Never again did he seem of this world. To me he was a completely different person; not even a vague shadow of himself.

Martin Kingsbury was another caller to be saddened by the situation, though he did find Malcolm 'disarmingly grateful' for the visit:

> It all seemed dark and gloomily institutional. Malcolm was very subdued and I have this image of him shuffling off, head down, up a long, soulless corridor …

He was luckier than Malcolm's niece, Jenny Gregory (Ruth's elder daughter), whose visit proved abortive:

> When I arrived – I think, in the afternoon – he was just very sleepy. I hung around for some time but in the end I just had to ask the nurse to tell him I had visited.

This was, however, a less distressing call than that made by Katherine's Irish friends, the Hilliards, who were so upset that when they returned to their car they both burst into tears:

> He had been so much the centre of attention, so famous and sought after, so much the giver, the creative centre of many lives, and there he was now in his little room. It broke our hearts to see how things had turned out for him.

---

[23] July 2003

He was very severely depressed. He was terribly unhappy. He was hunched over, and seemed heavily drugged. He was able to have a perfectly lucid conversation, but the fire inside him had gone out.[24]

Robert had the misfortune to visit his father, in October 1980, at a particularly bad period in which the violence and self-destructive urges of the Belsize Park period had returned.[25]

St Andrew's looked really attractive, but I guess it's not so attractive if you're stuck there! We found Dad in his room, looking dirty, with food and blood all down his front. His face was dirty too. I'm not suggesting that there was a lack of care going on in the hospital, because if he was being violently aggressive to them, there would be little they could do.

We chatted. He's always got something interesting to say. But he usually mixes something interesting with something horrible! That visit he begged me to take him out of the awful place. But there was nothing I could do! It was impossible to take him![26]

Robert ruminated over the situation on the way back to Skye with Anne. And the more he thought about it, the less he felt able to contribute. His father, he felt, was trapped and neglected in a mess of his own making, in a comfortable prison from which he seemed unlikely to achieve any breakout. And just as he had felt abandoned when his father went to Ireland without telling him, so now Robert felt his inability to see a way forward for his father as a kind of abandonment. But his visit had only caused great distress to both sides. It was a discouragingly long way to travel for a nil return...

Very gradually things improved. The hospital's policy of gradual reintegration into community life suited someone like Malcolm who, if he was ever to return to the musical world, needed to make some contact with it, however small. When he was a little better that winter, therefore, he was enthusiastically encouraged to accept an invitation to take a rehearsal with the Northamptonshire Youth Orchestra, who were preparing performances of his two *Little Suites*.[27] Malcolm duly turned up by taxi at the Northampton Music School one Saturday morning where the two orchestras, each ninety strong, were to meet. Unfortunately there had been snow overnight and many of the students, who came from all over the county, struggled to get in on time. The County's Music Adviser at this period, Malcolm Tyler, has vivid memories of a difficult occasion:

Malcolm started rehearsing with a small group, and, as the rehearsal progressed, more and more players filed in with Malcolm getting more and more ratty. In the end he had

---

[24] Betty Hilliard, August 2003
[25] 7 October 1980
[26] August 2003
[27] The invitation came from Denis MacManson, a former orchestral violinist who knew Malcolm from his London playing days and was now teaching at the Northampton Music School.

a vast orchestra, as the two groups were amalgamated, and took a good rehearsal for a while.

But as he became more tired, he became more and more cross and at one stage stamped his foot in fury. At this my dog bounded across the hall and grabbed him by the bottom of his trousers. 'Help! Help!' he cried in horror as the orchestra collapsed in merriment. The rehearsal carried on but his temper was understandably furious by then so we quietly interrupted, suggesting it was time for a cup of coffee in the staffroom, whereupon, as if he was back in the film studios, he tapped the music stand and said 'Thanks very much, chaps! Go and have a smoke and we'll record in ten minutes!' It caused a sensation! But we managed to get him away into the staffroom, and, once there, he fell immediately asleep.[28]

Malcolm's life in this traumatic period was enriched by renewal of contact with Lizzie Witts. Malcolm had not wanted his old nanny to know that he was in St Andrew's but when she eventually heard, in the summer of 1980, she at once insisted that he should take a taxi across town and join her each week for Sunday lunch. It was nearly two years since Pappy's death and Lizzie, now ninety and frail, was still living at the little bungalow built for her and Pappy at the bottom of the Craigmore garden. She was delighted to be able to fuss over him again, just as she had done some fifty years before, and provide him with old favourites, like roast beef and Yorkshire pudding. She also made sure that Malcolm had a liberal supply of Guinness.

Another important mother figure emerged at this period – the remarkable Sally Charlton. Fifty-seven-years-old and therefore a year younger than Malcolm, Sally ran the nearby Crown and Cushion pub with her husband Brian. Winifred Sarah Charlton, as she was really called, has been erroneously described as a social worker who befriended Malcolm while working in St Andrew's. In fact she was not connected to St Andrew's at all; it was Malcolm's inability to keep away from alcohol which led to their meeting. One of his fellow patients was the Irish pop star Ruby Murray, who in the 1950s had become everyone's sweetheart with songs like 'Softly, Softly', but whose later life was blighted by alcoholism. She used to be visited in St Andrew's by Jack de Manio, whom Malcolm knew through Isobel, and the three would sometimes walk the short distance down to the Crown and Cushion, one of Northampton's several 'Irish' pubs in a strongly working class area of town.[29] Malcolm had paid his first visit to the Crown and Cushion back in December 1979, when he was genuinely not drinking, but now, some months later, a friendship with Sally materialised. Sally herself soon took the initiative, writing into Malcolm's diary two important dates lest he forget them. On one they went out together to see a local production of *Brigadoon* and on the other she drove him down to a pre-Christmas party at the Crown and Cushion. A new phase in Malcolm's life was beginning.

---

[28] August 2003
[29] 276 Wellingborough Road

*Malcolm's 61st birthday party, 1982, with Brian and Sally Charlton (right)*
*and Alan Poulton (centre)*

In 1981, the year when Malcolm's contact with Katherine and Isobel became less frequent, the friendship escalated dramatically. Sally's daughter, Pat Fisher, who used to work at her parents' pub, remembers a convivial club atmosphere:

> Quite a lot of patients, some of them famous, used to come down from St Andrew's, a little clique that would use the back room and Mum would take them all under her wing. They'd sit and read the paper and talk. Malcolm fitted very easily into this group.[30]

In January he was celebrating 'Sally's birthday' with a pub lunch, though her birthday was in July, when it was duly celebrated again; in April he was having 'a day out with Sally'; and between the May and December of 1981 his diary was full of her, with over sixty different mentions. She had become the single most important person in his life.

Sally was a large woman of around sixteen stone with a personality to match. She came from Gloucester where her family had run a fruit and vegetable shop in the covered market. She had a lively intelligence, had worked as a shorthand typist for Armstrong-Siddeley and in her leisure moments would pound her piano in the honky-tonk style of Russ Conway and Winifred Atwell. A cheerful, no-nonsense character with a steely determination yet a kind heart, she both dominated and fascinated Malcolm from the outset. 'For Malcolm it was a real joy to get into Sally's warm world,' says Martin Kingsbury. 'It was instrumental in his rehabilitation at that time.' Sally was not

---

[30] November 2003

a drinker herself, preferring to sit on her high stool by the bar with a glass of lemonade, and she made it very clear to Malcolm that their friendship involved his moderation. She had been unsuccessful on this score, however, with her husband Brian, who drank heavily. In an embattled marriage, which had little left to it but the shreds of convenience, she was the dominant partner, though Brian himself was a mountain of a man. 'She ran the place,' maintains Frank McQuade, one of their barmen. 'She had Brian where she wanted him! He was under her thumb!'[31]

Malcolm's friendship with the Charltons soon led to his joining the Cheyne Walk Club, of which both Sally and Brian were members. The Club had been founded in 1929, not far from the Arnolds' home in Cliftonville, when local businessmen purchased a Victorian house which had been built for one of the great Northampton shoemakers, Alfred Church. It was a lively meeting-place with a membership of around five hundred, and Malcolm was to make good use of its restaurant and oak-panelled lounge bar.

Sally and Brian would go on to the club most nights after the Crown and Cushion's closing time, but initially Sally took Malcolm there from St Andrew's on a Sunday evening. It at once proved a big boost to Malcolm's morale. John Holles, Chairman of the Cheyne Walk Club for twenty years, saw much of them:

> Sally was a lovely person, and she looked after Malcolm well. On Sunday evenings we would be playing dice and Malcolm used to watch us and laugh. He never played himself, nor did he play the piano either. Sometimes he used to come down in the middle of the week with Sally. She was a great gambler and would play the machines. I never saw him the worse for drink, for Sally kept him under control.[32]

Another important aspect of Malcolm's new life with Sally was her bungalow, the White House, acquired a few years earlier as an alternative to living above the Crown and Cushion. Situated to the east of St Andrew's in Rushmere Road,[33] it was within easy walking distance of the hospital and, as an encouragement to his self-sufficiency, she would urge Malcolm to walk across to it. 'He spent a lot of time down Rushmere Road,' says Sally's daughter Pat. 'For a time he seemed to be in Rushmere Road more than he was at St Andrew's.' Sally soon created a music room for Malcolm. 'You're a composer!' she would say to him quite roughly. 'Sit down and compose!' Eventually he did.

Sally's were not the only efforts being made to encourage Malcolm to write again. Isobel had been trying for some time to persuade St Andrew's that he would benefit from having his much prized clavichord with him, the damage done to it in Holmefield Court having now been repaired. In May 1981, when Malcolm was given an adjacent room in Thornton Ward for use as a study, the clavichord was brought up, together with his trumpet, music and books.

---

[31] August 2003
[32] June 2003

St Andrew's staff were pleased to see that in this period of increasing stability he was soon making use of the new room. The charge nurse believed he was working on 'something for the Queen in celebration of her Silver Jubilee', though perhaps this was a joke of Malcolm's for that Jubilee was long since past. Amongst the music and papers Isobel had brought up was the first movement of the Trumpet Concerto he had intended for John Wilbraham and his wife, the harpist Susan Drake.

The first movement, with its striking 'John and Susan' second subject, needed writing out in coherent form, which proved a good way of focusing his mind again on the act of creativity. Later on, while impressing the nurse with the news that he was writing for the Queen, he began the second movement.

Malcolm's memory of the writing of the Trumpet Concerto is a little different. In an interview with the Kettering *Evening Telegraph* seven years later he attributed his brief return to creativity to a commission from the Queen Mother rather than the urging of Sally Charlton, and suggested the whole work was started in Isham Ward (in the autumn of 1979):

> St Andrew's was terribly expensive and lovely if you just wanted to wander round in your pyjamas not writing music. The turning-point came when I had a letter from Sir David Willcocks, Head of the Royal College of Music, saying the Queen Mother had put £1,500 of her own money commissioning me to write a trumpet concerto to mark the college centenary. I had met the Queen Mother before – she's a lovely lady. It was such a gracious offer, how could I refuse? I started writing there and then, working from a table in Isham Ward.[34]

Internal evidence supports the suggestion that the bulk of the first movement was written earlier, during the time Malcolm was seeing a great deal of John Wilbraham in Belsize Park before the final breakdown. The scoring of the second and third movements is much sparer than the first, and the ideas simpler. The Eighth Symphony, written in Belsize Park in 1978, shows Malcolm displaying all his usual musical faculties. But these had left him by 1981 and were never to return. Malcolm's writing, which was often spare, now becomes so to such a degree as to give every indication of a brain which has suffered some damage and can no longer cope with the kind of complex contrapuntal thinking and rich textures that were so much part of his style.

Any such damage would be entirely consistent with forty years of alcohol abuse. But it could also be the side-effect of medical treatment. Further applications of ECT could have calmed psychotic episodes at the expense of certain cerebral processes. The current is passed through the frontal lobes of the brain where the creative faculties reside. St Andrew's was not unusual in reserving electrical treatment 'for some very distressed patients who do not respond to

[33] The White House, 48 Rushmere Road, is part of a 1930s housing development at the top of a steep hill leading down to the River Nene.
[34] 6 April 1989

drug treatment',[35] a category to which Malcolm certainly belonged in 1980.[36] There is also the possibility of the side-effect of lithium, first taken in Ireland. Lithium has been a great boon in radically altering the treatment of manic-depressive illness and allowing patients to lead reasonably normal lives by flattening out the highs and lows. Many artists, however, have resisted such medication, partly in the belief that its side effects can interfere with the clarity and speed of their thought or dampen down their levels of energy and emotion.[37]

The Trumpet Concerto's second movement is wafer-thin. Malcolm simply presents a slow waltz melody, which he has borrowed from his *Fantasy for Brass Band*,[38] and repeats it three times. On the first and third occasions he gives the theme to the muted trumpet and offers some quiet, unobtrusive background to it from the harp and strings. On the second occasion, while the soloist takes a rest, hushed strings play the melody before a solo flute takes over, with harp accompaniment. It is such a surprising and dangerously fragile concoction that in the concert hall it is highly effective, the poignancy of the theme tellingly exploited by the unlikely alliance of trumpet and harp.[39]

In September 1981 Malcolm made a triumphant return to the Albert Hall, where a selection of his Dances was played as part of the Last Night of the Proms.[40] In the musical world he had been for some years as good as dead. His appearance was a revelation to many. He went there with nurses from St Andrew's as unobtrusive supports. Back at the hospital everyone watched the television broadcast anxiously.

> We all knew he was going to be welcomed to the Prom and mention would be made of the fact that he had been out of action through illness. Dr Arnold had a reputation

---

[35] Foss and Trick: *St Andrew's Hospital* (Granta, 1989) p.290

[36] Malcolm's sister Ruth had experienced ECT during her times there. Many years later, in 1998, her son-in-law felt impelled to resist when he was encouraged to undergo ECT during his five months as a patient: 'Every day the consultant and nurses would tell me that I should have ECT treatment. It was terrific pressure. All I needed was peace and quiet and time to recover, but every day the drugs were changed, never less than four major tranquillisers. The effects of ECT are dreadful. People would come out like zombies. Whole chunks of their former life would disappear from them and sometimes they never came back. It can change people.' Terry Pullen, August 2003.

[37] Jamison: *Touched with Fire*, p.7

[38] The *Fantasy* was played at the Proms on 7 September 1981, and this seems likely to have prompted Malcolm to appropriate one melody for the writing of the second movement of the Trumpet Concerto.

[39] John Wallace, who gave the work's first performance, writes: 'The very spare minimalist writing with the bare minimum of harmonic support perhaps reflects Malcolm's lifelong obsession with Berlioz. The movement also has an angelic feel and perhaps there is some correlation between the angels twanging their harps whilst Gabriel blows his horn.' (July 2003)

[40] This was a very rare moment of recognition from the organisers of the Proms. Despite the acclamation of Malcolm and his work on this occasion not one composition of his would be played throughout the next five seasons.

for being rather unpredictable, eccentric and witty at times, and we wondered what he might say! The moment of reference to him flashed by and he acknowledged it and looked fine.

Those who had known him in his prime reacted differently. Betty Hilliard, watching in Dublin, was saddened:

> He seemed to have lost a lot of life. He was being told to stand up, it seemed.

Weeks later, Malcolm was in Manchester for a rehearsal and first British performance of the Eighth Symphony by the ever-supportive BBC Northern Symphony Orchestra and Charles Groves.[41] Two nurses from St Andrew's again accompanied Malcolm and, despite a 6.30 start, the day went well. Later Malcolm gratefully presented the charge nurse with a signed copy of the score.

Throughout this period Malcolm was benefiting from Sally Charlton's smiling blandishments and, towards the end of 1981, he was at the bungalow in Rushmere Road most days. At last the cries of 'You're a composer! Compose!' were finally rewarded, when Malcolm settled down in the White House to the last movement of his Trumpet Concerto. It is a highly effective movement with moments of characteristic invention and humour, but it does depend heavily on repetition and sequence and much unison writing.[42] Malcolm was particularly enthusiastic about its ending. 'The thing which exercised his mind most at the time of the first performance,' recalls John Wallace, 'was the different tonal effect on the last note where you have the orchestral trumpets on a high B flat concert and the solo trumpet on concert D a third higher. Malcolm was really pleased about this.'[43]

Malcolm completed the Trumpet Concerto in January 1982 and in the euphoria of the moment he and Sally, who were spending many evenings together in the Cheyne Walk Club, agreed it would make sense if he made arrangements to leave St Andrew's permanently for the White House. Pat Fisher, Sally's daughter, believes Malcolm took the initiative:

> Malcolm was more at Rushmere Road than St Andrew's, and he decided it would be a good idea if he lodged there. He was getting on with his life. He would come round for lunch and be a perfect gentleman. A gentle soul really. I deal with alcoholics professionally these days and I know it was only social drinking he got up to while my mother was around. She monitored it.

The frequently made assertion that Malcolm was released by the Hospital to go and live in a pub is untrue. For the whole of his first year away from the hospital he was based at Sally's bungalow. So far as St Andrew's were concerned, the Charltons' offer represented what might well be Malcolm's best (or, indeed, only) opportunity for establishing himself back in the outside world. The

---

[41] 2 October 1981, at the Royal Northern College of Music.
[42] Malcolm scores both this and the first movement for a large orchestra but he uses it very sparingly. There is a strong similarity between the Beckus motif and the rondo theme.
[43] July 2003

*The Crown and Cushion, Northampton*

*Malcolm outside Elgar's birthplace, with Brian Charlton and Alan Poulton*

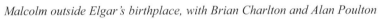

connection with the Crown and Cushion was a concern, but Malcolm was a voluntary patient and could do as he liked.

The Court of Protection similarly had no jurisdiction over where Malcolm lived. The fact that rent at the Charltons was less than his upkeep at St Andrew's was a recommendation. By contrast, Katherine and Isobel, who had heard very little of the Charltons up to then, were perplexed as to what to make of the sudden news, but neither was in a strong position to interfere. Katherine had recently had a second baby, while Isobel was exploring the possibilities of institutional help for Edward who, at nearly eighteen, was struggling to cope with all the pressures of life. The response of the Court's case worker, Graham Preston, to their enquiries was not particularly reassuring. He had recently visited Northampton, he said, and had a meeting with Malcolm, the Charltons, and representatives from St Andrew's:

> Whilst we all have misgivings about Malcolm's fitness to reside outside hospital, as he is an informal patient, the hospital authorities cannot stop his discharge and accordingly he will leave St Andrew's Hospital on Monday 1st March to reside with Mr and Mrs Charlton.

Brian Charlton, he declared, had given an undertaking that 'if he felt there was any deterioration in Malcolm's condition, Malcolm will immediately be referred back to St Andrew's'.[44] Isobel and Katherine for the moment kept their anxieties to themselves and hoped for the best.

Malcolm, meanwhile, was in good spirits. At the time of his official move to the bungalow he contacted several old friends. One of them was William Walton, who responded delightedly:[45]

> Dear Malcolm,
>
> What an UNEXPECTED pleasure to HEAR from you – and what is more to hear that you are WELL and feeling SO MUCH BETTER. I have tried to keep in touch but without success, except from Ruth Gipps who seemed to have heard about you, though not much.
>
> I look forward to receiving the CASSETTE of your 8th. How wonderful to have got as far as eight. I contemplate a third, but that is [as] far as I've got or likely to get! Keep well.
>
> With best love from us both,
> William

The letter was timely and so too the subsequent dispatch of the recording to Ischia, for just over a year later William Walton, perhaps the closest of all Malcolm's musical friends, was dead.

Another friend contacted at this period was Malcolm's former secretary, Dorothy Payne, who noted in her diary her delight at hearing from him after several years of silence:

---

[44] 23 February 1982
[45] 7 February 1982

> February 27th: Happy, happy! Malcolm telephoned and he is in Northampton, living with what seems a pleasant woman and her husband. He says he hasn't had a drink for six months and has lost four stone in weight. He says he attempted suicide again and Isobel put him in some form of chancery ...

The lie about his drinking and the confusion over who had invoked the Court of Protection both boded badly for the future. A muddled Malcolm, not knowing what was best for him and over-dependent on others, was dangerously vulnerable.

Shortly after his official release from hospital, Sally and Brian took him down to the Grand Hotel, Eastbourne, to spend a week with Dorothy Payne, who lived nearby.[46] Dorothy found Malcolm 'much thinner and a little grey, with the look of someone who has been through a lot'. He seemed 'a little child-like and simple', proudly putting on his D.Mus. robe and hat for her to admire. The Charltons and Malcolm visited Dorothy at her donkey farm the next day but he spent it 'hunched in a chair conversing in four-letter words and sulking if anyone else was spoken to'. On a return visit to the Grand Hotel she found Malcolm holding forth to dance band leader Henry Hall, and causing some embarrassment by singing to him his signature tune, 'Here's to the Next Time'. Later, however, he embarrassed her even more when 'he stripped off completely in his room and wandered about nude'. They met twice more for lunch but on each occasion Malcolm retired to bed immediately after the meal. Dorothy, though distressed at Malcolm's condition, was impressed by Sally's devotion to his cause. She also liked Brian Charlton, who reminded her of a Sergeant-Major. Sally she described as 'very fat with short, white hair standing up from her head'. She was wearing a 'tent-like' dress.

Dorothy's experiences were not untypical of Malcolm's see-saw existence, in which several good days might be followed by several bad. Pat Fisher shared Dorothy's admiration for the way her mother coped with it all. Malcolm, she says, was always quite fragile mentally. On the other hand she never saw him lose control.

> His depressive episodes were not very florid. His elated moods were nice, because he wasn't over-elated. He would have his depressed days when mum would chivvy him along as best she could. He would withdraw, not wanting to do anything, isolating himself, not being bothered with people. Yes, he could be irritable! But we all get like that!

Not everyone found him quite so easy. When Sally brought Malcolm down to London for working lunches with Faber, Sally Cavender, who had recently joined the publishing house, dreaded the occasions. They would generally lunch at the Italian Restaurant, Trattoria Verdi, which he used to call Joe Green's, and she still remembers her trepidation:

---

[46] From 28 March to 4 April, 1982

Though Malcolm was capable of great charm and was certainly charismatic, I found those twice-yearly meals unpleasant and very unsettling. He was clearly tormented. I was terrified by his face. His eyes were so dead. You didn't know if he would strike you. He was in fact over-friendly to me – as I think he was to most young women – and he was always ringing me up at that time if he felt amorous. When I took a young colleague to one of the lunches, his hand was soon fondling her knee! He was completely unpredictable. He sometimes could be funny but usually his humour was cruel. People would ask innocent questions and he would turn them round so as to make the questioner look stupid. Soon people stopped asking questions.[47]

Sally Cavender was impressed by the way Sally Charlton acted as a complete prop to Malcolm, organising him on the smallest points of detail, and how she tried very hard to counter his drinking. 'He used to try to get away from her, desperate for a drink.' On one occasion they were walking past a public lavatory, into which Malcolm suddenly darted. 'Watch out! Watch out!' cried Sally Charlton, galloping after him as fast as she could. 'He's trying to give me the slip!' There was, however, a certain inconsistency about what Malcolm was, and was not, allowed to drink. If he ordered a double brandy at the beginning of a meal, nobody seemed to mind. Malcolm's boisterous behaviour at some of those lunches was also kept under some kind of check by the presence of Donald Mitchell, whom he continued to respect. Sally Cavender remembers once asking Sally Charlton what she thought was wrong with him. 'His genius,' she replied. 'It's all to do with the moon!' Sally Charlton was optimistic that the Trumpet Concerto would reflect that genius. 'If this work is no good,' she announced, as she left the manuscript at Faber's, 'let me know and I'll tell him to do it again!'

It was during Sally's reign, in the topsy-turvy year of 1982, that Malcolm first met Alan Poulton, who was to become his Business Manager and work hard towards his re-emergence as a composer of stature. Alan Poulton was a young Sales Manager at British Oxygen and, as a devotee of Malcolm's work, had been in touch with Faber over the possibility of his providing a much-needed catalogue.

> I arranged to go over to Northampton and meet them in a pub. Malcolm was in the back room when I arrived, playing the piano. Brian Charlton was there too, and he led us back to the bungalow in Rushmere Road.[48]

Alan became a helpful, irregular visitor, supplying Sally with exactly what she was looking for, someone with a detailed knowledge of Malcolm's music, to act as an extra stimulus.

1982 was in many ways a good year for Malcolm, for, despite his uncertain moods, Sally boldly took him out and about. In addition to several concerts, for example, she organised visits to Cornwall (for the Gorsedd ceremonies), Grosvenor House (for the Ivor Novello Awards), Durham University (whose new

---

[47] July 2003
[48] September, 2003

Chancellor, Margot Fonteyn, was awarding Malcolm a Doctorate) and Ingrid Bergman's Memorial Service at St Martin's-in-the-Fields, where music from *The Inn of the Sixth Happiness* was played. They even went off as a family[49] for two weeks to Canada, where Sally's sister had settled. In between travels, Malcolm became godfather to Sally's grandson.

That he showed no interest in his own two grandsons distressed Katherine. Indeed in 1982 she struggled to make any contact with her father. At least one letter, which failed to elicit an answer, he claimed he had never received. Eventually Malcolm did come down to dinner at Highgate together with the Charltons and Mike, a Northampton taxi-driver who used to ferry them all around from time to time in Malcolm's Toyota Crown.[50] 'I just remember getting through it with no culinary or emotional disasters!' writes Katherine. 'Dad was OK but subdued. The whole occasion was extremely strange, though Sally and Brian Charlton were polite and friendly.'[51]

In November 1982 Katherine was told by the Court's Graham Preston that things were 'very sensitive' and her father was 'going through a period of being anti-family'. In his illness, he had swung against Katherine and Isobel again and was taking little interest in Edward and Robert. It would be disingenuous not to consider the possibility that Brian and Sally Charlton may have encouraged this anti-family swing. They had certainly made little effort to keep Malcolm's children or his ex-wife informed about him. At no stage, either before, during or after the trip to Canada, for example, had they contacted Katherine or Robert, who knew absolutely nothing of its occurrence. It is possible that they were simply taking the line of least resistance and going along with Malcolm's current inclinations. At all events, Katherine at this stage inadvertently exacerbated the situation by adopting the suggestion, given her by the Court of Protection's accountant, to apply for covenants for her children (which at the time could be set fully against tax). Malcolm, when approached, rejected Katherine's application out of hand, only to have the Court of Protection overrule him. Seeds of dissent had been sown.

Malcolm's mood of resentment towards his closest family could also have had some subconscious motivation from feelings of deep humiliation at his current condition and situation. To blame those closest to him, instead of himself, was a relief. There is an interesting parallel with the poet John Clare who in Victorian times had spent many years in St Andrew's and whose life Malcolm had studied.[52] One famous poem, 'I Am', written at St Andrew's, touches

---

[49] Brian did not in fact go. Malcolm was accompanied by Sally, Pat Fisher and Pat's daughter.
[50] Brian Charlton had made an endorsement deal, on Malcolm's behalf, with the local Toyota agency.
[51] April 2004
[52] He had set several of his poems to music back in 1955 in his *John Clare Cantata*.

significantly on the changed relationship, in Clare's mind at least, between himself and his closest family:

> I am: yet what I am none cares nor knows,
> My friends forsake me like a memory lost;
> I am the self-consumer of my woes,
> They rise and vanish an oblivious host.
> Shadows of life whose very soul is lost;
> And yet I am; I live, tho' I am tossed
>
> Into the nothingness of scorn and noise,
> Into the living sea of waking dream
> Where there is neither sense of life nor joys,
> But the huge shipwreck of my own esteem
> And all that's dear – even those I loved the best
> Are strange – nay, they are rather stranger than the rest …

Malcolm's shipwreck of self-esteem was worsened by the loss of creativity. 1982 was a disappointing year in that there was absolutely no follow-up to the Trumpet Concerto, although there were several projects to hand. Patric Dickinson's *Jericho*, for example, had been ignored for well over two years. Faber, meanwhile, were giving him every encouragement to start the series of sonatinas for brass instruments which he had been talking about ever since the completion of the Eighth Symphony. [53] Malcolm had also accepted a commission (and a cheque) from the Arts Council to provide a setting for the King's Singers of some lyrics by Patric Dickinson, entitled *Escape*. Nearly a year later, with its first performance planned and advertised, Martin Kingsbury was still urging him to start it.

> The King's Singers are anxiously awaiting their new piece … I do hope you will be able to provide them with a substantial part before they leave [on tour].[54]

But it never happened.[55] Some time later, Dickinson wrote to Alan Poulton:

> I had hoped that this commission meant he was really getting better … I've known Malcolm for ages, as a crony rather than intimately, and we've always got on splendidly. It was <u>awful</u> when I last saw him at a lunch Martin gave and he was simply not there … I had gathered from Martin that Malcolm was just <u>beginning</u> to write again, and then that he had been put on another course of medicine and wasn't …[56]

'Another course of medicine' suggests that Malcolm after he left St Andrew's was on a new regime of drugs of extra strength, to compensate the pressures of

---

[53] 'The idea of sonatinas for brass instruments with piano is a tremendously good one,' wrote Martin Kingsbury to him. 'Can I offer you strong encouragement to go ahead? How about the horn first?' (5 February 1982)

[54] 19 January 1983

[55] Even as late as February 1986, Simon Carrington of The King's Singers was querying with Martin Kingsbury: 'Has *Escape* died or is there still a chance? We're ready any time!'

[56] Undated but about late summer 1983

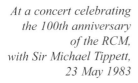

*At a concert celebrating the 100th anniversary of the RCM, with Sir Michael Tippett, 23 May 1983*

the outside world. 'Composition ideas flourished under Sally's regime!' comments Martin Kingsbury. Yet such was his medication, he was incapable of responding to them.

Despite the creative sterility, Sally's efforts on Malcolm's behalf throughout 1982 were truly remarkable, and all the more so in that she herself was no longer well. Dorothy Payne remembers that during the visit to Eastbourne, back in March, Sally had been complaining of stomach pains. In the later months of the year she made several visits to hospital, suffering from pains in her hip and, although she was well enough to travel with Malcolm to London for a Faber lunch just before Christmas, on Boxing Day she had what her daughter, Pat Fisher, believes was a stroke. The local doctor was called but 'it was the height of a 'flu epidemic and he was not sure quite from what she was suffering'. Sally's daughter then called a family friend, Dr Flynn, a hard-drinking Irish doctor and a leading member of the Cheyne Walk Club, who suggested Sally went in to St Matthew's Hospital, a small clinic near the Racecourse, for tests. That was on 2 January, and she was still having tests five days later when she suddenly died. She was fifty-nine. 'They said it was heart failure,' says Pat Fisher, 'but they also said there was an embolism on her hip that moved up.'[57]

Sally's death abruptly ended a special friendship which had lasted little more than two years. It was just ten months since Malcolm had officially left St Andrew's and moved into the bungalow. His presence as the Charltons' lodger had always been a somewhat odd one and now, under the sole care of Brian Charlton, it was even odder.

---

[57] November 2003

Brian Charlton was a man of many parts, though none of them particularly musical.[58] With his shaven head, heavy moustache and height of nearly six and a half feet, he presented the kind of tough façade needed to keep unruly Irish drinkers in order, but he also possessed a very charming side and was extremely well-spoken. He had served with the RAF[59] in the war and had afterwards been fluent enough linguistically to join the Special Investigation Branch in Italy. In peacetime he had been a police constable for a year[60] before transferring to industrial security and then Securicor. He was well qualified, therefore, to take direct control of security for Lord Spencer at Althorp. He had known Princess Diana since she was eight, acting as her 'minder' when she was at home right up to the moment of her engagement with Prince Charles in 1981. Such was the closeness of his relationship that the Princess not only showed off her engagement ring to the Charltons but took it off and let Sally's daughter try it on. Concurrently with his job at Althorp the indefatigable Brian had run the King's Head pub in nearby Northampton, before in 1972 taking over the Crown and Cushion.

At first little in Malcolm's routine altered. The regular excursions to concerts continued under the new regime, and only a few weeks after Sally's death Malcolm was sitting with Brian Charlton, Alan Poulton and Mike the chauffeur in a box at the Albert Hall, as John Wallace gave the first performance of the Trumpet Concerto. It was a big occasion, a celebration of the Royal College of Music's centenary, with the college orchestra conducted by Sir Alexander Gibson. But it must have been particularly saddening for Malcolm that the two people who had so inspired the concerto, John Wilbraham and Sally Charlton, were both missing.[61] Malcolm, nonetheless, was on top form. 'On the first performance night,' remembers John Wallace, 'we had great fun and he was in tremendously high spirits.' John Wallace has always found Malcolm 'strangely mischievous' whenever they meet, as if at the sight of his trumpet he is taken back to his own playing days. 'He seems to have an urge to be really naughty and do outrageous things!' At the same time there have usually been flashes of Malcolm's 'really quite disturbing' dark and acerbic side.

That side, however, was not particularly in evidence in these early public forays. Alan Poulton, who master-minded many of them, believes Malcolm's illness was far less in evidence than has sometimes been suggested:

---

[58] As a child his instrument was the banjolele.

[59] As a flight engineer he had flown in Liberators on many operations, notably over Tunis, El Alamein and Sicily.

[60] Before falling out with his Commissioner.

[61] John Wilbraham, who was engaged to play the concerto, had to withdraw, as he was going though a personal crisis, from which, happily, he would re-emerge. John Wallace reckons Wilbraham had spent the best part of twenty years urging Malcolm to write a trumpet concerto.

Most people think Malcolm was unconventional in this period, and couldn't be taken anywhere. This wasn't true. He was an absolute gent for most of the time. It was a rehabilitation for him to a certain extent, getting back into the swing of things in London. He was very generous with people. You didn't get much acid tongue.[62]

This was certainly true when, four months after the Trumpet Concerto's première, Malcolm returned to the Albert Hall with Brian and Alan, this time for the Royal College of Music's Centenary Charter concert, attended by Prince Charles and Princess Diana. They stayed overnight at the Kensington Palace Hotel where, says Alan, 'we had a very convivial time'. The afternoon concert proved a great success, Malcolm meeting John Lill and Julian Lloyd Webber again, both of whom asked him for new works.

In the interval he and Alan Poulton participated in a small royal reception along with David Willcocks, Michael Tippett and John Pritchard. Alan Poulton remembers Malcolm's behaviour as 'absolutely immaculate':

He went forward and was presented to the royal party in the mauve velvet dinner jacket we had dressed him in and then he introduced me. We had a long conversation with the Prince about his cello playing, talking of various pieces that had been written for him. The only piece he remembered was the one in which he played the cello in one hand and the trumpet in the other. The Princess was an absolute gem. She got on really well with Malcolm. She was just about to go off on a tour, she said, and was dreading it! She talked about gardening a lot of the time. Just before going back into the concert, which she was probably finding hard going, she said to Malcolm 'Where are you sitting?'

'Just below you, I think,' he replied.

'Then watch out!' she said. 'I might throw some peanuts at you!'

Afterwards they went across to the reception at the College, where two queues of guests had formed, one to meet Charles, the other Diana. When Malcolm reached Diana he introduced her to Althorp's former head of security, Brian Charlton. The Princess was amazed. 'Good God! What are *you* doing here?' she cried, adjusting his bow tie and chatting happily to him, to the growing frustration of the waiting queue.

Another expedition, with Mike-the-Driver at the wheel, took Malcolm, Brian and Alan, to Worcestershire and a concert at Ludlow School. A photograph taken outside Elgar's birthplace at Broadheath shows Malcolm looking plump and well. Malcolm was fascinated to discover in the museum a score of *Falstaff* used by Elgar when he conducted the first performance. 'He always used engraved scores at first performances,' he declared in awe, 'such was his confidence.' To his delight he discovered the score had been signed by all the members of the London Symphony Orchestra including Ernest Hall, about whom he had many memories:

[2] September 2003

There is a famous passage in the last movement of Elgar's Second Symphony where the composer has written a top B natural. One day at rehearsal Hall held the note over to the next bar with thrilling effect, and Elgar was so delighted he gave him permission to do that every time. I always used to hold it over when I played the work.[63]

Since Sally's demise Malcolm was drinking heavily again, whenever he had the money, spending more time in the Crown and Cushion than formerly and finding Brian more indulgent than Sally. He continued living in the bungalow, however, even when Brian Charlton suddenly remarried. This marriage, only four months after Sally's death, caused a considerable amount of local gossip. Brian was so obviously besotted with Mary Clancy, a lively Irish lady with curly, ginger hair, twenty years Brian's junior, that the wildest of rumours were circulating about Sally. Mary had been the apple of Brian's eye for some time. He had taken her, for example, to the Albert Hall concerts, though she had stayed in the background. Pat Fisher was so distressed at her father's hasty remarriage that she stopped working at the Crown and Cushion and for a long time had nothing more to do with him:

> My father was a womaniser and an alcoholic. You'd meet Dad and say 'What a charming, charming man!' Yet when he left us, it was with big problems. It was an awful time in our lives, really.

The wedding took place at the Northampton Town Hall Registry Office with Malcolm acting as Brian's best man.[64] A party followed at the Cheyne Walk Club in the course of which Bill Flynn somehow managed to pour a glass of brandy over Mary's head.

Brian Charlton in old age felt he had been misrepresented, believing in particular that he had done a great deal for Malcolm:

> I helped extract Malcolm from St Andrew's. It was a difficult process but Sally and I eventually persuaded them that we had a satisfactory option for him. Sally and I later encouraged him to write the Trumpet Concerto. I bought a piano for the Crown and Cushion as a present for Malcolm. He at once complained to me! 'That's no good! It must be properly tuned!' So we got it tuned, and he would play a lot of jazz on it, and, if he was pensive, the theme from *Dr Zhivago*. I really tried hard to give him a bit of a life.[65]

In all the confusion it was a timely move in July 1983 when the Court of Protection, in consultation with Katherine and Isobel as well as Malcolm, appointed Alan Poulton as his Business Manager. It gave his publishers welcome help in promoting the music at a most difficult period, and Alan's monthly bulletins, outlining his and their latest initiatives, gave a sense of communal purpose to the cause. Amongst the many items on the first bulletin, of September 1983, was the decision to send a copy of Patric Dickinson's *Jericho* to Malcolm.

---

[63] *Music & Musicians*, October 1986
[64] 11 May 1983
[65] October 2003

*Malcolm at Brian and Mary Charlton's wedding, Northampton,*
*with two guests (first left and fourth left)*

It was a comparatively insignificant item, yet it said a great deal, for it was four years now since Julian Elloway had first taken *Jericho* to him in St Andrew's. There was also mention in the bulletin of a letter from David Ellis challenging Malcolm to complete a short set of variations on a ground bass. Alan Poulton was bringing to his task large quantities of youthful vitality, but no amount of that admirable quality was going to disguise the fact that Malcolm could no longer write music and would not do so in the foreseeable future.

Some days it was quite hard to understand why this was so. Malcolm looked well. He could still be the life and soul of any party if he tried. But for all the glowing banter and anecdotes produced on the good days, he was not functioning at full intellectual capacity. From time to time, for example, he would ring up David Ellis in Manchester and David would often struggle at first to understand 'the strange, ethereal, mumbled voice' at the other end of the line. Then, for a while, there would be the familiar banter: 'Is that the bloody Scowse composer? Now look here, bloody Scowse composer...!' Malcolm would also usually ask after Cecily, his Manchester goddess, a particularly attractive sub-principal second violin in the BBC Northern Orchestra. But, when it came to it, he could not really hold a proper conversation: 'He struggled to have logical continuations,' remembers David. 'There would also be constant repetitions, questions already answered but asked again.'

Although Malcolm understandably enjoyed going to concerts and functions and on the whole gained much benefit from the experience, it was also true that the more he was paraded in public, the more vulnerable he was to making the wrong headlines or attracting the attention of those who might exploit him. By the summer of 1983 Katherine was worried enough to contact Dr Ferguson, a consultant at St Andrew's, to air her concerns. There seemed, she thought, an alarming lack of legal structure and protection in Malcolm's current situation. To whom was Brian Charlton answerable? By whom was he appointed as her father's guardian? What was the position about the administering of the daily drugs? Unfortunately, as Dr Ferguson's reply showed, there was no-one in a position of legal authority to ask these questions, let alone answer them. The state system of care utterly failed to embrace cases like Malcolm's. The letter also reveals the disturbing fact that, unknown to his family, Malcolm had suffered another psychotic episode that summer and briefly returned to St Andrew's:

> As you say, all of us are somewhat uneasy about the situation … As you know, Mr Charlton does bring your father very reluctantly to see me, and the visits, I think, have very little value in that it merely allows your father to be rude about his stay in hospital and Mr Charlton rather blandly reassuring that Dr Arnold is not drinking and seems happy and settled. Certainly, he looks all the happier having gained a considerable amount of weight, but I strongly suspect that he is indeed drinking again.
>
> I have reinforced to Mr Charlton each time I see him that it is entirely possible that Dr Arnold will have a further mood-type disorder of the excited type and, like the last time, he will have to bring him back to hospital so that it is absolutely essential that he takes the medication I prescribed …[66]

The problem all along for the doctors was that Malcolm could do as he liked. In the vital matter of medication Malcolm had become a patient of his friend Dr Bill Flynn. Often to be seen at the Cheyne Walk Club, Dr Flynn was full of delightful Irish blarney but a drinker of brandy in triples. Dr Ferguson seems not to have heard of him:

> The contact with his GP is, of course, unfortunately much reduced since he changed to Dr Flynn, whom I do not know and with whom I have had no exchange of correspondence. I can only hope Dr Flynn is being sensibly co-operative in continuing to provide Dr Arnold with the medication i.e. Priadel and Pimozide, which he should be taking …

Dr Ferguson was in a frustratingly helpless position, only able to put the best face on things and hope for a happy outcome:

> Although I may feel uneasy about the kind of support he is getting, I think there is little doubt that the quality of his life has improved since leaving Thornton Ward, and I console myself that this perhaps is the most important issue. Providing the Court of Protection can continue to exercise good control over financial matters, one hopes that no nasty abuse of your father's vulnerable position takes place …

---

[66] 9 August 1983

He ended with the news that one of the hospital's social workers would be visiting Malcolm shortly, although he held out little hope for this particular mission:

> She will find it difficult, I think, to penetrate the reassurances from both Dr Arnold and Mr Charlton.

Katherine also wrote to the Court of Protection, but found even less anxiety there. Graham Preston, the Court's case worker, had been down to Northampton, met Malcolm 'together with Mr and the new Mrs Charlton' and had suffered the fate Dr Ferguson anticipated for his social worker. Malcolm was 'very alert, well dressed, clean and tidy and was able to carry on a very sensible discussion.' Unlike Dr Ferguson, Graham Preston was totally taken in on the subject of drink:

> Whilst I was in Northampton I was in your father's company for about four hours during which time apart from a sip of a glass of wine, he drank no alcohol.

There was seeming reassurance on the subject of accommodation:

> I also informed your father that if he felt at any time he would like to leave the care of Mr and Mrs Charlton, the Court were prepared to purchase another property for him and set him up with a companion/housekeeper, but the only reply I received was that he was happy with the Charltons. I also discussed the same matter with Mr Charlton and again they seemed quite satisfied with him staying there.

But, as Katherine was about to discover, there was a subtext to the last paragraph and indeed the whole letter, for, earlier that year, just around the time of the death of Sally, Malcolm had made an application to the Court of Protection to change his will. It was no wonder that Dr Ferguson was somewhat uneasy about the situation and the kind of support Malcolm was getting, for that January he had been called upon to say whether or not Malcolm was able to make proper judgement on the changing of a will and had testified in the affirmative.[67] The new will gave over Malcolm's entire estate to Brian Charlton. Graham Preston's visit to Northampton, when Malcolm only sipped a glass of wine and Brian and Mary Charlton agreed to keep him on as their lodger, was the occasion when the new will was finalised.

Katherine, thoroughly alarmed by the naïvety of Graham Preston's letter and the situation developing in Northampton, travelled up there in early September. She did not yet know that she had been disinherited, nor would she have guessed, for (as she wrote to Graham Preston) she was received by her father in a friendly fashion. Preston replied in somewhat stilted tones:

---

[67] 'In my professional opinion based on two years' knowledge of him I would say that he is able to make judgement about personal matters as alterations in his will with clarity and self awareness. In other words, although he had problems of mood stability and has some limitations in the scope of his thinking ability, this does not take the form of insanity or unsoundness of mind which would in my opinion invalidate the legality of his decisions in any testamentary capacity.' (17 January 1983)

I was pleased to learn you had lunch with your father, and which was apparently a success. Any reconciliation between you will be to his advantage and I hope this will be the first meeting of many.

Perhaps he was feeling a little uncomfortable at the situation. But that is to suggest that the case worker actually either considered or cared about the long-term damage the disinheritance of Malcolm's three children could do to their relationship with their father. He had followed the letter of the law, spent four hours in Northampton and had been convinced by that visit and the psychiatrist's report from St Andrew's that Malcolm's request should be supported. It was a poor decision. It is clear that in September 1983 the Court failed to cope with a difficult situation, and did not give Malcolm the protection it was its business to provide. The repercussions of this decision were to reverberate between Malcolm and Katherine for the next twenty years.[68]

Quite why Malcolm wanted to change his will in favour of Brian Charlton will probably always be something of a mystery. Circumstantial evidence certainly suggests pressure could have been exerted upon him. But this might be wrong. While in St Andrew's Malcolm had formed a very strong friendship with a fellow patient with similar problems to his own. Elizabeth remained his 'girl-friend' for some time afterwards, Malcolm openly declaring at one stage that he was going to leave everything to her. And later on, the will in favour of Brian was altered and she, for a time, became a considerable beneficiary. It would seem, therefore, that Malcolm, in frustration at his current position of weakness, was getting his own back as best he could, emphasising one position of strength which still existed. He was again the mischievous pied piper, calling the tune, paying for the drinks, seeing how people responded to his generosity and lack of it. In his muddled state he would not have properly grasped the traumas he could be causing his children when they came to hear of this hurtful act of rejection.

That November Katherine eventually learnt that her father had changed his will. A new case worker, Bob Angel, had by now taken over and he, of course, refused to divulge its contents.[69] Wounded and frustrated, Katherine turned inwards to the family her father had seemingly rejected. By 1984 she had three small children, the eldest only five. She and Isobel also had the worry of Edward, now nearly twenty and being looked after in a home in Kent. Isobel was also now teaching in Hampstead. They had their own lives to lead, and though they

---

[68] Robert, further away from events, never felt party to any 'family rift', and he was never told at the time of the will change. 'I continued to be rung by Dad occasionally, often very awkward phonecalls to receive. Neither the Court nor the Charltons were in touch with me. The Charltons were never in touch with me about anything. But a person's will is his own affair. I have found Dad able to make bad decisions for years (usually with the help of drink), so I see my being disinherited at this time as one of these. It was his business.' (April 2004)

[69] 'It is not the practice of the Court to disclose a patient's will,' wrote Bob Angel to Katherine, 'and I am therefore unable to supply a copy.' (28 November 1983)

*Receiving the Fellowship of the RCM from the Queen Mother, November 1983*

*Ludlow, March 1983, two months after the death of Sally Charlton*

grieved for Malcolm in his solitariness and vulnerability, they struggled to know quite what they could do, while his back was turned so resolutely against them.

Malcolm was now struggling in Northampton. By the end of September, with the will signed in favour of Brian, Malcolm and the Charltons began falling out. Alan Poulton mentioned this in a letter to Katherine:

> I hear from Brian that recently things are getting a bit strained at the White House. It could be that his drugs are having an adverse effect on him, and I believe Brian is going to have a quiet word with his GP.[70]

Things were, indeed, strained. Mary had started married life by being very kind to Malcolm. She was amused by him and tolerant.

> He was no problem really – a bit awkward at times when he had had too many Guinnesses. He would pinch women's bums. 'Malcolm, you don't do that to the other 'women!' I told him. 'I like doing that!' he said.[71]

But he was not proving an easy lodger, the excessive drinking often leading to vomiting as well as belligerent behaviour. So four months into the marriage Mary told Brian that she wanted him out of the bungalow. He was given, instead, a small back room on the upper floor of the Crown and Cushion. Malcolm reacted with predictable anger. Violence, fuelled by drink, quickly escalated. Brian, in self-defence, resorted to the kind of strong-arm tactics he usually reserved for out-and-out trouble-makers in the pub, quickly asserting his authority with his massive physical presence.[72] Whenever Malcolm was difficult, he was locked in his room, to which he would sometimes respond by urinating out of the window and trashing it in the style of Holmefield Court. On one occasion he even set fire to it. A relationship which had promised a great deal had disintegrated appallingly. Alcohol was largely to blame.

For his final eight months at the Crown and Cushion Malcolm lived two lives. His private life was an ever-developing crisis. His professional life, by contrast, apart from the inability to write, offered some fulfilment. And for several months he kept the two departments so rigidly apart that it was extremely hard for people in one sector to understand what was going on in the other.

Alan Poulton, keen to promote Malcolm in public, continued to work with Brian Charlton to organise prestigious excursions, and, as outward appearances were important, usually only the best hotels and restaurants were involved. So Malcolm on occasions continued to re-sample the good life. For the British Film Institute's Jubilee Banquet at the Guildhall,[73] he and Alan stayed at the Savile Club:

---

[70] 24 September 1983
[71] April 2004
[72] 'He was a big guy,' says Alan Poulton. 'My kids were fascinated by a guy that size! He was enormous. You felt very safe when you were with him.' (August 2003)
[73] 5 October

Most times Malcolm and I did London, we stayed at the Savile. Mike drove us from the Savile Club to the dinner. We drew up and the lights were flashing, for all the stars were there. A flunkey opened the door and down a red carpet we went …

This particular event featured a televised champagne reception for seven hundred, as well as the dinner, the showing of a film and speeches.

Prince Charles was there and Malcolm had a quick word with him. It was marvellous because Malcolm was able to meet up with people like the Attenboroughs and a lot of guys he'd done films with. Sam Spiegel, for instance. He had a bit of a chat with Larry Adler. Tom Courteney was there, Anthony Hopkins, Joan Plowright… Malcolm got on fine. He probably wouldn't have been comfortable on his own but he was fine with me alongside. He liked talking to people. Eventually Mike came up to tell us the car was outside. Nothing could have been simpler. Back to the Savile. A late breakfast and then Mike drove him home to Northampton.

In late November they were in London again, staying at the Kensington Palace Hotel this time because of its proximity to the Royal College of Music, where at the President's Concert the Queen Mother, the President, bestowed a Fellowship on Malcolm. Two fellow recipients had had works written for them by Malcolm in recent years, James Galway and Philip Jones.

Alan Poulton, still only vaguely aware that all was not well at the Crown and Cushion, was now working hard on the comprehensive Catalogue of Malcolm's music which Faber would publish in 1986. This had the advantage of their taking more time away together. Shortly before Christmas the two of them stayed at the Savile[74] and Malcolm celebrated the New Year of 1984 with Alan and his family at the Overton Grange Hotel, Ludlow. Alan also arranged visits to old friends like Julian Bream.[75]

Early in 1984 came the most public foray of all, Malcolm's first reappearance on television. Sheridan Morley was doing a series of interviews for BBC East, networked onto BBC2, and Mike Purton, his producer, having already organised several writers and painters for Sheridan Morley, now wanted a suitable composer. His film editor, Karen Heward, who had known Malcolm from her days as a soundtrack layer on feature films, having worked with him on a whole raft of successes from *Kwai* to *Whistle Down the Wind,* suggested she might be able to track him down.[76] It was a selfless offer, because, as a young girl in films, she had found Malcolm's overbearing attitude to women intolerable. Nonetheless, she had volunteered to find him and find him she did:

---

[74] They attended a Gala Christmas concert at the Royal Festival Hall, in which the London Gabrieli Brass Ensemble celebrated the RNLI's 160th birthday. The Ensemble included *The Padstow Lifeboat* specially arranged for them by Alan Civil.

[75] 'It was wonderful seeing Malcolm again after such a long time', Julian wrote to Alan on 27 September 1983, 'far too long in fact, and he seemed in fine form.'

[76] Karen Heward visited Northampton on October 22. Malcolm had great admiration for Karen's father, the conductor Leslie Heward, and she asked him to write a short memoir of him. Malcolm agreed to do so, but it was beyond him.

Brian Charlton frightened the life out of me! And I felt Malcolm was frightened of him too. I was so worried about it that I phoned him from time to time to check up on him. 'Are you all right, Malcolm?' 'Yes,' would come the rather reluctant reply.[77]

Another visit soon followed, Mike Purton this time having an exploratory lunch with Malcolm, Brian, Mary and Alan at the Cheyne Walk Club.

> I discovered Malcolm had the most extraordinary memories. He knew everybody in the musical world and cinema and had a fantastic tale to tell and could, on a good day, tell it. But he was a marginal case as far as doing television was concerned. I didn't think he would cope with the pressures of a studio recording. I had to find somewhere where time would not be an issue ...[78]

The lunch proved memorable for one extra reason:

> I was counting Mary's considerable number of vodkas during that lunch! Fortunately the BBC was paying for it!

Mike Purton, following up the idea, hired a remote hotel in Norfolk, Bunwell Manor, for the shooting. In late February Alan Poulton drove Malcolm across to Norfolk, meeting up at the hotel for dinner with Sheridan Morley, Mike Purton, Karen Heward, the cameraman and sound technician. There could not have been a more homely atmosphere and Malcolm felt comfortable within it.

> The next morning we gently eased him into the shooting. Sheridan was so good, really clued up as always, yet highly sensitive to the situation. The day was carefully structured. We talked through each coming section just before we did it. Malcolm took it all on board. He was in a pretty bad way though. There were some slight *non sequiturs* and, sometimes, too big a jump in his thoughts. Even after twenty years, watching it, I have anxieties! Is he going to make it? He always did, remarkably! And he came out with some *bon mots* as well! The stories came trotting out. I think he knew it was important, his chance to begin to make his way back. And he took it. We didn't have a lot of retakes. It was fantastic, really.

The following day they drove out to do some location filming at Burgh Castle, where Nan's grandfather, the Revd. Thomas Hawes, had been Rector.[79] Malcolm was not equipped for the outdoors, borrowing Alan's white sweater and Mike's anorak before posing beside his grandfather's grave (triumphantly discovered, after a long search, by the sound technician) and later, at Breydon Water. Mike Purton wanted a shot of Malcolm 'writing' music. Alan accordingly found some manuscript paper on which Malcolm obligingly wrote out the opening bars of his First Symphony.

It was a highly successful film, with the Sarabande from *Solitaire* evocatively used with moody location shots by Breydon Water. Malcolm's quietly authoritative tones are ideal for television and lull the critical faculties. 'I did *all* his films,' he says cheerfully of David Lean, when in fact he did three. But he doesn't miss

---

[77] April 2004
[78] August, 2003
[79] He had been Chaplain of New College, Oxford for some years before retiring in Norfolk.

the punch line: 'I used to be known as Master of the Lean's music!' He blithely ignores the past five years, during which only the Trumpet Concerto had been completed, with the assertion 'I have never stopped writing concert music'. But again, the punch line is good: 'It's a life sentence with hard labour.' He rambles delightfully. Asked how the Oscar came about for *The Bridge On The River Kwai*, he replies:

> I went over to Paris to see it. It was finished in Paris. I thought it was a wonderful film. It's an anti-war film but Sam Spiegel, the producer, took it to Russia and they said 'It's an imperialist film' and wouldn't show it!

And, as always, Malcolm tries hard to please. Asked about the best conductors he played under, he at once brackets Karen's father, Leslie Heward, with Beecham, brazenly dubbing him 'the greatest British conductor who's ever lived'.

In public, therefore, Malcolm was beginning a modest comeback, always looked smart and lived in some style. It was all such a contrast to the last, traumatic months in the pub. John Holles of the Cheyne Walk Club believes 'the trouble started some time back':

> I think it is possible Malcolm got knocked about a bit. He was certainly under the thumb of Brian Charlton and I don't think we saw too much of him at the Cheyne Walk Club while all that was going on.

Frank McQuade was around at the most difficult time, the early months of 1984.[80] He tells lurid tales of drunken confrontation. No doubt it was intermittent rather than continual, but there were times when Malcolm was subjected to physical and mental abuse.

> When I'd come in at 7.30 in the morning to clear up, I'd sometimes find Malcolm going through the ash-trays collecting stubs. 'Why don't you buy your own?' I asked. 'He won't give me any money,' he replied. He was given his bare meals, five small cigarillos and that was that. He was a prisoner.
>
> One day I bought him some small cigars. Brian came in when he was smoking. 'Have you been at the till?' he shouted. 'No, I bought them for him,' I said. He nodded angrily at Malcolm. 'You get upstairs!' Malcolm at once obeyed, at the double.
>
> One day Malcolm had a great bloody eye. 'Where did you get that?' I asked. 'I was hungry last night,' he said, 'and came downstairs and opened the fridge. Brian caught me and beat me up.' Brian would have been drunk at the time, of course, and when he came down the next morning, he would not have remembered what had happened.[81]

Frank McQuade is full of stories of Malcolm playing the piano which Brian had bought for him in happier times. Some are cheerful ones. On occasion Malcolm would take Frank's little daughter on his lap and try to teach her how to play.

---

[80] During this period (February to April) Malcolm did attend many performances of his works and enjoyed meeting the players.

[81] August 2003

'I'm going to marry you, Michala, when you grow up!' he'd cry.

'Oh no you're not!' responded Michala's mother, hurriedly.

There were also less happy stories of Malcolm relentlessly playing for drinks, like old Eileen Braid at Goggins.

> He would often play his own music, cigar in mouth, everyone buying him a drink. He'd do anything for a drink. Sometimes of course it got rowdy. 'Knees up, Mother Brown' and so on! Brian didn't like that. He would enter at a rowdy time and shout 'Malcolm!' It would all go quiet. Malcolm would shut the lid on the piano and run upstairs.

Frank McQuade thought Malcolm essentially lonely, for all his outbursts of gaiety, a man of many acquaintances but few close friends.

The troubles at the Crown and Cushion came to a head towards the end of May 1984, when Malcolm and Brian were involved in a wild argument, in the course of which Malcolm is said to have accused Brian of killing Sally. He also had let it be known that he was contemplating moving elsewhere. He was thrown out onto the pavement and told not to darken the doors of the pub again. Once before Malcolm had had the door shut angrily in his face in Northampton. On that occasion his sister Ruth was living not far away, so his immediate problems were solved. This time, as he rose shakily to his feet on the busy pavement, he was not quite so certain in which direction to turn. Getting a taxi was out of the question because he had no money.

He would avoid St Andrew's, he decided, so he set off down the Wellingborough Road, past Stimpson Avenue, where Pappy and Nan had lived early in their marriage, before the move to Fairview. He walked painfully on, past Palmerston Road, which he had known well in the days of Frank Tomkins, musical instrument makers. A homing instinct took him down to the Billing Road, past the end of Cliftonville, with its thoughts of Fairview, and the little school which he had attempted to disrupt in the days of the two Miss Stricklands. He was passing the General Hospital and gathering his wits together.

Somehow succeeding in crossing the busy Cheyne Walk without being run over, he made his way to the Club's entrance. There, in front of him, in the hall was the welcome sight of Dr Bill Flynn, smiling concernedly. A triple brandy was quickly thrust into his bruised and shaking hand.

'Bill,' said Malcolm slowly. 'I think I'm in trouble.'

# 17
# Norfolk and the Ninth
## Bunwell and Wymondham, 1984-86

O NLY FOUR DAYS after stumbling into the Cheyne Walk Club, Malcolm was sitting quietly in the passenger seat of a Vauxhall Cavalier being driven away from Northampton to Norfolk. The last of the four main phases of Malcolm's life was about to begin. His first twenty years he had spent largely in Northampton, the next twenty in London, and the third on a series of travels from Surrey to Cornwall, Ireland, Belsize Park and finally back to Northampton. Now, as he left behind him the familiar streets of his birthplace, he could shed painful memories of Pappy and Craigmore and start to clear his mind of the puzzling last five years. He was bound for Norfolk and whatever that might hold, his future suddenly dependent on a new companion, a trained chef and hairdresser of thirty-four, Anthony Day.

It had been an exciting four days. On Malcolm's arrival at the Cheyne Walk Club, Dr Flynn had quickly summoned his friend John Holles, the Club Chairman. They agreed that there was no future for Malcolm at the Crown and Cushion and therefore booked him into the nearby Saxon Inn,[1] Holles lending him pyjamas and several changes of clothing. It was a Friday evening, so Holles was able to keep an eye on Malcolm throughout the weekend, giving him lunch at his farm outside Northampton. Malcolm was delighted to be in a smart hotel and was soon running up large bills on credit. John Holles thought his mood euphoric:

> Malcolm had had a rough ride for some time, and it was as if he had been let out of prison! Bill Flynn, who visited him each evening to see he was all right, said he'd never seen him so happy! I think he'd have still been there if they'd left him![2]

At the end of an anxious weekend John Holles was pleased to discover that Malcolm's Business Manager, Alan Poulton, had a possible solution to the problem of his next move. When, three months earlier, Alan Poulton had taken Malcolm to Norfolk for Mike Purton's film, Malcolm had enjoyed himself so much that he subsequently raised the possibility of moving there. Shortly after-wards, therefore, Alan had taken him back to Norfolk, where they met up with

---

[1] Today called The Moat House, an eight-storey modern hotel in the centre of town.
[2] June 2003

*Anthony Day*

Mike Purton and searched for a flat in Norwich. Purton had brought with him Anthony Day, a close neighbour from Bunwell village, who had said he might be able to look after Malcolm for a trial period, were he to come to Norfolk. So that Sunday night Alan rang up Anthony Day, alerting him to Malcolm's crisis. 'I was actually baby-sitting for Mike Purton when I got the call,' remembers Anthony, 'so the next day I got up and drove to Northampton.'[3]

Anthony had been looking for a new challenge since ending a nine-month stint as a barber on the *QE2* the previous January. Having left school at fourteen to train as a chef, he had enjoyed a wide variety of jobs. For two and a half years he was a steward on the *Oriana*; he also ran two different supermarkets, where he relished the hard work:

> We had opened every day apart from Christmas Day and I did virtually all of the serving – my friend Peter did the stock-room – I used to design and set all the windows up, buy all the fruit in the morning from the market. You start at six and close at six, after which you have to cash up …

He had worked as a companion once before, looking after Robert Strauss, an extremely rich stockbroker, for four and a half years. Strauss was in his seventies and in remission from serious illness. Anthony tended his every need, brightened up his life and became the most valued member of a staff of twenty-seven at Stonehurst, the Strauss estate in Ardingly. He much enjoyed this job, despite its very full-time nature and the sudden conclusion imposed on it by the Strauss family not long before the stockbroker's death.[4] For Anthony the whole experience was in itself an education, and he derived much pleasure from the foreign travel, the expert initiation into the stock market and an informed introduction to classical music. When Robert Strauss's increased illness led to loss of mobility, Anthony also acquired considerable nursing skills.

Malcolm must have experienced some serious mood change shortly before Anthony's arrival in Northampton, for although John Holles remembers Malcolm having 'the time of his life' in the Saxon, Anthony was confronted by something very different:

> I asked for Malcolm's room and was taken up. They knocked on the door. He wouldn't open it. So they opened it with a key. I was totally amazed. He was sitting on the floor in a corner of the room, looking absolutely terrified. He was bruised and he looked a terrified mess.

Surprised to discover that Malcolm had no possessions, Anthony escorted him to the Cheyne Walk Club, left him there, and drove on to the Crown and Cushion, where he found Brian and Mary Charlton behind the bar:

---

[3] July 2003

[4] Robert Strauss, he learned later, had left him a very large sum in his will providing he was with him at the time of his death. It gave a new significance to his being told he had three days to leave or Robert was going to be put in a home and his job would be finished.

They were not very pleased when I told them I'd come to pick Malcolm up. They told me all the horrible things he would do and how difficult and what a problem it would be. Most of what they said proved right in the fullness of time! I was shocked that the stuff he had there was virtually nothing. He had absolutely no clothes. I went back with what was there, and shortly afterwards Malcolm and I set off for Norfolk.

Two and a half hours later they reached Bunwell Manor Hotel, where Malcolm was staying for the immediate future. Situated not far from the Snetterton motor racing circuit, Bunwell Manor was an unpretentious country hotel, with just ten bedrooms, an old stone building of sixteenth-century origins, which had once been a rectory.[5] Malcolm's bedroom was on the ground floor next to the hotel bar. On their first night Anthony shared a meal with Malcolm, saw him to bed, and then went back to his parents' house in the village nearby, whereupon Malcolm put on his dressing-gown and spent the rest of the evening in the bar. This deception became a regular feature of his time at the hotel.

Shortly afterwards there were discussions over the telephone with the Court of Protection, which sanctioned the hotel costs and made arrangements with Anthony as regards salary and job description. His appointment as 'chauffeur and carer' was formalised with a contract six months later.[6]

Katherine is certain that nobody told her of the move to Norfolk. She struggles to understand how the Court, which was, in effect, entrusting her father into the care of a virtual stranger, could do so without any contact with his children. When she did eventually catch up with events, she was told her father would rather not have her know where he was now living.

Soon after their arrival in Bunwell Anthony signed Malcolm up with a GP, Dr Apthorpe of nearby Attleborough, who gave Anthony the grim news that Malcolm would be lucky to survive two years. A brain scan shortly afterwards confirmed serious damage. But what Anthony did not know was Malcolm's remarkable ability to defy medical opinion. Sheila had once been given the same prognosis thirty years before.

Malcolm settled very happily in his new surroundings, glad to be reviving the Norfolk connection of his mother's family. Rennie Law, who was running the hotel at the time, remembers him getting on well with his regular customers:

> He would often spend most of the day at the bar from about lunchtime. He'd like nothing more than to sit there and chat with the locals – he enjoyed this much more than meeting important people. On one occasion he got very drunk and then sat at the piano for hours entertaining us all with some very good playing, jazz mostly.[7]

But he also went out for long drives with Anthony, who usually found him quiet but co-operative.

---

[5] It is now a private house.

[6] 30 November 1984. The document was signed on Malcolm's behalf by the Principal of the Management Division of the Court of Protection, J R Ellis.

[7] June 2004

*In the garden of Old Mill Cottage, Wymondham*

Virtually every day in that summer of 1984 was a glorious exploration. He loved it! We went all over the place, the length and breadth of the county in the Cavalier and he loved it!

And as they travelled there was non-stop music, taped Malcolm Arnold, a recurring concert of *Peterloo* and the *English* and *Scottish Dances*. Highlights included a return visit to Burgh Castle (where he had been filmed by Mike Purton); butterfly watching on Thetford Chase; and idle hours in Sheringham, a resort they particularly liked, partly for its sheltered position but mostly for its high-class fish-and-chip shop.

Just occasionally the routine was broken for public appearances. In July Anthony drove Malcolm up to the Ludlow Festival, where after one of the concerts he spent a happy evening in the pub chatting to an old friend, jazz trombonist George Chisholm. Alan Poulton, who lived nearby and organised the visit, remembers Malcolm talking in 'full flow' to the organist of Ludlow Cathedral. That month there was also a return to Northampton, where, at the Derngate, Malcolm received a D.Mus from Leicester University.

One early problem was Malcolm's lack of clothes. He had come with none himself and the Court of Protection at this stage would not give Anthony permission to buy anything at all in Malcolm's name.[8] Fortunately Robert Strauss used to pass on to Anthony's father a large quantity of clothes each year.

---

[8] Robert Angel, operating at a distance, necessarily found himself in a difficult situation.

My father owns a garage, and you don't wear a stockbroker's suits for doing break-downs! So my mother had put them all away, and I was able to take them to a tailor to be remade to fit Malcolm. So for the first two years of our life together he wore my shoes, socks and ties and Robert's shirts and suits!

The Bunwell Manor experiment proved a great success. For Malcolm it was in many ways like a continuation of the Sally Charlton era, with someone around to organise him, give him companionship and discourage the drinking. For Anthony there was fulfilment of a need to be needed, which strengthened his ability to cope with Malcolm's swinging moods. At times of particular crisis he could always console himself with the thought that the job was only, at most, for two years. The one disappointment for him was Malcolm's - heterosexuality. Malcolm was at first bewildered at being cared for by someone openly gay. However, he soon found the humour of the situation appealing, and was not averse to encouraging the conclusions that were constantly being drawn.

As Anthony steadily reduced the intake of drugs, the fog in Malcolm's mind began to disappear, his strength grew, and so too his exasperation at the financial restrictions still imposed on him by the Court of Protection. It was, he declared, a 'considerable embarrassment'[9] and he blamed Katherine and Isobel all the more. Isobel had by this time followed Katherine to Crouch End and was now her next door neighbour, the hope being that, with more space and support around, Edward might be able to live there. He had not been able to settle in a Steiner home in Hampshire.

In July 1984, when Anthony and Malcolm began looking for a house of their own, the Court of Protection's case worker Robert Angel wrote to Katherine with the highly distressing news that Malcolm's whereabouts were to continue to be kept a secret:

> Your father has given me strict instructions that his family is not to be told of his present, or proposed, address until such time as he wishes a reconciliation to take place.[10]

Similar sentiments were expressed to Isobel:

> I write to let you know that there is a strong possibility that Dr Arnold will soon have a house of his own to live in. Unfortunately Dr Arnold has specifically asked me not

---

[9] Robert Angel (Court of Protection) to Katherine (26 July 1984): '[Your father] also made it quite clear to me that being under the Court's Jurisdiction is a considerable embarrassment to him.' The stigma of mental illness associated with the Court's involvement would have been an embarrassment. But over the past five years the Court had brought order and restraint into his finances, which had been in utter chaos. The invocation of the Court's help in 1979 was something for which Malcolm, had he been thinking straight, should have been grateful.

[10] 26 July 1984.

to disclose his present or proposed address to any member of the family for the time being.[11]

These acts of rejection, delivered second-hand through the Court, were accompanied by terse requests for the return of whatever paintings and personal effects Isobel and Katherine, at the Court's request, had collected from the Belsize Park flat three years previously and stored.[12]

Katherine's relationship with her father had thus, in four years, undergone an alarming metamorphosis. In 1980, when Malcolm was in St Andrew's and his illness at its worst, she was his closest ally. In 1981 and 1982, while she was involved in rearing a family (three children between 1979 and 1984), Sally Charlton took over her role, but more as a mother-figure than a daughter. Contact between father and daughter diminished at that time sharply. By 1983, when he was living with Brian and Mary Charlton, contact was further diminished and Malcolm disinherited Katherine and her brothers. And now, in July 1984, after two months in Bunwell Manor Hotel, Malcolm was still withholding his whereabouts from the family, something which he continued to do for over another year. The only known cause of disagreement for this extraordinary situation of estrangement between Malcolm and his family was the blame he attached to Katherine and Isobel for bringing him under the care of the Court of Protection and the payment by the Court of covenants for Katherine's children's education. This is hardly enough to justify total rejection. The equation of cause and effect does not balance. Something seems to be missing.

The Court, seemingly discounting Malcolm's mental instability, offered scant justification for its current stance. 'In order to perform my role as receiver,' wrote the Court's case worker to Katherine, 'it is necessary for me to retain his good-will as much as possible. I have no doubt that to disobey this instruction would seriously undermine any confidence he has in me.'[13] This obsequiousness had the unfortunate effect of further damaging the relationship between Katherine and her father, already undermined by the disinheritance of 1983. It also damaged her relationship with Anthony, for Katherine began to wonder if he was actively influencing her father against her. It seems disappointing that the Court's case

---

[11] 26 July 1984. As Robert Angel specifically states 'any' member of the family, this embargo must have included Robert. Robert remembers occasional telephone calls from his father, though he cannot be sure at what precise period they came. He does not believe they included discussion of his father's whereabouts. 'It was not something I ever asked.' He found his father unsettling, and had opted to create an independent life in Skye.

[12] Isobel was attacked further. By the final settlement of the divorce Malcolm had undertaken to contribute £6,000 towards Edward's education. Now that Edward was not at school, he no longer qualified for educational support, although his needs were still considerable. 'Appreciating Dr Arnold's affection for Edward,' wrote Robert Angel to Isobel, 'I am reluctant to consider ceasing the £6,000 a year altogether ... I must, however, give serious thought to reducing this figure to a more reasonable level and have in mind, say, £2,000 ...' (26 July 1984)

[13] 26 July 1984

workers should have supported rather than fought against what could be construed as a form of mental torture, a daughter being denied all knowledge of her sick father's whereabouts for over a year.

Anthony has stressed how much he tried to work towards family reconciliation, citing the comment of Dr Kitson, the Norwich psychiatrist to whom he had taken Malcolm, that reconciliation with the family was necessary for Malcolm's mental recovery. The psychiatrist, it seems, saw the rift as part of the illness. But Malcolm remained unmoveable.

Not long after Anthony and Malcolm started looking for houses to rent, they came across Old Mill Cottage[14] on the edge of Wymondham, not far from Bunwell. It was a large, rambling building of much antiquity, with a cellar said once to have been connected by underground passage to Wymondham Abbey. It was fully furnished, with enough space for Malcolm to have a study and guests their own private wing. It would cost a little less than the hotel, so the Court supported the move, which took place in August 1984. Anthony was particularly pleased with its secluded, two-acre garden:

> Every day, when the weather allowed, we would go out before and after breakfast and walk round the garden. I was amazed at Malcolm's wonderful knowledge of flowers. And he knows all the butterflies and moths by their Latin names! He is a real expert. It was in the Old Mill Cottage garden, I believe, that Malcolm began to rediscover a taste for life, as he totally loved the place.[15]

Though Malcolm was slowly re-finding himself, his improved physical and mental condition did not bring any warmer feelings towards his family. Of Katherine's three young children, he had only met the eldest, but he still told the Court he did not want her to know where he was living. Robert Angel wrote tantalisingly to Katherine,

> Your father has now moved into the house which I mentioned, and is again asking for his paintings, snuff boxes etc to be delivered.[16]

A few weeks later the case worker was commiserating with Isobel in her 'distress' at Malcolm's blanket rejection of his family:

> Dr Arnold has often told me how fond he is of Edward but, when he asked me to keep his address secret, he made no exceptions.[17]

Once he and Malcolm were well settled in the Old Mill, Wymondham, Anthony boldly returned to the Crown and Cushion to collect Malcolm's Toyota Crown from the Charltons, his father bringing it back on his car-transporter. The Toyota was soon in action, Anthony driving Malcolm down in it

---

[14] In Barnum Bridge Road

[15] July 2003

[16] 24 August 1984

[17] 10 September 1984. Anthony writes: 'Sadly, when Robert Angel was writing to Isobel, Malcolm was never asked if he wanted contact from Edward.' (June 2004)

*Malcolm with Janet Hilton, clarinet, at the recording of the First Clarinet Concerto in Bournemouth*

to Bournemouth, five years on from the ill-fated recording sessions there. Strangely, the visit was again for EMI recordings, though this time it was Norman Del Mar conducting the Bournemouth Sinfonietta.[18] The three-day visit began inauspiciously with an accident at some traffic lights in north London, when Anthony did an emergency stop and the car behind did not. Although no injuries resulted, the impact had been considerable and, soon after arrival, Anthony found himself hardly able to move. Free of his calming influence and enlivened by the heady Bournemouth ozone, Malcolm reverted to his old ways and, inevitably, with the drink came the bad temper. 'Malcolm was upset by Anthony's illness,' says Alan Poulton, 'and was a bit more difficult than normal.'[19]

The soloists of the four concertos being recorded, however, found him delightfully helpful. He was always joking with Alan Civil, an old friend and drinking companion, who also happened to come from Northampton. Janet Hilton, playing the First Clarinet Concerto, found him 'wholly helpful and always charming,'[20] John Wallace 'very supportive of my playing'.[21] John Wallace enjoyed the experience so much that soon after the recording he wrote to Malcolm's Business Manager asking about the possibility of a new concerto.[22] But Malcolm had not written any music since the Trumpet Concerto

---

[18] The recording was made at Christchurch Priory on 3 and 4 September.

[19] August 2003

[20] April 2004

[21] May 2004

[22] Letter to Alan Poulton, 23 September 1984

three years before, and for the moment there was no sign that he would ever do so again.

The Bournemouth recordings proved a helpful marketing exercise. But they were a misjudgement in financial terms, as Anthony explains:

> While it was taking place, we didn't know that Malcolm was paying for everything. The champagne was flowing. We were staying in the Royal Bath in a suite, and everybody was having a great time.

*With (clockwise from left) Norman Del Mar, Alan Poulton and John Wallace (trumpet) at Bournemouth*

*Listening to the playback of the Oboe Concerto with Gordon Hunt (oboe, left) and Norman Del Mar*

The Court of Protection had miscalculated Malcolm's finances that year, thinking there was an excess of income which could be reinvested, and Alan Poulton had accordingly been encouraged to go ahead on a promotional spending spree, which also included important recordings of chamber music.[23]

That November, after six months with Malcolm, Anthony took a day off, but returned to a series of crises. Malcolm had been out on a Wymondham pub crawl which had outraged the locals and led to a ban from several establishments. He had also managed a parting of the ways with Alan Poulton, who had made considerable efforts on his behalf.[24] It made Anthony realise that he could not leave Malcolm to fend for himself, and he never again took a day off.

It was soon widely noticed how much better behaved Malcolm was when he was with Anthony than when left alone. Robin Arnold, whose flat in Cambridge Anthony and Malcolm would visit, stresses the 'striking interdependence' of the two:

> If Anthony wasn't there, Malcolm got cross and the language showed it. Out came all the obscenities. He got really deranged one day, talking about the army, when Anthony was out of the room. Anthony's calming influence was hugely impressive.[25]

John Carewe[26] had similar experiences. He was first invited up to Wymondham after delighting Malcolm by the way he had conducted a broadcast performance of the *Concerto for 28 Players* for the BBC. Knowing Malcolm's reputation, Carewe accepted the invitation with some misgivings:

> But he was the complete English gentleman throughout the visit. His manners could not have been more correct or circumspect. That day he could have charmed the pants off the Queen![27]

Not long afterwards he was invited up to an Italian lunch at Wymondham's Sinclair Hotel to celebrate Malcolm's sixty-fifth birthday. Carewe found Malcolm over-excited and very difficult, behaving reasonably only when Anthony was on hand.

Mike Purton, who saw the pair regularly at this period, was under no illusions about Anthony's task.

> Malcolm could behave very badly! Almost made a career out of it! My wife found it very hard to cope, as a lot of women do, because of all the nonsense. He was very

---

[23] Three records by the Nash Ensemble did much to alert the public to many excellent, unknown chamber works.

[24] 'I had helped put him back on the musical map by accompanying him at all times when he had the opportunity to put himself about at key events, like the RCM centenary Concert and the BFI dinner. I had also enabled him to meet fellow musicians, which was a key motivator for him.' (June 2004) Above all, in researching his important Arnold Catalogue, Alan found several lost works and established a detailed chronology.

[25] July 2003

[26] Conductor and teacher, particularly associated with championing the works of Peter Maxwell Davies

[27] May 2004

fond of her but extremely pushy. Betty found it so difficult she would go off with Anthony and leave Malcolm with me.

Most of the time he'd be an absolute pain. He could be very spiteful, resentful probably at his situation. Every now and then, however, you'd strike gold. About twice a year I could have a sensible conversation with him, really riveting, interesting stuff. A lot of the rest of the time he was playing games, being thoroughly nasty. But there you are! The price of genius![28]

In all the circumstances Anthony could have been forgiven for turning Malcolm into a recluse, heavily sedated and kept out of sight in his retreat at the Old Mill. Instead, he pursued the very opposite policy, seeking opportunities from the very beginning to take him out into the local community. Wymondham College, a nearby boarding school, proved useful, Anthony taking Malcolm to several plays and musicals there, and it was not long before he was judging the House Music competition. He also became patron of the newly formed Wymondham Symphony Orchestra, which was run by the College's Director of Music, Ken Hytch, and played Malcolm's work regularly.[29] Ken found Malcolm extremely encouraging, though 'he didn't seem to like being asked things like "Is the tempo right?"' Anthony's presence he found crucial.

When Malcolm was with Anthony, he was OK. Without him he was a real handful.

Malcolm on one occasion conducted the Wymondham orchestra in a perform-ance of his *Cornish Dances*.[30] Knowing his volatile nature, the players awaited his appearance with some anxiety. As Malcolm emerged before them, smiling with all his old ebullience, Anthony sat down quietly at the back. The players turned to the first page of the first Cornish dance, reminding themselves nervously that it began on the third beat. Malcolm smiled at them roguishly, as he looked around, checking their readiness. There were one or two pretty violinists, but there was Anthony, too, catching his eye. 'Right, ladies and gentlemen,' he calmly began. 'I think the first two beats are mine.' And off they went.

Malcolm was also taken to concerts of the Norfolk Youth Orchestra at Norwich and he became a Patron of the West Norfolk Junior Youth Orchestra, based at King's Lynn. It was not long before, with Anthony on hand, he was conducting his own works with the Norfolk Youth Orchestra and he also conducted their wind band. He is said to have behaved impeccably, and he was always very generous if amateur standards faltered. 'They are playing it and

---

[28] August 2003. Anthony feels that this was because Mike tried to discuss things in which Malcolm was not interested. 'Malcolm always preferred to talk about music and resented probing questions.'

[29] There were notable birthday concerts. The WSO was one of several largely amateur orchestras showing a keen interest in Malcolm's symphonies at this period, in marked con-trast to the professional scene. Robin Page's Birmingham Philharmonic intended a complete symphonic cycle and Adrian Smith's Slaithwaite Philharmonic Orchestra (based in Huddersfield) for many years showed London what it was missing.

[30] For a sixty-fifth birthday concert, October 1986

enjoying it,' he would say to Anthony, 'and that's all that matters.' For Malcolm all these musical contacts were highly therapeutic. He was steadily regaining some important self-esteem.

Shortly afterwards Robert Angel was replaced at the Court of Protection by a new case worker, Emrys Lloyd-Roberts, who did much to sort out the debts but brought no new hope to the family. Isobel gave up at this stage, immersing herself in her teaching in Hampstead and helping Edward settle into a new care home in Kent. But Katherine persevered, refusing to send her father the items he wanted until he at least contacted her himself and told her where he was living. Eventually, that December, seven months after Malcolm's move to Norfolk, she discovered his telephone number and made several calls over the next ten days, trying to get her father to talk over their problems. The number was quickly changed, on the grounds that 'nuisance calls' were being received. Katherine doggedly went to see the Master of the Court of Protection[31] to find out why she could no longer get through.[32] The Master promised to look into the matter and Katherine in due course received a letter from Emrys Lloyd-Roberts.[33] The 'nuisance calls', he told her, were from herself:

> I hope that this information will enable you to decide on what best to do in the circumstances.

Katherine couldn't win.

> If I made no calls, I was 'neglectful'. If I made calls, I was 'harassing'.[34]

In February 1985 the Court sent its own 'Visitor', Dr Kenyon, to pay his annual visit to Malcolm. Emrys Lloyd-Roberts afterwards wrote to Katherine to summarise his findings, a sweeping endorsement of all that Anthony had achieved in the first nine months.

> The Visitor reported that Mr Anthony Day, although he had at times found Dr Arnold's behaviour extremely difficult to manage, was nevertheless coping well. The Visitor approved of your father's accommodation and found it pleasant, tidy and well-kept. Your father remembered Dr Kenyon from Northampton and said how glad he was to have got away from there. He had no particular complaints about his health and reported eating and sleeping well, although he has put on weight. In general, he

---

[31] 4 January 1985

[32] Anthony sees the sequence of events differently. Katherine refused to send her father the items, he writes, 'even when he asked her personally. She resisted several quite pressing reminders from Emrys Lloyd-Roberts and through her perseverance was given the Wymondham telephone number. She made four calls over ten days to her father, trying to get him to talk over their problems, but always returning to the old story of paying for his grandchildren's schooling which he disagreed with. The Trust he paid into, which was a settlement in the divorce from Sheila, paid for all of Robert's and Katherine's private schooling and universities, and he felt they should be responsible for their own.'

[33] 21 January 1985

[34] May 2004

seems to be well looked after and cared for and his general mental condition seemed to be much better than it had been in May 1984.

The doctor did, however, identify a persecution complex:

> Your father apparently views the future with some gloom and has a general paranoid attitude, believing himself to be exploited for the sake of his money.

This paranoia, which had years ago evidenced itself in his responses to the elderly Pappy, obviously contributed to Malcolm's current attitude to Katherine, causing him to misinterpret the invoking of the Court of Protection and resent helping his grandchildren financially.

The doctor's diagnosis of paranoia might have seemed a good moment for the Court of Protection to reassess its position on the relationship of Malcolm and his daughter. But instead, in the final paragraph of the very same letter, the case worker continued as if the paranoia had never been mentioned:

> Dr Arnold complained at some length to the Visitor about what he saw as unwarranted enquiries from you. Your father complained that you had been 'constantly ringing and harassing him' and he said that he did not want any more to do with you, and that he did not wish you to have any more money. He also grumbled about having to maintain his former wife, your stepmother.[35]

Katherine in a state of frustration sent off various items[36] requested by Emrys Lloyd-Roberts.[37] 'It was sad to hear how hostile my father is to me,' she replied. She grieved particularly in that his rejection of her never came directly but always through a third party. She pointed out the paranoia, identified by Dr Kenyon, and wondered whether the resultant delusions might not be taken into consideration by the Court. Her letter had no effect.

In May 1985 Anthony took Malcolm to a meeting with the Master of the Court of Protection as a first step in gaining release from its jurisdiction. The case worker reported back to Katherine:

> The Master told your father that the Covenants that have already been entered into in favour of your three children will not be stopped at present; but the Master pointed out to your father that if he were restored to the management of his own affairs the Covenants would lapse and their renewal would be entirely a matter for him. The Master asked me to say that your father expressed very firmly the view that since both yourself and your husband were working, your father could see no justification for the Court to have entered into the Covenants nor to continue them. The Master pointed out, however, that it was common occurrence for parents to help their children by providing for their grandchildren. Your father said he did not intend to be one of those grandparents.

---

[35] 19 February 1985

[36] Anthony identifies these as 'some of the snuff-box collection requested by Lloyd-Roberts, the rest coming from a storage place which had been paid for by Malcolm through the Court'.

[37] An open bookcase, an oak tallboy, two tea-chests packed with books and pictures and 11 other pictures (27 February 1985)

It was now exactly a year since Malcolm had been evicted from the Crown and Cushion and a clear indication of just how much he had improved under Anthony's care can be seen from the comments of the Master[38] in her own letter to Katherine explaining that meeting:

> Dr Arnold seemed very clear in his thinking and, had I not known the history, I don't think it would have occurred to me to consider that he might be suffering from mental disorder. He was coherent and comprehensible …

Katherine would have done better at this stage to relinquish the covenants for her children. But she saw Malcolm's contribution to them as something 'of over-riding importance'. It was, she told the Master, 'the only area in which we can perhaps salvage something from the wreckage he has created' of their family life. And when news came through that Malcolm had changed his will, Katherine involved herself in dialogue with the Master about it. But the more she fought against her exclusion from her father's life, the more she seemed to reinforce her father's long-held delusion that 'the family' was after his money. Things went from bad to worse.

With Malcolm's release from the Court's jurisdiction now imminent,[39] and with it the possibility of Malcolm buying a property of his own, the Court's case worker intensified his efforts to extract more possessions from Katherine. Under pressure, she sent to the Royal College of Music a number of musical scores which had been given to her and Robert at the time of the move from Meadowcroft, but when the College magazine stated that Katherine had made the gift of the manuscripts, Emrys Lloyd-Roberts was quickly in action:

> Your father is most adamant that an erratum should be made that he himself donated these manuscripts. I am instructing the College to make the necessary amendment.[40]

The Court has clearly moved well beyond its official brief of administering its patient's finances. Pressed again by the Court for her father's snuff-boxes, Katherine found and sent across a silver one. There should have been two, replied Emrys Lloyd-Roberts. If she had lost it, she should buy a replacement.

By September 1985 Katherine had finally, sixteen months on, learnt of her father's whereabouts, for that month Malcolm joined the fray himself, asking Katherine for possessions on the grounds that a further move was now under discussion:[41]

> Hello Katherine,
>     Thank you for your letter of the 5th September.
>     We have not moved yet but hope to in the near future, it will be nice to have a place of my own again. It would give me great pleasure to have the things back that

---

[38] Mrs A B Macfarlane
[39] Malcolm was finally released from the jurisdiction of the Court of Protection on 21 October 1986, seven years after Katherine and her husband Anthony had first sought its help.
[40] 9 June 1986
[41] 17 September 1985

you and your step-mother have looked after since I have left Ireland, and also the contents of my flat in London, as apart from having things around me that I would now appreciate, this would also save me considerable expense.

Perhaps you would be kind enough to let me have a list of things that you will return and I will make arrangements to have them collected either through the Court or personally if you prefer.

Dad

Katherine was curious about the letter. All her life her father had addressed her as 'Dear Katherine' or 'My Dear Katherine'. 'Hello Katherine' surprised her. The request was also muddled. She had been sent belongings by her father when he moved into de Vesci Terrace in 1976, not when he left it in disarray in 1977. Above all, it had never been her father's way to worry about material possessions. He had tended to fling them around with wanton abandon, to buy and to replace. She was curious at the change.

The snuff-box saga had not yet ended. Three months later, Katherine's Christmas post contained further correspondence on the subject from Emrys Lloyd-Roberts:

> I have recently received a letter from your father about his snuff-boxes. He says that he originally had six, one a silver snuff-box that was sent to him by yourself recently. The second, an oval pewter box, is with him at present. Of the four remaining ones there is a square pewter snuff-box, a large engraved silver snuff-box, an oblong rosewood snuff-box and an oblong mother-of-pearl snuff-box. I know how much your father would appreciate it if you could either find the original or obtain a copy.[42]

Katherine patiently replied that three of the missing items had probably been given away as gifts at Belsize Park. The one which she had spent time looking for, but could no longer find, was worth about £2.

Anthony meanwhile was getting on with the routine business of life with Malcolm at the Old Mill. There were many good times.

> He started to come back from his solitariness very quickly. Soon we were able to have dinner parties regularly. He would be on great form and chat quite happily. There would be, amongst others, Mike and Betty Purton, coming over from Bunwell; Ron Gilroy, a piano tuner, and his wife Eileen, a piano teacher; Ken and Janine Hytch from Wymondham College; and Emrys Evans, the Head of Music for Norfolk, with his wife, Judith…
>
> At all these occasions, as when he was in the Savile Club, Malcolm would hold court and because his knowledge was so diverse, his audience sat enthralled. I was totally amazed to watch and see what he was capable of …[43]

It was at the Old Mill Cottage that Anthony noticed several idiosyncracies, which he connected to Malcolm's time at St Andrew's, but more probably reflected his problems at the Crown and Cushion.

---

[42] 20 December 1985
[43] June 2004

I found that if I put out a big bowl of fruit, he wouldn't touch it. However, if I turned the light out and he thought he couldn't be seen, he would take it to a corner and start eating.

He had obviously not been allowed to go into the kitchen. At the Old Mill the ground floor lavatory was the far side of the kitchen, but instead of approaching it directly, through the kitchen, he would go out of the front door, go all the way round the house, and come in the back door.[44]

His smoking habits too were peculiar:

He had obviously got used to being limited in the number of cigarettes he could have, and, after he'd have one, he'd carefully hide the stub. If he was smoking upstairs and heard me coming, he'd put it in the bed, so that's when I banned upstairs smoking. He was burning the quilts. Malcolm always respected my rules, as I kept to them myself.

Anthony's battle to limit Malcolm's drinking was a difficult one. 'It could be a nightmare!' he recalls. One of the problems was the encouragement he would be given at certain favourite venues, like the Sinclair Hotel:

He got on with everyone very well there, and went there a lot. People loved him because he would spend, spend, spend. That was my big problem. A lot of people were highly encouraging to him because he spent so well, and the problem was he was spending money we hadn't got. Also, when the money ran out, they would ring me to come and get him home, but always before he had finished the drinks he had paid for, saying he was being a nuisance.[45]

Old friends occasionally visited, which was a mixed blessing for Anthony, as old habits persisted. Lawrence Leonard, for example, who was running a course at Wymondham College, came to see Malcolm and was surprised to find that someone always so generous at the bar had been limited to mere pocket money. However, he ensured they had a really good evening together and they arrived back at the Old Mill very drunk. Anthony was understandably upset and let them both know it.

Anthony had now realised that the drinking was not going to be solved by gentle reasoning, so he went round all the pubs at Wymondham begging the landlords to eject Malcolm if he appeared. Malcolm, however, knew how to charm his way back into favour, and Anthony, frustrated by the problem, resorted to an eccentric response:

I got a reputation at Wymondham because I used to go down and, if he were drinking heavily and being offensive to other customers, I would toe him up the backside and then he would start off for home at a jogging pace, with me walking at a fast pace behind him. But it slowly started to work and he started to drink less …[46]

[44] June 2003
[45] June 2004
[46] June 2004

Sometimes, very disconcertingly, Malcolm would suddenly vanish from the house and take the train to Norwich. Eventually Anthony would receive a telephone call and have to go and collect him.

> He was always difficult at these times, but I think that was because he felt guilty that I had been called out.[47]

One evening Malcolm disappeared from the Old Mill Cottage but neither returned nor telephoned.

> I waited up and waited up. By the morning he still had not returned. I searched all over the town but couldn't find him. Eventually I called the police. They searched everywhere, all over the town but found no sign of him. When they started searching the waste ground, I fell apart …

But the anticipated tragedy did not materialise. The story has a bizarre dénouement:

> He had walked past a house in Wymondham, seen the television on, knocked on the door, and chatted to the occupants, who had invited him in. He was still there the next day! He's a rogue, but he's so loveable! There are two sides to him! People love him and make him welcome![48]

Malcolm's schizophrenic nature did not make him easy to work for, but in 1985 he was lucky to be introduced to someone strong enough to cope with him, his new agent, Georgina Ivor. Howard Blake believes her appointment did much to help re-establish Malcolm's reputation:

> Georgina was spiky, pushy, dominating, a cutting-edge agent, exactly what was needed! I think she did a fantastic job! All the time she was telling me 'I can't go on! He's so bloody rude!' but she stayed on for nine years, which in itself was phenomenal![49]

She had been introduced to Malcolm, she recalls, at a Faber lunch.

> I seem to remember going to the Chagall Exhibition at the Royal Academy afterwards – Anthony must have let me loose with him – a dangerous move![50]

On this first meeting she found him 'rather gentle'. Subsequently she grew familiar with his chameleon-like moods.

> You could never tell what would happen from one moment to the next. Sometimes he'd be brilliant. There was a party once in my house after a school prom. He spoke so warmly and fluently. But there were bad times too. If the music hadn't been so wonderful, there's no way I'd have stuck it out.

Georgina's arrival took some pressure off Anthony, and he again turned his thoughts to travel, his original therapy for Malcolm. In 1985 they took the first

---

[47] June 2004
[48] June 2003
[49] July 2003
[50] July 2003

of many holidays abroad, at Hammumat in Tunisia.[51] The same year he also took him back to Cornwall, where Malcolm was able to revisit several old friends, including Tony and Hilary Giles and Beatrice Gregory.[52] Malcolm's enjoyment of travel encouraged Anthony to organise a reunion with Robert, which took place in the summer of 1985, when Anthony drove up to Skye in the Toyota.

They stayed at the small and friendly Skeabost Hotel, frequented by the fishing fraternity and pleasantly sited by a river, about twelve miles from Robert. During the three-day visit Robert and Anne entertained them in their home, took them on a walk to Stein, a nearby village on the sea, spent a day at Portree and had a meal in the Skeabost Hotel:

> I found it quite tense, as I was accustomed to Dad behaving very embarrassingly in public. I don't think he did, but there were a few near misses! I think at one stage we walked aboard a naval minesweeper which was on a courtesy visit to Portree and there was some banter with the crew...[53]

They survived a formal tea at a 'rather gloomy' Portree hotel.

> Dad was fairly bored by it all. He behaved like royalty expecting everything to be provided for him. Anthony was easy and helpful, if rather surprising. For example, we usually wore Wellingtons but he had patent leather shoes and kept explaining how practical they were for wet Scottish moors. You could just wipe them and they were fine again!

Robert found his father much improved from the days of crisis:

> He was able to be sharp and cutting, but seemed happy to be organised by Anthony and was quite chatty with us. But he was also quite bored with things and a bit distant.

The departure was somewhat tense, as the Toyota Crown had been parked in the track to Robert's house with its radio left on.

> When they finally left the house, it was raining and their battery was flat. So Dad sat in the back of the car taking no notice of anything while I got totally soaked in driving rain jump-starting their car!

Robert had not found it an easy visit, but was grateful to Anthony for organising it all. He was glad his father had now seen his young grandson Tim and that they had all been together for a while.

Having visited Robert in the summer of 1985, Malcolm decided he would now like to visit Edward, whom he had not seen for four years, but was frustrated to find that Isobel and Edward were not immediately keen on the idea. A letter from Edward, now twenty-one and well settled in his home in Kent, survives from this period:[54]

---

[51] This was followed in 1986 by El Kantoui in Tunisia.

[52] Charles Gregory's wife

[53] April 2004. 'Robert and Anne were very nervous and tense to start with,' remembers Anthony, 'but slowly relaxed as time went on. Anne is a potter as well as a homeopath and I bought some of her pottery.' (June 2004)

[54] October 1985

Dear Dad,

How are you? I hope you are well. The garden in Holden is in better shape than before and I have been working hard at weeding again.

Lots of love

From Edward

PS I enclose photos of my 21st Birthday party, where I had grasshopper pie for pudding.

Later that month Edward sent his father a card on his sixty-fourth birthday, but he continued to resist suggestions of a visit. Anthony eventually wrote to him, suggesting he might reconsider this decision. Edward replied to his father carefully:

I have now reconsidered my decision, and although I like you very much I would rather have phone-calls and letters from you than you visiting me, because a visit would upset me a lot.

Mrs Mann who runs the home agrees that contact with you should be limited to letters and phone-calls. All the other staff agree with me on this point. If possible, could you arrange a meeting with Mrs Mann, my mother, Mr Day and my social worker, Mrs McKenna, if Mrs Mann thinks this is a good idea.

In late 1985 Malcolm began to think about the possibility of writing again. It is said – and it is partly true – that he was inspired in this thought by the young Danish recorder virtuoso Michala Petri, whom he happened to see one day on television. 'He just went on and on about her!' remembers Anthony. As luck would have it, Anthony discovered from the local paper shortly afterwards that Michala Petri would be appearing in a concert at Wingfield College, Suffolk. So Anthony rang up beforehand, and an arrangement was made for Malcolm to meet Michala at the end of the concert:

I invited Michala and her mother back to the house the following day, and I entertained her mother downstairs and she went upstairs to Malcolm's office and showed him everything she could do on the recorder.

Within a matter of days [55] Malcolm had produced an eleven-minute *Fantasy for Recorder*, which, on Michala's next visit from Denmark, they took down to her at the New Barbican Hotel.

They sat in the tea-room and she read through the score several times, then picked up her recorder and played it through. She said it was fantastic and she would guarantee 150 performances in the next three years, which she did indeed achieve...

Malcolm was so encouraged by Michala Petri's sincere delight in this fine miniature that within days of its completion he was collecting together for Donald Mitchell the complete set of *Irish Dances* which he had actually finished a month before the *Fantasy*. Although he had been writing music again before he

---

[55] The *Fantasy* was completed on 9 June 1986, two years after the move to Norwich.

*Receiving the Wavendon award from Princess Anne.*
*With John Dankworth and Ned Sherrin, 1985*

met Michala, undoubtedly it was she who inspired him to take himself seriously again.

The *Irish Dances*, which Donald Mitchell had been urging ever since the move to Ireland, were only started after Malcolm left there and was living in Belsize Park. He just had time to complete the first dance,[56] shortly after the Eighth Symphony, before the onset of his mental collapse. This dance, he told Martin Kingsbury, was a tribute to Sam Kelly, the taxi-driver-raconteur who had acted as help-mate on many a glorious expedition and inglorious binge. Now, in Wymondham in April 1986, seven years later, he began to work again on this old project. Somewhere there had been sketches of a second movement, a tribute to Dymphna.[57] No matter if he had lost them. He remembered the theme: Dymphna in one of her serious moments, stately as the Wicklow mountains, Dymphna when she wasn't giggling or playing tricks on him. And after Dymphna, for the

---

[56] It was dated 1978/79 on the manuscript.
[57] Martin Kingsbury was told that the second dance was a tribute to Dymphna.

third dance, he would include raven-haired Irene. Her movement would be *Piacevole*, expressing her prettiness and willingness always to see the best in him. *Graceful and agreeable*, that was Irene. He could begin the third dance, therefore, with an allusion to her theme, first used in the *Fantasy for Brass Band* and later restated in the slow movement of the Trumpet Concerto. Nobody would notice, and it would get him going. That was the all-important thing, for he had not written for a full orchestra for five years. He could not, as yet, sit down and write continuously. His inability to concentrate meant an intermittent approach. In mid-April he spent two days on Dymphna's movement, and then, after a pause of three weeks, he wrote Irene's dance.[58] This only took him a day, as did the fourth dance, written a week later.

The *Irish Dances* clearly illustrate the damage Malcolm had suffered in the course of his long breakdown. There is a considerable loss of sophistication between the first dance, of 1979, and the final three of 1986. The first dance may be simplistic and repetitive, but the writing is fuller than in anything that follows. It is clear that the brain damage, identified by the medical scan of 1984, impaired Malcolm's creative abilities. But even though the ideas are simple and the textures spare, the *Four Irish Dances* still generate enough atmosphere and changes of mood in their brief eight minutes to be considered something of a success.

Donald Mitchell, to whom Malcolm had dedicated the work, was surprised by their spareness, but wrote back encouragingly:

> I cannot tell you, dear Malcolm, how touched and honoured I am by the dedication of the *Irish Dances*. This means a very great deal to me and, as you can imagine, I shall much look forward to the first performance of the Dances and to the very many performances that I know will ensue. They are marvellous pieces and I am already carrying them around in my mind. I feel very lucky indeed that my name will be associated with this quite special score. A thousand thanks.[59]

And his belief in the *Dances* was strong enough for him to send a score to John Drummond at Broadcasting House with the suggestion that they might be included in next year's Proms, preferably on the last night:

> I can't help being profoundly touched by the dedication. You know it is a very long time since Malcolm put pen to paper and I am rather moved by being associated with a work which, as it were, is a signal of his return to musical life and creativity. Let's hope this new phase endures.[60]

---

[58] He wrote the second dance on 19/20 April 1986; the third on 13 May; and the fourth on 19 May.

[59] 1 July 1986. Malcolm had also taken the *Recorder Fantasy* to Donald who described it as a 'stunning addition to the Recorder repertoire'.

[60] 11 July1986. Donald Mitchell's letter had some effect, the second set of *English Dances* being included in the Last Night of the next season. Mitchell's letter does not betray his frustration that there had been three barren seasons before that for Malcolm. Two more barren seasons would follow the year of the *English Dances*.

In the same letter Donald Mitchell suggests to Drummond that Malcolm should also be invited to conduct the work. Not many months later[61] Faber were suggesting to Malcolm that perhaps he might lecture and conduct in America. It came to nothing, which may have been just as well, but it is an indication of how improved everyone found him.

An interesting insight into Malcolm's creative abilities at this time comes from Ken Hytch, who was involved in mounting at Wymondham College the first stage production of Malcolm's television musical, *Parasol*, since its first and only performance in 1960. There was a problem with the overture, the BBC only managing to discover a piano score, so Ken asked Malcolm to orchestrate it for him:

> It was arranged that I should go there, have lunch and then work with Malcolm. Up to his room we went. I thought it would be wonderful watching the great man put all the notes down, but no such thing! He looked at the score and read it through. 'Blimey, bombastic bugger, aren't I!' He sat down at the far end of the room and indicated I should sit at the desk. There's the paper,' he said. 'Get on with it!'

Perhaps Malcolm was simply playing games, seeing what reaction he would get from Ken, but more probably he felt inadequate to the task himself. In the end the orchestration was worked by collaboration:

> 'What shall we start with?' I asked. 'Try the tune in violins,' he said. So I wrote it in. 'And the bass line?' 'Oh, give it to the double basses and the cellos and the harp.' So I wrote it down and got to the trumpets last, for this opening. 'What do the trumpets do, Malcolm?' 'Oh, just let them fill in the harmony'. So I pondered over it for a bit. 'Malcolm! I think it will work out very nicely! They'll go in thirds and they'll go down by step.' And he said, 'Yes, I thought they would.' Of course, he'd worked it all out in his head! He knew damn well it would work!

Malcolm's leisurely return to composition over the past six months hardly suggested a major work was in the offing, but the recorder *Fantasy* and the *Irish Dances* proved to be the prelude to the Ninth Symphony, the highlight of Malcolm's Norfolk period. Ever since the completion of the *Irish Dances*, in May 1986, he had been thinking about this long-discussed project.[62] As usual, although ideas were flowing, he would not commit one note to paper until he had worked out everything in his head. He no longer favoured the use of ciphers, the

[61] January 1987
[62] David Ellis had asked Malcolm in 1977 if the BBC Northern could have his Ninth Symphony and Malcolm had agreed, but it was never an official BBC commission. Ratification from London never came. Later, when all the BBC orchestras had been invited to nominate two composers to write works for 1985 (European Year of Culture), Manchester (which had nominated Peter Maxwell Davies and Malcolm) was the only region to be cut back to one. 'Max was commissioned to write his Third Symphony, but the commission for Malcolm was rejected ... London decided it just didn't want a Malcolm Arnold Symphony.' It proved, in the event, an unnecessary veto, for Malcolm's health would not have allowed him to complete the work for 1985.

artificial device which had helped sustain much of his writing in the Irish period, and, as in earlier days, was again relying entirely on his own imagination. In the peace of the Wymondham garden that summer the musical jigsaw began to fit together and on Anthony's birthday, 12 August, he started to write it all down.

Anthony, at thirty-seven, was no longer keen on birthdays. Malcolm was well aware of this and was taking great pleasure, that morning, in not letting him forget the occasion. 'For God's sake,' said Anthony at last, 'stop all this Happy Birthday nonsense and just go upstairs and write me a bloody piece of music!' Malcolm paused, pondered, left the breakfast table without another word, went upstairs to his study and took up his blue biro.

The Ninth Symphony did not follow the same compositional method as the preceding eight, because he flinched at the prospect of writing into full score. Instead he began in short score, just sketching on two staves. He had struggled for concentration when completing the *Irish Dances*, but this time there was no problem and he worked non-stop, for around fourteen hours each day, only pausing for meals and sleep. He was calm and thoughtful, absolutely absorbed in his own world, which Anthony took care to protect. He had no need for alcohol, but instead Anthony plied him with cups of coffee. By 26 August, having made very few alterations, he had completed the short score and, elated by what he had so far accomplished, pressed on with the orchestration. In ten more days he had orchestrated the symphony, proudly dedicating it on 5 September 'To Anthony With Love'.

The Ninth Symphony stands starkly apart from its eight predecessors. From the opening bars of the first movement we are in an unfamiliar sound world, immediately unsettling, distinctly surreal. It is marked *Vivace* but what liveliness there is sounds artificial and anxious. The main themes, repeated continually in different formations of two-part writing, have the potential for jollity, but the unstable tonality and the constant dissonance between the two parts never allow them to shake off the shackles of distress. This is music of an alien world, a bleak lunar landscape; a landscape with enough dramatic features to encourage exploration, yet a harsh environment, bereft of humanity, with a repetition of imagery which makes for a sense of disorientation. The movement's strength is its mesmerising inexorability, demanding our attention as it proceeds on its seemingly unstoppable way. It is with some relief when we eventually arrive, cymbals crashing, at a dramatic restatement of the opening theme, taken more slowly, and, for the first time, scored for full orchestra,[63] followed by an anguished coda of rising intensity, thundering in long notes to a surprisingly assertive conclusion.

---

[63] But the writing is still in two parts only with much doubling. The first part is given to the piccolo, flutes, oboes, clarinets, trumpets, glockenspiel and first and second violins, and the second canonic-like part, beginning two bars later, is given to the bassoons, horns, trombones, tuba, violas, cellos and basses.

The writing throughout is of startling simplicity with page after page of mainly empty bars. The lack of sophistication is the very antithesis of Malcolm before the long silence, but the simplicity breeds an arresting intensity. The Ninth Symphony reminds us of a late Picasso drawing, created by only a couple of lines; or a late Matisse, with scraps of paper cut out and stuck to a canvas, the simple materials and method still creating a work of great art.

The second movement, *Allegretto*, takes us further away from orthodoxy and further into the lunar landscape, its plaintive little tune, first announced solemnly

*The first draft of the Ninth Symphony*

on the bassoon, being repeated no less than sixteen times, leavened only by a variety of equally fragile counter-melodies. The writing is entirely in two parts, as if it were the work of an inexperienced composition student. But, as in the first movement, what looks unfinished on paper, sounds surprisingly well in performance. The melody, so simplistic in its constant repetition, is nonetheless presented with such subtle, gentle craftsmanship that the movement haunts the memory long after the solo bassoon has brought it to a desolate conclusion. Like a slender sculpture, seen from different angles and in different lights, it bemuses and fascinates.

Had the cheery third movement, *Giubiloso*, been orchestrated with all of Malcolm's old authority, it would have been a great crowd-pleaser. As it is, there is not enough invention in the orchestration and too much dull unison writing to bring the witty ideas fully to life. But within the context of the whole work it doesn't matter that there is little in this movement that is truly *giubiloso*. Malcolm is offering us a further aspect of that alien world which preoccupies him, the lunar landscape dead to humanity, where sounds intended to be joyful echo back from craters in hollow mockery. In doing this, the eerie *giubiloso* presents an attractive contrast to its adjacent movements, and, above all, sets the scene well for the most important movement in the symphony.

Malcolm's concluding *Lento* has strong parallels with Mahler's *Adagio* at the end of his Ninth Symphony, both composers making their final statements with funereal slow movements. Mahler, like Malcolm, had suffered from the premature deaths of close family and friends, and both were gloomily preoccupied all their lives with their own mortality. Mahler wrote his Ninth Symphony in the knowledge of his imminent death, Malcolm in the hope of it.[64] And there are certain similarities in the music. Both slow movements are dominated by a strong theme in the strings, have moments where, such is the emotion, the music almost stops, and both end in peaceful acceptance of the inevitable,[65] Mahler with a strong chord of D flat major, Malcolm of D.[66] Malcolm's is much the more ascetic of the two finales. As in the symphony's second movement he is at complete variance with accepted symphonic form, elevating simple devices like repetition and sequence and eschewing development, the traditional symphonic prerequisite. Although he avoids Mahler's lush sounds, Malcolm nonetheless manages to achieve a similar intensity of emotion, the sadness of the melodic outline and the dour inevitability of the repetition making it a sombre, highly cathartic experience.

---

[64] 'I didn't want to live to be seventy,' said Malcolm on television in 1991. 'I'm very sad I have done.' (Kriss Russman's programme for BBC *Omnibus*)

[65] Malcolm orchestrates the final chord in a similar fashion to the 'heavenly sounds' of the Fifth Symphony's first movement second subject – harp and glockenspiel predominating.

[66] 'It's a long chord held low and dying,' explained Malcolm (BBC *Omnibus*, 1991), 'so that at the end there should be no applause and then you know you've just won through.'

But the means he uses to achieve his mesmerising ends are hardly those of the practical composer. He employs a large orchestra yet many players are silent for most of this long movement. The piccolo and the trombones sit inactive throughout its length, joining in only on the very last note. The second trumpet plays in only twenty of its three hundred and twenty-seven bars. The *Lento* is scored so sparely there is almost a childish feeling about it. Only in performance does the childishness melt away. And the more the work is heard, the more meaningful it becomes. An artist of genius can still express himself inimitably, even if an impaired capability limits the extent of the canvas. For all the alienation of this barren lunar landscape, the artist is still clearly, quintessentially Malcolm Arnold.

The Ninth Symphony has come to be identified specifically with Malcolm's 'lost years' and the 'escape' to Norfolk. Commentators have suggested that in the first two movements Malcolm is suffering incarceration at St Andrew's; in the third he is enjoying the delights of freedom from his prison; and in the fourth he finds safety and contentment with Anthony. And Malcolm's own declaration[67] that the last movement 'is meant to be complete serenity' has been an encouragement to read the symphony this way.

There is one late comment of Malcolm's,[68] however, which suggests that his experiences of 'to hell and back'[69] were merely the starting-point: the Ninth Symphony, he said, was an amalgam of all his knowledge of humanity.[70] In other words, he is looking back on his whole life. Although it would be too fanciful to extract precise identifications – Malcolm and Gerard Hoffnung, for example, in the duet of trumpet and tuba in the second movement – the most important people in his life would certainly be those who most shaped this 'amalgam'.

Ruminating upon 'humanity' could not have been a particularly comfortable experience for him. For all the extravagance of his life-style, for all his prodigious shows of generosity, it was the broken relationships which stood out in starkest relief, the present just as painful as the past, current estrangements particularly bitter. He had turned his back on Katherine, Isobel and Edward, and was largely out of touch with Robert. Sheila, too, who had never remarried but dedicated herself to her violin teaching, was resolutely distant again. Love seemed to breed estrangement. How ironic that the five people once closest to him, those he had held dearest, had no part to play in his current life.

Ruminating upon humanity also meant ruminating on the dead. Sweet Sally Charlton, dead these three years now, his paragon of devotion. Devotion of

---

[67] BBC *Omnibus*, 1991

[68] Made to Andrew Penny in the conversation recorded by Naxos, 1996

[69] The phrase, referring to Malcolm's problems in Northampton and revival in Norfolk, seems to have been coined in an article in the *Independent* celebrating Malcolm's 75th birthday.

[70] In an earlier interview with composer Peter Paul Nash for the BBC (1991), Malcolm had described the symphony as 'an affirmation of the constant running of life'.

another kind from Pappy. Eight years now since the end of that long vigil, that sadly obsessive preoccupation with 'my talented son'; and thirty years since the devotion of Nan, who took her leave of the family in an elaborate ritual in the front room of Craigmore. 'Please don't bother Malcolm. He won't want to come.' He did, in the end. Devotion too meant Lizzie, holding on till her nineties, and longing to see him, when she could not hold on any more. 'Malcolm will be coming, won't he?' He wouldn't.

There had been five of them, back in Fairview, four brothers and a sister, for ever being paraded before their father's camera. What could he write of poor Ruth, so loved yet neglected? Ruth, with her poetry, poverty and dreams! 'Will Malcolm be coming? He does know, I take it?' He did, yet he didn't. Or Clifford, the golden! Everyone's favourite, yet dying like Nan in the Craigmore front parlour after formal farewells. 'We've rung Malcolm, Cliff. He'll be here to see you.' They did, yet he wasn't.

Or Aubrey and Wyn, no leave-taking there, just dark oblivion in the damp Salcey Forest. Or Philip, the hero – no pilot was safer – till falling to earth, bruised and ablaze. Only weeks before, on his last leave, there had been French Cricket on the Racecourse. 'You're out, Philip, you're bloody well out! Let go of the bat!'

There was just one left, sitting tired and bemused in a garden of butterflies, sweet peas and roses, still coming to terms with his knowledge of humanity, patiently waited upon by the soft-footed Anthony. Anthony, both an acquisition and an enigma, offering a devotion he didn't comprehend, a life he wasn't sure he wanted, and a symphony he had never thought would be written.

An amalgam of humanity. All that he had learnt in sixty-four bitter years. The writing had not been easy, but he had seen it through, this amalgam of four movements. Despite a diminished capability which riled and frustrated him, he had achieved his goal of a Ninth Symphony. It had not exactly been a pleasure. More a purgation.

# 18
# Sir Malcolm
## Wymondham and Attleborough, 1986-96

WHEN DONALD MITCHELL examined the new symphony at Faber, he was perplexed by the emptiness of the score, with page after page of just two parts. In a life devoted to music he had seen nothing like it. There had been hints of a diminished mental capacity in the later movements of the Trumpet Concerto and *Irish Dances*, but this long symphony, written so sparingly, was very different. Something had happened in the period of his breakdown and Malcolm was no longer himself. There were some encouraging signs now of Malcolm's growing rehabilitation as a serious composer after the many years of neglect, and Donald Mitchell felt loath to jeopardize all these gains by the publication of such an extraordinary work.[1]

When Georgina Ivor consulted others about the symphony, she met with similar disappointment. John Amis thought it 'one of the most depressing documents you can find'. And the BBC's reader, Edwin Roxburgh, rejected it. A strong adherent of Malcolm's music, Roxburgh had immediate reservations:

> I felt rather sad, concerned and disappointed. There was something missing in the piece. It was a curious work and I wondered what had happened, with its two-part counterpoint, occasional four-part chords and simple Beethovenian rhythmic figuration. I was reminded of Oscar Wilde's quotation 'the last refuge of complexity is simplicity'. But this seemed a strange kind of simplicity.[2]

Although David Ellis was no longer at Manchester, Georgina had hoped that Edward Downes would conduct the work there with the BBC Philharmonic. The gloomy reply came back that neither he nor Peter Marchbank, David Ellis's successor, believed the work would ever be played. She responded by sending the score to David Ellis, from whom she received a somewhat mixed reply. He felt its length and sparseness were incompatible and wondered whether Malcolm might be persuaded to support the linear simplicity with some substance.

---

[1] That October, for example, Malcolm's sixty-fifth birthday was to be marked by a three-day festival in Manchester at the RNCM; an English Chamber Orchestra concert at the Queen Elizabeth Hall; *Tam O'Shanter* by the LPO at the Festival Hall; *Beckus* at the RCM; and a recorded relay of major works by the BBC Philharmonic Orchestra. He would also be Composer of the Week on Radio 3.

[2] November 2003

It's rather like a delicate mobile hanging from the ceiling; but without the ceiling it could not exist in intention: it would simply fall to the floor.[3]

However, despite these misgivings, he told Georgina Ivor that he could see no reason for BBC Manchester avoiding the work 'out of hand' and undertook to telephone Edward Downes:

I asked him 'What's the problem with the Ninth Symphony?' 'Well, it's not finished,' he said. 'There are pages of nothing.' 'But does it make sense?' I queried. 'Yes, it makes sense, but it's not finished. There's nothing going on. Just one line and something supporting it down below. It's as if he's turned the page before he's finished it.'[4]

David Ellis was asked to suggest to Malcolm that he might fill out the work.

I had lunch with Malcolm in a hotel in Salford and broached the subject. It was a very short conversation, brought to a swift conclusion by Malcolm. 'If I had wanted to do something different,' he said, 'I'd have done something different.'

There had been the same reaction at an earlier meeting at Faber, where Donald Mitchell had invited Malcolm to talk about the score over lunch. It was a difficult occasion, as Martin Kingsbury remembers:

Malcolm and Anthony came up to Donald's room, and Malcolm sat down in a chair and refused to move. He said he didn't want to go out to lunch, so we sent out for some sandwiches. A complete monologue from Malcolm ensued. It was all about his life, and it was fascinating. It was spoken in measured tones, he wasn't inveighing against anybody, he wasn't in one of his waspish moods, he was simply telling us the story of his musical life. It went on for over an hour, perhaps ninety minutes. But he would not talk specifically about the symphony.[5]

Donald Mitchell nervously tried to lead the conversation back to it.[6] He asked Malcolm about the thinking behind the long flute solos. 'I like the flute,' was the laconic reply. Why so many long duets? 'I like the sound.' The repetitions in the second movement? 'I wrote it like that, because that's how I wanted it.' The meeting ended with nothing resolved. Faber said they would be in touch. Martin Kingsbury explains:

We were in a dilemma. In the end we told him that, since we still had other works of his to publish, we wanted to get up-to-date with them first, after which we would think about the symphony again. I suppose it was a bit of a cop-out!

Few would have disagreed with Faber's decision at the time. There were only isolated cries of support. One, predictably, came from Charles Groves, who had rung Faber's Sally Cavender most excitedly:

---

[3] 9 September 1987
[4] August 2003
[5] August 2003
[6] 'Donald was terrified he would go out and kill himself,' says Sally Cavender.

I've got a towel round my waist and I've just come out of the shower, but the postman's just arrived with the symphony! Yes, I can see there are problems, but I definitely want to get this performed for Malcolm's sake!

Georgina Ivor worked hard with him in setting up a première with the Bournemouth Symphony Orchestra at the Northampton Derngate, but David Richardson, in charge of the orchestra and himself a strong supporter of Malcolm's, eventually decided it would do Malcolm's reputation a disservice and so changed the programme. Charles Groves then approached the Royal Liverpool Philharmonic and the BBC Scottish Orchestras, but to no avail.

Georgina had almost given up hope when she received a very positive response from Howard Blake. The further he went through the score, the more he had been fascinated by its extraordinary power. He picked up the telephone.

You've got to get this work performed, Georgina! It's not like his other works. It's very sparse and meditative, but it will work fine. It should be *played*! If nobody will do it, it's the sort of thing you could do in the Roundhouse and have young people all sitting on the floor meditating! You must get it put on! It's a very significant work. It's from the deep inner recesses of Malcolm.[7]

On receiving this encouragement, Georgina tried even harder to find an outlet for the unwanted symphony. But, despite her best efforts, there continued to be no immediate prospect of a performance.

Just two months after he had completed the controversial Ninth Symphony, Malcolm, on his sixty-fifth birthday, was released from the jurisdiction of the Court of Protection.[8] His relationship with the Court in the months preceding his release had not been very cordial, both Malcolm and Anthony believing there had been financial mismanagement and that a mortgage which they had requested for the purchase of the Old Mill should have been granted.

A letter from Malcolm to the Master of the Court of Protection survives from February 1986, its unpredictable spelling suggesting that it was written in the heat of the moment:

I am writing to you because I have now been with the Court seven years[9] and I am distressed to find that because of the obviously wrong discisions [sic] taken by the court on my behalf, [I] now find myself in a financially embarrassing condition. How can this happen? What can be done about this?

The 'wrong decisions' refer to the expensive recording forays with EMI and Hyperion; the payment to a part-time Business Manager of £17,000 a year (while the full-time Anthony received just £6,000); and covenants which the Court was paying for Katherine's small children, a grievance referred to in more detail:

One thing I find hard to understand is that even in these difficult times, although I have made it clear that I do not wish covenants made to Mrs King's children, they still go

---

[7] As remembered by Howard Blake, June 2003
[8] 21 October 1986
[9] The Court had taken over his finances on 26 July 1979.

ahead even when it means I have to go without. What does 'Court of Protection' mean? Is it that I shall go without to provide for everybody else?

Does what I want count? I would like to be settled in my own property and to be able to travel again. I desire very much to go back to India among other places, as it brings back many happy memories of when I was writing the score for 'nine days to Ramah'.[10] I admit freely that in the past I have not helped my position but I have worked hard during my lifetime and I think I am entitled to enjoy some of the benefits of my work.

Malcolm then moves on to the possibility of his release from the Court's jurisdiction once the Norwich psychiatrist, Dr Kitson, has given his support:

My improvement in the past year is obvious and to confirm this I saw Dr Kitson last Monday and he was very impressed with the progress I have made. My memory of the last few years is returning quite quickly and I have started basic working again …

Quite what had caused this serious memory loss is hard to say. Further treatment of ECT after the last psychotic episode (of 1983) is a possibility. 'Basic working' refers to his return to composition, the *Irish Dances* being written only two months after this letter.

Malcolm next puts forward a possible solution to the Court's unwillingness to take out a mortgage for the Old Mill, ('a delightful place', which could have been bought for £84,000).

Obviously for financial reasons I need a £30,000 morgage [sic] but I do not want to be in debt for the rest of my life and therefore would like you to give the following idea consideration. I am not sure what my family have left of my possessions but I know you hold what I do have in store, [and] as I get no pleasure from these things I would like a list of the things sent to me and I can decide what I would like sold to raise some capital.

The acerbic comment 'what my family have left of my possessions' resolutely ignores the fact that they were sent – at the time of the move from Meadowcroft – as gifts. That he 'gets no pleasure' from old possessions is in character but makes the constant requests to Katherine by the Court case workers on his behalf in 1985 all the more surprising.

The letter's final complaint concerns the Court's lack of support for Anthony:

Another thing I cant [sic] understand is the attitude taken to Mr. Day without whom there would have been no hope for me, he has done all he can over the last year to ease the financial burden on myself. And yet when he allows me to hang his pictures in my house, which by the way are giving me great pleasure, and asks if they can be covered by my insurance gets no consideration at all. It dosent [sic] look good to me when to save my dignity he allows me to distribute all his Christmas gifts and yet the first little thing he asks for, gets a flat refusal.

The letter ends, as it began, very challengingly.

---

[10] *Nine Days to Rama*, a film about the assassination of Gandhi, made twenty-four years previously.

Very kindly last year you offered to release me from the court providing you had the necersary [sic] assurances from Dr Kitson but I certainly will not consider this till you have returned my affairs to good order.

Malcolm, who treated money like confetti all his life, is unlikely to have written such a business-like letter without some active encouragement. Anthony's shrewd business sense would seem to have inspired him. Having earlier been denied money by the Court to buy Malcolm basic necessities like clothes, and having now been thwarted over a mortgage on a house which showed every likelihood of being an excellent investment, Anthony would understandably be sympathetic to the tone of such a letter.

Four days later Malcolm was writing again, this time to Katherine, furthering the same campaign to raise money from the sale of former possessions:

Dear Katherine,

I am sure you will be pleased to know that I saw Dr Kitson last Monday and he is very pleased with my progress. My memory of the last few years has now returned apart from a small amount of vagueness and I have started basic working again, answering letters and doing criticisms.

I am writing to you because I am hoping you can help me track down my three bronzes which I had in the London flat. Originally there were five, but I gave two to Ania, the three which I still should have are 1. Icarus 2. Mantic figure 3. Daedalus by Michael Ayrton. Please let me know where they are.

I am very happily settled in Wymondham which I am sure you will be pleased to hear.

Dad X

Katherine in her reply resisted any temptation she might have had to remind him of the Belsize Park free-for-all:

Dear Dad,

Thank you for you letter. I am glad things are going well for you. I don't recall a Daedalus, but I do remember the Icarus and mantic figure. I am afraid I don't know where they are now. I'm sorry not to be able to help more,

Best wishes,
Katherine

The letters are curiously formal, with no mention of the three grandchildren, now aged between two and six, in whose future education Malcolm so much resented the Court's investment.

In June that year, shortly after the completion of the Recorder Fantasy for Michala Petri and just two months before the start of the Ninth Symphony, Anthony took Malcolm across to Ischia to stay with Lady Walton, an invitation which had come about after the donation of her late husband's letters to Malcolm for the archive she was organising in William's memory at La Mortella. Anthony remembers a happy visit:

We had a lovely time, and Susana was charming once we safely arrived. It was lovely looking around the delightful garden she had created and seeing the hill where William's ashes are on his beloved Ischia.

Malcolm got a nasty shock, however, while we were doing a tour of the house. Going along one of the corridors he noticed a painting of William that William had given him. He asked Susana how it came to be there and the curt reply came back 'Your daughter sold it to me and I bought it to prevent it going to auction'.[11]

It was, in fact, a Michael Ayrton drawing, which Malcolm had bought from the artist in the early 1960s and had included in the many gifts he sent off to Katherine and Robert in 1976 at the time of his Dublin move. But Malcolm was in a muddled state at the time of this visit of June 1986, as Lady Walton's memories suggest:

> Malcolm came to visit, as he said he wished to see again the property at which he had often stayed when William was alive. It was not a success, as Malcolm's brain was deteriorating and he couldn't remember if he had just finished breakfast or was starting to have it. He stood by my cook for an hour a time watching her cook, and did the same to Maureen Murray who was working on the archive. He unnerved the household, so I had to tell Anthony that Malcolm was not in a fit state to take as a guest to stay at a private house.[12]

Just four months later Malcolm's long-awaited release from the Court was achieved. Although Malcolm had satisfied his psychiatrist's requirements, he had not been able to organise the submission to the Court himself – it was done for him – and the Court, in ending its seven-year administration, was in effect passing over Malcolm's business affairs to Anthony. Robin Arnold has pointed out the enormity of the task: 'Malcolm in 1986 was in no fit mental state to handle any financial matters or take any decision on his lifestyle. Anthony listened to his views, but basically took over the total running of Malcolm's life and had full control over budgets and accounts.' It was a large undertaking, but Anthony embraced all the extra work willingly, and his success in handling the budgets and accounts was notable, his fierce devotion to the management of Malcolm's finances playing a considerable part in their rejuvenation. But his contract with the Court had been as chauffeur and companion, and technically this contract remained in place, so his new responsibilities put him in an ambiguous position.

Within a couple of weeks of her father's release from the Court of Protection Katherine wrote to Malcolm,[13] asking whether he would consider keeping on the covenants which had been set up, against tax, for her children's future school fees. Although she now knew his Wymondham address, she was still essentially out of touch with him. 'I'm apparently not meant to have your phone number,' she wrote, suggesting it would be helpful if they talked again to each other:

---

[11] July 2004
[12] July 1986
[13] 17 November 1986

I also do not understand why I am to be refused the chance to communicate with you, when you seemed to me to feel strongly that parents and children needed to keep in touch, with which I would agree. I would be glad if you could explain why some of these things have happened, as I am sure there is a lot we need as a family to consider and I am very puzzled by many of these things.

Malcolm in response not only rejected the covenants but did so in a highly critical manner. Katherine replied carefully:

Dear Dad,

Thank you for your letter, and for replying to some of my questions. I am sorry you feel that I and the children deprived you of so much and I cannot quite see how it could possibly be so.... I think you gave us one twentieth, or thereabouts, of your income, and I cannot see how that accounts for your going without anything, as you are a very successful person.

After thanking him for what he had done and for her own education, she again expressed her puzzlement as to the current turn of events:

I am sorry you feel bitter, and that Isobel and I have deprived you of anything. It was certainly not the intention, as I hope you know. I am very glad things are better now. I think that some of your feelings about me are puzzling – I don't understand why if I had your phone number I would threaten your good health, for instance. Thank you for trying to explain though.

Her final paragraph contained family news, including that of Edward:

I saw Edward last week and wondered if you would like to hear about him ... He has had a difficult time recently though Holden House seems a very good place ...

Katherine had little option but to try to forget the bitter rebuff she had received and devote all her energies to the bringing up of her young family. It was now two and a half years since Dr Kitson had declared that Malcolm needed reconciliation with his family for his own full recovery, but as yet there were only limited signs of it.

He continued to make efforts to re-establish his relationship with Edward both by letter and telephone. Edward was not ready for a visit, but wrote to him from Southborough in April:

The garden here is a fusion of colours, and it is lovely and hot. I will be going to Brighton on Saturday and my mum and I will be taking a picnic. If there is time, we will go on the VER, the Volks Electric Railway, which is the first electric railway to be built in Britain ...

And in June:

My mother has brought me some tapes of your symphonies and dances. One of the tapes has the Peterloo overture on it and Beckus the Dandipratt. I am glad you are writing music again because that shows you are well ...

And in August, shortly after Malcolm had started the Ninth Symphony:

> The weather down here has been atrocious. I have been to Camber Sands with my mother. I have been shopping in Tunbridge Wells and bought some records and tapes. I have got some tapes of your Dances ... I hope to hear from you soon ...

Edward was right in believing that the new burst of creativity showed his father was getting better. Although Malcolm took time to recover from his efforts on the Ninth Symphony, a couple of months later he began the first of two successful solo works. The *Three Fantasies for Piano*, dedicated to a Norfolk friend, Eileen Gilroy,[14] have similarities with the Ninth Symphony in mood, melodic invention and texture. These evocative and fascinating pieces, in which two dark slow movements frame a deceptively cheerful central movement, were written entirely in two parts, just a single line being given to each hand. They were completed not long before the Christmas of 1986, as Anthony vividly remembers:

> Just after Malcolm had finished writing the piano pieces, Eileen Gilroy arrived at the house. He had his £70 weekly pocket money and off they went to Norwich, and he did not return till the evening, as usual penniless. I said to him 'You must have bought me a Christmas present!' He turned round, went out of the front door, reappearing half an hour later. He removed a disposable lighter from his pocket, slammed it on the table and said, 'Now don't say I don't buy you any bloody thing!'[15]

Shortly afterwards Malcolm wrote a second solo piece, this time a *Fantasy for Cello*, commissioned by Julian Lloyd Webber.

> I had long wanted Malcolm to write me something and I was there at the Albert Hall when the Trumpet Concerto was given its première. I particularly liked the slow movement – and it was there I asked Alan Poulton to ask Malcolm for a piece.

He was delighted with the result.

> Not one note had to be changed – it's a very good piece of cello writing – typical as it veers from melancholy to buffoonery. It contains some unusual and effective ideas – almost minimalist in style – almost hypnotic. The slow section is desperately sad – a really deep sadness that is very difficult to recreate in performance.[16]

After the première[17] at London's Wigmore Hall there was a small party at a nearby pub, where Malcolm was his enigmatic self, chatting happily one moment, and the next turning to Lloyd Webber with an aggressive 'Why don't you fuck off?' Shortly afterwards he was his charming self again. He also made several irritating passes at Julian Lloyd Webber's wife, but 'she forgave him, because she liked the music!'

By 1987 Malcolm's health had dramatically improved. Three years of living under Anthony's determined regime had had its effect. The careful administration of his medication had cleared his head, steadied his moods and increased his vitality. He became, in Anthony's words, 'sparkling'.

Something of this new sparkle can be seen in a television feature of 1987, when, interviewed by Anne Gregg on Anglia, he is self-assured and conversationally adroit. Looking slightly raffish, smart in a well-cut suit and elegantly using a small cigar like a theatrical prop, he is clearly delighted to be back in the limelight. Having been introduced as 'the great composer in East Anglia's midst', he is first questioned not about music at all but how he shot himself in his foot. This insulting start he parries adeptly with a joke. 'I've got big feet so I could hardly miss!' Shown conducting a local school choir and brass band[18] in extracts from *Song of Freedom*, he seems totally in control of the sixty young children, even if an oddly isolated figure, jacket off, spectacles on, hunched and intense, more aware of the music than the occasion.

He is on his best behaviour in the interview, constantly using Anne Gregg's first name, his manner almost obsequious in its graciousness. Yet the friendliness feels brittle, with perceptible tensions just beneath the surface. Irked perhaps by feeling he is being patronised, Malcolm mercilessly picks on any errors. No, he had not got an Oscar but a Novello award for *The Inn of the Sixth Happiness*. No, he was not lead trumpet of the LPO ('that's in jazz, dear') but principal trumpet. No, he did not take only ten days on *Kwai*, he was only given ten. He also surprises Anne Gregg with some mischievously unexpected answers. Would he be rude about modern music? No, it's a free world. Would he say film music was restricting? No, it was liberating. When she declares his music 'hummable' he briefly fixes her with a beady stare. 'I take that as a compliment!' After a further sally at his film music, he is less honeyed. 'I'm not ashamed of it!' In 1984 at Bunwell Manor Malcolm had needed the help and prompting of Sheridan Morley; in 1987 he is back in control, and woe betide an interviewer, even a pretty one, who meets him not completely briefed!

He had rediscovered his zest for life and Anthony found him often tremendous fun. In public his infectious enthusiasm more than compensated for his unpredictability. At the King's Lynn Festival, where he was conducting a programme of his own and other people's music, a member of the audience noted that all his old effervescence was back with that very special ability to enthuse others by his own evident enjoyment. When he came onto the platform at the beginning of the concert, he raised quite a laugh by reaching behind him and flicking up his tails.

> I'm not sure to this day whether he was making fun of the pomposity of the clothing or he was still not totally right.[19]

---

[14] November 1986. Malcolm gave them to Eileen Gilroy as a Christmas present in December; one of her pupils, Kate Setchell, gave the first performance in 1988. Malcolm, who was in the audience, was so moved that he presented Kate with the bouquet he himself had been given.

[15] June 2004

[16] July 2004

[17] 13 December 1986

[18] The choir of Hewett School and the Youth Brass Band of the Norwich Brewery.

[19] Barry Forshaw, August 2003

*Malcolm, Composer in Residence at the Perth Festival, 1987*

It was probably Malcolm's sense of fun predominating, for in May 1987 Anthony was able to take Malcolm up to Perth, where they stayed for the eleven days of the Festival at which Malcolm was a very busy 'Composer in Residence'. In addition to attending a large number of musical events[20] Malcolm was the guest speaker at a lunch, gave an interval talk at a concert, met the staff and pupils of various schools and conducted a choir of two hundred children in *Song of Freedom*. As if this was not enough, on the way up to Scotland a stop was made at Sunderland, where Stewart Craggs[21] had organised a small festival in Malcolm's honour. The Perth Festival's director, Iain Halliday, still remembers the impact Malcolm made:

> It was a huge coup to get him to come. He was a very engaging character – fairly red-blooded! During a lunch in his honour, hosted by the President who was a lady, he gave her knee a tweak or two. We had several local choirs to combine, which he conducted well – he had a marvellous rapport with the younger players and singers. We did a very absorbing interview; he was talking about his music and composing in general. It was a wonderful time.

---

[20] During the course of the Festival there were many performances of his work: Janet Hilton played the lst Clarinet Concerto; the Endymion Ensemble, the Quintet, Opus 7, and Trio, Opus 6; Hakan Hardenberger was the soloist in the Trumpet Concerto; and the Scottish National Orchestra played the Second Symphony.

[21] Stewart Craggs was later to compile *Malcolm Arnold: A Bio-Bibliography* (Greenwood Press, 1998)

He has been back on occasion since. The curtains in the street always flutter when the limousine with the Arnold crest turns up outside our house! [22]

Howard Blake was also in Perth in 1987, Malcolm attending Blake's oratorio *Benedictus* at the John Knox Church.

It was a very polite and proper occasion. Malcolm liked the *Benedictus* and came up to me afterwards in great enthusiasm. 'A terrific piece, a marvellous piece! But it's got a lot of sexuality in it!' 'I don't know what you mean by that,' I replied. 'Oh ho!' he said and winked at me. Later, we were waiting to be introduced to a Scottish VIP, whose pretty daughter was standing nearby. Malcolm suddenly went up to her, squeezed her by the bum and said 'How about a quick one?' I stepped in as fast as I could. 'For God's sake, Malcolm,' I said, moving him away ...[23]

Towards the end of 1987 Malcolm and Anthony finally left Wymondham and moved to nearby Attleborough, where Anthony had found a three-year-old house, which Malcolm, freed from the Court, was able to buy on a mortgage. Although it lacked its predecessor's old-world charm, it was easier to manage and that, for Anthony, with his growing responsibilities, was an important consideration.

The day of the move [24] was marked by a reminder that even though the house might be easier to run, the same might not be the case with Malcolm. In the morning, while Anthony was supervising removal vans, Malcolm quietly slipped out of the Old Mill and took a train to Norwich. Many hours later, with Anthony about to report his absence to the police, Malcolm caught an evening train to Attleborough, walked the lengthy distance from the station to the new house, let himself in and went straight to bed. It showed an extraordinary homing instinct, for he had only visited the house once before, but in all other respects this bizarre behaviour was an indication of a mind no longer readily accommodating other people's points of view.

Malcolm was to write five works in his first year at Attleborough, including a Recorder Concerto for Michala Petri and a Cello Concerto for Julian Lloyd Webber. The therapeutic value from this was immense, but his impaired capability, which he had somehow miraculously transcended in the Ninth Symphony, led to a lack of invention and substance. The Cello Concerto with its pages of scales and arpeggios was a worry for Julian Lloyd Webber as it was scheduled to be played at the Festival Hall.[25] He eventually decided to go ahead with it, not wanting to upset Malcolm, and was thankful the critics were kind. But it was not an easy occasion:

---

[22] June 2004

[23] Howard Blake sees Malcolm's outrageous nature as a late flowering of the tradition of bohemianism prevalent between the wars: 'Like Gully Jimpson in *The Horse's Mouth*! Malcolm goes back to Warlock, Moeran, Lambert, those kind of people!' (August 2003)

[24] 2 November 1987

[25] On 9 March 1989 with the Royal Philharmonic Orchestra conducted by Vernon Handley.

Malcolm insisted on shaking hands with all the players, which they found embarrassing because the work was obviously so poor. He was clearly still drinking, and, though not like the Malcolm of old, he much appreciated having some fun.[26]

Lloyd Webber played the first part of the *Fantasy* as an encore, 'to ensure there was good Arnold at the concert'. Malcolm was delighted, and listened to it from the leader's chair. After the concert Faber quickly decided they could not publish the Concerto and Lloyd Webber did his best to see that it was quietly forgotten.

It has re-emerged recently, however, in a revised version by David Ellis, commissioned by Anthony. David's comments are instructive:

> As soon as I saw the score I could see the muddle in Malcolm's mind. As in the *Fantasy for Recorder and String Quartet*,[27] another disaster of this period, he was turning the page before he had finished.

The slow movement, for example, started with a sombre little theme, after which there was a bare section with the cello playing arpeggios.

> They're nice arpeggios, but clearly there should be a tune in the orchestra going on at the same time. Malcolm would have heard it, but forgot to write it down. So I've written one in, springing, as it would have done, from the first subject.

While filling in the empty score David also reduced the orchestra, which helped tone down a number of exaggerations, which David believed were the result of muddled thinking.

> There were also some silly things. A piccolo and two flutes, for example, which were hardly used. The second flute only played one note, the very last of the first movement! That's not the real Malcolm. He would never have done that.

The alterations and additions are not simply Arnold pastiche, David at one stage giving a solo to an instrument Malcolm strongly disliked, the cor anglais, 'simply because it suited the music'. More than just an effective repair job, the Arnold-Ellis Cello Concerto is an attractive work in its own right, but, being something of a hybrid, it has so far struggled to find favour.[28]

In 1988 Charles Groves made an important move on behalf of the Ninth Symphony, which was still languishing in neglect two years after its completion. Booked to spend a week working with the students of the now-defunct Centre for Orchestral Studies, Groves arranged with the course's organiser, Basil Tschaikov, that he would rehearse the symphony with the students for a whole morning and then play it through. Anthony was alerted and hurriedly brought Malcolm down to London. There was an 'audience' of about a dozen at the Greenwich

---

[26] May 2003

[27] Written two years later and one of his very last works.

[28] After three years of waiting it was given its première in Schneppenbaum, Germany, 15 June 2003, by the Musica Art Orchestra of Sofia, conducted by Martin Panteleev, the soloist Stoian Razhkov. The printed score declares an 'amended version by Sir Malcolm Arnold in collaboration with David Ellis'.

*With Charles Groves at the first play-through of the Ninth Symphony, 1988*

Borough Hall, for, although Charles Groves had tried to persuade several concert managers to attend, none turned up. 'It was not in any sense a special occasion,' remembers Basil Tschaikov. 'A piece had been thrown on the scrapheap and this was simply an opportunity to let the composer hear it.'[29] Malcolm sat alone upstairs in the gallery. 'Malcolm behaved curiously. He seemed strangely detached, wandering off during the rehearsal, not really listening, and unusually jocular.'

It sounds like a defence mechanism, masking his eagerness and anxiety at hearing for the first time his deeply tragic summary of life. For Anthony too it was a highly emotional occasion. Malcolm was never good at thanking him for his devotion, but the symphony had been dedicated to him with love, and, as such, it was a present to cherish:

---

[29] March 2004

When he began writing the symphony, which I thought was to be about me, I went up to his study and wrote out things like 'happy; moody; angry; optimistic…' – all of my various facets! And after the run-through in Greenwich I said to Malcolm 'It doesn't sound like me at all. It's so bloody miserable!' 'It's not about you,' he replied, 'it's for you. It's the story of my recent life in Northampton till I got to Norfolk.' Hence, of course, that long slow movement at the end.

I sat beside Lady Groves at the run-through. She loved it, said it was heart-wrenching. We agreed it was like somebody trying to climb out of a barrel, but as they got to the top they kept slipping back, but in the end they finally escape, and that is what it was. He was in Northampton. He was going through total hell and he escaped.[30]

Robin Boyle, who had become Chairman of Faber Music on the recent retirement of Donald Mitchell, was present at the run-through, but unimpressed. Believing the symphony would damage Malcolm's reputation, Boyle decided not to publish the score. 'It seemed kinder to protect him.' This decision largely contributed to Georgina Ivor, Malcolm and Anthony turning to Novello, ending a collaboration of over twenty years.[31] As his professional reputation had plummeted and he had gone from one personal crisis to another, Faber's friendship and support had been unwavering.[32]

In April 1988, not long after the run-through, Malcolm suffered a heart attack, which led to a week in West Norwich Hospital and some important consequences. Told by the specialist that he must either give up alcohol or smoking, he opted to stop drinking. Anthony enthusiastically enforced the ban:

It was quite easy! I had discouraged him, and he'd been drinking less and less. He just stopped! Once he makes his mind up he just does it. It's not a problem. Yes, there was a problem when we went to receptions and concerts. He would always be looking out of the corner of his eye to see if I was watching. If I was, he took orange juice.

Anthony's fierce crusade against his drinking was an enormous help, but some mental or physical change had also occurred in Malcolm at the time of this illness, during which he lost seven stone. Suddenly, at the age of sixty-six, he found the all-consuming need to drink had gone.

Anthony was also given a choice by the doctors. Malcolm could stay in hospital, they told him, which could well disturb his mental equilibrium, or leave with Anthony, who would then have to bear the burden of some very unpleasant nursing for several weeks. Anthony without a moment's thought took Malcolm home.

---

[30] June 2003

[31] Anthony points out that Novello were offering a better financial deal for Malcolm.

[32] One of Faber's most recent endeavours on Malcolm's behalf had been to commission a sympathetic critic, Hugo Cole, to write a detailed analysis of his music, to help increase awareness of Malcolm's more serious works. Published in 1989, it did not include the Ninth Symphony. Faber also paid for the parts used in the 1988 run-through.

Malcolm still found the concentration needed for writing hard to muster, and he produced just one new piece in 1989, the *Welsh Dances*.[33] The misleading title is just one of several oddities raised by this fascinating work. Apart from the presence of a harp and the dedication to Emrys Lloyd-Roberts, the Court of Protection's Welsh case worker, there is nothing specifically Welsh about it. Instead there is more than a hint of the Arabian Nights. Nor is it really a set of dances at all, but a melodramatic suite of four movements, and one which so galvanized Malcolm's interest that his textures were a little fuller than usual for this period, though there is still much unison writing and not all the melodic ideas are original. The first dance, for example, begins with the same (Irene) theme which he had used three years earlier in the third *Irish Dance* and which originated in the *Fantasy for Brass Band*. There are also some charming eccentricities, such as the ending of the first dance, which (in the manner of the *Grand, Grand Overture*) threatens to go on *ad infinitum*. But there is wit and sparkle, particularly in the fine second dance, and overall the *Welsh Dances* reflect Malcolm's improved spirits and greater emotional stability.

This still did not extend, however, to a desire for reconciliation with Katherine and Isobel. Interviewed by a local reporter in April 1989, Malcolm was happy to misrepresent Isobel grotesquely:

> Malcolm Arnold no longer suffers from the deep depressions he sank into after his second wife, Isobel, walked out on him in 1978.[34] 'It is a painful memory,' he said. 'She took my son with her and I was forced to sell a beautiful house and pension off the gardener and housekeeper. I then went through a terrible illness and three times[35] tried to commit suicide with amphetamines.'[36]

Later in the year, however, he had made peace sufficiently to be able to see Edward in Kent. Anthony takes responsibility for this peace-making:

> It was a long time before Isobel would give way and let him see him, although I had tried and tried to persuade her. People just didn't realise how much Malcolm was changing. But eventually, when we did go down, there were wonderful visits. Edward was thrilled to see his father, and used to take him round the garden of the home, showing him all the things he himself had been doing. He was very artistic. He had this wonderful picture he'd made with lentils, sweet corn and things. It really was beautifully done and Malcolm was very taken with it.[37]

---

[33] Commissioned by the Hallé, they were completed on 8 April 1989 and premiered in Manchester on 19 July.

[34] In fact 1976

[35] He is referring, it seems, to the attempts of 1975 (before Isobel's departure) and 1977 in Dublin and 1979 in Belsize Park. To blame Isobel, by inference, for these is to make a mockery of the truth.

[36] *Evening Telegraph*, Kettering, 6 April 1989

[37] June 2003

In the year of the *Welsh Dances* Malcolm appeared in another television feature, Central's *An Act of Friendship*.[38] The film was structured around a visit to Birmingham,[39] where Malcolm listened informally to the Fine Arts Brass Ensemble playing one of his recent works, the Second Brass Quintet.[40] Malcolm comes over charmingly. He is relaxed and softly spoken, quick to smile, often dissolving into peals of laughter. His relationship with the young brass quintet is very cordial. And though, as ever, what he says is not always as impressive as the way he says it, it is overall a splendid performance.[41] It is so good, in fact, that it partly masks the fact that the new work for brass quintet is disappointingly naïve.[42]

Anthony remembers this Birmingham excursion as a great success. Piers Burton-Page, the film's unseen interviewer, is a little more cautious.

> My memory of the sessions is that they were very hard work. We recorded for two solid days which, for a thirty minute programme, is an absurd ratio and an indication of how difficult it was.[43]

The director, Terry Bryan, who initiated the project, discovered 'that you couldn't relax with Malcolm' and that his interest in listening to the Quintet was only fleeting.

> But on the whole I found him very co-operative, articulate and interesting. Just once, when he was under some pressure, he exploded and went off on an extremely rude and cutting tirade. So I sat him down in a chair and laid things on the line to him. 'We've invested a lot of money in this programme, we're on a very tight schedule and if you go on talking like that, I'll simply walk out.' Malcolm thought about this for a moment, lit a small cigar, and quietly resumed the interview.[44]

A year later Malcolm was in front of the cameras yet again, this time for Anglia's *A Portrait of Malcolm Arnold*.[45] As in Birmingham, he is very relaxed, sitting in a wing-backed chair in his braces, smoking the inevitable cheroot, and, between puffs, speaking softly and with oracular certainty, giving each tendentious generalisation real authority:

> If you don't hear film scores inspired by Berlioz, they're no damn good.

> If music doesn't reflect the man, it's no good!

---

[38] 7 February 1989

[39] Woodbrook College at Bourneville

[40] The Ensemble, for whom it was written, had given its first performance in the summer of 1988 at the Pittville Pump Room, Cheltenham.

[41] He states, for example, that the *Grand, Grand Overture* is 'a parody of those Victorian overtures in the Proms before Sir Henry Wood'.

[42] In marked contrast to his splendid Quintet for Brass of 1961

[43] March 2004

[44] April 2004

[45] Directed by Richard Fawkes, for the *Notes on Norfolk* series, 1990

In the most interesting section he is shown gazing with admiring eyes at Michala Petri, as she talks about their collaboration. It is an insight into just how agreeable Malcolm can make himself in the presence of an attractive young lady. Even when he tells Michala – now in her mid-twenties, and already at the top of her profession – that she still has things to learn on her instrument, he manages to do it graciously. He is, we are told, about to write her a new concerto for a concert at the Carnegie Hall. 'Michala. It's a very great compliment,' he says to her mellifluously, 'and I shall not disappoint you.'[46]

For all the charming urbanity, Malcolm does not always answer questions directly. Taxed, for example, as to whether or not he could work when depressed, he replies, 'You have to', but then embarks on an account of the suicide of Grimaldi, 'the greatest clown who ever lived', which totally demolishes his point. He gives a graphic description of Grimaldi's uncompromising end:

> He hung himself in Drury Lane Theatre. He must have climbed up into the flies, put a rope around his neck and jumped, and I don't think he was found till he was wanted for the pantomime the next evening. 'Where's Grimaldi?' [Malcolm points.] 'He's up there! Dead!'

Then comes the moral:

> So although we're clowns, we're all serious at heart, dear.

All of Malcolm's long experience in spinning yarns with a pint in his hand pays off on such occasions. Grimaldi's suicide is so convincingly told that it is hard to grasp that it is, in fact, entire fantasy, for Grimaldi died, many years after retirement, in a Pentonville tavern. But Malcolm was never one to let historical accuracy spoil a good story.

Nor was he one to disappoint his public. And in 1990, in addition to Michala Petri's commission, he completed three other works: an overture for the Norfolk Youth Orchestra;[47] a suite for the Manx Youth Orchestra;[48] and *Flourish For Battle*, a commission for the RAF Band for a celebration in the Festival Hall of the Fiftieth Anniversary of the Battle of Britain. All three were threadbare works, damaging to his reputation, the *Flourish* having to be rewritten by Christopher Palmer. Malcolm's Norfolk period had produced one major work and three or four good minor ones. In all the circumstances this was something of a miracle. But he had nothing more to offer.

When the United States Air Force asked for a work, therefore, in March 1991, a long and not particularly edifying saga resulted, which somehow culminated dramatically in Anthony invoking the aid of President Clinton:

---

[46] In the event he was to do so. The *Fantasy for Recorder and String Quartet* (which he wrote instead of a second concerto) was to prove a weak work.

[47] *The Robert Kett Overture* Op 141, first performed by the Norfolk Youth Orchestra under Simon Halsey on 25 July 1990.

[48] *A Manx Suite (Little Suite No 3)* Op 142 first performed by the Manx Youth Orchestra on 8 December 1990, Malcolm conducting.

While we were in New York for the première of Michala Petri's Fantasy, an official from an airbase in Washington DC came to see Sir Malcolm and me, asking for a Fanfare and Wind Band Suite. He said they could not afford much money, but would give us a first-class trip and treat us like royalty when we came over for the première.

Malcolm did the Fanfare, it was sent over and they were thrilled with it.[49] He then had his first stroke and was unable to do the second piece, which Christopher Palmer did, and it was sent over, but proved a non-starter.[50] They then agreed to a wind band version of *The Sound Barrier*, which was achieved by a collaboration between Malcolm and Martin Ellerby.[51] Sadly the guy who had invited us over had been made redundant and they would not honour their agreement. They offered us two economy flights to Chicago and 25 dollars a day expenses. I declined, and wrote to Bill Clinton, complaining.[52]

Malcolm all his life had rarely left a work unfinished, because he knew exactly where he was going before he started, but in these final desultory years he abandoned several projects. Having been inspired by hearing Nigel Kennedy on television, Malcolm began a Violin Concerto, only to give up after working on it for three days.[53] A work commissioned by the Incorporated Association of Preparatory Schools Orchestra and scheduled for a concert at the Barbican only ever got as far as a title, *A Flavour of Ischia*.[54] A *Sinfonia Concertante* for flute, clarinet, horn, bassoon and strings was begun and then restarted for violin, cello, oboe and horn, before being changed to a *Sinfonia Duo Concertante* for horn, viola and strings, in which guise it was promised to Ross Pople and the London Festival Orchestra.[55] But Malcolm simply could not produce it. Anthony later showed what Malcolm had done to a young composer, Philip Wood:

> It was a scribbly, untidy score. It was just not Malcolm Arnold. He had run out of ideas; it was repetitive and the textures were thin. I had to tell Anthony there was nothing I could do with it.[56]

[49] Christopher Palmer was actively involved, in fact, re-using ideas from the *Farnham Festival Fanfare* and the last movement of the Sixth Symphony. It was published as *Forces' Fanfare*.

[50] Christopher Palmer, who arranged several suites from Malcolm's films, on this occasion manufactured a *Dance Suite* from Malcolm's ballet *Elektra* and his sketches for *The Three Musketeers*.

[51] 'I ended up arranging *The Sound Barrier*,' writes Martin Ellerby, 'for which I was paid by Novello. We agreed that the terminology would be 'This arrangement was commissioned by the U.S.A.F. (Washington DC) and the adaptation made by Martin Ellerby under the close guidance of the composer'.' The first performance was given by the United States Air Force Band in Chicago, December 1995.

[52] July 2004

[53] There are just over seven pages of sketches of the first movement of the Violin Concerto. It is in A minor and Malcolm intended the work to be 'approximately 20 to 23 minutes'.

[54] There are also the first 13 bars of a Saxophone Concerto.

[55] It was even advertised for the concert he was giving in the Queen Elizabeth Hall on Malcolm's seventieth birthday.

[56] August 2003

Philip was one in a long line of young composers to whom Malcolm had given encouragement. He had written to Malcolm, expressing interest in some composition lessons. After a meeting in Northampton,[57] where he brought along some of his work, Philip was invited up to Attleborough, Anthony organising the occasional visits enthusiastically, largely in the interests of Malcolm's morale.[58] But Philip found them a disappointment:

> Malcolm's health was unfortunately not up to it. He was often irascible! I would take him scores and, in the mornings, he would comment on them. Then we would go out to lunch and afterwards there would possibly be further chat, before he disappeared early to bed.

Philip was involved when Malcolm finally gave up the struggle to compose. He had been asked to write a Fanfare for the Norwich Festival, something which he would have been able to do in his heyday in a few minutes in the back of a taxi. However, it was now causing such a problem that Anthony asked Philip Wood if he would help write it. Philip sat down with Malcolm and they prepared the manuscript paper for three trumpets and three trombones.

> Malcolm wrote down the time signature of 2/4 and then some root position chords of C major. Then a chord of Bb D F A. It was a very typical Malcolm Arnold chord, the kind of thing he would fling out in *The Heroes of Telemark*. But as he did it, I could see him visibly tire. There was a long pause. 'Can I stop now?' he enquired.

Malcolm's new publishers, Novello, had been getting more and more anxious. They had originally been sent several scores by Georgina Ivor, including the Ninth Symphony, the Cello Concerto and the Serenade for Tenor and Strings,[59] which they agreed to publish although concerned about their content. Leslie East, the publishing director, thought the Ninth 'shockingly stark'[60] but that 'it might just about hold together in performance'. The rest, he thought, were 'a pale shadow of earlier Arnold pieces'. However, the Novello situation was complicated by a takeover[61] which involved their acquisition of Paterson's catalogue, containing many of Malcolm's important works. Believing that to refuse to take new items could sour relations with Anthony and Malcolm at this very early stage, Novello published all the latest work despite reservations.

---

[57] At the Lime Trees Hotel. Philip was studying at Nene College; Malcolm and Anthony had come up for a concert.

[58] Anthony adds: 'Carl Vincent was another of the young composers to whom Malcolm gave encouragement. They came and stayed at the house and worked with him each day and were charged nothing. I organised this enthusiastically as I loved to see Malcolm doing what he enjoyed most, talking about music. I think they learnt most from his talent of orchestration.' (July 2004)

[59] Published under the title of *Contrasts*

[60] May 2004

[61] They were taken over by Filmtrax.

Eventually, Leslie East arranged a meeting with Anthony on 8 January 1991, at which he explained that in Novello's considered view Malcolm was unlikely to produce any more work of passable quality.

> Anthony, though disappointed, recognised that he wasn't in a position to judge and accepted the suggestion. He had been encouraging Malcolm to write something every day by way of therapy.

It was agreed that no further commissions would now be accepted but that Anthony would still encourage Malcolm to write for his own pleasure.

Another important meeting took place in 1990, this time at the Savile Club, where both Malcolm and Anthony were members. Although the club was an all-male preserve, Katherine had been invited to meet there for tea. Katherine had been largely out of touch with them since the flurry of letters in 1986, and there was much to discuss, as that summer Malcolm made Anthony his Attorney.[62] In the event a long-lasting reconciliation was not effected, although, as Anthony writes, 'Malcolm set off afterwards happily to his solicitor to put Katherine in his will for the first time since his marriage to Isobel'. The meeting ended in predictable disarray when a club steward politely suggested they should carry on their discussion off the premises.

Katherine's memories of the meeting are largely of her father's wish to cause a stir by ostentatiously breaking club rules, and not for the first time. 'They didn't blame Malcolm at all!' remembers Anthony. 'All the blame naturally descended on me!' It has to be possible from the choice of venue that Malcolm was deriving some amusement from the whole stressful situation of confrontation. And psychiatric theory would certainly suggest the chances for reconciliation were minimal now that Malcolm was no longer writing music. For creation and destruction are seen as closely related to each other, the act of creation often involving the act of destruction. It is also suggested that 'a key motive for engaging in creative activity is often an attempt at unearthing and working through the sources of destructive feelings'.[63] Artists 'frequently create in order that they do not destroy...' Malcolm's relationship with his family is consistent with this, the uneasiest times being those when he was not writing.

There was much happening in 1991 to keep Malcolm's mind off his disappointment at Novello's decision. A 70th birthday was an admirable promotional tool and Georgina Ivor made the very best of it, Malcolm's return to public esteem gathering real momentum in 1991. On 21 October, Malcolm's birthday, Ross Pople's London Festival Orchestra featured some of his most important works at the Queen Elizabeth Hall[64] and five days later, at the same venue, Barry Wordsworth and the BBC Concert Orchestra gave a lighter

---

[62] In 28 June 1990 Anthony was appointed Malcolm's sole attorney.
[63] Albert Rothenberg: *Creativity And Madness*, Johns Hopkins University, 1990.
[64] The programme included the Fifth Symphony, *Third Sinfonietta*, the Double Violin Concerto and the First Flute Concerto.

*With Ross Pople at the 70th birthday celebrations, 21 October 1991*

programme, which was also broadcast.[65] Throughout November an Arnold/ Haydn Festival took place, centred on Manchester. The Hallé Orchestra, the BBC Philharmonic, David Ellis' Northern Chamber Orchestra, the Medici String Quartet and John McCabe were among those participating in the twenty-five concerts, at a wide variety of venues. John McCabe recalls:[66]

> It was a great occasion for me, if a little scary, to play Malcolm's *Variations on a Ukrainian Folk Song* at a mid-day concert, broadcast live, and for him to be there! But he was extremely generous with his reception of my performance. And the warmth he expressed was especially pleasing from someone who has always been one of my musical heroes.[67]

Anthony took Malcolm to celebratory events all over the country. In Canterbury, where several 'Mozart and Arnold' concerts were held, Malcolm did

---

[65] This included the *Harmonica Concerto*, the *Concerto for Two Pianos* and Christopher Palmer's new suite from *The Bridge on The River Kwai*.

[66] July 2003

[67] John McCabe, meeting Malcolm later at a dinner around this period, was struck by his 'tremendous knowledge of the repertoire, orchestras and conductors. One got all sorts of insights into conductors, many confirming one's own instincts!'

a pre-concert talk with John Amis. He also made a personal appearance at the Harrogate Festival, where the public were invited to 'Meet the Composer'. Such events, though good for Malcolm's morale, strained to the limit his ability to cope. John Amis had to bring his interview to a hurried close.

Another encouragement to Malcolm in his seventieth year was a rare appearance at the Proms, Julian Bream giving a performance of the Guitar Concerto[68] in a televised concert. It was greeted with great enthusiasm and Malcolm enjoyed coming onto the platform at the end, though David Ellis believes this damaged his relationship with John Drummond, the Controller of Radio Three and Director of the Proms:

> When Malcolm appeared the audience were cheering madly and his body language (with arms raised high) communicated 'I'm back!' John Drummond up there in his box would have been fuming. Anthony had said to Malcolm, 'For God's sake don't do anything stupid! Don't take your trousers off! Don't pee on the prommers! Just go out there and wave!' But unfortunately he couldn't have foreseen that he was going to walk on so arrogantly and stand there rather like Napoleon or Mussolini! The prommers loved it! But as an 'Up yours, pal!' to Drummond it was a disaster.

Malcolm's seventieth birthday may not have endeared him to John Drummond, but it did encourage many expressions of affection from the musical world.

Among the tributes was a letter from Yehudi Menuhin:

> Dear Malcolm,
>
>    It is nice to know that the gods have been with us, because by sheer coincidence and good fortune I am conducting your *Tam O'Shanter* in Zurich a day after your 70th birthday. May there be many more near-perfect timings as this which allow me to present my tribute so shortly after the very important day.
>    Devotedly,
>    Yours Admiringly,
>    Yehudi

The celebratory year of 1991, therefore, was in many ways the climax of the 'sparkling' era of regained vigour, a chance for Malcolm to realise just how much he had returned into public favour. And it was particularly encouraging for him that core works were both being played and appreciated. The Fifth Symphony, for example, thirty years on, sounded just as fresh and challenging in the Ross Pople concert as it had ever done. The core works were standing the test of time.

Unfortunately 1991 also brought further illness, a first stroke, which, although causing no paralysis, aged Malcolm considerably. Malcolm is very gaunt in the BBC's *Omnibus* film, directed by Kriss Russman, celebrating his seventieth birthday. *Malcolm Arnold at 70*, in rebutting the question 'Has Arnold's neglect been justified?', shows Malcolm conducting the BBC Concert Orchestra in several orchestral excerpts, taking the Matthews Norfolk Brass Band through the

---

[68] 20 July, with the BBC Concert Orchestra conducted by Barry Wordsworth

*Padstow Lifeboat* on the beach at Great Yarmouth, and revisiting the hangar where *Three Shanties for Wind Quintet* had first been performed.[69] Throughout all the location footage Malcolm shows little sparkle. On Yarmouth beach, as he flails away madly before the brass band, he is wild-eyed and seems scarcely of this world at all.

Kriss Russman, in trying to open up debate on the music, invited the *Observer*'s Peter Heyworth, but disappointingly the most vociferous of Malcolm's past adversaries restricts himself to some dull generalisations.

> I don't tremendously warm to Arnold's music. I must say I don't think much of it will last. But who can say?

It was likewise disappointing that the current Controller of Radio Three and Director of the Proms, John Drummond, declined to participate, though his predecessor, Robert Ponsonby, did agree, adroitly declining to get drawn on the music and making a convincing rebuttal of the suggestion of a 'conspiracy' against Malcolm. Lined up on Malcolm's side were some articulate supporters, led by Julian Lloyd Webber, Piers Burton-Page and Norman Lebrecht, but Kriss Russman allowed the music to be the main advocate.

Very boldly the decision was taken to let the programme culminate in the unknown and unwanted Ninth Symphony, on whose behalf Piers Burton-Page made an emotional appeal:

> It seems to me a scandal that the score, now five years old, has never been played. It's a challenging work, and in some ways an eccentric work, but this is a great composer speaking to us from deep in his heart and it needs to be heard.

Malcolm then took the BBC Concert Orchestra through the closing bars of the *Lento*. Kriss Russman remembers it as a moment of great drama:[70]

> The orchestra had been a little apprehensive before the recording sessions, knowing that Malcolm wasn't well, and with Barry Wordsworth standing by just in case. But he behaved well and when they got to the Ninth, they realised they were involved in something special. They weren't sure quite what it was all about, but there was a real tension in the air.

This was captured beautifully by the camera. As the *Lento* makes its slow, inexorable progress, Russman moves from one thoughtful face to the next, giving a powerful visual endorsement to everything Piers Burton-Page had said. And such is the power of television that within months a slot had been found for the Symphony in a broadcast before a studio audience, given by Charles Groves and the BBC Philharmonic.[71] The long wait was over.

*Malcolm Arnold at 70* is as much about Malcolm as his music, and has at its heart a series of monologues, shot in painful close-up. The buoyancy seen

---

[69] Or so it seemed. It was, in fact, a similar hangar in Norfolk.
[70] May 2004
[71] 20 January 1992 (Radio Three)

in earlier television programmes has totally gone. Malcolm speaks slowly, in sombre tones, as if weighing his words very carefully. Yet here again appearances are deceptive, for what we see on the screen does not begin to reflect the emotional mayhem which Kriss Russman experienced behind the scenes:

> The film was very difficult to make, because Malcolm was not well mentally, and, indeed, hadn't been well for many years. Malcolm was always very difficult during the filming and behaved in a manner that I can only assume was that of someone mentally disturbed. His regular outbursts of verbal abuse to everyone, mixed with moments of extraordinary calm and politeness, made us all react with a combination of nervousness, incredulity, fascination and deep sadness.[72]

The fascination also extended to the relationship between Malcolm and Anthony, Russman being most impressed by Anthony's overall authority. When Malcolm, for example, was conducting the 'Annetta theme' in the Fifth Symphony at an exaggeratedly slow tempo, holding up on every sound, Russman asked Anthony to ask Malcolm to speed up. The message was immediately implemented.

> Anthony told me that he administered medication to Malcolm every day and altered the dose depending on Malcolm's behaviour or state of mind. Looking after Malcolm was clearly a thankless task and I wondered why Anthony would want to do it – especially, as he himself admitted, a fair amount of physical aggression was required to persuade Malcolm to 'behave' … It was certainly clear that Anthony had complete control over Malcolm and that Malcolm did what he was told …

Even Anthony's encouragement, however, failed to elicit co-operation over the five weeks of filmed interviews:

> Most of our interviews produced nothing which could be used. It was only on the very last day of filming when, coincidentally, Anthony was out of the room for the first time (he'd decided to mow the lawn), that Malcolm gave us not only coherent material but material that was extraordinarily moving and shockingly revealing.

The problems experienced by Russman's film crew make Anthony's achievement in coping with Malcolm on a daily basis all the more remarkable:

> I've filmed in two war zones since making that documentary, but nothing compares with the daily apprehension and extreme anxiousness that filled my whole being whilst working with Malcolm.

In seeking to produce a rounded portrait, Kriss Russman persuaded Katherine to participate, neatly inserting her comments on the Seventh Symphony after an extract of the first movement:

> I can see my brothers in the last two movements but as regards the one about me – it's very energetic and even violent – I think I see my father in that.

Isobel was also encouraged to make a contribution. In the previous *Omnibus* programme, made in Cornwall over twenty years earlier, Isobel had been

---

[72] December 2003

virtually ignored, only momentarily sighted with Edward on a beach and with Malcolm and the Duke of Kent at the lifeboat launch. Now, for the first time, at fifty-eight, she was being allowed to speak her mind and she did so with characteristic generosity, strongly condemning Malcolm's treatment by the musical press:

> The critics used either to dismiss him or not bother to show up at the concerts where his music was being played. If his music was in the second half, they would leave at the interval and wouldn't mention it at all. It wasn't what they said about his music that upset him, that they didn't take it seriously, it was what they said [that] was personal about him. He thought very deeply about what he was doing, he put a lot of thought into the technique part, he put a lot of thought into what he was trying to say. He longed to communicate, he thought that was what his work was for.

Her mouth puckered with emotion as the injustice of it all struck her afresh, and the film was tactfully cut at this point.

Isobel discreetly alluded to the drinking as if it was purely the result of his lack of acceptance by the musical establishment:

> He got angry about the situation he found himself in because his music, he felt, was not being properly appreciated. When he was feeling particularly depressed he went off to the pub, which if you're in a situation you can't deal with because you're help-less in the hands of others, it seems to me a reasonable thing to do.

Without divulging any details, she simply described her marriage as 'a very interesting experience' but something she would not want to repeat.

Around the time of the film Isobel had enjoyed a reconciliation with Malcolm, when she contacted Anthony and suggested they meet in Norfolk. It was eight years since Malcolm had taken against her, but the reunion passed off very happily, as Anthony recalls:

> We had a wonderful day, with a fine lunch at the Sinclair Hotel, Wymondham, for which she insisted on paying! We also visited Wymondham Abbey. She was charming, a lovely woman.

Nine years earlier, at the time Malcolm was settling in at the White House with Sally Charlton, Isobel had begun a new life, as one of only two teachers starting off a Pre-Prep department for Hampstead Hill School. Her colleague was Jenny Martin:

> Isobel had done a post-graduate course at St Margaret's, but this was a whole new beginning. She was wonderful from the start! Such a placid, giving nature! Her philosophy was that children should learn through play, and by meeting poetry, good music and song. We made all our own resources, and as well as doing the teaching, at first we even did the lunches and answered the telephone! For both of us it was a glorious adventure![73]

---

[73] May 2004

Isobel had kept Edward with her as long as she could. Bernadette Maugham, who also worked with her at Hampstead Hill, recalls:

> He was quite a handful. He was extremely focused. He would get an idea in his head and just follow it, and Isobel did her best to assist.[74]

He was very interested in tea at one point, knowing everything there was to know about it; Isobel took him to every tea-house in London and even to the old docks which the tea clippers had used. 'He was a lovely boy,' Jenny says, 'on the brink of genius because that's how focused he was.' But unfortunately, as he grew older, he inevitably became more of a handful:

> There were a few physical struggles, and she decided, for his sake, to find somewhere he could be looked after. She really didn't want him away from her. She had hated boarding school herself. But it was only through her great love for him that she was able to keep him with her as long as she did.

Isobel had some very deserved happiness at Crouch End. She had always adored Katherine and Robert and so it was a great joy to her to be living so close to Katherine and her children, two of whom she taught at Hampstead Hill. She delighted in her garden, making it exciting for Katherine's children with a marsh and pond. She never spoke anything but well of Malcolm, often saying that she would have stayed on with him if it hadn't been for Edward. At school every Burns Day she would read the poem of 'Tam O'Shanter' and then play the children Malcolm's overture. She went to concerts whenever his music was being played. Life with Malcolm had reduced her to smoking sixty cigarettes a day and drinking heavily, but in her new life she no longer needed either. She had too many interests ever to be lonely, loving books, taking evening classes (in advanced cooking and elementary bee-keeping) and was always going off to art exhibitions.

Her love for Scotland had never left her and many holidays had been spent there. She was much looking forward to retiring in 1993, when she would have been sixty, and had acquired a little cottage near Galloway.[75] But she never reached retirement, for in 1992 she was struck down very suddenly by lung cancer. It was diagnosed in February and she was dead by May.

Jenny went to live with her to delay hospitalisation.

> It got so bad that physically she couldn't walk up the stairs so she and I would play a game. I used to get behind her and we'd sing 'It's a long way to Tipperary' and she would take it step by step ... Edward was all she talked about. What would happen to Edward? She loved him so much ... She had a grandfather clock and, looking at it one day, she said 'I know I'm dying. It has only ever stopped once before – when my mother was dying. And look! It's stopped again!'

---

[74] May 2004
[75] Called 'The Tack Room' at the Cairn Smore Stables, close to Newton Stewart, where her parents had lived for many years.

Right at the end, when she went into Whittington Hospital, she put on the wedding ring which Malcolm had lovingly given her nearly thirty years before. Despite everything, she had really never stopped loving him.

Bernadette would visit every afternoon from school.

> They tried to drain her chest of fluid but finally she said 'No more!', winking at the nurse at the same time.

Katherine was with her when she died. 'Enough's enough,' Isobel had whispered to her.

At the funeral the church was overflowing with grieving friends, testimony of her great popularity in the school and locally. 'She hadn't a bad bone in her body,' says Jenny, simply. A few days later, Katherine and her son Sebastian scattered Isobel's ashes in the sea at Cornwall.

For Edward it was a devastating blow. He was now twenty-seven and still living in care in Kent. Although Southborough was some distance from Crouch End Isobel had visited him with devoted regularity. Katherine now took over as Edward's guardian, doing her very best to help him through a turbulent period which involved several unsatisfactory moves.

Malcolm did not attend Isobel's funeral, though he was shocked at the news of her death. Not long afterwards he had a second stroke, which weakened him a little on his right side. He could well be dead in two months, Anthony was told. Yet again, however, he rallied, confounding medical opinion, and a year later he was in his finery at Buckingham Palace being knighted. Supported by many friends and admirers [76] – and with the Arts Minister, David Mellor, able to present his case to the Prime Minister, John Major – Malcolm at last received the award he had long coveted. Anthony remembers the occasion with pride:

> We stayed at the Tara Towers Hotel in Kensington. We drove through to the inner quadrangle of the palace. Malcolm was then shown to a separate room to be briefed on the procedures, while my sister Wendy and I took our seats in the gallery. It was a wonderful moment for us when Malcolm came into the room through the left-hand entrance, walked across and knelt in front of the Queen. After she had knighted him, he rose, exchanged a few words with her and then left by the right-hand door. He behaved perfectly, as always on the big occasions. After the ceremony we proceeded to the courtyard where Malcolm was waiting and we had our photographs taken. He was really happy and excited to have had his contribution to British music recognised in this way. [77]

The following day was something of a contrast. There was a crisis at the Savile where Malcolm and Anthony were lunching:

> He was having Scotch Woodcock, and dropped some scrambled egg on his trousers. I went to wipe it, whereupon he picked up his plate and threw it at me.

---

[76] Notably Mike Purton, John Kehoe, Neville Marriner, John Lill, Larry Westland and John Woolf.
[77] June 2004

They were sitting at the club's large dining table and the egg went not only over Anthony but his next door neighbour, a journalist. Next day there appeared in the *Daily Telegraph* the heading 'Recently knighted composer throws his lunch'. Anthony was displeased:

> The Savile is a private club and what goes on there should have been private. Both of us therefore resigned our membership in protest. They accepted mine, but made Malcolm an honorary member!

In 1993, the year of the knighthood, Malcolm made a nostalgic return to Dublin to attend the mass for his friend of Camelot days, John Ryan. John's widow, Deirdre, who eighteen years earlier had saved his life when she arrived with a copy of John's book at Meadowcroft, was impressed with the effect of Anthony's care.

> He was very beautifully dressed. He looked fantastic. Well-kept! So much better! Stunning! He was not drinking at all and was very sociable. It was a sunny day and we were out in the garden and Malcolm took a shine to a girl there, Evelyn McGonagall. He liked a woman beside him, to talk to. Later we had a really pleasant dinner at Jury's.[78]

On such informal social occasions an odd lapse by Malcolm did not really matter, whereas professionally it could have serious repercussions. There was talk, for example, of a Swiss recording of Malcolm's wind music, and an executive interested in the project had come to Attleborough to assess the possibilities. Malcolm behaved impeccably as they listened to recordings of various pieces of chamber music for some time. But not long after it had finished Anthony left the room and Malcolm seized his moment. 'Now you've heard the music,' he said to the executive, 'you can piss off!'

The extent of Malcolm's illness for a number of years was a loyally guarded secret, with Anthony the chief custodian. Somehow, by the sheer strength of his personality, Anthony managed to encourage Malcolm to say and do the right things in public, more often than not. He used the medication sparingly and expertly. And if anything went wrong in the daily round and a Swiss executive happened to be told to 'piss off', then it was made very clear that this was simply a question of Malcolm having 'a bad day'. It was never to be acknowledged publicly that Malcolm's periods of lucidity were shortening. The bad days simply became a little more frequent. The fierceness with which Anthony had fought early on to rescue Malcolm's finances was now matched by that with which he countered whispered suggestions that Malcolm had 'lost it'.

By limiting the extent to which Malcolm's illness was generally known, Anthony has ensured his own contribution to Malcolm's welfare has been underestimated. Without Anthony, Malcolm would long ago have been consigned to a mental hospital, where his hold on reality would have speedily

---

[78] August 2003

slipped. When in the 1990s the 'sparkle' finally left Malcolm and the illness gained a greater hold, it was only Anthony's gritty determination which kept him in touch with reality. Two things in particular helped greatly: listening to his own music and being taken out into the musical world. Just as in the past Malcolm had only found respite from his demons in the writing and making of music, so now in the 1990s he found similar respite in listening to it, Anthony intuitively realising early on how much comfort Malcolm might draw from it. Anthony's decision to involve Malcolm in both amateur and professional music-making was likewise important for his mental well-being, minimising his feelings of rejection by the musical world.

For Anthony, therefore, who had fought hard to convince everyone that Malcolm was generally still 'in good form', it was very distressing when, in 1995, an article in a national newspaper suggested the exact opposite. Alexander Waugh's interview[79] in the *Sunday Telegraph*[80] painted the domestic scene in Attleborough realistically rather than in idealised tints. Although he had set out to write an article shaming the musical establishment for its lack of support of a composer whose music he had always admired,[81] he found the Attleborough ménage so interesting it claimed most of his space.

Waugh's first shock was Malcolm's home. Great composers have tended to live in ample and romantic settings. There was Walton's La Mortella on Ischia; Elgar's rustic retreat at Broadheath; Britten's sixteenth-century Red House, with its swimming-pool and tennis court; Gerald Finzi's sprawling village home on the top of a Berkshire hill; and Michael Tippett's huge timber-framed house with far-reaching views of Wiltshire. Malcolm's situation was very different.

> The first surprise was not 74-year-old Sir Malcolm himself but his house – a plain, ordinary detached dwelling on a modern housing estate – a most unlikely residence for a composer of such driven and spirited music … How could the ruminative splendour of the Ninth Symphony have possibly been conceived by the same brain that chose to live in a place like this? But he seems not to care about his environment. His mottled pink sitting room, it turned out, had been furnished and decorated entirely by Anthony Day.

The interview itself began quite promisingly, Malcolm offering the usual stock responses. Out again came the runaway red-haired art student and the wartime foot-shooting. ('Most people would be anarchists if they had the choice,

---

[79] Son of Auberon and grandson of Evelyn Waugh, Alexander was opera critic of the *Evening Standard* at the time. 'I love Malcolm's music and believe in it. I thought the article was warm and affectionate.' (July 2004)

[80] *Faithful in his Fashion*, 17 September 1995. It was in the very first Sunday Magazine the newspaper produced, so it attracted considerable attention.

[81] 'More than 120 composers have been represented in this year's Proms,' he began, 'but Sir Malcolm Arnold is not among them. The BBC Symphony Orchestra has not played a note of his music in twelve years …' It was a well-intentioned article.

*Malcolm and Anthony relax on holiday in Dubai, 1998*

wouldn't they, dear?') It was only when, inevitably, they reached *Kwai* and the Oscar that the interview went wrong:

'Did you go to Hollywood to collect your Oscar?'

'No I bloody didn't, my daughter used it as a doorstop.'

Pointing at Waugh, Malcolm then declaimed lugubriously, 'I have been faithful to thee, Cynara! in my fashion.' Asked what he meant by this, he refused to say. And every time Waugh attempted a further question, Malcolm interrupted with the same quotation. He was clearly having a 'bad day' and it got worse:

> Whenever Anthony left the room, even for an instant, Sir Malcolm bared his teeth like a chimpanzee, muttered, swore, stared at me with fearful hatred, and twitched like a tropical bird. As soon as Anthony returned, peace was restored, and he resumed a pose of benign and sophisticated good humour.

There was much more that Waugh could have included, to show the extent of Malcolm's malaise that day:

> He was shuffling around a lot in a quite scary way, sometimes looking as if he wanted to kill me. He wandered around the room, stopped and stared at me from different angles. He had an extraordinary waspishness about him. Sometimes he was quite benign and then suddenly quite vicious.[82]

Of the many interviews of the 1990s Alexander Waugh's is the one which chronicles Anthony's devotion most tellingly. Anthony, for example, was asked to chart a typical day:

> In the morning I give Malcolm a shave and a bath, I make his breakfast, bring him downstairs where he sits and listens to music on CD or watches one of his films. Lunch is always out: we usually go to the Dunstan Hall Hotel[83] fourteen miles away. We come back, have a rest, and then listen to more music. We never have dinner.

---

[82] July 2004

[83] An attractive Victorian manor house in the country, it had only recently been converted into a hotel. Malcolm frequently would play at the piano there before lunch. Regular lunches at Dunstan Hall went on for many years.

Impressed, Waugh asked Anthony why he was devoting his life to Malcolm.

> The previous person I was looking after became the love of my life, but he died. I like older men; and when I was asked if I would look after Malcolm, I thought 'Oh good! Here we go again!'

It was hardly a complete answer, but it gave an insight into the uncomplaining love which was keeping the Attleborough ménage intact through good times and bad.

Another outside view of Malcolm at this period comes from Matthew Taylor, a young composer and conductor. In 1996 Matthew, about to conduct the Fifth Symphony and already a great enthusiast of Malcolm's music, was invited by Anthony to have lunch with them.

> They kindly picked me up by car. Malcolm was sitting in the front passenger seat and at first totally ignored me. 'Here's Matthew Taylor,' said Anthony. Malcolm muttered something. He seemed to be living in his own world. But once we started talking about music, Malcolm became interested, left his own world, and became a very friendly and engaging companion. The key thing was to stop him being bored, when he would drift away again. It was a memorable meeting, but not a comfortable one. We were talking about Robert Simpson, his contemporary. 'Do you know the symphonies?' I asked. 'Yes,' he replied. 'Which is your favourite?' 'The twelfth.' 'But he only wrote eleven!' 'Yes, I know!'

Matthew is still unsure whether it was a joke or a jibe, but, as Malcolm later spoke generously about Simpson, it was probably the former. Later, the conversation turned to religion.

> He asked me what my beliefs were and I said I was an agnostic. So I asked him the same question. 'Why don't you mind your own fucking business?' he growled.[84]

That same year, in 1996, Malcolm's seventy-fifth birthday brought another promotional jamboree[85] with two hundred and eighty concerts around the country and a celebration patrons' list which included the Duchess of Kent, Yehudi Menuhin, Edward Downes, Neville Marriner and Richard Attenborough. In April there was an all-Arnold concert at the Barbican, given by Richard Hickox and the LSO, combined with a study day and an exhibition. On his birthday the Ninth Symphony was part of an all-Arnold programme with Andrew Penny and the Royal Liverpool Philharmonic at the Derngate, Northampton. Two days earlier Ross Pople's Festival Orchestra also played the Ninth Symphony at the Royal Festival Hall, where Yehudi Menuhin conducted the Double Violin Concerto.

---

[84] July 2003

[85] Georgina Ivor was no longer working for Malcolm by this time, and the seventy-fifth birthday celebrations were organised by an old friend and colleague, Stan Hibbert. Among many promotional successes he persuaded the BBC to issue a double CD of some of Malcolm's broadcast performances.

*With Anthony, c.1996*

The critics' response to the Ninth was cautiously welcoming,[86] a reminder that a new generation had emerged with catholic tastes and open minds. Nicholas Williams of *The Independent* described it as a kind 'of a musical Alzheimer's, a picture in sound of a creative death'. But he also thought it was, in its own weird way, a masterpiece:

> It was the funereal finale that capped the experience. With its echoes of the Fifth Symphony, a slow march cliché collapsed into single bass notes that drew themselves into vaulting arches of inactivity. The sense of emptiness, prolonged over many minutes, was clearly palpable to the several members of the audience who left the hall. Yet in the end it all made sense.[87]

Ross Pople was delighted to have given what was the first public performance.

> It's surreal. Like a black hole. I felt at times it's extraordinarily beautiful. When we started rehearsing the players were saying 'What's this?' 'What's going on?' But after

---

[86] So too the musicians'. Yehudi Menuhin, for example, wrote cautiously to Ross Pople after the concert, 'I, too, loved working with that wonderful orchestra you have assembled. They did put their heart and soul particularly into the 9th symphony. One would have to know it much better to assess it as it no doubt deserves, but I was most impressed with the performance.' (23 November 1996)
[87] 22 October 1996

the concert there was not a musician in the house who didn't say to me 'That was profound! That was so meaningful for us to play!'[88]

Malcolm enjoyed it all the more because he was sitting next to Irene Duffy who had come across from Ireland specially for the concert and had spent most of the evening with him. And afterwards, at the Festival Orchestra's headquarters close to the Festival Hall, there was a party with Malcolm at the piano till 2.00 a.m. Not only did he have Irene there but also Hayley Mills, who had earlier been playing a vacuum cleaner in the *Grand, Grand Overture*. 'He was so sweet,' she remembers, 'very cosy, very warm. He insisted on playing *Whistle Down the Wind* for me and did so delightfully.'[89]

Katherine also attended the concert, together with her husband and children, though, as usual, she had received no invitation. Not that she was out of touch with her father. At this time she was having telephone conversations (which tended to be rambling monologues) and was seeing him in Norfolk every two or three months.

> The visits were sometimes enjoyable, when there would seemingly be close contact and he would talk with affection of places and people; other visits would usually just about be all right, but he would often be lost and odd and talking rubbish, with bursts of aggression always a possibility.

After the concert they went to wish him a happy birthday.

> Ross Pople was friendly, and Irene said 'Hello'. Dad seemed to me to be elsewhere psychologically. Anthony was busy. We'd made a bit of an effort. I'd brought Dad's three grandchildren along to see him on his birthday, but they were just ignored.

It was somewhat discouraging, but Katherine still collected a copy of *The Gramophone*'s supplement, *Arnold at 75*. It was something to read on the train home.

She thumbed through it, absorbing its flavour. Beneath all the gloss and predictable journalistic set pieces, where, alas, was the *reality* of her father? The longer he lived, the harder he was to define. Did other daughters find their fathers more elusive at each passing year? To what extent had the illness affected his ability to maintain one consistent personality? Maybe the drink had long since sapped his reality? All his life he seemed to have spoken with so many voices, been so many people, offered so many different answers to the same question. She found him as muddling as muddled. When she was a child, at least he had been more obvious: an ebullient, confident shell of a father with all the fear locked bravely inside. But throughout her adult years he had been more elusive, and since the illness had overwhelmed him, he was impossible to read. Did he *need* the support of other people's strength to get through each day, or was he a prisoner, masking his own vulnerability with a classic display of the Stockholm

---

[88] February 2003
[89] December 2003

Syndrome? She longed to know. It was odd to see him, as today, close yet distant, so difficult to identify with the loving, dominant father who had explored the rock-pools of Newtrain, set the holiday agendas and called the tunes. The tunes, perhaps, in the end were the only reality. As inconsistent as he was, and as hard to categorise, yet possessing a viewpoint which was easier to understand, less multi-stranded and changeable. Perhaps she had lost her father because of the music, the calling he had had to answer, the only real truth in his life?

She stared at the cover, a moody photographic close-up of the composer in old age, with four-fifths of his face in total shadow, a fine photograph but distinctly glum. Inside, the booklet told of Malcolm's 'sheer enjoyment of his music-making' and compositions which had 'created laughter and happiness' and 'bright, colourful and gloriously melodic music'.

There surely should be some hint of mirth on that elderly face?

But there was none.

# 19
# Continuation
## Ten Scenes in the Life of an Octogenarian

## I

*A BIRTHDAY CONCERT*
*Malcolm continues to be fêted.*
*The Scene: The Derngate, Northampton*
*The Time: 21 October 2001*

Leaning heavily on Anthony's arm, Malcolm enters the Derngate. They pass through the long foyer, Anthony greeting various familiar faces, but not stopping, for Malcolm is too frail to stand. At the Mayor's pre-concert reception in the Harlequin Suite, Malcolm and Anthony sit at a central table, receiving greetings from friends and well-wishers. One admirer gives Malcolm a gaudy tie with a large trumpet on it. His eyes flicker with interest, but he remains quiet, looking tired. The faces of the dignitaries on nearby tables seem strained. Not realising that Malcolm no longer indulges in sequential conversation easily, they struggle to disentangle disability from rudeness. They are, after all, clutching programmes in which 'Malcolm' has written a message to them, suggesting an intellectual coherence he does not really possess. The brave pretence that things are better than they are has its inevitable drawbacks.

In the concert hall, as the Royal Liverpool Philharmonic Orchestra await their conductor Douglas Bostock, Anthony and Malcolm take their seats in a box with the Mayor and Mayoress. Anthony radiates confidence and pleasure. He has worked hard towards the organisation of this eightieth birthday concert and is determined it will be a success.

Malcolm's sight is not particularly good, but he can see that the hall is virtually full. The tiredness begins to slip off him. He is once more in the habitat he best understands, in a relationship that is totally secure. There is just he himself and the music.

The highlight is the Second Symphony. The *Lento* still stirs the emotions with the same intensity it did nearly fifty years before. He loves the way it starts: a hauntingly beautiful bassoon solo over shimmering strings, with violas taking up the theme over chords in the woodwind. He listens in awe to the pure song of lamentation which is the first half of the movement, no longer a comment on his own personal unhappinesses, but more a universal threnody, a cry of woe for all the hurt, pain and grief in this unhappy world. The funeral cortège enters and passes, the lamentations continue, calmed at length by the gentle tolling of bells and bitter-sweet cries from the flute. As the *Lento* sinks to its peaceful conclusion, Malcolm looks around with satisfaction. The audience is gripped. In the pause between movements there is hardly a cough or a whisper.

Later, at the symphony's conclusion, the audience cheer, quite wildly. The conductor is pointing smilingly in his direction and Anthony is suggesting another wave of the hand. Malcolm complies. More noise, more smiles, more happiness. The players in the orchestra are now standing and applauding, a gesture which moves him greatly. It was what he had done, trumpet in hand, all those years ago for Henry Wood ...

# II

## *DISPUTES CONTINUE*
### *Alongside the music.*
### *The Scene: The Wigmore Hall    The Time: 23 October 2001*

The third eightieth birthday concert in three days has left Malcolm dazed but delighted. First Northampton, then Manchester, now London and the Wigmore Hall.

He had not expected Katherine, but she has come with her new husband, Adrian, and Sheila too, and has found him in the interval.

Briefly he holds Sheila's hand. It is forty years or so since the divorce, half his lifetime. She also is in her eighties now, but still looks beautiful. Briefly, too, he holds Katherine's hand. There is a great deal to say, but where does he begin? And finding the right words has long since ceased to be easy.

There is little time for conversation anyway, for an argument has broken out between Anthony, on his left, and Katherine, Adrian and Sheila on his right. Accusations and rebuttals, hard to understand, fly over his head. It seems to have something to do with the power of Attorney, an enduring power which Anthony is presently registering. The row is clearly serious, but it is really far too late for him to worry about such minutiae. And the audience is returning, the second half of the concert soon to start. John Amis is turning round and waving. And could that be John Gardner? Suddenly Katherine and Sheila are no longer there.

Of all the items in the second half of the programme it is the Flute Sonata he particularly enjoys. It is the one he somehow wrote for Jimmy Galway in de Vesci Terrace, salvaged from the débris of his collapse in the aftermath of Isobel's departure.

Karen Jones is playing it quite beautifully, and Richard Shaw's accompaniment is all that one could wish. It is a marvellous little work, which has defiantly withstood the test of time. But in the sadness of the *Andante* thoughts of Isobel well up uncomfortably. 'Fancy a night out, Iso? Fancy a night out?'

# III

## *A HOLIDAY BROADCAST*
### *Malcolm continues to meet the media.*
### *The scene: A 'Radio Sultanate of Oman' Studio*
### *The Time: May 2002*

Anthony sits beside Malcolm a little anxiously in the studio. Malcolm usually has much to say in such situations but his thoughts from time to time can be erratic. It has been agreed, therefore, that the edited interview will be preceded by some cautionary words:

> As you may notice in this programme, Sir Malcolm does not always give a direct answer to a question. His mind is so active and his thoughts full of his music and experiences ... Now and again he is prompted by his carer and companion of eighteen years, Anthony Day ...

Malcolm, gaunt but tanned, is by contrast extremely relaxed, in distinct holiday mood. Besides, he has always been a performer, always felt a quickened pulse at the sight of a microphone.

He needs little prompting at the start. Asked about his orchestral days, he responds at once with cheerful inaccuracy:

'I was in the London Philharmonic for twenty-four years ...'

They move on to ballet, where he pontificates happily:

'You can't attempt ballet unless you know every darned step in the repertoire of boys and girls – and they call them boys until they're one hundred years old! You usually have to attend every bloody rehearsal, if it's a man like Ashton ...'

Asked if he can see an Arabic influence ever happening to Western music, he is unstoppable:

'I think it would be very much to the good, would it not? Because Arabic means "mathematical" and mathematic precision is what is required in music particularly with conductors. It's better without a baton, dear!

'Arabic music is entirely different because it uses quarter-tones and even eighth-tones. The diatonic scale of C which is really the Ionian mode is very limiting, but I think to go back to the ecclesiastical mode, which is Byzantine in its origin, is correct, and you'll find the meaning of *numes* which is the Turkish name for notes. The Arabic instruments are more varied than the Indian musical instruments and the most interesting of the Indian instruments is the rudraveena, which has steel on the 'been' to make them vibrate, dear, and is played on the floor from an upright position.

'When I went to Delhi I said "Have you ever heard of Yehudi Menuhin?" They said, "No! Who is he?" I said, "Well, he's supposed to be an expert on Hindustani music" and they said, "No! he's never been here!"'

'Can you see English musicians playing Arabic music?'

'Not very often!' Malcolm guffaws heartily at the thought. 'No!'

The interviewer momentarily bridles. 'Do you think it's too difficult for them?'

'No I don't, dear. Louis Armstrong played the trumpet when he was a very old man.'

This unexpected answer brings things to a temporary halt. There is a brief flurry of *Nick Nack Paddy Wack*, by way of illustrating 'this great composer' (we have already heard *Colonel Bogey*), and then the interview resumes.

'Now let's find out how he composes this fantastic music for films! Please tell us!'

'Well it's a different process.'

'What's the process?'

'Oh dear, you are an inquisitive little girl! You have to read the *script* – You've *heard* of a *script*? – whether it is in Arabic or English or someone... You have to read the *script*, dear!'

It is time for Anthony to leap in:

'It was the twelfth of August, my birthday, in 1986 and I'd just asked Sir Malcolm to write me a piece of music ...'

# IV

## MALCOLM'S NEW BIOGRAPHY
### *Anthony continues to give guidance.*
### *The scene: Attleborough     The time: Summer 2002*

Malcolm has been brought downstairs by Anthony, wrapped up in a blanket and made comfortable in the best armchair. He has already been bathed, shaved and dressed a little earlier than usual because of a visit from the latest biographers. But interviews most days are burdensome for him. The hoops he has jumped through so many times are no longer attractive. And he is not even sure he can see them clearly, so he pulls a fierce grimace, guaranteed to drive interlopers away. 'I know who you are, you shit!' he says to his questioner with some belligerence. 'You're Benjamin Britten!' Delighted with the surprised reaction, he drifts away from current irritations into more pleasant reverie ...

'I'm so grateful for what you're doing on the boy's behalf,' says Anthony in the adjacent room. 'He's normally much better than this. It's just a bad day. He was up late watching the Eurovision Song Contest, which of course he loves.'

He lights a cigarette with careful elegance, ponders a moment, and begins again.

'I feel I have probably concentrated too much on the negatives rather than the glorious times we have had over the past eighteen years. Like the great trip to Miami University, Oxford, Ohio for the Doctorate of Arts and Humane Letters, where he was fêted and treated to a week of superb performances of his music. Piers wrote his speech, and he delivered it perfectly. Or like going to the Double Violin Concerto at the Menuhin Festival in Switzerland, and the trip up the Nile.

'Can you please destroy the myth that Sir Malcolm does what *I* want when in fact it is the other way round? When he says "no", he means "no"! Like staying in this house when I spent years finding a dream home only for him to refuse to move into it. Likewise the hell when we are at home or in London ready to go to a concert and he decides he won't go, which, with a manic-depressive, is a problem, as you can never predict the come-down, when they are on a high, and you cannot adjust the medication due to lack of time for it to take effect. Or the time he decided that he did not want to go out to hotels for lunch any more, after which we stayed at home and I cooked. Fortunately I enjoy cooking, but I still miss going out daily and meeting people …'

# V

## *MALCOLM IN HOSPITAL*
### *Puzzling Katherine.*
*The Scene: Norwich Hospital*     *The Time: Early 2003*

Katherine sits beside her father for a while. He has been seriously ill with pneumonia, his life for a time in the balance. But he is not particularly pleased with her today, for she has grown up and is no longer his little girl.

Though conscious, he is largely silent. For some time he stares at her watch and eventually moves a weak arm and points at it.

'A rich man gave you that!'

Katherine smiles. He catches her eyes challengingly, before focusing on a new, absorbing topic of interest, Katherine's wedding ring.

Again it takes a little time for the words to formulate.

'Take off your ring!' he says eventually. 'You're not married!'

# VI

*MALCOLM'S MUSIC INTERESTS A NEW GENERATION*
*His biographers meet a young admirer.*
*The Scene: The Railway Inn, Gipsy Hill      The Time: Summer 2003*

Matthew Taylor, an authority on Robert Simpson, is also fascinated by Malcolm's position in twentieth-century music. He is typical of an emerging younger generation which can view Malcolm's lifework objectively, without subjective interference from past allegiances in the battle of musical taste begun in the 1960s. He knows Malcolm's music well, has studied the symphonies with great care, and is founder of the Arnold Ensemble.

It is a fine late summer evening and the pub's garden is crowded. Most of the chatter nearby is of Crystal Palace Football Club, but as Matthew develops his arguments with a growing passion, interested neighbours put down their pints and start to listen in.

> You're going to have to give some sort of overview of his music. All biographies do that sort of thing. Put him in his landscape! Trouble is, he's in a very desolate landscape. There's just this rock-like figure in twentieth-century music – as Berlioz was in the Nineteenth Century – there's nobody else really like him – this rock-like figure that is Malcolm Arnold. And, like a rock, he has never looked to right or left …
>
> His music hasn't really deepened; it has darkened. It hasn't gained in wisdom, or depth. He was too angry to do that. There was an extraordinary anger inside the man, an anger that sometimes bordered on bombast…!
>
> There's nothing in an Arnold score that doesn't work. So many composers don't know the instruments they're writing for, but Arnold did. He is always writing naturally and fluently, embracing you with open arms, even on those occasions when the fire and imagination are less obviously there … His craft was supreme.
>
> In this time of plurality, where there is so much mediocrity and the term 'greatness' applied far too readily and without sufficient justification, it may be significant that those who support Arnold most fervently are the orchestral players themselves …

He pauses. The Crystal Palace supporters wait expectantly.

> Yes! That might be it! You could start your overview by posing a question: Why *is* it that most orchestral players you meet *love* and *rate* Malcolm Arnold's music?

The supporters look blankly worried. It is not a question to which they had previously given much thought.

# VII

## *THE FAMILY CONTINUE THEIR INDEPENDENT LIVES*
### *Robert and Edward in middle age.*
### *The Scene: Skye          The Time: August 2003*

It is so warm and cloudless we could be in Ischia rather than the north-west of Scotland, where Robert and Anne have lived for many years. Sheila has recently come to join them here, after four years in a flat next door to Katherine in London.

There is an engaging diffidence and generosity of spirit in Robert, honed perhaps by the peace of the Scottish isles, as he seeks to define the ironies of his father's life:

> Dad's always had this idea that music could be capable of bringing something special to the world: socialism, fairness, tolerance, world peace, things he passionately believed in all his life and towards which he thought music could genuinely contribute. Then crises like the Vietnam War came along, which deeply disappointed him. But worst of all was what happened after he'd been drinking.
>
> You can have great ideas about tolerance and peace, but have a few drinks and you start shouting at people! If your great idea is that the world is *rid* of aggressive monsters but you've *become* an aggressive monster yourself, then it's all gone badly wrong! And what do you do then? You kill yourself, because you yourself are responsible for bringing your own great ideals crashing down!
>
> He's got this motto 'Music Unites'. It's a wonderful *ambition*. But it isn't something he's managed to *achieve* in his own life!

Around the time Malcolm was dangerously ill, Robert had visited Edward, now rising forty and living in a new care home:

> I offered to take him to see Dad, but he said. 'No thank you. I don't think so. I'll stay here.' He's concerned about the fact he's ill and how long he's going to live. But he still calls him 'The Waspish'. Anthony says they used to get on well, and I'm sure they did for a short time, but it's many years now since they've seen each other, ten years or so. I can't see Dad not saying something hurtful or waspish to him. And Edward really can do without that kind of distress.
>
> He has a pleasant room overlooking a garden. He collects stereo equipment; he has all the latest digital technology and is a real expert on it, for he loves music. He's especially into very peaceful music of the sea: the waves and wind, and so forth. Katherine visits him regularly, and Anne and I come down to see him when we can.

# VIII

*MALCOLM'S 82nd BIRTHDAY*
*In a Wymondham nursing home.*
*The Scene: Ogden Court      The Time: 21 October 2003*

Further illness and hospitalisation have led to Malcolm spending a period of recuperation in Ogden Court, Wymondham. Katherine meanwhile has applied to take her father out of Anthony's control. Doctors and lawyers, even the police, have been involved, and, several months later, it is still not yet known whether Malcolm will return to Attleborough or a home near Katherine. He is in Ogden Court, physically and mentally very weak, when his eighty-second birthday comes round.

Anthony spends much of each day with Malcolm, taking him fruit, helping him with his meals, showering him, getting him in and out of bed, changing his pads, even attending to his dentures. His smiling presence does much to brighten Malcolm's room, and he is intent to endow the birthday with an extra sparkle and sense of occasion.

Malcolm sits in a dressing gown, hunched in a chair, a rug over his knees, fruit and flowers on a table in front of him. Most days he will be listening to classical music on the radio, or, at least, it will be playing in the background. Today, however, the television, moved within close range, is blaring. Anthony tactfully turns it off. 'Malcolm, visitors! You recognise them, don't you! They've come to wish you Happy Birthday!' Malcolm stares impassively. His eyesight is impaired and, although he seems to focus on his visitors and has no trouble in locating the slices of orange on the table before him, he has been registered as officially blind.

Though the visitors try to talk of the past, aware that that is where he is mostly living, his mind flits inconsequentially, rarely settling. Malcolm tends to take a contrary view on most subjects, and clearly dislikes mention of those who have been closest to him, resorting at such moments, by way of defence, to absurdities. These, however, may not be deliberate, for coherent thought seems only to survive in patches.

Those patches are always when Anthony is around. Anthony's deftness of touch, born of long experience, still conjures up from Malcolm precious respect. It is a respect which comes from the knowledge that, try as he might, Malcolm has met defences which he cannot pierce. When he goes for the weakest point, as he always must, he is met with a resisting barrier never previously encountered: kind yet tough. Anthony defers, cajoles, questions and banters with masterly adroitness as he seeks to maintain coherence in the relationship. On occasion, if necessary, he will raise his voice to re-establish calm. His optimism is a greater medication than anything officialdom can produce. He is full of laughter and his repartee with the nurses and sad old ladies is uninhibited and engaging. He is wearing himself out. But he endures it stubbornly, knowing only too well that he is Malcolm's solitary, though tenuous, grip on life.

The visitors, running out of conversation, get up to leave. A flicker of regret shows on Malcolm's face, suggesting that his perplexing verbal parries may stem from mischievous intent.

'Nice to see you!' cries Anthony, as they depart.

'To see you nice,' mutters Malcolm.

The eighty-second birthday is nearly over. It is raining hard outside and dusk is gathering around the well-kept gardens. As he tidies the room in preparation for putting Malcolm to bed, Anthony rearranges a large variety of cards set out on a chest of drawers, testimony that, although most of Malcolm's generation have gone before him, he has not been completely forgotten, even in the obscurity of a Norfolk nursing home. One card has a picture of a large, lugubrious dog, wearing the smartest of hats and scarves. 'Happy Birthday,' runs the legend, 'to someone with style.' Anthony chortles. 'That's a good one, Malcolm! Appropriate!' Inside is a simple handwritten message. Anthony looks up.

'Have you seen this one, Malcolm?'

'What?' comes gruffly back.

'Do you know what it says?'

A shrug for an answer.

Anthony crosses the room and sits down beside him, pointing to the message with a radiant smile.

'It says "Thank you for the music!" Malcolm. "Thank you for the music!"'


# IX

*ANTHONY CONTINUES AS MALCOLM'S ATTORNEY*
*A battle in the Courts.*
*The Scene: The Court of Protection, London.*
*The Time: December 2003.*

Katherine has applied to the Court to cancel Anthony's registration of enduring powers of Attorney. One of the most vexed areas is Anthony's control over Malcolm's finances, on which Anthony responds with vigour:

When I took Sir Malcolm in 1984, he was £150,000 in debt. In October 1986 when he left the Court of Protection he had £192 in the bank. He now has his own house (though he gave me half in 1989, when I paid the mortgage off, and the other half in 1997), over £300,000 in shares, £30,000 in premium bonds, and some £200,000 has been spent converting it for his day to day care, such as a lift instead of stairs and a bedroom converted into a double bathroom and shower-room, as the space is now necessary for his needs ...

Another vexed area is Malcolm's relationship with Katherine. Opinions from various interested parties are read out, and The Master of the Court of Protection, in attempting clarification, introduces the Seventh Symphony as an insight into the relationship. He quotes from a critic who had explained that each movement was a loose portrait of each child, found the symphony 'replete with dissonance and unrest' and concluded that 'Arnold didn't particularly enjoy parenthood'. It is a somewhat simplistic response. The critic had not included any mention of Malcolm's emotional state at the time of writing the symphony. He mentioned neither the mayhem of Meadowcroft nor the imminent Irish breakdown, which led to the madness of Belsize Park. The Seventh Symphony is not presented in its overall context.

Much is made of the initial decision to invoke the Court of the Protection's aid at the height of the Belsize Park nightmare in 1979. This the Master seemingly sees as something against Malcolm's best interests:

> Sir Malcolm has had professional receivers before ... for seven years between 1979 and 1986. By all accounts Sir Malcolm hated being the subject of receivership proceedings, and bitterly resented Katherine Arnold's action in instigating them ... The papers reveals that her first husband applied for the appointment of a receiver, but ... Katherine Arnold appears to be the *éminence grise*, lurking behind the scenes, loading bullets for others to fire.

Anthony's enduring powers of attorney are confirmed. The Court endorses Anthony's full control. After eight months in Ogden Court Malcolm returns to Attleborough. For Katherine it is another battle lost.

# X

*FINALE*

*On the telephone.*
*The Scene: Attleborough   The Time: March 2004*

Anthony receives an unexpected telephone call.

'Hallo! It's Sheila. Can I speak to Malcolm, please?'

It takes time for Anthony to explain to Malcolm who it is who is most unexpectedly wishing to speak to him, for Malcolm is having a 'bad' day.

'Hallo, Malcolm, is that you?' Sheila pauses momentarily.

'I've been listening to the First Symphony on the radio and I just want to tell you how very moved I was by it.'

She pauses again, uncertainly.

'It was quite a surprise hearing it on the radio, and it was so marvellous I just had to tell you.'

This time from the other end comes a noise, half cough, half strangled sob.

'Goodbye, Malcolm. I was so moved by it. I really was.'

# THE WORLD'S TEARS

A sad heart
Is a bright jewel in the fabric of Immortality:
A merry heart is but a bubble,
Gaily coloured outside,
   But a barren substance at the core.
It breaks eventually –
And Wisdom gathers the memory of it in her breast,
To keep until the Time of using it.

No heart has blossomed
Till love's tears have succoured it,
And no heart finds happiness
Till it has born sadness;
For, with the benison of sorrow
Comes the triple blessing of understanding,
And that is the wisdom of all races,
      And all ages.

So open wide the gates of sacrifice,
And let the world's tears
Find solace within your own poor heart.

*RUTH ARNOLD, 1939*

# Chronological List of Works

*Note:* Concert works are listed in the year of composition; works for films or television (both *in italics*) in the year of the film's release and first televised transmission.
TV = Television; D = Documentary;
R = Radio; d. = director

**1936**
Haile Selassie – March for piano (lost)

**1937**
Allegro in E minor for piano
Serenade in G for piano
Theme and Variations for piano
Three piano pieces

**1938**
'Beauty Haunts the Woods' for voice and piano
Day Dreams for piano
Dream City for piano
Grand Fantasia for flute, trumpet and piano, Op. 973
Kensington Gardens – song cycle for voice and piano

**1939**
Rhapsody for piano (lost)
Two part songs
Violin Sonata (lost)

**1940**
Overture for wind octet
Trio for flute, trumpet and cello (lost)
Suite Bourgeoise for flute, oboe and piano

**1941**
Phantasy for String Quartet, 'Vita Abundans'
Sonata for flute and piano in C (Sonata poor [sic] flute)
Two Pieces for piano
Two sketches for oboe and piano

**1942**
Divertimento for Orchestra, Op. 1 (lost)
Wind Quintet, Op. 2
Three Shanties for Wind Quintet Op. 4
Piano Sonata
Sonata for flute and piano

**1943**
Larch Trees – Tone poem for orchestra, Op. 3
Beckus the Dandipratt – Overture for orchestra, Op. 5
Trio for flute, viola and bassoon. Op. 6
Three Pieces for piano

**1944**
Quintet for flute, violin, viola, horn and bassoon, Op. 7
Two songs for voice and piano ('Neglected', 'Morning Moon'), Op. 8
Variations on a Ukrainian Folk Song for piano, Op. 9

**1945**
Duo for flute and viola, Op. 10
Concerto No. 1 for horn and orchestra, Op. 11
Symphonic Suite for Orchestra, Op. 12 (lost)
Prelude for piano

**1946**
Symphony for strings, Op. 13

**1947**
Festival Overture for Orchestra, Op. 14 (lost)
Sonata No. 1 for violin and piano, Op. 15
Children's Suite for Piano, Op. 16
Sonata for viola and piano, Op. 17
Two Bagatelles for piano, Op. 18
*Avalanche Patrol (D)*
*Seven RAF Flashes (D)*

**1948**
Sonatina for flute and piano, Op. 19
To Youth – Suite for Orchestra (lost, but published in altered form as Little Suite No. 1 Op. 53)
Concerto No. 1 for clarinet and strings, Op. 20
*(continued)*

**1948** *(continued)*

The Smoke – Overture for orchestra, Op. 21
*Badger's Green (d. John Irwin)*
*Accident Prevention Concerning You (D) –*
  *RAF*
*Charting the seas (D) – Admiralty*
*Every Drop To Drink (D) – Metropolitan*
  *Water Board*
*Gates of Power (D)*
*Lancashire's Time for Adventure – This*
  *Modern Age (D) – Cotton*
*Mining Review series (D)*
*Report on Steel (D)*
*Queen of the Border – Harwick  (D)*
*The Struggle for Oil (D)*
*Women in our time – This Modern Age (D)*

**1949**

**SYMPHONY No. 1, Op. 22**

String Quartet No. 1, Op. 23
Henri Christophe – unfinished opera in four
  acts
*Britannia Mews (d. Jean Negulesco)*
*Your Witness (d. Robert Montgomery)*
*Julius Caesar*
*Antony and Cleopatra*
*The Beautiful County of Ayr (D)*
*Dollars and Sense (D)*
*Drums for a holiday (D)*
*This Farming Business (D)*
*Fight for a Fuller Life – This Modern Age (D)*
*The Frasers of Cabot Cove (D)*
*The Riddle of Japan – This Modern Age (D)*
*Terra Incognita (D)*
*Trieste: Problem City – This Modern Age (D)*
*When you went away – This Modern Age (D)*

**1950**

Divertimento No. 2 for orchestra, Op. 24
  (revised as Op. 75)
Psalm 150 (Laudate Dominum) for SATB
  chorus and organ, Op. 25
Serenade for small orchestra, Op. 26
English Dances (Set 1), Op. 27
*Up for the Cup (d. Jack Raymond)*
*Airways (D)*
*Alien Orders (D) – Malaya*
*Fifty Acres – Green Park (D)*
*Man and Machines (D)*
*Oil Review No. 5 – Green Park (D)*
*Power for all (D)*
*'This is Britain' series (D)  [title unknown]*
*Science in the Orchestra (D) (Hearing the*
  *Orchestra; Exploring the Instruments;*
  *Looking at Sounds)*
*Where Britain Stands (D)*

**1951**

Sonatina for oboe and piano, Op. 28
Sonatina for clarinet and piano, Op. 29
Symphonic Study 'Machines', Op. 30
A Sussex Overture for orchestra, Op. 31
Concerto for piano duet and strings, Op. 32
English Dances (Set 2), Op. 33
Up at the Villa – sketches for opera in one act
*Home at Seven (d. Ralph Richardson)*
*Home to Danger (d. Terence Fisher)*
*No Highway (d. Henry Koster)*

**1952**

The Dancing Master – Opera in one act,
  Op. 34
Two Ceremonial Psalms for unaccompanied
  SSA boys' chorus, Op. 35
Eight Children's Piano Pieces, Op. 36
Divertimento for wind trio, Op. 37
The Sound Barrier – Rhapsody for Orchestra,
  Op. 38
Concerto for oboe and orchestra, Op. 39
*Curtain Up (d. Ralph Smart)*
*The Holly and the Ivy (d. George O'Ferrall)*
*It Started in Paradise (d. Compton Bennett)*
*The Ringer (d. Guy Hamilton)*
*The Sound Barrier (d. David Lean)*
*Stolen Face (d. Terence Fisher)*
*Wings of Danger (d. Terence Fisher)*
*Copenhagen, City of Towers (D)*
*The Local Newspaper (D)*
*Channel Islands (D)*
*The Island (D) – Kent Oil Refinery*

**1953**

**SYMPHONY No. 2, Op. 40**

Sonatina for recorder and piano, Op. 41
Homage to the Queen – Ballet, Op. 42
Homage to the Queen – suite from ballet, Op.
  42a
Sonata No. 2 for violin and piano, Op. 43
Flourish for a 21st birthday, Op. 44
*Purple Dust – incidental music*
*Albert R.N. (d. Lewis Gilbert)*
*The Captain's Paradise (d. Anthony Kimmins)*
*Four Sided Triangle (d. Terence Fisher)*
*The Story of Gilbert and Sullivan (d. Sidney*
  *Gilliat)*
*Hobson's Choice (d. David Lean)*
*Man of Africa  (d. Cyril Frankel) (semi-*
  *documentary)*
*Powered Flight: the story of the century (D)*

**1954**

Concerto for flute and strings, Op. 45
Concerto for harmonica and orchestra, Op. 46

Concerto for organ and orchestra, Op. 47
Sinfonietta for chamber orchestra, Op. 48
Rinaldo and Armida – Ballet, Op. 49
The Tempest – incidental music
*The Royal Tour – New Zealand (D)*
*War in the Air (TV) (i The Fated Sky; iv*
   *Maximum Effort)*
*Welcome the Queen! (D)*
*The Beautiful Stranger (d. David Miller)*
*The Belles of St Trinian's (d. Frank Launder)*
*The Constant Husband (d. Sidney Gilliat)*
*Devil on Horseback (d. Cyril Frankel)*
*The Sea Shall Not Have Them (d. Lewis*
   *Gilbert)*
*The Sleeping Tiger (d. Joseph Losey)*
*You Know What Sailors Are! (d. Ken Annakin)*
Paddy's Nightmare – revue number

**1955**

Serenade for guitar and strings, Op. 50
Tam O'Shanter – Overture for orchestra, Op. 51
John Clare Cantata for SATB chorus and piano
   duet, Op. 52
Little Suite No. 1 for orchestra, Op. 53
Electra – Incidental Music, stage play
Fanfare for a Festival for brass and percussion
*The Deep Blue Sea (d. Anatole Litvak)*
*I am a Camera (d. Henry Cornelius)*
*The Night My Number Came Up (d. Leslie*
   *Norman)*
*A Prize of Gold (d. Mark Robson)*
*Value for Money (d. Ken Annakin)*
*The Woman for Joe (d. George O'Ferrall)*
*1984 (d. Michael Anderson)*
*Let go For'ard (D)*
*War in the Air (TV) (x Operation Overlord)*

**1956**

Piano Trio, Op. 54
Song of Praise for unison voices and piano,
   Op. 55
Fanfare for a Royal Occasion
The Open Window – opera in one act, Op. 56
A Grand, Grand Overture for orchestra, Op. 57
Concerto No. 2 for horn and orchestra, Op. 58
Solitaire – Ballet (sarabande and polka)
*The Barretts of Wimpole Street (not used)*
*A Hill in Korea (d. Julian Amyes)*
*Invitation to the Dance (d. Gene Kelly) (One*
   *of the three items, not used)*
*Port Afrique (Rudolph Maté)*
*Tiger in the Smoke (d. Roy Baker)*
*Trapeze (d. Carol Reed)*
*Wicked As They Come (d. Ken Hughes)*
*Roses Tattoo (D)*
*Fanfare (TV) for ABC TV launch*

**1957**

Four Scottish Dances, Op. 59
H.R.H. The Duke of Cambridge – March for
   military band, Op. 60
Oboe Quartet, Op. 61
Toy Symphony, Op. 62
**SYMPHONY No. 3, Op. 63**
Commonwealth Christmas Overture for
   orchestra, Op. 64
Richmond Fanfare for brass
*Blue Murder at St Trinian's (d. Frank*
   *Launder)*
*The Bridge on the River Kwai (d. David Lean)*
*Island in the Sun (d. Robert Rossen)*
*For Mr Pye An Island (R) – incidental music*
*Royal Prologue (TV)*
*Music For You (TV) – Theme tune*

**1958**

Sinfonietta No. 2 for chamber orchestra,
   Op. 65
Concert Piece for percussion and piano
'Katherine, Walking and Running' for two
   violins [date uncertain]
United Nations for 4 military bands, organ and
   orchestra
*Dunkirk (d. Leslie Norman)*
*The Inn of the Sixth Happiness (d. Mark*
   *Robson)*
*The Key (d. Carol Reed)*
*The Roots of Heaven (d. John Huston)*
*Coupe des Alpes (D) – 1958 Alpine Rally*

**1959**

Five William Blake Songs for contralto and
   strings, Op. 66
Concerto for guitar and chamber ensemble (or
   orchestra), Op. 67
Sweeney Todd – Ballet, Op. 68
Song of Simeon – Nativity masque, Op. 69
March: 'Overseas' for military band, Op. 70
Four pieces for chamber ensemble
Kingston Fanfare for brass
*The Boy and the Bridge (d. Kevin McClory)*
*Solomon and Sheba (d. King Vidor) (Funeral*
   *music sequence only)*

**1960**
**SYMPHONY No. 4, Op. 71**
Carnival of Animals for orchestra, Op. 72
A Hoffnung Fanfare
*The Angry Silence (d. Guy Green)*
*The Pure Hell of St Trinian's (d. Frank*
   *Launder)*
*(continued)*

**1960** *(continued)*
*Suddenly, Last Summer (d. Joseph*
    *Mankiewicz)  (opening credits only)*
*Tunes of Glory (d. Ronald Neame)*
*Parasol  (TV)*

**1961**
Brass Quintet No. 1, Op. 73
**SYMPHONY No. 5, Op. 74**
Divertimento No. 2 for orchestra, Op. 75
Grand Concerto Gastronomique, Op. 76
Fanfare for the Farnham Festival
Leonora No. 4 Overture for large orchestra
Fantasy for Flute and Guitar  [date uncertain]
*No Love for Johnnie (d. Ralph Thomas)*
*On the Fiddle (d. Cyril Frankel)*
*Whistle Down the Wind (d. Bryan Forbes)*

**1962**
Concerto for two violins and strings, Op. 77
Little Suite No. 2 for orchestra, Op. 78
Theme for 'Players'
*The Inspector (d. Philip Dunne)*
*The Lion (d. Jack Cardiff)*
*Nine Hours to Rama (d. Mark Robson)*

**1963**
The Peacock in the Zoo for unison voices and
    piano
Elektra – Ballet, Op. 79
Little Suite No. 1 for brass band, Op. 80
*Tamahine (d. Philip Leacock)*
*Gala Performance (TV) – theme*
*Espionage (TV) 14 episodes, extended over a*
    *year*

**1964**
Sinfonietta No. 3 for chamber orchestra,
    Op. 81
Water Music for wind and percussion, Op. 82
Water Music arranged for orchestra, Op. 82b
A Sunshine Overture for orchestra, Op. 83
    (lost)
Five Pieces for violin and piano, Op. 84
*The Chalk Garden (d. Ronald Neame)*
*The Thin Red Line (d. Andrew Marton)*
*A Free Agent (TV)*

**1965**
Duo for two cellos, Op. 85
Fantasy for bassoon, Op. 86
*The Heroes of Telemark (d. Anthony Mann)*

**1966**
Fantasy for clarinet, Op. 87
Fantasy for horn, Op. 88

Fantasy for flute, Op. 89
Fantasy for oboe, Op. 90
Four Cornish Dances, Op. 91
'Jolly Old Friar' for unison voices and piano
Theme and variation – for Severn Bridge
Variations on a Welsh Folk Song for orchestra
*Africa Texas Style (d. Andrew Marton)*
*The Great St Trinian's Train Robbery (d.*
    *Launder & Gilliat)*
*Sky West and Crooked (d. John Mills)*

**1967**
*The Turtle Drum – incidental music (TV),*
    Op. 92
Little Suite No. 2 for brass band, Op. 93
The Padstow Lifeboat – Mach for brass band,
    Op. 94
**SYMPHONY No. 6, Op. 95**
Trevelyan Suite for ten instruments, Op. 96
Peterloo – Overture for orchestra, Op. 97
This Christmas Night for unaccompanied
    SATB chorus
A Salute to Thomas Merritt for two brass
    bands and orchestra, Op. 98
*North Sea Strike (D)*

**1968**
Anniversary Overture for orchestra, Op. 99
Savile Centenary fanfare for two trumpets
St Endellion Ringers – canon for voices
This Christmas Night – carol for
    unaccompanied SATB chorus
*Divertimento (D) – British Petroleum [used*
    *Divertimento Op. 37]*
*The First Lady (TV)*

**1969**
Fantasy for trumpet, Op. 100
Fantasy for trombone, Op. 101
Fantasy for tuba, Op. 102
The Song of Accounting Periods for voice and
    piano, Op. 103
Concerto for two pianos (3 hands) and
    orchestra, Op. 104
*Battle of Britain (d. Guy Hamilton) [last part*
    *of 'Battle in Air'; helped William Walton,*
    *whose score was otherwise rejected]*
*The Reckoning (d. Jack Gold)*

**1970**
Concerto for 28 players, Op. 105
Fantasy for audience and orchestra, Op. 106
Fantasy for guitar, Op. 107
Fanfare for Louis for two trumpets
*David Copperfield (d. Delbert Mann)*

**1971**

Concerto for viola and chamber orchestra, Op. 108

Fanfare for one, eighty years young for solo trumpet

**1972**

Song of Freedom for SA chorus and brass band, Op. 109

The Fair Field Overture for orchestra, Op. 110

Concerto No. 2 for flute and chamber orchestra, Op.111

A Flourish for Orchestra, Op. 112

Popular Birthday for orchestra

**1973**

**SYMPHONY No. 7, Op. 113**

Fantasy for brass band, Op. 114a

**1974**

Two John Donne Songs for tenor and piano, Op. 114b

Concerto No. 2 for clarinet and chamber orchestra, Op. 115

**1975**

Fantasy on a theme of John Field for piano and orchestra, Op. 116

Fantasy for harp, Op. 117

String Quartet No. 2, Op. 118

Railway Fanfare for 6 trumpets

The Three Musketeers – incomplete sketches for a ballet

**1976**

The Return of Odysseus – Cantata for SATB chorus and orchestra, Op. 119

Philharmonic Concerto for orchestra, Op. 120

**1977**

Sonata for flute and piano, Op. 121

Variations for orchestra on a theme of Ruth Gipps, Op. 122

**1978**

Symphony for brass instruments, Op. 123

**SYMPHONY No. 8, Op. 124**

**1982**

Concerto for trumpet and orchestra, Op. 125

**1986**

Four Irish Dances, Op. 126

Fantasy for descant recorder, Op. 127

**SYMPHONY No. 9, Op. 128**

Three Fantasies for piano, Op. 129

**1987**

Fantasy for cello, Op. 130

Little Suite No. 3 for brass band, Op. 131

Brass Quintet No. 2, Op. 132

**1988**

Concerto for recorder and chamber orchestra, Op. 133

Serenade for tenor and strings (Contrasts), Op. 134

Divertimento for two B flat clarinets, Op. 135

Concerto for cello and orchestra, Op. 136 (Revised 2000, David Ellis)

Divertimento for Wind Octet, Op. 137

**1989**

Four Welsh Dances, Op. 138

**1990**

Flourish for a Battle for wind band, Op. 139

Theme and variations: Fantasy for recorder and string quartet, Op. 140

Robert Kett Overture for orchestra, Op. 141

A Manx Suite for orchestra, Op. 142 (Little Suite No. 3)

# Index